THE ST. JAMES

fashion

ENCYCLOPEDIA

THE
ST.
JAMES

fashion

Richard Martin

ENCYCLOPEDIA

A Survey of Style from
1945 to the Present

DETROIT

The St. James Fashion Encyclopedia:

A Survey of Style from 1945 to the Present

By Richard Martin

Copyright 1997 by Visible Ink Press™

Visible Ink Press™
42015 Ford Rd. #208
Canton, MI 48187-3669

Visible Ink Press is a trademark of Visible Ink Press LLC.

Most Visible Ink Press books are available at special quantity discounts when purchased in bulk by corporations, organizations, or groups. Customized printings, special imprints, messages, and excerpts can be produced to meet your needs. For more information, contact Special Markets Director, Visible Ink Press, at www.visibleink.com.

Cover Photo: From Unzipped, 1995. Courtesy of the Kobal Collection.
Cover Design: Tracey Rowens

Library of Congress Cataloging-in-Publication Data
              p.   cm.
    Rev. ed. of: Contemporary Fashion, 1995.
    ISBN 0-7876-1036-4 (alk. paper)
    1. Fashion designers—Biography—Encyclopedias. 2. Costume design—History—20th century—Encyclopedias. 3. Fashion—History—20th century—Encyclopedias. I. Martin, Richard (Richard Harrison). II. St. James Press. III. Contemporary fashion.
TT505.A1S7 1996
746.9'2'03—dc20
                                    96-22878
                                    CIP

ISBN 0-7876-1036-4
Printed in the United States of America
All rights reserved
10 9 8 7 6 5

CONTENTS

fashion

Introduction . . . .*vii*

Fashion Chronology . . . . *ix*

Entries   1

Appendix 423

Nationality Index 433

Notes on Contributors 435

INTRODUCTION

fashion

Ironically, fashion needs an encyclopedia. Lately, many people have wanted to market their advice on what we wear, but with little credibility other than to clone a personality, depend upon one designer, demand minimalism (or extravagance), or pick a style of the moment. We do not need a manual; we need a more reliable measure and a larger perspective. We need to know the designers and important names of fashion to get our bearings in the visual, creative, and merchandising phenomenon that defines modern culture. Fashion—in its full spectrum of design, garments, people-watching, advertising, retailing, and consumption—is the quintessential modern experience.

Yet some have assumed that fashion is too ephemeral to be worthy of a basic reference book. The testimony of the *St. James Fashion Encyclopedia* is, of course, to the contrary. This book records some fads and notes some business failures, but it is overwhelmingly a document of fashion's power to surpass the momentary and to lay claim in a very effective way to permanence and to our imagination. In more than 200 essays on designers of the period since 1945, we see that fashion is not given to erratic change, but is instead a far steadier course than many have imagined. Fashion is connected to impulses of the moment, whether those are retro desires of the current culture or current standards of beauty, but fashion is also a strong force of continuity. Fashion's willingness to change is part of what makes us modern and what draws us to fashion as a paradigm of the new and innovative. But fashion is also a powerful connection to the past—memories, mementoes, personal values, and history.

Fashion is always hard to grasp. It is a visual art of immense creativity, challenged to accommodate art to the human body. It is a pragmatic business of addressing and dressing consumers in clothing that flatters and pleases and sells.

It is a complex system, involving advertising—including the most controversial advertising of our time—and commerce. It is a social system in which wearers and designers are not merely expressing themselves but using apparel to negotiate daily contacts with one another and with the larger social contract.

Fashion is so central to our culture that we must consider it. In addition to facts, this encyclopedia is composed of critical essays by insightful scholars and writers on fashion. Their thoughts are valid, but they are not absolute; their ideas and tastes are subjective, not incontrovertible. As a result, this is a very special kind of encyclopedia—never, dry, doctrinaire, or uninteresting. It is, I believe, the right kind of encyclopedia for fashion because it is not dictatorial, but rather more democratic, like contemporary fashion. This book is filled with facts, but it is also elevated by ideas and enthusiasms. Its pleasures are like those of fashion, except for the touch: this is a book with a lot of truths and some splendid opportunities for dispute and judgment, personal choice that is now informed. This is a book that takes us to the modern practice and pleasure of fashion with no secret formula and no hidden guilt, just the information that makes fashion more interesting and more compelling than ever.

Richard Martin

FASHION CHRONOLOGY

fashion

1946
Louis Réard's bikini shown at Piscine Molitor, Paris

1947
Dior New Look

1950
First Pierre Cardin collection

1952
Sala Bianca, Italian fashion shows, launched in Florence

1953
Norman Hartnell designs Queen Elizabeth II coronation gown

1954
Chanel reestablishes couture business (closed since 1939); Dior H-Line; Bermuda shorts popular, first for men, later for women

1957
Balenciaga Chemise or "Sack"; Dior's death; appointment of Saint Laurent as Dior designer

1958
McCardell awarded Coty Hall of Fame posthumously in year of her death

1961
Kennedy inauguration, with Jacqueline Kennedy pillbox hat by Halston; *Breakfast at Tiffany's* film with Audrey Hepburn wardrobe by Givenchy

1962
Karl Lagerfeld designs Fendi furs

1963
First Geoffrey Beene collection

1964
Gernreich topless bathing suit

1965
Saint Laurent Mondrian dress

1965-66
Quant and Courrèges miniskirts

1966
Nehru jackets for men, first by Cardin

1967
Gernreich on cover of *Time*

1968
Balenciaga retirement; Calvin Klein establishes business; Saint Laurent transparent blouse

1970
Miyake Design studio established; Kenzo opens Jungle JAP Boutique, Paris

1971
Death of Chanel; Vivienne Westwood "Let It Rock" collection; jeans on Warhol/Rolling Stones album cover *Sticky Fingers*; Diane Von Furstenberg wrap dress

1972

Norell retrospective, Metropolitan Museum of Art, and designer's death

1973

Balenciaga exhibition, first directed by Diana Vreeland, at Metropolitan Museum of Art; "The T-shirt is the year's number one counter-culture status symbol." —*Women's Wear Daily*

1974

First Armani menswear collection; death of Anne Klein, Donna Karan and Louis Dell'Olio direct design; Beverly Johnson is first black woman on cover of *Vogue* (USA)

1977

Carter White House: President in cardigan and jeans; *Annie Hall* with Diane Keaton wearing clothes by Ralph Lauren; Stephen Burows wins Coty Award

1979-82

Designer ("status") jeans

1980

First Alaia collection; Calvin Klein/Richard Avedon advertising with Brooke Shields

1982

Rei Kawakubo "lace sweater" for Comme des Garçons

1983

Karl Lagerfeld begins at Chanel

1984

Perry Ellis collection inspired by Sonia Delaunay; Katharine Hamnett wears protest T-shirt to 10 Downing Street

1985

Donna Karan established

1987

Patou by Lacroix pouf dresses; Lacroix initiates his own business; bicycle messenger chic

1988

Council of Fashion Designers of America (CFDA) Lifetime Achievement award to Nancy Reagan

1992

Versace "bondage" collection; Donna Karan "cold shoulders" dress

1993

Gaultier "hasidim" collection

1995

Givenchy retirement; Versace Atelier polyvinyl-chloride transparent dresses; Calvin Klein "kids" advertising withdrawn

Abboud, Joseph

American designer

Born   *Boston, Massachusetts, 5 May 1950.*

Education   *Studied comparative literature, University of Massachusetts, Boston, 1968-72; also studied at the Sorbonne.*

Family   *Married Lynn Weinstein, 6 June 1976; children: Lila Faith, Ari Rachel.*

Career   *Buyer, then director of merchandise, Louis of Boston, 1968-80; designer, Southwick, 1980; associate director of menswear design, Polo/Ralph Lauren, New York, 1980-84; launched signature menswear collection, 1986; designer, Barry Bricken, New York, 1987-88. J.A. (Joseph Abboud) Apparel Corporation, a joint venture with GFT USA, formed, 1988; Joseph Abboud Womenswear and menswear collection of tailored clothing and furnishings introduced, 1990; opened first retail store, Boston, 1990; collections first shown in Europe, 1990; JA II line introduced, 1991; fragrance line introduced in Japan, 1992, in America, 1993; introduced J.O.E. (Just One Earth) sportswear line, 1992; designed wardrobes for male television announcers for 1992 Winter Olympics, Albertville, France, 1992; Joseph Abboud Environments bed and bath collection launched, 1993; Joseph Abboud Fragrance launched, 1994.*

Awards   *Cutty Sark Award, 1988; Woolmark Award, 1988; Menswear Designer of the Year Award from Council of Fashion Designers of America Award, 1989, 1990; honored by Japanese Government in conjunction with the Association of Total Fashion in Osaka, 1993; Special Achievement Award from Neckwear Association of America Inc., 1994.*

Address   *650 Fifth Avenue, New York, New York 10019, USA.*

Joseph Abboud has said that his clothing is as much about lifestyle as design. Since 1986, after breaking away from Ralph Lauren, he has filled a niche in the fashion world with his creations for both men and, more recently, for women. For the contemporary individual seeking a façade that is as casual, elegant, and as international as the accompanying life, the Abboud

Joseph Abboud: Spring 1995; band-collar jacket, linen bib-front shirt, and crochet vest.
Photograph by Randall Mesdon.

wardrobe offers comfort, beauty, and a modernity that is equally suitable in New York, Milan, or Australia. Abboud was the first menswear designer in the United States to revolutionize the concept of American style.

Born in Boston, Abboud is hardly provincial. Something of an outsider, he did not come to fashion through the usual design school training and had no pre-established world in which to fit. Instead he made his own. His approach to fashion was via studies in comparative literature, followed by study at the Sorbonne in Paris. His fall 1990 menswear collection, Grand Tour, pays homage to that experience with its romantic 1930s and 1940s designs, reminiscent of Hemingway, while his own rich ethnic background provided the depth of appreciation for global culture inherent in his work. Coming of age in the 1960s, Abboud began collecting early Turkish *kilims* (flat woven rugs) with their salient handcrafted quality and stylized geometric patterns. These motifs form a recurring theme in his work, from the handknit sweaters to the machine knit shirts. The rugs themselves, in muted earthtones, complement the calm, natural environment of the Abboud stores. For Abboud, the presentation of the clothing mimics the aesthetics of the garments: soft, casual, and elegant in its simplicity.

Color, texture, and the cut of Abboud fashions express a style that lies between, and sometimes overlaps, that of Ralph Lauren and Giorgio Armani. The palette of the Joseph Abboud and the 1992 J.O.E. (Just One Earth) lines for both sexes is more subtle than the traditional Anglo-American colors of the preppie or Sloane Ranger genre, yet more varied in tone and hue than the sublimely unstated Armani colors. Neutrals from burnt sienna to cream, stucco, straw, and the colors of winter birch, together with naturals such as indigo and faded burgundy, are examples of some of the most alluring of Abboud dyestuffs.

The Pacific Northwest Collection, fall 1987, manifested rich hues, from black to maroon, but even these were harmonious, never ostentatious. The black of his leather jackets, fall 1992, appears like soft patches of the night sky due to the suppleness and unique surface treatment of the skins. The fabrics for Abboud designs represent the artist's diligent search for the world's finest materials and craftsmanship. His respect for textile traditions does not mean that his work is retrospective but that his inventiveness is grounded in the integrity of the classics. His interpretation of tweed, for example, although based on fine Scottish wool weavings, which he compares to the most beautiful artistic landscapes, differs from the conventional Harris-type tweed. Silk, alpaca, or llama are occasionally combined with the traditional wool to yield a lighter fabric.

Unique and demanding in his working methods, Abboud is at the forefront of contemporary fashion-fabric design. His fabrics drape with a grace and elegance that is enhanced by the oversize cut and fluid lines of his suits. His characteristically full, double-pleated trousers, for example, are luxurious. The romantic malt mohair gossamer-like fabrics for women in the fall 1993 collection are cut simply with no extraneous details. Even the intricate embroideries that ornament the surfaces of many of his most memorable designs, from North African suede vests with a Kashmiri *boteh* design to the jewel-like beadwork for evening, have a wearability uncommon in the contemporary artistic fashion.

Nature is Abboud's muse. Beyond the obvious J.O.E. line appellation, the theme of the bucolic environment provides inspiration for the garments. Country stone walls, pebbles on a beach, the light and earthtones of the Southwest are interpreted in exquisitely cut fabrics that embrace the body with a style that becomes an individual's second skin.—MARIANNE CARLANO

Adolfo

American designer

Born *Adolfo F. Sardiña in Cardenas, Cuba, 15 February 1933.*

Education *B.A., St. Ignacious de Loyola Jesuit School, Havana, 1950. Immigrated to New York, 1948, naturalized, 1958.*

Military Service *Served in the United States Navy.*

Career *Apprentice millinery designer, Bergdorf Goodman, 1948-51; apprentice milliner at Cristobal Balenciaga Salon, Paris, 1950-52, and at Bergdorf Goodman, New York; designed millinery as Adolfo of Emme, 1951-58; also worked as unpaid apprentice for Chanel fashion house, Paris, 1956-57; apprenticed in Paris with Balenciaga; established own millinery salon in New York, 1962, later expanding into women's custom clothing; designer, Adolfo Menswear and Adolfo Scarves, from 1978. Perfume Adolfo launched, 1978. Closed custom workroom to concentrate on his Adolfo Enterprises licensing business, 1993.*

Exhibitions *Fashion: An Anthology, Victoria & Albert Museum, London, 1971.*

Collections *Metropolitan Museum of Art, New York; Smithsonian Institution, Washington, D.C.; Dallas Museum of Fine Arts; Los Angeles County Museum of Art.*

Awards *Coty Fashion Award, New York, 1955, 1969; Neiman Marcus Award, 1956. Member of the Council of Fashion Designers of America.*

To make clothes that are long-lasting and with subtle changes from season to season—this is my philosophy.—Adolfo

In April of 1993, Adolfo closed his salon on New York's East 57th Street, after more than 25 years of producing his classically elegant knit suits, dresses, and eveningwear. The outcry from his clientèle was emotional and indicative of the devotion that his clothes inspired in his "ladies":

"It's just a tragedy for me. He has such great taste, style, and manners. I don't know what I'm going to do. I've been wearing his clothes for years; they suit my lifestyle. He designs for a certain way of life that all these new designers don't seem to comprehend."—C.Z. Guest

"I'm devastated. . . . It's terrible. I adore him. He's the sweetest most talented man. You know when ladies say, 'Oh I just don't know what I'm going to wear!' With Adolfo, you always have the right thing to wear."—Jean Tailer.

These loyal clients were among the many who returned to Adolfo season after season for clothes that they could wear year after year, clothes that looked stylish and felt comfortable, style and comfort being the essence of his customers' elegant and effortless lifestyle.

Adolfo began his career as a milliner in the early 1950s, a time when hat designers were accorded as much respect and attention as dress designers. By 1955, he had received the Coty Fashion Award for his innovative, often dramatic hat designs for Emmé Millinery. In 1962, Adolfo opened his own salon and began to design clothes to show with his hat collection. During this period as women gradually began to wear hats less often, Adolfo's hat designs became progressively bolder. His design point of view was that hats should be worn as an accessory

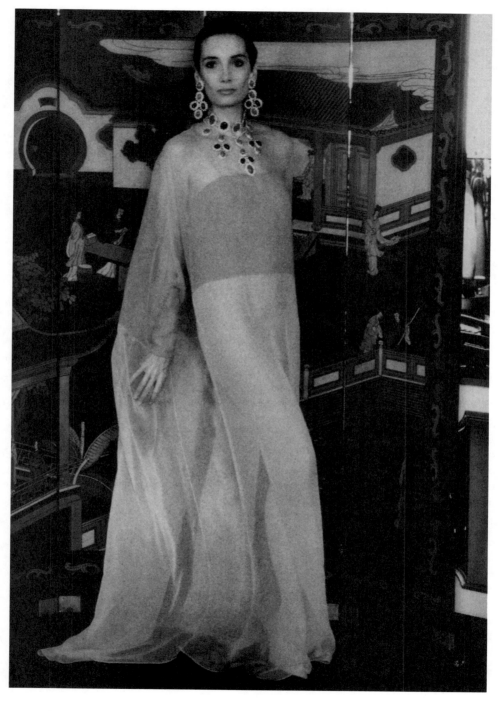

Adolfo: Yellow to red mousseline, round-neck, long-cuffed sleeve caftan and red slip.

rather than a necessity, and this attitude was carried over into his clothing designs as well. His clothes of the late 1960s had the idiosyncratic quality characteristic of the period and, most importantly, each piece stood out on its own as a special item. This concept of design was incongruous with the American sportswear idea of coordinated separates but was consistent with the sensibility of his wealthy customers who regarded clothes, like precious jewelry, as adornments and indicators of their social status. Among the garments that captured the attention of clients and press during this period were felt capes, red, yellow, or purple velvet bolero jackets embroidered with jet beads and black braid, studded lace-up peasant vests, low-cut floral overalls worn over organdy blouses, and extravagant patchwork evening looks.

Adolfo remarked, in 1968, that "today, one has to dress in bits and pieces—the more the merrier." By 1969, he described his clothes as being "for a woman's fun and fantasy moods—I don't think the classic is appealing to people any more." Just one year later, however, he changed his point of view and at the same time increased the focus of his knits that had been introduced in 1969. In a review of Adolfo's fall 1970 collection Eugenia Sheppard, writing in the *New York Post,* declared that "he has completely abandoned the costume look of previous years." Adolfo was always responsive to his customers' needs and this sudden change of direction probably reflected their reaction to the social upheavals and excesses of the last years of the 1960s.

By the early 1970s, the 1930s look, inspired by films such as *Bonnie and Clyde* and *The Damned,* swept over fashion, drowning out the kooky individualism of seasons past. His explorations of this look led Adolfo, in 1973, to hit on what would become his signature item. Taking his cue from Coco Chanel's cardigan style suits of the 1930s, Adolfo translated the textured tweed into a pebbly knit, added a matching silk blouse, and came up with a formula that his clients came to him for over and over again until his recent retirement. These revivals of a classic became classics in their own right and the look became associated, in America, with Adolfo as much as with Chanel. Adolfo's collections were not limited to suits. When other American designers abandoned dresses for day in favor of sportswear separates, Adolfo continued to provide his customers with printed silk dresses appropriate for luncheons and other dressy daytime occasions. Adolfo's clients also relied on him for splendid eveningwear that often combined luxury with practicality. Typical evening looks included sweater knit tops with full satin or taffeta skirts, fur trimmed knit cardigans, silk pyjamas, and angora caftans.

The designer has remarked that "an Adolfo lady should look simple, classic, and comfortable." Adolfo brought those modest and characteristically American design ideals to a higher level of luxury and charm, combining quality and style with comfort and ease.—ALAN E. ROSENBERG

Adrian, Gilbert

American designer

Born *Gilbert Adrian Greenburgh in Naugatuck, Connecticut, 3 March 1903.*

Education *Studied at Parsons School of Design, New York and Paris, c.1921-22.*

Family *Married Janet Gaynor in 1939; son: Robin.*

Career *Film and theater designer, New York, 1921-28; designer, MGM studios, Holly-wood, 1928-39; ready-to-wear and custom clothing salon established, Beverly Hills,*

Gilbert Adrian: Jean Harlow in Adrian's bias-cut gown from the film *Dinner at Eight* (1933).
Photograph: MGM, courtesy of The Kobal Collection.

1942-52; fragrances Saint and Sinner introduced, 1946; New York boutique opened, 1948; retired to Brasilia, Brazil, 1952-58; film designer, Los Angeles, 1958-59.

Exhibitions *Retrospective, Los Angeles County Museum, c.1967; retrospective, Fashion Institute of Technology, New York, 1971.*

Awards *Coty American Fashion Critics Award, 1944.*

Died *(in Los Angeles, California) 14 September 1959.*

By the time MGM costumer Gilbert Adrian went into business for himself in the middle of World War II, his potential customers were already familiar with his work. For over a decade American women had been wearing copies of the clothes he had designed for some of the most famous movie stars of all time. Adrian's ability to develop a screen character through the progression of costumes, be they period or modern, was translated into costuming the modern woman for her new role as career woman while men were away at war.

Adrian was primarily an artist, having trained in France, and was able to perceive Greta Garbo's true personality—aloof, mysterious, earthy—and change the way the studios dressed her, insisting upon genuine silks, laces, and jewels to lend authenticity to her performances. For all the stars he dressed, Adrian believed that the quality of materials that a woman wore affected how she behaved in the clothes, even if the details were not immediately obvious. He brought the same philosophy to his custom and ready-to-wear creations. Of course the copies MGM permitted to be made of Adrian's costumes, timed to coincide with the releases of the films, were not always of the same fine quality as the originals, but the overall looks were what women were after. While films provided a great escape from the dreariness of the American Depression, a dress such as the famous white organdy with wide ruffled sleeves that Adrian designed for Joan Crawford in the movie *Letty Lynton* offered cheer and flattery. Macy's New York department store alone sold nearly half a million copies in 1932. The artist's eye perceived the need to balance Crawford's wide hips, thus the broad shouldered typical "Adrian silhouette" started a fashion revolution in America and abroad.

For Jean Harlow in *Dinner at Eight,* Adrian created another widely copied sheer white bias-cut satin ballgown. Though Madeleine Vionnet invented the bias cut and Elsa Schiaparelli was credited with padded shoulders, at least in Europe, Adrian had the awareness to bring high fashion and glamor to the screen. Joan Crawford praised Adrian's emphasis on simplicity to make a dramatic point, as in the suits she wore in her later films. Even in lavishly costumed period dramas, Adrian was able to stop short of excess. Often, as in Garbo's *Mata Hari,* the character's evolution into purity of spirit would be expressed through increased simplicity of costume. Adrian's understanding of light and shadow made possible dress that, due to clarity of line, looked as well in monochrome film, as later black and white photographs of his commercial designs would show. His eye for perfect cut was impeccable. A day suit consisting of a beige wool jacket trimmed with loops of black braid, paired with a slim black skirt, black gloves, and beige cartwheel hat, looks as crisp and smart today as it did when featured in *Vogue* in 1946. Fluid floor-length crêpe gowns would dramatically yet whimsically be decorated with asymmetrical motifs of horses, cherubs, or piano keys, or else his taste for modern art would be indulged in gowns made up of abstract jigsaw puzzle shapes in several colors.

Just as in films Adrian worked within themes, so did his collections for Adrian, Ltd. develop according to such themes as Grecian, Persian, Gothic, Spanish, or Americana. For the latter he appliquéd Pennsylvania Dutch designs on gowns and made tailored suits and bustled evening gowns out of checked gingham, echoing the gingham checks worn by Judy Garland in *The Wizard of Oz*. Adrian costumed Garbo as the essence of romance in *Camille*, not only in 19th-century crinolines, but in a death scene white nightgown which could have been any female viewer's late day dinner dress. For his average American customer, Adrian recommended clothes like the "costumes worn by the heroines of light comedies laid in moderate-sized towns." Katharine Hepburn in *The Philadelphia Story* was dressed by Adrian as the ideal girl next door, while conservative Norma Shearer in *The Women* mirrored the sophisticated simplicity of Adrian's future well-heeled Beverly Hills clients.

The spare, padded-shouldered, narrow waisted and skirted silhouette of the 1940s was the ideal medium for Adrian's artistry with fabric, while conforming to the wartime L-85 restrictions on materials—the U.S. government limitation on the amount of fabric used in a civilian garment for public consumption. The color inserts, appliqués, mitering of striped fabrics and combinations of materials in one ensemble allowed for savings in rationed fabrics, while creating the trademark Adrian look that was desired then and is still sought after by vintage clothing collectors. Old time movie glamor would resurface in some of Adrian's elegant columns of crêpe, diagonally embellished by beaded bands of ancient motifs, or thick gilt embroidery on dark backgrounds. Diagonal lines and asymmetry also lent interest, as in a short sleeved wartime suit that was sewn half of plaid fabric—one sleeve and half the bodice culminating in a bow at the opposite hip, the other half of plain wool—completed by a hat trimmed with the plaid used as edging. Having grown up observing his father's millinery trade, Adrian had included hats in his movie stars' costumes, such widely copied designs as Garbo's slouch, cloche, and Eugenie in the 1930s.

Adrian unsuccessfully resisted Dior's round-shouldered New Look. Women returned to the home. Thirty years later, with the resurgence of women into the workforce, Adrian's broad shouldered looks enabled women to compete confidently with men, as designers resurrected the masterpieces of this truly American fashion virtuoso.—THERESE DUZINKIEWICZ BAKER

Agnès B
French designer

Born Born Agnès Troublé in Versailles, France, 26 November 1941.

Family Married Christian Bourgois, 1958 (divorced); married Jean René Claret de Fleurieu, 1980; has five children from her marriages.

Career Junior fashion editor, Elle magazine, Paris, 1964; designer, press attaché and buyer for Dorothée Bis, Paris, 1965-66; free-lance designer for Limitex, Pierre d'Alby, V de V and Eversbin, Paris, 1966-75; set up CMC (Comptoir Mondial de Création) holding company for Agnès B., 1975; established first Agnès B. boutique in Les Halles, Paris, April 1975; opened second-hand shop in same street as boutique, 1977; created American subsidiary of CMC, and first American boutique in SoHo, New York, 1980; opened men and childrens' boutique Agnès B. Enfant, Paris, 1981; licence with Les Trois Suisses for mail order of selected items, 1982; opened Agnès B. "Lolita" boutique for teenagers, also opened la Galerie du Jour art gallery/bookshop, Paris, with ex-husband, 1984; launched perfume, Le B, skincare and cosmetics range and also a maternity collection, 1987; launched ranges of sunglasses and watches, 1989; launched perfume for children, Le petit *b.b., 1990; launch of perfume Courant d'air, 1992; has also established many shops in France and worldwide, including 26 in Japan, two in London, and four in USA.*

Collections *Musée des Arts de la Mode, Paris; Musée du Louvre, Paris.*

Awards *Order of Merit for Export, Paris.*

Address *17 rue Dieu, 75010 Paris, France.*

Agnès B. is a French sportswear designer who has catapulted herself to fame by challenging the need for fashion in clothing design. She denies that clothes must be stylized, highly detailed, and ephemeral in order to catch the public imagination. Her ascent began in the mid-1970s when, after only a few years in the fashion business, first as junior editor at *Elle* magazine and then briefly as an assistant to Dorothée Bis, she opened her own boutique in a converted butcher shop in Les Halles, Paris, to sell recut and redyed French workers' uniforms, black leather blazers, and T-shirts in striped rugby fabric. Her reputation grew as one of the first young French clothing designers to sell fashion to those who do not want to look too fashionable. In fact, her clothes, while identifiably French in their no-nonsense cut, simple, subdued colors (often black), and casual mood, have a timeless quality that keeps them current. The wrinkling common to natural materials and the already worn look that characterized the hippie ethos were translated by Agnès B. into a timeless chic, combining common sense with flair.

In the age of name identification and personal marketing, Agnès B. is as respected for her business sense as for her relaxed fashion designs. The spontaneous, childlike hand with which she quickly fashioned the logo for her stores belies a sophisticated business sense. Retaining her own independent boutique rather than being swallowed up in larger department stores, she astutely perceived that the non-design of her clothes was too inconspicuous, that they would blend in with other, trendier lines and be lost. She has opened over a dozen shops in France, of which seven are in Paris, with branches in Amsterdam, London, Tokyo, and the United States: two in New York, one in Boston, and one in Los Angeles.

Her understated approach to design for real people (men and children, as well as women) extends to her shows, which she calls working sessions, where professional models are rarely used, and her stores, in which casual and friendly salespeople mix their own antique or mod clothes with her separates. All the stores exude the same comfortable look, with pale wooden floors, white walls, and the occasional decorative tile. The flimsy curtain that separates the display area from the communal dressing rooms is an implication of the marginal distinction between Agnès B. clothes and what everyone else is wearing.

Agnès B. strikes a commercial and creative balance—a radical chic. "I have no desire to dress an elite," she states. "It's all a game. I work as if I were still in my grandmother's attic, dressing up. Clothes aren't everything. When they become too important, when they hide the person wearing them, then I don't like them. Clothes should make you feel happy, relaxed, and ready to tackle other problems."—SARAH BODINE

Alaia, Azzedine

French designer

Born *Tunis, Tunisia, c.1940.*

Education *Studied sculpture, École des Beaux-Arts, Tunis.*

Career *Dressmaker's assistant, Tunis, then dressed private clients before moving to Paris in 1957; part-time design assistant, Guy Laroche, Thierry Mugler, 1957-59; also housekeeper and dressmaker for the Marquise de Mazan, 1957-60, and for Comtesse Nicole de Blégiers, 1960-65; designer, custom clothing, from 1960; introduced ready-to-wear line, Paris, 1980, and New York, 1982; opened boutiques, Beverly Hills, 1983, Paris, 1985, and New York, 1988-92.*

Exhibitions *Retrospective, Bordeaux Museum of Modern Art, 1984-85.*

Awards *French Ministry of Culture Designer of the Year Award, 1985.*

Address *7 rue de Moussy, 75002 Paris, France.*

Dubbed the King of Cling by the fashion press in the 1980s, Azzedine Alaia inspired a host of looks that energized high street fashion, including the stretch mini, Lycra cycling shorts, and the body suit.

His designs were renowned for the display of the female body they afforded and, accordingly, bedecked the bodies of off-duty top models and stars such as Tina Turner, Raquel Welch, and Brigitte Nielson. Alaia's clothes caught the mood of the times when many women had turned to exercise and a new, muscled body shape had begun to appear in the pages of fashion magazines. Many women wanted to flaunt their newly toned bodies, helped by recent developments in fabric construction that enabled designers to create clothing that would accentuate the female form in a way unprecedented in European fashion.

Following in the footsteps of the *ancien régime* of Parisian haute couture, Alaia is a perfectionist about cut, drape, and construction, preferring to work directly onto the body to achieve a perfect fit. Tailoring is his great strength—he does all his own cutting—and, although his clothes appear very simple, they are complex in structure. Some garments contain up to 40 individual pieces linked together to form a complex mesh that moves and undulates with the body. The beauty of his design comes from the shape and fit of the garments, enhanced by his innovative use of criss-cross seaming.

His method of clothing construction includes repeated fitting and cutting on the body. His technique of sculpting and draping owes much to Madeleine Vionnet, the great *tailleur* of the 1920s, famed for the intricacies of her bias-cut crêpe dresses that moulded closely to the body. Vionnet applied the delicate techniques of lingerie sewing to outerwear, as has Alaia, who combines the stitching and seaming normally used in corsetry to achieve the perfect fit of his clothes. Combined with elasticated fabrics for maximum body exposure, his garments hold and control the body yet retain their shape.

Although at first sight his clothes seem to cling closely to the natural silhouette of the wearer, they actually create a second skin, holding in and shaping the body by techniques of construction such as faggoting. This body consciousness is further enhanced by using materials, such as stretch lace over flesh-coloured fabric, to give an illusion, rather than the reality, of nudity.

Alaia introduced his first ready-to-wear collection of minimalist clothes in 1980, and continued to work privately for individual customers until the mid-1980s. Although his clothes are indebted to the perfection of the female body, and indeed at times expose great expanses of skin, he manages to avoid vulgarity with muted colours and expert tailoring.

Based in Paris, Alaia shows regularly but nevertheless seems above the whims and vagaries of the fashion world, producing timeless garments rather than designing new looks from season to season, and inspiring the adulation from enthusiastic collectors that was once reserved for Mariano Fortuny.—CAROLINE COX

Albini, Walter

Italian designer

Born *Born Gualtiero Albini in Busto Arsizio, near Milan, 9 March 1941.*

Education *Studied fashion and costume design, Istituto Statale di Belle Arti e Moda, Turin, 1959-61.*

Career *Illustrator for Novità and Corriere Lombardo periodicals, Milan, and free-lance sketch artist, Paris, 1961-64; free-lance designer for Krizia, Billy Ballo, Basile, Callaghan, Escargots, Mister Fox, Diamantis, Trell, Mario Ferari, Lanerossi, Kriziamaglia, Montedoro, and Princess Luciana, Milan, 1964-83; established Walter Albini fashion house, Milan, 1965; signature ready-to-wear collection introduced, 1978; Walter Albini Fashions branches established, London, Rome, Venice.*

Died *(in Milan) 31 May 1983.*

In William Shakespeare's *Richard II*, "report of fashions in proud Italy" are the vanguard for what comes to England only in "base imitation." Walter Albini epitomizes the brilliant epoch of Italian fashion in the 1970s, when it seized the international imagination. At least as much as any other designer, if not more, Albini had the Italian spirit *con brio*. Journalists compared him to Yves Saint Laurent and Karl Lagerfeld, designers whose careers outlasted Albini's flash of brilliance. Albini brought his obsession with the 1920s and 1930s to the elongated line and youthful energy of the 1970s; his collections of 1969 and 1970 tell the story of his encapsulation of the time: Gymnasium and Gypsy and China in 1969; Antique Market, The Pre-Raphaelites, Safari, Military, and Polaroid in 1970.

Sadly, Albini so brilliantly embodies the 1970s for Italy (as one would perhaps say of Halston in the United States) because of the détente of his work by 1980 and his death in 1983, just after his forty-second birthday. His Gatsby-like style and passion for life were fulfilled in prodigious achievement—once even, in five simultaneous collections, in romantic brevity, and in the youthful exuberance immortalized by his early death.

Isa Vercelloni and Flavio Lucchini described Albini's mercurial and gifted personality and habits: "From adolescence he still retains the capacity of dreaming, but with the ability of giving body or a semblance of reality to his world of dreams. He has the rare quality of even doing this without spoiling it. This is why women like his dresses so much. They recognize immediately that imagination is given power" (*Milano Fashion*, Milan 1975). It was a wide-ranging imagination, indicative of the 1970s in its travelogue-inspired wanderlust, that captured the vivacity of Diana Vreeland's *Vogue* of the 1960s. Like Vreeland, Albini loved the 1920s and extolled the freedom of women and reminded them of their liberation during that period. Also like Vreeland, Albini was smitten with North Africa and the potential for exoticism. He played with paisley and was fascinated by the pattern and design asymmetry as well as the mysterious women of China. His pragmatic exoticism is evident in a spring 1980 T-blouse and party skirt combination, described in advertising copy in *Harper's Bazaar* (March 1980) as "the mystique of madras. A bit sophisticated for midnight at the oasis . . . but divine for sunset on the patio."

So many collections were produced in his own name and others between the late 1960s and 1980 that he touched upon many themes, but he returned consistently to the 1920s and 1930s. He had moved to Paris because of a lifetime preoccupation with Chanel, whom he had glimpsed during her late years, but he more substantively used her as a touchstone for his collections. His fall 1978 knits, as photographed by David Bailey, intensified the luxury of Chanel tailoring, although slightly oversized, in a palette of bronze and browns. For his Mister Fox line in beautiful geometrics, he approximated Sonia Delaunay, but echoed the feeling of Chanel. His movie and fashion magazine passions would encompass Katharine Hepburn and Marlene Dietrich, but for Albini these merely confirmed the role of Chanel in freeing women to be comfortable in sportswear- and menswear-derived styles that were luxuriously tailored for women.

Besides Chanel, Albini's other passion was for ancient Egypt, for which he felt mystical affinity and which served as an inspiration for his men's and women's fashions—especially his fashion drawings. By the mid-1970s, Albini's style was predominately an amalgam of ancient Egyptian motifs (although often attributed elsewhere in the East) and Chanel, using the Chanel suits and proportions with the accommodations of wrapping *à la Egyptienne* and the excuses of Venice, North Africa, and India for billowing harem pants and other pantaloons of which Chanel would scarcely have approved. In 1978 a riding skirt, with its fluid drape, was teamed with a short cropped jacket, combining tradition with contemporary 1970s style.

In some ways, Albini was the precursor of Gianni Versace. His intensely personal style respected many historical exemplars and was passionately defended and highly expressive. Like Versace, Albini combined a studious infatuation with the past with a passion for his own synthesis of styles and a comprehensive style attainment and conviction that was his own; he created this with a fervor approaching fanaticism that reinforced the sense of abiding adolescence and keenest ebullience for the work.

Vercelloni and Lucchini asked Albini what his motto was. He said, "Enjoy today and leave unpleasant things for tomorrow." For Albini and the extravagant fashion that he created, fate held no tomorrow and no unpleasantness.—RICHARD MARTIN

Alfaro, Victor

American designer

Born *Mexico, c.1965.*

Education *Attended Univeristy of Texas, 1982; graduated from Fashion Institute of Technology, 1987. Immigrated to the United States, 1981.*

Career *Assistant to Mary Ann Restivo, late 1980s, and Joseph Abboud, 1990; established own business, early 1990s.*

Awards *Best new talent award, 1995, Council of Fashion Designers of America.*

Address *130 Barrow Street, New York, NY 10014, USA.*

Bare simplicity and an equally frank sexuality inform Victor Alfaro's dresses for cocktail and evening. Bridget Foley predicted in *W* (March 1994): "The heir apparent to Oscar and Bill?

Perhaps. Victor Alfaro may be New York's next great eveningwear designer." If Alfaro is the torchbearer of style for New York nights, his role betokens a shifting sensibility, one that pointedly exalts the body and seeks out youth and one that takes risks. Skilled in the vocabulary of separates (he worked for Mary Ann Restivo and Joseph Abboud), Alfaro eagerly draws upon the street for inspiration and demands a body consciousness that has made some call him the American Alaïa. In a first recognition as designer for celebrities, photographed by Francesco Scavullo for covers of *Cosmopolitan* in New York, Alfaro flirted with attention-getting vulgarity, though his collections have come to represent a more natural, but nonetheless wilfully seductive, sensuality.

Amy Spindler reported in the *New York Times* (2 April 1993), "Victor Alfaro's clothes come with plenty of attitude." The attitude is, of course, of post-feminist women's individuality and options, including a very 1990s reexamination of the possibilities of seductive, relatively bare clothing in the most luxurious fabrics. One needs a self-confidence approaching attitude to wear dresses and outfits of such body-revealing form, but one also needs a distinct segregation of Alfaro's partywear from day-to-day clothing. His clothes are not for the timid, but neither are they for showgirls. Amy Spindler refers to his "sex-kitten clothes," but their relative austerity, depending entirely upon textile and shape, keeps them from being vitiated by Las Vegas.

In fact, Alfaro raises provocative issues of women's overt and self-assured physicality and sexuality more than of sexual license. To be sure, short skirts, bared shoulders, lace in direct contact with skin, leather notes, and sheer, skimming fabrics suggest fetishes, but there is always something strangely wholesome about Alfaro's sensibility. The singer Mariah Carey is quoted as saying very aptly that Alfaro's "clothes are fierce." Their ferocity resides in the fact that they define strong women.

According to Ricky Lee (*New York Times,* 2 August 1992), Alfaro was counseled by one buyer from Chicago that in order to succeed he should add more suits to his line. But Alfaro rightly declined, knowing that he is not creating professional clothes or daywear basics. He eschews sobriety and, with it, tailoring. Rather, he is responding to sexuality's siren and creating the sexiest siren dresses for young New Yorkers of the 1990s. He is dressmaker to the legendary "Generation X." At least at this moment, Alfaro is defining a strong personal style and a clientèle that is generationally, visually, and libidinously nurtured on MTV and informed by multicultural street smarts. Woody Hochswender reported in the *New York Times* (9 April 1992) that Alfaro's collection "suggested sex—in a voice loud enough to clear a disco. There were lace chaps and fake snake chaps, worn over bodysuits. Skintight snakeskin jeans were zipped all the way from front to back, reason unknown. Rib-knit sweater dresses were worn with harnesses of metal mesh, Mr Alfaro's version of the bondage look that is sweeping fashion."

Explaining his relative restraint and deliberate avoidance of vulgarity in his fall/winter 1993-94 collection to Bridget Foley, Alfaro explained: "I didn't want it to look cheap. Buyers see every trick in the book, and they want clothes that are wearable." Alfaro has consistently made unencumbered clothing, emphasizing minimalist sensibility and cut and employing luxurious materials. In these characteristics, he is a designer in the great American tradition. His distinctive deviation from that tradition might seem to be his hot sexuality, the body-tracing and body-revealing simplicity of his clothes. But again and again 20th-century American designers have been dressing advanced new women of ever-increasing power and self-assurance.

Alfaro is creating the post-feminist fashion sensibility, consummately beautiful in execution, infinitely skilled in construction, and assertively avant-garde. Even as some critics dismiss his work as offensive, Alfaro is a true fashion risk-taker and visionary. He is defining and dressing today, and will dress hereafter, the bravest woman of the future.—RICHARD MARTIN

Allard, Linda

American designer

Born *Akron, Ohio, 27 May 1940; grew up in Doylestown.*

Education *Studied Fine Arts, Kent State University, Kent, Ohio, 1958-62.*

Career *Design assistant, Ellen Tracy, New York, 1962-64, then director of design, from 1964; Linda Allard label introduced, 1984; design critic, Fashion Institute of Technology, New York; visiting professor, International Academy of Merchandising and Design, Chicago; board of directors, Kent State University; member of The Fashion Group International, Inc., Council of Fashion Designers of America.*

Awards *Dallas Fashion Award, 1986, 1987.*

Address *575 Seventh Avenue, New York, NY 10018, USA.*

Linda Allard is the woman behind Ellen Tracy. In fact, there is no Ellen Tracy—there never was. The company was founded in 1949 by Herbert Gallen, a juniors blouse manufacturer, who invented the name Ellen Tracy for his fledgling firm. Gallen hired Allard in 1962, fresh out of college, as a design assistant. Quickly, she expanded the line to include trousers and jackets. Two years later, she was made director of design and a new Ellen Tracy was born. Since then, under Allard's artistic leadership, Ellen Tracy has become synonymous with top quality fabrics, clean lines, and the concept of a complete wardrobe for the working woman.

Linda Allard grew up in Doyleston, Ohio in a hundred-year-old farmhouse with five brothers and sisters. Like many women Allard was taught to sew at the age of ten by her mother and quickly began designing garments for her dolls. "Even before I could sew, I was always designing clothes for my paper dolls," she said. After receiving a Fine Arts degree from Kent State University in 1962, she moved to New York, where she received her first job offer from Gallen.

Shortly after Allard joined the firm, Ellen Tracy moved away from junior clothing to apparel designed for the newly established female workforce of the 1960s. Allard was one of the first designers to address the new shifting demographics, creating a professional look, stylish yet appropriate for the workplace. Eventually, by the mid-1970s, the company moved into the bridge market. The bridge collections—which fill the gap between upper-end designer lines and mass-market brands—have since become the fastest-growing area of the women's fashion market, key to Ellen Tracy's success, with the company's volume nearly tripling over the following decade.

As the creative force behind Ellen Tracy, Allard has transformed the company into one of the key anchor designers in the bridge market. To give the collection more of a designer feel, Allard's name was placed on the Ellen Tracy label in 1984. Nonetheless, Allard believes high fashion has little relevance to most women's lives. "The extreme end of fashion is over-rated," she said. "It gets a lot of coverage by the press, but it doesn't mean anything to a lot of women. We mean more to real women."

Linda Allard for Ellen Tracy: Fall 1996.

Today, working with a 12-person design team, Allard is responsible for the entire Ellen Tracy line. For Allard, designing begins with an emphasis on high-quality fabrics and specific color grouping. "We start with color and a sense of the flavor of the collection. Will it be fluid or rigid, soft and slouchy or tailored? The focus is on easy dressing and effortless shapes. We develop the fabrics first, finding the texture that expresses the attitude we feel, and then comes the styling. Fabrics make the collection unique." There are three Ellen Tracy collections each year. To ensure the clothes work well with each other, each garment is sold separately. "The modern woman buys a wardrobe of jackets that work well in a variety of pairings," says Allard.

One of the keys to Allard's success has been her ability to diversify. In 1981, Ellen Tracy launched a petites division and in 1985 a successful dress division. To cater to the more leisure-oriented customer, Ellen Tracy launched its latest extension, a sportswear line, Company, in the fall of 1991. Allard says her intent is to provide "the same level of quality for the woman who doesn't need strictly career clothes, or whose career offers more fashion choices than the tailored suits we're known for." In 1993, the company introduced a large-sizes division and sophisticated evening dress collection. A perfume line was launched in 1992. Ellen Tracy also has licensing agreements to produce scarves, shoes, eyewear, hosiery, and handbags.

Allard lives and works in Manhattan and spends weekends in her new country home in Washington, Connecticut set on 60 acres of rolling countryside. She designed the house with her brother David Allard, an architect. The house is a 5,500 square feet Palladian-inspired villa, complete with studio and guest quarters. "When we were designing my new house, I challenged my architect brother to take strong classical designs of the past and make them livable for today," she explains.

When asked in an interview with *Women's Wear Daily* if there were a missing ingredient in her life, she replied, "I've always thought about the idea of having children, but I think children need to be nurtured, and I don't think you can do that from five to six at night." In another interview she said, "from the age of ten I always wanted to design. I never excluded having a family, but my work is so demanding. I'm happy that I have a lot of nieces and nephews, so I can enjoy family life and kids, and that's a lot of fun."—JANET MARKARIAN

Amies, Hardy

British designer

Born *Edwin Hardy Amies in London, 17 July 1909.*
Education *Studied at Brentwood School to 1927.*
Career *School teacher, Antibes, 1927; office assistant, Bendorf, Germany, 1928-30; trainee, W. & T. Avery Ltd., Birmingham, England, 1930-34; managing designer, Lachasse, 1934, managing director, 1935-39. Served in the British Army Intelligence Corps, 1939-45; lieutenant colonel; head of Special Forces Commission to Belgium, 1944. Designed for Worth and for the British government Utility Scheme during the war; established own couture business, Hardy Amies Ltd., 1946; introduced ready-made line, 1950; dressmaker by appointment for HM Queen Elizabeth II, England, from 1955; added menswear, 1959; firm owned by Debenhams, 1973-81, re-purchased by Amies, 1981.*

Also menswear designer for Hepworths, from 1961. Vice-chairman, 1954-56, and chairman, 1959-60, Incorporated Society of London Fashion Designers.

Awards *Named Officier de l'Ordre de la Couronne, Belgium, 1946; Royal Warrant awarded, 1955; Harper's Bazaar Award, 1962; Caswell-Massey International Award, 1962, 1964, 1968; Ambassador Magazine Award, 1964; The Sunday Times Special Award, London, 1965; Commander of the Royal Victorian Order, 1977; Personnalité de l'Année (Haute Couture), Paris, 1986; British Fashion Council Hall of Fame Award, 1989; Knight Commander of the Victorian Order, 1989.*

Address *Hardy Amies Ltd., 14 Savile Row, London W1X 2JN, England.*

Hardy Amies began his career as a couturier when he was brought in as managing designer at Lachasse, in London, after the departure in 1933 of Digby Morton. He acknowledges that by examining the models left by Morton he learnt the construction of tailored suits. The 1930s was an auspicious time for the new generation of London couture houses that had begun to emerge, for the British tailored suit reigned supreme in America. Amies's contribution to the construction of the tailored suit for women was to lower the waistline of the jacket, which he believed Morton had always set too high, thus giving the "total effect of a more important-looking suit." His fashion philosophy, that elegant clothes must have a low waistline, has characterized his work ever since and his clothes are always cut just above the hipline rather than on the natural waistline. Working on his theory that fashion design should be a process of "evolution rather than revolution," Amies concedes that his duty as a designer is to vary the cut and design of the tailored suit to make it as feminine as possible, without departing from the canons of good tailoring.

Like his counterparts in the London couture, Amies's work was always tempered by the requirements of the private couture customer who formed the main part of the business. Unlike the Paris couture houses who enjoyed the support of large textile firms, who saw the link with couture as a beneficial form of publicity, as well as backing from the French Government for its *industrie de luxe,* the London couture houses did not benefit from such aid. Thus the main role of the London couture was not to create what Amies has described as avant-garde clothes for publicity purposes but to design for the individual customer.

Amies is perhaps best known for his work for Queen Elizabeth II for whom he began a long association as a royal dressmaker in 1950 when he made several outfits for the then Princess Elizabeth's royal tour to Canada. Although the couture side of the Hardy Amies business is the less financially successful area today, it has nonetheless given his house a degree of respectability as a royal warrant holder. One of Hardy Amies's best known creations is the gown he designed in 1977 for Queen Elizabeth's Silver Jubilee portrait which, he says, has been "immortalized on a thousand biscuit tins." However, while Amies's royal patronage has clearly enforced his international image, the couture side of his business is less financially successful than his menswear and related fashion spin-offs such as licences. These include small leather goods, ties, knitwear, and shirts which are produced under licence in various countries including America, Canada, Australia, and Japan where the Hardy Amies label has become a household name with his association with Diatobo.

Another side of Hardy Amies's work is seen in his designs for corporate uniforms for the service industries, such as hotels and airlines, where his reputation both as a designer of tailored clothes and his royal association have undoubtedly made him an appealing choice.

Hardy Amies is one of Britain's best known establishment designers. He has weathered the transformation of London's fashion image as the home of the thoroughbred tailored suit to a veritable melting pot of creativity, during the course of a career which has spanned more than half a century.—CATHERINE WORAM

Anthony, John

American designer

Born *Gianantonio Iorio in New York, 28 April 1938.*

Education *Studied at the Accademia delle Belle Arti, Rome, 1956-57; graduated from Fashion Institute of Technology, New York, 1959.*

Family *Married Molly Anthony; son: Mark.*

Career *Designer, in New York, for Devonbrook, 1959-68, and Adolph Zelinka, 1968-70; John Anthony, Inc., established in New York, 1971-79, and from 1986.*

Awards *Maison Blanche Award, New Orleans, 1964; Silver Cup Award, Kaufmann's Department Stores, Pittsburgh, 1964; Mortimer C. Ritter Award, Fashion Institute of Technology, New York, 1964; "Winnie" Coty Award, 1972; Coty Return Award, 1976.*

John Anthony believes that designing clothes is a fusion of function and purpose. The function appears to be his logical, wearable approach. The purpose lies in his pared-down minimalist ideas. He edits collections down to their bare essentials and, whilst other designers often show over 100 styles per collection, he makes his statement in under 50. His subtle, understated clothes are designed for a young, sophisticated woman. He uses natural fabrics like wool crêpe, chiffon, jersey, satin, and menswear fabrics. He is particularly noted for his cardigan sweaters or pullovers teamed with skirts and his pared-down gala evening gowns, in contradictory daywear fabrics.

Educated at the Accademia delle Belle Arti in Rome, and the Fashion Institute of Technology in New York, Anthony worked for several wholesale companies before opening his own house with the manufacturer Robert Levine in 1971. He immediately marketed his look towards the top end of ready-to-wear, establishing a glossy, up-to-the-minute fashion image and selling to leading retail stores.

John Anthony's first collection was an edited Marlene Dietrich look, featuring masculine tailoring in pinstripe and herringbone wools, softened with blouses underneath, or pleated and smocked crêpe dresses. By 1976 he was showing the soft, liquid separates that became his trademark; ice cream colours seemed to melt into clothes that were so light they almost floated.

His modern understatements have brought him commissions from high profile clients like US presidents' wives Betty Ford, Rosalynn Carter, and Jacqueline Kennedy Onassis, who needed to attract attention through impeccable taste rather than outrageous overstatement. Performers Lena Horne and Audrey Meadows have also been customers, comfortable with the John Anthony style philosophy.

Muted colour is another strong feature of his work. He believes the colour palette in a collection should intermingle, so that one item can easily go with everything else. His first collection was predominantly black with white, navy, and red. He claims to hate shock colours like turquoise or fuchsia and has usually been faithful to a range of beiges, christened with names such as peanut and cinnamon.

Anthony considers the designer's job to be to make things easy for the customer. However, behind this ease lies a renowned skill for cutting, tailoring, and overall dedication to developing a specialist style, which has won the designer Coty Awards.

Born Gianantonio Iorio in Queens, New York, to a metalworker, John Anthony has evolved into a dress designer who uses the most luxurious fabrics in the simplest shapes with unequalled taste. He was one of the first designers to promote the idea of easy-to-travel clothes that can be rolled up in a ball and thrown into a suitcase, with no danger of wrinkling. He recommends that his customer buys a few things that work for her each season, then interchanges and adapts these garments to create several different looks.—KEVIN ALMOND

Armani, Giorgio
Italian designer

Born *Piacenza, Italy, 11 July 1934.*

Education *Studied medicine, University of Bologna, 1952-53; also studied photography.*

Military Service *Served in the Italian Army, 1953-54.*

Career *Window display designer, La Rinascente department stores, 1954; stylist, menswear buyer, La Rinascente stores, 1954-60; menswear designer, Nino Cerruti, 1960-70; free-lance designer, 1970-75; introduced Armani menswear collection, 1974; introduced womenswear collection, 1975; introduced Emporio Armani and Armani Jeans, 1981; introduced less expensive womenswear range, Mani, c.1987; introduced Giorgio Armani Occhiali and Giorgio Armani Calze, 1987; introduced sportswear range, and Emporio Armani shops selling younger collection launched in London, 1989; Giorgio Armani USA company formed, 1980; AX, Armani Exchange, boutiques introducing lower-priced basic quality clothes launched in the United States, 1991. Fragrances include Armani le Parfum, 1982, Armani Eau pour Homme, 1984, and Gio, 1992.*

Exhibitions *Intimate Architecture: Contemporary Clothing Design, Massachusetts Institute of Technology, Cambridge, 1982; Giorgio Armani: Images of Man, Fashion Institute of Technology, New York, 1990-91, travelled to Tokyo, Paris, London; retrospective Armani: 1972-92, Palazzo Pitti, Florence, 1992.*

Awards *Neiman Marcus Award, 1979; Cutty Sark Award, 1980, 1981, 1984; Gentlemen's Quarterly Manstyle Award, 1982, Grand'Ufficiale dell'Ordine al Merito Award, Italy, 1982; Gold Medal from Municipality of Piacenza, 1983; Council of Fashion Designers of America International Designer Award, 1983, 1987; L'Occhio d'Oro Award, 1984, 1986, 1987, 1988, 1994; Cutty Sark Men's Fashion Award, 1985; Bath Museum of Costume Dress of the Year Award, 1986; named Gran Cavaliere della Repubblica, Italy, 1987; Lifetime Achievement Award, 1987; Christobal Balenciaga Award, 1988; Media Key Award, 1988; Woolmark Award, 1989, 1992; Senken Award, 1989; Honorary Doctorate from the Royal College of Art, 1991; Fiorino d'Oro award, Florence, 1992; Golden Effie Award, United States, 1993; Aguja de Oro Award, Spain, 1993; Academia del Profumo Award, Italy, 1993.*

Giorgio Armani: Men's collection, Spring/Summer 1995.

Armani

Address *Via Borgonuovo 21, 20122 Milan, Italy.*

Giorgio Armani is a design colonialist responsible for the creation of an aesthetic in both menswear and womenswear that had a firm grip on international style in the 1980s. Renowned for his use of fabric and expertise in tailoring, he is a world leader in menswear design who was responsible for the wide shouldered look for executive women. His pared-down unstructured silhouette moved away from the standard tailored look that had epitomized menswear since the 19th century. By eliminating interfaces, linings, and shoulder pads, Armani restructured the jacket, creating a softly tailored look.

Although Armani produces entire ranges of these functional, adaptable, flexible items of clothing that seem almost throwaway in their simplicity, they are, in fact, luxurious designs made of high quality cloth. His clothes, however, although expensive, have their own understated glamour and could never be described as ostentatious. Neither trend nor tradition, the Armani style draws a fine line between the two. His designs seem to have little to do with fashion. Notwithstanding, each season he introduces understated alterations, albeit irrespective of the more compulsory fashion changes that affect other designers. Eschewing change for its own sake, he believes in quality rather than invention. Correspondingly, his collections are redefinitions of a soft, unstructured style, playing with layers of texture and colour but constantly renegotiating proportions. Elegant, understated rather than "important" clothes, they have a timeless quality, a classicism emphasized in the nostalgic advertising campaigns that use images by the Italian photographer Aldo Fallai.

Born in Piacenza, Italy, in 1934, Armani's first taste of the fashion industry was with La Rinascente, a large Italian department-store chain where in 1954 he worked on the window displays. He then transferred to the Office of Fashion and Style where he had an invaluable training in the use of fabrics and the importance of customer profiling and targeting. After seven years he left to design menswear for Nino Cerruti, a textile and garment firm, and for a month worked in one of their textile factories where he learned to appreciate fabric, the skills that went into its production, and the techniques of industrial tailoring.

In 1974 Armani launched his own label, which was to become incredibly successful—the biggest-selling line of European design in America. His first designs revolved around the refining of the male jacket, which he believed to be the most important invention in the history of dress being both versatile and functional and suited to all social occasions. His idea was to instill the relaxation of sports clothing into its tailored lines. He later applied similar notions to womenswear, evolving a new way of dressing for women that was not just a simple appropriation of items from the male wardrobe but the use of them as a source upon which to build. He developed a style for the working woman that had an understated, almost androgynous chic that was so discreet in its detailing that it was almost perverse.

At this time his designs were very expensive, being made out of the most luxurious materials such as alpaca, cashmere, and suede. To expand his customer base and to meet the increasing demands of a fashion conscious public for clothes with a designer label, he produced a cheaper womenswear range entitled Mani, made out of synthetics so advanced they could not be copied, together with the popular Emporio Armani range of sportswear. His styles for women include Peter Pan collars on simple blouses, classics such as navy blazers and matching skirts, or tailored trousers whose cut may change slightly each season while the range of garments remains essentially the same. For men he produces items such as the same definitive navy blazers, crumpled linen jackets, leather blousons, which he introduced in 1980, and oversized overcoats and raincoats. Impeccably tailored, with faltering cut, easy lines, and subtle textures, patterns, and colours, he introduces twists such as lowslung button placement on double breasted suits for men and experimental blends of fabrics such as viscose with wool or linen with silk.

Armani's clothes seem anonymous, suited to life in the city—the epitome of post-modern style.—CAROLINE COX

Ashley, Laura

British (Welsh) designer

Born *Laura Mountney in Dowlais, Glamorgan, Wales, 7 September 1925.*
Education *Attended Marshall's School, Merthyr Tydfil, Wales, until 1932; mainly self-taught in design. Served in the Women's Royal Naval Service.*
Family *Married Bernard Albert Ashley in 1949; children: Jane, David, Nick, and Emma.*
Career *Worked as secretary, National Federation of Women's Institutes, London, 1945-52; founder and partner, with Bernard Ashley, Ashley-Mountney Ltd. printed textiles, 1954-68, in Kent, 1956-61, and in Carno, Wales, from 1961; established Laura Ashley Ltd. in 1968; opened first retail outlet, London, 1967, then Edinburgh, Bath, Cheltenham, Cambridge, Norwich, Oxford, Aix-en-Provence, Munich, Vienna, etc.; opened first United States shop, San Francisco, 1974; New York shop opened, 1977; established 185 retail outlets worldwide by 1985.*
Awards *Queen's Award for Export Achievement, 1977.*
Died *(in Coventry, Warwickshire) 17 September 1985.*
Address *27 Bagley's Lane, London SW6 2AR, England.*

Welsh designer Laura Ashley developed and distilled the British romantic style of neo-Victorianism, reflecting past eras in clothing, textiles, accessories, and furnishings and demonstrating classic country styling.

Her approach to design was inspired by her environment, the surrounding Welsh countryside, and her yearning to return to all things natural. Integrating ideas adopted from the designs and qualities of past eras, she combined elements to create a look of nostalgic simplicity and naive innocence. Floral sprigged cotton fabrics, often directly adapted and developed from 18th- and 19th-century patterns, paisleys, and tiny prints worked with romantic detailing to create a style that was original and easily recognized.

Her style possesses old world charm with individual rustic freshness, reflected in traditional beliefs of bygone days. Victorian nightshirts, Edwardian-style dresses, the introduction of the long smock in 1968, delicately trimmed with lace, pin tucked bodices, tiered skirts, and full puffed sleeves are her trademark, aimed at the middle market and retailing at affordable prices.

Laura Ashley rose from the modest beginnings of a small cottage industry, producing a simple range of printed headscarves and table mats in her kitchen, to the development of a company that became a huge enterprise of international renown. It was a fairy story in itself.

A fashion

Laura Ashley: Spring/Summer 1996.

Her self-taught skill produced ranges of womenswear, childrenswear, bridalwear, accessories, and furnishings. She established home interiors consisting of coordinated ranges of bed linens, wall tiles, curtains, cushions, and upholstery. Her brilliant concept of fabrics, her discerning research of past eras for new inspiration, and her study and re-interpretation of antique textiles led to the success of the Laura Ashley label.

Traditional floral prints combined together, printed in two colours and various colour combinations, distinguished her work. However, through the technical expertise and experimentation of Bernard Ashley, Laura's husband and business partner, new developments and improved machinery extended versatility: new and subtle colour combinations were produced, often to Laura's own design. Natural fibres, crisp cottons, and lawn fabrics expanded to include ranges in twill, silk, wool, crêpe, velvet, corduroy, and eventually jersey fabrics.

Along with the 1960s youth revolution came a move towards romanticism, conservation, and world peace, an alternative to modern living, pop culture, mass-produced clothing, and vivid Parisian fashions. Due to her convincing beliefs in past values, quality, and the revival of romantic simplicity, Ashley's success has been overwhelming. Bernard Ashley's perceptive business brain and Laura Ashley's determination and enterprising mind led to the development of excellent marketing techniques. Retail settings, complementary to the old world style of neo-Victorianism, promoted a look of individuality and quality.

Throughout the 1980s and into the 1990s, the style retains its unique and easily recognizable image. The style, however, has evolved, extending to all ranges to incorporate contemporary fashion ideas, including the introduction of jersey for practical and easy-to-wear clothing. The Laura Ashley style remains unchanged, incorporating the same ingredients, but with a newer, fresher approach.

The phenomenal success of this closely knit family firm, from a chain of boutiques to a multi-faceted company expanding from Europe to Canada, the United States, and Australia, has continued to grow after Laura Ashley's tragic accidental death in 1985, with the style maintaining its international appeal. Her legacy is a multi-million-dollar empire in clothing and coordinated furnishings, constantly updated but withstanding the passage of time.—CAROL MARY BROWN

A
fashion

Badgley Mischka

American design team

Mark Badgley born in East Saint Louis, Illinois, 12 January 1961; raised in Oregon; studied business, University of Southern California, to 1982; graduated from Parsons School of Design, New York, 1985. James Mischka born in Burlington, Wisconsin, 23 December 1960. Studied management and art history, Rice University, Houston, Texas, to 1982; graduated from Parsons School of Design, 1985. Before forming own company, Badgley designed for Jackie Rogers and Donna Karan, New York, 1985-88; Mischka designed for Willi Smith, New York, 1985-88; Badgley Mischka Company established, New York, 1988; financed by Escada USA, from 1992.

Awards *Mouton Cadet Young Designer Award, 1989; Dallas International Apparel Mart Rising Star Award, 1992.*
Address *525 Seventh Avenue, New York, NY 10018, USA.*

Lilly Daché (couture hat and style maker of the 1950s) writes in her 1956 *Glamour Book* (Daché, Lilly and Dorothy Roe Lewis, New York 1956) that glamour "means making the most of what you have" and "the consciousness of looking her best often touches off a woman's inner mainspring of joyous self-confidence and—presto!—all of a sudden she is glamorous." Designers Mark Badgley and James Mischka say of their clothing, "one zip and you're glamorous." Dee-luxe and de luxe, their clothing radiates youthful confidence. Fanciful but realistic, their designs recall the elegance of an age when one dressed for evening. The two young designers, who introduced their first collection in 1988 in New York, make glamour attainable by demystifying and simplifying it.

Uptown diners and downtown executives alike would find something appropriate and pleasing in Badgley Mischka designs. Evening suits and dresses are refined and uncontrived: form fitting wool jersey, cotton brocade, faille, re-embroidered lace, silk, and baby bouclé are

**Badgley Mischka: Fall 1994; bronze beaded Byzantium cocktail dress (left);
Hematite beaded Chaucer vest tunic, black tuxedo crepe skirt (right).**

used to create suits with long fitted jackets (worn underneath: sexy, long silk scarves instead of the predictable blouse), and pencil-thin or swingy full short skirts. One versatile wool jersey dress, perfect for career dressing, looks like two pieces, with a rib knit turtleneck and either a permanently pleated or straight wrap skirt, in gray or pale yellow. The combination of fine crisp and softly draping fabrics (bouclé and silk, velvet trimmed wool, organza and silk chiffon) adds dimension and drama. Fitted, empire, or lowered, waistlines are superbly shaped. Expertly mixed cocktail dresses—with evocative cocktail names such as the Tom Collins, the Delmonico, the Bacardi—are off-the-shoulder, *décolleté,* bowed, lacy, or beaded and above the knee. All are subtly provocative, feminine, and flirtatious. The bridal gowns almost make you want to be wed, soon, just so you may show off your never-seen-so shapely shoulders and waist in a V-backed ivory lace and silk-crêpe dress, or choose the off-white silk brocade coatdress, with front wrap and jeweled buttons. The bridal dresses are for the grown-up sweet tooth, confections which allow the beauty of the wearer to shine through the frills.

American *Vogue*'s Dodie Kazanjian (July 1991) looked to six designers (including Bill Blass, Donna Karan, and Michael Kors) for the perfect "little black dress," and found hers at Badgley Mischka, which "felt new without straining for newness." Frances Lear agrees, choosing a Badgley Mischka wool jersey as *Lear*'s "Relevant Dress," stating that it is ". . . reminiscent of other seminal dresses, yet is perfectly contemporary. . . ." and "as comfortable as your own skin" (New York, September 1991). There is a sense of ease and balance in Badgley Mischka designs. They create something expertly vital without superfluidity or trendiness; the design team is restrained in their creation, offering designs appealing in their modernity and lack of excess.

Lilly Daché further states, "real fashion begins with simplicity." Mark Badgley and James Mischka employ this mandate, creating clothing that is beautifully made and beautiful and glamorous to wear. Badgley Mischka make glamour easy.—JANE BURNS

Balenciaga, Cristobal

Spanish designer

Born *Guetaria, San Sebastian, 21 January 1895.*
Education *Studied needlework and dressmaking with his mother until 1910.*
Career *Established tailoring business, with sponsorship of the Marquesa de Casa Torres, San Sebastian, 1915-21; founder, designer, Elsa fashion house, Barcelona, 1922-31, and Madrid, 1932-37; director, Maison Balenciaga, Paris, 1937-40, 1945-68; spent war years in Madrid; fragrances include le Dix, 1948, Quadreille, 1955, and Pour Homme, introduced by House of Balenciaga, 1990; couture house closed, 1968. Retired to Madrid, 1968-72. House of Balenciaga managed by German group Hoechst, 1972-86; Jacques Bogart S.A. purchased Balenciaga Couture et Parfums, 1986; Balenciaga ready-to-wear collection launched, 1987; reopening of Balenciaga stores launched, 1989.*
Exhibitions *Balenciaga, Bellerive Museum, Zurich, 1970; Fashion: An Anthology, Victoria & Albert Museum, London, 1971; The World of Balenciaga, Metropolitan Museum of Art, New York, 1973; El Mundo de Balenciaga, Palacio de Bellas Artes, Madrid, 1974; Hommage a Balenciaga, Musée Historique des Tissus, Lyon, 1985; Balenciaga, Fashion Institute of Technology, New York, 1986; Cristobal Balenciaga, Fondation de la Mode,*

Balenciaga

Cristobal Balenciaga: Summer 1994.

Tokyo, 1987; Homage to Balenciaga, Palacio de la Virreina, Barcelona, and Palacio Miramar, San Sebastian, Spain, 1987.

Awards *Chevalier de la Légion d'Honneur; named Commander, L'Ordre d'Isabelle-la-Catholique.*

Died *(in Javea, Spain) 23 March 1972.*

Cristobal Balenciaga's primary fashion achievement was in tailoring, an art that was for the Spanish-born couturier a virtuoso claim to knowing, comforting, and flattering the body. He could demonstrate tailoring proficiency in a *tour-de-force* one-seam coat, its shaping created from the innumerable darts and tucks that shaped the single piece of fabric. His consummate tailoring was accompanied by a pictorial imagination that encouraged him to appropriate ideas of kimono and sari, return to the Spanish vernacular dress of billowing and adaptable volume, and create dresses with arcs that could swell with air as the figure moved. There was a traditional Picasso-Matisse question of post-war French fashion: who was greater, Dior or Balenciaga? Personal sensibility might support one or the other, but it is hard to imagine any equal to Balenciaga's elegance, then or since.

Balenciaga was a master of illusion. The waist could be strategically low, it could be brought up to the ribs, or it could be concealed in a tunic or the subtle opposition of a boxy top over a straight skirt. Balenciaga envisioned the garment as a three-dimensional form encircling the body, occasionally touching it and even grasping it, but also spiraling away so that the contrast in construction was always between the apparent freedom of the garment and its body-defining moments. Moreover, he regularly contrasted razor-sharp cut, including instances of the garment's radical geometry, with soft fragile features. A perfectionist who closed down his business in 1968 rather than see it be compromised in a fashion era he did not respect, Balenciaga projected ideal garments, but allowed for human imperfection. He was, in fact, an inexorable flatterer, a sycophant to the imperfect body. To throw back a rolled collar gives a flattering softness to the line of the neck into the body; his popular seven-eighths sleeve flattered women of a certain age, while the tent-like drape of coats and jackets were elegant on clients without perfect bodies. His fabrics had to stand up to his almost Cubist vocabulary of shapes, and he loved robust wools with texture, silk gazar for evening, corduroy (surprising in its inclusion in the couture), and textured silks.

Balenciaga's garments lack pretension; they are characterized by self-assured couture of simple appearance, austerity of details, and reserve in style. For the most part, the garments seem simple. American manufacturers, for example, adored Balenciaga for his adaptability into simpler forms for the American mass market in suits and coats. The slight rise in the waistline at center front or the proportions of chemise tunic to skirt make Balenciaga clothing as harmonious as a musical composition, but the effect is always one of utmost insouciance and ease of style. Balenciaga delved deeply into traditional clothing, seeming to care more deeply for regional dress than for any prior couture house. As Marie-Andrée Jouve has demonstrated, Balenciaga's garments allude to Spanish vernacular costume and to Spanish art: his embroidery and jet-beaded evening coats, capelettes, and boleros are redolent of the *torero,* while his love of capes emanates from the romance of rustic apparel (*Balenciaga,* New York 1989). Chemise, cape, and baby doll shapes might seem antithetical to the propensities of a master of tailoring, but Balenciaga's 1957 baby doll dress exemplifies the correlation he made between the two. The lace cage of the baby doll floats free from the body, suspended from the shoulders, but it is matched by the tailored dress beneath, providing a layered and analytical examination of the body within and the Cubist cone on the exterior, a tantalizing artistry of body form and perceived shape.

The principal forms for Balenciaga were the chemise, tunic, suit—with more or less boxy top—narrow skirt, and coats, often with astonishing sleeve treatments, suggesting an arm transfigured by the sculptor Brancusi into a puff or into almost total disappearance. Balenciaga perceived a silhouette that could be with or without arms, but never with the arms interfering. A famous Henry Clark photograph of a 1951 Balenciaga black silk suit focuses on silhouette: narrow and high waist with a pronounced flare of the peplum below and sleeves that billow from elbow to seven-eighths length; an Irving Penn photograph concentrates on the aptly named melon sleeve of a coat. Like a 20th-century artist, Balenciaga directed himself to a part of the body, giving us a selective, concentrated vision. His was not an all-over, all-equal vision, but a discriminating, problem-solving exploration of tailoring and picture-making details of dress. In fact, Balenciaga was so very like a 20th-century artist because in temperament, vocabulary, and attainment, he was one.—RICHARD MARTIN

Balmain, Pierre

French designer

Born Saint-Jean-de-Maurienne, Savoie, 18 May 1914.

Education Studied architecture, École Nationale Supérieure des Beaux-Arts, Paris, 1933-34.

Military Service French Air Force, 1936-38, and French Army Pioneer Corps, 1939-40.

Career Free-lance sketch artist for Robert Piguet, Paris, 1934; assistant designer, Molyneux, Paris, 1934-38; designer, Lucien Lelong, Paris, 1939, 1941-45; founder, director, Maison Balmain, Paris, 1945-1982, Balmain Fashions, New York, 1951-55, Balmain Fashions, Caracas, 1954; Director General, Balmain S.A., Paris, 1977-82; ready-to-wear line launched, 1982. Fragrances include Vent Vert, 1945, Jolie Madame, 1953, Miss Balmain, 1967, Ivoire, 1980; fragrance business purchased by Revlon, 1960. Also stage and film designer, from 1950.

Exhibitions Pierre Balmain: 40 années de création, Musée de la Mode et du Costume, Palais Galliera, Paris, 1985-86.

Awards Neiman Marcus Award, Dallas, 1955; Knight of the Order of Dannebrog, Copenhagen, 1963; Cavaliere Ufficiale del Merito Italiano, Rome, 1966; Officier de la Légion d'Honneur, 1978; Vermillion Medal, City of Paris.

Died (in Paris) 29 June 1982. Firm continued after his death.

Address 44 rue Francois-1er, 75008 Paris, France.

"Dressmaking is the architecture of movement." This was the philosophy of French couturier Pierre Balmain. His mission, as he saw it, was to beautify the world just as an architect does. The relationship between architecture and couture was emphasized throughout Balmain's career. He initially studied to be an architect. The beauty of couture, Balmain often argued, was when it was brought to life on the human form. He also stated, "nothing is more important in a dress than its construction."

The House of Balmain opened, with great acclaim from the fashion press, in 1945. Alice B. Toklas wrote, "A dress is to once more become a thing of beauty, to express elegance and grace." Prior to opening his own house, Balmain apprenticed with couturier Captain Edward Molyneux, in Paris, for five years. It was these years with Molyneux that taught him about the business of couture. Molyneux was at the height of his success during that time and Balmain defined him as a true creator. He learned there about the elegance of simplicity which is so evident in his later designs under his own name. After leaving Molyneux, Balmain joined the firm of Lucien Lelong, where he worked from 1939 to 1944 off and on during the war and the German Occupation. In 1941, the House of Lelong reopened and Balmain returned to work with a newly hired designer, Christian Dior.

Balmain credited himself with the now famous "New Look" and cited his first collection (1945), pictured in American *Vogue,* as evidence. These designs did illustrate the feminine silhouette of longer, bell-shaped, higher bustlines, narrow shoulders, and smaller waists. The collections of Jacques Fath and Balenciaga were also reflective of the New Look silhouette with which Christian Dior was ultimately credited.

Pierre Balmain believed that the ideal of elegance in clothing was achieved only through simplicity. He detested ornamentation for the sake of making a garment spectacular and offended the American fashion press by stating that Seventh Avenue fashion was vulgar. As a couturier he was not interested in fashion *per se;* rather he sought to dress women who appreciated an elegant appearance and possessed sophisticated style. Balmain once stated, "Keep to the basic principles of fashion and you will always be in harmony with the latest trends without falling prey to them."

The basic Balmain silhouette for day was slim, with that for evening being full-skirted. He was credited with the popularization of the stole as an accessory for both day and evening. Balmain also used fur as trim throughout his collections. He was also remembered for his exquisite use of embroidered fabrics for evening.

After the war, Balmain toured the world giving lectures on the virtues of French fashions. He promoted the notion that French couture defined the ideal of elegance and refinement. The French couture was virtually shut down during the war and these visits did much to revive the industry. As a result of these lectures, Balmain recognized the potential of the American market and opened a boutique in New York, offering his distinctly French fashions.

Balmain was one of the few French couturiers of his generation to also design for the theatre, ballet, and cinema, and also for royalty. Balmain was commissioned by Queen Sirikit of Thailand in 1960 to design her wardrobe for her official visit to the United States.

Pierre Balmain died in 1982. His high standards of elegance were well regarded in the world of couture and he did much to revitalize the French couture industry abroad.—MARGO SEAMAN

Barnes, Jhane

American designer

Born *Jane Barnes in Phoenix, Maryland, 4 March 1954.*

Education *Graduated from Fashion Institute of Technology, New York, 1975.*

Family *Married Howard Ralph Feinberg, 1981 (divorced); married Katsuhiko Kawasaki, 1988.*

Career *Menswear company established as Jhane Barnes Ltd, 1977; President, Jane Barnes for ME, New York 1976-78, and Jhane Barnes Inc., from 1978; introduced women's collection, 1979; neckwear line by Zanzara introduced, 1989; footwear collection launched, 1991; clothing licensed by American Fashion Company, San Diego, California, from 1990; leatherwear licensed by Group Five Leather, Minneapolis, Minnesota, from 1994. Also designs furnishing fabrics marketed by Knoll International, from 1989.*

Awards *Coty American Fashion Critics Award for Menswear 1980; Cutty Sark Most Prominent Designer Award, 1980; Cutty Sark Outstanding Designer Award 1982; Coty Return Menswear Award, 1984; Council of Fashion Designers of America Award, 1981, 1984; Contract Textile Award, American Society of Interior Designers 1983, 1984; Product Design Award, Institute of Business Designers, 1983, 1984, 1985, 1986, 1989.*

Address *575 Seventh Avenue, New York, New York 10018, USA.*

DNR (11 August 1994) reported of Jhane Barnes's 1995 collection, "Jhane Barnes's spring sportswear collection is designed for a city sophisticate, one who appreciates unstructured silhouettes, rich textures, and cerebral prints for shirts." In fact, Barnes's work has been consistently about a cosmopolitan view of texture, bestowing on menswear a stony, flecked range of earth, grain, and granite hues.

Describing her work for interiors with Knoll, *The New Yorker* (29 October 1990) chronicled: "And the main thing about the Jhane Barnes approach is that it is a modernist approach to nature. For instance, she decided on the design for one fabric, called Aerial View, while she was noticing how the earth looked from an airplane. She has also been influenced by time spent in her country house, in South Salem [New York]." One imagines the inspirations coming so effortlessly from Barnes's observations of informal beauty, whether the aerial landscape or ripe plums or passages of deteriorated façade. Barnes's design exudes its humanism, its earthy and natural bent, and its sense of the easygoing and comfortable. Her knit sweaters are never the artistic geometries of Missoni; instead, they suggest leafy surrounds and irregular patterns in nature. Her propensity to loose, even amorphous, shapes, along with the organics of color, would settle any of her garments into a comfortable camouflage at Walden Pond. In a menswear world of aggressive self-assertion and power, Barnes speaks quietly and with nature's sweet sounds. Her scumbled knits seem like the residue from an artist's palette and her wondrous colors could forecast overcast skies more than any Pantone swatch. Her name could hardly be more apt, her colors and interest suggesting the nostalgic, weathered old barns of rustic life now bygone and prized by urban recollection.

Barnes attempted to re-do menswear from the foundation, accepting none of the conventions or principles of power when she began in the late 1970s. As she admitted to Michael Gross (*New York Times,* 5 January 1988), "I was way too early," though Barnes can be said to anticipate many of the softened, cozy changes to menswear tailoring and palette in the late 1980s. "Now," she told Gross, "I try to be innovative and interesting, but not trendy or classic. I like a man to be noticed across the room, but not across the street." In fact, Barnes is a chastened designer even in the era of dress clothing for men being more and more reconciled with casual wear. Her clothing always has great dignity and reserve; her beckoning nature seems always to be flinty, cautious New England, not the epic Great Plains of Ralph Lauren or the steamy tropics of Gianni Versace.

Touch and the tactile are leitmotifs of Barnes's work: among menswear designers, she is uncommonly sensitive to hand and feel. Barnes's work—often esteemed almost as much as works of art as garments—has attracted an ardent and loyal clientèle, even if her efforts to reach a mass market have always been strangely out of synch with market trends. Perhaps too urban and unconventional for some and too modest for others, Barnes is making a menswear that may never be wholly mainstream. Nonetheless, her rich earthy design is as fresh, colorful, and splendid as a sunrise garden.—RICHARD MARTIN

Barrie, Scott

American designer

Born _Nelson Clyde Barr in Philadelphia, 16 January 1946._
Education _Studied applied arts at Philadelphia Museum College of Art, and fashion design at Mayer School of Fashion, New York, mid-1960s._
Career _Designer, Allen Cole boutique, New York, 1966-69; co-founder, Barrie Sport, Ltd., New York, 1969-82; menswear collection and Barrie Plus collections introduced, 1974. Also designed dresses for S.E.L., mid-1980s, loungewear for Barad, and furs for Barlan. Moved to Milan, 1982; formed Scott Barrie Italy SrL, in partnership with Kinshido Company, Ltd., of Japan, 1983; designer, Milan D'Or division for Kinshido, 1983-91; designer, signature line for Kinshido, 1983-91; free-lance designer, Krizia, Milan, 1986-88._
Died _(in Alessandria, Italy) 8 June 1993._

Scott Barrie was one of a group of brassy and vibrant black designers and models to establish themselves on New York's Seventh Avenue in the late 1960s. Influenced by his godmother, who had designed and made clothes for the sonorous and volatile jazz singers Dinah Washington and Sarah Vaughan, Barrie began designing in 1966. Although he graduated from the Philadelphia College of Art and the Mayer School in New York, his mother was not initially encouraging about his future in fashion designing for Seventh Avenue. "Blacks don't make it there," she warned her son—Barrie quickly proved her wrong.

Describing himself in the 1970s as being midway between the crazy extremes of Zandra Rhodes and Herbert Kasper, Barrie quickly established himself as a designer of sexy, often outrageous clothes. His eveningwear was particularly noteworthy: skinny gowns sprinkled with _paillettes_ and dangerously high splits, or jersey slips that slid tantalizingly over the figure.

He began making clothes in his New York apartment, with a makeshift cutting table and domestic sewing machine. His first orders were from small independent boutiques but success came when prestigious stores Henri Bendel and Bloomingdale's in New York placed orders for his sparse and revealing jersey dresses. By 1969 he had christened his company Barrie Sport and moved into spacious workrooms at 530 Seventh Avenue.

Barrie's forte was the sensuous use of jersey, cut in inventive and unexpected ways, from which he created elegant and often risqué eveningwear. Popular devotees of the Barrie look have been Naomi Sims, an extravagantly beautiful black model, who always ordered her clothes in white, and Lee Traub, wife of the president of Bloomingdale's.

Barrie also designed ranges of loungewear, furs, and accessories and was involved in costume design, creating clothes for films and the costumes for the Jeffrey Ballet's production of *Deuce Coupe*.

The intermingling of culture and race on New York's Seventh Avenue in the 1960s brought a new sort of creative energy that challenged accepted standards. Barrie's models did not parade the catwalk with elegance; instead they boogied wildly and arrogantly, with a streetwise brashness. It was a testimony to the changing times that the clothes were accepted at the higher end of the ready-to-wear market.

Scott Barrie enjoyed being a fashion designer, but acknowledged the hard work and competitive nature of the business. In the 1980s he ceased designing under his own name, taking a position with the dress firm S.E.L. as a designer.—KEVIN ALMOND

Bartlett, John

American designer

Born *Cincinnati, Ohio, c. 1964.*
Education *Graduated from Fashion Institute of Technology and Harvard College.*
Career *Worked for Ronaldus Shamask and WilliWear; established own menswear line, 1992; clothing sold at Barneys New York, Bergdorf Goodman Men, and Saks Fifth Avenue.*
Awards *Perry Ellis Award for New Fashion Talent, 1994, Council of Fashion Designers of America.*
Address *48 W. 21st St., New York, NY 10011, USA.*

John Bartlett's fashion is driven by ideas—astute ideas—about men and about clothes. For example, his spring-summer 1994 collection was for a man, as Bartlett said to Amy Spindler, "day-dreaming about cashing in his Gucci loafers for a lean-to on Easter Island" (*New York Times*, 3 August 1993). Bartlett's volitional Robinson Crusoe would have assembled an elegant mix of tribal tattoos, gauze tunics, and rough silk-twine jackets. As Spindler noted, "It is an ambitious designer who will take on Jean-Jacques Rousseau, but Mr Bartlett did it with fervor." Bartlett never lacks fervor: he is determined—with a missionary's zeal—to make clothing meaningful.

Bartlett is a designer of convictions and of compellingly suggestive and allusive menswear. His spring-summer 1995 collection demonstrated the designer's learned and connected awareness of culture. A runway show that began with clothing inspired by the summer 1994 movie *Forrest Gump* in its nerdish normalcy, in distinctive mint greens, continued into navy-and-white evocations out of Jean Genet (Edmund White's biography had just been published), sharp sharkskin two-button suits, and *tour de force* cross-dressing. Bartlett is a reader, observer, assimilator of contemporary culture in the best sense, bringing his acute sensitivity to contemporary culture into his design. His earlier shapeless structures were being updated into piquant reinterpretations of earlier silhouettes with trousers either cigarette thin or perfectly tubular and shown on models as high-water pants. *Daily News Record* (29 July 1994) enthused about the 1995 collection, "In just four short seasons, this glamour-boy designer has established himself as

John Bartlett: Spring 1996.

the *enfant terrible*—the Gaultier, if you will—of American men's wear." If there is a fault to Bartlett's work, it is that he is the best and consummate stylist of his own clothing. Few menswear customers will actually carry off the clothing with the full styling and intellectual jolt Bartlett imparts. But, of course, one might say the same of the ever-influential and beguiling Gaultier. One could easily imagine Bartlett fully assuming the Gaultier role of polite *provocateur,* a function woefully absent from American fashion. Bartlett's 1995 ventures into womenswear will expand the designer's capacity.

Dan Shaw (*New York Times,* 5 December 1993) calls Bartlett's design "a sort of no-fashion fashion for men who don't dress to impress." To call Bartlett no-fashion is like calling conceptual art no-art. His design is cerebral and yet he delights in the cut, materials, and masculinities of menswear. Clearly, though, Bartlett is not out to impress in any ostentatious way. However, to create monks' robes, paradise fantasies, uncompromised sarongs for men, and fictional heroes is, in its own way, most impressive. Rather than flamboyant, Bartlett's clothing is pensive and passionate. His historicism is enlightened: his 1995 argyles are light and pastel and his sheer nylon knee socks make both hairy legs and the 1950s into an irresistible irony. Bartlett's lively, optimistic intelligence does not, however, ever become the impediment that Vivienne Westwood's punk pessimism or John Galliano's melancholic historicism is. Rather, Bartlett relishes the menswear visual and structural options that make clothing wearable and comfortable as much as he adds concept to menswear: as a designer, he thinks through wearing the clothing even as he offers trenchant ideas and provocative allusions. If Bartlett's Harvard education honed his lampooning and imaginative wit, the Fashion Institute of Technology, Williwear, and Ronaldus Shamask added a Seventh-Avenue savvy. Bartlett's logo is the pear that plays on his surname: he practices the Surrealist and dandy inventions that obsessed Magritte, but still keeps the clothing foremost and wearably wonderful.

On winning the Council of Fashion Designers of America's 1994 Perry Ellis Award for New Fashion Talent (presented by actors Joe Mantello and Stephen Spinella of *Angels in America*), Bartlett showed at the awards ceremony a video paean to men's bodies in motion, including nudity and his own nudity, culminating in the dress of a man. His clothing addresses such a fundamental and ritualistic assessment of clothing in which Bartlett, more than any other major American designer in menswear, is examining the basic tenets of men's bodies and their identity in dress. Bartlett's "become yourself" philosophy is inexhaustibly optimistic. His clothing is so idiosyncratically shrewd and seductive that one could wish that many more would choose either to become themselves or, perhaps even better, to realize the ideal, thinking men that Bartlett creates.—RICHARD MARTIN

Beene, Geoffrey

American designer

Born *Haynesville, Louisiana, 30 August 1927.*

Education *Studied medicine, Tulane University, New Orleans, 1943-46, University of Southern California, Los Angeles, 1946; studied fashion, Traphagen School, New York, 1947-48, Chambre Syndicale d'Haute Couture and Académie Julien, Paris, 1948.*

Career *Display assistant, I. Magnin, Los Angeles, 1946; apprentice tailor, Molyneux, 1948-50; assistant to Mildred O'Quinn, Samuel Winston, Harmay, and other New York*

Geoffrey Beene: Winter 1995. *Photograph by Andrew Eccles.*

fashion houses, 1950-51; assistant designer, Harmony ready-to-wear, New York, 1951-58; designer, Teal Traina, New York, 1958-63; founder-director, Geoffrey Beene Inc. fashion house, beginning in 1963; showed first menswear collection, 1970; Beenebag sportswear collection introduced, 1971; established Cofil SpA, 1976, to manufacture for Europe and the Far East; first free-standing boutique opened, New York, 1989; home furnishings collection introduced, 1993. Fragrances: Gray Flannel, 1975; Bowling Green, 1987.

Exhibitions *Geoffrey Beene: 25 Years of Discovery, Los Angeles, 1988, Western Reserve Historical Society, Cleveland, Ohio, 1988, National Academy of Design, New York, 1988, and Musashino Museum, Tokyo, 1988; Geoffrey Beene Unbound, Fashion Institute of Technology, New York, 1994.*

Awards *Coty American Fashion Critics Award, 1964, 1966, 1968, 1974, 1975, 1977, 1981, 1982; National Cotton Council Award, 1964, 1969; Neiman Marcus Award, 1965; Ethel Traphagen Award, New York, 1966; Council of Fashion Designers of America Award, 1986, 1987, 1989, Special Award, 1988.*

Address *550 Seventh Avenue, New York, New York 10018, USA.*

"Among the fashion *cognoscenti,* [Geoffrey] Beene has long been acknowledged as an artist who chooses to work in cloth," reports Carrie Donovan in the *New York Times* (9 May 1993). "Every season his work astounds as he ingeniously shapes the most modern and wearable of clothes." For some, the designation of fashion as art is simply an encomium, a way of saying "the best." Geoffrey Beene is one of the best designers today—arguably the greatest American designer living—but also one of the most artistic. His art resides in certain principles and preoccupations: reversibility and alternative reading in Yin-Yang twins; surgically clean cutting, but a fluidity of cloth to body in the manner of Vionnet; an origami-like three-dimensionality that approaches sculpture; a propensity for Cubism, piecing the garment from regular forms in a new tangency and relationship one to another as if in the simultaneity of Cubism; and a modernist indulgence in the medium, relishing the textiles both of tradition and of advanced technology that he selects.

Such abiding elements of art in his work do not mitigate other elements. History may be seized, as in a remarkable Confederate dress inspired by the gray uniform of the Southern Army in the American Civil War. Sensuous appreciation of the body is ever present in Beene's work (he initially went to medical school and always demonstrates his interest in the body and ergonomics). His lace dresses expose the body in underwear—defying gyres of inset lace, a *tour de force* of the exposure of the body and of the security of the wearer in the dress's perfect and stable proportions. In 1988 his virtuoso single-seam dress was minimalist in design, but one never forgot that it was sensuous and clinging on the body. He shifts, conceals, and maneuvers the waist as no other designer has since Balenciaga.

Born in the South, Beene's personal style is of utmost charm, and his clothes betray his sense of good taste, though often with gentility's piquant notes. His 1967 long sequined football jersey was sportswear with a new goal in the evening and played with the anomaly of the simple style with its liquid elegance. Sweatshirt fabric and denim would be carried into eveningwear by Beene, upsetting convention. A brash gentility combines leather and lace; a charming wit provides for circus motifs. In particular, Beene loves the genteel impropriety of stealing from menswear textiles (shirting fabrics and gray flannel) for women's clothing.

Beene has a profound affinity with his contemporary Southerner Jasper Johns, who practices consummate good taste in art but with the startling possibilities of popular-culture appropriations, new dispositions to familiar elements, and a strong sense of contemporary cultural pastiche. Like Johns, Beene is always fascinated by *trompe l'oeil* and continually plays with illusions. Specific illusions of a tie and collar on a dress are the most obvious, but other wondrous tricks of illusion in clothing are found in three-dimensional patterns replicated in textile and vice versa. His bolero jackets so effectively complement the simplicity of his dresses that jacket and dress become an indistinguishable ensemble. Even his preoccupation with double-faced fabrics and reversible abstract designs are sophisticated illusionism.

Optically, Beene demands both near- and far-sight. Even before the most fluid forms emerged for Beene in the 1970s and 1980s, he had been influenced by Op Art to create apparel that was graphically striking. His frequent use of black and white is a treatment that can be read across a room and acts as sign. But one can approach a Beene composition in black and white close up with the same scrutiny of a Frank Stella black painting: there is a fascination up close even more gratifying than the sign from afar. In Beene's case, texture is an important element, and the distant reading of graphic clarity becomes far more complex when disparate textures are mingled. Like reversibility, the near-far dialectic in Beene is provocative: utter simplicity from a distance becomes infinite technicality up close. In the 1990s Beene has often eschewed the catwalk showing of new collections, preferring to display the garments on static dress forms, thus allowing the viewer to examine the garment attentively and immediately, as one might appreciate painting or sculpture.

Art, to describe Beene's clothing, is not vacuous or striving to compliment. Rather, art recognizes a process and suite of objectives inherent in the work. In a discipline of commercial fulfillment, Beene displays the artist's absolute primacy and self-confidence of design exploration.—RICHARD MARTIN

Bellville Sassoon-Lorcan Mullany

British couture and ready-to-wear firm, Bellville Sassoon & Bellville Sassoon-Lorcan Mullany, respectively

Belinda Bellville founded own company, 1953, joined by designer David Sassoon to form Bellville Sassoon, 1958; Bellville retired from company, 1983; Bellville Sassoon-Lorcan Mullany founded, 1987. David Sassoon born in London, 5 October 1932. Attended Chelsea College of Art, 1954-56, and Royal College of Art, London, 1956-58. Served in the Royal Air Force, 1950-53. Lorcan Mullany born 3 August 1953. Trained at Grafton Academy, Dublin. Worked for Bill Gibb, Hardy Amies, and Ronald Joyce in London before producing collection under his own name in 1983. Joined Bellville Sassoon in 1987. Ready-to-wear collection sold in, among others, Sak's Fifth Avenue, Bloomingdale's, and Henri Bendel, New York, and Harrods, Harvey Nichols, London. Also flagship store in Chelsea, London.

Exhibitions   *Fashion: An Anthology, Victoria and Albert Museum, London, 1971.*
Address   *18 Culford Gardens, London SW3 2ST, England.*

Bellville Sassoon-Lorcan Mullany: 1991.

I like clothes that flatter a woman and are sexy. If a woman feels good in the clothes I design, she looks good.

I enjoy designing cocktail and eveningwear with my co-designers Lorcan Mullany and George Sharp. We work together as a team to produce ready-to-wear dresses, sometimes in a romantic mood, sometimes whimsical or sexy. I do not like unkind clothes that are ugly and do not flatter a woman.

I love colour and beautiful fabrics. Each season we try to do something different, but always with a distinct Bellville Sassoon-Lorcan Mullany handwriting, which our buyers always look for. Our collection is sold internationally and each country looks for a different fashion concept, so our collections are always varied, never sticking to one theme. I do not like to philosophize about clothes; they are, after all, only garments to be worn and discarded as the mood of fashion changes.—David Sassoon

The company of Bellville Sassoon-Lorcan Mullany is currently jointly run by David Sassoon who owns the company, designing the couture, and Lorcan Mullany who joined in 1987 and is responsible for the ready-to-wear. Together they provide a very English version of glamorous occasion dressing and eveningwear, uncomplicated, clear, and immensely flattering clothes worn by society ladies and the international jet set: the Princess of Wales, Ivana Trump, Shakira Caine, Dame Kiri Te Kanawa, and The Countess von Bismarck, to name but a few. The company is also renowned for its glamorous and romantic wedding dresses, designed to order, and the selection of designs available in the *Vogue Pattern Book*'s designer section, which are on sale internationally.

"You have to find your own niche," declared David Sassoon when questioned about his approach to design. "You cannot be all things to all markets. My philosophy of fashion is that I like to make the kind of clothes that flatter. I am not interested in fashion for its own sake. If you make a woman feel good, she looks good automatically" (*Tatler* [London], September 1992). On leaving the Royal College of Art fashion school in the late 1950s David Sassoon was recruited as Belinda Bellville's design assistant. She recognized in him a designer who had a strong, distinctive signature and a simple approach that was romantic in style but dramatic and very feminine. Together they became business partners, naming the company Bellville et Cie, to capitalize on the prevalent conception that all smart clothes were French. From the start it attracted vast attention from press and buyers. "We gave our first show in my grandmother's house in Manchester Square and the next day there was a queue outside the shop, with Bentleys blocking the street," declared Belinda Bellville.

Sassoon identifies the peak of his career as being the period between the late 1960s and 1970s when he believed that the taste for high romanticism and fantasy clothes endorsed his style. The company was constantly featured in the pages of glossy magazines, sharing the stage with contemporaries such as Zandra Rhodes, Gina Fratini, and Bill Gibb. Sassoon regrets the fact that the British fashion press often flippantly discards designers as no longer newsworthy, comparing this with the American press who always acknowledge good design. Bill Blass and Oscar de la Renta, he declares, may no longer be in the forefront of fashion but the press still regards them as newsworthy.

In the 1970s emphasis on couture was dwindling and the company realized that in order to survive, the ready-to-wear line had to be built up. This was verified by Sassoon's belief that couture runs the risk of turning into a little dressmaker. The decision proved correct as business for the company is very large in America and is promoted with fashion shows across the United States and at trade fairs in London, Paris, New York, Munich, and Dusseldorf. Their agents have had little problem building a strong and impressive clientele.

Lorcan Mullany, who joined the company on Belinda Bellville's retirement in 1987, has a strong background in occasion and eveningwear. He trained at the Grafton Academy in Dublin and, before joining David Sassoon, worked for Bill Gibb, Ronald Joyce, and Hardy Amies. The label now bears the joint name Bellville Sassoon-Lorcan Mullany, justifiably crediting all designers for the product.

Today, Bellville Sassoon's clothes represent the top end of British occasion dressing, from sumptuous ballgowns to flirty cocktail dresses. Frills, sinuous draping, ruching, streamlined side splits, and plunging backs evoke memories of Hollywood in its glamorous heyday. Tulle, encrusted embroideries, taffetas, duchesse satin, mink, and double silk crepes are representative of the luxurious fabrics used. Unlike some eveningwear, the clothes are never gaudy and overstated; their success is reliant on a streamlined sense of style.—KEVIN ALMOND

Biagiotti, Laura

Italian designer

Born *Rome, 4 August 1943.*

Education *Studied literature and archeology in Rome, 1960-62.*

Family *Married Gianni Cigna in 1992; daughter: Lavinia.*

Career *Worked in Biagiotti family ready-to-wear firm, Rome, 1962-65; free-lance designer for Schuberth, Barocco, Cappucci, Heinz Riva, Licitro, and others, 1965-72; founder-designer, Laura Biagiotti Fashions, Rome, from 1972; took over MacPherson Knitwear, Pisa, 1974; established headquarters in Guidonia, 1980; Rispeste collection introduced, 1981; Laurapiu collection introduced, 1984; diffusion knitwear collection for Biagiotti Uomo introduced, 1985; Biagiotti jeans collection introduced, 1986; Biagiotti Uomo collecton introduced, 1987; launched perfumes Laura, 1982, Night, 1986, Roma, 1988, and Venezia, 1992; signed licensing agreement for Biagiotti shops in China, 1993; opened LB shop in Beijing, China, Bangkok, Thailand, 1994, and in Moscow, Russia, 1994.*

Awards *Golden Lion Award for achievement in linen, Venice, 1987; named Commendatore of the Italian Republic, 1987; Marco Polo Award for high achievement in diffusing Italian style worldwide, 1993; Frenio Fragene for fashion achievements, 1994.*

Address *Biagiotti Export S.p.A., via Palombarese Km, 17.300, 00012 Guidonia, Rome, Italy.*

Indisputably Italian, trained by her tailor-mother to admire the couture of France but also witness to the quality of her mother's work and employed early on in Schuberth's elegant Italian ready-to-wear, Laura Biagiotti might seem the quintessential European. Her devotion to fine materials, almost eponymously as she is sometimes called the Queen of Cashmere, may also seem devotedly Italian. Close family ties reinforce the image and Biagiotti's selection of Isabella D'Este as her ideal would seem to substantiate the nationalism of this designer's spirit. One Biagiotti fragrance is named *Venezia*.

When one looks at Biagiotti's clothes, however, one cannot help but think of America. Like Giorgio Armani, Biagiotti bespeaks Italian fashion, but is redefining Italian fashion in the last quarter of the 20th century in a sense of sportswear, separates, menswear influences, and quality materials for the standardizing templates of clothing. Biagiotti tells the story that at the time of her first show in 1972, she had so few pieces that she showed one white jacket three times, once with a skirt for morning, once with a day dress, and finally with a shiny skirt for evening. "Unintentionally I had invented the use of only one item for morning to evening," she said. If Biagiotti was, as she professes, initially inadvertent, her concept has become canny and global; her invention is necessarily as smart as it is coy. Her collections in the 1980s and 1990s have sustained a sense of the marketably traditional, always freshened with insights and style inflections to become one of the most effective designers of the era.

Biagiotti's spring-summer 1990 collection, built around navy, red, and white (admittedly with other pieces as well, but carefully constructed around the red-white-and-blue core), not only anticipated 1993 merchandising of Carolyne Roehm, but offered its clothes as wardrobe builders as well as dramatic outfits. In exposition of her work, Biagiotti told Valerie Steele, "Elegance, taste, and creativity have belonged to the Italian tradition and character for centuries and I share this privilege with all other Italian designers" (_Women of Fashion: Twentieth-Century Designers,_ New York 1991). Biagiotti has studied archaeology and now is much engaged with the arts and architecture through generous support of archeology and conservation. Yet again, her work is as much divorced from the historical past as one could imagine. It is as if she has chosen to restore the edifice (and she does live and work in what Gillian Skellenger, in _Contemporary Designers,_ rightly calls the factory-castle of Marco Simone near Rome, a Romanesque-era edifice), but her decision is a gutted rehabilitation, putting everything new inside. There are no marks of historicism in her clothing, even in the fall-winter 1985-86 collection when her monastics seem as much about Claire McCardell as about medievalism; her abiding preference for white is symbolic of her _tabula rasa_ in her clothing, so clean, notably modern in style; her sensible knits address manifold uses for contemporary working women; and, as Skellenger has noted, "Biagiotti reveals a mania for research," committed to new fabric study.

Biagiotti has spoken of her work as a personal projection, thus inevitably being fit for a modern, self-confident, and business-aware woman. If she is the ideal client for her own clothing, her personal sensibility is toward simple, almost reductive, shape carried in luxury materials, an ethos sounding like three generations of American sportswear-to-evening designers. The women's clothing can be slightly flirtatious in the American mode while her evening looks express her Roman sophistication, always with a reserve and sense of good taste. Biagiotti has come to represent decorum and fashion nuance unerring in its mainstream elegance, again a characterization she would share with Armani. What she does not share with Armani is his intense interest in menswear _per se;_ while Biagiotti has designed menswear for many years, it seems even safer than her women's clothing and the epitome of conservative good taste.

Biagiotti has said, "There are some beautiful dresses designed by others that are so important that you cannot always wear them. If you are in a bad mood or tired, if you have some problems, everyone understands that what you are wearing is simply dressing you up. But this does not happen with my designs. In fact, I would define my creations with the slogan, 'A dress for when you want to be yourself.'" Biagiotti has rendered the specific garment unimportant, but she attaches utmost importance to clothing as a value-laden social frame to the portrait of the modern woman. In fact, Biagiotti creates a spare, quiet, comfortable clothing, the essence of late 20th-century dressing, even as she inhabits and works from a medieval castle. The combination is mesmerizingly romantic.—RICHARD MARTIN

Bikkembergs, Dirk

Belgian designer

Born   *Flamersheim, Germany, 3 January 1962.*

Education   *Studied fashion at the Royal Academy of Arts, Antwerp.*

Military Service   *Served with Royal Belgian Army, in Germany.*

Career   *Free-lance designer for Nero, Bassetti, Gruno and Chardin, Tiktiner, Gaffa, K, Jaco Petti, 1982-87; launch of Dirk Bikkembergs-Homme Co., with DB shoe line for men, 1985; knitwear introduced, 1986; first complete menswear collection introduced, 1988; first womenswear line Dirk Bikkembergs-Homme Pour La Femme presented in Paris, 1993.*

Awards   *For menswear collection, winter 1985-86, several Belgian fashion industry awards, including Golden Spindle.*

Address   *Dirk Bikkembergs Hommes BVBA, Kidorp 21, Belgium.*

I design clothes for men and women that have a special, strong attitude. For a younger, future-minded generation for whom fashion has become a way to express themselves; to give shelter and strength and the feeling of looking good. A generation that has risen above the question of fashion, sure about its quality and style and their own; celebrating life.

I design collections that give one whole strong look, a vision of life, men and women with items that are nonchalant and easy to mix, give freedom and don't restrict the wearer; but there are always special pieces that are stronger and more defined, marking a certain period of time and setting a sign.

My clothes are never retro. I hate the idea of looking back. I don't have any idols from the past. I do strongly believe in tomorrow and the future of the human race. To achieve this I devote a lot of attention to the cut and fabric that I use. Yes, I tend to think about my clothes as fashion and I'm not afraid of that, nor are my clients.

I design strong clothes for strong individuals rather than wrapping up pretentious nerds in sophisticated cashmere. Nothing is so boring as a "nice and neat" look. Life is just too good and too short for that.—Dirk Bikkembergs

Heavyweight fabrics and macho imagery quite literally dominate Dirk Bikkembergs's work. His best designs convey a solidity through their layering of leather and thick knitwear, while still retaining the feeling of minimalist restraint which has come to be associated with Belgian fashion. Bikkembergs, although not the most prominent of the designers who formed the Belgian avant-garde of the later 1980s, is nonetheless a significant purveyor of their ideals. His clothing consists of dark and muted toned separates which provide strong images of modern

Dirk Bikkembergs: Fall/Winter 1995/96. *Photograph by Marleen Daniels.*

living: although his own work does not so frequently contain the deconstructed edge of his counterparts.

The most influential area of his work has been footwear. A specialist in the field, he has brought together the traditions of well made hardwearing shoes made up for him by Flanders craftsmen, with the late 1980s/early 1990s obsession with workwear. His designs are inspired by classic functional styles. He constantly reworks the clearly defined shapes of 1930s football boots, making them into neat, round-toed lace-up urban footwear in 1987. In 1993 he tampered with the weighty infantryman's boot, stripping it of its utilitarian status, when, with a deconstructivist flourish, he removed the eyelets which normally punctuate the boot and accommodate the distinctive high lacing. Instead a hole was drilled into the sole through which the laces had to be threaded and then wrapped around the boot's leather upper to secure it to the foot. The style soon became *de rigueur* for both men and women in fashion circles, with copies being sold in High Street chains.

Like all his work, they were based on familiar designs which convey traditional notions of masculinity, conjuring up images of sporting and military heroics. Such ideals pervade his menswear.

His carefully styled shows send musclebound models down the catwalk, clad in the obligatory biker boots and black leather which have now become a staple of the late 20th-century male wardrobe. This machismo continues in his signature knitwear range. Heavy rib V-necks are worn with lightweight jogging bottoms or matching woollen leggings. His work may not show the more slimline feminine notes which have been gradually breaking through the previously limited spectrum of menswear designs, but have still had influence. He helped to widen the scope of knitwear with witty takes on classic Aran jumpers and cardigans, and by using decorative detailing to add interest to simple designs: in 1992 with bright blue zips on either side of burnt orange sweaters, and in 1987 by adding them to high necked jumpers which were popular at the time.

Although he works best with these winter weight fabrics, he still adds twists to his summer collections. In 1988 he produced collared linen waistcoats which could be layered over long sleeved shirts, or worn alone to give interest to plain suits. It was in the late 1980s that his designs were most attuned to the *Zeitgeist*. He provided the overblown masculine imagery which was popular then. This was encapsulated in his distinctive marketing, which demonstrated the same eye for detail. The catalogues produced for each range show in grainy black and white his tough masculine ideals with his commandeering of popular stereotypes like the biker.

Despite this concentration on menswear, his work has extended to a womanswear range. In 1993 his first collection was warmly received, bringing together both his love of strong silhouettes and a deconstructed minimalism to provide a twist to basic shapes. The natural counterpart to his masculine lines, it carried through his use of sturdy footwear and accessories which had always been popular with women as well.

As part of the rise in status of Belgian fashion since the late 1980s, Bikkembergs's work appeals to the fashion *cognoscenti*. The overt masculinity of his designs is combined with a knowledge and exploitation of traditional styles to provide stark modern imagery. If not as well known as contemporaries like Dries Van Noten, he has still carved a niche for his work and heralded a fresh slant to his output with his recent divergence into womenswear.—REBECCA ARNOLD

Blahnik, Manolo

Spanish footwear designer

Born *Santa Cruz, Canary Islands, 27 November 1942.*

Education *Educated at home, then at the University of Geneva, 1960-65; studied art in Paris, 1965-70.*

Career *Jeans buyer for Feathers Boutique, London, early 1970s; encouraged to design shoes by Diana Vreeland; first collections for Zapata Boutique, London and for Ossie Clark, early 1970s; opened London firm, 1973 with subsequent shops in New York and Hong Kong. Also furniture designer.*

Awards *Fashion Council of America Award, 1988, 1991; British Fashion Council Award, 1991; Balenciaga Award, 1991; American Leather Award, New York, 1991; Hispanic Institute Antonio Lopez Award, Washington, DC, 1991.*

Address *49-51 Old Church St., London SW3, England.*

Established in the 1970s, Manolo Blahnik is world famous. His beautiful shoes exude a level of craftsmanship which has become a rare commodity in today's age of mass production, and he has a wonderful sense of line and silhouette. These talents, combined with the other footwear sense that he displays and exploits, have ensured his rightful position as a true genius in his field, worthy of sharing the mantle worn by the other brilliant shoe designers of the 20th century, Yanturni, Vionnet, Perugia, Ferragamo, and the genius he most admires, Roger Vivier.

Manolo Blahnik was born in 1942 in Santa Cruz, in the Canary Islands, of a Czech father and Spanish mother. This slightly exotic and romantic start to his life possibly determined the pattern his future was to assume. His awareness of shoes was an early memory. His mother, who had a fondness for satin and brocade fabrics, had her footwear made by Don Christino, the island's leading shoemaker. Blahnik inherited her love of the unconventional and remembers seeing a trunk containing shoes by Yanturni, the Russian designer and one-time curator of the Cluny Museum in Paris. The shoes, in brocades, silks, and antique lace, trimmed with buckles, were elegant and light; attributes which Blahnik later sought to achieve in his own creations.

Blahnik studied law, literature, and Renaissance art in Europe before settling in London in 1970. His portfolio of theatrical designs was seen by the photographer Cecil Beaton, and Diana Vreeland of American *Vogue* who particularly admired his shoe designs and encouraged him to concentrate on this aspect of his work. His subsequent footwear collections were to prove how astute had been their instincts for this extraordinary talent.

The mood of the 1970s was lively, adventurous, and colourful. The advent of the mini skirt had focused attention on the legs and consequently on original interpretations of footwear. Creative thought had produced new materials for shoes and a climate in which fresh ideas could flourish, and Blahnik dramatically interpreted these trends. Flowers appeared at the ankles, there were cutout shapes and appliqués. Purple was the "in" colour; ankle boots, lace-ups with small, chunky heels in stacked leather or shiny veneer, crêpe soles and a new craze for "wet-look" leather, all appeared in his collections. Footwear was zany, feet were in fashion and it required endless imagination to stay in front.

Blahnik chose "Zapata" as the name of his first shop, opened in London in 1973. He now uses his own name but, from the beginning, his tiny, personalized salon has continued to be a mecca for devotees from all over the world. His shoes are worn by friends and socialites and always attract media attention.

A shoe designer's handwriting is as distinctive as that of a couturier. It will evolve and embrace the newest developments of fashion but, once established, it will not radically change and will continue to be instantly recognizable. Manolo Blahnik has a deep understanding of contemporary trends and a genuine feeling for his clientèle and what they seek in a shoe. Constantly featured in the world's most prestigious fashion magazines, it is easy to see why his imagination and ability to translate fantasy into delectable and desirable foot coverings have won him such acclaim. His designs are always immensely complimentary to the feet. His philosophy is that fashion should be fun and his ebullient and energetic designs have always reflected this. He considers shape, material, and decoration with great care and combines hand-craftsmanship with modern techniques. A master of materials, he handles leather, suede, velvets, silks, and the unconventional and unexpected with equal flair and panache, paying exact attention to detail and creating fine, elegant footwear with glamour and refinement. His shoes have a weightless quality and a seemingly ethereal atmosphere often pervades his collections.

Many styles are deliberately kept exclusive, with only small quantities produced, and his instantly recognized style remains constant, regardless of the fashion climate. Over the years he has designed collections to enhance the work of, amongst others, Yves Saint Laurent, Emmanuel Ungaro, Calvin Klein, Perry Ellis, Bill Blass, Fiorucci, Isaac Mizrahi, Ossie Clark, Zandra Rhodes, Jean Muir, Jasper Conran, and Rifat Ozbeck. One of his most famous individual clients is the fashion eccentric, Anna Piaggi. She invariably selects a pair of Blahnik's shoes to complement the other wonderful items in her wardrobe. The following is a typical description of her appearance: "Black velvet coat by Lanvin, c.1925; T-shirt in cotton jersey by Missoni, c.1975; Harem trousers made out of a silk kimono; Grey suede shoes trimmed with mink by Blahnik; the jewel, a crystal iceberg with an orange bead by Fouquet."

Wherever they are featured, Blahnik's shoes are a copywriter's dream. Frequently executed in vivid colours, magenta, deep purple, bright scarlet, orange, emerald green, or saffron yellow, they retain a certain theatrical fantasy—"Red mules with high, knotted vamps;" "jewelled satin shoes for the summer collection;" "Ribbon wrapped ankles for watered silk dancing shoes;" "Sketch for the glove shoe;" "The Siamese twin shoe." Completely original combinations of wit, sex, and allure. With their reference to history they nevertheless remain entirely contemporary whilst catching the spirit of both.

Manolo Blahnik is a distinctive personality, much travelled, intelligent and well educated, in demand for his opinions, wit, energy, and style. Like many true originators, he could probably have been a successful designer in another field. His distinctive sketches, for example, transmit a real feeling for his shoes and are used for his company publicity. They serve to underline how very individual his work is. He clothes some of the world's best dressed feet. He makes shoes for all occasions. He has an international reputation and a clientèle worldwide. His shoes are worn, and adored, by film stars, celebrities, socialites, and those who just love what he offers. He has an intrinsic feeling for the moment, and a foresight into what will come next. His shoes are provocative and dashingly extrovert; almost, but not quite, too beautiful and desirable to be worn.—ANGELA PATTISON

Blass, Bill

American designer

Born *William Ralph Blass in Fort Wayne, Indiana, 22 June 1922.*
Education *Attended Fort Wayne High School, 1936-39; studied fashion design, Parsons School of Design, New York, 1939.*
Military Service *Served in the United States Army, 1941-44: Sergeant.*
Career *Sketch artist, David Crystal Sportswear, New York, 1940-41; designer, Anna Miller and Company Ltd., New York, 1945; designer, 1959-70, and vice-president, 1961-70, Maurice Rentner Ltd., New York; Rentner company purchased and re-named Bill Blass Ltd., 1970; Blassport sportswear division introduced, 1972; signature perfume introduced, 1978. Licensed products include menswear, women's sportswear, candies, furs, swimwear, jeans, bedlinens, shoes, perfumes, and an automobile.*
Awards *Coty American Fashion Critics "Winnie" Award, 1961, 1963, 1970, Menswear Award, 1968, Hall of Fame Award, 1970, and Special Citations, 1971, 1982, 1983; Gold Coast Fashion Award, Chicago, 1965; National Cotton Council Award, New York, 1966; Neiman Marcus Award, Dallas, 1969; Print Council Award, 1971; Martha Award, New York, 1974; Ayres Look Award, 1978; Gentlemen's Quarterly Manstyle Award, New York, 1979; Cutty Sark Hall of Fame Award, 1979; Honorary Doctorate, Rhode Island School of Design, 1977; Council of Fashion Designers of America Award, 1986.*
Address *550 Seventh Avenue, New York, New York 10018, USA.*

"Like most people who seem to be most typically New York, Bill Blass comes from Indiana," wrote native Midwesterner Eleanor Lambert in an early press release for Blass when he worked at Maurice Rentner. Blass reigns as an American classic, the man who abidingly exemplifies high style because his work plays on the sharp edge of glamour, but never falls into the abyss of indecency. Likewise, it defines sophisticated style because it has elements of the naive and the crude in impeccable balance. Blass is the perfect example of fashion's deconstructivist internal oppositions of real, hyper-glamour, and style synthesis.

Although Blass believes in eliminating the superfluous and stressing the essentials of clothing, he is no Yankee skinflint or reductive modernist and aims to beguile and flatter, adding perhaps a flyaway panel, not necessary for structure, that would never appeal to a Halston or a Zoran. He aims to create a fanciful chic, a sense of glamour and luxury. It may be that these desires are fashion's game, but it is undeniable that Blass is the expert player. Everything he does is suffused with glamour, and he creates evening gowns that would stagger Scarlett O'Hara. His shimmering Matisse collection, embroidered in India, transformed the client into the conveyer of masterpiece paintings.

Blass is an indisputable enchanter, a man who loves being with the ladies he dresses. Correspondingly, they love being with him, but the relationship is not merely indicative of the elevation of fashion designer from dressmaker to social presence. Blass learns from his clients and, in learning, addresses their needs and wishes. In designing separates, he describes what he likes with a certain top, admits that one of his clients prefers to wear it otherwise and acknowledges that it looks better as she wears it. The client is supreme not in a manner of subservience, but in adaptability, as if the composer of modern music sought fulfillment in the musical interpretation through performance and some degree of improvisation.

There are essential leitmotifs in Blass's work. Recalling Mainbocher, he invents from the sweater and brings insights of daywear into the most elegant night-time presentations. Blass imports menswear practicality and fabrics to womenswear. His evening gowns are dream-like in their self-conscious extravagance and flattery to the wearer. He can evoke Schiaparelli in the concise elegance of a simulated wood embroidered jacket. A succulent slice of watermelon for a rever may emulate Schiaparelli, but there is also something definably Blass about the gesture. In a very old-fashioned way, he celebrates life with none of the cynicism of other designers. He is audacious in mixing pattern and texture, though generally with the subtlety of his preferred palette of dove, gray-green, and muted color. Texture is equally important, a red wool cardigan resonant to a red silk dress or the complement of gray flannel trousers to fractured, shimmering surfaces for day and evening. Layering is essential to Blass: whether it is a cardigan teamed with a blouse or sweater or gauzy one-sleeve wraps for evening, Blass flourishes in layers.

It is conventional wisdom to say that Blass has become the superb licensing genius and dean of American fashion designers, implying an inconsequential creative impulse. Blass's attainment, however, is to imagine. His is an intensely pictorial imagination, one that conjures up the most romantic possibilities of fashion. He maintains an ideal of glamour and personal aura, redolent of socialites and stars of screen and stage. He plays with the reconciliation of nonchalant comfort for the wearer and the impression his clothing conveys to the spectator.

There is little in Blass's work that is truly unique to him and not practiced by any other designer, yet one would never mistake a Blass for a Mainbocher or a Schiaparelli, nor for any of his contemporaries. The characteristic glamour and star-quality grandeur that he gives to clothing, while maintaining a level of refinement, is distinctively Blass. He is, as Eleanor Lambert said of him when he was still at Rentner, quintessentially New York. A crossroads city, a striving place, and a dreaming desire inform Blass's work. Beguiling charm and glamorous seduction are perhaps easy to envy and easier still to criticize, yet the extraordinary consistency and quality of Bill Blass is not easily achieved.—RICHARD MARTIN

Bodymap

British design team

Owned by Stevie Stewart and David Holah. Stewart born in London, 1958; studied at Barnet College. Holah born in London, 1958; studied at North Oxfordshire College of Art. Both studied fashion at Middlesex Polytechnic, 1979-82; graduation collection purchased by Browns, London. Firm founded in 1982, expanded from 1985 to include Bodymap men's and women's collection, B-Basic junior line, Bodymap Red Label, and Bodymap swimwear.

Awards *Martini Young Fashion Award, 1983; Bath Museum of Costume Dress of the Year Award, 1984.*

Address *93 Fortress Road, London NW5 2HR, England.*

"Barbie Takes a Trip," "Querelle Meets Olive Oil," "The Cat in the Hat Takes a Rumble with the Techno Fish," are just some of the bizarre titles of previous Bodymap collections. The company, a male-female partnership between Middlesex Polytechnic graduates, David Holah and Stevie Stewart, was one of the brightest design teams to emerge during the 1980s. By the middle of the decade London was being promoted by the media as a trendy hothouse of bright young things. Bodymap was regarded as being amongst the brightest of all, turning the Establishment upside-down with wild, young, and unconventional clothes. Fashion editors were clamouring for more, declaring Bodymap to be the hottest fashion label of the decade.

Founded in 1982, the name of the company was inspired by the Italian artist Enrico Job, who took over a thousand photographs of every part of his anatomy, then collaged them together, creating a two-dimensional version of a three-dimensional object; in other words, a body map. A similar philosophy was adapted in Stewart and Holah's approach to pattern making and garment construction. Prints, knits, silhouettes, and shapes were restructured and reinvented to map the body. Stretch clothes had holes in unexpected places, so that the emphasis was transferred from one place to another. Pieces of flesh were amalgamated with pieces of fabric in an effort to explore new areas of the body, previously considered unflattering.

Awarded the Individual Clothes Show prize as the "Most Exciting and Innovative Young Designers of 1983," Bodymap clothes have always been for the young, avant-garde, and the daring. Working predominantly in black, white, and cream, a familiar theme involves the layering of prints and textures on top of one another, to create an unstructured look, redefining traditional body shapes, overemphasizing shapeliness or shapelessness so that both the overweight and underweight, plain or beautiful can wear and be comfortable in an outfit.

Bodymap described themselves in the 1980s as being a young company that employed other young people to mix creativity with commerce. They worked very closely with textile designer Hilde Smith, who has created many Bodymap prints and has helped bridge gaps between fashion and textile design. The film and videomaker John Maybury was responsible for Bodymap's outrageous fashion show videos, featuring dancer Michael Clark, singers Boy George and Helen Terry, and performance artist Leigh Bowery. Photographer David La Chappelle was responsible for many of the visual stills used in magazines.

While still at Middlesex Polytechnic, Bodymap recognized the importance of moving in a circle of talented, creative people. Holah and Stewart were part of the young 1980s generation that attracted worldwide attention for London as a vibrant centre for creative energy and ideas, not only in fashion but music, painting, video, and dance.—KEVIN ALMOND

Bohan, Marc

French designer

> **Born**   *Marc Roger Maurice Louis Bohan in Paris, 22 August 1926.*
> **Education**   *Studied at the Lycée Lakanal, Sceaux, 1940-44.*
> **Family**   *Married Dominique Gaborit in 1950 (died, 1962); married Huguette Rinjonneau (died); daughter: Marie-Anne.*
> **Career**   *Assistant designer in Paris to Robert Piguet, 1945-49, and to Molyneux, 1949-51; designer, Madeleine de Rauch, Paris, 1952; briefly opened own Paris salon, produced*

one collection, 1953; head designer for couture, Maison Patou, Paris, 1954-58; designer, Dior, London, 1958-60, and head designer and art director, Dior, Paris, 1960-89; fashion director for Norman Hartnell, London, 1990-92.

Awards *Sports Illustrated Designer of the Year Award, 1963; Schiffli Lace and Embroidery Institute Award, 1963; named Chevalier de la Legion d'Honneur, 1979; Ordre de Saint Charles, Monaco.*

"N'oubliez pas la femme," Marc Bohan's much quoted comment in *Vogue* magazine in 1963, is the tenet which underscores all his work. It has brought his success throughout his lengthy couture career, his design always based on the grown-up female form and a recognition of his customers' needs rather than an overriding desire to shock and provoke headlines in his name. From his early days at Molyneux he learned a sense of practicality, as well as an appreciation of the flattering potential of luxurious fabrics and good fit. His perfectionist zeal and attention to detail, and especially in the 1960s and 1970s at Christian Dior, a good fashion sense, have been at the foundations of his reputation.

It was at Dior that Bohan's talents were established, winning him international acclaim. He enabled the house to remain at the forefront of fashion while still producing wearable, elegant clothes. To achieve this end, Bohan combined innovation with repeated classic shapes and styles, reworked to express the current mood. In 1961, Dior included some of the briefest skirts of the couture collections, but the neat black and white tweed fabric of these little suits enabled Bohan to please the established clientèle, as well as attracting new customers with use of wit and modernity. His suiting always showed the most directional styles and cut, which others would follow.

This ability to ease normally cautious clients towards new, more radical styles by carefully balancing all the elements of a design was seen again in his 1966 collection, when he showed the by then *de rigueur* mini with longer coats, promoting a shift in hemlines gradually rather than dictating a change.

It is this desire to coax and flatter which distinguishes his couture work. His sensitivity to the needs of women has prevented him from trying to mould them into ever-altering silhouettes, or forget their desire to look grown up and elegant even when fashion promoted girlish styles in the 1960s. His use of decoration is equally discreet. He prefers the demure wit of pussycat bows on simple silk blouses and shirtwaist dresses or naturalistic floral prints to add interest to his creations, rather than any overblown gestures that might render the garments less easy to wear, making the client self-conscious.

He has always been unafraid to tell his customers what is most flattering for them and they appreciate his honesty; his rich and famous client list remained faithful even when he switched from one house to the next. His eveningwear is, with his clever suiting styles, his greatest strength, with an understated sense of style allowing the luxurious fabrics and subtle detailing to shine through the simple forms he prefers.

This was seen both in his work of Dior and his later creations for Norman Hartnell. At the former he presented stark modernist shapes, like the angular ivory silk evening tunic and matching cigarette trousers (1965), with rich red floral design creeping over its surface. At Hartnell he again excelled at reviving the spirits of an established couture name. He developed his pared-down style to fulfill the house's design brief, attracting a younger audience with his first collection, combining flirtatious shaping with classic styles. In 1991, he showed the sophisticated chic of black sheath dresses with diamanté buttons next to witty fuchsia silk scoop-necked dresses with short, very full skirts that harked back to the bubble dresses that had reinvigorated his work for Dior in the late 1970s. Again he provided choice for his customers and commercial designs which were well received by the press.

Bohan's time at Hartnell was brief, curtailed by the recession of the early 1990s which caused the decline in interest in couture, precipitating the demise of several of the smaller houses and leading to cutbacks in all areas of fashion. His sense of elegance remained undiminished. If his suits were the most innovative area of his work, he balanced their fashion-led cut with well-constructed, feminine separates and striking eveningwear which had the lasting appeal characteristic of all good design.—REBECCA ARNOLD

Brigance, Tom
American designer

Born   *Thomas Franklin Brigance in Waco, Texas.*

Education   *Attended Waco Junior College; studied in New York at the Parsons School of Design, 1931-34, and the National Academy of Art; studied in Paris at the Sorbonne and at the Académie de la Grande Chaumière, Paris.*

Military Service   *Served in the United States Air Corps Intelligence Service, South Pacific, 1941-44, decorated for bravery.*

Career   *Worked in Europe as free-lance fashion designer, designed in London for Jaeger and for Simpson's of Piccadilly, late 1930s; designer, Lord & Taylor, New York, 1939-41 and 1944-49; opened own firm, 1949; also designed in New York for Frank Gallant, and free-lanced for Fonde, Sportsmarket, and designed swimwear for Sinclair and Gabar, Water Clothes, 1950s.*

Awards   *Coty American Fashion Critics Award, 1953; International Silk Citation, 1954; National Cotton Award, 1955; Internazionale delle Arti Award, Italy, 1956.*

Died   *(in New York City) 14 October 1990.*

Eleanor Lambert's 1951 press release for Tom Brigance quotes the young designer: "Good American clothes should be able to go anywhere. They should not be designed with a single town or section in mind. They should be appropriate for the American woman's mode of living, expressive of her individual personality, and suitable for the climate she lives in." Brigance spoke and designed with the plain common sense of Will Rogers and the utmost simplicity of the American ethos. No one could more readily have epitomized the main-street ideal of an American fashion designer than Brigance. From Waco, Texas, slim, dark, and charming, Brigance became a recognized designer in 1939, while still in his twenties, as part of Dorothy Shaver's campaign to create American designer identities at Lord & Taylor.

His first success was in active sportswear and beachwear. In an advertisement in *Vogue* (15 May 1939), Lord & Taylor boasted of its new American hero, "When you come to the World's Fair be sure to visit our Beach Shop on the fifth floor, home of creations by Brigance, one of our own designers, whose ideas enchant even the blasé Riviera." Anne-Marie Schiro reports in Brigance's obituary in the *New York Times* (18 October 1990) that the Duchess of Windsor bought half a dozen outfits from his first beachwear collection in 1939, a formidable endorsement for any young designer. Brigance remained a designer at Lord & Taylor until 1949. Although he later designed a full spectrum of clothing, including eveningwear, his forte through his retirement in the late 1970s was sportswear, especially playsuits, beach- and swimwear. At Brigance's death in 1990 Schiro reported: "He retired in the late 1970s after a two-year stint with Gabar whose owner, Gabriel Colasante, said this week that a Brigance-designed skirted swimsuit is still one of his company's best-selling styles. 'It sells no matter what print I do it in,' he said."

Brigance was at his best when at his most simple. His employer Lord & Taylor boasted of Brigance in advertising in the *Herald Tribune* (14 September 1947): "His suits and coats have the distinctively American lines that inspire individuality with accessories." Like Claire McCardell, Brigance used fabric ties and sashes to shape waists and create form; his coats and suits were uniformly unadorned, but inflected with relatively large buttons in interesting placement. By the late 1940s, he was acknowledging the New Look, not in its extreme forms, but in a modified version in which the skirt or peplum flared with pockets, adding practicality to the gesture of the wider skirt. His play clothes were his most imaginative, suggesting the spectrum of leisure from beach pajamas through halter tops and playsuits with shorts and skirts. For summer, his preference was generally for colorful cottons, often with dots. His swimwear presaged the American idiom of dressing in warm climates in clothes as suitable for the street as for the beach and swimming.

Distinctively, Brigance enjoyed pattern mixes more than most of his contemporaries. Today his surprising combinations of florals, geometrics, and exotics are strikingly bold and seem more advanced as textile fusions than others of his generation. While his ideological interest was reductive, his style was always to supply plenty of material and ample coverage. He kept a loyal, even aging, clientele because he flattered the body with informal exposure that was never scanty, even in swimwear and playsuits. One could be unfailingly modest and self-assured in Brigance. His design sensibility for minimalism was aided in another way by his interest in fabric technology: his nylon swimsuit of 1960 exploited the fast-drying material. In 1955 he was the only man among seven American designers, including Anne Fogarty, Pauline Trigère, and Claire McCardell, to style interiors for Chrysler Corporation cars.

Eugenia Sheppard, writing in the *Herald Tribune* (28 October 1947), claimed that Brigance had Aristotle's phrase "nothing is permanent but change" set over the mirror in his design workroom at Lord & Taylor. Change for Brigance was ever modest; sportswear was also a credo, believing in the practical aspects of clothing. Less adventurous than McCardell or Cashin, Brigance (along with John Weitz) anticipated the emergence of great male designers in the 1970s and 1980s era of American sportswear. Like them, he was his own best salesperson and a kind of native hero, the man who not only dressed the American ideal woman of suburban chic, but also the man for whom she dressed. His 1949 dinner separates in pleated jersey exemplify Brigance's contribution to design: a quintessentially American look that is informal, sporty, innovative, open, and yet demure.—RICHARD MARTIN

Brooks, Donald

American designer

Born *New York City, 10 January 1928.*

Education *Studied art, Syracuse University, Syracuse, New York, 1947-49, and fashion design and illustration, Parsons School of Design, New York, 1949-50.*

Career *Designed for a series of New York ready-to-wear firms, c.1950-56; other work in New York includes designer for Darbury, 1956; partner and designer, Hedges of New York, 1957-59; designer, own label for Townley Frocks, 1958-64; designer, custom apparel, Henri Bendel department store, 1961; owner and designer, Donald Brooks, Inc., 1964-73; launched Boutique Donald Brooks line, 1969. Designed sweaters for Jane Irwill, 1965; shoes for Newton Elkin, 1966; furs for Coopchik-Forrest, Inc., 1967; furs for Bonwit Teller department store, 1969; robes and sleepwear for Maidenform, shoes for Palizzio; drapery fabrics and bedlinens for Burlington, 1971; DB II line introduced, c.1980; Donald Brooks ready-to-wear, 1986; consultant for fabric and colour design, Ann Taylor stores, from 1990. Also: theatre, film, TV, and custom clothing designer from 1961.*

Awards *Coty American Fashion Critics Award, 1958, 1962, 1967, 1974; National Cotton Award, 1962; New York Drama Critics Award, 1963; Parsons Medal for Distinguished Achievement, 1974; Emmy Award, 1982.*

Address *c/o Parson's School of Design, 66 Fifth Avenue, New York 10011, USA.*

Staying power characterized Donald Brooks every bit as much as the simply cut, easy fitting dresses in distinctive fabrics for which he is best known. A summer job in the advertising and display department at Lord & Taylor let him into ready-to-wear, first as a sketch artist and subsequently as designer for a series of undistinguished manufacturers. After a stint as designer at Darbury and Hedges of New York, where his work was admired by the fashion press, Brooks moved to Townley Frocks as successor to Claire McCardell. There, Brooks was given his own label as well as the chance to develop his own prize-winning printed fabrics.

By the mid-1960s, Brooks was one of the few American designers to have financial control of his own business. From that base he diversified along the usual lines, designing sweaters, shoes, swimsuits, furnishing fabrics, and other items under a multitude of licensing agreements. At the same time he built a secure base for his custom-made clothes that would stand him in good stead throughout the recession years of the 1970s and 1980s. Brooks also developed a parallel career, interpreting the contemporary scene for television, film, and the theater, beginning in 1961. His many stage credits include the musical *No Strings,* which earned him a New York Drama Critics Award, 1963, and a nomination for the Antoinette Perry, or "Tony," Award. For his film design Brooks received four Oscar nominations. The parallel careers often supported one another, as when Brooks's clothes for the film *Star,* set in the 1920s and 1930s, provided the direction for his 1968 ready-to-wear collection.

Donald Brooks's clothes are known for their clean lines, often surprising colors, and for their distinctive fabrics, most of which he designs. There is a boldness about a Brooks design that makes an impact and makes his contemporary dresses for the stage particularly successful.

The Parsons Medal for Distinguished Achievement has been awarded less than half a dozen times in almost as many decades. Brooks received it in 1974, to join a roster that singles out Adrian, Norman Norell, and Claire McCardell as especially noteworthy American designers.—WHITNEY BLAUSEN

Bruce, Liza

American designer working in London

Born *New York, 1955.*
Family *Married Nicholas Barker.*
Career *Designed high-end bathing suits, c.1982; began designing ready-to-wear, 1988; works in London.*
Address *37 Warple Way, London W3, England.*

Lean, pared-down shapes, devoid of decoration or unnecessary seams dominate Liza Bruce's work. Shaped with Lycra, her clothes cling to the body. She has removed tight clothing from its conventional daring context and defined the mid-1980s notion of simple stretch garments as the basis for the modern wardrobe. Her designs are founded on the flattering silhouette they produce, emphasizing shape while narrowing the frame.

Her background in swimwear design, which continues in her collections, has given her a confidence in working with the female form. Although at first her stretch lustre crêpe leggings made some women feel too self-conscious and underdressed, they became the ultimate example of this 1980s innovation and were soon a staple in the fashion world, taken up by the 1984 revival interest in synthetics.

Minimalist shape was one of the early examples of her highly recognizable style. She has built on the garments that supplement her streamlined swimwear range, originally modelled on bodybuilder Lisa Lyons, who embodied the toned strength of Bruce's design. Her swimming costumes and closely related bodies produce the characteristic smooth line that pervades her work, some in stark black and white with scooped out necklines, in 1989, others more delicate and decorative. In 1992, soft peach bodies were sprinkled with self coloured beads across the bust area.

Bruce's detailing maintains the aerodynamic line of her clothes, while adding definition and interest to their usual matt simplicity. In 1992 she also produced column-like sheath dresses and skirts that clung to the ankle like a second skin, punctuated by beads at regular intervals down their sides, which were quickly copied in the High Street. The subtle sophistication of such tubular styles avoided the pervasive retro fashion of that year. Indeed, Bruce's work, based as it is on easy-to-wear, timeless separates, pays only lip service to current trends. In 1990 this took the form of black crêpe and Lycra mix catsuits with fake fur collars, while her 1993 collection nodded towards deconstructionist styles, with shrunken mohair jumpers, crumpled silk shifts, and narrow coats with external seams. It was perhaps inevitable that her work would incorporate such touches as her outerwear range, begun in 1989, expanded.

Bruce's signature is most strongly stamped on the lean, sculptured stretchwear she consistently produces. It presents an ideal of modernity in its streamlined design, confident shape, and essential minimalism. She has been able to build on these basic garments as her confidence as a designer of outerwear grew, enabling her to incorporate contemporary fashion preoccupations into more tailored pieces that complement and expand upon the post-modernist tenets of her style. Her popularity in the fashion world is established and her appeal to confident, independent women who appreciate simple yet sexy clothes bereft of unnecessary detail continues to grow.—REBECCA ARNOLD

Burrows, Stephen

American designer

Born *Stephen Gerald Burrows in Newark, New Jersey, 15 September 1943.*
Education *Studied at Philadelphia Museum College of Art, 1961-62; studied fashion design, Fashion Institute of Technology, New York, 1964-66.*
Career *Designer, Weber Originals, New York, 1966-67; designer, Allen & Cole, c. 1967-68; co-founder, proprietor, "O" boutique, 1968; in-house designer for Stephen Burrows' World boutique, Henri Bendel store, New York, 1969-73; founder-director, Burrows Inc., New York, 1973-82; also, designer, Henri Bendel, 1977-82, 1993; returned to ready-to-wear design, 1989, and to custom design, 1990; designed knitwear line for Tony Lambert Co., 1991.*
Exhibitions *Versailles Palace, 1973.*
Awards *Coty American Fashion Critics "Winnie" Award, 1973, 1977, and Special Award, 1974; Council of American Fashion Critics Award, 1975; Knitted Textile Association Crystal Ball Award, 1975.*

Phoenix and fire bird of New York fashion, Stephen Burrows is one of the most audacious and auspicious talents in contemporary fashion. As Bernadine Morris (*New York Times,* 3 April 1990) said of Burrows, he is "incapable of making banal clothes." When creating custom-made clothes in the 1990s, Burrows insisted he would make only one dress of a kind. He told Morris (*New York Times,* 1 May 1990), "Why not? I have plenty of ideas—I don't have to repeat myself."

With the Henri Bendel (New York) 1970 launch of Stephen Burrows' World, Burrows was recognized for his remarkable color-block, fluid, flirting with the *non-finito,* sexy separates that typified the assertive woman of the 1970s. Spectacularly successful in the 1970s, Burrows has enjoyed periods of triumph and quiescence in the subsequent years with forays into sportswear in the early 1990s, custom-made clothing in the 1980s, and eveningwear in 1993, again for Henri Bendel. He has come and gone and come again in the public gaze, partly for business reasons, but his design sensibility has been consistent. He sees bold color fields and tests color dissonance to achieve remarkable new harmony. His great mentor Geraldine Stutz, erstwhile president of Bendel's, commented (*New York Times,* 12 August 1970) that he "stretches a rainbow over the body." But Burrows's rainbow has never sought a Peter Max popularity; his rainbow is extraordinary and unexpected, juxtaposing the strongest colors.

Serviceable separates have always been a large part of Burrows' look. Even his flirtatious dresses of the 1970s, often with his characteristic lettuce edging, seem to be parts when broken by color blocks and zones. As a result, his clothing always seems unaffected and young in the tradition of American sportswear. Clinging jersey, curving lines, and off-setting of easy drape by tight cling make Burrows' clothing both comfortable and very sexy. Of his 1990 collections, the designer himself said: "The dresses are sexy. Women should have an escort when they wear them." (*New York Times,* 9 January 1990).

Like Giorgio di Sant'Angelo and, to a lesser degree, Halston, Burrows was the quintessential fashion expression of the 1970s in a disestablishment sensibility, young nonchalance, and unfailing insistence on looking beautiful. Native American themes (also explored by di Sant'Angelo in 1969 and 1970), bold color fields in jersey with exposed seams as edges, and the unfinished appearance of puckered lettuce edging seemed almost careless in 1969 and 1970 when invented by Burrows, but they can also be recognized as hallmarks of a truthful, youthful culture that demanded no deceit in dress and a return to basics. If Burrows never yielded the sensuality of the body, he again prefigured the last quarter of the century as the body becomes the inevitable discourse of a society of a century freed of Victorianism only at its end. His honesty in technique is an "infra-apparel" trait, betokening a strong feeling for clothing's process, not merely a superficial result. Ricki Fulman suggested in the *New York Daily News* (4 October 1971) that "you've got to have a sense of humor to understand Stephen Burrows' clothes."

If the clothing offers an immediacy and vivacity, Burrows himself and his recognition in his twenties are a comparable phenomenon. Emerging from among the Bendel's designers in 1969, Burrows was a world-class Coty-Award winning talent in the early-to mid-1970s and was one of the five designers selected to represent American fashion in the epochal showing at Versailles in November 1973. One of the first African-Americans after Ann Lowe to achieve stature as a designer, Burrows may have offered fresh ideas in palette and color combination, but he was also sustaining a sportswear ideal. Even his laced cords and snaps have affinity with Claire McCardell's germinal work. Many designers after Burrows have looked to African-American, African, and Latin styles for inspiration and especially to the sexy zest he found there for his designs.

Elsa Klensch argued that the name "Stephen Burrows' World" was more than a store sign. "It is his own world—a philosophy, a life style, an environment," one that is composed of astute street observation, a lively sense of contemporary living and its impatience with rules and convention, and of a non-verbal self-communication through clothing. As much as Halston and di Sant'Angelo, Burrows was the avatar of new styles accorded to a cultural transfiguration in the 1970s. Perhaps he so personifies the early 1970s that his later erratic career is inevitable: we have sacrificed our fullest appreciation of him to another sexy lady he dressed, Clio.—RICHARD MARTIN

Byblos
Italian fashion house

> *Founded in 1973 as a division of Genny SpA; independent company formed c. 1983; designers include Versace, 1975-76, and Guy Paulin. Principal designers, since 1981, Alan Cleaver and Keith Varty; collections include Byblos Uomo, 1983, Byblos USA, and Options Donna, 1985, Vis à Vis Byblos, 1986, and Options Uomo, 1988.*

> **Address**   *Via Maggini 126, 60127 Ancona, Italy.*

Byblos takes its name from a hotel in St. Tropez, France. Since its inception in 1973, it has been a kind of international grand hotel of design, starting with a group of stylists, then engaging the Milanese Gianni Versace as designer 1975-76, then Frenchman Guy Paulin, and finally Keith Varty called from the Royal College of Art in London, via a period in Paris at Dorothée Bis, with Alan Cleaver. Varty and Cleaver have become the personification of Byblos objectives: a young line, international, with panache, and a carefree, optimistic nonchalance. In the 1980s the market-acute colorful palettes and relaxed resort-influenced informality of Cleaver and Varty for Byblos became a young *lingua franca* in fashion for the twenty-something and twenty-something generations. Together, Varty and Cleaver are as irresistible in person as their clothing design has proved to be: they seem to step out of a Somerset Maugham story, precocious and perspicacious English schoolboy adventurers travelling the world and absorbing ideas and visual design into an exuberant cultural colonialism at once laconic and vigorous, a passion about clothing evident in successive Byblos collections and manifest in the joy of the clothes, now available for women and men.

What Varty and Cleaver lack is any sense of the sinister or cynical: they are intent upon making clothing that is fun and exuberant. Varty described their design challenge to *Women's Wear Daily* in 1987, "Our product has to be salable, in the right fabrics with this young image and it's got to be fresh every season." The crux of the Cleaver-Varty achievement is color: they bring Matisse colors to clothing, can capture aubergines and gingers with a greengrocer's discrimination, and know the earth colors of every part of the globe with a geologist's imagination. *Daily News Record* (11 January 1989) rightly described the menswear: "Gold at the end of the rainbow. If anyone can make color successfully commercial, it's Keith Varty and Alan Cleaver for Byblos." They are to contemporary fashion what David Hockney is to contemporary art: British travel, observation, effervescence, and child-like delight in the world's bright colors. The American fashion press loves to call Varty and Cleaver "the Byblos boys" and they warrant the name in an irrepressible cheerfulness and delight that gives their clothing an upbeat mood that is its commercial success as well as its artistic signature.

Travel and exoticism is an important theme in Cleaver and Varty's work, reflecting their vacationing in Marrakech, their flirtations with Hawaii and the South Pacific, a recurring spirit of the American West (cowboys and Indian themes alike in womenswear, with cowboys especially applied in their menswear), menswear with the swagger of old-Havana *machismo,* and their love of tropical colors and refreshing prints inspired by southeast Asia, Oceania, and South America. In 1987 resort collections, the voyage was specific, with big skirts featuring postcards from the Bahamas and maps of islands. Fiesta brights are almost invariably featured in the spring and resort collections, with options for khaki, chocolates, mud, and tobacco brown. If the spring 1987 collections seemed like the British in India, their colonialism was mellowed by supple shapes, fluid lines, and khaki silk poplin. In 1988, the trek was to Russia in a savagely romantic display of fake fur, folkloric embroidery and motifs, and grand silhouettes that *Women's Wear Daily* (29 February 1988) called "Anna Karenina comes to Milan . . . ." Even their Russian collection, however, was no mere historicism or tourism: rich fabric combinations, pattern, and flamboyant shapes. It was as if all the extreme elements of peasant and Tsarist Russian fashion were distilled in select garments, redolent of the Russian novel, but also translated to the modern consumer in fake fur.

It seems unlikely that the sun will ever set on these two brilliant adventurers who have done so much to establish the Byblos style.—RICHARD MARTIN

Cacharel, Jean

French designer

Born *Jean Louis Henri Bousquet in Nîmes, 30 March 1932.*
Education *Studied at École Technique, Nîmes, 1951-54.*
Family *Married Dominique Sarrut in 1956; children: Guillaume and Jessica.*
Career *Cutter and stylist, Jean Jourdan, Paris, 1955-57; founder and director, Société Jean Cacharel, women's ready-to-wear, from 1964; children's line added, early 1970s; perfume and jeans lines added, 1978; men's line added, 1994; fragrances: Anaïs Anaïs, 1978; Loulou, 1987; Cacharel pour Homme, 1991; Eden, 1994; cosmetics range introduced, 1991.*
Awards *Export Trade Oscar, Paris, 1969.*
Address *3 Rue du Colisée, 30931 Nîmes, France.*

Jean Cacharel became an established designer name in the mid-1960s when his fitted, printed, and striped shirts for women became fashion "must haves." So much so that by the end of the 1960s, French women did not go into a shop and ask for a shirt, they asked for a Cacharel. The reason for this was because until Cacharel began designing for women no one else had managed to produce a shirt that was flattering, comfortable and easy to wear.

Cacharel, Jean Louis Henri Bousquet, came to Paris from Nîmes in the mid-1950s, where he had apprenticed in men's tailoring. Adopting the name of Cacharel, which was taken from the Camargue's native wild duck, he moved into womenswear as a designer/cutter for Jean Jourdan, Paris. At that time womenswear was dominated by Parisian haute couture and the mass market took second place. Cacharel was one of the first designers to foresee a fashion future beyond the old monied clientèle and catered to an emerging new monied and fashion-conscious mass market. The strong emergence of youth culture in the 1950s and 1960s strengthened this vision.

Cacharel opened his own business at the end of the 1950s and employed Emmanuelle Khan as a stylist and designer. Together they created an image for the company that was very French, young, and sporty in fresh matching separates that were colourful, pretty and wearable.

Success was sealed in 1965 when Cacharel began working with Liberty of London. He rescaled and recoloured traditional floral prints so that they became softer and more flattering. Prints that had previously been scorned as frumpy and homely were transformed by Cacharel's cut and taste into snappy, feminine, and wearable clothes. Liberty of London has subsequently stocked and sold the Cacharel label for many years.

Further developments at Cacharel have included moves into licensing, mainly in jeans, socks, and bedlinen. Cacharel's sister-in-law, Corinne Grandval, joined the firm as designer in 1966. Continuing the feeling for young, trendy clothes, she also helped to introduce a successful mini couture line for children. This idea has since been widely copied and adapted by the mass market.

Jean Cacharel has the affable air of a country vet and enjoys spending much of his spare time at his country house. He is greatly inspired by travel and the cultures found in places like Japan, Mexico, Chile, and Paraguay. These cultural fusions are then softly moulded and filtered, to create his feminine, gentle yet sporty, looks. They are worn predominantly by a customer who is romantic and individual, who does not want to wear aggressive extremist fashion but adapts her Cacharel separates to express her individual taste and personality.

Cacharel is secure in his belief that his established customers recognize the essential classicism in his garments. When the fashion element has become superfluous, the ease and versatility of his clothes ensures a permanent place in any woman's wardrobe. This perhaps signifies Jean Cacharel's overriding contribution to fashion.—KEVIN ALMOND

Calugi e Giannelli

Italian design house

Founded in Florence, 1982, by Mauro Calugi (born 27 November 1941) and Danilo Giannelli (born 21 April 1957; died 13 May 1987). Incorporated, 1984; renamed Danilo Giannelli, SpA, c.1987. Principal designer, Mauro Calugi.

Exhibitions *Pitti Immagine Uoma, Fortezza da Basso, Florence, 1985; A Dress Beyond Fashion, Palazzo Fortuny, Venicew, 1991.*
Awards *Ecco L'Italia (New York), 1985.*
Address *Via Catalani 28—Zona Industriale Bassa, 50050 Cerreto Guidi, Florence, Italy.*

Since beginning in 1982, Calugi e Giannelli has invented and re-invented clothing—menswear in particular—as if it were conceptual art. Arguably, Calugi e Giannelli clothing is an advanced art of the idea, often conveying avant-garde principles, frequently invoking and investing language and word play, and always bringing an edge to clothing. Formal properties matter, especially as they are developed from the properties of fabrics and fabric technology, most notably stretch, but the essence of a Calugi e Giannelli garment is its idea, or what 1993 press materials describe as "ironic temperament, a strong core and decisive taste." As playful as

Calugi e Giannelli: Fall/Winter 1992/93.

the Milanese Franco Moschino and as avant-gardist at the Parisian Jean-Paul Gaultier, Calugi e Giannelli's erudite conceptualism is accompanied by an equally strong sense of libido and sensuality. Transparency applied to textiles and the body becomes a *tour de force* of ideas for Calugi e Giannelli, but it also serves as a grand tour of erogenous zones. Pop Art is remembered, especially in the spring/summer 1991 collection, but when consumerism's systems and labels end up on tight swimwear and biker shorts, the equation of sex and consumption is only heightened. Both the Church and masculinity are special targets of Calugi e Giannelli satire and wit. A *leitmotif* of the collections is an interest in clerical dress subverted to secular clothing, with crosses and vestment details appearing again and again with schoolboy irreverence. Studded leather jackets are an over-the-top *machismo* that can only be interpreted as tongue-in-cheek. Calugi e Giannelli's work is always winning and not subject to the tiresome jokes of some sportswear: it is a fashion animated by fresh ideas and interpretive energy.

Learned and yet fun referencing to both dollar signs and hammer-and-sickle (spring/summer 1989), Arab motifs and script (spring/summer 1991), mocking motifs of ecclesiastical hats (fall/winter 1988-89), Tahiti and tattoos (spring/summer 1993), and tough biker leathers (fall/winter 1993-94) establish clothing as a widely referential, all-encompassing art. Singularly characteristic of the design's sartorial surrealism is the fall/winter 1988-89 anamorphic jacket with two lapels in which the exterior and interior, jacket and waistcoat, shell and marrow are purposely confused with resulting asymmetry and winsome disorder. A spring/summer 1988 double-collared shirt plays with the same uncertainties of the *doppelganger*. Art-like in its proposition, knowledgeable in its deliberate discords (snakeskin and lace together in spring/summer 1989), supremely sexy in its orientation, Calugi e Giannelli clothing sets a distinctive style in menswear.

While partner Danilo Giannelli died in 1987, the sensibility continued by Mauro Calugi has been seamless with the design duo's original objectives. Clothing is subject to aesthetic consideration. The fall/winter 1988-89 collection included a series of jackets with barbed wire motifs, introducing *faux* barbed wire at the shoulders or around the waist. In the seeming disparity of soft clothing and the fictive brutalism of barbed wire, Calugi e Giannelli displayed characteristic wit and irrepressible irony. In the same season, the "Violent Angels" leather jacket set metal plates with letters in continuous reading on a leather jacket: its diction is the continuous language of computer input; its effect is to put language onto the supposedly inarticulate form of the leather jacket. By such paradox, Calugi e Giannelli offers contradiction and incongruity about clothing, but also with an ideal of harmony and reconciliation. Even the language, redolent of Bruce Naumann and other artists, of the "Violent Angels" title, suggests the combination of the ferocious and the chaste.

Despite heady artistic purpose, Calugi e Giannelli clothing is well made and is never wearable art or craft. In fact, the interest in the basic templates of clothing arises in part from the preference in silhouettes for standard types, perfectly executed, and the knits and performance sportswear have the integrity of quality clothing. Detailing of embroidered suits, knit jackets with representational scenes, and sweaters with a range of illustration and image are consummately made; the lace T-shirts and jackets, and the tailored clothing with sudden apertures, have been copied in expensive and inferior versions, but the Calugi e Giannelli originals are beautifully made. The spring/summer 1988 block cutouts with sheer panels are a body peek-a-boo inflected with the design language of Piet Mondrian or Mark Rothko.

Menswear is the forum for Calugi e Giannelli ideas, though womenswear has also been produced. Perhaps menswear's accustomed reserve from fashion controversy and aggressive aesthetics lends itself to Calugi e Giannelli's definitive work in Mauro Calugi's insistence that fashion is an art of compelling dissent and dissonance that leads toward significant social and personal statement.—RICHARD MARTIN

Cardin, Pierre

French designer

Born *Son of French parents, born in San Andrea da Barbara, Italy, 2 July 1922.*

Education *Studied architecture, Saint-Etienne, France.*

Career *Worked as a bookkeeper and as a tailor's cutter, Vichy, 1936-40; Apprentice, Manby men's tailor, Vichy, 1939; served in the Red Cross, World War II. Design assistant, working for the Madame Paquin and Elsa Schiaparelli fashion houses, Paris, 1945-46; head of workrooms, Christian Dior fashion house, Paris, 1946-50, helping to design "New Look" in 1947; founder-director and chief designer, Pierre Cardin fashion house, Paris, from 1950, presented first collection, 1951; opened up market in Japan, 1958; first ready-to-wear collection introduced, 1959; marketed own fabric, Cardine, 1968; children's collection introduced, 1969; holds more than 600 licenses. Also film costume designer from 1946; founder, Espace Cardin, 1970.*

Exhibitions *Pierre Cardin: Past, Present and Future, Victoria and Albert Museum, London, October-January 1990-91.*

Awards *Sunday Times International Fashion Award (London), 1963; Dé d'Or Award, 1977, 1979, 1982; named Chevalier de la Légion d'Honneur, 1983; Fashion Oscar, Paris, 1985; Foundation for Garment and Apparel Advancement Award, Tokyo, 1988; named Grand Officer, Order of Merit, Italy, 1988; named Honorary Ambassador to UNESCO, 1991.*

Address *82 rue Faubourg Saint-Honoré, 75008 Paris, France.*

The shrewd entrepreneurial skills displayed by Pierre Cardin throughout his career have made him the world's richest fashion designer and a household name. A global phenomenon, he was the first designer to open up markets in Japan in 1958, China in 1978, and more recently Russia and Romania, applying the Cardin name to hundreds of products, from ties to alarm clocks and frying pans.

Cardin was the first designer to understand the potential of the business of fashion. His move into ready-to-wear in 1959 scandalized the Chambre Syndicale, the monitoring body of haute couture in Paris, and he was expelled from its ranks for what was essentially an attempt to make designer clothes more accessible, and also displaying an astute sense of where the real money to be made in fashion lay.

From his earliest work for the House of Dior up to the 1950s, Cardin displays an interest in the sculptural qualities of cut and construction that are still his trademarks in the 1990s. Cardin produces garments of a hard-edged minimalism, backed up by exquisite techniques of tailoring that he manipulates to produce sparse, geometric garments offset by huge collars and bizarre accessories such as the vinyl torso decoration he introduced in 1968.

Pierre Cardin. *Photograph by Sergio Altieri.*

His designs resist the rounded curves of the traditional female body, aided by his use of materials such as heavyweight wool and jersey rib, creating clothing that stands away from the body thereby producing its own structural outline. From the balloon dress of 1959 that delineated the body only at the pull of a drawstring at the hem, through the geometrically blocked shifts of the 1960s to his series of hooped dresses in the 1980s, Cardin describes the underlying form of the body obliquely, creating planes that intersect with, yet somehow remain disconnected from, the body itself.

Cardin's embrace of the romance of science and technology, together with the notion of progress that seemed so inherent in the two in the 1960s, was expressed in his 1964 Space Age Collection, which featured white knitted catsuits, tabards worn over leggings, and tubular dresses and more generally in his interest in man-made fibres. He created his own fabric, Cardine, in 1968, a bonded, uncrushable fibre incorporating raised geometric patterns.

Cardin's curiously asexual designs for women in the 1960s remained so even when making direct reference to the breast by the use of cones, outlines, cutouts, and moulding. Similarly, the exposure of the legs afforded by his minis was desexed by the models wearing thick opaque or patterned tights and thigh-high boots. Experiments with the application of paper cutout techniques to fabric with which Cardin was preoccupied in the 1960s were replaced in the 1970s by more fluid materials such as single angora jersey and the techniques of sunray and accordion pleating. A spiralling rather than geometric line began to be more noticeable and Cardin became renowned for his frothy evening dresses of layered, printed chiffon while continuing his experimentation with a series of unusual sleevehead designs.

Cardin was the first post-war designer to challenge London's Savile Row in the production of menswear. The high buttoned collarless jackets worn by the Beatles became *de rigueur* for the fashionable man in the 1960s and provided a relaxed yet elegant look when combined with a turtleneck sweater. Cardin, by paring away collars and relinquishing pockets, broke with tradition to create a new look for men realizing that the male suit, once a bastion of tradition, could be high fashion too.

Although merchandising and licensing his name may have overshadowed his influence as a fashion designer in recent years, Cardin's inventiveness and technical flair should not be underestimated.—CAROLINE COX

Carnegie, Hattie
American designer

Born   *Henrietta Kanengeiser in Vienna, 1889.*

Family   *Married third husband, John Zanft, in 1928.*

Career   *Left school at age 11 and moved with parents to New York, 1900; established as Carnegie—Ladies Hatter, 1909; opened custom dress-making salon, 1918; offered Paris models after first buying trip to Europe, 1919; opened East 49th St. building to sell own label, imports, and millinery, 1925; added ready-to-wear, 1928; Hattie Carnegie Originals carried in stores throughout the United States by 1934; custom salon closed, 1965.*

Awards   *Neiman Marcus Award, 1939; Coty American Fashion Critics Award, 1948.*

Carnegie

Died *(in New York City) 22 February 1956.*

For decades Hattie Carnegie's personal taste and fashion sense influenced the styles worn by countless American women. Whether they bought her imported Paris models, the custom designs, the ready-to-wear collections, or the mass market copies of her work, women welcomed Carnegie's discreet good taste as a guarantee of sophistication and propriety. Carnegie's business ability and fashion acumen enabled her to build a small millinery shop into a wholesale and retail clothing and accessory empire and made her name synonymous with American high fashion for almost half a century.

Carnegie's place in fashion history is assured not because of her own designs, but because of her talent for choosing or refining the designs of others. Between the World Wars, the list of couturiers whose models she imported included Lanvin, Vionnet, Molyneux, and Mainbocher—classic stylists—but also select creations for Chanel and Patou, Schiaparelli, and Charles James. In fact, Carnegie claimed in a *Collier's* article (16 April 1949) to have had a three-year unauthorized exclusive on selling Vionnet models in the early 1920s, a few years before Vionnet started selling "to the trade."

The Custom Salon was generally considered to be the heart of the Hattie Carnegie operation, since it was with made-to-order fashion that Carnegie began. The focus of her business was to interpret European style for American consumers, but the sense of dress that she chose to champion was not contained in the minutiae of design. It was instead an approach to fashion that emphasized consummate polish in every outfit. Norman Norell, who was with Carnegie from 1928 to 1940 (primarily as a ready-to-wear designer), remarked in *American Fashion* (Sarah Tomerlin Lee, ed., New York 1975) that he often worked from models that Miss Carnegie had brought back from Paris. He could legitimately claim, however, that he had imprinted his own signature on his designs for the firm, and it is often possible to make an informed attribution of Hattie Carnegie styles to her other designers. Certainly one gown featured in a 1939 magazine layout is recognizably the work of Claire McCardell, who spent two years with the firm. Others who worked for Carnegie were Emmett Joyce, Travis Banton, Pauline Trigère, Jean Louis, James Galanos, and Gustave Tassell.

Carnegie was already established as a taste-maker by the time she added the ready-to-wear division to her company in the 1920s. "Vogue points from Hattie Carnegie" contained her style tips and forecasts for *Vogue* readers. At the Hattie Carnegie salon, a customer could accessorize her day and evening ensembles with furs, hats, handbags, gloves, lingerie, jewelry, and even cosmetics and perfume, everything, in fact, but shoes.

The Carnegie customer, whatever her age, seems to have been neither girlish nor matronly, but possessed of a certain decorousness. Even the casual clothing in the Spectator Sportswear and Jeunes Filles ready-to-wear departments was elegant rather than playful. The Carnegie Suit, usually an ensemble with dressmaker details in luxury fabrics, traditionally opened her seasonal showings. She often stressed the importance of black as a wardrobe basic, both for day and evening, but was also famous for a shade known as "Carnegie blue." Perhaps Carnegie's preference for 18th-century furnishings in her home relates to the devotion of formality so clearly expressed in her business.

During World War II Carnegie was an impressive bearer of the standard of the haute couture. French style leadership was unavailable, and designs from her custom salon took pride of place in fashion magazines and on the stage, as in the original production of *State of the Union* by Lindsay and Crouse. Carnegie's leadership was also important to other fashion industries. She had always used fabrics from the best American textile companies, and continued to patronize specialty firms such as Hafner Associates and Onondaga Silks, which were not immersed in war work. She also used fabrics designed and hand printed by Brook Cadwallader, and continued to do so after French materials again became available. Only after Carnegie's death did the company claim to use exclusively imported fabrics.

Hattie Carnegie died in 1956. The fashion empire she had built survived into the 1970s, but in 1965 the custom salon was closed and the company concentrated on wholesale businesses. The informal youth culture of the 1960s and 1970s was ill suited to the type of clothing and client that had made Hattie Carnegie's reputation. The strength of her personal identification with the company made it difficult for the company to succeed without her at its head, and it quickly lost ground to the younger taste-makers who emerged in the 1960s.—MADELYN SHAW

Carven

French fashion house

Established by Mme Carven Mallet in Paris, 1945; Carven Scarves and Carven Junior lines launched, 1955; Kinglenes and Kisslenes sweater collections introduced, 1956; neckwear collection introduced, 1957; swimwear collection introduced, 1965; fur collection introduced, 1966; jewelry collection, Ma Fille line for children and line of blouses introduced, 1968; Monsieur Carven boutique opened, Paris, 1985. Perfumes: Ma Griffe, 1948, Robe d'un Soir, 1948, Chasse Gardée, 1950, Vetiver, 1957, Vert et Blanc, 1958, Madame, 1980, and Guirlandes, 1982. Also designed uniforms for Air India, 1965, S.A.S., 1966, Aerolineas Argentinas, 1967, and Air France, 1978.

Exhibitions *retrospective, Paris, 1986.*
Awards *Chevalier de la Légion d'Honneur, 1964, Grande Medaille des Arts et Lettres, 1978.*
Address *6 rond-point des Champs-Elysées, 75008 Paris, France.*

In 1949, when Jacqueline François sang of "Les robes de chez Carven" in her immortal song, *Mademoiselle de Paris,* the clothes of Madame Carven embodied all the charm, gaiety, and beauty of the city of Paris and its fabled women in the magical period after the war. The 1950s are seen as the Golden Age of the haute couture in Paris and Carven is regarded as having been one of its primary practitioners. She is still actively designing and while Carven's vast array of licensed products, from perfume to golfwear, have been distributed throughout the world, her name is not one that is immediately recognized in America. Perhaps this is because she has never sought to shock or create trends or to follow the whims of fashion. The single conceptual basis for her work has always been to create beautiful clothes for all women, but in particular women of petite size: "I felt that I was small, and the contemporary taste for tall mannequins combined with my own admiration for Hollywood stars ended up giving me a complex. At the age of 25 I was a *coquette.* France was learning to dance again after the war and I wanted to be slinky. This desire to be attractive inspired a few reflections. First I noticed that I wasn't the only petite woman I knew, and that the grand couturiers weren't very interested in us. But I had a feeling for proportion and volume. All that remained for me to do was to create, with the help of friends who were scarcely taller than I was, dresses that would allow us to be ourselves. . . . I'd found an opening where there was no competition and a moment when Paris was overflowing with happiness."

Carven's designs from the late 1940s through the early 1960s, while conforming to the prevailing stylistic tendencies of the period, are distinguished by the delicate decorative detail that flatters the wearer without overwhelming her. Trims at collar and cuff are frequently executed in all variations of white lace and embroidery. Occasionally coolly plain white linen collar and cuffs assert the propriety of the wearer while enhancing an image of chic self-assurance. White on white is a recurring theme in Carven's designs as evident in an evening dress of 1950 in which an embroidery of white *fleurs de Mai* completely covers a white bustier and asymmetrical long skirt, supported by a white halter and pleated underskirt. A bouffant skirted afternoon dress with a closely fitted top from 1954 is executed in white linen subtly embroidered with white flowers, almost as if the dress were created from a fine tablecloth. Another recurring design motif is the use of fabrics and embroideries that shade from light to dark (*dégrader* in French), thus subtly enhancing the wearer's figure and stature.

Madame Carven.

Carven was one of the first designers to promote her clothes in foreign countries, presenting her collections in Brazil, Mexico, Egypt, Turkey, and Iran. These travels greatly influenced her designs. After a trip to Egypt she introduced a tightly gathered type of drapery to her evening designs which mimicked ancient Egyptian gowns: a design of 1952 shows a bodice of sinuous gathers closely outlining the body in white jersey that, under beaded fringe at the hip reminiscent of a belly dancer's jeweled belt, breaks loose into a long flowing skirt. Another dress of 1952 is covered with an all-over design of Aztec inspired motifs. An entire collection in 1959 was inspired by the beauties of Spain, as seen in paintings by Velazquez.

Today the Carven label can be found throughout the world as a result of extensive distribution of licensed products and especially Carven's perfume *Ma Griffe*, in its familiar white and green packaging. Madame Carven always includes a signature white and green dress in her collections which, to this day, stand for a tasteful style of charm and beauty that complements the wearer no matter her proportions.—ALAN E. ROSENBERG

Cashin, Bonnie

American designer

Born *Oakland, California, 1915.*

Education *Studied at the Art Students League, New York, and also in Paris.*

Career *Costume designer, Roxy Theater, New York, 1934-37; designer, Adler and Adler sportswear, New York, 1937-43 and 1949-52; costume designer, 20th Century Fox, Los Angeles, California, 1943-49; designer, Bonnie Cashin Designs (with partner Phillip Sills), New York, 1953-77; established The Knittery, 1972; founder, Innovative Design Fund, c.1981.*

Exhibitions *Brooklyn Museum, 1962 (retrospective).*

Awards *Neiman Marcus Award, Dallas, Texas, 1950; Coty American Fashion Critics Award, New York, 1950, 1960, 1961, 1968, 1972; Sporting Look Award, 1958; Philadelphia Museum College of Art Citation, 1959; Woolknit Associates Design Award, 1959, 1961; Lighthouse Award, 1961; Sports Illustrated Award, 1963; Detroit Business Association, National Award, 1963; The Sunday Times International Fashion Award, London, 1964; Leather Industries American Handbag Designer Award, 1968, 1976; Kaufmann Fashion Award, Pittsburgh, 1968; Creator Citation, Saks Fifth Avenue, 1969; Mary Mount College Golden Needle Award, 1970; I. Magnin's Great American Award, 1974; The American Fashion Award for Furs, 1975; Drexel University Citation, Philadelphia, 1976.*

An awareness of the body in motion informs Bonnie Cashin's design style. Her earliest efforts were created for dancers: as a California high school student, Cashin costumed the local ballet troupe. Only two years later she became the house costumer for New York's famed Roxy Theater. There, her brief was to design three sets of costumes a week for the Roxy's chorus of 24 dancing showgirls. With minimal budgets, Cashin used her ingenuity, a little paint, and a knowledge of cut learned from her dressmaker mother to transform inexpensive fabrics into striking costumes that looked equally graceful in motion or in repose. Whether for stage or street, Cashin's work has always been styled for the active woman on the move, who prefers an easy, individual look with a minimum of fuss. The May 1970 issue of *Current Biography* (New York) quotes her: "All I want is to speak simply in my designing; I don't want the gilt and the glamour."

A 1937 production number, in which the Roxy dancers emerged smartly dressed from between the pages of a fashion magazine, sent Cashin in a new direction. Louis Adler, co-owner of the sportswear firm Adler and Adler, saw Cashin's designs and recognized her potential importance to the fashion industry. Wary of the garment district's regimentation, Cashin initially played it safe. She stayed on in the familiar collegial world of the theater and free-lanced for Adler. Eventually she signed with the firm for whom she designed for approximately 12 years before and after World War II. In 1950, during her second stint at Adler and Adler, Cashin won both the Neiman Marcus Award and the first of five Coty Awards for a prototype of her signature *Noh* coat, an unlined, sleeved or sleeveless T-shaped coat with deeply cut armholes to wear singly, in combination, or under a poncho or cape.

Despite this success, Cashin sensed that she would never achieve her creative best working under contract in the profit oriented canyons of Seventh Avenue. In 1953 she began designing on a free-lance basis from her studio. Unusual for the time, she worked on a royalty basis, creating complete coordinated wardrobes—accessories, knits, capes and coats, dresses and separates—to be combined in layers to suit the climate or the event.

Cashin typically worked years ahead of the market, pioneering clothing concepts which today seem part of fashion's essential vocabulary. In the 1950s, when most women's clothing was concerned with structure, the Cashin silhouette was based on the rectangle or the square and called for a minimum of darting and seaming. Bonnie Cashin showed layered dressing long before the concept became a universal option; she brought canvas boots and raincoats out of the show ring and into the street in 1952 and she introduced jumpsuits as early as 1956.

Signature pieces include her *Noh* coats, funnel-necked sweaters whose neck doubles as a hood, classic ponchos and such innovations as a bicycle sweater with roomy back pockets. Other Cashin hallmarks are her use of toggle closures and leather bindings. Indeed, Bonnie Cashin is often credited with having revived leather and suede as materials suitable for couture.

Very likely because of her early work in the theater, both color and especially texture play a starring role in Cashin's designs. An organza *Noh* coat may be trimmed with linen and shown over a sweater dress of cashmere. A jersey sheath may be paired with an apron-wrap skirt cut from a boisterous tweed. Her palette is both subtle and controlled: earth tones, sparked with vivid accents.

Bonnie Cashin worked to her own brief, forming a collaboration with women who were smart, active, and, like herself, of independent mind. She designed for the self-aware woman who asked that her clothes be practical, comfortable, and stylish.—WHITNEY BLAUSEN

Cassini, Oleg

American designer

Born *Oleg Loiewski in Paris of Russian parents, 11 April 1913; raised in Florence; adopted mother's family name, Cassini, in 1937.*

Education *Attended English Catholic School, Florence. Studied at Accademia delle Belle Arti, Florence, 1931-34; political science, University of Florence, 1932-34.*

Oleg Cassini: Floor-length sheath gown stitched with white sequins.

Military Service *Served five years with U.S. Army Cavalry during World War II.*

Family *Married Merry Fahrney in 1938 (divorced); married the film actress Gene Tierney in 1941 (divorced, 1952); daughters: Daria and Christina.*

Career *After working in mother's Maison de Couture in Florence, opened own Maison de Couture in Rome; sketch artist, Patou, Paris, 1935; immigrated to the United States in 1936, naturalized, 1942; design assistant to couturier Jo Copeland, New York, 1936; designer, William Bass, New York, 1937, and James Rotherberg Inc., New York, 1938-39; New York salon, Oleg Inc., established, 1937-39; owner of Cassini fashion studio, New York, 1939-40; designer, Paramount Pictures, Los Angeles, 1939-42; designer under contract with Twentieth Century Fox, Los Angeles, 1940. Owner of Cassini Dardick fashion firm, New York, 1947-50: established Oleg Cassini Inc., New York, 1950; appointed official designer to U.S. First Lady Jackie Kennedy, early 1960s; established ready-to-wear business, Milan, mid-1963; returned to New York, designed tennis clothes for Munsingwear and swimwear for Waterclothes under own label, 1974; introduced new fragrance line, A Love That Never Ends, 1990.*

Awards *Has received numerous awards, including five first prizes, Mostra della Moda, Turin, 1934; Honorary Doctor of Fine Arts, International College of Fine Arts, Miami, 1989.*

Address *3 West 57th Street, New York, New York 10019, USA.*

Oleg Cassini has had an extremely varied, glamorous, and exotic career but is perhaps best known for the personal style and clothing he developed when official designer for the U.S. First Lady Jacqueline Kennedy in 1961. He worked closely with Mrs. Kennedy, a personal friend, and together they created many widely copied garments that have since become American fashion classics and that firmly established Kennedy as a style leader. She frequently wore a fawn wool two-piece outfit, a dress and a waist-length semi-fitted jacket or coat with a removable round neck collar of Russian sable, often topped by the famous pillbox hats created by Halston. Another outfit was a high-necked silk ottoman empire-line evening gown that gently flared in an A-line to the floor. Jacqueline Kennedy's vast public exposure proved a huge boost for Cassini's profile and brought worldwide attention to American fashion in general.

Cassini was born a count and was brought up by Italian/Russian parents in Florence, where his mother ran an exclusive dress shop. He began his career in 1934 by making small one-off designs sold through his mother's shop. He moved to New York in 1936 and worked for several Seventh Avenue manufacturers before joining Twentieth-Century Fox in Hollywood as a costume designer in 1940. He worked for several major film studios and created glamorous clothes for many film stars, even marrying one, Gene Tierney.

In 1950 the designer opened Oleg Cassini Inc., his ready-to-wear dress firm in New York, with 100 thousand dollars worth of backing. Femininity quickly became the keyword when describing his work. He produced dresses made from soft, romantic fabrics like lace, taffeta, point d'esprit, and chiffon. He popularized ladylike fashion innovations, such as the A line, the smart little white collared dress, the sheath, the knitted suit, and dresses with minute waistlines. Military details such as brass buttons and braid were also popular features. In the 1960s the Cassini look evolved to incorporate ease and simplicity. The straight, lined cocktail and evening dresses popularized by Jackie Kennedy were customer favourites, as were his plain and boxy jacket suits.

Retiring from his ready-to-wear and couture business in 1963, Cassini's next venture was a ready-to-wear business in partnership with his brother Igor. He presented a menswear collection for the first time, breaking tradition by introducing colour to shirts that had previously nearly always been white, and teaming them with traditional three-piece suits.

Today Cassini is president of a vast organization, exporting to over 20 countries. The company produces innumerable accessory products including cravats, luggage, children's clothes, make-up, shoes, umbrellas, and perfumes.—KEVIN ALMOND

Castelbajac, Jean-Charles de

French designer

Born *Of French parents in Casablanca, Morocco, 28 November 1949.*

Education *Attended Catholic boarding schools in France, 1955-66; studied law, Faculté de Droit, Limoges, 1966-77.*

Family *Married Katherine Lee Chambers, 1979; children: two sons, Guillaume and Louis.*

Career *Founder and designer, with his mother Jeanne-Blanche de Castelbajac, of Ko and Co, ready-to-wear fashion company, Limoges, beginning in 1968; free-lanced for Pierre d'Alby, Max Mara, Jesus Jeans, Etam, Gadgling, Julie Latour, Fusano, Amaraggi, Carel Shoes, Ellesse, Hilton, Levi-Strauss, and Reynaud, beginning in 1968; director, Jean-Charles de Castelbajac label, Paris, 1970, and Societe Jean-Charles de Castelbajac SARL, Paris, 1978; established boutiques in Paris, New York, and Tokyo, 1975-76. Also designed for film and stage, including Elton John, Talking Heads, and Rod Stewart, beginning in 1976; interior and furniture designs, beginning in 1979. Member of Didier Grumbach's Les Createurs group of designers, Paris, 1974-77.*

Exhibitions *Centre Georges Pompidou, Paris, 1978; Forum Design, Linz, Austria, 1980; Laforet Museum, Belgium, 1984.*

Collections *Musée du Costume, Paris; Fashion Institute of Technology, New York.*

Addresses *188 rue de Rivoli, 75001 Paris, France; 55 rue de Lisbonne, 75008 Paris, France.*

If color produces optimism, then Jean-Charles de Castelbajac is the most optimistic designer in existence. Void of lux rhinestones or glitz, his collection features color to luxuriate the world. The designer will not only clothe people in color but create an environmental lifestyle, with everything from sofas, to crystal, to carpets.

Castelbajac is a man of passions—for form and function, for color, for comfort and protection—and therein lies the basis of this humanistic designer. Castelbajac began his obsession by cutting his first garment out of a blanket from boarding school. Because the material already existed, he was left to play only with the form. Many times each year he returns to this first gesture, cutting the cloth, so he remains close to its essence and function.

Recently titled Marquis, Castelbajac has erected the first monument to celebrate the living in Paris: one hundred and fifty thousand names of young people are inscribed on a steel totem pole to support Castelbajac's project to give inspiration and a sense of worth to a generation so used to growing up with war memorials celebrating the dead. Despite his interest in youth, he has always been involved with heroes and heritage, but he is never archaic in his designs. Castelbajac is a man of the future, but he does not make futuristic clothing. His designs fulfill the need for practical and unassuming fashion of maximum quality. While favoring natural textures and fibers, Castelbajac creates designs that are innovative but respectful of the classics; he has been called a modern traditionalist. And now, designing the collections of André Courrèges, the futuristic designer who marked the 1960s, Castelbajac has managed successfully to rejuvenate the original spirit of Courrèges clothes.

Castelbajac's fondness for architecture is apparent in the harmonious, architectonic shapes that flow through every collection. He has a great affinity with painters, with whom he spends much time to strengthen his creative impulses. Having a strong revulsion to prints on garments, he humorously solved the predicament by using large scale motifs of Tom and Jerry, or phrases from Nerval or Barbey d'Aurevilly inscribed on silk, for very simply shaped dresses. At other times his garments are filled with angels, or medieval and heraldic motifs, or childlike inscriptions drawn with the skill of an artistic adult but with the imagination of a child.

The inscription of Cervantes in Jean-Charles de Castelbajac's book published in 1993 reads: "Always hold the hand of the child you once were." His clothing and his art are identifiable by his manner of being true to himself, that is, by being profoundly human and knowing something that is not only style.—ANDREA ARSENAULT

Cerruti, Nino

Italian designer

Born *Biella, Italy, in 1930.*

Career *General manager for family textile firm (founded 1881), Cerruti Brothers, Biella, from 1950. Hitman men's ready-to-wear line introduced, 1957; knitwear line introduced, 1963; first menswear collection presented in Paris, opened Cerruti 1881 boutique, Paris, and launched unisex clothing line, 1967; women's ready-to-wear added, 1976. Fragrances include Nino Cerruti Pour Homme, 1978, Cerruti Fair Play, 1984, Nino Cerruti Pour Femme, 1987, and 1881, 1988.*

Awards *Bath Museum of Costume Dress of the Year Award, England 1978; Cutty Sark award, 1982, 1988; Pitti Uomo award, Italy, 1986.*

Address *3 place de la Madeleine, 75008 Paris, France.*

Nino Cerruti's life could be the most dramatic narrative of the post-World War II Italian renaissance. *L'Uomo Vogue* (November 1990) declared: "Nino Cerruti, a name synonymous with modern restraint. Industrialist-designer, one of the founding fathers of Italian fashion. . . ." Assuming control of his family's mills as a young man of 20, he transformed the staid business of textile mills that had been significant for generations in the textile-producing region of Biella, Italy. Cerruti saw the quiet revolutionary possibility of a vertical operation, a kind that other Italian textiles companies would later pursue with astounding success, following Cerruti's model. According to Adriana Mulassano (*The Who's Who of Italian Fashion,* 1979), in the 1950s "he earned the fame as a fashion madman for his ventures and publicity in textiles and fashion denounced as cheap Americana." His sensibility was immediately for fashion, rather than for the traditionalism of textiles manufacturing. In fashion, Cerruti prefers the streamlined, near-industrial design in tailoring applied to richly textured fabrics.

Ironically, Cerruti's fashion madness was short-lived. His first men's ready-to-wear line Hitman was launched in 1957, he showed unisex clothing in 1967, and opened his Cerruti 1881 boutique in Paris on the Rue Royale, off the Place de la Madeleine, in 1967. His icons are distinguished dates and places; tradition abides in the stable factors of 1881 and his elective association with Paris. Mulassano argues for a kind of vanguard genius about Cerruti: "Among those working for him (and perhaps even outside) there might be those who still think he's crazy. Perhaps it is the fate of the avant-garde, of those who know that the mind guides the hand, to be perennially misunderstood." It is Mulassano, however, who misunderstands Cerruti. He is the businessman-designer, not the raw-talent creative; he displays the tempered intelligence of vertical operations and commercial acumen. He is involved today in the fragrances and advertising not out of unremitting creativity but out of the controlling perspicacity of business. The raging revolutionary of the 1950s and 1960s has mellowed into the judicious businessman of the 1980s and 1990s as his model has been so fully copied by others, both in menswear and in women's clothing. He reflected to *Esquire* (September 1987): "I like to describe my operation as a modern version of the handcraft *bodegas* of centuries ago. It is important to know each link in the chain. I consider myself still very close to the theory of industrial design: using modern technology to reach the market. It's a very modern challenge: the continuous harmonization between the rational or scientific world and the emotional or artistic world." Cerruti projects an impeccable harmony.

His fall-winter 1993-94 menswear collections were shown in Paris with none of the histrionics of some menswear presentations. He kept in his tailored clothing to his simple principle: "A man should look important when he wears a suit," allowing for the unconstricted jackets of the period, but rendering them with sufficient solidity to avoid being too limp for the office. He showed the prevailing elongated three-button single-breasted look of Giorgio Armani and others. One can always tell, however, that Cerruti is a man of cloth: his menswear fabrics are so textural, in pebbled and oatmeal grains, and so luxurious in their handling. The touch of history that the dates of the mills' foundations convey is one of traditional authority, one that is palpable in the clothing. Cerruti has experimented with dandies and even designed Jack Nicholson's costumes in the movie *The Witches of Eastwick* and costumes for *Philadelphia* (1993), but anyone can experiment. Nonetheless, Cerruti has made his mark with the restraint of his clothes. His principal effort in menswear takes advantage of the thriving vertical operations that he commands from mills to clothing to advertising and promotion and related products. Mulassano is, in fact, much more on target when she recognizes Nino Cerruti is what is commonly known as an "enlightened businessman." To wit, there is Cerruti's 1987 statement to *Esquire:* "I think that innovation and fancy are essential to daily life. But my clothes are designed to be real. It's easy to indulge in decadence in fashion, but I don't think that's meaningful. The world has been full of enough of that."

If Cerruti exemplifies post-war Italy, perhaps in his judiciousness, cautious good taste, and reversion to his own basic values, he exemplifies Everyman. He foresaw menswear's future in *L'Uomo Vogue* in 1990: "A fashion that will be more refined and yet at the same time more everyday. In other words, a greater desire for authenticity, a traditionally elegant simplicity that doesn't smack too much of fashion."—RICHARD MARTIN

Chanel, "Coco" Gabrielle Bonheur

French designer

Born *Saumur, the Auvergne, France, 19 August 1883.*

Education *Educated at convent orphanage, Aubazine, 1895-1900, and at convent school, Moulins, 1900-02.*

Career *Clerk, Au Sans Pareil hosiery shop, Moulins, 1902-04; café-concert singer, using nickname "Coco," in Moulins and Vichy, 1905-08; lived with Etienne Balsan, Château de Royalieu and in Paris, 1908-09; established millinery and women's fashion house with sponsorship of Arthur "Boy" Cappel, in Paris, 1913, later in rue Cambon, Paris, 1928; established fashion shops in Deauville, 1913, Biarritz, 1916; fragrance, No. 5, marketed from 1921; other fragrances include No. 22, 1921, Cuir de Russie, 1924, No. 19, 1970, and from House of Chanel, Cristalle, 1974, Coco, 1984, and Egoïste for men, 1990. Rue Cambon headquarters closed during World War II, re-opened, relaunching Chanel's work, 1954, and continued after her death. Also stage costume designer, 1912-37, and film costume designer, 1931-62. Lived as exile in Lausanne, 1945-53.*

Exhibitions *Les Grands Couturiers Parisiens 1910-1939, Musée du Costume, Paris, 1965; Fashion: An Anthology, Victoria and Albert Museum, London, 1971; The Tens, Twenties, Thirties, Metropolitan Museum of Art, New York, 1977.*

Awards *Neiman Marcus Award, Dallas, 1957; Sunday Times International Fashion Award, London, 1963.*

Died *(in Paris) 10 January 1971.*

Address *29-31 rue Cambon, 75001 Paris, France.*

A woman of ambition and determination, Gabrielle Chanel, nicknamed "Coco," rose from humble beginnings and an unhappy childhood to become one of this century's most prominent couturiers, prevailing for nearly half a century.

In contrast to the opulent elegance of the *belle époque,* Chanel's designs were based on simplicity and elegance. She introduced relaxed dressing expressing the aspirations of the 20th-century woman, replacing impractical clothing with functional styling.

Chanel's early years tend to be vague in detail, being full of inaccuracies and contradictions, due to her deliberate concealment of her deprived childhood. It is generally accepted that Chanel gained some dressmaking and millinery experience prior to working in a hat shop in Deauville, France. Using her skills as a milliner she opened shops in Paris, Deauville, and Biarritz with the financial assistance of a backer. Chanel was an astute businesswoman and skilful publicist, quickly expanding her work to include skirts, jerseys in stockinette jersey, and accessories.

Chanel, recognized as the designer of the 1920s, initiated an era of casual dressing, appropriate to the occasion, for relaxed outdoor clothing created to be worn in comfort and without constricting corsets, liberating women with loosely fitting garments. Her style is that of uncluttered simplicity, incorporating practical details. She dressed the modern woman in clothes for a lifestyle.

In 1916 Chanel introduced jersey, a soft elasticated knit previously only used for undergarments, as the new fashion fabric. Wool jersey produced softer, lighter clothing with uncluttered fluid lines. She made simple jersey dresses in navy and grey, cut to flatter the figure rather than to emphasize and distort the natural body shape. The demand for her new non-conformist designs by the wealthy was so great and the use of jersey so successful that Chanel extended her range, creating her own jersey fabric designs, which were manufactured by Rodier.

Highly original in her concept of design, Chanel ceaselessly borrowed ideas from the male wardrobe, combining masculine tailoring with women's clothing. Her suits are precise but remain untailored, with flowing lines, retaining considerable individuality and simple elegance. Riding breeches, wide-legged trousers, blazers, and sweaters were all taken and adapted.

A major force in introducing and establishing common sense and understated simplicity into womenswear, Chanel's coordination of the cardigan, worn with a classic straight skirt, has become a standard combination of wearable separates. Chanel produced the cardigan in tweed and jersey fabrics, initiating the perennially popular "Chanel suit." It usually consisted of two or three pieces: a cardigan-style jacket, weighted with her trademark gilt chain stitched around the inside hem, a simple easy-to-wear skirt, worn with a blouse, the blouse fabric coordinated with the jacket lining. Her work offered comfort and streamlined simplicity, creating clothes for the modern woman, whom she epitomized herself. The key to her design philosophy was construction, producing traditional classics outliving each season's new fashion trends and apparel. Whilst other designers presented new looks for each new season, Chanel adapted the refined detailing and style lines.

Her colours are predominantly grey, navy, and beige, incorporating highlights of a richer colour palette. Chanel introduced the ever popular "little black dress," created for daywear, eveningwear, and cocktail dressing and a firm fixture in the fashion world today.

Attentive to detail, adding to day and eveningwear, Chanel established a reputation for extensive uses of costume jewelery, with innovative combinations of real and imitation gems, crystal clusters, strings of pearls, and ornate jewelled cuff links, adding brilliant contrast to the stark simplicity of her designs. The successful development of *Chanel No. 5* perfume in 1922 assisted in the financing of her couture empire during difficult years. An interesting aspect of Chanel's career was the re-opening of her couture house, which was closed during World War II. After 15 years in retirement, Chanel relaunched her work in 1954 at the age of 71, re-introducing the "Chanel suit," which has formed the basis for many of her collections and become a hallmark. The look adopted shorter skirts and braid trimmed cardigan jackets.

Despite her work and individual style, Chanel craved personal and financial independence, and was ruthless in her search for success. She was unique in revolutionizing the fashion industry with dress reform and in promoting the emancipation of women.

Her influence has touched many American and European designers, who continue to reinforce her concept of uncomplicated classics that inspire many contemporary designers' ready-to-wear collections—a homage to Chanel's essential modernist styling and her legacy to the world of fashion.—CAROL MARY BROWN

Chloé

French deluxe ready-to-wear house

Founded by Jacques Lenoir and Gaby Aghion, 1952; company acquired by Dunhill Holdings, plc, 1985, and by Vendome, 1993. Karl Lagerfeld, designer, 1965-83, and again from 1992; Martine Sitbon, designer, 1987-1991.

Address *54-56 rue du Faubourg St-Honoré, 75008 Paris, France.*

Style, modernity, and a strong sense of femininity have been the key elements of Chloé since its inception. It has maintained a quiet confidence among the Parisian ready-to-wear houses, relying on the abilities of various already-established designers to produce fresh and vibrant clothing which reflected and, in the high points of its history under Karl Lagerfeld, defined the *Zeitgeist*.

Riding the wave of prêt-à-porter companies set to challenge couture in the 1950s, Chloé was keen from the start to produce wearable clothes which conveyed the immediacy of modernism in clear, strong styles. The house's identity remains true to the design tenets of its early days, producing simple garments made from fluid fabrics. These promote a sense of elegant movement, enlivened by the artistic sense of colour which distinguishes French fashion; a constant feature at Chloé, despite the varied nationalities of its designers.

Chloé and its peers provided a lively, frequently directional alternative to haute couture, whose dictatorial status was diminishing. It was able to headhunt inspirational designers with the talent to translate the Chloé design image into clothing which would remain distinct to the label, while consistently evolving to embrace contemporary styles.

In the 1960s this meant keeping pace with the youth-orientated look in London, with clothes imbued with a futuristic vitality. In 1966 this sense of freedom through technology was assimilated into Jeanne Do's design for Chloé of the slim, straight-falling Empire line dress in stark white. This was decorated with metallic geometric shapes which marched down the dress, seeming to emanate from the slatted silver squares that made up the shimmering cropped bodice. This modern armour as eveningwear was a current fashion trend, picking up on the sci-fi trend of this early period of space exploration. The dress also pinpointed the introduction that year of maxi skirts, reinforcing Chloé's place at the cutting edge of fashion.

Indeed, it has continued to occupy this place, rarely absent from the fashion pages, despite temporary dips in status due to a loss of direction between designers. This reliance on different names to pursue Chloé's viability has, however, enabled a chameleon-like adaptability to the contemporary fashion temperature, calling upon such catalytic free-lancers as Karl Lagerfeld, at the height of his creative powers, to invigorate the house's image.

From the late 1960s Chloé's name became synonymous with Lagerfeld's, as he gave their line strongly conceived evening- and daywear of modernity and direction without compromising the supple femininity of the luxury fabrics employed.

The house style remained pared-down sheath dresses, hovering around the figure, adorned with minimal decoration, which distilled the late 1960s fashion directive. Under his guidance, the label moved with ease into the pluralistic 1970s, absorbing and refining the myriad of reference points with which fashion toyed. He was as adept at witty reinterpretations of the multi-ethnic gypsy look of pop festivals, referred to in patterned bordered skirts, as the more artistic classics popular the following year, when he turned two poster-paint bright patterned circles into versatile skirts and shawls which emphasized movement as they swirled onto the figure.

The success of his work for the label is indisputable, reinforcing its ready-to-wear dominance. It is unsurprising that Chloé languished after his departure. Having spent the previous decade pushing fashion forward, the label could only mark time until Martine Sitbon was chosen to reinject a sense of originality and verve in 1988.

Sitbon embodied facets of Chloé's style which had been established in the 1960s: uncluttered designed, which drew on popular culture to provide distinct themes for each collection, translated into classic shapes for women confident of their own identity.

Sitbon toned down the more overtly 1970s rock-influenced styles of her own named line to produce masculine tailored suits. These were softened by a dandyish swing to their cut and by delicately coloured silk chiffon blouses which blossomed into curving frilled collars. She defined Chloé's look during the 1980s, rounding the edges of the decade's often over-extravagant silhouette with well placed decoration and rich fabrics that drew on the glamorous mood which spilled into the first years of the 1990s.

In fall/winter 1991, shortly before she left the label, this sense of feminine swagger was shaped into scarlet textured silk evening dresses, cut short to mid-thigh and standing out from the hips to add a mobile swing from the fitted high collar bodice. The bold impact of the dress was tempered by the tantalizing gold bead strands, which hung in a bunch from the back fastening zip.

The desire to remain in the forefront prompted the return of Lagerfeld in 1992, when he captured the mood for unstructured, easy-to-wear styles in his fluid slip dresses in faded prints which harked back to the heights of his Chloé collections of the 1970s and tapped the nostalgia for the flower child look upon which they drew. He adorned them with dressing-up-box flair, throwing long strings of beads around the models' necks and silk blooms in their hair. Although the initial reaction was uncertain, Chloé had judged the fashion moment for change well, and Lagerfeld continues to fit comfortably into their mould.

Chloé's place in prêt-à-porter history has been ensured by the house's ability to allow designers to flourish under its auspices. Lagerfeld, particularly, has encapsulated its ideals of femininity and sophistication through pure distinct designs which enhance the figure in a contemporary way.—REBECCA ARNOLD

Claiborne, Liz

American designer

Born *Elizabeth Claiborne in Brussels, 31 March 1929, to American parents from New Orleans. Moved to New Orleans, 1939.*
Education *Studied art at Fine Arts School and Painters Studio, Belgium, 1947, and at the Nice Academy, 1948. Self-taught in design.*

Family *Married Ben Schultz in 1950 (divorced); son: Alexander. Married Arthur Ortenberg, 1957.*

Career *Sketch artist and model, Tina Lesser, 1950; design assistant to Omar Kiam for Ben Reig, Seventh Avenue, New York; designer, Youth Guild division of Jonathan Logan, 1960-76; founder and partner with Art Ortenberg, Liz Claiborne Inc., 1976; went public, 1981. Petite Sportswear line, 1981; dress division formed, 1982; shoes, 1983; purchased accessory firm Kaiser-Roth Corporation, 1985; Lizwear label featuring jeans, 1985; men's sportswear, Clairborne, 1985; Liz Claiborne perfume, 1986. Dana Buchman and Claiborne Furnishings inaugurated, 1987-88; larger-size line, Elizabeth, introduced, 1988; First Issue inaugurated, 1988, currently 38 stores throughout USA. Liz & Co. knitwear division formed, 1989; men's fragrance, Claiborne, launched, 1989; Elizabeth Dresses introduced, 1990; Sports Shoes and Suits, 1991; Sport Specific Activewear and Liz Sport Eyewear introduced, 1992; Russ and Crazy Horse labels purchased from Russ Toggs, 1992.*

Awards *Winner, Harper's Bazaar Jacques Heim national design contest, 1949; Hecht and Company Young Designer Award, Washington, D.C., 1967; Woolknit Association Award, 1973; Entrepreneurial Woman of the Year, 1980; Council of Fashion Designers of America Award, 1985; award from Barnard College, 1991; High School of Fashion Industries Award, 1990; award from Marymount Manhattan College, 1989.*

Address *1441 Broadway, New York, New York 10018, USA.*

Liz Claiborne is founder, president, and chief executive officer of Liz Claiborne Inc., by December 1991 a publicly held company posting sales increases of 17.6 percent to two billion dollars. With 19 divisions and three licensees, the company ranks fourth on *Fortune*'s "America's Most Admired Corporations."

In 1976, after a 25-year career as a designer, Liz Claiborne founded her own company to provide innovative design in women's working clothes. By 1988 her designs for the new market needs of the rapidly expanding women's workforce earned her the title of "The Wizard of the Working Woman's Wardrobe" in the series "Women Who Have Changed the World" in the journal *Working Woman* (June 1988). Liz Claiborne views herself as her down-to-earth client, "the Liz Lady . . . a working woman like myself," who now makes up 45 percent of the US workforce. Her original concept was, as she explained in a *Vogue* (New York) interview in August 1986, "to dress the women who didn't have to wear suits—the teachers, the doctors, the women working in southern California and Florida, the women in the fashion industry itself."

In 1980 her innovative designs were so successful that she became the first woman in the US fashion industry to be named Entrepreneurial Woman of the Year and in the following year her firm went public, prospering financially to such a degree that it has been described by Merrill Lynch as "a case history of success."

The phenomenal growth of the company has been spurred on by diversification from the two original basic lines—active sportswear and a slightly dressier collection—to include a dress division in 1982, and a unit for shoes in 1983. In 1985 Liz Claiborne Inc. bought the Kaiser-Roth Corporation, the company it had licensed to produce accessories, including handbags, scarves, belts, and hats. In the same year a collection of men's sportswear, Claiborne, was introduced and 1986 saw the launch of a perfume *Liz Claiborne*, described by its eponymous designer as appealing "to a woman's idealistic version of herself. . . . She's active, whatever her age. It's the same feeling we try to give in the clothes" (*Vogue*, New York, August 1986).

Claiborne's designs worked on the premise that what she needed, other American women needed, and the company's links with their consumers are strengthened by such devices as the questionnaires to encourage customers to express their views and provide accurate and timely customer feedback which are a feature of the 18 US stand-alone Claiborne shops. They provide Liz Claiborne Inc. with near-instantaneous information on market trends.

Liz Claiborne Inc., which already controls an estimated one-third of the two billion dollar US market for upmarket women's sportswear, sells through some 3,500 retailers in the United States alone. The company also sells products to stores in Great Britain, Spain, Ireland, and the Netherlands and has recently established its first free-standing retail licensee in Singapore.—DOREEN ERLICH

Courrèges, André
French designer

> **Born**   *Pau, Pyrenées Atlantiques, 9 March 1923.*
>
> **Education**   *Studied engineering at École des Pont et Chaussées; studied fashion in Pau and Paris.*
>
> **Family**   *Married Jacqueline (Coqueline) Barrière in 1967; daughter: Marie-Clafoutie-Ustoa.*
>
> **Career**   *Cutter, Cristobal Balenciaga, Paris, 1945-61; independent fashion designer, Paris, 1960-61; founded Courrèges fashion house, boulevard Kléber, Paris, 1961-65; first haute couture collection, 1965; business sold to l'Oréal, 1965; resumed designing, 1967, with Prototype custom line, Couture Future high priced ready-to-wear line introduced 1969; first fragrance line Empreinte introduced, 1971; men's ready-to-wear line and men's fragrance introduced, 1973; Hyperbole lower priced ready-to-wear line, 1980; company purchased by Itokin, 1983; produced collection with Jean-Charles de Castelbajac, spring-summer 1994 and 1995. Also: designed own boutiques from 1970, accessories, leather goods, watches, belts, bathrooms, furniture, stationery, automobiles, windsurfing equipment and others, from 1979.*
>
> **Awards**   *Couture Award, London, 1964.*
>
> **Address**   *40 rue François Premier, 75008 Paris, France.*

One of a generation of strikingly innovative designers working in Paris in the 1960s, André Courrèges was one of the first since Chanel to understand the potential for womenswear of using the items which make up the male wardrobe. His goal became to provide the same simple range of garments for women, not by mere appropriation of male adornment, but inventing a totally new modernistic aesthetic.

Courrèges regarded the 1950s silhouette of a tightly boned and wasp-waisted mannequin, teetering on impossibly high stiletto heels, as completely alien to the needs of the modern woman of the 1960s, even though he had worked for Balenciaga for 11 years, from 1950 to 1961,

Courrèges

André Courrèges: 1969.

as chief cutter. Courrèges subsequently left to set up his own business with his wife Coqueline. Their first collection, using tweeds and soft wools, had yet to shake off Balenciaga's influence.

Ultimately Courrèges saw the male wardrobe as more logical and practical than a woman's because of its unadorned and reductionist nature, resulting from its being pared down to the barest essentials over the passage of time. Thus he responded as an engineer well versed in the functionalist aesthetics of architectural practitioners such as Le Corbusier and, utilizing the skills he had learned and finely honed at Balenciaga, and his own modernist tendencies, Courrèges conceived a new look of femininity entirely different from that of Balenciaga.

Cutting skills were used to free rather than contain the body, emphasized by short trapeze skirts for extra movement. By 1964 Courrèges was producing spare but not spirited ranges of clothing, such as his monochromatic pinafore dresses and suits with hemlines well above the knee, all in crisply tailored, squared-off shapes. Renouncing the stiletto as an item of clothing symbolizing women's subordination, Courrèges provided his models with flat-heeled white glacé boots and accessorized his honed-down clothes with extraordinary headgear such as futuristic helmets and strange baby bonnets.

Courrèges believed that the foundation of successful design was in understanding function; correct form would automatically follow. Aesthetics was only the wrapping. In fact, the only decoration to be found on Courrèges clothes is either directly allied to its construction, as in the use of welt seaming, or is minor such as the small half belt on the back of his coats. One decorative device he revels in and which was copied extensively within mass market fashion was his use of white daisies made out of every conceivable material such as sequins, lace, or used as patches.

It is still debated whether or not Courrèges invented the mini skirt, but he was indisputably responsible for making trousers and matching tunic tops *de rigueur* for every occasion, overturning the taboo of trouser wearing by women, creating versions slit at the seam to give an exaggerated elongation to the female body and emphasizing this clean streamlined look by using lean, well-muscled female models.

Courrèges displays his love of construction in his use of chevron stitching, such as that used in 1965 at the hips of dresses and trousers, and his use of devices such as the bib yoke, keyhole neckline, and patch pocket. Hip yokes and welted seams with top stitching emphasize the lines of the garment, the stitching occasionally deployed in contrasting colours, such as orange on white, to exaggerate the details of assembly.

Courrèges collections were copied and disseminated worldwide, although the taut outline of the originals was lost when cheaper materials were used. Consequently he refused to stage shows for the press or retail buyers and would only sell to private clients, biding his time until he was ready to produce his own ready-to-wear collection, entitled Couture Future, in 1969. However, by this time his hard-edged style had become dated in comparison with the hippie, ethnic style of the 1970s and his seminal structured A-line dresses with welt seams and square-cut coats on top seemed out of step with contemporary fashion.

By 1990 Courrèges was again designing successfully, spurred by a 1960s revival as the architectural lines of his short trapeze dresses were rediscovered by a new generation.—CAROLINE COX

Cox, Patrick

Canadian footwear designer working in London

Born *Edmonton, Canada, 19 March 1963.*

Education *Studied at Cordwainers College, Hackney, London, 1983-85.*

Career *Established firm in London and designed collections for Bodymap, Vivienne Westwood, John Galliano, and others, from 1987. London shop opened, 1991.*

Address *8 Symons Street, London SW3 2TJ, England.*

"My early shoes stick in people's minds," says Patrick Cox, "but things are getting more refined." Those who may remember him as the devoted nightclubber of the early 1980s might be surprised to find him, a decade later, presiding over the salon atmosphere of his shoeshop-cum-antiques emporium in London. Patrick Cox has grown up, but he has also gone beyond the image of the shoemaker with "street credibility," designing for Vivienne Westwood, John Galliano, *et al.* He has survived the designer decade of the 1980s and emerged with his ability to wittily re-interpret traditional styling, still constantly in tune with contemporary fashion.

Cox's fascination with the British fashion scene brought him to London, rather than the obvious footwear design centres of Italy. He enrolled at Cordwainers College, Hackney, London to study, but soon found that college life was less rewarding than meeting and making contacts within the London club world. His involvement with the music and fashion scene brought him the chance to design for Vivienne Westwood's first solo collection, whilst he was still at college. He recalls: "I used to shop at Westwood's quite a lot and my flatmate David was her assistant. Six weeks before the show someone realized that nothing had been done about shoes and David suggested that I could probably help . . . my gold platform shoes with large knots went down a treat. Everyone noticed them—you couldn't miss them really—and my other commissions have followed from there."

Indeed they did. In no time at all he was designing shoes to accompany the collections of the young English designers who were then flavour of the month on the international fashion circuit. Cox shod the feet to fit the wilful perversities of Bodymap, the calculated eccentricity of John Galliano, and the ladies-who-lunch chic of Alistair Blair.

Cox went on to design his own label collections with such delightfully named styles as Chain Reaction, Rasta, and Crucifix Court. These were typical, hard-edged classic women's silhouettes given the Cox treatment—chain mesh, silk fringes and crucifixes suspended from the heels. Witty and amusing as these styles were, they had limited appeal and Cox would not have attained his current prominence had he not sought a larger audience.

The launch of his own London shop in 1991 gave him the opportunity to show his collections as a whole, displaying the brash alongside the sophisticated. His audience now came from both the devotees of the off-the-wall fashion experimentation of the King's Road and the classic chic of the Sloane Square debutante. Cleverly, his shop was geographically situated between the two.

Selling shoes alongside antiques was a novelty that appealed to the press and boosted Cox's profile. There was something delightful in the presentation of shoes balanced on the arms of Louis XVI gilt chairs or popping out of the drawers of beautiful old dressers. The shoes gained

Patrick Cox.

an aura of respectability; a sense of belonging to some tradition, which perfectly complemented Cox's re-interpretation of classic themes.

No longer is there a typical Cox customer. They include the young and not so young. Cox takes great delight when elderly ladies appreciate his now subtle styling and women's shoes now rival those of Manolo Blahnik in their sophistication; a calculated move.

In contrast, the development his men's footwear is less obvious. Cox has always loved traditional English styling, and says: "I believe that British men's shoes are the best in the world, so mine are just an evolution from those classic ideas." This evolution has kept him close to the spirit of British footwear, if not to the colourways. He reproduces the weight and proportions of the styles whilst exaggerating the soles and fastenings.

Patrick Cox is the shoe designer who admits that there is not a lot you can do with shoes. The very nature of footwear imposes constraints upon the designer, where there are fewer problems for the clothing designer. Cox sees shoes as more architectural than clothes; a free standing form with an inside and out. Yet these restrictions do not stop him producing fresh contemporary styles which still work within the perceived framework of what a classic silhouette should be.—CHRIS HILL

Daché, Lilly

American millinery designer

Born *Bèigles, France, c.1904.*

Education *Left school at 13.*

Family *Married Jean Desprês in 1931; daughter: Suzanne.*

Career *In Paris, apprenticed with Reboux, later worked for Maison Talbot and Georgette. Immigrated to New York, 1924. Designer, Darlington's (Philadelphia); millinery saleswoman, Macy's, 1924; saleswoman, The Bonnet Shop, New York, 1924; purchased shop from owner and established own millinery business, 1924; expanded and moved business in 1925, 1928; built Lilly Daché Building, East 56th St., New York, 1937; added dresses and accessories, introduced fragrances, Drifting and Dashing, 1946; launched own clothing line, 1949; added coats, stockings, cosmetics, early 1950s; ready-to-wear millinery collections Mlle. Lilly and Dachettes introduced, early 1950s; closed business, 1968.*

Awards *Neiman Marcus Award, Dallas, 1940; Coty American Fashion Critics Award, 1943.*

Died *(in Louvecienne, France) 31 December 1989.*

Lilly Daché was the archetypal flamboyant immigrant beloved of Americans and so often taken to their hearts. In approved rags-to-riches fashion, she arrived in New York with a few dollars in her pocket (13, henceforth her lucky number) in the heady days of the mid-1920s. Twenty years later, her name was as much a household word as any milliner's could be.

Daché's heyday coincided with a period in fashion history, the mid-1930s to the mid-1940s, during which one's hat—one always wore a hat—was often more important than one's frock. Great heights of chic and absurdity were achieved by the milliners of the day: tiny doll's hats perched over one eye, two-tone "Persian" turbans stuck with jewelled daggers, pom-poms of mink or marabout; Daché's hats were amongst the most outrageous of all. Her "complexion

Lilly Daché. *Photograph courtesy of the Costume Institute, Metropolitan Museum of Art.*

veil" was tinted green across the eyes, and blush-rose across the cheeks. For Beatrice Lillie, she made a "hands-across-the-sea" hat, with two clasped hands on the front, for the actress to wear both in England and America.

Daché's verve and skills attracted a high-profile clientele of stage and film stars: Marlene Dietrich, Carole Lombard, Joan Crawford, Marion Davies, Gertrude Lawrence—all the big names. She worked with Travis Banton on Hollywood films, providing the hats to top his costumes, as many as 50 for one star for one movie. Often it was she who stuck Carmen Miranda's towering turbans with birds and fruit, and yet more birds and more fruit.

At her New York headquarters, Daché created a setting for herself which now seems the essence of kitsch glamour. Her circular salon was lined with mirrors; she had a silver fitting-room for celebrity brunettes, and a golden one for blondes. For wholesale buyers, she had another circular room padded with tufted pink satin, where she reigned from a leopard-skin divan wearing a leopard-skin jacket and leopard-skin slippers with bells on (to warn her girls of her approach, a job later undertaken by her armful of jingling bangles).

Not an early riser, Daché conducted her morning's business from her bed, in the style of an 18th-century *levée,* dictating letters, buying supplies, designing, and interviewing employees whilst wrapped in a leopard-skin rug (she had a robe made from the skins of more of these unfortunate cats, lined with shocking-pink felt). Occasionally business would be conducted from the reasonably modest depths of a neck-high bubble-bath. But Daché, like so many fashionable New Yorkers of her day, professed herself never so happy as when digging around in the garden of her upstate Colonial home.

Daché was one of the so-called Big Three New York milliners of her day, the others being John Fredericks and Sally Victor, and as such exerted a powerful influence on the American millinery trade, designing for wholesale manufacturers as well as for personal clients. Her designs sold worldwide and she embarked enthusiastically on promotional tours, accompanied by mountainous luggage and concomitant publicity.

At the height of her fame, Lilly Daché had shops in Chicago and Miami Beach, Florida and employed 150 milliners at her flagship building off Park Avenue, New York. Daché was a great self-publicist and epitomized the kind of woman to whom her smart American customers aspired. She was chic, dressy, and flamboyant, and presented herself with self-assured bravado—"I like beautiful shoes in gay colours, with thick platforms and high heels. I like splashy jewellery that clinks when I walk, and I like my earrings big. I am . . . Lilly Daché, milliner de luxe."—ALAN J. FLUX

Dagworthy, Wendy
British designer

Born   *Gravesend, Kent, England, 4 March 1950.*
Education   *Northfleet Secondary School; studied at Medway College of Design, 1966-68, and at Hornsey College of Art (now Middlesex University), London, 1968-71; first-class honours.*
Family   *Married Jonathan Prew in August 1973.*

Wendy Dagworthy: Check short jacket with stripe classic shorts. *Photograph by Jon Prew.*

D
_____
fashion

Career *Designer, Radley, 1971-72; founder, designer, Wendy Dagworthy Ltd, 1972-88; joined London Designer Collections, 1975; director, 1982-90. Lecturer in fashion from 1972, including Royal College of Art, London; course director on Fashion BA course at Central St Martin's College of Art and Design, London, 1989; free-lance designer and consultant, Laura Ashley, 1992. Exhibitor Victoria and Albert Museum, London; member of British Fashion Council management committee; speaker at The Fashion Conference, Lagos, Nigeria, 1992; participates in many charity fashion shows and awards.*
Awards *Fil D'Or International Linen Award, Monte Carlo, 1985.*
Address *18 Melrose Terrace, London W6, England.*

For nearly 20 years Wendy Dagworthy produced bright, easy, wearable separates and established herself as one of the most successful British designers in the wacky world of 1980s fashion. Her style was always distinctive and colourful, incorporating cheerful mixtures of fabrics, colours, patterns, textures and an attention to fine detail; "You wear them, they don't wear you," was Dagworthy's fashion philosophy.

She formed her company in 1972 after one year as a designer for the wholesale firm Radley and a year after graduating from the Hornsey College of Art fashion course, with a first-class honours degree. There was an immediate consumer demand for Dagworthy's designs, and prestigious international stores soon placed orders. Italy, in particular, proved a lucrative outlet for her very English look and during the early 1980s she was exporting nearly half of her total output to that country.

Dagworthy loved to use vibrant colours and prints, embroidered Caribbean style *batiks*, mixed with stripes or swirling floral designs in fuchsia, scarlet, and orange. Favourite fabrics were mohairs, strongly textured woven wools, and wool baratheas. Her most popular, signature garments were oversize wool coats, back buttoning smocks, circular skirts, and gathered skirts with boldly tied waists, teamed with easy cardigans or wide cropped jackets. The menswear collections, introduced in the early 1980s, adhered to the same lively, colourful themes and quickly emulated the success of the womenswear, being comfortable and easy to wear.

Dagworthy has always been a strong supporter of British fashion design. In 1975 she joined the London Designer Collections, a prestigious collaboration of British designers, supporting and promoting their industry, and became a director in 1982. She has always been active in British fashion education, both as a lecturer and assessor, participating in design competitions like the Royal Society of Arts Awards and the British Fashion Awards. She has also appeared regularly as fashion consultant to television shows like *The Clothes Show, Frocks on the Box,* and *Good Morning America.*

Wendy Dagworthy Ltd exhibited their seasonal collections at trade shows in London, Milan, New York, and Paris. Her international reputation went from strength to strength each season and her work was recognized with several awards including the Fil d'Or International Linen Award in 1985. The Victoria and Albert Museum in London display a Wendy Dagworthy outfit in their permanent costume collection.

Wendy Dagworthy closed her business in 1988 and in the following year became the course director for the BA fashion course at London's Central St Martin's College of Art and Design. Since then she has devoted herself to fashion education but has not completely forsaken commercial designing. She still accepts consultancies, her most recent being in 1992, as free-

_ _ _ _

lance designer and consultant for Laura Ashley. She is also an active member of the British Fashion Council's Management Committee.—KEVIN ALMOND

De la Renta, Oscar
Dominican designer working in New York

Born *Santo Domingo, 22 July 1932.*

Education *Studied art, National School of Art, Santo Domingo, 1950-52; Academia de San Fernando, Madrid, 1953-55.*

Family *Married Françoise de Langlade in 1967 (died, 1983); married Annette Reed in 1989; adopted son: Moises.*

Career *Staff designer under Balenciaga, Madrid, from 1949; assistant designer to Antonio Castillo, Lanvin-Castillo, Paris, 1961-63; designer, Elizabeth Arden couture and ready-to-wear, New York, 1963-65; partner, designer, Jane Derby Inc., New York, 1965-69; designer, chief executive, Oscar de la Renta Couture, Oscar de la Renta II, de la Renta Furs and Jewelry, Oscar de la Renta Ltd., from 1973; signature perfume introduced, 1977, followed by Ruffles, 1983, and Volupté, 1991; also owner, de la Renta specialty shop, Santo Domingo, from 1968; designer, couture collection for Balmain, from 1993.*

Exhibitions *Versailles 1973: American Fashion on the World Stage, Metropolitan Museum of Art, 1993.*

Awards *Coty American Fashion Critics Award, 1967, 1973; Coty Return Award, 1968; Neiman Marcus Award, 1968; Golden Tiberius Award, 1969; American Printed Fabrics Council "Tommy" Award, 1971; Fragrance Foundation Award, 1978; named Caballero of the Order of Juan Pablo Duarte, and Gran Comandante of the Order of Cristobal Colón, Dominican Republic, 1972.*

Address *550 Seventh Avenue, New York, New York 10018, USA.*

Although he was born in the Dominican Republic and moved to New York at the age of 30, Oscar de la Renta has become a great ambassador for American fashion. His recent appointment as designer to the French couture house of Pierre Balmain in early 1993 was an historic occasion; the first time an American designer had been commissioned by the French couture. This choice in many ways reflects the growing eminence of New York as a fashion force and the international status of American designers.

As a designer, de la Renta has inspired many international trends. During the 1960s his clothes were elaborate and witty parodies of experimental street fashion: jackets and coats of bandanna printed denim, embroidered hotpants under silk mini dresses, or caftans made out of silk chiffon and psychedelic silk saris. He was largely responsible for initiating the ethnic fashion of the 1970s with gypsy and Russian fashion themes incorporating fringed shawls, boleros, peasant blouses, and full skirts. In recent years, de la Renta has been popular for his romantic evening clothes, glamorous, elegant, and made from richly opulent fabrics such as brocade, transparent chiffon, fox fur, ermine, and embroidered *faille*.

All through his career de la Renta has concentrated on simple shapes and silhouettes that have created dramatic and flashy statements. He has an inherent feeling for women's femininity and has established fashion classics, such as variations of his portrait dresses in taffeta, chiffon, or velvet with ruffled necklines or cuffs, or his ornate luncheon suits, embroidered in costume jewellery and gold.

Since founding his own company in 1967 to produce luxury women's ready-to-wear, de la Renta has expanded to create jewellery, household linens, menswear, and perfumes. These products are marketed and sold all over Europe, the Orient, South and North America.

De la Renta had a well travelled international fashion pedigree before establishing his own label business. He studied art at the Academia de San Fernando in Madrid and began sketching for leading Spanish fashion houses, leading to a job at Balenciaga's Madrid couture house, Eisa. A move to Paris in 1961 brought him work as an assistant to Antonio De Castillo at Lanvin-Castillo. He moved with Castillo to New York in 1963 to design at Elizabeth Arden. Joining Jane Derby Inc. as a partner in 1965 he began operating as Oscar de la Renta Ltd. in 1973.

The designer's first marriage to the late Françoise de la Langlade, the editor-in-chief of French *Vogue,* in 1967 was an undoubted asset to his business. Together they created *soirées* that were the equivalent of 18th-century salons. This environment enhanced the wearing of an Oscar de la Renta creation and provided valuable publicity, with frequent mentions in society columns.

De la Renta has not forgotten his Dominican associations and has been honoured as its best known native son and one of its most distinguished citizens with the Orden de Merito de Juan Pablo Duarte. He also helped build a much needed school and day care centre in the republic for over 350.

De la Renta continues to design in New York today, redefining American elegance with his famous womenswear line, Signature, the couture line, Studio, the ready-to-wear line and a range of sophisticated dresses and suits known as Miss.—KEVIN ALMOND

Demeulemeester, Ann

Belgian designer

Born *Kortrijk, Belgium, 29 December 1959.*

Education *Studied at the Royal Academy of Fine Arts, Antwerp, 1978-81.*

Family *Married Patrick Robyn; son: Victor.*

Career *Showed first collection of women's ready-to-wear, 1981; free-lance designer for international ready-to-wear men's and women's collections, 1981-87; has also designed shoes, handbags, sunglasses and accessories since 1987, outerwear since 1989, knitwear since 1991. Founded B.V.B.A. "32" company, with husband, 1985. Opened Paris showroom, 1992.*

Exhibitions *La bienale de venise avec Rodney Graham, Anvers, 1993.*

Awards *Golden Spindle Award, Belgium, 1983; Golden T Award, Spain, 1992.*

Address *B.V.B.A. "32," Populeerenlaan 34, B-2020 Antwerp, Belgium.*

Linked to a group of designers to come out of Belgium in the mid-1980s, Demeulemeester's deconstructed style has come into its own as the 1990s have progressed. Her work, with its monochromatic colour schemes and matt layering onto the body of flowing columns of fabric, encapsulates the contemporary *Zeitgeist.*

Ann Demeulemeester: Winter 1995/96.

The impact of this Belgian avant-garde designer's pared-down structure, combining rough edges with more traditionally cut suiting, has been comparable to that of Japanese designers Kawakubo and Yamamoto a decade earlier. Both superseded more overtly designed fashions in favour of purer silhouettes that combine references to antique clothing with the worn-in patina of their fabrics and a disregard for the more conventional notions of fit.

Demeulemeester's work represents (along with Margiela, Dries Van Noten *et al.*) a recognizable 1990s approach to clothing and designer style. It overtakes the often directionless attempts to integrate the sportswear styles of the late 1980s into a high fashion context and the myriad of 1970s reworkings in the early 1990s. Dedicated to this more experimental strain of fashion, Demeulemeester, having won early accolades for her designs while still at college, pays great attention to detail. From the start she used local craftsmen to make up her work. In the late 1980s her designs were more attuned to fashionable classic garments. In 1987 short black sunray pleated skirts were shown with cross-over braces and crisp white shirts, worn with stark gabardine coats. Even at this stage, however, she showed concern for proportion, constructing skirts and dresses with adjustable waistlines that could be worn high or low, altering the emphasis of the design to suit the figure of the wearer and give a different sense of balance to the overall outfit.

The appeal of designs which are at the cutting edge of fashion and yet ultimately still wearable has ensured Demeulemeester's success, and, as her work has grown in confidence, so have her sales. The strong lines of her signature long coats and dresses are punctuated by more deconstructed styles like the frayed-edged lacy knit top shoe showed in 1993. This, with its shrunken fit, married the resurgent punk ethos of rough, makeshift anti-fashion to the languorous swing of Gothic-inspired floor-skimming coats.

Her autumn-winter collection for 1993 continued in this vein. Shroud-like white dresses with overlong cuffs and black velvet and brocade coats were set against fitted crêpe sheaths, their differing textures giving a sense of shade and light to provide interest and definition to each outfit. The trumpet cuffs and jet crucifixes with which these were teamed gave a religious aspect to the show which was echoed amongst her contemporaries.

Although there will inevitably be a backlash against such austerity, Demeulemeester's work is strong enough to outlive short-term trends and consolidate her name as a designer of avant-garde independent styles, incorporating an artistic use of fabric and texture and an attention to detail.—REBECCA ARNOLD

Desses, Jean

French designer

> **Born** *Jean Dimitre Verginie, in Alexandria, Egypt, 6 August 1904.*
> **Education** *Studied law, then design, in Paris.*
> **Career** *Designer, Mme. Jane in Paris, 1925-37; opened own house in Paris, 1937; launched Jean Dessès Diffusion line in America, 1950; in Paris, opened boutique Les Soeurs Hortenses, 1951, and made-to-measure dress shop, Bazaar, 1953; closed couture house, 1960; closed ready-to-wear house, 1965; free-lance designer in Greece, to 1970.*
> **Died** *(in Athens, Greece) 2 August 1970.*

Desses

Jean Dessès belongs to the small group of couturiers, such as Vionnet, Balenciaga and Grès, whose clothing combines technical skill with sculptural aesthetic. Although he began as a designer for a small couture house in Paris in the 1920s, and opened his own house in 1937, it was not until the post-war years of the 1940s and 1950s that his work gained its greatest acclaim.

The hallmarks of his post-war fame are evident in his pre-war work. Draped and twisted sashes and bodices, cape or kimono sleeves, a fondness for asymmetry, and ornament derived from the architecture of the garment rather than applied as surface decoration, were all elements of both his day and evening wear in the late 1930s. Magazine coverage during that period suggests that he favored jerseys and crêpes, with the jersey dresses in particular anticipating the draping skill which Dessès would use to such advantage after 1945.

Immediately after the war Dessès began to explore his own heritage for design themes which would best use his cutting expertise. He showed a collection inspired by ancient Egyptian costume in 1946 and returned to that theme in the mid-1950s, while the costume of ancient Greece provided a continuous thread through his work. Today his reputation rests primarily on the pleated and draped silk chiffon evening dresses which most notably express Dessès's historical interests.

Dessès's transition from jersey to chiffon may have been mandated by the fuller silhouettes of the 1940s, or perhaps by the fact that Madame Grès was the acknowledged master of the draped jersey column, but the change set him on a path which made his name. In September 1951 New York *Vogue* lauded Dessès's chiffon gowns as the "Fords" of his collection, "good for a lifetime." By 1958 they were termed "classic." The variations on the theme seemed endless, but there are several important common factors. Appearances notwithstanding, the dresses were not always simple Grecian draperies. The understructures were formal and the cuts were complex, with swags, sashes, bows, and scarves twisted and pleated into shapes that seem effortless, and defy analysis. In lesser hands they might simply seem contrived. The dresses also show his sensitive, if somewhat conservative, color sense. Cream or ivory, always flattering, are constants, but Dessès often used two or three shades of one hue, or used three different hues, but of equal value, to maintain harmony. It is also worth noting that the garments are impeccably made; every yard of hem in the double- or triple-tiered chiffon skirts has a hand-rolled finished.

Dessès was equally deft with crisp silks, rough tweeds, and fine dress wools, and his most skilful and inventive draping and cutting techniques were often allied with these fabrics. Dropped shoulder lines, raglan or kimono sleeve variations, and draped collars softened voluminous mohair coats and tweed suit jackets. Tucks, godets, and intricate seaming molded crêpe and gabardine dresses to the contours of the figure. Skirt fullness was swept to the back, folded in at the side, or turned into tiers of flounces which spiraled from hem to hip—all through manipulation of the grain in one piece of cloth.

The most successful of his silhouettes, such as the Streamlined and Winged collections of 1949 and 1951, may not have set trends, but they interpreted the trend with elegance. He favored asymmetry and oblique lines, which gave the garments a sense of movement even in repose. Bold, architectural details such as stand-away pockets and cuffs were used like punctuation marks, adding drama and intensity to a silhouette. Dessès made clothes which were complex but not fussy, and, on occasion, did set the trend in 1950 when he introduced a one-sleeved stole.

Dessès made an easy transition to the 1960s. His stylistic talents were well suited to the cutting possibilities of the stiffer fabrics and simpler silhouettes in vogue at the time. He was also able to devote more of his attention to the ready-to-wear "Dessès Diffusion" line he had started in 1949, and licensed to two US manufacturers—one for suits and one for evening clothes. Dessès closed his couture operation in 1965, apparently due to poor health. His influence on fashion has outlived him, however, figuring even today in the work of Valentino, who was with Dessès's house for several years in the 1950s.—MADELYN SHAW

Dior, Christian

French designer

Born *Granville, France, 21 January 1905.*

Education *Studied political science at École des Sciences Politiques, Paris, 1920-25.*

Military Service *Served in the French Army, 1927-28, mobilized, 1939-40.*

Career *Art dealer, 1928-31; free-lance designer and sketch artist, 1934-37; assistant designer, Piguet, 1937-39; lived in Provence, 1940-42; designer, Lelong, 1941-46; Maison Dior opened, 1947; Christian Dior-New York opened, 1948; Miss Dior boutique opened, 1967; fragrances: Miss Dior, 1947, Diorama, 1949, Diorissima, 1956, Diorling, 1963.*

Exhibitions *Christian Dior et le Cinéma, Cinémathèque Francaise, Paris, 1983; Dessins de Dior, Musée des Arts de la Mode, Paris, 1987; Gruau: Modes et publicité, Musée de la Mode et du costume, 1989; Réne Gruau pour Christian Dior, Musee des Beaux Arts, 1990; Christian Dior: The Magic of the Fashion, Powerhouse Museum, 1994.*

Awards *Neiman Marcus Award, Dallas, 1947; Remise de la legion d'honneur a Christian Dior, 1950; Parsons School of Design Distinguished Achievement Award, New York, 1956; Fashion Industry Foundation Award, to the House of Dior, New York, 1990.*

Died *(in Montecatini, Italy) 24 October 1957.*

Company address *30 avenue Montaigne, 75008 Paris, France.*

Christian Dior is still one of the most famous fashion designers of the 20th century. In the years after the debut of his first collection in 1947 he was a legendary figure and the world press developed an extraordinary love affair with him, increasing their enthusiasm with each new collection. Dior never disappointed them, constantly creating clothes that were newsworthy as well as beautiful.

Dior was middle-aged when he achieved fame. A sensitive and gentle personality, he had previously worked as a fashion illustrator, then as a design assistant for both Robert Piguet and Lucien Lélong in Paris. In 1946 the French textile magnate Marcel Boussac offered to finance the opening of Dior's own couture house and secured the lease on 30 avenue Montaigne, Paris.

The first collection was revolutionary, heralded as the "New Look" by the fashion press— Dior himself had christened it the "Corolle Line." It was a composition of rounded shoulders, shapely emphasis of the bust, cinched waist, and curvaceous bell-shaped skirt in luxurious fabric. The concept of the collection was not new, bearing a striking resemblance to French fashions of the 1860s. Dior himself attributed his inspiration to the pretty, elegant clothes he had remembered his mother wearing to the Deauville races in the 1900s.

Christian Dior: Fall/Winter 1948/49.
Photograph by Willy Maywald; © 1997 Artists Rights Society (ARS), New York/ADAGP, Paris.

Even though several other designers had experimented with or predicted the new silhouette, Dior's luxurious version reawakened the world to the importance of Parisian couture. At a standstill during World War II, Paris had lost its way as the world's fashion capital. Dior reestablished it as a centre of excellence, creating what Janey Ironside of the Royal College of Art in London described as "a new chance in life, a new love affair."

There were many criticisms of the New Look. Feminists have argued that it was an attempt to return women to an oppressed, decorative role with its emphasis on the restrictive padding, corset, and crinoline. Others were shocked by the extravagant use of ornament and fabric metreage when clothes were still being rationed. The New Look, however, rapidly became a postwar cultural symbol for what Dior himself described as "Youth, hope, and the future."

After creating a furor with his first collection, Dior established himself as a cautious, methodical designer. Each collection that followed was a continuation of the New Look theme of highly constructed clothes. They were christened with names that described their silhouettes, the Zig Zag Line, A Line, Y Line, Arrow Line, etc. All the collections were realized with the finest tailoring and the most sumptuous fabrics: satins, traditional suiting, fine wools, taffetas, and lavish embroideries.

Throughout Dior's ten years of fame, none of his collections failed, either critically or commercially. The only threat to his run of success occurred when Chanel made a fashion comeback in 1954 at the age of 71. Chanel's philosophy, that clothes should be relaxed, ageless, dateless, and easy to wear, completely opposed Dior's philosophy. "Fifties Horrors," was how she described male couturiers, deploring them for torturing bodies into ridiculous shapes. Dior's reaction was to introduce his most unstructured collection, the "Lily of the Valley Line," was young, fresh, and unsophisticated. Relaxed, casual jackets with pleated skirts and sailor-collared blouses, clothes that "Couldn't be easier," described *Vogue*.

By the time Dior died his name had become synonymous with taste and luxury. The business had an estimated turnover of 20 million dollars a year, thanks in part to Dior's own shrewdness. Dior organized licence agreements to manufacture Dior accessories internationally. By the time Dior died, perfume, furs, scarves, corsetry, knitwear, lingerie, costume jewellery, and shoes were being produced.

Many of Dior's associates have said that his death was timely and that his work and fashion philosophy were entirely suited to his period. It would be interesting to speculate how Dior would have adapted to the excesses of fashion in the 1960s, 1970s and 1980s, because, as his former personal assistant, Madame Raymonde, once said, "If Dior had lived, fashion would not be in the state it is in now."—KEVIN ALMOND

di Sant'Angelo, Giorgio
American designer

Born *Count Giorgio Imperiale di Sant'Angelo in Florence, 5 May 1933. Raised in Argentina; immigrated to the United States, 1962.*

Education *Studied architecture in Florence, industrial design in Barcelona, and art at the Sorbonne.*

di Sant'Angelo

Career Animator, Walt Disney Studios, Hollywood, 1962-63; textile and jewelry designer, 1963-67; designer, Sant'Angelo, New York, 1967-89; company incorporated, 1968.

Awards Coty American Fashion Critics Award, 1968, 1970; Inspiration Home Furnishings Award, New York, 1978; Knitted Textile Association Designer Award, New York, 1982; Council of Fashion Designers of America Award, 1987; Fashion Designers of America Award, 1988.

Address 611 Broadway, New York, New York 10012, USA.

Died (in New York) 29 August 1989.

Giorgio di Sant'Angelo was a child of the 1960s. Unlike many of that decade's talented new designers—including Pierre Cardin, André Courrèges, and Rudi Gernreich—who suffered symptoms of career burn-out as the 1960s came to a close, di Sant'Angelo soared on a creative high. His formative years, leading up to his move to New York, included an education in the arts in Florence and a studio apprenticeship with Picasso who urged di Sant'Angelo to trust his own restless creativity and to keep trying new artistic ventures.

Di Sant'Angelo, who had an affinity for the new plastics developed with Space Age technology, designed lucite jewelry and accessories in colorful geometric shapes. Diana Vreeland, editor of *Vogue* from 1963-71, found di Sant'Angelo's designs to be in step with her own ideas and gave him carte blanche as a stylist. The results of their association during the late 1960s are stunning examples of the breadth of di Sant'Angelo's originality. His concoctions of colored Veruschka were the peak of fashion fantasy. This option of make-believe went beyond mere merchandise shown in a magazine layout. Di Sant'Angelo's work was theatrical, exotic, and on some level could be considered performance art. This taste for escapism through dress coincided with the escalation of the Vietnam War in 1968-69.

Inspired by hippie and street fashions, di Sant'Angelo also translated ideas that would fit the marketplace. His love of ethnic clothing was evident, and his gypsy looks included elements of romanticism. Introducing a modern component, di Sant'Angelo also incorporated Lycra body suits with these varied influences. He offered women a chance at self-expression through dress.

In 1972, di Sant'Angelo left behind his gypsy and American Indian inspirations and concentrated on body-conscious designs that combined knits and wovens. His collection of 33 pieces was shown at the Guggenheim Museum further emphasizing di Sant'Angelo's commitment to fashion design as an artform. Calling the group "Summer with Soul," Sant'Angelo stated: "To me, soul means freedom and inner confidence. I express it in happy, bright colors, and in simplicity of design." He presented matching knit shirts, tops, trousers, and bra that folded into an envelope for travel. These pieces were based around a body stocking and formed the 1970s American fashion silhouette.

A 1978 advertisement read: "Giorgio di Sant'Angelo Spoken Here." He saw his work as a new language in fashion. Di Sant'Angelo admired the ideas of Rudi Gernreich, whose work also contributed key elements to modern design. He also respected the work of Halston, Elsa Peretti, Betsey Johnson, Stephen Burrows, Oscar de la Renta, Yves Saint Laurent, Pierre Cardin, and Valentino. Throughout the 1980s' shifts in fashion, di Sant'Angelo worked on classical refinements of his own concepts. Poised for a timely re-emergence as a name in fashion, di Sant'Angelo died in 1989. A truly original free spirit was lost forever.—MYRA WALKER

Dolce & Gabbana

Italian ready-to-wear firm

Established by Domenico Dolce and Stefano Gabbana, 1985. Dolce born in Polizzi Generosa, near Palermo, Italy, 13 August 1958. Gabbana born in Milan, Italy, 14 November 1962. Opened fashion consulting studio, 1982. First major women's collection shown at Milano Collezioni, 1985; knitwear collection first shown, 1987; lingerie and beachwear introduced, 1989; menswear collection first shown, 1990; women's fragrance line launched, 1992; D&G line for young people, men and women, 1994; men's fragrance and home collection also 1994; men's and women's jeans lines and eyewear collection, 1995. Opened showrooms in Milan, 1987, 1993, and 1995; and in New York, 1990.

Awards *Woolmark Award, 1991; International Prize of the Perfume Academy for best feminine fragrance of the year, 1993, for best masculine fragrance, best packaging, and best campaign, 1995; Oscar de Parfums Award for best men's fragrance, 1996.*
Address *Via San Damiano, 7 20122 Milan; Press Office: Via Santa Cecilia, 7 20122 Milan; Commercial Departments: P.zza Umanitaria, 2 20122 Milan, Italy.*

Since their first womenswear collection in 1985, Dolce & Gabbana have evolved into perhaps the definitive purveyors of sexy clothes for women who want to revel in their voluptuous femininity. They have taken items like satin corset bodies, black stockings, fishnets, and maribou-trimmed babydolls out of their previous *demi-monde* existence and put them together in such a way that they have become representative of the new glamorous image of the 1990s, an escape from the pervasive unisex sporty styles.

Loved by fashion editors and film stars alike, this partnership revives the Southern Italian sex bomb look, inspired by the films of Roberto Rossellini and Luchino Visconti, as well as the adoration of the strongly romantic Mediterranean ideals of Sicily the pair grew up with. They have been the driving force behind the rise in images of the fashionable woman empowering herself by reclaiming sexual stereotypes and using them to her own benefit.

They brush aside the preoccupations of other Milan-based designers with mix-and-match separates and revamp potent images previously deemed degrading to women—the baby doll, the scantily clad starlet—and give them a new lease of life. Confidence and irony are key for Dolce & Gabbana: their women are very much in control, whether in one of their glittering rhinestone-covered bodices—notably chosen by that post-feminist icon Madonna to make an impact at the 1991 Cannes Film Festival and subsequently filtered down into every High Street chain—or a slightly more sober, but nonetheless sexy, stretch velvet Empire cut jacket and leggings.

Although they originated from opposite ends of Italy, Dolce & Gabbana's shared interests and influences give their collections a sense of unity and an instantly recognizable look. Their use of film imagery, and obvious love of the fiery beauty of stars like Sophia Loren and Anna Magnani, has imbued their advertising with an unforgettably glamorous style of its own. They combine supermodels with screen stars to create images which ooze an earthy sexuality.

Dolce & Gabbana

Dolce & Gabbana: Spring/Summer 1992.

The same key elements of sexiness mixed with traditional details are applied to the menswear collections, first shown in January 1990 and designed to complement Dolce & Gabbana's women's line. Skilled Sicilian craftswomen and tailors, supervised by Dolce's father, are employed to produce the internationally acclaimed menswear collections which espouse a more laid-back, witty approach to the 1990s, after the brasher, more rigid styles of the previous decade. Muted shades of earthy browns are used alongside blacks with flashes of scarlet to produce modern-day versions of Sicilian men, with bandannas around their necks, and bikers in tattoo-covered leather jackets, lightened by the leggings used so frequently by Dolce & Gabbana. Current fashion influences are often absorbed, the tie-dyed 1970s feel of their 1992 summer collection being a prime example, but there is always a more timeless selection of unstructured suits, often based on a 19th-century high-buttoned tighter cut style, and knitwear which explores all its textural possibilities to give it a very tactile appeal.

Both Dolce & Gabbana's men's and womenswear are international bestsellers. Influential and innovative, the clothes express a confident, sexy glamour which, however potent, never overpowers the wearer's personality, making them one of the most important design forces to emerge from Italy in recent years.—REBECCA ARNOLD

Ellis, Perry

American designer

Born *Perry Edwin Ellis in Portsmouth, Virginia, 30 March 1940.*

Education *Bachelor of Arts, business, College of William and Mary, Williamsburg, Virginia, 1961; Master of Arts, retailing, New York University, New York City, 1963.*

Family *One daughter: Tyler Alexandra.*

Military Service *Served in the US Coast Guard, 1961-62.*

Career *Sportswear buyer, Miller and Rhodes department stores, Virginia, 1963-67; design director, John Meyer of Norwich, 1967-74; vice-president, sportswear division, 1974, and designer, Vera sportswear for Manhattan Industries, 1975-76; designer with own Portfolio label, Manhattan Industries, 1976-78; president and designer, Perry Ellis Sportswear, Inc., 1978-86; Perry Ellis International menswear line launched, 1980; Portfolio label, lower priced sportswear revived, 1984; fragrance collection launched, 1985. Licenses include furs, coats, shoes, bedlinens, household textiles, toiletries, and clothing patterns for Levi Strauss, Greif, Martex, Visions Stern, etc., from 1978. Council of Fashion Designers of America Perry Ellis Award established in memoriam, 1986.*

Awards *Coty American Fashion Critics Award, 1979, 1980, 1981, 1983, 1984; Neiman Marcus Award, Dallas, 1979; Council of Fashion Designers of America Award, 1981, 1982, 1983; Cutty Sark Award, 1983, 1984; California Men's Apparel Guild Hall of Fame Award, 1993.*

Died *(in New York City) 30 May 1986.*

Address *575 Seventh Avenue, New York, New York 10018, USA.*

The house of Perry Ellis has seen some tumultuous times. From the early days things had never been particularly easy, with Ellis continuously battling over finances with the parent company, Manhattan Industries. Problems with stability continued after Ellis's death in 1986, when Robert McDonald assumed the helm of Perry Ellis International, only to die four years later.

Recent problems have arisen from Salant's $100 million takeover of Manhattan Industries and its subsequent bankruptcy filing. Obstacles with direction, especially within the menswear divisions, with the death of designer Roger Forsythe in 1991 from AIDS, to the recent disjointed running of Perry Ellis Group and Perry Ellis International, have done nothing to remedy the company's disarray.

Through all the problems and despite the fickle nature of the fashion world, the fashions of Perry Ellis's men's and women's collections have remained relatively consistent, true to the tenets and goals in which, as a designer, Ellis believed and aspired to.

Perry Ellis was known as a flirtatious, fun-loving man with a great sense of humor. According to Claudia Thomas, former chair of Perry Ellis International, it is hard to characterize Ellis, except to describe him as whimsical. There was, however, an air of seriousness about him when it came to creating and fulfilling his objectives, as reflected in his personal philosophy of "never enough." It was the playful side of his personality, however, that was reflected in his fashions. When his company arrived on the scene in the 1970s, it was a time of increasing emphasis on American designers and designer name merchandise. Perry Ellis did his best to create a mystique about himself and his lifestyle that would attract fans.

The Perry Ellis look began as a playful, relaxed and comfortable look that was exclusively American in feeling and sportswear-like in its practicality. So playful and relaxed was it that at shows, the models would skip down the catwalk. As Ellis matured as a designer, his clothing occasionally took on a more serious tone, but even his most formidable collections were considered easy-dressing by fashion industry standards.

Inspiration came in many forms—California; the movie *Chariots of Fire;* artist Sonia Delaunay; the Broadway show *Dream Girls*—all retained the casual ease for which Americans are known internationally and the sense of proportion and freedom from fashion conformity which was the hallmark of Perry Ellis. The company's subsequent womenswear designer, Marc Jacobs, and menswear design director, Andrew Corrigan, appeared to create their collections with the feeling that Perry Ellis had tried to instil into a consumer's mind when buying clothing.

Ellis once said, "Always provide the clothes needed for daily life. Never be afraid to take risks and, most importantly, never take the clothes you wear too seriously." It is to this statement one should refer when trying to understand the essence of Perry Ellis designs.—LISA MARSH

Emanuel, David and Elizabeth

British designers

Born *David—Bridgend, Wales, 17 November 1952; Elizabeth—born Elizabeth Weiner in London, 5 July 1953.*
Education *David—Attended Cardiff School of Art, Wales, 1972-75, and Harrow School of Art, Middlesex, 1974-75; Elizabeth—Attended Harrow School of Art, 1974-75. Both David and Elizabeth studied fashion in post-graduate courses at the Royal College of Art, 1976-77.*

Family *Married in 1976; (divorced). Children: Oliver and Eloise.*
Joint Career *Partners and directors of Emanuel, in London, 1977-90; ready-to-wear line 1977-79; designed custom clothing only, 1979-90; established The Emanuel Shop, Beauchamp Place, London, 1987-90; collections also sold at Harrods and Harvey Nichols, London, and Bergdorf Goodman, Henri Bendell and Neiman Marcus, New York. Also: ballet and stage production designers, from 1985. Fellows of Chartered Society of Designers, London, 1984; Partnership dissolved, 1990.*
Individual Careers *David—Formed David Emanuel Couture, autumn 1990. Fellow of The Society of Industrial Artists and Designers. Elizabeth—Launched Elizabeth Emanuel Couture fashion label, 1991; designed complete range of Virgin Airways uniforms and accessories, 1991; Sew Forth productions established 1993; launched range of wedding dresses for Bridal Fashions, London, 1994. Also; costumes for Ballet Rambert, London Contemporary Dance Theatre, and Royal Ballet productions, London, 1990-94, and for musical theatre production of Jean de Florette, London, 1994-95.*
Address *David Emanuel Couture, 13 Regents Park Terrace, London, England; Elizabeth Emanuel, Sew Forth Productions, Studio 7, 44 Grove End Road, London, England.*

The romantic Renaissance revival came to life in the early 1980s in the music world and in films. Nowhere, however, was it more apparent than in certain fashion circles.

The announcement of the engagement of Charles, the Prince of Wales, to Lady Diana Spencer made this an even bigger trend than it would normally have been. Lady Diana's penchant for ruffles created a need for this type of apparel, as she was already becoming a woman many wanted to emulate fashion-wise.

It is appropriate that she chose the design team of David and Elizabeth Emanuel to design her wedding dress as romance is the underlying theme to all they designed. Ruffles are the rule for the Emanuels, used on everything from gowns to pant suits and even swimwear.

This duo, the only married couple to be accepted at the Royal College of Art, had operated their dressmaking shop in London since 1977 and in 1979 took the unusual step of closing their ready-to-wear business to concentrate on the made-to-order business.

Although it was the Princess of Wales's ivory silk taffeta wedding dress that brought the Emanuels international fame, they had a firmly entrenched business catering to what Americans would call the carriage trade. It also enabled the Emanuels to enter into licensing agreements for items such as linens, sunglasses, and perfume.

Princess Anne and Princess Michael of Kent have both worn Emanuel designs for portraits. Her Royal Highness the Duchess of Kent joins these women and the Princess of Wales in their love of the Emanuels' work.

Each dress was created for each individual, taking into account where it would be worn and the style of the wearer. Next, a suitable reference in art would be determined and work would progress from there. Creations by artists from Botticelli to Renoir and Degas were used as influences, as were photographs of some of the more romantic women in history. The garments seen on Greta Garbo in *Camille,* Vivien Leigh in *Gone with the Wind,* and Marlene Dietrich in *The Scarlet Empress* were all recreated to some degree.

In this respect, David and Elizabeth Emanuel were more stylists than designers, recreating a mood or image. However, they usually reinterpreted the design rather than copied it, adding a fresh dimension through fabric or hidden detail. A wedding dress, for example, had subtly glittering mother-of-pearl sequins for a woman who was marrying in a dark church. The sequins picked up the light, allowing the bride to glow luminously. The Princess of Wales's veil also incorporated these sequins, drawing attention to the star of the show. David and Elizabeth Emanuel are nothing if not retrospectively romantic and all they do reflects this.—LISA MARSH

Escada

German fashion house

Founded by Wolfgang and Margarethe Ley (died 1992), 1976. Lines include Laurel, Crisca, from 1984, Escada leather goods, from 1990, and Apriori bridge line, from 1991. Escada Beauté company formed, 1990; fragrance, Escada by Margarethe Ley, introduced in USA, 1990, and in Germany and United Kingdom, 1991. Michael Stolzenburg named designer to succeed Ley, 1992.

Awards *Fragrance Foundation Award, 1990.*
Address *Karl Hammerschmidt Strasse 23-29, Dornach, 80ll Munich, Dornach, Germany.*

The Escada group was founded in 1976 by Wolfgang and Margarethe Ley and is currently based in Dornach, near Munich. The group designs, produces and distributes high quality women's fashion, marketed worldwide to leading fashion stores and own name boutiques. Apart from Escada by Margarethe Ley, which includes apparel, luggage, fragrance and accessories, the group's other labels are Cerruti 1881, Crisca, Kemper, Laurel, Apriori, Seasons, Natalie Acatrini, Marie Gray, Schneberger, and St John.

Margarethe Ley was the chief designer for the group until her death in 1992. She strongly adhered to the belief that a designer must never rely solely on creative talent to be a success; creativity must be balanced by a strong market appeal. Ley created a highly distinctive identity for Escada, clean, slick, and sophisticated. She also pioneered the development of exiciting new fabric combinations and colour schemes.

Ley was succeeded by Michael Stolzenburg who has brought a younger, more modern perspective to the company. Taking his influence from daily life, he believes that the balance of a collection relies on the mix of tried and true design and fresh new ideas. He is backed by a strong team of designers, chiefly from British and German fashion schools.

Bright, bold colour statements have always been integral to the Escada look: geometric blocks of colour that contrast with vibrant prints, embroideries, and appliqué. Stripes often appear, one season in sharp nautical blocks of navy and white, the next in black and gold, teamed with black and gold leather for a glitzy evening look. Other strong themes have included Animal Rustics—country gentry and pure nature; High Society—a colour cocktail of purple and pink. Overall, Escada provides a complete ready-to-wear look for a high-salaried, professional woman, sexy, sharp, and sometimes overstated.

As a design group all Escada operations share a common objective, to be market leaders producing fashions that set the highest quality standards in the fashion industry.

The company's commitment to quality production has resulted in the installation of advanced technology equipment. Computer-assisted pattern-making equipment, automated cutters, and state-of-the-art knitting machines contribute to continued development and leave the design team greater time to concentrate on the creative development of innovative collections, for their specific market segments.

The Escada group sees the whole world as its market place. The products are sold in over 55 countries with an overall objective to achieve the leading market share in each country in which the products are sold, as determined through market analysis into the disposable income available at the top of the market in each country. Escada's success relies on the canny entrepreneurial spirit first instilled into the business by Wolfgang and Margarethe Ley.—KEVIN ALMOND

E
fashion

Fath, Jacques

French designer

Born *Lafitte, France, 12 September 1912.*

Education *Studied bookkeeping and law, Commercial Institute, Vincennes, France.*

Family *Married Geneviève Boucher de la Bruyère, 1939; son: Philippe.*

Military Service *Completed required military service and served again in the artillery during World War II.*

Career *Bookkeeper, then trader at the Paris Bourse, 1930-32. Showed first collection, Paris, 1937; reopened salon, 1940; designed ready-to-wear collection for American manufacturer Joseph Halpert, 1948; formed own company in the United States, 1951; developed ready-to-wear collection in Paris, 1954, including Fath scarves and hosiery. Business sold, 1957.*

Exhibitions *Jacques Fath Création-Couture des Années 50 (retrospective), Palais Galleria, Paris, 1993.*

Awards *Neiman Marcus Award, Dallas, 1949.*

Died *(in Paris) 13 November 1954.*

Address *3 rue du Boccador, 75008 Paris, France.*

Jacques Fath had a short career—from 1937 until his death in 1954—and after he died his name fell into obscurity. In contrast to his great contemporaries, Christian Dior and Cristobal Balenciaga, Fath has been largely forgotten, but he deserves to be rediscovered as a talented creator.

Fath was born in 1912 into a Protestant family of Flemish and Alsatian origin. His great-grandmother had been a dressmaker to the empress Eugène and, from an early age, he showed an interest in designing clothes. He also toyed with the idea of becoming an actor, a craving that he later indulged in private theatricals and costume parties.

Fath had "the showy elegance of a character from a Cocteau play and the charm of an *enfant terrible,*" recalled Célia Bertin (*Paris à la Mode,* London 1956). But fashion editors like Bettina Ballard and Carmel Snow (of *Harper's Bazaar*) tended to dismiss him as "a good-looking child prodigy . . . with slightly theatrical fashion ideas not worthy of the hallowed pages of *Vogue* or *Harper's Bazaar.*"

His career was interrupted by the outbreak of World War II. Taken prisoner in 1940, he was, however, soon back in Paris, where he reopened his couture house with his wife Geneviève. A recent book on fashion during the Nazi Occupation notes that scruples of conscience did not embarrass Fath, who was closely associated with various Franco-German groups and whose clientèle consisted heavily of Germans, wealthy collaborators and black marketeers. Unlike Chanel, however, whose reputation as a Nazi sympathizer temporarily injured her post-war career, Fath's image emerged intact, and after the war, his international career took off.

His glove-fitted dresses glorified the female form, and some have said that he even inspired Dior's New Look. Certainly, Fath designed some of the sexiest and most glamorous dresses to come out of Paris. The typical Fath dress featured a fitted bodice that moulded a slender waistline and emphasized the swelling curves of bosom and hips. Sleeve and collar treatments were important to Fath, and he favored irregular necklines that drew attention to the breasts. Skirts were either very slim or very full, characterized perhaps by a whirlpool of pleats or interesting draped effects.

If Dior and Balenciaga were known for the architectural beauty of their designs, Fath's style was praised for its glamour and vivacity. He often used diagonal lines, asymmetrical drapery, and floating panels to give a sense of movement. Nor was he afraid of color, even using such daring combinations as bright blue and green. (He himself liked to wear a red tartan jacket.) Whereas Dior's career was characterized by striking shifts of silhouette (the A-line, the H-line, etc.), Fath maintained an unswerving fidelity to the female form divine, focusing on sexy lines and novel decorative details, such as rows of nonfunctional buttons. Fath's style of wearable glamour had a wide appeal, and in 1948 he signed an agreement with the American manufacturer, Joseph Halpert. Henceforth, in addition to his own couture collections, Fath also produced a low-priced American line.

Fath was increasingly regarded as the "heir apparent to Dior's throne." As *Life Magazine* said in 1949: "Dior is still generally acknowledged to be the head man, so to speak, of the fashion world, but Fath has recently had a spectacular rise in prestige, and it now seems likely that the next look to confront and impoverish the U.S. male will be the Fath look." Carmel Snow, editor of *Harper's Bazaar,* revised her earlier opinion of Fath, and now declared that, "He makes you look like you have sex appeal—and believe me, that's important."

Fath himself had tremendous personal appeal, with his blond wavy hair and slender physique (a 28-inch waist, claimed one source). He was also very much a social personality; he and his pretty wife loved throwing lavish and imaginative parties, which had the pleasant side-effect of providing excellent publicity. "An atmosphere of glitter, chic, and perfumed excitement permeates both his personal and business affairs," observed *Life* (October 1949). Yet behind the scenes, Fath was struggling with illness. Only a year before his death in 1954, the American press had hailed him as the "fabulous young French designer who . . . is out to make every woman look like a great beauty." Now that promise was cut short.—VALERIE STEELE

Fendi

Italian design firm

Established as a leather and fur workshop by Adele Casagrande (1897-1978), Rome, 1918; renamed Fendi with her marriage to Edoardo Fendi, 1925. Current principals are daughters Paola (born 1931), Anna (born 1933), Franca (born 1935), Carla (born 1937), Alda (born 1940), their husbands and children. The firm designs leather and fur clothing and accessories, a ready-to-wear line, knitwear and beachwear; bridge line introduced, 1990; jewelry line licensed, 1991; Fendi Uomo perfume introduced, 1988. Karl Lagerfeld has collaborated with Fendi for over 30 years.

Awards *National Italian American Foundation Award to Paola Fendi, 1990.*
Address *Fendi Paola e S.lle S.A.S., Via Borgognona 7, 00187 Rome, Italy.*

Like many Italian firms producing luxury goods, the Fendi company is a family dynasty that owes a great deal of its success to the strong blood links which are an intrinsic part of the business. Fendi is unique in that it is run not by male members of the family (of which there are none, except by marriage), but by five sisters, daughters of Adele and Edoardo Fendi, who became involved in the business after the death of their father in 1954. The firm of Fendi originally specialized in producing high quality furs and leather goods on the via del Plebiscito in Rome in 1925. It was at this point that the firm moved towards a more high fashion profile, with the first Fendi fashion show being staged in 1955.

Although Fendi produces a ready-to-wear sports line, the name is probably best known in the fashion arena for its dramatic fur collections, which have been designed by Karl Lagerfeld since 1962. It was the company's relationship with Lagerfeld that brought the name of Fendi to the attention of the fashion press, where it has since remained. Lagerfeld was also responsible for designing the double-F *griffe* that is almost as well-recognized among the fashion *cognoscenti* as the double-C and double-G symbols of Chanel and Gucci.

Lagerfeld's innovative treatment of fur is both witty and, at times, shocking and has kept the Fendi company at the forefront of this particular field. In Lagerfeld's capable hands, real fur has taken on the appearance of fake fur; it has been perforated with thousands of tiny holes to make the coats lighter to wear; it has been printed to look like damask and other similar fabrics. Denim coats are lined with mink by Lagerfeld, who has also employed unorthodox animal skins such as squirrel and ferret in his creations. More recently, Lagerfeld has covered an entire fur coat with woven mesh and created completely reversible fur coats as his stand against the anti-fur movement that has created great problems for the trade. Another design he produced for autumn-winter 1993-94 consisted of a small zipped bag that unfolded into a calf-length fur coat. Whatever one's personal beliefs regarding the wearing of animal furs, the partnership of Karl Lagerfeld and the Fendi company has undoubtedly broken barriers in the field of fur design. In Italy, the fur sales continue to constitute a major part of the company's business—where the Fendi sisters claim to have changed the age-old tradition of fur as being a status symbol, to being a covetable high-fashion garment.

Like many luxury goods companies, Fendi has capitalized upon its name, with the usual plethora of accessories, gloves, lighters, pens, glasses and perfumes that have become a natural

Fendi

Fendi: Fall/Winter 1996/97; summer ermine fur coat
with the new "column" shape in brushwood colors.

progression for a well-recognized label. However, in terms of design, the house of Fendi will be remembered for its innovative treatment and development of luxury furs that has occurred as a result of its successful working partnership with designer Karl Lagerfeld.—CATHERINE WORAM

Feng, Han

Chinese designer

Born *Hangzhou, China.*

Education *Graduated from Zhejiang Art Academy, South-East China.*

Career *Began career designing scarves in the United States, in the 1980s.*

Address *2109 Broadway, New York, NY 10023, USA.*

Amy Spindler has said of Han Feng that she "offers a few lines of the poetry of Romeo Gigli and Issey Miyake, but for much lower prices" (*New York Times*, 3 November 1993). Spindler rightly perceives the affinities of the gossamer pleated, yet practical, clothing and accessories that Feng designs, but it may be that a touch of poetry is just the levitating apparition we need in the midst of practical clothing. Feng creates unremittingly real clothing, wearable and practical, but with a concise, *haiku*-like hint of the historicist romance conveyed by Gigli and of the Cubist authority suggested by Miyake. There is something about Feng's inventiveness that is so radical a disposition for clothing that, like Miyake's pleats, it will either be a significant historical interlude in reform dress for an avant-garde margin of the population or a revolution in the way in which all people dress. There is a poetry to Feng's minimal natural structures for clothing.

One wonders, however if clothing is the ultimate or exclusive goal of a designer who, growing up in Hangzhou, China, a great silk city, has become a devotee of the extraordinary organic materials that, with human intervention, yield even more possibilities of organic shapes. A graduate of the Zhejiang Art Academy in South-East China, Feng approaches her work as an artist. She began her work in the United States in the 1980s creating scarves, and the effect of the clothing is still a wondrous wrapping and veiling uncommon in the tailored West. Her clothing wraps the body as the clouds enclose a mountain; her "smoke rings" are wraps of the kind that Charles James and Halston made, allowing a gentle helix of cloth to fit from hand to hand and sheathe the shoulders in an arch out of nature. In as much as Feng is using materials that are, as Wendy Goodman described, "magic out of silk" (*House and Garden* New York, June 1993) the organic compositions are only reinforced by the pliant materials, diaphanous delicacy, and classic shapes, often defying clothing as ceremony. She all but ignores tailoring and, in fact, uses many of the same experiments in textiles for her home furnishings. Not bothering with tailoring and instead assembling the garment as a light sculpture on the body, Feng fulfils the most predicted expectations in the West of design from the East. Spindler notes, "Her most beautiful dresses were of organza, which was gathered in little puffs, as if filled with helium. Han Feng's vision is so romantic that the clothes look dreamily feminine even when draped over the tattooed form of the auto mechanic-cum-model Jenny Shimizu." The mystery of the clothing is that Feng is offering soft shells of body wrap and comfort that return us to the most primitive, pre-tailored sensibility for dress.

In delving into clothing at the fundamental principle of wrapping, Feng is offering an alternative to the evolved forms of Western dress. It would be unlikely that a relatively young, unknown designer will have the opportunity to transform so thoroughly and effectively the principles of fashion, yet Feng's work has the visionary impact to cast a wide and important influence. Even as her dresses and jackets gradually achieve acceptance, her work in home fashion, including table linens, pillows, and bed covers, is perhaps the most likely to be broadly accepted. Even in apparel, pleated, weightless ringlets do not seem to be the stuff of insurrection, but in this case they may be an anticipation for clothing of the 21st century. It is not surprising that Feng's work was prominently featured in the Christmas 1994 mail-order catalogue of the Museum of Modern Art (New York).—RICHARD MARTIN

Féraud, Louis

French designer

Born *Arles, France, 13 February 1921.*

Family *Married Zizi Boivin in 1947 (divorced, 1963); married Mia Fonssagrièves in 1964 (divorced, 1972).*

Military Service *Served as lieutenant in the French Resistance.*

Career *Opened first couture boutique in Cannes, 1955; moved to Paris, entered ready-to-wear; first menswear line launched, 1975; costumer designer for films and television, has designed over 80 films; perfumes Justine, introduced, 1965, Corrida, 1975; Fantasque, introduced, 1980, Fer, 1982; Jour de Féraud/Vivage, introduced, 1984; sportswear line introduced, 1989; New York flagship store opened, 1990; accessories line introduced, 1992. Also painter. Also author of novels, The Summer of the Penguin, 1978, and The Winter of the Mad.*

Exhibitions *Exhibition of paintings in Paris, 1988, 1989, 1992, 1993, 1994, and in Japan, 1989; Gallery Urban, New York, 1990.*

Awards *Légion d'Honneur; Golden Thimble Award, 1984; Dé d'Or Award, 1978, 1984.*

Address *88 rue Faubourg Saint-Honoré, 75008 Paris, France.*

It has been said of Louis Féraud that he is a man who loves women. Indeed, he describes himself as "Louis Féraud who adores women, Louis Féraud who admires women." This no doubt inspired this former lieutenant from the French Resistance to pursue a career in the rarefied worlds of French haute couture and ready-to-wear.

Féraud designs for a seductive woman who lives in harmony with life and herself, a woman looking for comfort and freedom. He declares himself fascinated by the different personalities of women and how this inspires him to create different moods and themes. For women, he says, "Fashion is an opportunity to be chic, to conspire between reality and desire."

Louis Féraud creates glamorous, luxurious clothes at ready-to-wear prices; he also designs for couture. Among his clients are Joan Collins, for whom he designed some of the clothes worn in the television series *Dynasty* and Madame Mitterand, wife of the French President. The collection is divided between the prêt-à-porter Louis Féraud Paris collections and the less expensive Louis Féraud set.

A strong team backs up the Féraud business. The creative team is led by Féraud himself and consists of ten international designers, colour specialists, and stylists who work together to form what he describes as a weather forecast that predicts trends. Féraud has also designed clothes for film and television. As well as suits and dresses for *Dynasty* and *Dallas,* he has designed clothes for Brigitte Bardot, 1955, Paulette Goddard, 1959, Kim Novak, 1963, Catherine Deneuve, 1965, Mireille Mathieu, 1970, and Sabina Anzema, 1983. However, when asked if, given the chance to design clothes for women from another era, which era he would choose he declared: "Tomorrow. I am often seriously asked what fashion will be doing next year. I am like an art medium for these people, who has the ability to look into the future."

Féraud lists painting as being amongst his passions; it inspires him to develop colour in his work. "Colours are fantasies of light," he claims. "However, all colours are diffused in black, memories of the sun, the indispensable, and the perfect that is beauty." He selects specific colour ranges each season, but declares himself unaffected by fashion trends. "The only thing that we must know in our business is what doesn't exist as yet." Colour is developed within the team, which also creates new ideas for fabric trims.

When asked how, out of the French Resistance in World War II, emerged one of the leading fashion designers of the world, Féraud replied: "Fashion does not separate people but holds them together. One can also describe fashion as the meeting place out of love."—KEVIN ALMOND

Ferragamo, Salvatore
Italian footwear designer

Born   *Bonito, near Naples, Italy, June 1898.*

Family   *Married Wanda Miletti in 1949; children: Fiamma, Giovanna, Ferruccio, Fulvia, Leonardo, Massimo.*

Career   *Apprentice shoemaker, Bonito, 1907-12; immigrated to the United States, 1914; with brothers, opened shoemaking and shoe repair shop, Santa Barbara, California and also created footwear for the American Film Company, 1914-23; relocated to Hollywood, 1923-27; returned to Italy, established business in Florence, from 1929; bankrupted in 1933; back in business by late 1930s. Business continues.*

Exhibitions   *Salvatore Ferragamo 1898-1960 (retrospective), Palazzo Strozzi, Florence, 1985; The Art of the Shoe (retrospective), Los Angeles County Museum, 1992.*

Awards   *Neiman Marcus Award, 1947; Footwear News Hall of Fame Award, 1988 [Fiamma Ferragamo].*

Died   *(in Fiumetto, Italy) 7 August 1960.*

Address   *Salvatore Ferragamo SpA, Palazzo Feroni, Via Tornabuoni 2, 50123 Florence, Italy.*

A master craftsman, Salvatore Ferragamo was known as one of the world's most innovative shoe designers, transforming the look and fit of the shoe. He broke away from conventional footwear designs, exploring not only innovative design, but also the technical structure of the shoe.

Ferragamo acquired the basic skills of shoe production whilst apprenticed to the local village cobbler in Bonito. Ambitious for success, he emigrated from his home town in Naples to America, where he studied mass production in shoe design. The years in the United States assisted him in fully understanding the technical procedures implemented in manufacturing his unique design. Owing to his excellent grounding in shoe design exploration and study, Ferragamo fully understood all the technical aspects of shoe production, the anatomy, and the balance of the foot. Eventually he set up in business in Santa Barbara, California, where his original, inventive designs caught the regard of many famous customers. Private commissions came from actors, actresses and celebrities including Sophia Loren, Gloria Swanson, the Duchess of Windsor, and Audrey Hepburn.

Initially a designer and creator of hand-made one-off shoes for individual customers, Ferragamo introduced the possibility of creating shoes that were exotic and beautiful, yet supportive to the foot and ankle. Function and comfort, together with an understanding of good design, were the essential elements behind his success.

His name is synonymous with style, glamour, ingenuity, and quality. Ferragamo diverged from the restrictions of conventional shoe design and manufacture, exploring the realms of fantasy and creating footwear well advanced of contemporary classic designs. Ferragamo produced shoes for every occasion; ankle boots, moccasins, laced shoes, Oxford brogues, stilettoes, shoes for evening and daywear, including classic traditional styles.

The shortage of leather and quality skins during the war years encouraged Ferragamo to explore new materials, continually searching beyond the realms of traditional materials for aesthetically attractive alternatives. Cork, crochet, crocheted cellophane, plaited raffia, rubber, fish skins, felt, and hemp were successful if unconventional alternatives.

His designs were brilliant in concept and craftsmanship, creating many unique and outrageous styles. He was inspired by past fashions, cultures, Hollywood, oriental clothing and classical styling. He created over 20,000 styles in his lifetime and registered 350 patents, including oriental mules with a unique pointed toe, patented by Ferragamo at the end of the 1930s. From the late 1930s his amusing, ambitious, and extreme designs involved the use of perforated leathers, raffia checks, elasticated silk yarns, appliqué motifs, needlepoint lace, sequined fabrics and patchwork.

In 1938 he launched the platform shoe which has re-emerged in varying forms ever since. His "invisible shoe," created in 1947, was produced with clear nylon uppers and a black suede heel and Ferragamo produced many variations on this design.

His innate sense of colour extended from traditional browns and beiges to vivid contrasting colours of ornate richness. The technical knowledge attained whilst developing new dyeing techniques assisted him in combining technical knowledge with his creative colour flair.

In 1927 Ferragamo returned to Italy, setting up a workshop in Florence, a city which was to become the fashion centre of Italy. He continued to produce custom-made shoes, many of his customers' individual lasts still being in existence today, maintained in collections in Feroni. Using modern production methods his made-to-measure shoes had quality, durability, and style. He was modern in his approach to design, taking advantage of new technology to improve his output, without jeopardizing standards. Through ambition and ingenuity his productivity and creativity improved greatly, leading to the industrialization of his work, producing 60 per cent hand crafted shoes and 40 percent mass production. Ferragamo maintained high standards by overseeing all aspects of production. The mass produced shoes were manufactured under the label Ferrina Shoes, produced in England.

After his death in 1960 his family continued to produce quality shoes. Ferragamo's biography, published in 1957, three years before his death, titled *Shoemaker of Dreams*, aptly describes his work. His innovative masterpieces in shoe design and his quality accessories contributed to and inspired the world of couture and introduced respectability to the craft of shoe making, raising its importance in the concept of fashion.—CAROL MARY BROWN

Ferré, Gianfranco

Italian designer

Born *Legnano, Italy, 15 August 1944.*

Education *Graduated in architecture from Politecnico, Milan, 1969.*

Career *Free-lance jewellery and accessory designer, Milan, 1969-73; designer, Baila, Milan, 1974; launched own label for women's fashions, Milan, 1978; introduced secondary Oaks by Ferré line, 1978; introduced men's collection, 1982; introduced perfume line, 1984; introduced watch collection, 1985; introduced glasses collection and perfume and bath line for men, 1986; introduced haute couture collection, 1986-88; introduced furs collection, 1987; signed agreement with Marzotto for the Studio 000.1 by Ferré lines for men and women, 1987; introduced Ferrejeans, 1989; introduced Forma O by GFF, 1989; introduced feminine fragrance, Ferré by Ferré, 1991; introduced house-hold linens collection, 1992. Named artistic director for the House of Dior, 1989.*

Exhibitions *Italian Re-Evolution, La Jolla Museum of Art, California, 1982; Intimate Architecture: Contemporary Clothing Design, Massachusetts Institute of Technology, Cambridge, 1982; Design Italian Society in the Eighties, La Jolla Musuem of Contemporary Art, 1982; Creators of Italian Fashion 1920-80, Osaka and Tokyo, 1983; Il Genio Antipatico: Creatività e tecnologia della Moda Italiana 1951-1983 (The Unpleasant Genius: Creativity and Technology of Italian Fashion 1951-1983), Rome, 1984; Tartan: A Grand Celebration of the Tradition of Tartan, Fashion Institute of Technology, 1988; Momenti del design italiano nell'industria e nella moda, Seoul, 1990; Japonism in Fashion, National Museum of Modern Art, 1994.*

Awards *Tiberio d'Oro Award, 1976; Best Stylist of the Year Award by Asahi Shimbun and Women's Wear Daily, 1983; Modepreis for women's fashions, Monaco, 1985; Cutty Sark Men's Fashion Award, New York, 1985; Medal of Civic Merit, Milan, 1985; named Commendatore dell'Ordine al Merito della Repubblica Italiana, 1986; Dé d'Or prize for first haute couture collection for Dior, 1989; named "Milanese of the Year" by the Famiglia Meneghina, 1989; I Grandi Protagonisti prize from the Italian Furs Association, 1990; Lorenzo il Magnifico award from the Medicean Academy, Florence, 1990; Occhio d'Oro prize, 1983, 1983/84, 1985, 1986/87, 1987/88, 1989; Il Fiorino d'Oro Award, 1991; Pitti Immagine Uomo Award, 1993.*

Address *Via della Spiga 19a, 20121 Milan, Italy.*

Fashion is a reality connected with the changes of our society, of which it is an attentive interpreter.

Gianfranco Ferré: Women's Collection, Fall/Winter 1996/97.

Artistic trends, new expressive languages, individualistic or mass behaviour and any other event which marks our society or determines its choices, also determine trends or, at least, fashion changes. A fashion designer has to be an attentive interpreter of these events; he has to be able to prophecy, without forgetting the realities of industry and commerce.

My role as a fashion designer comes from a complex process, where creativity and imagination play an important role, but are supported by a firm rational analysis.—Gianfranco Ferré

Gianfranco Ferré has been dubbed by *Women's Wear Daily* (New York) as the "Frank Lloyd Wright of Italian Fashion." Trained initially as an architect, his work bears many references to this early discipline. He draws up a plan for each collection based on a philosophy that his customer wants functional, classic yet powerful clothes, constructed in the highest quality materials. The clothes are then created with a distinct eye for dramatic proportion and purity of line.

There is nothing understated about Ferré's womenswear. His minimalist approach has often made opulent, theatrical statements on the catwalk, bearing many references to the film star glamour projected by Anita Ekberg in the film *La Dolce Vita*. The clothes reflect a glamorous, fantasy dressing, combined with architectural symmetry. Ferré often exaggerates proportions in tailoring and dressmaking. Classic shirt shapes often have extreme cuffs or collars; coats and jackets are always defined by silhouette. An extravagant use of luxury fabrics like fur on dresses or long evening coats, leather, and taffeta often in the distinctive, stark colours of red, black, white or gold reinforce this definition of modern glamour.

His menswear collections are less extravagant, based on tradition but designed with his characteristic modernist approach. Ferré sees his customer as a man who appreciates traditional cloth and a classic line. He has developed new tailoring techniques to create a more relaxed, expansive shape for men, a reaction to the hard-edged lines so prevalent in 1980s power dressing. Ferré often looks to London for inspiration, believing that the British capital is a key point in the world of fashion. As he explained to journalist Liz Smith, "There is an in-bred eccentricity in London which allows clothes to be worn in original and completely modern proportions."

Ferré has a reputation for being a realist, with a practical approach to projects. His assistant Airaghi confirmed this when she described the designer as going to work with everything in his head—market requirements, manufacturing schedules, financial limitations, development of themes, advertising. Brought up in a secure family environment, his mother instilled in him an obsessive sense of duty and responsibility; she was strict when it came to homework and passing exams. This level-headed approach even caused him to react with economic sense to Diana Vreeland's famous fashion quote, "Pink is the navy blue of India," made during the course of a conversation with Ferré. He replied judiciously, "Naturally pink is the navy blue of India because it's the cheapest of all dyes."

In 1989 Ferré was appointed as designer for Dior, with a brief to supply the house with an image for the 1990s. His first collection made no reference to Dior's illustrious past. Dior's extravagant and romantic tradition and the coquettish style of Marc Bohan, designer for the house since 1960, were ignored. Instead, Ferré introduced a refined, sober, and strict collection inspired by Cecil Beaton's black and white Ascot scene from the film *My Fair Lady*. Black and white herringbone and checked tweed suits, sprinkled with embroidered pearls, jet, and jewels, opened a show that ended with a series of evening dresses in russet red and grey, edged in fox, combined with lace stoles and rose corsages with sweeping trains.

Ferré is easily identifiable as an Italian designer. His clothes are well shaped, confident, and powerfully feminine or masculine. Through his own label collections, he has developed such hallmarks as the crisp white shirt with stand-up collar or in his signature colour, red. However, as a designer he has adapted to a variety of customers and markets from French haute couture to the larger-size jeans market. The Ferré product, whether it be prêt-à-porter or leather goods, glasses, furs, or shoes, has become synonymous with precision and elegance, an identity which he feels has strongly increased the cachet of "made in Italy."—KEVIN ALMOND

Fezza, Andrew

American designer

Born *New Haven, Connecticut, 1955.*

Education *Graduated from Boston College, 1976; traveled in Europe, summer, 1976; studied at the Fashion Institute of Technology, New York, 1976-77.*

Family *Married Marilyn Cousa Fezza in 1985; two children.*

Career *Assistant designer for womenswear, Schrader Sport, New York, 1977-78; free-lance designer, selling to Camouflage and other New York menswear stores, 1977-78; formed own company, Andrew Fezza, Ltd, 1979; also designer, Firma by Andrew Fezza for Gruppo GFT from 1986, and designer, Andrew Fezza Company, joint venture with Gruppo GFT, from 1990; maintained Assets by Andrew Fezza boutique to 1991.*

Awards *Chrysler Stargazer Award, 1981; Cutty Sark Award, 1982, 1984, 1985; Coty American Fashion Critics Award, 1984.*

Address *300 Park Avenue, New York, New York 10022, USA.*

Andrew Fezza's design is based around unchanging elements that have characterized his men's clothing throughout changing labels and businesses: relaxed drape, soft silhouette in all garments but never at a loss of proportion, are combined with an interest in unusual materials, whether in leather or fabric, luxurious richness in fabric more often associated with womenswear and mellifluous color harmony in individual collections, always including neutrals and earthbound tones. Respect for American sportswear is challenged and complemented by a sensibility that is not provincially American or traditional, often with influences from Italy.

In such intensity of conviction and integrity of sensibility, Fezza is unusual in menswear (while he trained for and has designed womenswear, he is chiefly a menswear designer) and has inevitably been called an "American Armani," so sincere and sustained are his design objectives. Menswear is seldom thought of as a profession for purists with distinct aesthetic marks, given the market-driven practicality of the field, but Fezza has flourished with an uncompromising crusade for male attire. He suffers, however, from the Armani characterization. So reminiscent is his style of the Milanese master that some have chosen, especially after he entered into production agreements in 1990 with Gruppo GFT, to call Fezza a poor man's Armani. In fact, almost all advanced menswear designers in the 1990s have been displacing collars, mutating jackets into longer and softer shapes, and watching the textile industry for both innovation and the most sumptuous materials to bring to men in that indeterminate arena between contempo-

Andrew Fezza: Spring/Summer 1992.

rary office and home. Similarly, Fezza has created tailored clothing with the unconstructed effects of the Armani-inspired contemporary jacket, for casual living as well as the conventional office, but so have almost all other menswear designers of the past decade.

Fezza's aesthetic, however close at times to Armani's, is nonetheless his own. That he began in knitwear and leather, as Armani had some five or six years earlier, is partly a matter of how designers can get started in small-scale production and partly an example of parallelism, but not of derivativeness. Points of differentiation include Fezza's deep colors, consistent in his collections, his reliance on sportswear, and a keen sense of comfort for the American male body, large and athletic.

Fezza brings his own style to each achievement, beginning with his first sweaters, made free-lance and delivered by hand to Camouflage when still working in womenswear at Schrader Sport, soon after graduating from the Fashion Institute of Technology, New York. Subsequently, his leathers, of which *DNR* wrote in 1981: "Andrew Fezza is a leather innovator. In his approach to color, silhouette, and texture, Fezza has consistently broadened the scope of American leather design, which is rapidly catching up with the European market," generated excitement and esteem for their directional colors, embossed treatments, and knowledgeable shapings: unconventional for leather, but not extreme. Fezza has likewise brought a lifetime interest in luxurious textiles and the traditional designs of textiles into menswear, often making a garment seem even softer and more costly by virtue of the fabric. Even his earliest collections, in the early 1980s, brought together linens, cotton, silk-wool blends, and knits with leather and suede. Arguably, Fezza brings elements of womenswear sensibility to menswear with such emphases as proportion and luxury in textiles. In such a characteristic, he indicates the great shift in menswear in the 1980s and 1990s.

Few menswear designers possess Fezza's unity and clarity of vision. Business shifts, which might have diverted or deflected most other designers in the big-business climate of menswear, have not deterred Fezza. In his second decade as a still-young designer, Fezza is pursuing the relaxed new look, acknowledging Europe but affirming America. When he says that he entered the menswear business because he was uninspired when looking for clothing for himself, he anticipates some characteristics of his designs: so purposeful they are elegant, so unassuming that they become the nonchalance of high style in menswear, and so luxuriously casual that they fit the lifestyles of men in the 1980s and 1990s. He has deliberately avoided, with one or two exceptions in the early 1980s (with some justice, Melissa Drier in *DNR* attacked his spring 1984 collection as overworked), any of the excesses of menswear, with extraneous detailing or extreme proportions, but he has insisted upon clothing with texture and an interest in color and shape. A 1983 press kit for Fezza reports: "Andrew's unique hand with fabric, shape, and color reflects a designing mind that is both thoughtful and provocative, without surrendering to fashion 'trends' either here or in Europe. But from the beginning, Andrew Fezza's trademark has been his individuality." In this instance, a press kit is true. In the fixed and fascinating domain of menswear, Andrew Fezza has offered a highly consistent and individual aesthetic in the 1980s

and 1990s.—RICHARD MARTIN

Fiorucci, Elio

Italian designer and manufacturer

Born *Milan, 10 June 1935.*

Career *Founder, Fiorucci shoes, Milan, 1962-67; director, Fiorucci fashion shop, Galleria Passerella, Milan, selling clothes by Ossie Clark, Zandra Rhodes and others, from 1967; began wholesale production of jeans, fashion and home accessories, 1970; founder, Fiorucci SpA, 1974, and Fiorucci Inc., New York, 1976; first American boutique opened, New York, 1976, Boston and Los Angeles, 1978; stores opened throughout Europe, USA, Japan and Southeast Asia, from 1978. Also founder, Technical Design School, Milan, 1977. Contributor to Donna magazine, Milan.*

Exhibition *Italian Re-Evolution, La Jolla Museum of Art, California, 1982.*

Address *Fiorucci SpA, Galleria Passerella 2, 20122 Milan, Italy.*

Visitors to Milan in Italy during the late 1960s could not fail to notice a constant crowd trying to enter a narrow fronted shop in the centre of the city. The birth of Elio Fiorucci's boutique caused consternation amongst the elders and delight in their offspring. Those who travelled the European city circuit in pursuit of fashion and footwear inspiration now ensured that this was one retailer who could not be missed.

Visiting manufacturers and designers fought over the limited stock with local customers. Italy, the accepted home of stylish clothing, had seen nothing like it. It was Fiorucci, more than any other single entrepreneur of the time, who possibly created a worldwide market for the youth culture that first expressed itself in music, then in clothing. In the mid-1960s it was the young people who were creating and dictating the fashions they wanted to wear. It was the skill of this man, who had his finger on the pulse and brought it into reality, that created the visual dreams and recognized the aspirations of this new and hitherto untapped market.

Fiorucci had inherited a shoe store from his father. In 1967, at the age of 32, he added mini skirts brought from the then "swinging" London. Designs by Ossie Clark, Zandra Rhodes, and other young English talents soon followed and the store was gradually enlarged to accommodate a vast range of assorted items. From this embryonic beginning grew a world famous chain of boutiques, culminating in outlets in New York, Boston, Beverly Hills, Rio de Janeiro, Tokyo, Hong Kong, Zurich, and London. Conceived for the youth culture, the stores were constantly filled with new ideas and exciting styles. The atmosphere was unique and the presentation always witty and original. Shopping for clothes was suddenly a different and stimulating experience. The sales assistants were teenagers, too, who helped the customer to put together the latest looks in fashion clothing, accessories, and even make-up.

Fiorucci was a constant traveller, collecting ideas from around the world, including the original hippie woven bags from Morocco which became so synonymous with the spirit of Flower Power. A team of designers translated ideas, seeming always to capture the moment, for example, recycling the themes of the 1950s with plastic shoes in riotous colours, fluorescent socks, or graffiti T-shirts. Possibly best remembered of all were the tightly cut, streamlined jeans which established Fiorucci as a label in the marketplace for many years. At one time they even replaced Levi's as the most desirable and fashionable shape of the moment.

Elio Fiorucci. *Photograph by Oliviero Toscani.*

One of the company's greatest strengths and the reason for its place in fashion history was the ability to control all aspects of advertising, packaging, store design, and merchandising in a clever and original way. It should not be forgotten that Elio Fiorucci was the first to establish what has subsequently become an indispensable part of so many success stories, a Total Concept.—ANGELA PATTISON

Fogarty, Anne
American designer

Born *Anne Whitney in Pittsburgh, Pennsylvania, 2 February 1919.*

Education *Attended Allegheny College, Meadville, Pennsylvania, 1936-37; studied drama at Carnegie Institute of Technology, Pittsburgh, 1937-38; studied design at East Hartman School of Design, 1939.*

Family *Married Thomas E. Fogarty in 1940 (divorced); children: Taf, Missy; married Richard Kollmar (widowed, 1971); married Wade O'Hara (divorced).*

Career *Worked as a fit model and copywriter in New York; designer for Sheila Lynn, New York; fashion stylist, Dorland International, New York, 1947-48; fashion designer, with the Youth Guild, New York, 1948-50, and with Margot Dresses Inc., New York, 1950-57; designer, Saks Fifth Avenue, 1957-62; managed own business, Anne Fogarty, Inc., New York, 1962-74; lines included Anne Fogarty Boutique, Clothes Circuit, Collector's Items; closed business, c.1974; free-lance designer to 1980; final collection designed for Shariella Fashion, 1980.*

Awards *Coty American Fashion Critics Award, 1951; Neiman Marcus Award, Dallas, 1952; Philadelphia Fashion Group Citation, 1953; International Silk Association Award, 1955; Cotton Fashion Award, New York, 1957.*

Died *(in New York) 15 January 1980.*

Anne Whitney Fogarty designed the American look, creating clothes that were youthful, simple and stylish. Although Fogarty studied drama at the Carnegie Institute of Technology in Pittsburgh, Pennsylvania, her real love was for the costumes she wore. Moving to New York she worked as a fitting-model for Harvey Berin while looking for acting parts. When she received the offer of an acting job, Berin encouraged her to think about becoming a stylist instead and in 1948 Fogarty began designing clothes for Youth Guild. Youth Guild's market was teenagers, who were perfect for the narrow waist and full skirts of the "New Look," a style Fogarty used.

In 1950 Fogarty began designing junior-size clothing for Margot, Inc. She still favored the "paper-doll" silhouette for both day and evening wear, with its full skirt, narrow waist, and fitted bodice. To help create this shape, she adopted the idea of crinoline skirts from the Edwardian age. These stiffened petticoats made of nylon net, frilled or trimmed in lace, helped to hold out the skirt and Fogarty encouraged wearing two at a time to enhance the silhouette. She herself had an 18-inch waist.

Fogarty wrote a book called *Wife Dressing* in 1959, a guide for "the fine art of being a well-dressed wife with provocative notes for the patient husband who pays the bills." In the book she recognized that women led varied lives working, as students, wives, and mothers and she encouraged women to find their own style and color, recommending an understated, natural look that did not slavishly follow the fashion of the day.

Fogarty continued to design for Margot, Inc., and eventually for Saks Fifth Avenue. In 1962 she opened her own business, Anne Fogarty, Inc., and added misses' sizes to her line of clothes. Although she began with full skirts, and fitted bodices, she adapted her designs to suit the times. After the paper-doll silhouette came the tea cozy dress in which the full skirt fell from a dropped, rather than natural waist. She used a narrow silhouette without fullness, the Empire line, with its emphasis on the bust line, and she introduced the "camise," a chemise which falls from a high yoke. Fogarty designed separates and long dresses, quilted skirts over hot pants, and mini skirts. She produced designs in a peasant style, blouses with ruffles, long skirts with ruffled hems, and ethnic styling. Whatever the silhouette or fashion type, her interpretation was youthful, with details like puffed sleeves and round collars. She avoided the use of trims.

Fogarty produced different design collections under the names of A.F. Boutique, Clothes Circuit, and Collector's Items. In 1950 she was selected as one of the Young Women of the Year by the magazine *Mademoiselle*. In 1951 she received the Coty Award and in 1952 the Neiman Marcus Award.

Although she closed her own business in the 1970s, Fogarty continued to design. In 1980, she finished a collection for Shariella Fashion shortly before she died. During her career Fogarty worked with a variety of silhouettes and fabrics, in a broad range of sizes. She was a prolific designer who was able to adjust to a changing market, responding with designs that typified the all-American look.—NANCY HOUSE

Fontana

Italian fashion house

Founded in Rome, 1944, by sisters Zoe (1911-78), Micol (1913-) and Giovanna (1915-) Fontana. The sisters began working in their mother's tailoring business. Zoe and Micol worked in Milan, early 1930s; Zoe moved to Paris after her marriage, returning to Italy, to work for Zecca in Rome, 1937; Nicol and Giovanna moved to Rome, 1940; Zoe, Micol and Giovanna open the Fontana studio in Palazzo Orsini, Rome, 1943, designing and producing gowns for the Roman aristocracy and many film stars; participated in first catwalk presentation of Italian Alta Moda, Florence 1951; studio moved to present address, 1957; designed first ready-to-wear collection, 1960. Incorporated as Sorelle Fontana Alta Moda SrL by Micol Fontana, Rome, 1985. Also: Costume designers for many films, including The Barefoot Contessa, *1954,* The Sun Also Rises, *1957,* On The Beach, *1959, and* La Bibbia (The Bible), *1966.*

Exhibitions *retrospective, University of Parma, 1984; evening dresses, Venice, 1985; Castel Sant'Angelo Museum, Rome, 1985; Munich, March 1986.*

Collections *Metropolitan Museum of New York; Metropolitan Museum of San Francisco; Museo Fortuny, Venice.*

Awards *Silver Scissors Award, Pittsburgh Fashion Group, 1956; Silver Mask Award, Rome, 1960; Fontana sisters named Cavaliere della Repubblica, Rome, 1965; Fashion*

Fontana: Sorelle Fontana Collection, 1991.

Oscar Award, St Vincent, 1968; Stella di Michelangelo Award, Rome, 1985; Polifemo Prize, Sperlonga, Italy, 1985; Minerva Prize, Rome, 1985; Attraction 1986 Prize, Italy; Europe Plate, 1987; Europe Gold Plate, 1988.

Address *Via San Sebastianello 6, 00187 Rome, Italy.*

Fontana created fantasy dresses, wedding gowns, and ball gowns, and the glamour of movie stars. In the 1950s, in particular, the Fontana style was a rich excess and ideal of the sumptuous dress. For the client, these were the most flattering kinds of party dresses cognizant of the New Look, buoyant in full skirts, and attentive to the bust. To the observer, theatrical high-style 1950s was crystallized in the internationally known clientèle including Linda Christian for her wedding dress on marrying Tyrone Power, Audrey Hepburn, and preeminently Ava Gardner. Gardner, in particular, was the perfect Fontana client and model: unabashedly and voluptuously sexy and known for high-style glamour. Gardner wore Fontana for film roles in *The Barefoot Contessa* (1954), *The Sun Also Rises* (1957), and *On the Beach* (1959). Whereas American film had its own specialty costume designers such as Edith Head and Travis Banton, post-war Rome re-ignited its status as a glamour capital by the conflation of life and film. Sisters Zoe, Micol, and Giovanna Fontana had begun their business in 1936, but seized the public imagination when American films were made on location in Italy using their costumes and, to a lesser degree, with the Italian film industry. The popular appeal internationally of the Power/ Christian wedding and Ava Gardner's paparazzi-trailing fame brought vast international visibility and recognition.

If waning Hollywood glamour found its ideal Trevi Fountain wardrobe in Fontana, Fontana came to Middle America and intellectual America with the demure but unequivocally rich lace wedding dress designed for the 1956 wedding of Margaret Truman, daughter of the ex-President of the United States, and Clifton Daniel, *New York Times* journalist and editor. Long-time celebrity Margaret Truman Daniel, famous as the apple of her father's eye and as a television performer, put the good-girl seal of approval on Fontana for America that Gardner's sultry glamour, Elizabeth Taylor's buxom beauty, or Loretta Young's dream-girl radiance had been unable to provide. Roman grace and opulence of materials were, for Americans, more accessible in many ways, including cost, than the couture of Paris. By the late 1950s, the strong silhouettes of Balenciaga and Dior (under Yves Saint Laurent) were so immediately and carelessly processed into American clothing that Roman dress, with its conspicuous extravagance of lace and taffeta and aura of luxuriance, seemed ineffably richer than Paris design. The preference of the Fontana sisters for wedding dresses, eveningwear, and full-skirted cocktail dresses through the 1950s and 1960s, made their style seem especially colorful, a kind of pre-*La Dolce Vita* for Americans covetous of Italian flair.

So much a part of the Italian post-war renaissance that Rome designated one street Via Zoe Fontana, the work of the Fontana sisters testifies to Italy's command of magical aura, dressmaking skill, and international glamour in the 1950s. Later work assumes more tubular silhouettes of the 1960s and 1970s and some similarity to Princess Irene Galitzine, but the definitive work of the Fontana sisters is the bust-enhanced, narrow-waisted, full-skirted resplendence of their style in the 1950s. Their extravagance walked a fine line between vulgarity and richness, one to which Americans felt a keen affinity. The Fontana sisters created a Roman Empire of post-war fashion; they enjoyed an influential and unforgettable decade of style sovereignty.—RICHARD MARTIN

Fortuny (y Madrazo), Mariano

Spanish designer

Born *Granada, Spain, 1871.*

Family *Married Henriette Negrin, 1918.*

Career *Produced Knossos printed scarves from 1906; produced Delphos gowns, 1907-52; Delphos robe patented, 1909; method for pleating and undulating fabric patented, 1909; methods for printing fabrics patented, 1909, 1910; 18 other patents received, 1901-33. Opened showroom for sale of textiles and clothing, Venice, 1909; established Società Anonima Fortuny, factory for printed textiles, 1919; opened shops in Paris and Milan, 1920. Also: inventor, stage designer, painter, photographer.*

Exhibitions *A Remembrance of Mariano Fortuny, Los Angeles County Museum, 1967-68; Mariano Fortuny (1871-1949), Musée Historique des Tissus, Lyons, and Brighton Museum, 1980, Fashion Institute of Technology, New York, 1981, and Art Institute of Chicago, 1982; Exposition Fortuny y Marsal y Fortuny y Madrazo [etchings], Biblioteca Nacional, Madrid, 1952; Mariano Fortuny y Madrazo [drawings and paintings], Galeria Dedalo, Milan, 1935, Galerie Hector Brame, Paris, 1934.*

Died *(in Venice, Italy) 2 May 1949.*

Mariano Fortuny was an artistic genius with an insatiable curiosity. This led him to pursue a variety of disciplines, which evolved through an interesting series of interconnections. Always a painter, he turned to etching, sculpture, photography, lighting design, theatre direction, set design, architecture, and costume design, ultimately to be a creator of magnificent fabrics and clothing. Through painting he learned the subtle uses of color that would enable him to produce unequalled silks and velvets from which he made exquisite gowns. Fortuny's work as a fabric and dress designer was determined by a combination of external and internal influences: externally by Modernism and the English Aesthetic movement, during the early part of the 1900s, as well as Greek and Venetian antiquity; internally by a love inherited from his father of everything Arabic and oriental. During all these creative experiences he maintained a keen artistic sense and the mind of an inventor.

Fashion, as we know it, did not interest Fortuny and he rejected commercial fashion and the couture houses. First and foremost a painter who happened to create stage scenery and lighting effects, as well as clothes, Fortuny's initiation with fabrics and fashion was through costumes for the theatre designed in conjunction with his revolutionary lighting techniques. His first textile creations, known as the "Knossos scarves," were silk veils, printed with geometric motifs (inspired by Cycladic art) which were made in any number of variations until the 1930s. This scarf was, essentially, a type of clothing—a rectangular piece of cloth that could be wrapped, tied, and used in a variety of ways—always allowing for freedom of individual expression and movement. His sole interest was the woman herself and her personal attributes, to which he had no wish to add any ornamentation. These simple scarves allowed Fortuny to combine form and fabric as they adapted easily into every kind of shape, from jackets to skirts, and tunics.

Fortuny's most famous garment was the Delphos gown. It was a revolution for the corseted woman of 1907 in that it was of pleated silk, simply cut, and hung loosely from the shoulders. Fortuny regarded his new concept of dress as an invention, and patented it in 1909. The dress was modern and original and numerous variations were produced—some with short sleeves, some with long, wide sleeves tied at the wrist, and others that were sleeveless. The original Delphos gowns had batwing sleeves. They usually had wide *bateau* necklines and always, no matter what the shape, a cord to allow for shoulder adjustments. They were invariably finished with small Venetian glass beads that had a dual purpose: not only did the beads serve as ornamentation, they also weighed the dress down, allowing it to cling to the contours of the body rather than float. The pleats of the Delphos were achieved through Fortuny's secret, patented invention. However unconventional for the time, these dresses were extremely popular for at-home women entertaining and considered primarily tea dresses. It was not until the 1920s that women dared to popularize them as clothing acceptable to be worn outside the home. Fortuny's techniques were simple but effective. Today the Delphos dress has pleats that are as tight and crisp as when they were new. Storing them as rolled and twisted balls makes them convenient for travel and eliminates the need for ironing.

In addition to his work in silk, Fortuny began printing on velvet, first with block prints followed by the development of a stencil method that was a precursor of the rotary silk screen. The velvet found its use in dresses, jackets, capes, and cloaks to cover the Delphos gowns, as well as home furnishing fabrics, still available today. Due to the fact that his work in silk and velvet never radically changed into anything different, it is almost impossible to establish a chronology of his garments.

To Mariano Fortuny fashion was art, an unchanging fashion outside the world of fashion. Although many of his contemporaries were innovative designers, their designs were created for a specific time and season with built-in obsolescence. By contrast, Fortuny's clothes are timeless. The elegant simplicity, perfection of cut, and unusual sensuality of color is where their beauty lies. Perfectly integrating these elements and placing them on the female figure makes a Fortuny garment a work of art.—ROBERTA H. GRUBER

Galanos, James

American designer

Born *Philadelphia, Pennsylvania, 20 September 1924.*

Education *Studied at the Traphagen School of Fashion, New York, 1942-43.*

Career *General assistant, Hattie Carnegie, New York, 1944-45; sketch artist for Jean Louis, Columbia Pictures, Hollywood, 1946-47; apprentice designer, Robert Piguet, Paris, 1947-48; designer, Davidow, New York, 1948-49; designer, Galanos Originals, from 1951; licenses include Galanos Furs, introduced in 1984, and Parfums Galanos, 1980.*

Exhibitions *Galanos Retrospective, 1952-1974, Costume Council of the Los Angeles County Museum of Art, 1975; Galanos—25 Years, Fashion Institute of Technology, New York, 1976; Smithsonian Institution; Metropolitan Museum; Brooklyn Museum; Philadelphia Museum; Ohio State University; Dallas Museum of Art.*

Awards *Coty American Fashion Critics Award, 1954, 1956; Neiman Marcus Award, Dallas, 1954; Filene's Young Talent Design Award, Boston, 1958; Cotton Fashion Award, 1958; Coty American Hall of Fame Award, 1959; Sunday Times International Fashion Award, London, 1965; Council of Fashion Designers of America Lifetime Achievement Award, 1985; Stanley Award, 1986.*

Address *2254 South Sepulveda Boulevard, Los Angeles, California 90064, USA.*

Dedication to excellence, in craftsmanship and design, is the foundation of James Galanos's career. The quality of workmanship found in his clothing is unsurpassed in America today. It may seem a contradiction that his sophisticated, mature, and elegant clothing is designed and produced in southern California, traditionally the land of sportswear. But Galanos is satisfied to remain where he began his business in 1951, a continent away from New York and the center of the American fashion industry.

Galanos knew what he wanted to do early in life and he pursued his dream to design school, an internship in Paris and several design positions with companies in New York. When

James Galanos.

the opportunity arose for him to open his own company, he created a small collection, which was immediately ordered by Saks Fifth Avenue. From that first collection his clothing has been admired for its particularly high quality, especially considering that it is ready-to-wear, not custom-made. His chiffon dresses in particular made his reputation in the early 1950s, with their yards of meticulously hand-rolled edges.

Galanos had gathered some of the most talented craftspersons available in his workrooms; many were trained in Europe or in the costume studios of Hollywood. If his work is compared to that of anyone else, it is compared to the French haute couture. Indeed, his business is more comparable to a couture house than a ready-to-wear manufacturer; there is an astonishing amount of hand work in each garment and all of his famous beadwork and embroidery is done by his staff. Galanos chooses his fabrics and trimmings personally during several trips to Europe each year. It is acknowledged that he often lines dresses with silks that other designers use for dresses themselves. He is a firm believer in the importance of hidden details, such as exquisite silk linings. These details make a difference in the feel of the clothes on the body and the hang of the fabric, and his clients all over the world are happy to pay for them. Many of the world's most socially prominent women are Galanos customers. In the 1980s, he made national headlines as one of former First Lady Nancy Reagan's favorite designers. The fact that Mrs. Reagan wore a 14-year-old Galanos to her first state dinner at the White House attests to the timelessness and durability not only of his workmanship, but more importantly, of his design. This type of occurrence is commonplace among his faithful customers.

His silhouette has remained narrow with a fluid ease and he continues to refine his shapes. If his design has changed in more than 40 years of business, it has become more simple and refined. Not one to be satisfied with past success, he still relishes the challenge of creating the perfect black dress. But despite his fondness for black in design, he is also known for his brilliant and unusual combinations of darker shades. His masterful handling of chiffon and lace tends toward the softly tailored, staying away from excess fullness of any kind. Galanos is not necessarily synchronized with the rest of the fashion world; if the themes of his collections bear similarities to others from year to year, it is coincidental.

Galanos prefers to work somewhat in isolation, both geographically and ideologically. His goal has always been to make the most elegant clothing possible for a select group of the world's most sophisticated women. The number of women who are what he considers truly elegant may be smaller than it was when his career began, but he has certainly succeeded in his goal of providing the clothing that they require. His designs are collected by his customers, like other objects of artistic value, and they are represented in museum collections around the United States.—MELINDA WATT

Galitzine, Irene

Russian designer working in Rome

Born *Tiflis, Russia, 1916.*
Education *Studied art and design in Rome.*
Family *Married Silvio Medici.*

Career *Assistant, Fontana, c.1945-48; established own import business, Rome, 1949; first collection, 1959; business closed 1968; worked as free-lance designer, 1968-70; designer for own business, reopened as Princess Galitzine, from 1970.*

Awards *Filene Award for new talent, Boston, 1959; Designer of the Year Award, Italy, 1962; Sunday Times International Fashion Award, 1965; Isabella d'Este Award, Italy, 1965.*

Nathaniel Hawthorne and Henry James were Americans who dreamed of Italy; after World War II, the dream was a film, *Three Coins in a Fountain,* eventually superseded by the Italian-made *La Dolce Vita.* Italian freedom and innate style held romance; Italian nobility in the fashion and beauty industries such as Emilio Pucci, Princess Marcella Borghese, and Princess Irene Galitzine were fairy-tale heroes.

In the 1950s and 1960s (launching her business in 1949), Princess Irene Galitzine exemplified Roman high style and the princely life. Diana Vreeland, then of *Harper's Bazaar,* dubbed Galitzine's full, liquid trousers for at-home leisure (introduced to a standing ovation at the Palazzo Pitti fashion showing in 1960) "palazzo pajamas" and every aura of Renaissance and romantic (and erotic) Italy flooded the American imagination. Galitzine's palazzo pajamas were, in fact, not wholly an invention, but they became in Galitzine's countless versions of uncompromising luxury a silken reverie. The silks of Italy were a factor, but Galitzine was especially inventive in the elaboration of the palazzo pajamas, bringing to the leisure trousers expressions of *alta moda* embellishment. She treated the drapey silks as a scrim for attached necklaces in the manner of Mainbocher and created other illusions of encrusted ornament and articulated hems and sleeves with beads in a manner reminiscent of Fortuny's Murano bead edges, but even more of Renaissance paintings. Even with the comfort and casualness of palazzo pajamas, the wearer seemed to step out of a lustrous, bejewelled world of Renaissance art. Similarly, her decoration of hems, collars, and cuffs articulated countless Pierrots (often with long tops over either palazzo trousers or narrow trousers). Galitzine used these applied effects not only to establish the grandeur of what might otherwise lapse into a too casual mode, but also to apply a countervailing weight to the almost fly-away big cutting of her styles. Weight and the illusion of weight was an effective punctuation of the clothing. Likewise, in her signature toga top over trousers, the elaborate *fibula* at the shoulder not only secures, but gives a solid balance to the loose drape.

Roman grandeur led rather dramatically, in the 1960s, to the Cardin-like futurism in Galitzine's work. A quilted vinyl jumpsuit with matching helmet on the cover of the May 1966 *Harper's Bazaar* is of *Brave New World* anticipation, but continues to observe Galitzine's dress rationalism. In the same era, she was converting her palazzo pajamas into ensembles with Empire-waisted tops and boxy jackets in reinforcement of the new geometry. In fact, her clothing had always understood lifestyle and the reductivism of the 1960s. After a brief hiatus in the late 1960s, Galitzine reopened to show for spring/summer 1970. In that collection, she used bold graphics for trousers and dresses to be worn with sleeveless tunics, again a device that could seem to step out of a Renaissance painting or step forward into fantasies of outer space.

For a fashion designer able to trace her Russian ancestry back to Catherine the Great and insistent on her Russian style even as much as her Roman, Galitzine became the epitome of Roman style. "I've always tried to design new outlines that feel good on the body. . . . I don't care for clothes that you have to think about after you've put them on. No elegant woman ever looks ill at ease." Galitzine's formula for easy and comfortable dressing managed to combine the avowed comfort of the clothing with an unmistakable pomp of Roman refinement and the abiding presence of Italian Renaissance lustre. Always adding to the aura of Galitzine's design was her remarkable client list, the best of Italy and an international clientèle that discovered Italian clothing in the 1950s and 1960s. *Architectural Digest* (September 1988) noted, "As Eleanor Lambert once remarked at a Galitzine showing: 'The audience is snob, not mob.'" Yet, the supreme evidence is Galitzine's clothing: luxurious and inventive high-style casualness with grace.—RICHARD MARTIN

Galliano, John
British designer

Born *Gibraltar, 1960.*

Education *Studied design at St Martin's School of Art, London.*

Career *Graduation collection, Les Incroyables, sold to Brown's. Free-lance designer, establishing John Galliano fashion house, London, from 1984.*

Awards *British Fashion Council Designer of the Year Award, 1987; Bath Costume Museum Dress of the Year Award, 1987.*

Address *Passage du Cheval Blanc, 2 rue de la Roquette, 75011 Paris, France.*

Experimental and innovative, John Galliano has become internationally renowned as one of Britain's most exciting designers, acclaimed from the start for his brilliance in cut and magpie-like ability to take inspiration from diverse sources to create a completely new look. Although his clothes are often difficult to understand when on the hanger—with collars that seem to be bows or halter necks that actually fit over the shoulders—they are frequently ahead of the current fashion trends and eventually filter down the clothing chain to the High Street, as well as being picked up by other designers. A favourite among fashion aficionados, Galliano was spotted as soon as his first student collection was completed and has continued to develop since, despite repeated problems with backers that have hampered his career.

As part of a new breed of avant-garde British designers, Galliano led the way in the mid-1980s with his historically influenced designs. This fascination for period detail and adaptation of traditional styles into highly contemporary pieces has continued throughout his work. Studying surviving garments in museums to learn about construction methods and different ways to cut and drape fabric to create new shapes inspired his innovative 18th-century Incroyables collection for his degree show. He has suffused this knowledge with other diverse influences to produce collections always exciting and different. His great belief in the necessity to push fashion forward by learning from the past, coupled with his skill at balancing his designs with modern ideals, has earned him the reputation of a prodigy.

Every outfit is thought out to the last detail, producing a series of completely accessorized looks as he constantly strives for perfection. His love of bias cut gives added fluidity to the asymmetrical hemlines of many of his designs, with a taste of 18th-century dandyism thrown in, always with a surprise twist—often in his use of fabric, another area where Galliano loves to experiment and challenge. In one collection he presented Napoleon-style jackets in bright neoprene, in another, *devoré* velvet bias-cut dresses which clung to the body, giving the element of sexiness that pervades his work. His love of shock gave us the camped-up glamour of his "underwear as outer wear," with satin knickers worn with feathered bras and leather caps, tapping the trend for drag in the London clubs.

With Galliano's Girl and, perhaps to an even greater extent, the largely denim and Lycra-based line Galliano Genes, the designer demonstrates his ability to redefine existing subcultures to develop clothes for the younger, funkier sisters of his mainline buyers. Produced at a cheaper cost by using less exclusive fabrics, these designs are nonetheless inventive. Three-way jackets can be worn with attached waist-coats outside or inside, and there are more basic items that are more commercial, confronting occasional claims from his critics that his work is too avant-garde and less popular than other European names.

The sheer breadth of vision of Galliano's designs, which frequently rethink form and shape, and the great inventiveness of his cut surely earn him his reputation as one of the best of British designers. The research he does before forming a collection—bringing together influences and details from the French Revolution to Afghan bankers to Paul Poiret—and his experimentation with fabrics demonstrate his dedication to pushing fashion and dress forward, yielding excitement and surprise in every collection.—REBECCA ARNOLD

Gaultier, Jean-Paul

French designer

Born *Arcueil, France, 24 April 1952.*
Education *Educated at the École Communale, the College d'Enseignement, and at the Lycée d'Arcueil, to 1969.*
Career *Design assistant, Pierre Cardin, 1972-74; also worked for Esterel and Patou; designer, Cardin United States Collection, working in the Philippines, 1974-75; designer, Majago, Paris, 1976-78; founder, Jean Paul Gaultier S.A., from 1978; menswear line introduced, 1984; Junior Gaultier line introduced, 1987; furniture line introduced, 1992; licenses include jewelry, from 1988, perfumes, from 1991, and jeans, from 1992.*
Awards *Fashion Oscar Award, Paris, 1987.*
Address *70 Galerie Vivienne, 75002 Paris, France.*

By injecting kitsch into couture, Gaultier has redefined the traditionally elegant trappings of Paris fashion. He is a playful, good-natured iconoclast, glamorizing street style and cleaning it up for the haute couture. By turns surreal but never completely bizarre, rebellious but always wearable, he produces seductive, witty clothes which redefine notions of taste and elegance in dress.

His eclectic source material, inherited from punk via the fleamarket, and an astute sense of the origins of style mean his clothes make constant historic and literary references, as opposed to the cool modernism of contemporaries such as Issey Miyake, displayed in his use of heraldic motifs in the late 1980s or a collection based on Toulouse-Lautrec in 1991.

Gaultier challenges orthodox notions of the presentation of gender through both male and female dress and ignores the stereotypical femininity normally paraded on the catwalks of traditional Parisian haute couture. During his employment at Jean Patou, Gaultier recognized how most couturiers ignored the female form at the expense of the construction of a particular

Jean-Paul Gaultier: Corset evening dress, 1991.
Photograph courtesy of the Metropolitan Museum of Art; gift of Richard Martin.

line. He was, on one occasion, horrified to see a model having to wear heavy bandages to suppress her breasts in order for the dress she was modelling to hang properly. This impulse eventually culminated in a controversial series of negotiations of the corset, stemming from his interest in the exaggerated definition of the female form it produced. In the 1980s he redefined this usually private, hidden garment, whose traditional function is to provide a structure from which to hang the more important outerwear, by recreating it as outerwear itself. One of these, the Corset Dress of 1982, commented astutely on femininity, constructing the breast less as a soft malleable object of passive attraction and more as an object of power, a female weapon, whilst at the same time alluding to the conically stitched bras of the 1950s sweater girl—a particularly tacky glamour. These ideas achieved mass attention when Gaultier designed the costumes for Madonna's Blonde Ambition tour in 1990.

By 1984 Gaultier had decided to move more directly into menswear. Through personal experience he could find nothing he really wanted, particularly in terms of sizing, and even unstructured Armani jackets seemed too small. He noticed that men had been buying his women's jackets because of the unusual fabrics and cut, so he began his seminal reworking of the pin-striped suit for both men and women. He displayed a traditional male wardrobe by redesigning such classics as the navy blazer and Fair Isle jumper and dismantling clichés of masculine styling by producing skirts, corsets, and tutus for men. During one notorious catwalk show female models smoked pipes and men paraded in transparent lace skirts. This acknowledgement of male narcissism and interest in the creation of erotic clothing for men, as shown in the Man-Object Collection of 1982, has influenced designers such as Gianni Versace into the 1990s.

Gaultier is perhaps best associated with the rise of popular interest in designer clothing in the mid-1980s. His redefinitions of traditional male tailoring made his clothes instantly recognizable amongst so-called fashion victims in most of the major European capitals, using details such as metal tips on collars and extended shoulder lines. Structured, fitted garments like jackets were reworked, being cut long and slim over the hips to mid-thigh to give an hourglass shape to the wearer's physique.

Gaultier has always been interested in new developments in fabric and intrigued by the design possibilities of modern, artificial fibres, and is known for using unconventional fibres like neoprene. He uses fabrics outside of their usual context, such as chiffon for dungarees, resulting in a utilitarian garment being produced out of a delicate material traditionally associated with eveningwear. This juggling with expected practice directs him to produce items such as a willow pattern printed textile incorporating the head of Mickey Mouse and Aran sweaters elongated into dresses with the woollen bobbles taking the place of nipples.

Gaultier rebels against the old school of Parisian couture but, because of his years of training within its system under Pierre Cardin, Jacques Esterel and Jean Patou, he is a master craftsman. However avant-garde his collections may seem, they are always founded in a technical brilliance based inventive tailoring and are able to convince because of the technique.—CAROLINE COX

Genny SpA

Italian ready-to-wear manufacturer

Founded in Ancona by Arnoldo and Donatella Girombelli in 1961. Lines include Genny Moda, Complice, Byblos (introduced 1973, became independent company, 1983), Malisy (to 1993), Montana Donna and Montana Uomo (to c.1992). Chief designers for Complice include Gianni Versace, from 1975; Claude Montana, from 1980; Dolce e Gabbana, from 1990. Designers for Byblos include Versace, 1975-77; Guy Paulin, 1977-80; Keith Varty and Alan Cleaver, from 1980.

Address *Strada Statale 16, 60131 Zona Pip (Ancona), Italy.*

Named after their first-born child, Genny was the brainchild of Arnoldo and Donatella Girombelli, who founded the company in 1961. Genny Holding has since become one of Italy's foremost fashion companies, designing, manufacturing, and distributing its own ranges which include Genny, Genny Due, Complice, and Byblos among others. From relatively humble origins as a small clothing factory based in Ancona, Italy, the company was operating at an industrial scale by 1968. During the 1970s it experienced rapid growth when its founder made radical changes in the company structure, steering it towards a more fashionable product in terms of garment styling. These changes did not, however, alter the company's original commitment to the production of high quality, predominantly tailored garments. As an early protagonist of the "Made in Italy" label, Genny assumed a leading role during the 1970s when the Italian fashion industry took its first steps toward becoming a serious competitor with French ready-to-wear fashion.

Genny Holding is typical of a number of Italian fashion companies who manufacture high fashion lines designed for them by leading names in the industry, yet launched under the company's own label. Fashion writer Colin McDowell has described this very successful, as well as lucrative, format as a form of "moonlighting." Considerable financial reward, coupled with the high quality of the Italian ready-to-wear product, has meant that there is no shortage of well-known designers willing to supply their creative talent for such companies. Genny's earliest working relationship with an outside designer was with the young Gianni Versace (then relatively unknown) who designed his first collection for Genny in 1974. Versace was also responsible for designing the early Byblos collections, a younger range introduced in 1973 to complement the classic Genny image.

After the death of Arnoldo Girombelli in 1980, his wife, Donatella, assumed a leading role in the company and now chairs its board of directors. Described by fashion retail entrepreneur Roberto Devorik as "a rare catalyst for design talent," Donatella Girombelli has continued her husband's policy of employing top designers to create lines for the Genny labels. These include Dolce e Gabbana, who design for Complice, and Alan Cleaver and Keith Varty who have designed the Byblos collection since 1980.

The position of Genny and its other labels, including Complice and Byblos, is not a real cutting edge of fashion. They are not dramatically avant-garde or barrier-breaking, but rather producers of top quality ready-to-wear clothing with a strong design element. It is this that has led to the company's widespread success in the international market. In 1992 Genny Holding produced over 2,050,000 items under its different labels, which were distributed worldwide through the company's boutiques, and under carefully controlled licensing agreements.—CATHERINE WORAM

Gernreich, Rudi
American designer

> **Born**   *Vienna, 8 August 1922. Immigrated to the United States, 1938, naturalized, 1943.*
>
> **Education**   *Studied at Los Angeles City College, 1938-41; Los Angeles Art Center School, 1941-42.*
>
> **Career**   *Dancer, costume designer, Lester Horton Company, 1942-48; fabric salesman, Hoffman company, and free-lance clothing designer, Los Angeles and New York, 1948-51; designer, William Bass Inc., Beverly Hills, 1951-59; swimwear designer, Westwood Knitting Mills, Los Angeles, 1953-59; shoe designer, Genesco Corp., 1958-60; founder, GR Designs, Los Angeles, 1960-64; designer, Rudi Gernreich Inc., 1964-68. Designs featured in first fashion videotape, Basic Black, 1966. Designed furnishings for Fortress and Knoll International, 1970-71, lingerie for Lily of France, 1975, cosmetics for Redken, 1976. Also designed knitwear for Harmon Knitwear, kitchen accessories, ceramic bathroom accessories, and costumes for Bella Lewitzky Dance Company.*
>
> **Exhibitions**   *Two Modern Artists of Dress: Elizabeth Hawes and Rudi Gernreich, Fashion Institute of Technology, New York, 1967.*
>
> **Awards**   *Sports Illustrated Designer of the Year Award, 1956; Wool Knit Association Award, 1960; Coty American Fashion Critics Award, 1960, 1963, 1966, 1967; Neiman Marcus Award, Dallas, 1961; Sporting Look Award, 1963; Sunday Times International Fashion Award, London, 1965; Filene's Design Award, Boston, 1966; admitted to Coty American Fashion Critics' Hall of Fame, 1967; Knitted Textile Association Award, 1975; Council of Fashion Designers of America Special Tribute, 1985.*
>
> **Died**   *(in Los Angeles) 21 April 1985.*

Son of a hosiery manufacturer, born into an intellectual Viennese family in the 1920s, Rudi Gernreich was to become one of the most revolutionary designers of the 20th century. After fleeing the Nazis in the late 1930s he settled in Los Angeles, becoming an American citizen in 1943. Perhaps because of this geographic detachment from the centres of fashion and the fact that he refused to show in Paris, Gernreich is a name which is not spoken in the same breath as Balenciaga, Dior, or even Courrèges, although Gernreich had just as much influence on women's appearance, especially during the 1960s and 1970s.

Gernreich studied dance before entering the world of fashion and, using as inspiration the practice clothes of dancers, particularly leotards and tights, he produced pared down body-clothes in the 1960s, aimed at what seemed to be the new woman of the era. To cater to this popular construction of femininity, Gernreich attempted to produce a new version of women's clothing, freed of all constraints.

Influenced by Bauhaus functionalism, Gernreich conceived a body-based dressing with coordinated underwear, celebrating the unfettered movement of the body based on his early involvement with Lester Horton's modern dance troupe. This interest in liberating the body from the limitations of clothing surfaced in his early swimwear designs of 1952 in which he eliminated the complicated boned and underpinned interior construction which had been obligatory in the 1950s. He revived the knitted swimsuit or *maillot* of the 1920s, which he elasticized to follow the shape of the body. These experiments were continued in his knitted tube dresses of 1953.

Gernreich was interested less in the details and decorations of clothes and more in how they looked in motion. In the 1950s he was designing relaxed, comfortable clothes fabricated out of wool, jersey, and other malleable materials, usually in solid colours or geometric shapes and checks. During the next decade he went on to use unusual fabrics and bold colour disharmonies such as orange and blue or red and purple.

In the early 1960s Rudi Gernreich opened a Seventh Avenue, New York, showroom where he showed his popular designs for Harmon knitwear and his own more expensive line of experimental garments. During the 1960s he acquired a reputation for being the most radical designer in America. His designs included the jacket with one notched and one rounded lapel, tuxedos made of white satin, and the topless bathing suit of 1964, which reflected the new vogue for topless sunbathing.

Gernreich's freeing of the breasts was a social statement, somehow part of the emancipation of women, and a portent of the unfettering of the breast by the women's movement in the 1970s. Gernreich invented the "no bra" bra in 1964, a soft nylon bra with no padding or boning in which breasts assumed their natural shape, rather than being moulded into an aesthetic ideal. He went on to display overtly his sympathy for women's liberation with his 1971 collection of military safari clothes accessorized with dogtags and machine guns.

Gernreich was also responsible for developing the concept of unisex, believing that as women achieved more freedom in the 1960s, male dress would emerge from the aesthetic exile into which it had been cast in the 19th century. He conceived of interchangeable clothes for men and women such as floor length kaftans or white knit bell-bottom trousers and matching black and white midriff tops, and even, in 1975, Y-front underwear for women. Other designs included the first chiffon T-shirt dress, see-through blouses, coordinated outfits of dresses, handbags, hats, and stockings, mini dresses inset with clear vinyl stripes, and the thong bathing suit, cut high to expose the buttocks. He experimented constantly with the potentials of different materials using cutouts, vinyl, and plastic, and mixing patterns such as checks with dots.

His clothing was part of a whole design philosophy which encompassed the designing of furniture, kitchen accessories, rugs, and quilts—even, in 1982, gourmet soups. His notion of freeing the body was taken to its logical extreme in his last design statement, the pubikini, which appeared in 1982, revealing the model's dyed and shaped pubic hair.—CAROLINE COX

Ghost

British fashion house

Founded in 1984 by Tanya Sarne.

Awards   *British Apparel Export Award, 1992.*
Address   *The Chapel, 263 Kensal Rd., London W10 5DB, England.*

The British label Ghost was founded in 1984 by Tanya Sarne and has since become a firmly established name in the fashion industry. The company's signature use of flowing fabric, with its softly crinkled look cut in loose, flowing shapes, has always formed the basis of each collection. Ghost designs are not usually viewed as the cutting edge of fashion. This was particularly true during the power-dressing period of the 1980s, when strict tailoring and padded shoulders were a major element in fashion. A label such as Ghost offered an individual and alternative way of dressing.

Fabrics are the hallmark of each Ghost collection and 99 per cent of them are woven from viscose yarns derived from specially-grown soft wools that have a fluid, crêpe-like texture. An intricate process of washing, shrinking, and dyeing is applied to each garment, which is constructed from the unfinished material or "grey cloth" and dyed at the final stage. These "grey cloth" garments are cut several sizes bigger to allow for the ensuing process of shrinking that occurs when the viscose is boiled to the consistency of vintage crêpe fabric. The traditional process employed by Ghost of garment dyeing at the final stage is rarely used in production today, due to its cost and the fact that it is extremely time-consuming. Another feature of each Ghost collection is its richly varied use of colour, which can achieve great depth on the viscose fabric and changes each season from softest pastels and pale powdery shades to rich autumnal and spicy tones. The signature fabric is also treated with surface decoration such as heavy embroidery, cutwork, and *broderie anglaise* lace effects. Due to the soft, fluid nature of this fabric, Ghost was initially perceived as being primarily summerwear. However, over the past few seasons, new fabrics have been introduced, in particular to the autumn-winter collections, and which have included quilted satin, velours, and mohair wool mixes.

Like many of its British counterparts, more than 80 percent of Ghost's business is export, of which America and Japan represent around 50 percent of sales volume. This was one of the main reasons that prompted Sarne to start showing her collections in New York in 1993, where the company had been selling successfully since 1987. In 1992, Ghost was awarded the British Apparel Export Award when the company exports rose from 60 percent to over 70 percent of the company business. However, although Sarne has abandoned London as a base for her catwalk shows, her design studio and offices remain in Britain. While the United States remains the largest export market for Ghost, others markets include Japan, Europe, Australia, the Caribbean, and the Middle East.

According to Sarne, her philosophy of creating clothes, which she describes as "By Women, For Women," is the key to the considerable success of the Ghost label and its consequential appeal to a wide-ranging age group. Each new garment is tried on by the design team before it goes into production. The revolutionary nature of each Ghost collection, which means that existing pieces can be added to each season, is another appealing feature of the company's designs and may be the key to dressing in the 1990s. "It's a unique product and very feminine," says Sarne of the Ghost label. "It also has a very 'antipower dressing' stance—a look that I believe will only increase in importance as the decade progresses."—CATHERINE WORAM

Gigli, Romeo
Italian designer

Born *Castelbolognese, Faenza, Italy, 12 December 1949.*

Romeo Gigli: Summer 1996. *Photograph by Javier Vallbonrat.*

Education   *Studied architecture. Travelled internationally for ten years.*

Career   *First collection for Quickstep by Luciano Papini; small collection of handknits, 1972; designer, Dimitri Couture, New York, 1978; Romeo Gigli label, from 1981; designer, Romeo Gigli for Zamasport, from 1984; designer to 1989, then consultant, Callaghan for Zamasport; signature fragrance launched, 1991; lower priced G Gigli sportswear line introduced, 1990.*

Address   *Via Marconi 3, 20129 Milan, Italy.*

Romeo Gigli produces clothes that are always subtle and sophisticated. He blends a spectrum of muted colours with a fluid sense of cut and drape to the body to give a feeling of balance and harmony to all his designs, perhaps as a result of his architectural training. His prime influences are fine art and travel, both apparent in the Renaissance luxury of the fabrics he uses in some of his pieces and the mix of cultural influences discernible in their shaping and decoration. A soft sculptural beauty pervades both his day and eveningwear, with a talent for shaping clothes to the body in an elegantly flattering way without ever clinging too tightly or restrictively.

His womenswear encapsulates these qualities and has been very influential, having taken its cue from the elastic fluidity of dancewear to produce garments that are soft and feminine. Although Gigli's clothes are obviously designed for the busy modern woman, they are never merely a series of mix-and-match separates, nor indeed are they as ostentatious as the work of some of his Italian counterparts. His use of stretch fabrics and rich warm woollen suiting have inspired many imitators with their purity of cut and sensuous, body-skimming fit. The classical virtues of the body which pervade Gigli's work give a feeling of an evolutionary process to fashion, rather than a slavish following of seasonal dictates, and it is perhaps this innate classicism that gives his clothes a timeless air. Some garments, like his richly enveloping embroidered coats, seem destined to become treasured collectors' items, passed on like heirlooms rather than falling victim to the fickleness often associated with fashion. His use of detailing is subtle and uncluttered, as in the minimal silhouette of the Empire line dresses and ballet-style wrap tops he introduced and popularized during the mid-1980s. When decoration is used it follows his restrained ideals of iridescent beauty: golden thread embroidered around the edge of a soft bolero jacket, evoking a feeling of the East, dull amber gold beads making a shimmering glow of fringing from waist to floor, or thousands of glittering gunmetal blue beads on a cocoon-like evening dress.

If Gigli's strength is perhaps his gently romantic womenswear, his menswear is nonetheless notable for the same kind of muted colours and sinuous cut, giving it a feeling of luxury without any obvious show of wealth. Suiting is again unstructured, working with the shape of the body rather than against it. His jackets are often high-buttoned, with an extra sense of depth and texture given to their rich wools by the subtle range of mossy greens, dull aubergine and bitter chocolate browns used to stripe the fabric. It is this kind of colour sense which, combined with clever mixing of shiny and matt fabrics, marks out all his work. Even his most formal menswear has an effortless elegance, and a fluidity of cut, which has made it unfailingly popular with discerning male customers.

Gigli has followed the increasingly popular notion of the diffusion range with the more practical daywear basics of his Gigli line, launched in 1990. Here the silhouette is bulkier, with rich berry coloured chenilles and sage and golden corduroys being used to produce a collection of classic zip-style cardigans, hooded tops, trousers, and soft leggings for men and women. Although less ethereally beautiful than much of his main collection, there is still the same signature use of contrasting fabrics and muted colours to produce a very tactile appeal through texture and shade.

An intelligent balance of all elements of design and choice of textiles makes Gigli's work uniquely sophisticated and beautiful. His subtlety of touch and soft sculptural forms have influenced all levels of design from the High Street up, especially during the last half of the 1980s, when his elasticated wrapped styles and pure tailoring were seen in every fashion magazine. His work has continued to develop along his self-assigned tenets of harmony and balance, while always retaining a feeling of sensuous luxury.
—REBECCA ARNOLD

Girbaud, Marithé & François

French design team

Born *Marithé Bachellerie born in Lyon, France, 1942. François Girbaud born in Mazamet, France, 1945.*

Career *Business formed in 1965; showed first collection, 1968, first boutique selling Girbaud-designed jeans opened, Paris, 1969; Halles Capone boutique opened in Paris, from 1972; first US shop opened, Nantucket Island, Massachusetts, 1984. Jeaneration 21 line introduced, 1993; HiTech/HiTouch line developed, 1993; other lines include Complements for women, Closed for men, Reproductions for children, Complete Look accessories, Kelian-Girbaud shoes, Maillaparty, Compagnie des Montagnes et des Forêts, 11342, and Millesimes.*

Address *12 bis rue des Colonnes du Trône, 75008 Paris, France.*

Marithé and François Girbaud have created fashion that emanates from the street; that revels in design problems of cylinders, mutation, and reversibility; and that brings high-style aspirations to casual materials and effects. Their proclivity to oversizing seems akin to Japanese design and Middle Eastern and East Asian peasant garb. Their futurist vocabulary of tubes and metamorphosis can seem a highly conceptual eventuality worthy of Marinetti or Balla, but it also functions as fluid streetwear. Their deconstructivist bent, exposing the elements of garment manufacture, parallels Karl Lagerfeld at Chanel, but their medium is a more accessible casual wear that is almost hip-hop homeboy style in New York and *insouciant* flair for the "week-end" in Paris. In the casual jeans-based "look that they almost invented" (*Daily News Record,* New York, 11 February 1987), the Girbauds have been consistently the most innovative, experimental, concept-driven designers.

They have, in fact, commanded the avant-garde position in casualwear, customarily characterized by stasis, in the manner of high-fashion designers such as Jean-Paul Gaultier or Issey Miyake, thriving on conceptual development and change, yet never failing to represent the irrefutable leadership position in the field. Ruth La Ferla (*Daily News Record,* 20 September 1982) called François Girbaud "three parts fashion technician, one part theoretician," yet the Girbauds are also savvy interpreters, bringing cascades of Ninja-inspired pantaloons to the contemporary wardrobe with the practical note of snaps to gather the trousers at the ankles, rugged survival wear for fall 1983, and sophisticated 1940s and 1950s revival for spring 1988. Beginning in retailing, the Girbauds are as street smart as they are conceptually witty and ingenious. François Girbaud told Irene Daria (*Women's Wear Daily,* 21 December 1984), "We design from the streets. We start at the bottom and move up."

Their streets are global. Roomy drawstring trousers, loose shirts worn over the waist, and other styles evade traditional European and American notions of fit. The Amerasian collection for summer 1984—featuring Moudjahadin outfits with drawstring jackets and wide tubular trousers inspired by the Middle East and Afghanistan as well as boxy jackets inspired by China— typifies the eclectic, globe-trotting ethos of the Girbauds' design. For summer 1985, the Jet Laggers collection showed no straggling or fatigue: trousers called "Kaboul/Champs Elysées" could be worn in the Middle East or in Paris in their amplitude, cargo pockets adding to the engorged size, with a rustic combination of buttons and drawstrings. For fall 1986, big *dhoti* trousers and exotic cummerbunds and kilto-pants with voluminous tops and tapered legs combined East and West, exercise and boudoir. Shirts and jackets can flow with the simple grace of Brancusi and sensuous volume of balloon shapes in the couture, but the virtuoso accomplishment of the Girbauds is their repertory of trousers options for men and women, international in possibilities and strikingly original and inventive in realization.

The Girbauds are also aware of the history of Western dress. In menswear, their high-waisted Hollywood style for fall 1987 evoked the glamour era of movies in the 1940s. Their interest is also in materials, the softness of fabrications that lend themselves to the tubes and cones of form that they prefer, including quilting, fabric-backed leather, and a soft stonewashed denim. Another conceptual element of the Girbaud style is the didactic display of the garment's construction, one Momento Due jacket revealing its pattern components, other garments inscribed with all their wearing options. In addition to the language of clothing, the Girbauds also play with language itself, vocabulary, hieroglyphs, and alphabets appearing again and again in the collection. In interview, the designers like to suggest that their work is a perfect synthesis of their childhood preoccupations, she with creating doll clothes, he with American pop culture, films, and military outfits. There is a truth to that proposition, yet it also is unlikely that these two designers who began as retailers are only pursuing personal desires. The casual clothing they have created is imbued with heritage, even if that legacy is working clothing, while brought to the present in technical and even futuristic ways. In the evident conceptualism of their clothing (and in their bridge lines), they have expanded the market of casual clothing beyond the young, so that their clothes are as appropriate to the market of persons in their 30s and 40s as they are to the primary market for jeans of teens and 20s. They face many competitors in stylish casual wear for the young; they command the market for an abiding casual style for an older market, ever-increasing. *California Apparel News* (11-17 July 1986) reported accurately, "In an industry where fashion changes with each season, the Girbauds' clothes have kept the image of comfort while growing in style and versatility to become 'concept dressing.'"—RICHARD MARTIN

Givenchy, Hubert de

French designer

Born *Hubert James Marcel Taffin de Givenchy, in Beauvais, 21 February 1927.*
Education *Studied at the Collège Felix-Fauré, Beauvais and Montalembert; École Nationale Supérieure des Beaux Arts, Paris; Faculty of Law, University of Paris.*

Career *Worked in Paris for Lucien Lelong, 1945-46; for Piguet, 1946-48; for Jacques Fath, 1948-49; for Schiaparelli, 1949-51; established Maison Givenchy, 1952; president, Société Givenchy Couture and Société des Parfums Givenchy, from 1954. Fragrances include De, 1957; L'Interdit, 1957; Givenchy III, 1970; L'Eau de Givenchy, 1980; Vetyver; Ysatis, 1984; Xeryus, 1986; Amarige, 1991.*

Exhibitions *Givenchy: 30 Years, Fashion Institute of Technology, New York, 1982; Givenchy: 40 Years of Creation, Palais Galliera, Paris, 1991.*

Address *3 avenue George V, 75008 Paris, France.*

In 1992 Hubert de Givenchy celebrated his 40th anniversary as a couturier. Givenchy chose his vocation at the age of ten, and as a youngster admired the designs of Elsa Schiaparelli and Madame Grès. Later, after stints with Jacques Fath, Robert Piguet, and Lucien Lelong, he spent four years working for Schiaparelli, during which he designed the clothes sold in her boutique, many of them separates, an American idea new to Paris in the early 1950s, for which Givenchy gained a following. Although he is now appropriately acclaimed as a classicist and traditionalist, it was as an *enfant terrible* of sorts that Givenchy burst upon the couture scene in 1952, just weeks before his 25th birthday, with a novel collection based on separates, in which even eveningwear was conceptualized as a series of interchangeable pieces. Also noteworthy in that first collection was his generous use of white cotton shirting, which had an economic as well as an aesthetic rationale: the shirting was as inexpensive as it was fresh-looking. The Bettina blouse which Givenchy has recently used as his signature was part of that cotton group; it had a convertible stand-up collar and ruffled sleeves with scalloped black eyelet trim. A few years later the blouse reappeared, in white organdie without trimming, a metaphor for the direction Givenchy's work would take: Simplify and refine were the watchwords.

Again and again in Givenchy's early years as a couturier, the appeal of his designs to young women was remarked upon. The symbol of that youthful appeal was Audrey Hepburn, an actress whose rise to fame paralleled his. Givenchy created the clothes worn by Hepburn in several of her most beloved roles, starting with *Sabrina* (1954) for which Edith Head won the Oscar for costume design and Givenchy received no credit. Although Head designed some of Hepburn's *Sabrina* wardrobe, the very soigné black tailleur and hat in which Sabrina returned from Paris, and the strapless white organdie gown embroidered with black and white flowers which was the envy of every young woman who saw the film, were both from Givenchy's collection. Typically, these were clothes which transformed Hepburn from charming gamine to paragon of chic sophistication. Similar transformations were at the heart of *Love in the Afternoon* (1957), *Funny Face* (1957), and *Breakfast at Tiffany's* (1961). By 1963, when *Charade* appeared, the gamine had finally grown into the sophisticate, and "the world's youngest couturier" had become the most elegant of classical couturiers. Hepburn remained Givenchy's muse for almost 40 years, the quintessential Givenchy client, flying into Paris from Switzerland to sit in the front row for his collections until shortly before her death.

Givenchy shared the ideal of creating a perfect, simple dress from a single line with his idol, Balenciaga. When the two men finally met, by accident, in 1953, they developed a relationship that was perhaps unique in the annals of couture, with Balenciaga giving Givenchy unprecedented access not only to his sketches, but also to his fittings and his workrooms. Starting in 1959, after Givenchy moved to 3 avenue George V, almost across the street from Balenciaga, they conferred daily, critiquing each other's sketches and collections. Their aesthetic affinity was such that when Balenciaga closed his couture salon, he referred his most valued clients to Givenchy.

Because of the emphasis on line rather than decoration, Givenchy's designs were easy to adapt, endearing him to the many American manufacturers who interpreted them. Givenchy himself helped to make his clothes accessible to a much wider market in the early, pre-licensing years, designing junior sportswear to be made by American manufacturers with American fabrics, for *Seventeen* and *Glamour* magazines. The caption for *Glamour's* December 1955 cover, featuring a Givenchy sweater, speaks directly to the appeal of his designs: "The Givenchy marks: its young chic, . . . meant for long, lean people in pipestem skirts . . . for when they want to look casual in a worldly way."

Today Givenchy continues to enjoy designing fashions that make a woman look beautiful; his oeuvre bespeaks restraint and refinement, with gradual transitions from one season and style to the next. Although Givenchy still designs cotton separates, including some with Matisse-inspired patterns in his 40th anniversary collection, his designs have matured along with his original clientèle. Givenchy's creations begin with the fabric; his forte is choosing or developing Europe's most luxurious, yet tasteful, fabrics and embroideries in an expansive range of colours. From these he creates exquisite couture clothes that complement the lifestyles of a clientèle which has included several of the world's most elegant women. He is known for deceptively simple day dresses, superbly tailored suits, coats that are marvels of line and volume, sumptuous cocktail dresses or suits, extravagant evening dresses that are nevertheless eminently wearable, and hats that reveal his sense of whimsy and fantasy.—ARLENE C. COOPER

Grès, Madame

French designer

Born   Germain "Alix" Barton in Paris, 30 November 1903.

Education   Studied painting and sculpture, Paris.

Family   Married Serge Czerefkov, late 1930s; daughter: Anne.

Career   Served three-month apprenticeship with Premet, Paris, 1930; made and sold toiles using the name Alix Barton, Paris, 1930s; designer, Maison Alix (not her own house), 1934-40; sold rights to the name Alix and adopted Grès, from husband's surname, 1940; director, Grès Couture, from 1942; accessory line introduced, 1976; ready-to-wear line introduced, 1980; retired, 1988. Perfumes include Cabochard, 1959, Grès pour Homme, 1965, Qui Pro Quo, 1976, Eau de Grès, 1980, Alix, 1981, Grès Nonsieu, 1982, and Cabotine de Grès, 1990.

Exhibition   Madame Grès, Metropolitan Museum of Art, New York, 1994.

Awards   Named Chevalier de la Légion d'Honneur, 1947; Dé d'Or Award, 1976; New York University Creative Leadership in the Arts Award, 1978.

Died   (in the South of France) 24 November 1993 (death not made public until December 1994).

Company Address   422 rue du Faubourg Saint-Honoré, 75008 Paris, France.

According to many who attended, the Madame Grès showings were exquisite anguish. With emendations up to the last minute by the designer, models would be delayed, garments

Grès: Fall/Winter 1996/97. *Photograph by Patrice Stable.*

could appear trailing strings, and long intervals might occur between the display of individual garments. At the very end, a flurry of models in the flowing draped jersey evening dress would come out on the runway in rapid succession, an abrupt finale to a halting presentation. Known for designing with the immediacy of draping with cloth, Grès was the self-committed and consummate artist, never the agreeable couturière. Her white salon bespoke her austerity in engineering and her clarity in grace.

Grès shunned the promotional grace and personal identification of many fashion designers, insisting instead on rigorous attention to the clothing. First a sculptor, Grès depended upon sculptural insight even as she, in her most famous and signature form, brought the Louvre's statue of the *Nike of Samothrace* to life in clothing form. Grès's draped and pleated silk jerseys flatter the body with the minimalist and rationalist radicalism of 1930s design, but provide a classical serenity as well. The real achievement of the draped dresses is not their idyllic evocation, but their integrity. They are a unified construction, composed of joined fabric panels continuously top to bottom, fullest in the swirling flutes of the skirt, tucked at the waist, elegantly pinched through the bodice, and surmounted at the neckline—often one-shouldered—with the same materials resolved into three-dimensional twists and baker's-like *volutes*. Thus, Grès was creating no mere look-alike to classical statuary, but a reasoning exercise in formal abbreviation and a characteristically modern enterprise in imparting the body within clothing.

Grès, however, was never a one-dress designer. Her 1934 black Cellophane dress with a black-seal-lined cape (photographed by Hoyningen-Heuné) is, as *Vogue* described, a scarab, but with the cling of bias cut. Following a trip to the Far East in 1936, Grès created a brocaded "Temple of Heaven" dress, inspired by Javanese dance costume. Throughout the 1930s, she took inspiration from North Africa and Egypt. An exuberant *chinoiserie* evening coat of the 1930s, in an exquisite reversible textile by Raoul Dufy with embroidered hummingbirds, flares into shaped pagoda extensions. In the 1940s, after managing to keep her business alive through most of the war, Grès became interested in tailoring and created some of the most disciplined tailoring of suits for day in the 1940s and 1950s. By the 1960s and 1970s, Grès was translating the planarity of regional costume into a simplified *origami* of flat planes, ingeniously manipulated on the body to achieve a minimalism akin to sportswear. Ironically, she who exemplified the persistence of the couture treated the great dress with the modernist lightness of sportswear, and she who held out so long against ready-to-wear turned with a convert's passion to the possibilities of ready-to-wear in the 1980s, when she was in her late 80s. The personalizing finesse of a plait or wrap to close or shape a garment is as characteristic of Grès as of Halston or McCardell; her ergodynamics can bring fullness to the chest simply by canting sleeves backward so that the wearer inevitably creates a swelling fullness in the front as arms force the sleeves forward, creating a pouch of air at the chest.

For evening, Grès practiced a continuous antithesis of disclosure of the body and hiding the body in cloth. Even the Grecian "slave" dress, as some of the clients called it, seemed to be as bare as possible with alarming apertures to flesh. But the Grès draped dress, despite its fluid exterior, was securely corseted and structured within, allowing for apertures of skins to seem revealing while at the same time giving the wearer the assurance that the dress would not shift on the body. Conversely, more or less unstructured caftans, clinging geometries of cloth, could cover the wearer so completely as to resemble dress of the Islamic world, but in these instances the softness of structure complemented the apparent suppleness. Never is a Grès garment, whether revealing or concealing, less than enchanting. The slight asymmetry of a wrap determined by one dart, the fall of a suit button to a seaming line, or the wrap of a draped dress to a torque of shaping through the torso, is an invention and an enchantment in Grès's inventive sculptural vocabulary.

History, most notably through photographers such as Hoyningen-Heuné and Willy Maywald, has recorded Grès's sensuous skills chiefly in memorable black-and-white images, but the truth of Grès's achievement comes in garden and painterly colors of aubergine, magenta, cerise, and royal blue, along with a spectrum of fertile browns. Her draped Grecian slaves and goddesses were often in a white of neo-classicism, but an optical white that has tended, with exposure to light, to yellow over time. Grès's streamlined architecture of clothing reminds us of the optimism of pure white dreaming, languorous physical beauty, and apparel that is perfect in comfort and image.—RICHARD MARTIN

Gucci

Italian fashion and accessory house

Founded in Florence, Italy, as saddlery shop by Guccio Gucci (1881-1953), 1906, after family millinery business failed; became retailer of accessories, 1923. Subsequently became Società Anonima Guccio Gucci, 1939, Guccio Gucci srl, 1945, and Guccio Gucci SpA, 1982. Component companies include Gucci Shops, Inc. (USA), from 1953; Guccio Ltd, (UK), from 1961; Gucci et cie (France) and Gucci Boutique, from 1963; Gucci Ltd (Hong Kong), from 1974; Gucci Parfums, formed 1975, became Gucci Parfums SpA, 1982. Gucci shops opened in Florence, 1923; Rome, 1938; Milan, 1951; New York, 1953; Paris, 1963; Hong Kong, 1975. Sons: Aldo, Ugo, Vasco, and Rodolfo part of Gucci firm; Aldo Gucci (1909-90) head of firm, from 1960s; Maurizio Gucci (1948-1995) president of Gucci shops, beginning in 1989. Design/creative director: Dawn Mello, from 1990-91; Richard Lambertson, 1989-92; Tom Ford, 1994; firm acquired by Investcorp, 1993.

Exhibitions *Costume Archive, Metropolitan Museum, New York.*
Address *73 Via Tornabuoni, Florence, Italy.*

The illustrious name of Gucci began as a mark on leather goods produced in Florentine workshops for the young Guccio Gucci. Inspired by the grandiose luggage transported by wealthy guests to the Ritz Hotel in London, where Gucci worked in the kitchens, the young Italian returned to his native country where he began making leather luggage.

The characteristic double-G motif printed on the canvas that was introduced after World War II due to a shortage of leather—with its bold red and green bands on suitcases, bags, satchels, wallets, and purses—has become one of the most copied trademarks in the world, along with France's Louis Vuitton. The Florence-based company grew to international proportions in the post-war period, expanding its range to include clothing, perfume, household items such as decanters and glasses painted with the distinctive red and green bands, scarves, and other accessories. It was this indiscriminate expansion that ultimately proved to be detrimental to the name of Gucci for, as Yves Saint Laurent's director Pierre Bergé once said, "A name is like a cigarette—the more you puff on it the less you have left." Added to this, the proliferation of Gucci imitations which reputedly cost the company a fortune in legal fees, along with infamous conflicts between the volatile members of the Gucci clan, were detrimental to the high profile image the company needed to maintain. However, there were many Gucci items that became status symbols in their own right—namely, the Gucci loafer with its unmistakeable gilt snaffle trim which, according to the *New York Times,* was what carried the company to fortune. Biographer Gerald McKnight notes in his book *Gucci* (New York 1987) that the loafer even became the subject of well-worn jokes in the 1970s, when the name Gucci became as well known as household items such as the Hoover and Sellotape.

Having lost a great deal of the prestigious aura that is a vital element to the success of a luxury brand, the house of Gucci suffered bad press during the 1980s, as journalists hungered after stories of bitter rivalry between family members and their legal battles. It was an American woman, Dawn Mello, who would restore the luxurious image of Gucci when, in 1989, she was appointed executive vice-president and creative director of the company. Under control, the existing Gucci lines have been edited and refined and new items have been introduced. A clever combination of just the right balance of historical relevance (essential to a status name brand) with a real sense of modernity has restored Gucci to its former glory as a "must have" name. The Gucci clog was a sell-out item among the fashion *cognoscenti* in the summer of 1993. This became the most copied shoe style that season, and established the Gucci name not only as a purveyor of luxury goods but also as a serious contender in the high fashion stakes. In 1994, Gucci relocated all officers from Milan to Florence in another sign of renewal of tradition; Mello left to rejoin Bergdorf Gordman in New York.—CATHERINE WORAM

Halston

American designer

Born   *Roy Halston Frowick in Des Moines, Iowa, 23 April 1932.*
Education   *Studied at Indiana University, Bloomington, and at the Art Institute of Chicago to 1953.*
Career   *Free-lance milliner, Chicago, 1952-53; window dresser, Carson-Pirie-Scott, Chicago, 1954-57; designer and hats division manager, Lilly Daché, New York, 1958-59; millinery and clothing designer, Bergdorf Goodman, New York, 1959-68; founder, designer, Halston Ltd, couture, New York, 1962-73; with Henry Pollack Inc, established Halston International, ready-to-wear, 1970; established Halston Originals ready-to-wear with Ben Shaw, 1972; Halston Ltd renamed Halston Enterprises, 1973, and company, design services and trademark sold to Norton Simon; menswear and signature fragrance introduced 1975; company sold to Esmark, Inc, and Halston III collection initiated for JCPenney Company, 1983; company sold to Revlon, 1986; company has been owned by Halston Borghese Inc. since 1992.*
Exhibitions   *Fashion Institute of Technology, New York, 1991 (retrospective).*
Awards   *Coty American Fashion Critics Award, 1962, 1969, 1971, 1972, 1974.*
Died   *(in San Francisco, California) 26 March 1990.*
Address   *Halston Borghese Inc.; 767 Fifth Ave., 49th Floor, New York, New York 10153, USA.*

The life of Roy Halston Frowick was marked by deeply American directness. He became one name known internationally. But it was, after all, his name in a concise form. In a nonchalant elegance that stripped away all that was superfluous in his life and art, Halston was the creation of his own obsessive, workaholic achievements. In the markedly public world of fashion and in his own dialectic between gregarious social extrovertism and sincere, almost hermetic, privacy, Halston provided a personal contradiction. Gatsby in fashion sovereignty, laconic but inexorable personal charisma, and tragic acumen to cultural need and moment, Halston was in the 1970s and early 1980s not only the supreme American fashion designer, but the quintessential one.

Again and again, Halston would say to the press, as he told Eugenia Sheppard in the *New York Post* (7 February 1973), "Women make fashion. Designers suggest, but it's what women do with the clothes that does the trick." While this modest disavowal is, in part, canny public relations, granting to the client or potential client the creativity of dress, Halston believed his statement. He recognized and accounted for the women who would wear the clothing as much as for his own creation and acknowledged a partnership between designer and wearer. One aspect of the partnership was Halston's continuous synergy with important clients, beginning with his millinery work which, after all, started from the top to reconcile personal attitude and physiognomy with apparel. Later, even as the "total designer" he strove to be and so successfully became, Halston's personal affection for and connections to clients in show business, design, dance, and public life gave him an intimate and abiding affiliation with the wearer. And when he sought to dress every woman, there was a grounded, natural aspect to Halston that readily reminded the wearer that this cryptically simple, *soigné* designer was born in Des Moines, Iowa and raised in Evansville, Indiana.

If Halston ascribed the social function to the wearer, he himself was the consummate creator of the garment in formal terms and his work corresponds to the taciturn discourse of minimalism in American arts. His geometry of design, employing bias as the three-dimensional element that causes the geometry to drape splendidly on the body, was as conceptual as that of Vionnet, if even more abstemious. Some design problems were played out in paper origami, as he created twisted forms in white paper on a black lacquer tray. Discovering such form, Halston projected it onto the body with absolute integrity, cutting as little as possible, and allowing the simplicity of the two-dimensional design to be felt, even as it assumes form on the body.

Likewise, Halston's colours were as selective as Mondrian's, preferring ivory, black, and red, but knowing that fuchsia, electric blue, or deep burgundy could provide accent and emphasis. Of textiles, he worked with cashmere, silk and rayon jerseys, double-faced wools, and Ultrasuede as chosen aesthetic media. His Ultrasuede shirtwaist, which sold 60,000 copies, was one of the most popular dresses in America in the 1970s: in its utmost simplicity, the same dress could be worn in a multitude of ways (collar up or down, sleeves down or rolled, front buttoned or unbuttoned) to allow each woman to wear it in her own personal style. Its success was in that *tabula rasa* plainness and the attraction of contributing one's own style to the garment, as well as the probity of Halston's colour choices and the putative convenience of Ultrasuede, even to its claim of being able to be tossed into the washing machine. His rich double-faced wool coats were the luxury of colour fields, an art brought to apparel; his athletic looks in bodysuits and sports-inspired dressing were as much an ancipation of the late 1980s American fashion as they were renewals of 1940s and 1950s Claire McCardell. He could dress a Martha Graham dancer as readily as he could create a mass-market dress.

Halston's eveningwear was acclaimed for its glittery, gossamer shimmer, but often unacknowledged for the same principles of simplicity. Working on the bias, Halston caressed the body with spiralling scarfs of form. His one-piece, held-at-the-shoulder "orange-peel" dress was the product of a deft hand, like that of the fruit peeler. His evening jackets were often nothing more than rings of material twisted into cocoon fantasies. As Liza Minnelli has said of Halston, he made one feel comfortable and feel beautiful.

Merging the special chic of a custom business and a vast ambition to dress everyone in the world was Halston's high goal, briefly achieved in the late 1970s and early 1980s. But business changes ignited the American Icarus's wings and he plummeted to earth, a loss and an angel ahead of his time to all who might later reconcile high fashion and mass marketing.—RICHARD MARTIN

Hamnett, Katharine

British designer

Born *Gravesend, 1948.*

Education *Studied at Cheltenham Ladies College and at St Martin's School of Art, London, 1965-69.*

Family *Children: Samuel and William.*

Career *Co-founder, Tuttabanken Sportswear, London, 1970; free-lance designer, London, Paris, Rome and Hong Kong, 1970-79; Katharine Hamnett, Ltd founded, London, 1979; menswear line introduced, 1982; launched "Choose Life" shirts, 1983; flagship London shop and three others opened, 1986.*

Awards *International Institute for Cotton Designer of the Year Award, 1982; British Fashion Industry Designer of the Year Award, 1984; Bath Museum of Costume Dress of the Year Award, 1984; Menswear Designer of the Year Award, 1984; British Knitting and Clothing Export Council Award, 1988.*

Address *202 New North Road, London N1 7BJ, England.*

A British designer as much recognized for her political and environmental beliefs as she is for her catwalk collections, Katharine Hamnett designed some of the most plagiarized fashion ideas in the 1980s. Hamnett set up her own company in 1979 after freelancing for various European companies for ten years. Although the designer claims she never intended to become involved in the manufacturing side of the fashion industry, preferring to concentrate solely on design, she was often, as a free-lancer, badly treated. In 1979 she produced her own collection under the Katharine Hamnett Ltd label, of which six jackets were taken by the London fashion retailer, Joseph Ettedgui, and which subsequently sold out. Hamnett's early collections utilized parachute silk, cotton jersey, and drill, which she cut as functional unisex styles, based on traditional workwear that became her hallmark and, like many of her designs, spawned a thousand imitations.

Her nomination as British Fashion Industry Designer of the Year in 1984 testifies to her influence in the early years of that decade. One of Hamnett's most influential designs was the idea of the slogan T-shirt bearing statements about political and environmental issues in bold print on plain white backgrounds. Perhaps the most famous is the one which read "58% Don't Want Pershing" that Hamnett wore when she met Margaret Thatcher at a Downing Street reception in 1984. Like Coco Chanel before her, Hamnett sees imitation as a form of flattery—particularly in the case of her slogan T-shirts which, she says, were meant to be copied to help promote her cause. Another example of Hamnett's obsession with politics was seen in the launch of her own magazine, *Tomorrow*, in 1985, in which the designer attempted to portray both fashion and political views. Unfortunately this combination was not a great success and the magazine folded after the first issue.

Katharine Hamnett: 1984.

By 1986 a change was evident in Hamnett's design as she embraced the theme of sex as power with her Power Dressing collection aimed at the post-feminist woman. Since that time her collections have become decidedly less workwear-oriented, to which critical reactions have been somewhat mixed.

Although the slogan T-shirts are no longer part of her collection, Hamnett's devotion to environmental issues continues to play an important role in her approach to fashion design. One project in which Hamnett became involved is the Pesticides Trust Sustainable Cotton Project, launched in 1990, which is concerned with the environmental costs of cotton production, most specifically the use and misuse of chemical pesticides (insecticides, herbicides, fungicides) and other artificial chemical inputs such as fertilizers and defoliants. The power of the media is seen by Hamnett as a vital instrument in her personal campaign for the protection of the environment, and her fashion has provided an ideal vehicle. Hamnett admits that she has more publicity than she needs to sell the clothes themselves, and can afford to use her influence as a designer to promote her own causes. However, while undoubtedly a major force in British fashion during the 1980s, along with John Galliano and Vivienne Westwood, her influence as a designer has declined in recent years.

Hamnett's most important contribution to fashion, and the one for which she will best be remembered, is her use of clothing as a vehicle for political and environmental concerns. Her success as a fashion designer has enabled her ultimately to pursue her commitment to these issues.—CATHERINE WORAM

Hardwick, Cathy

American designer

Born *Cathaline Kaesuk Sur, in Seoul, Korea, 30 December 1933.*

Education *Studied music in Korea and Japan. Immigrated to the United States, 1952; naturalized, 1959.*

Family *Married Anthony Hardwick in 1966 (divorced); four children.*

Career *Free-lance designer and boutique owner, San Francisco, c.1966-70; knitwear designer, Alvin Duskin, San Francisco, 1960s, and Dranella, Copenhagen; moved to New York, 1960s; sportswear designer, Pranx, New York; designer, Cathy Hardwick 'n' Friends, New York, 1972; president, designer, Cathy Hardwick Ltd., New York, 1975-81, and Cathy Hardwick Design Studio, New York, from 1977; company reorganized, 1988; also, sportswear designer for Sears Roebuck and Co., from 1990.*

Awards *Coty American Fashion Critics Award, 1975.*

Address *215 West 40th Street, New York, New York 10018, USA.*

Cathy Hardwick designs ready-to-wear for the audience she knows best—the modern career woman with an active lifestyle. There is a certain spirit and success about Hardwick's designs that come from this defining relationship to the clothing and its purpose. Hardwick's collections consistently offer women clothing with ease and simplicity, appealing to the young and young-minded spirit of the confident, self-assured businesswoman. Her clothing is not merely a somber uniform, but rather it has an air of wit and sophistication that makes it fun, worn by the stylish young woman who is secure with her life and is moving in a positive direction.

Cathy Hardwick was recognized early in her career as a talented young designer involved in creating simplistic, modern clothing. In the late 1960s she began designing knitwear for Alvin Duskin in San Francisco. The designs were well received and commercially successful. Soon after, she developed her own company and continued to design knitwear as a part of her collections throughout the 1970s and 1980s. She continues to design under her own label in New York, using natural fibers almost exclusively.

"Know your physical type and personal style, and be true to it. Any current look can be adapted in silhouette, scale and color so it's right for you. You have to feel comfortable. The most fabulous clothes won't work if you're self-conscious," says Cathy Hardwick (*Harper's Bazaar*, February 1978).

Hardwick's design success is a result of the masterful execution of her pure and basic principles—neutral colors and simplicity of form. By centering her collections around basic, neutral colors and relating the colors of current collections to previous ones, the wearer can develop a wardrobe of pieces that work together. Her designs recognize fashion trends but always retain a clean, simplistic style that is distinctly her own. Hardwick's clothing is associated with the modern woman's ability to go from an effective day at work to an evening out with minimal changes.

A 1980 advertisement for B. Altman and Co. shows her collection coordinating in different ways to suit the style of the potential wearer. The ad reads: "Hardwick's done a forward looking collection that lets you choose the new length you like, a little or a whole lot shorter. Another fine fashion point you should notice: These separates are all cut and colored (in magenta and black) so you can build your own new-decade pants-set." The philosophy of personal style and selection is one that is apparent in Hardwick's collections throughout her career.

Hardwick's collections are based on strong, simple shapes reminiscent of traditional Korean clothing. She was born to a Korean family of diplomats and financiers including her grandfather, who was ambassador to France. Hardwick's clothing reflects her life-long exposure to and depth of understanding of the fusion of Eastern and Western styles. The *chinoiserie* elements in the designs seem to be a part of the total vision and philosophy that she has about clothing rather than a motif that is applied on Western fashion. In her first formal show in New York in 1974, Hardwick showed *obi* style wrapping in the closures of her skirts and trousers along with oriental prints and accessories. In 1975, she showed the effectiveness of shaping a "Big Dress" with an *obi*-inspired tie. Earlier Hardwick incorporated frog closures in her mandarin collared jacket for a more direct use of the Eastern look. The mandarin collar and frog closures are used again in her spring 1994 collection on light and easy shaped tops.—DENNITA SEWELL

Hartnell, Norman

British designer

Born *London, 12 June 1901.*

Education *Studied at Magdalen College, Cambridge, 1921-23.*

Career *Assistant to Court Dressmaker, Mme. Désiré, 1923; opened own dressmaking studio, London, 1923; first Paris showing, 1927; appointed dressmaker to the Royal Family, 1938; designed women's uniforms for the Royal Army Corps and the Red Cross;*

introduced ready-to-wear lines, from 1942; also designed for Berkertex, from the late 1940s, for Women's Illustrated magazine, 1950-60s, and lingerie line for Saks Fifth Avenue, 1950s; theatrical designer, 1923-60s.

Exhibitions *Norman Hartnell, 1901-1979 (retrospective), London, 1985; Norman Hartnell (retrospective), Brighton, 1985; Hartnell: Clothes by the Royal Couturier, 1930s-1960s (retrospective), Bath, 1985-86.*

Awards *Officier d'Academie, France, 1939; first Royal Warrant received, 1940; Neiman Marcus Award, 1947; appointed Member of the Royal Victorian Order, 1953; appointed Knight Commander of the Royal Victorian Order, 1977.*

Died *(in Windsor, Berkshire), 8 June 1979.*

Norman Hartnell began his fashion career working as an assistant to the extravagant society couturière Lucile. Through his exposure to this rarefied world of fashion, gossip, decoration, and illicit romance, he was inspired to open his own dressmaking business in 1923, establishing what has become one of the best-known and longest-running couture houses in Britain. Situated in the heart of London's Mayfair, the house on Bruton Street has always had an air of splendour. A graceful staircase, panelled with mirrors, leads up to the splendid salon where gilt mirrors and two giant crystal chandeliers create an air of tranquillity. Seated on their gilt-encrusted chairs, society hostesses, actresses, film stars, debutantes, and royalty have watched countless collections float elegantly by.

The early collections shown in both London and Paris quickly established Hartnell's reputation for lavishly embroidered ballgowns in satin and tulle, fur trimmed suits, and elegantly tailored tweed day ensembles. His first wedding dress fashioned from silver and gold net was a showstopping finale to an early collection and was described as "the eighth wonder of the world" when worn by the bride of Lord Weymouth. Other early commissions included a 1927 wedding dress for romantic novelist and socialite Barbara Cartland, and informal clothes for actress Tallulah Bankhead who scandalized 1920s London with performances both on and off-stage.

Hartnell's clothes often stood apart from fashion, owing a greater allegiance to costume. This was no doubt fuelled by his early experience designing theatrical productions whilst at Cambridge University. He drew inspiration from the saucy French paintings of Watteau and Boucher, purity of line from Italian masters like Botticelli and painters such as Renoir and Tissot for what he described as a touch of "chi chi." Summoned to Buckingham Palace on the succession of King George VI to discuss designs for the coronation dresses of the maids of honour, the King led them through the hall of Winterhalter portraits. This gave him the inspiration for the crinoline dresses that would later become a symbolic royal look for the two monarchs—Queen Elizabeth the Queen Mother and Queen Elizabeth II. The dresses also influenced the silhouette of Dior's New Look of 1947, a line that came to epitomize a post-war return to femininity.

Hartnell was officially appointed dressmaker to the royal family in 1938 and subsequently designed for various royal occasions, eventually being acknowledged for creating a stylistic royal image that remains today. He was responsible for both the wedding dresses of Queen Elizabeth II and Princess Margaret. In 1953 he created the Queen's historic coronation dress, embroidered with the emblems of Great Britain and the Commonwealth. The House of Hartnell is today still responsible for the personal wardrobe of Queen Elizabeth the Queen Mother.

It could be argued that Hartnell limited himself as a designer by his work for British royalty and aristocracy. He created to promote and protect an establishment, encasing it in a grandiose aura of ornament and glamour, a service that was honoured by a knighthood in 1977. However, it should be remembered that Hartnell also produced ready-to-wear collections, sold through department stores from 1942 onwards. He also designed for Berkertex and created the uniforms of the British Red Cross and the Women's Royal Army Corps during World War II.

Although Norman Hartnell died in 1979 his legacy is continued today by the French couturier Marc Bohan, who is responsible for the design of the haute couture collections and maintaining the Hartnell name as a major force in contemporary fashion.—KEVIN ALMOND

Heim, Jacques

French designer

Born *Paris, 8 May 1899.*

Family *Married; one son: Philippe.*

Career *Manager, Isadore and Jeanne Heim fur fashion house, from c.1920; initiated couture department for coats, suits and gowns, c.1925; opened own couture house, 1930; Heim Jeunes Filles collection introduced, 1936; Heim sportswear boutiques established in Biarritz and Cannes, from 1937; Heim-Actualité girlswear collection introduced, 1950; fragrances include Alambie, 1947, J'Aime, 1958, Shandoah, 1966; house closed, 1969. President, Chambre Syndicale de la Couture Parisienne, 1958-62. Also: owner and publisher, Revue Heim, 1950s.*

Died *(in Paris) 8 January 1967.*

"An innovator by nature," says Caroline Rennolds Milbank of Jacques Heim (*Couture: The Great Designers,* New York 1985). Few would agree. The *New York Times* obituary (9 January 1967) read: "Mr Heim's fashion house designed and made clothes of a modest style. He was never in the front ranks of the big houses that radically changed the looks of women by offering new silhouettes in the manner of Balenciaga, Chanel or Saint Laurent." Perhaps the median truth was expressed in *Women's Wear Daily's* obituary (9 January 1967): "Heim was basically an innovator in business. He didn't want to be called a designer, but rather an editor of clothes." He was aggressive in conceiving of ways in which the couture might be vital to new audiences (his Heim Jeunes Filles brought garments to a young audience, even before the boutiques of other couture designers, and engendered early client loyalty) and an impeccable (until he broke with the couture schedule for delayed photographs in summer 1962) spokesman for the fashion industry of France. He was an editor of many design ideas, beginning with the possibilities of fur, continuing through beach and play outfits, even the two-piece swimsuit, and the plane and planar simplifications of design in the youth-conscious 1960s.

If he was not driven by the market, he was at least keenly sensitive to it. In *Femina* in April 1928, spring Heim fashions are casual and sportswear-inspired, with low waists and combinations of fur and textile. In autumn 1950, day suits swing out from the waist with Balenciaga equilibrium; spring 1950 evening gowns and a two-piece shantung suit are indebted to Dior. Heim was a smart, eclectic designer of many styles. In that consistent sales sensitivity he had transformed the fur business of his parents Isadore and Jeanne Heim, founded in 1898, and persevered and prospered as a designer for nearly four decades. But his commerce was clearly his passion and his *métier,* not the design itself. The *New York Times* obituary said, "Jacques Heim, a tall good-looking man with a cheery disposition, seemed more like a businessman or banker than a couturier. He exhibited none of the flamboyance or temperament of competitors like Yves Saint Laurent or Christian Dior." But, of course, design is made by acumen as well as by inspiration.

Heim's fashion breakthrough was to realize that fur could be worked as a fabric. Wool and fur combinations, geometries of fur and textiles, and fur accents became hallmarks of the Heim fashion in the 1930s. At the same time, along with Chanel and Patou and others, Heim was alert to the possibilities of elegant sportswear and observed bathing and sports costumes as inspiration. According to Milbank, Heim was inspired by the Tahitian exhibits in the Paris colonial exhibition of 1931 to create *pareos* and sarongs. Later, his 1950 two-piece swimsuit Atome came considerably after the bikini incident and invention, but addressed a broader public.

Through the 1950s, Heim addressed American needs for sportswear in innovative and utilitarian fabrics, while still remaining, in the vocabulary of the day, very ladylike. Moreover, his Heim *Actualité* diffusion line, launched in 1950, extended his influence into ready-to-wear along with the young styles of Heim Jeunes Filles. From 1958 to 1962 he was President of the Chambre Syndicale de la Couture Parisienne, "probably the last effective president of the couture's professional body," according to *Women's Wear Daily.* When, however, he permitted immediate release of collection photographs to the press in July 1962, in advance of the agreed-upon delayed release, he precipitated a furor among designers still eager, in the old way, to preserve the design's secret until their slow dissemination. Heim was steadfastly modern and business-oriented. In this decision, he anticipated the couture's gradual *détente* in the 1960s, but did it so abruptly that he lost the confidence of his colleagues. Patricia Peterson reported, "Photographs were not to have been published in the United States until August 26. For Europe the release date was to have been August 27. When Heim allowed photographs to run even before the opening, the chase was on to find photographers. Men used to shooting wars, riots, and dignitaries were suddenly faced with swirling models. Other couture houses were besieged with queries." (*New York Times,* 23 July 1962). Perhaps it always takes an insider to bring the certain news of change, but Heim was as wounded as any messenger with the apparent bad tidings that couture's control was over and the camera and the press held sway.

Favored by Mme. Charles de Gaulle and a designer for Mrs. Dwight D. Eisenhower, Heim would have understood the expression "old soldiers never die." He had never married a style or become one form's advocate. Instead, he had insisted on the business principle that fashion would thrive in change and adaptation. "The life of a couturier is a magnificent and continuous torture," Heim said. But he was probably only expressing a businessman's shrewd romanticism and a leader's quixotic belief in fashion's anguish.—RICHARD MARTIN

Heisel, Sylvia

American fashion designer

> **Born** *Princeton, New Jersey, 22 June 1963.*
> **Education** *Barnard College, New York, 1980–81.*

Heisel

Career Designed and sold costume jewelry, 1981-82; designed collection of coats for Henri Bendel, New York, 1982, and exclusive line of womenswear for Barney's, New York, 1987; first full catwalk collection shown, 1988. Also film costume designer mid-1980s.

Awards Chicago Gold Coast Award, 1993.

Address 580 Broadway, New York, New York 10012, U.S.A.

I think fashion is about who you are right now. What you're wearing says who you are at that moment in time. It's the first thing you communicate to another person.

My favorite clothes are easy, comfortable, creative, and beautiful because that's what I'm attracted to in people. What we wear is a combination of reality and what is in our minds. The reality is where we have to go, what we have to do, and what we can afford. The dream is who we want to be, what's beautiful and exciting to us, and what we desire. I try to design clothes with a combination of these qualities: wearability in the real world with an aesthetic of dreams.

Sylvia Heisel: Front-slit dress in eggplant silk crepe with green lining, 1992.

H
----
fashion

Inspiration comes from everything in the world, more often from the *Zeitgeist* than from other pieces of clothing or designed items. Historically, fashion is interesting because of what it says about any particular moment in history. What looks good, new, and exciting one day looks old and tired the next. It is the most transient of art and design fields.

The clothes I design combine skills of construction and manufacturing with the communication of my ideas.—Sylvia Heisel

Sophisticated elegance is perhaps the most distinguishing characteristic of Sylvia Heisel's collections. Heisel's use of exquisite fabrics, colors and the simplicity of cuts have assured her favorable recognition by fashion buyers and critics alike. As one of New York's young contemporary fashion designers, Heisel has instinctively avoided catering to recent trends. Her approach to fashion combines an "aesthetic of dreams" with the reality of modern wearability and affordability.

Heisel studied art history briefly at Barnard, leaving college eventually to pursue a free-lance career designing costume jewelry, theatre costuming, and fashion display. With no formal training in fashion design, Heisel launched her first coat collection for Henri Bendel in New York, followed by an exclusive line for Barney's first women's store in New York in 1987. Her first independent collection appeared in the spring of 1988.

Heisel is interested in communicating ideas intrinsic to particular moments in history. The 1980s emphasis on body consciousness led Heisel to embrace the notion of executing a controlled draping of her now signature slip and tank dresses. Constructed in fabrics such as jersey, mesh, and silk, these dresses are contoured, accentuating the body with deep cut backs and high slits. They are simultaneously wearable and feminine.

The growth of professional American women in the job market highlighted the fashion designers' need to accommodate this new status with garments both practical and timeless. Heisel addressed these needs with small, tightly edited collections, including "sportswear inspired suits, separates for day and sophisticated dresses and coats for evening." Her jackets range from waist-length to sleek over-the-hip styles. The selected fabrics, such as silk and wool crêpe, are comfortable and travel well. Her garments are architectural, employing both body-fitting silhouettes and a boxy construction in her coats and jackets. Heisel's color selection is based on instinct rather than forecasts and she often uses black for balance. The use of solids highlights the minimalist cut, drape, and texture of each garment. At the same time, simplicity allows for a variety of ways of wearing each piece.

Heisel's awareness of contemporary culture was successfully transferred into costume designs for the 1985 film *Parting Glances*. In 1985 Heisel was included by the *New York Times* in the list of young designers—including Carol Horn, Cathy Hardwick, and Mary Jane Marcasiano—who are "currying favours with American women and retailers." Heisel has on several occasions deviated from collections based on minimalist constructions—fake pony-fur coats, lizard prints, and McFaddenesque dresses. She still maintains a consistent approach, stressing that how a woman feels in her clothes is as much a part as how the clothes look.—TEAL TRIGGS

Herrera, Carolina

Venezuelan designer working in New York

Born *Maria Carolina Josefina Pacanins y Nino in Caracas, Venezuela, 8 January 1939.*

Education *El Carmen School, Venezuela.*

Family *Married Reinaldo Herrera in 1957; children: Mercedes, Ana Luisa, Carolina, Patricia.*

Career *Showed first couture collection, 1981; introduced fur collection for Revillion, 1984; launched CH diffusion line, 1986, Couture Bridal collection, 1987, Carolina Herrera Collection II sportswear line, 1989, Herrera for Men, Herrera Studio bridge line and W by Carolina Herrera, 1992; Carolina Herrera fragrances introduced, 1988; jewelry collections introduced, 1990, 1991;*

Awards *Pratt Institute Award, 1990.*

Address *501 Seventh Avenue, New York, NY 10018, USA.*

When Carolina Herrera introduced her first fashion collection in 1981, *Women's Wear Daily,* New York dubbed her "Our Lady of the Sleeve." Her early interest in the shoulder area has remained constant throughout her many lines and seasons. The Herrera look is characterized by strong, fitted shoulders, tight bodices, straight lines and slightly pushed-up sleeves.

Though she has often been referred to as a socialite turned designer, her contributions to the industry are many. Prior to beginning her career as a designer, Carolina Herrera was on the International Best Dressed List for over ten years and was then nominated to the Best Dressed Hall of Fame. Her personal style influenced how women dressed around the world. Her affluent, South American background exposed her to the work of the best couturiers and dressmakers in the world. She cites Balenciaga as her greatest influence. It was a natural transition from socialite to fashion designer, as Herrera is a member of the world for which she designs. She understands her customer's lifestyles and needs because she is one of them. Her friends, impressed with her design quality, fabric selection, attention to detail, construction and drape, also became her clients.

Herrera's designs have been described as being for the "quintessential woman of the 1980s who has consummate style and taste as well as an active lifestyle." Her clothes have a couture element, feminine detail, and genuine ease. Herrera herself believes that her clothes are feminine, elegant and, most importantly, comfortable. Though she loves to mix and match expensive Italian and French fabrics, she maintains the importance of the cut of the clothes. Herrera states, "You don't have to buy very expensive materials if the clothes are well cut." In terms of color, Herrera favors the combination of black and white and black and brown.

Becoming a designer seemed a logical evolution in Herrera's life. She married and had four children. She came to symbolize the upper-class South American lifestyle. When her children were grown, she decided, with the financial backing of a wealthy South American publisher, to open a design house in New York.

Like many designers, Herrera expanded her business to include other lines. The CH Collections, introduced in 1986, are less expensive versions of her high-fashion lines, similar silhouettes in cut and finish but made of different fabrics. Herrera also launched a successful

Carolina Herrera: Fall/Winter 1995/96; Persian blue re-embroidered lace halter gown with tulle skirt.
Photograph by Patrice Casanova.

bridal line in 1987 after designing Caroline Kennedy's wedding gown. A perfume for both women (1988) and men (1991) also followed.

In the early collections, Herrera's strengths were in her day dresses and luncheon suits. They expressed femininity through their beautifully tailored hour-glass design. In more recent collections, Herrera has ventured into the downtown New York scene for inspiration, showing chiffon split skirts topped with satin motorcycle jackets, thus illustrating her ability to interpret and combine the surrounding culture with her own design sense. Most importantly Carolina Herrera's clothes are about style and elegance achieved by her trademark of shoulders, sleeves, line, and construction.—MARGO SEAMAN

Hilfiger, Tommy

American designer

Born *1952.*

Career *Owner and designer, People's Places, New York, until 1979; founder, designer and vice-chairman, Tommy Hilfiger Corporation, New York; company floated on Stock Exchange, 1992. Member of Council of Fashion Designers of America.*

Address *25 West 39th St, New York, NY 10018, USA.*

In an article titled "Throwing Down the Trousers" (*Newsweek*, 11 July 1994), Calvin Klein and Tommy Hilfiger are rendered in a showdown over men's underwear, the former having long occupied Times Square (New York) billboard space with provocative underwear ads. Hilfiger, seen standing on Broadway and 44th Street with his boxer-clad male models, meekly states, "My image is all about good, clean fun. I think Calvin's image is about maybe something different." Hilfiger is smart. He juxtaposes his hunky models in boxers in flag and stripe designs at surfer jam length with the implied enemy in bawdy, black, sopping promiscuity. Hilfiger has been right—in design and business—in promising "good, clean fun" in an unabashed American style that has achieved phenomenal success. America has wanted a menswear mainstream, neither aristocratic nor licentious. Emerging first in the 1980s with a clever campaign announcing himself among established designers, he has come to fulfil his own declaration to become one of the leading names in American design, certainly in menswear.

Acknowledging "I'm both a designer and a businessman" (*Amtrak Express*, September-October 1993), Hilfiger divides his own successful role into its two components that he himself has rendered indivisible. Hilfiger has indubitably learned from older American designers Ralph Lauren and Calvin Klein that fashion is a synergy of business, aspiration, and classic design—with the image and craving that constitute aspiration perhaps the most important element. Hilfiger has shrewdly and wonderfully chosen a particular place for himself in American menswear imagery. Whereas Lauren has pre-empted old-money WASP styles and Klein has successfully created a sexy vivacity, Hilfiger has come closer to Main Street, a colorful Americana that still waves flags, that still loves button-down collars, that appreciates classics, that adores his "good, clean fun" along with family values and may even abhor pretence or promiscuity, that strives for college and collegiate looks but would never rebel too much even on campus, and that dresses a little more modestly and traditionally than those who prefer his designer-commerce confreres. His closest kinship (or competitor) in the market is David Chu's similarly brilliant work for Nautica, likewise reaching into the small-town, cautious American sensibility for roots and imagination.

The "real people" effectiveness of Hilfiger is, of course, both real and illusory: he is stirring the deep-felt American conservative sensibilities of the late 20th century at the very moment at which culture is annulling any vestigial *Our Town* sentimentalities. The "feel good" ethos of Hilfiger's design is not image alone, for his intense commitment to value-for-price and quality materials confirms the joy in his design. His colorful, sporty, comfortable clothing appealed preeminently in the 1980s to the middle-class in America. By the 1990s, Hilfiger was a clothing symbol of African-American and Hispanic urban youth, engendering immense street-smart urban loyalty along with his classic Main-Street constituency. Hilfiger's clothing is readily identified, with logo crest on shirttails, pockets, or even boxer waistband center-front; green "eyes" (green-lined buttonhole on the breast pocket flap near the heart) on pockets; and contrasting linings within collars.

Hilfiger has associated himself with two other popular American images, both with special appeal to youth: sports teams and rock music. He has captured a 30-something client who is ageing into his 40s, and yet Hilfiger is also building his young following. Hilfiger's great success has defied much élitist fashion skepticism. Ruth La Ferla reported unforgivingly, "As a 'name' designer Mr Hilfiger sprang full grown from the mind of his sponsor, Mohan Murjani, in the mid-80s. Explicitly promoted as a successor to Perry Ellis or Calvin Klein or Ralph Lauren, Mr Hilfiger achieved a degree of fame, or notoriety. But the stunt never came off; Mr Hilfiger's fashions and image did not gel" (*New York Times,* 31 July 1990). Of course, American enterprise is full of "stunts," from P. T. Barnum to Henry Ford to Dr Kellogg, all with origins in harmless chicanery and old-fashioned *chutzpah*. Despite detractors, Hilfiger has consistently created his own dynamic and vigorous vision. After Murjani's backing, Hilfiger took his business public on the New York Stock Exchange in 1992, a rare instance of a designer name business trading with success.

In 1994, Hilfiger added tailored clothing to his line, confident that the men who have already associated him with comfort and clean-cut exuberance would carry those same ideals to a full-cut American suit or jacket for business. In 1988, Hilfiger had spoken in his own advertising, "The clothes I design are relaxed, comfortable, somewhat traditional, affordable and . . . simple. They are the classic American clothes we've always worn, but I've reinterpreted them so that they fit more easily into the lives we live today." His sensitivity to casual wear (and his sympathetic American ethos of inclusiveness) can be brought to the business side of the male wardrobe, especially as it is already inflected by casual and sports-influenced notes. Part of his business acumen and pragmatism is expressed in his statement to Joseph Younger that he wants to dress men from head to toe before beginning to dress women (though his full-bodied shirts and oversized trousers are often borrowed). But, of course, there is no end to a wish as empowered and desirable as Tommy Hilfiger's distinct and determined American dream.—RICHARD MARTIN

Hulanicki, Barbara

British designer

Born *Warsaw, Poland, 8 December 1936. Raised in Palestine, immigrated to England in 1948.*

Education *Studied fashion and fashion illustration at Brighton College, 1954-56; winner in the Evening Standard Design Competition, beachwear division, 1955.*

Family *Married Stephen Fitz-Simon in 1961; one son: Witwold.*

Career *Illustrator for Helen Jardine Artists, London, c.1956-59; free-lance fashion illustrator, 1961-64; opened Biba's Postal Boutique, 1963; established first Biba emporium, Abingdon Road, London, 1964; moved and expanded to Church Street, London, 1965; opened branch location in Brighton, 1966; launched mail order catalogue, 1968; moved Biba to High Street, Kensington, London, 1969; introduced line of Biba cosmetics, 1969; cosmetics distributed nationally through Dorothy Perkins shops, 1969; introduced line of footwear, 1969; 75% interest in company sold to consortium of investors, 1969; Biba boutique established at Bergdorf Goodman, New York, 1970; purchased Derry and Toms Department Store for "Big Biba," 1972; control of firm passed to British Land, 1972; Big Biba opened, 1973, closed, 1975; firm declared bankruptcy, 1976. Fashion designer in Brazil, 1976-80; relocated to Miami Beach, Florida, 1987; designer of hotel and club interiors, videos, ready-to-wear children's clothes, theatre costumes, from 1988.*

Exhibitions *Retrospective, Newarke Houses Museum, Leicester, England, 1993.*

Awards *Bath Museum of Costume Dress of the Year Award, 1972.*

Address *1300 Collins Avenue, Suite 205, Miami Beach, Florida 35139, USA.*

In the decade from 1964 to 1974, Barbara Hulanicki's design and entrepreneurial skills contributed to the development of an entirely new ethos in British fashion which responded to ideas generated by the rising youth culture of the period. Hulanicki and her husband Stephen Fitz-Simon created a series of fashion businesses, under the name of Biba, perfectly suited to the spirit of change and adventure which characterized the Mod movement originating in London during the early 1960s. Unlike the English establishment rag trade, Hulanicki understood that fashion ideas would, henceforth, originate in the streets of British cities, rather than in couture houses across the Channel. She styled her shop as a meeting spot and a place of entertainment for those interested in a lifestyle represented by the clothes and other goods designed by Hulanicki.

Following a year at art school, Hulanicki set up Biba's Postal Boutique in the early 1960s, with herself as designer and Fitz-Simon as business manager. The success of their business was assured when an early design for a simple smock dress was worn by Cathy McGowan, "Queen of the Mods," on the popular television programme *Ready, Steady, Go*. The first Biba shop was opened in 1964 in a small, old-fashioned chemist's shop on a corner of Abingdon Road, Kensington, London. Hulanicki concentrated on generating a unique atmosphere through décor, music, and the glamour of the young shop assistants—all of which turned her shop into an instant "scene," a gathering place for a hip, young clientèle who knew where to go for the latest ideas in clothing, without even the benefit of a sign over the shop-front.

Hulanicki's early clothes were short, simple dresses, the "Biba smock" which became the uniform for an era. Her little girl look was given a major boost when Julie Christie selected her wardrobe for the film *Darling* from the Biba shop. Other early customers included Sonny and Cher, Twiggy, and Mick Jagger. The typical Biba dolly girl would have a slim, boyish figure, huge eyes and a child-like pout, updating the Audrey Hepburn gamine look of the 1950s. She would wear a simple mini dress selected from a wide range of muted colours, blueberry, rust, plum, which Hulanicki called Auntie colours, as they had previously been associated with the wardrobes of old ladies. At this time, she also introduced the first fashion T-shirts, distinguished from their ordinary equivalent by the range of Auntie colours in which they were dyed. The T-shirts initiated the unisex appeal of Biba goods.

In 1966, the shop moved to larger premises in Kensington Church Street. The new shop sported a black and gold art nouveau logo and was decorated in an eclectic mix of late 19th-century decadent motifs, Victoriana and art deco. Hulanicki expanded her range of clothing to include fashion accessories, including bangles and feather boas displayed on old-fashioned bentwood hatstands, cosmetics, menswear, and household accessories. The Church Street Biba became an internationally known symbol of Swinging London in the mid-1960s.

In the early 1970s, the Biba style developed in the direction of retro glamour and glitter. Hulanicki introduced a line of children's clothing which followed the styles and colours of the adult ranges. She featured items such as straw hats with veils and artificial flowers, velvet and lace, all enhanced by a new element of innocent eroticism and un-childlike glamour. Her cosmetics had, by the late 1960s, become big business, the range of colours corresponding to the Auntie colours of her clothing and including bizarre hues such as blue, green, purple, and black lipstick, eye-shadow and powder.

Rapidly increasing sales forced Biba to move again, in 1969, to a larger shop in Kensington High Street where art nouveau and art deco fused into a single style which became Biba's own. During the early 1970s, Hulanicki and Fitz-Simon expanded their operations to the United States through New York's Bergdorf Goodman, which set up a Biba boutique in its flagship store.

The final phase of expansion came in 1973 when Hulanicki opened the Biba department store in the former Derry and Toms premises in Kensington High Street, London. This enormous art deco building housed a huge enterprise which provided a complete setting, including an all-day restaurant and nightly entertainment in the glamorous Rainbow Room, exotic roof gardens, and a kasbah for the elegant and exotic retro style clothes, all designed by Hulanicki. The Biba store was, for a short time, a mecca for fashionable young Londoners looking for a setting in which to parade the elegant and eclectic clothing of the period. Management difficulties forced Hulanicki to leave Biba in the mid-1970s. She eventually moved to Brazil and thence to Florida, where she began to design under the Hulanicki name.—GREGORY VOTOLATO

H
fashion

Jackson, Betty

British designer

Born *Bacup, Lancashire, 24 June 1949.*

Education *Studied at Birmingham College of Art, 1968-71.*

Family *Married David Cohen in 1985; children: Pascale and Oliver.*

Career *Free-lance fashion illustrator, London, 1971-73; design assistant to Wendy Dagworthy, London, 1973-75; chief designer, Quorum, London, 1975-81. Director and chief designer, Betty Jackson Ltd., London, from 1981; Betty Jackson for Men collection introduced, 1986; opened flagship shop in the Brompton Road, London, 1991.*

Awards *Woman Magazine Separates Designer of the Year Award, London, 1981, 1983; Cotton Institute Cotton Designer of the Year Award, 1983; Bath Museum of Costume Dress of the Year Award, 1984; British Designer of the Year Award, 1985; Harvey Nichols Award, 1985; International Linen Council Fil d'Or Award, 1985, 1989; Viyella Award, 1987; Honorary Fellow, Royal College of Art, London, 1989; Fellow, Birmingham Polytechnic, 1989; Honorary Fellow, University of Central Lancashire, 1992; Member of the British Empire, 1987.*

Address *33 Tottenham Street, London W1P 9PE, England.*

My work is understated and easy. I do not like formal dressing and I always try to achieve a relaxed and casual look. The mix of texture and pattern is very important and we work with many textile designers to have specialness and exclusivity on fabrics. Unexpected fabrics are often used in simple, classic shapes.—Betty Jackson

"What makes you most depressed?," Betty Jackson was once asked by a fashion editor. Her reply was that it was only when work was going badly and that in such situations strength of character and conviction became important assets. It comes as no surprise therefore to find that

Betty Jackson: Autumn/Winter 1996.

she admires strong women, "Bold and casual like Lauren Bacall." A stoic, no-nonsense fashion approach underpins a business that Jackson declares began in a recession only to find itself in one again when the company celebrated its tenth anniversary in 1991.

Betty Jackson began her career at Birmingham College of Art in 1968, working in London as a free-lance fashion illustrator until 1973 when she joined Wendy Dagworthy as her design assistant. She moved to further positions at Quorum, then Coopers, before setting up her own design company with husband David Cohen in 1981. Success was quick to come, culminating in several awards including The Cotton Institute Designer of the Year in 1983 and the Fil d'or Award from the International Linen Council in 1985, the year she was also named British Designer of the Year; two years later she was awarded the MBE in the Queen's Birthday Honours list for services to British industry and export as well as becoming an elected member of The British Fashion Council.

Betty Jackson has gained an international reputation as a designer of young, up-to-the-minute clothes. "I've never liked prettiness much," she is quoted as saying, and this is reflected in her designs. She rescales separates into larger and unstructured proportions. Loose, uncomplicated shapes with no awkward cuts are often made up in boldly coloured and patterned fabrics. Jackson loves bright prints and knits, often working in conjunction with the textile designers Timney Fowler in colours that complement the warm, smoky, and earthy base colours of the collections. The oversized printed shirts and hand knit sweaters are always popular and usually the first garments to sell out. Previous print and knit themes have been inspired by Sonia Delauney, oversized paisleys or abstract painterly shapes and textures reminiscent of Matisse or Braque.

The rescaled sporty shapes give the clothes an androgynous feeling which was reflected when the menswear collection was launched in 1986. However Jackson never uses androgyny to shock or alienate her established customer or to make a fashion statement. Instead her themes evolve each season, incorporating the newest shapes, lengths, and fabrics. She tends to favour expensive, supple fabrics like linen, suede, or viscose mixes, crêpes, chenilles, and soft jerseys.

She has said that she prefers not to follow trends set by other designers or predictions from fashion forecasters. Instead she prefers to source her own ides for inspiration; ideas that are relevant to her and her own design philosophies. "There's nothing like taking a colour you love, making something wonderful, and seeing a beautiful girl wearing it. I think if you ever tire of that feeling, then it's time to think again," she says.

The most recent developments at Betty Jackson Ltd have been the opening of a shop which she describes as her greatest extravagance. She was quick, however, to deny that extravagance implied recklessness ". . . and it's certainly not reckless as it's part of a well laid plan." She has also turned her talents to accessories; chunky jewellery in bright colours encased in bronze and silver, soft suede gloves, belts, bags, and printed scarves.

Jackson declares that the single thing that would most improve the quality of her life would be more time. "I organize myself badly and never have enough time to do anything." It is the dilemma of many creative people, forced to sacrifice precious creative time to the day-to-day practicalities of running a business. However, lack of time has not halted Betty Jackson's achievements; her business is thriving and she has recently been made honorary fellow of both the Royal College of Art, London, and the University of Central Lancashire.—KEVIN ALMOND

Jacobs, Marc

American designer

Born *New York City, 1964.*
Education *Graduated from Parsons School of Design, New York, 1984.*
Career *Designer, Sketchbook label, for Ruben Thomas Inc., New York, 1984–85; managed own firm, 1986–88; named vice-president for womenswear, Perry Ellis, 1988; head designer, Perry Ellis, New York, 1989–93, Marc Jacobs, 1994–.*
Awards *Parsons School of Design Perry Ellis Golden Thimble Award, 1984; Council of Fashion Designers of America Perry Ellis Award, 1988; Womenswear Designer of the Year Award, 1992.*
Address *113 Spring Street, New York, New York 10012, USA.*

Marc Jacobs was from the start a fashion legend, a prodigy of mythical talent, tribulation, and triumph who attains unequivocal success and authority. The legend is indisputably true, but the clothing tells a similar and instructive story in which a special genius is realized in clothing—encyclopedic in its sources, poignantly romantic, remarkably sophisticated, and yet imperturbably impudent and joyous. Through a succession of labels and collections, Jacobs has consistently demonstrated a strong personal sensibility of the kind that marks clothing definably and, in his case, the history of clothing forever.

Jacobs's first collection was hand-knit sweaters produced by Charivari, the New York clothing store where he worked as stock boy. Fatefully, those sweaters earned him the Perry Ellis Golden Thimble Award at Parsons. Upon graduation in 1984, he designed Sketchbook for Ruben Thomas through fall 1985. There, he created a memorable collection based on the film *Amadeus*. In 1986, he began designing his own label, first with backing from Jack Atkins and later from Onward Kashiyama. In fall 1988, Jacobs was named vice-president for womenswear at Perry Ellis, succeeding Patricia Pastor who had worked with and succeeded Ellis. Along the way, there were Homeric afflictions and distress, ranging from a major theft at the Ruben Thomas showroom to a fire that gutted his Kashiyama studio and destroyed his fall 1988 collection and fabrics two months before showings. The appointment at Perry Ellis was, of course, only another trial for a then-25-year-old designer. As Peggy Edersheim wrote in *Manhattan, Inc.,* "Instead of staying one step ahead of the bill collector, he now has to worry about keeping up with Calvin Klein," a prodigious challenge in leadership for one of the principal sportswear houses in America. However, Jacobs made a great critical success of Perry Ellis, re-instilling the firm with the bountiful energy and excitement of its founder.

Significantly, Jacobs's works reflect Ellis's design. Jacobs did not perpetuate Ellis, but expanded on fundamental traits. For example, Ellis's imaginative, imagistic, even painterly palette was hauntingly revived in Jacobs's work, including extraordinary colors of fall in ocher, pumpkin, plum, camel, and rust, renewing the vitality of the Ellis spectrum. In fall 1991, Jacobs showed a grape princess coat over a brown cardigan, and a tangerine car coat with a butterscotch sweater and trousers with complete coloristic self-confidence. Ellis's sensuous fabrics are transmuted into Jacobs's hallmark sophistication: cashmere, camel, wool and angora, and mohair are soft, sumptuous materials. Moreover, Jacobs returns again and again to a basic vocabulary of design, treating each new interpretation of stripes, American flag, tartan, or gingham with a renewing luxury. His tailoring is also refined, returning to such classics as a Norfolk jacket or the eight-button double-breasted camel wool flannel suit for fall 1990 that appeared on the front page of _Women's Wear Daily._

Jacobs's special interests include homages to designers he admires. His "hugs" sequined dress of 1985 remembers Schiaparelli and his spring 1990 English sycamore sequined short sheath "for Perry Ellis" was a touching condensation of the workroom and showroom environment of Perry Ellis, with its silver accents on a blond sycamore. Jacobs loves the 1960s and returns not only in the early sweaters with happy faces, but also in his voluminous mohair balloon sweaters for fall 1989. Suzy Menkes, reviewing his first collection at Perry Ellis, noted "Jacobs's own-label collections have also been all-American, but much less innocent—celebrations of Miami Beach kitsch, sendups of the 1960s hippies and wacky versions of patchwork and down-home gingham." New York-bred and unquestionably street-smart, Jacobs knows so much and is so nimbly, naturally witty that some cynicism blends with the joy in his clothing. A spring 1990 red-and-white tablecloth cotton shirt and jacket is accompanied by embroidered and beaded black ants. His early "Freudian slip" was a simple dress imprinted with the face of the Viennese master, a play on words. In fall 1991, Jacobs showed sweaters with aphorisms borrowed from the tart embroideries of Elsie de Wolfe. Language crops up even in Jacobs's fall 1990 "fresh berries and cream" collection that included blueberry herring-bone patterns on a cream field in wool jackets and the same design in short chiffon flirt skirts. His spring 1992 collection, focused on the Wild West and southern California, was a smart synthesis of Hollywood glamour (including an Oscar dress with the Academy Award statue) and boot-stomping country-and-western cowgirls, a perfect combination of rodeo and Rodeo Drive.

The legend of fashion prodigy is probably inseparably attached to Jacobs; that he has performed prodigiously as a leading master of American style in an immediate and seamless transition from child prodigy is indeed a marvel.—RICHARD MARTIN

James, Charles
American designer

Born _Camberley, England, of Anglo-American parentage, 18 July 1906._
Education _Self-taught in design._
Family _Married Nancy Lee Gregory in 1954 (separated, 1961); children: Charles, Louise._
Career _Moved to United States, established as Charles Boucheron, milliner, Chicago, 1924-28; milliner and custom dressmaker, New York, 1928-29; custom dressmaker, using the name E. Haweis James, London and Paris, 1929-c.1939; also sold designs to wholesale manufacturers in New York, 1930s; relocated to New York, 1939; established as Charles James, Inc., primarily for custom designs, from 1940; became permanent resident of the United States, 1942; designer, couture collection, Elizabeth Arden salon, New York, 1943-45; worked as independent designer, 1945-78. Charles James Services, Inc., licensing company established, 1949; Charles James Associates, limited partnership for manufacture of custom clothes, established, 1954, then merged with Charles James Services; Charles James Manufacturers Company established, 1955._
Exhibitions _A Decade of Design, Brooklyn Museum, 1948; A Total Life Involvement (retrospective), Everson Museum, Syracuse, New York, 1975; The Genius of Charles James_

(retrospective), Brooklyn Museum and Art Institute of Chicago, 1982-83; Charles James, Architect of Fashion, Fashion Institute of Technology, New York, 1993.

Awards *Coty American Fashion Critics Award, 1950, 1954; Neiman Marcus Award, Dallas, 1953; Woolens and Worsteds of America Industry Award, 1962; John Simon Guggenheim fellowship, 1975.*

Died *(in New York) 23 September 1978.*

"Charles James is not only the greatest American couturier, but the world's best and only dressmaker who has raised it from an applied art form to a pure art form." From anyone other than their author, and James's closest professional equal, Cristobal Balenciaga, these words would seem potentially pretentious and inflated. Instead they constitute a balanced and deserved evaluation.

Charles Wilson Brega James was of Anglo-American parentage and possessed an incredibly sharp mind. He could have excelled in any number of fields but a foray into millinery in Chicago of the 1920s led to a career devising intellectually refined and devastatingly beautiful women's garments. James's lifetime career was devoted not to producing quantities of either designs or products but rather to refining and evolving concepts. His clièntele in Britain, France, and the United States was dedicated: they put up with his unpredictability and his inflated costs. When they ordered a garment there was no guarantee of its delivery, or its permanence in their wardrobe as the designer would freely play roulette with his clients' clothes.

Why did clients remain loyal? Why is the word "genius" applied so frequently in describing James? Because James saw the female form as an armature on which to fashion sculpture, not just cover with clothes. He did not just sketch or drape a model. He approached the craft of dressmaking with the science of an engineer, often studying the weight distribution of a garment. Like an artist he analyzed the interacting elements of proportion, line, color, and texture. Construction details were not merely important, they were an obsession. He spent a vast sum on perfecting a sleeve. He turned a four-leaf-clover hat into the hemline of a ballgown which he then built up into the garment he designated as his thesis in dressmaking.

A cruciform became a circular skirt. An evening dress (with matching cape of antique ribbons) which made its debut in 1937 was still offered 20 years later, the finesse of the ribbon replaced by other yardgoods of silk, but the detailing to infinity remaining. James was such a perfectionist that clients never banked on wearing either a new or old James to a function. Even his well-known quilted jacket designed in 1937, and now in the Victoria and Albert Museum, London, bears witness to his challenge to perfect. One can follow his tortured, ghost-like tracts of stitching and restitching.

As brilliant as his design sense is James's subtle sensibility of color. Open a coat or jacket of subdued hues and be confronted with a lining of an unexpected range. Follow his curvilinear pattern configurations and note that inset sleeves and darts are not part of either his design or construction vocabulary. His lines are seductive and intellectually intriguing. Rarely did he employ patterned materials, relying rather on the most revealing, unforgiving plain goods. While he is perhaps best remembered for his spectacular eveningwear his tailored daywear was equally original. It was with his coats that he attempted to enter what he perceived to be the more lucrative ready-to-wear market. However, this didn't suit his temperament or methods of working.

James dressed many of America's best-dressed women of the generation. They patronized the couture salons of Paris and could easily have been dressed abroad. Instead they had the courage and determination to support a unique creator of fashion: Charles James.—ELIZABETH A. COLEMAN

Javits, Eric

American milliner

Born *New York, 24 May 1956.*

Education *Choate School, 1970-74; graduated from Rhode Island School of Design, 1978.*

Career *Co-founded company, Whittall and Javits, Inc., 1978, creating women's hats and later separates and T-shirts. Sold out to partner, 1985. Founded Eric Javits, Inc., specializing in women's hats and occasionally hair accessories, 1985. Licenses include Maximilian Furs, 1991-93, and Kato International, Japan. Also designs hats for films, including Bonfire of the Vanities, for television shows, including Dynasty and Dallas, for many advertising campaigns and for runway collections of other designers, including Carolina Herrera, 1984-93, Caroline Roehm, 1988, Mary McFadden, 1988-93, Pauline Trigère, 1990-93, Adolfo, 1990-91, Louis Féraud, 1989-90, and Donna Karan, 1991-92.*

Exhibitions *Mad Hatters, Women's Guild of the New Orleans Opera Association, 1989; Current Trends in Millinery, Fashion Institute of Technology, New York, 1990; The Art of Millinery—20th Century Hat Design, Philadelphia Museum of Art, 1993.*

Collections *Metropolitan Museum of Art Costume Institute, Fashion Institute of Technology, New York.*

Awards *"Millie" Award, Hat Designer of the Year, 1991, 1992.*

Address *406 West 31st St, 3rd Floor West, New York, NY 10001, USA.*

My design work is only one aspect of involvement with owning my own hat company, and it remains the only part where I am not relying on the team's abilities but on my own.

Whenever an inspiration hits me, I make a note of the idea by sketching a small diagram. This provides a springboard from which many things can later develop. Using this method, I can have the concepts for an entire collection outlined within a few days. Sometime later in the process, when the designs are actually being fabricated, I will consider them from a production and marketing viewpoint. Those issues are quite complex given today's woman's varied needs, and the ever-changing nature of the fashion business.

Many of my ideas are the result of an evolution, synthesizing and reworking bits and pieces of my most effective ideas and occasionally going off to test a completely new direction which, if successful, could eventually become part of the line's core.

Eric Javits: Summer 1994, "Pagoda Planter" hat (two-tone Milan braid, woven chin ties with clay beads).

J

When a design arrives successfully, most of my developmental energy is not evident. What remains, seemingly, is an object which has its own logic and which appears to have been plucked effortlessly from our collective subconscious.—Eric Javits

Eric Javits is, as *New York Magazine* (16 September 1991) assessed, "quite simply, tops." In an era in which the hat is a style anachronism and a definite statement of individuality, if not idiosyncrasy and exhibitionism, Javits has created hats of distinct and discreet identity, the designer's and the potential wearer's.

Upon graduation as a painter and sculptor from the Rhode Island School of Design in 1978, Javits began his millinery career as a sculptural improvisation. Javits creates a wide range of hats: United Airlines flight attendant caps, private-label millinery for many American department stores and specialty chains, Louis Féraud hats, his own label, and its diffusion line, Lily J., named for his grandmother. But even as he is dubbed "crown prince" by Peter Stevenson in *Manhattan, inc.* (August 1989), Javits is not making hats for grandmothers. He is almost Spartan in millinery adornment and has concentrated on hats that are not agglomerations and concoctions, but are modest one-statement sculptures for the head. Javits's restraint is his focus on one important statement in each hat, seldom adding secondary elements. Often the interest is, in fact, in the shape as he has searched the past for a wondrous array of traditional shapes to frame the face. Yet, even as shape is of critical importance to Javits, one of the millinery myths is he or the archetypal hat designer whips a perfect hat out of his pocket, as Javits is said to have done for Carolina Herrera. The legerdemain of the hat in his pocket notwithstanding, Javits plays with a softening of shape so that even his military inspirations and his menswear derivations work as softer versions of the source, though never collapsing into Oldenburg flaccidity.

Defending his decision to enter millinery, as he did somewhat serendipitously, Javits describes the early hat-making as a relief from painting and sculpture. "Hatmaking was playful, there was no pressure. A weight was taken off, and it snowballed into something more serious." Javits's play is quite serious, a *Bauhausian* caprice rather than Carmen Miranda theatrics. While some of Javits's hats can compete at the races and in the evening sweepstakes, his most important contribution is hats that can serve for day and cocktail hours. He makes one of the most convincing arguments for the possible return of millinery to daily attire in dealing with classic shapes, giving a velour beret, for example, a luxury, or offering a most refined form of basic derby. His red tophat with poinsettia photographed on the cover of *Town & Country*, New York (December 1990) is indicative: Dickensian tradition is manifest in a time-honored silhouette, but made fresh with a feminine and flattering red as well as the single note of the white poinsettia adornment. Javits excels in such distilled grace notes, projecting the hat as a deliberate statement for and upon the wearer.

Simple enough for the working day, special at the cocktail hour, and still splendid for evening, Javits's hats afford the contemporary woman a *raison d'être* and repertory for returning to the systematic wearing of hats. Fantasy and special-occasion hats will probably never serve to revive the custom of wearing hats; Javits's reasoned, history-invoking hats may, in the same manner in which American (and subsequently Italian) luxurious minimalism in the 1970s and 1980s restored the faith of women in elegant dress. Moreover, in the late 1980s and 1990s, Javits has also designed headpieces and hair accessories that extend the possibility of millinery.

Fred Miller Robinson argues for the bowler hat as a salient sign of the modern spirit (*The Man in the Bowler Hat,* Chapel Hill, 1993). He points out that it is ever and increasingly filled with the semantics of its origin. What happens in an Eric Javits hat? Customarily, saving most of the over-the-top extravagance for the Louis Féraud line, the Javits hats have the snappy stateliness of a wonderful tradition fittingly renewed. Without succumbing either to arid art or to a conceptual base alone, Javits's fundamentals of hatmaking likewise give the hat its historical function and purpose and offer it as a basic vessel adaptable to modern lives. Few milliners have been as conscientious as Javits in reconfiguring the hat in accordance with its historical templates and modern comforts. Few milliners have taken a modernist sculptural responsibility and talent in honing in one element of the hat to make it converse with the apparel to give presence to the face of its wearer.—RICHARD MARTIN

Joan & David

American footwear and fashion firm

Begun by Joan and David Helpern in Cambridge, Massachusetts, 1967; Joan & David label introduced, 1977; David & Joan menswear division launched, 1982; Joan & David Too lower priced line of shoes and accessories introduced, 1987; first women's apparel collection produced by Sir for Her, 1983-85; second women's ready-to-wear collection produced by Gruppo GFT, from 1988. Maintained licensing agreement with Ann Taylor chain of fashion shops, 1967-92; producer and distributor, Calvin Klein Footwear, from 1990, and Calvin Klein accessories, 1990-91. New York flagship shop opened, 1985; in-store boutiques opened at Harvey Nichols, London, and Ogilvey's, Montreal, 1987; freestanding Paris and Hong Kong boutiques opened, 1988.

Awards *American Fashion Critics Coty Award, 1978; Footwear News Designer of the Year Award, 1986; Cutty Sark Award, 1986; Fashion Footwear Association of New York Award, 1990; Michelangelo Award, 1993.*

Address *4 West 58th Street, New York, New York 10019, USA.*

Joan & David, Inc. is responsible for making flat shoes for women fashionable. The company developed because Joan Helpern wanted a comfortable, stylish shoe that would not become dated through its design. When Joan married David Helpern in the 1960s, she was a student in child psychology working on her PhD at Harvard University. In her multiple roles of wife, mother, teacher, and student, Joan wanted a shoe that was not a gym shoe, loafer, or stiletto, the only readily available styles for women at the time. She needed a shoe that would look stylish, yet allow her to get about the city in comfort. The solution was to design the shoe she needed herself, an oxford style which is still available in a modified form today.

While editing academic manuscripts, Joan created footwear designs for department stores and private labels, including Harvard Square and Foreign Affairs. She began designing under the name of Joan & David in 1977. Today, Joan serves as president and David is the chairman of the company.

Joan & David designs are found throughout the world. The shoes are manufactured in Italy, because it was there that Joan found craftsmen willing to produce limited editions of her designs, numbering from 12 to 120, to her specifications. Joan & David, Inc. produce shoes specifically for women under the name Joan & David, Joan & David Too, and Joan & David

Joan & David: Spring/Summer 1995; from the Joan Helpern Signature Collection.

Couture. Men's footwear is designed under the names David & Joan and David & Joan Couture. Through the years the product line has expanded to include purses and other accessories, as well as women's ready-to-wear.

Helpern's entry into the design field was not planned and she had no formal design training. However, she knew what she wanted in a shoe, so she researched the market and technology involved in their manufacture. She was able to produce footwear which met the needs of active women like herself, who race through the day serving in many different roles: women who are not self-consciously fashionable, but value good quality and style. Joan has a less-is-more philosophy when it comes to design. She concentrates on classic, usable styles such as oxfords and patent pumps with designs that evolve from year to year. The colors she uses are subtle, and the emphasis in on interesting textures. Comfort is essential. Neither flat shoes nor shoes with low heels have extraneous details or extreme designs. In 1978 she was given the Coty Award for her designs.

Joan Helpern has been influential in the field of shoe design. By successfully creating shoes that were both stylish and comfortable, she helped open up a new way of thinking about shoe design for women. Women who work as professionals wanted what Joan herself originally searched for: a stylish, yet comfortable shoe that would not be an obsolete design the next season. They needed a shoe more stylish than sneakers, and more comfortable than stilettos. By providing herself with a comfortable shoe to wear, Joan Helpern was able, with her husband David, to fill this need and develop the successful business named Joan & David.—NANCY HOUSE

John, John P.

American milliner

Born *John Pico Harberger in Munich, 14 March 1906. Immigrated to the United States, 1919.*

Education *Studied medicine, University of Lucerne, and art at the Sorbonne and l'École des Beaux Arts, Paris.*

Career *Milliner, Mme Laurel, dressmaker, New York, 1926; partner (with Fred Fredericks), John Fredericks, milliners, 1929-48, with shops in New York, Hollywood, Miami and Palm Beach; formed independent company, Mr John, Inc., New York, 1948-70; designed for private clients, from 1970.*

Awards *Coty American Fashion Critics Award, 1943; Neiman Marcus Award, 1950; Millinery Institute of America Award, 1956.*

Died *(in New York) 25 June 1993.*

"My business," John P. John told *Good Housekeeping* (June 1957), "is strictly an individual business. When I go, there will be no more Mr John. I have only one worry. When I do go, should I reach heaven, what will I do? I know I cannot improve on the halo." Ironically, John, who had made almost every kind of head covering other than a halo, saw the demise of his kind of milliner on earth; by the time of his death in 1993, perhaps even the halo was obsolete. As early as 1957, he was already on the defensive, arguing, "A hat cannot actually give one golden curls if the hair is mouse-colored and stringy; it cannot lift a face, pay overdue bills, subtract ten years from one's age, or transform a plain soul into a reigning princess. But it *can* lend practically any woman a temporary out-of-herself feeling. For *the right hat creates a desired mood,* and that isn't fiction or fancy, but fact, fact, fact."

Like his contemporary Lilly Daché and Halston who would follow later (translating the concept to apparel, but retaining John's contradictory modes of shape reductivism and theatrical sparkle), John successfully combined the glamor of a custom business with a wide-reaching appeal. He could create extraordinary hats for exceptional women. At the same time, he was a hero to countless middle-class women who copied his styles or had them copied by local milliners. John's hats were on the cover of *Vogue* many times, including 15 June 1943, 15 October 1944, 15 January 1946, 1 August 1946, and 15 February 1953.

From the opening of his own business in the 1920s, after apprenticing with his mother, through the 1960s, John was an important milliner, never fixed in one style but producing eclectic variations of romantic picture hats, snoods, subdued cloches, and other forms. Indeed, it was form that was essential to John: his hats were sculptural, shaped to flatter the face, outfit, and presence. His historicist pieces, in particular, could use surface decoration, but the effect of a Mr John hat nonetheless always resided in the shape. As Anne-Marie Schiro (*New York Times,* 29 June 1993) described, "In the 1940s and 1950s, the name Mr John was as famous in the world of hats as Christian Dior was in the realm of haute couture. At a time when other milliners were piling on flowers, feathers, and tulle, Mr John was stripping hats naked, relying on pure shape for effect." Turbans, berets, and snoods, a specialty, were supple shapes in favor with John and were often shown in the fashion magazines with American fashion. He could, however, also cut crisp shapes and bow a brim to flatter the face and forehead to accompany Dior, Schiaparelli, and Balenciaga. For all the flamboyance of his own life and all the drama that he could vest in a suite of picture hats that ever seemed to belong at Tara, John could also create what *Vogue* (15 October 1951) called a "strict" black hat of utmost simplicity. Even at their most whimsical and wild, John's hats were flattering to the wearer and to the ensemble of dress.

Eugenia Sheppard (New York *Herald Tribune,* 2 July 1956) called him "the artist among milliners" and he self-consciously courted the rubric of art, including collections with the themes of modern art and style history, and a sense of the avant-garde. However, it was one piece of historical recreation that made John most famous: his millinery for Vivien Leigh in *Gone with the Wind.* Widely copied, the *Gone with the Wind* hats confirmed John's long-time association with Hollywood and women of style, including Mary Pickford, Greta Garbo, Gloria Vanderbilt, Gloria Swanson, Jacqueline Kennedy Onassis, and the Duchess of Windsor. His hats were also worn in films by Marilyn Monroe in *Gentlemen Prefer Blondes* and Marlene Dietrich in *Shanghai Express.* By the time Mr John closed in 1970, hats were largely *démodé.*

Custom-made millinery is a matter of extreme co-dependency between client and milliner. If it is the purpose of the hat to flatter, the milliner, too, must practice a psychology of intervention and flattery. When Pierce Fredericks dubbed John the "Mad Hatter" in *Cosmopolitan* (April 1951), the madness was only of energy; rather, clients enjoyed John's "diplomatic manner." John used only one house model, a Miss Lynn, for many years: she was his type for countless hats, many of which he made directly on her head. He was also famous for his miniature hat collection, prototypes for his own hats and historical recreations based upon his study in museums and historical references. John lived in and defined the golden age of millinery. Once, in the 1950s when I was a child, my mother and I were on train from Philadelphia to New York. John walked by and complimented my mother on the picture hat she was wearing. She never forgot Mr John's approval.—RICHARD MARTIN

Johnson, Betsey

American designer

Born *Weathersfield, Connecticut, 10 August 1942.*
Education *Studied at Pratt Institute, Brooklyn, New York, 1960-61; B.A., Phi Beta Kappa, Syracuse University, Syracuse, New York, 1964.*
Family *Married John Cale in 1966 (divorced); daughter: Lulu; married Jeffrey Oliviere in 1981.*
Career *Guest Editor, Mademoiselle, New York, 1964-65; designer, Paraphernalia boutiques, New York, 1965-69; partner in boutique Betsey, Bunky & Nini, New York, from 1969; designer, Alvin Duskin Co., San Francisco, 1970; designer in New York for Butterick patterns, 1971 and 1975; Alley Cat, 1970-74; Jeanette Maternities, 1974-75; Gant, 1974-75; Betsey Johnson's Kidswear division of Shutterbug, 1974-77; Tric-Trac by Betsey Johnson, 1974-76; Star Ferry by Betsey Johnson and Michael Miles, 1975-77; head designer, President and Treasurer, B. J. Vines, from 1978; owner, Betsey Johnson stores, from 1979.*
Awards *Mademoiselle Merit Award, 1970; Coty American Fashion Critics Award, 1971; American Printed Fabrics Council Tommy Award, 1971, 1990.*
Address *209 West 38th Street, New York, New York 10018, USA.*

For the youthquake generation, the names Betsey Johnson and Paraphernalia symbolized the hip, young fashions of mid-1960s America just as Mary Quant and Biba did for the equivalent age group in Great Britain. In the early 1970s, a second wave of young women with a taste for affordable style discovered the flippant body-conscious clothes Johnson designed for the ready-to-wear firm Alley Cat. Throughout the 1980s and into the 1990s Johnson's clothes have been characterized by her sense of humor and an innocent, tongue-in-cheek sexiness. Wearing a Betsey Johnson dress is like putting on a good mood.

After graduating Phi Beta Kappa, magna cum laude from Syracuse University, Syracuse, New York, Johnson won a guest editorship at *Mademoiselle* magazine. There, colleagues put her name forward to Paul Young who was scouting out fresh new design talent to launch his Paraphernalia boutiques. It was a good match. Young encouraged experimentation and Johnson had begun to develop what was to be a long-standing interest in such unorthodox materials as vinyl, sequin sheeting, and the then new stretch fabrics. Her "kit" dress, for example, was of clear vinyl with a trim-it-yourself package of stars, dots and ellipses cut from reflective adhesive foil. The "noise" dress had a hem fringed with loose grommets.

Johnson's approach to clothing is very much influenced by her early days as a dancer. "I am basically about a ballerina torso and a full skirt," she told a reporter for the *Soho News* (New York), in 1982, "a dancing school dress-up craziness." Johnson's emphasis on tight, stretch bodices also grows out of her dancing school background. Not surprisingly the shift in the 1970s to a subdued, tailored look was incompatible with Betsey Johnson's style as a designer. She continued to have her own label with a variety of manufacturers, but it was not until the end of that decade that Johnson's real *joie de vivre* emerged again, this time for her own company.—WHITNEY BLAUSEN

Jones, Stephen

British millinery designer

Born *West Kirby, Cheshire, England, 31 May 1957.*

Education *Studied at High Wycombe School of Art, 1975-76; B.A. (with honors) in fashion from St Martin's School of Art, London, 1979.*

Military Service *Served as chief petty officer in the Royal Navy, 1974-76.*

Career *Chairman and designer, Stephen Jones Millinery, from 1981; S.J. Scarves and Miss Jones lines introduced, from 1988; Jonesboy and S.J. Handkerchieves, from 1990; S.J. Kimonos, from 1991; handbag line introduced, 1993. Also colour creator, Shiseido Cosmetics, 1988.*

Exhibitions *Headspace by Stephen Jones, Isetan Museum, Tokyo, 1984; Fashion and Surrealism, Victoria and Albert Museum, London and Fashion Institute of Technology, New York, 1988; Mad Hatter, Australian National Gallery, Canberra, Sydney, 1992; Hats: Status, Style, Glamour, The Collection, London, 1993; Rococo Futura, Ginza Artspace, Tokyo, 1994.*

Address *29 Heddon St, London W1R 7LL, England.*

Hats for me are an expression of the spirit. They can parallel the whole range of human emotions and may exaggerate them to dramatic effect. The expression of an eye can be enhanced by the particular line of a brim, a Roman profile concealed or enhanced by twists of fabric, or the wearer can be veiled with mystery. Whatever effect my hats achieve, they must have, as Diana Vreeland would have said, "Pizazz." Therefore the balance between them and the wearer is all-important; too much emotion in the curl of a feather or the glint of a *paillette* is vulgar and dominating, too little and the exercise is pointless.

Unlike clothing, novelty is the *raison d'être* of millinery. I must rewrite the score in every hat I make. Making a hat should be like dancing; as one's body follows the beat, so must one's hands be in rhythm with the tempo of the particular hat. Hats make themselves, I merely help them along.—Stephen Jones

When Stephen Jones left St Martin's School of Art, London in 1979 hats were yet to become high fashion news for the young. Ethnic styles had spread from the mid-1970s onwards, drably cloaking the fashion-buying public with Serious Good Taste and leaving little room for wit or fantasy.

In the late 1970s, however, there was a glimmer of change. Waists, hips, and padded shoulders were beginning to emerge from shapeless chemises and sloppy knits. What better to complete this new silhouette than an amusing and frivolous piece of headgear. Many of London's young clubgoers had first appeared on the scene wearing the spikily aggressive trappings of punk. They were new to this glamour born of Hollywood retro-kitsch and embraced it wholeheartedly; and Jones entered right on cue.

Jones was a champion of the eccentric, the stylish, and the innovative. He could be seen emerging from the morning train at Paddington, dressed like the other commuters in smart pinstriped suiting, but with black patent stilettos emerging from his immaculate turn-ups. He was a great ornament to the clubs and parties of the era, usually wearing one of his own

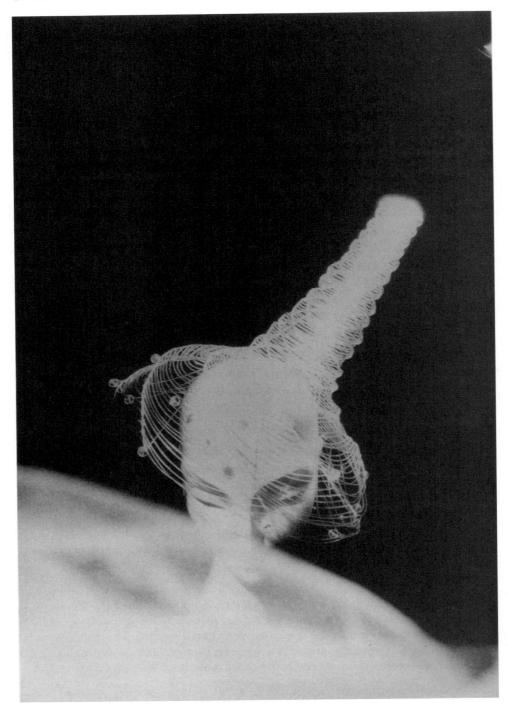

Stephen Jones: Fall/Winter 1994, "Helix" hat. *Photograph by Peter Ashworth.*

asymmetric and intriguing hats, perched on his bald head. An enthusiastic self-publicist, his charm and good humour endeared him to many.

Jones's salons—the first in Covent Garden's P.X.—were unique environments, swathed in lush fabric and dripping with gilt cupids, where one might gaze leisurely at his always astonishing and delightful creations. He re-interpreted the chic and quirky styles of the past, cleverly draping, moulding and trimming his hats in a way so personal as to be entirely of its own time. Moreover, Jones's hats are well-crafted—a reflection of early work at the traditional couture house of Lachasse.

Jones was soon a fast-rising star in the heady London galaxy of the early 1980s; his talent, and that of his peers—Bodymap, Stephen Linard—burst on the scene like a vivid firework display, drawing the world's fashion buyers and press as moths to the British flame.

During the following decade, Jones's esoterically titled collections—Sunset on Suburbia, Ole' Steamy, Passport to Pleasure—have continued to delight and inspire; and he must take due credit for the current popularity of hats amongst the young. Millinery is once more a popular subject on fashion course timetables, whereas a decade or so ago it was fast becoming an endangered species.

Jones's talents have naturally taken him abroad; he continuously designs for top French fashion houses—Gaultier, Montana, Mugler—and enjoys much success in Japan, where genuinely innovative design skills allied with Western charisma are justly lauded. Other young milliners have arisen, some to stay and some to go; but Stephen Jones was the first of this new breed, and remains one of its most influential and quixotic practitioners.—ALAN J. FLUX

Joop, Wolfgang
German designer

Born *Potsdam, Germany, 18 November 1944.*
Family *Married Karin Bernatzky; children: Henriette, Florentine.*
Career *Journalist, Neue Mode; free-lance designer for Christian Aujard, Brecco and others. Showed first fur collection under own label, 1978; Joop! ready-to-wear line added, 1981; menswear line added, 1985; Joop! boutiques opened, Hamburg and Munich, 1986; fragrances introduced, 1987; Joop jeans added, 1989; ready-to-wear fur collection introduced, 1990.*
Address *Harvestehuder Weg 22, 2000 Hamburg 13, Germany.*

Photogenic Wolfgang Joop is at least as recognizable as his fashion and fragrance products. Along with Jil Sander, one of the major figures of German fashion in the 1990s, Joop is as much a national anomaly as he is an international celebrity. Until Sander and Joop, Germany had few designers of sexy clothing achieving world-class status: suddenly, after years in Germany, both came into international recognition in the early 1990s.

Joop, the design identity with an exclamation point, is the hyper-real, hyperbolic badge of the designer. He has brought the American concept of the designer to Germany, with its strong sense of personal identification and the projection of style. Again and again, he appears charismatically, if a little too prominently, in his own imagery. Further, as he describes in a 1993

Wolfgang Joop: Winter 1995.

press release, "When it comes to designing the men's collection, the man I have in mind for the clothes is myself." When Joop bought an apartment in New York in 1993, it was the former apartment of Bill Blass, for Joop has cleverly understood the impulse of contemporary fashion marketing to personification and projection. He has expressed his admiration for the work of American minimalists and marketing prodigies Donna Karan and Calvin Klein. Like Blass, Joop projects utmost self-confidence in style, an aplomb that allows him the polymath aptitude to design for menswear, women's apparel, and fragrance. In examining himself, he gives some surety in the ambiguous realms of style.

In telling his own story in a 1993 press release, with a merchant's beguiling fluency, Joop cites as an important influence growing up on a farm near Potsdam: "As the city of Philip the Great it was one of the poorest of the European courts, but the one with the most style," thus enjoying both a simple life and a proximity to high style. His statements on fashion lean to the populist though his clothing is always on the well-mannered side of democracy (he called a fragrance _Joop! Berlin_ after the fall of the Berlin Wall in 1989). He avers: "Fashion should not just be a blatant expression of money. It should be humorous and give dignity to the individual wearing the clothes."

Among his greatest successes have been jeanswear, likewise in the optimistic spirit of American style and ready-to-wear populism. But the Joop denim collections are not standard: fit, size, and style distinctions bring to the lowly subject of jeans at least a rudiment of tailoring and individuation. Joop's principle is that the ready-to-wear client, even in denim, must be served with a kind of customized distinction and satisfaction, again very much in the ethos of traditional American sportswear. Contending that "jeans are fashion's _alter ego_," Joop adumbrates his view of fashion as an alien force and his conviction in jeans and other products that are wholly part of a daily life. The effect is both real and marketing strategy. A denial of fashion, thus avoiding any purport of excess or exploitation, is fashionable in the 1990s for reasons of economics and lifestyle, but Joop has consistently been a lifestyle designer. Joop attributes to his upbringing in circumstances both rustic and stylish his range of occasion. Thus, the collections work for both casual dress and contemporary high style.—RICHARD MARTIN

Jourdan, Charles

French shoe designer

Born 1883.

Career _Foreman at Établissements Grenier, shoe leather cutters, 1917; independent shoe manufacturer, 1919. Seducta, a luxury range, introduced in Romans sur Isère, France, 1921. In the 1930s, extended distribution to all of France; other shoe lines introduced. After World War II, sons Rene, Charles, and Roland took over factory, adding shoe lines in the mid-1940s. First Charles Jourdan women's boutique in Paris launched, 1957, launched in London, 1959. Dior contract with international distribution of shoes under Dior label, 1959. Perugia began designing for Jourdan in early 1960s. First New York boutique launched, 1968. Bags and ready-to-wear clothing line launched in 1970s. By 1975 there were 21 franchises. Firm continued after Jourdan's death; sons launched menswear and Un Homme fragrance in early 1980s. Company bought over by Portland Cement Werke in 1981. Chief designer: Bernard Sucheras. Outside designers are commis-_

sioned, including Hervé Leger for accessories. Company specializes in shoes, leather goods, accessories, jewelry, scarves.

Exhibitions *Charles Jourdan: 70 Years, Galeries Lafayette, Paris and The Space, Tokyo, both 1991.*

Collections *Musée de la Chaussure, Romans sur Isère, France; Charles Jourdan Museum, Paris, including 2000 creations by André Perugia.*

Address *28, Avenue de New York, 75116 Paris, France.*

Died *1976.*

Charles Jourdan, a shoe manufacturer, made the name Jourdan synonymous with couture by licensing and diversifying in the manner of the Paris haute couture houses. No other footwear company has so successfully marketed its image, and 75 years later Jourdan still symbolizes luxury, international fashion, and the best of couture.

The founder of the company, Charles Jourdan, was both a skilled craftsman and creative businessman. His aim was to produce shoes of quality, made with the best materials and the traditional skills of a *bottier*. He also recognized that many of these bespoke skills could be translated into the much larger ready-to-wear market, producing affordable luxury shoes. Jourdan believed in the power of advertising. As his business expanded during the 1930s he used

Charles Jourdan: Autumn/Winter 1992/93.

a network of commercial travellers to introduce his brands across the whole of France, backing up this sales force with advertisement in popular magazines—a new concept at the time.

His styles were not trendsetting, but their classic luxurious look succeeded. He produced perfectly hand-crafted ladies shoes that could be worn in harmony with elegant outfits. Not that these first simple styles were influenced by the direction of Parisian fashion. The only thing that Jourdan had in common with his contemporaries Poiret, Schiaparelli, and Chanel was that he also used only the finest materials. He did, however, benefit from the new higher hemline which raised the visibility of shoes, making them a much more important accessory in the modern woman's wardrobe.

The economic crisis of the 1930s followed by the war, drastically affected the couture market, which could not cheapen its products. Jourdan, ever ready to diversify, recognized that price was an important selling factor at all levels of the market, and he introduced new lines at lower prices. He sold to the newly emerging chain stores, and the Jourdan empire grew.

In the 1950s Jourdan's three sons began managing the business. The youngest son, Roland Jourdan, who was responsible for design and development, has been described as "the most able man in the shoe industry." He was fully aware that it was simplicity and quality, not wild innovation, that sold Jourdan shoes. When Jourdan's first boutique opened in Paris in 1957, Roland Jourdan only offered a small range of styles. But each style was available in 20 colours, all sizes, and three widths. At Jourdan, not only would the shoe fit, but it would also perfectly accessorize any shade of outfit.

The ultimate connection of the luxury shoe brand to haute couture came with the contract between Jourdan and the house of Christian Dior in 1959. Jourdan created, manufactured, and distributed shoe models for Dior worldwide. It was the ultimate seal of approval. The next two decades saw Jourdan at their most successful and creative. They launched a series of seminal advertising campaigns that profoundly influenced both fashion and advertising. In the 1960s they commissioned Guy Bourdin, a young Parisian photographer who produced a series of surreal, witty, and often visually stunning advertising photographs. The images usually had nothing to do with shoes, and the name "Charles Jourdan" appeared as a small caption in one corner. It is difficult now to imagine the impact of this campaign, but its success was such that for a time the brand became associated with a sense of innovation and modernity that the shoes themselves, perfect creations though they were, did not really possess.

The Jourdan shop design helped to perpetuate this innovate image. The ultra modern interiors and striking window displays of the first Paris boutique became a blueprint for a chain in every fashion capital of the world. It was the environment that created the Jourdan look, that extended at its peak in 1979 from neckties to sunglasses, allowing the dedicated customer to be completely Jourdan accessorized.

Jourdan achieved a level of product diversification unsurpassed in the footwear industry. Borrowing the haute couture strategies of licensing and franchising, and creating a global presence, Jourdan became the couture accessory. This success attracted competition. New names such as Bruno Magli and Robert Clergerie were concentrating solely on footwear. The diversity that had made Jourdan so big now threatened to dilute the brand names exclusivity. Finally, the loyal customer base was growing older, and a new generation of women found alternative designers outside the classic couture mould.

Jourdan

In 1981 the family's dynastic control of the empire ended with the retirement of Roland Jourdan. The name survives, confident in the knowledge that a luxury brand will never be out of fashion. New and younger lines have been launched. Charles Jourdan remains an important name because its enduring strength is the recognition that all a woman really wants in a shoe is the perfect accessory, with the perfect fit. Simple.—CHRIS HILL

Kahng, Gemma

American designer

Born *Masan, Korea, 21 May 1954.*

Education *Immigrated to the United States, 1969. Graduated from the Art Institute of Chicago, 1979.*

Family *Married Charles Chang-Lima in 1984 (divorced in 1994).*

Career *Design assistant, Cathy Hardwick, New York, 1981-84; designed free-lance before establishing own business in 1989.*

Address *550 Seventh Avenue, New York, New York 10018, USA.*

The inspiration for each of my collections comes from my desire to create clothing that is sexy, witty, glamorous, comfortable, and most importantly, practical. I reflect on my own personality and lifestyle and think of things I would like to wear and what I need to expand my wardrobe.

Each of my collections begins with high quality fabrics, an important tool for good design. Mostly I choose wools, silks, cottons, and linens that are luxurious yet basic, so that my design aesthetic becomes more prominent than the fabric itself. The details of clothing from the historical past are a good influence for my ideas. I am fascinated by the cultures of different time periods, especially the Victorian era, and find it challenging to combine them with the look of today.

This design sensibility appeals to my customer, a consistently busy woman who doesn't have the time to experiment with her image. She is a person who has enough confidence to incorporate a sense of humor in her style and can rely on my clothing and accessories for a complete look. Over the past five years, my image has become a recognizable one throughout the United States and is rapidly growing in foreign markets, especially in Hong Kong and Taipei where I have freestanding boutiques.

Gemma Kahng: Fall 1994.

My goal is to perfect upon what it is that my customers like about my clothing and create something new. Design is a growing process and each season I experiment further by bringing more of my self-expression to a collection. What makes it exciting for me is the challenge and risk involved in taking the next step. No one can tell me what to bring to the future. I just have to be aware of the everyday world we live in.—Gemma Kahng

"She's a lot like her designs—a winning mix of playfulness and practicality, forthrightness and charm," said Barbara Phillips of Gemma Kahng (*Wall Street Journal*, 6 August 1991). Kahng's fashion design is practical and tries hard to meet price points appropriate for a relatively new designer, while at the same time the chief trait of her work is to render a classic idea slightly askew or fresh with a theme of whimsy, exaggeration, or notice. The charm of the work is its perturbed normality: it is all just right, but for that one eccentricity or detail that seems gloriously juvenile or marvelously anomalous in the template of a traditional garment.

Kahng's clothing is undeniably serious, addressed paramountly to an American working woman of some means, but always with a note of self-expression. Buttons can be almost as whimsical as those of Schiaparelli; pockets are unexpectedly given colorful flaps in accent colors; and pockets bounce with asymmetry. Schiaparelli is Kahng's soul-mate in fashion history, not for the flamboyant garment, but rather for those most restrained tailored suits that Schiaparelli created with nuanced absurdities and minor amazements. Kahng's identifying style resides in such quirky twists on classics, attention inevitably being drawn to the garment by an outstanding detail, but restrained in every other aspect of the composition.

Kahng, who collaborates with her former husband Charles Chang-Lima, oversees production in a new, yet traditional, way employing the resources of the Seventh Avenue garment district in New York. Rather than seeking large-scale production elsewhere, Kahng has preferred to do all her production in the garment-district neighborhood of Manhattan. It is a matter for Kahng of quality and control, not flag-waving. After all, Kahng was born Shin Kyong in Korea; Chang-Lima was born in Venezuela of Chinese parents. Instead, they are attempting to guarantee production standards by watching the process, an old tradition of the garment industry now abandoned by many bigger companies. Of course, there may be reason in a designer and her partner, neither born in the United States, appraising American traditions and Western dress with a reasoning, potentially ironic, eye. Kahng recalls that in her Korean childhood there were no store-bought dolls and that she had to fantasize and create clothing for her paper dolls.

"Classic with a twist" is a conventional goal of many young designers who take a minimal risk in construction and allow one lovely or bizarre note to make a memorable difference. In fact, the concept is difficult to carry out as one disturbance from the norm can seem to be an unwelcome aberration, especially in clothing that depends upon our sense of recognition of formality. Kahng has demonstrated an unusually sure and decisive sense of distorting or contributing enough in the gesture of discrepancy, but without destroying the practical validity of the garment. When a tweed jacket is trimmed with red, the effect is at first of the most diabolically arresting house-painting on the block, but the combination settles into a rather winsome palette of clothing for the hunt. A pea jacket that is modified by horses on the pockets and jeweled buttons on the front assures that it will not be worn by Popeye, but deliberately softens the military regimen into a feminine and whimsical jacket. The anomaly for Kahng is never mere kitsch or cuteness: it is a feature that alters our perception (whether color or content) of the entire garment, an abnormality that makes us see the normal in a wholly new way.

Kahng described her collaboration with Chang-Lima to Barbara Phillips in a way that may show the matched capacities of Kahng's clothing: "Most lines we design together. He thinks women should be glamorous and sexy. And I think women should be charming and practical. We make, together, a combination." The combination is, in fact, very effective: never unduly impulsive, the design is nonetheless different and enchantingly whimsical: Kahng honors the great traditions in dress and yet gives a happy surprise with each garment.—RICHARD MARTIN

Kamali, Norma

American designer

Born *Norma Arraes in New York City, 27 June 1945.*

Education *Studied fashion illustration at Fashion Institute of Technology, New York, 1961-64.*

Family *Married Mohammed (Eddie) Houssein Kamali in 1967 (divorced, 1972).*

Career *Free-lance fashion illustrator, New York, 1965-66; airlines reservation clerk, 1966-67; free-lance fashion designer and partner, with Eddie Kamali, Kamali Fashion Imports, New York, 1967-78; opened first retail store, Kamali, in New York, 1968; established OMO (On My Own) Norma Kamali boutiques in New York, from 1978; ready-to-wear line introduced, 1981; also produced sportswear for Jones Apparel Group, 1981, children's sportswear for Empire Shield Group, 1982, sportswear for Renown Corporation, Japan, 1983, bags and footwear for Vittorio Ricci, 1983-84, headwear for Stetson, 1983, and belts for Raymon Ridless, 1985; signature fragrance collection introduced, 1985; OMO home collection introduced, 1988; 1-800-8-KAMALI line of casual wear introduced, 1993; cosmetics line introduced, 1994. Also: Designer of costumes for the Emerald City in film, The Wiz; designed and opened Norma Kamali Building, New York, 1983; producer and director of video, Fall Fantasy; designer of costumes for the Twyla Tharp dance in The Upper Room.*

Exhibitions *Parachute designs displayed at Metropolitan Museum of Art, New York, 1977.*

Awards *Coty American Fashion Critics Award, 1981, 1982, 1983; Council of Fashion Designers of America Award, 1982, 1985; Fashion Institute of Design and Merchandising Award, Los Angeles, 1984; Fashion Group Award, 1986; Distinguished Architecture Award from New York Chapter of American Institute of Architects; Outstanding Graduate Award from the Public Education Association of New York; Award of Merit, Video Culture International Competition; American Success Award from the Fashion Institute of Technology in New York, 1989.*

Address *Norma Kamali Building, 11 West 56th Street, New York, New York 10019, USA.*

In a highly original way, Norma Kamali has been designing with uncanny foresight for the modern woman's multifaceted lifestyle. The sensational success of her sweatshirt fleece fabric line in 1981 brought Kamali clothes into the mainstream, while she continued to design experimental, one-of-a-kind fashions for wealthier clients. The mass produced sweats offered good design in comfortable clothes, with a touch of the eye-catching elements that distinguish Kamali. Inspired by the late 1960s British clothes she brought back from England to sell in the New York Norma Kamali boutique, the retro Biba clothing of Barbara Hulanicki in particular, Kamali began offering her own designs to keep up with the demand. When she opened her New York OMO (On My Own) boutique in 1978 after her divorce, Kamali symbolized all newly independent women.

As early as 1972 Kamali designed bathing suits according to her own vision: gold lamé *maillots,* structured or spare bikinis, decorated or plain, introducing the then-startling high-thigh styles with cutouts to show off a well-toned body—beach fashions that have become mainstream as the 1980s progressed. In the late 1960s Kamali was credited with the hot pants craze. A sense of playfulness combined rhinestones with stretch leotard material, pleasing the celebrities who patronized the Madison Avenue store. In 1974 Kamali changed to a more refined look, lacy and delicate, specializing in well-made suits and dresses.

It was in the West Side OMO store that Kamali came into her own. Cosy down-filled coats became popular after she introduced them, spurred by the necessity of sleeping in a sleeping bag after her divorce. Drawstringed jumpsuits made of colorful parachute material resulted in her inclusion in the *Vanity Fair* Exhibition at the Costume Institute of the Metropolitan Museum of Art. She showed draped 1930s-styled jerseys, and exaggerated broad shoulders on garments from coats to sweatshirt dresses to evening gowns, always a little before her time. She also utilized suede in bright colors before it became trendy. Kamali 1950s-style "Ethel Mertz" dresses were fabricated in plaid flannel, certainly different than anything else on the streets in the early 1980s. Her short cheerleader skirts were the first popular mini skirts in a decade. Dramatic lamé accents appeared on special occasion sweats and she designed sweatshirting for children.

Kamali epitomizes the shy person who allows her clothes to speak for her, yet there is an inner strength that has led to successful business enterprise and the willingness to take risks. Using her boutique as an *atelier,* Kamali has been producing one-of-a-kind garments from unusual fabrics in versatile shapes that could be worn in a number of ways. She was one of the first to present unitards or bodysuits as serious fashion staples. As in French couture, Kamali listens to her customers, on whom she has waited in person in her boutique, to get their honest opinions. She has described herself as relying upon intuition, taking inspiration from the street, but making it her own result as if in a creative trance. Her credo has been to make attractive the functional aspects of clothing, taking inspiration from the unique qualities of each fabric, always designing for the woman who will wear the clothes.

Throughout her career Kamali has inspired other designers, and has been considered one of the most original designers in New York. She has brought the inventiveness that used to be allowed only in couture salons to versions affordable to working women, although many of her more exclusive designs remain high priced. Kamali has also introduced revolutionary marketing techniques to fashion merchandising. Twenty-four hours a day, fashion videos play in the windows of OMO. Unlike ordinary catwalk videotapes, Kamali videos are actually mini-movies, often as long as 30 minutes, with story lines and character development, showing various situations in which Kamali fashions might be worn. Kamali also advertised through the use of billboards and by staging fashion shows in New York's Central Park. By 1993 she was offering a toll-free number for ordering her new lower priced label, while retaining the OMO Norma Kamali label for her expensive line. Plans for expansion to Los Angeles, Europe, and Japan as well as 1-800-8-KAMALI shops all over the country attest to her mission to bring well-designed fashion to all women.

Kamali clothes continue to be timeless in evoking past fashion eras while representing a modern outlook in interpretation, use of new materials and technology. The newest innovation has been a non-perishable fiber, soft yet impervious to wrinkling and staining, to create an entire wardrobe of interchangeable pieces. In 1991 Kamali presented bell-bottomed trousers, then scoffed at by the fashion press, which have now become standard in the revival of the 1970s. She herself revived her own fake leopard print coats to combine in the eclectic individualistic mood of the 1990s with other garments having vintage and ethnic overtones. Soft flowing floral tunics, Edwardian and 1930s detailing, hip-huggers, lace dresses all in spirit with the times denote the experimentation that has always been the hallmark of Kamali's style and has at last caught up with her fashion forward attitude. Shiny Lurex bathing suits feature underwire cups and a direction toward a more covered-up look in response to the new consciousness about the dangers of sunlight. Her own best model, Kamali epitomizes the 1940s vamp that is a characteristic classic expression of her aesthetic. She has made self-expression seductive.—THERESE DUZINKIEWICZ BAKER

Karan, Donna

American designer

Born Donna Faske in Forest Hills, New York, 2 October 1948.

Education Studied at Parsons School of Design, New York.

Family Married Mark Karan in 1973 (divorced); daughter: Gabrielle; married Stephen Weiss in 1977; stepchildren: Lisa, Cory.

Career Assistant designer, Anne Klein & Co., and Addenda Company, New York, 1967-68; designer, Anne Klein, 1968-71; designer and director of design in association with Louis Dell'Olio, Anne Klein & Co., 1974-84; launched Anne Klein II diffusion line, 1982. Designer, Donna Karan New York (DKNY), from 1985; added swimwear line, 1986; hosiery collection, 1987; DKNY bridge line, 1988; DKNY menswear collection, 1991; founded Donna Karan Beauty Company, fragrance and cosmetic division, New York, 1992; lingerie, and children's line, DKNY Kids, from 1992.

Awards Coty American Fashion Critics Award, 1977, 1981, 1984, 1985; Fashion Footwear Association of New York Award, 1988; Council of Fashion Designers of America Award, 1985, 1986, 1990, 1992; Woolmark Award, 1992; Honorary Degree, Bachelor of Fine Arts, Parsons School of Design, 1987.

Address 550 Seventh Avenue, New York, New York 10018, USA.

Donna Karan can be considered the designer who has made it fashionable to be voluptuous. She has based her corporate philosophy on clothes that are designed to hug a woman but also hide bodily imperfections. "You've gotta accent your positive, delete your negative," she declared in a press release, emphasizing the fact that if you're pulled together underneath, you can build on top of that. Karan firmly relates designing to herself and her role as a woman. She sees design as a personal expression of the many roles she has had to balance, being a wife, mother, friend and business person. She believes that her sex has given her greater

Donna Karan: Fall 1996; sapphire double constructed wool wing- collar jacket and flare pant.

insight into solving problems that women have with fashion, fulfilling their needs, simplifying dress to make life easier and to add comfort, luxury, and durability. Originating as a womenswear label, the company now also produces menswear, childrenswear, accessories, beauty products, and a perfume that perpetrate the lifestyle and philosophy instigated by the womenswear line. Donna Karan stresses that she has not drawn the line there. "There's so much to be done. DKNY underwear, swimwear, home furnishings . . . the designs are already in my head, it's just a matter of getting them executed."

Karan was born and raised on Long Island, New York. Both her mother and father were involved in fashion careers so it seemed inevitable that Donna should follow in their footsteps. After two years studying fashion at Parsons School of Design in New York she was hired by Anne Klein for a summer job. She later became an associate designer until Anne Klein died in 1974. Her next lucky break was to shape the rest of her career. She was named successor to Anne Klein and together with Louis Dell'Olio, who joined the company a year later, designed the collection.

Shortly after the launch of the diffusion line, Anne Klein II, in 1982, Karan felt ready to go it alone. Together with her husband, Stephen Weiss, she launched the first Donna Karan collection in 1985 and since then the company has grown at a dizzying pace. Karan is inspired by New York. She believes that its energy, pace, and vibrance attracts the most sophisticated and artistic people in the world, the type of people and lifestyle for whom she has always designed. Her principle is that clothes should be interchangeable and flexible enough to go from day to evening, summer to winter. Fashion should be a multi-cultural language, easy, sensuous, and functional, a modern security blanket. This explains perhaps why her fundamental trademark items, the bodysuits, unitards, black cashmere, stretch fabrics and sensuous bodywrap styles, owe great allegiance to the innate style and taste of the artist.

There is a great sense of urgency about Donna Karan; to say that there are not enough hours in a day would be an understatement. Her interviews are always frenetic, emotionally charged yet human and blatantly honest. When asked by journalist Sally Brampton to describe her life, she replied, "It's chaos, C.H.A.O.S."

Karan's magic touch is a combination of creative flair and marketing know-how. She designs for human needs, people who live, work, and play. She conceptualizes a customer and wardrobe and can then merchandise a line, applying her designer's eye for colour, proportion, and fit. In many ways she is like a contemporary American Chanel in that she analyses women's needs with a question to herself: "What do I need? How can I make life easier? How can dressing be simplified so that I can get on with my own life?"—KEVIN ALMOND

Kasper, Herbert
American designer

Born *New York City, 12 December 1926.*

Education *Studied English at New York University, 1949-53; studied fashion at Parsons School of Design, New York, 1951-53, and l'École de la Chambre Syndicale de la Couture Parisienne, 1953.*

Family *Married Betsey Pickering in 1955 (divorced, 1958); married Jondar Conning in 1979.*

Military Service   *Served in the United States Army.*

Career   *Spent two years in Paris working for Fath, Rochas, and at Elle; designer, Arnold and Fox, New York, 1954-64; designer, Kasper for Joan Leslie division of Leslie Fay, New York, 1964-85; designer, J.L. Sport, and Kasper for Weatherscope, 1970-85; vice-president, Leslie Fay; designer, Kasper for ASL, from 1980.*

Awards   *Coty American Fashion Critics Award, 1955, 1970, 1976; Cotton Fashion Award, 1972; Maas Brothers Pavilion Design Award, 1983; Cystic Fibrosis Foundation, Governor of Alabama Award, 1984; Ronald MacDonald House Award, 1984.*

Address   *32 East 64th Street, New York, New York 10021, USA.*

Over a lifetime of designing I've evolved a philosophy that comes from creating clothes for a particular kind of American woman. (Who, by the way, I very much admire.) This woman is adventurous and vital with a lifestyle that demands she play many different roles throughout the day. It's the confident spirit of this kind of woman that inspires me most.

Whatever she's doing, running a home, a career, entertaining, mothering, traveling, I deeply believe that this woman remains an individual. No one is going to tell her exactly what she has to wear, no matter what's currently in style. She wants and needs high style, high quality, fashion-conscious clothes that can last for more than one season. That's what I believe I offer her. And because I think I have an exceptional ability to anticipate trends, my clothes always have a "today" spirit. They're high fashion . . . in the mood of the moment. I'm constantly refining, improving, interpreting . . . trying to capture the essence of the times without being trendy.

I design sophisticated clothes for women who are spirited and young . . . whatever their age. And I believe in the concept of wardrobe dressing—being able to mix clothes—which is the basis of American sportswear, so my pieces are often mixable. A jacket from one suit may work wonderfully with the skirt of another, or look great with an odd pair of trousers.

In fact, interesting mixes of color and fabric have become my signature . . . it's what gives them their individuality. My inspiration comes from many sources. Ideas come from the streets, museums, from my own way of twisting an idea around. I remember once being at a beach in the south of Italy and seeing a woman wearing a long black tunic. This inspired me to do a resort collection based on black and gold which at the time was very different from the more traditional navy for beachwear.

Another time I went to a Matisse exhibition in Paris and built an entire collection using Matisse prints on many different kinds of fabrics. But from whatever source my ideas come from, I always keep in mind that lively, energetic, smart looking woman who is my customer. She's my motivation and my ultimate inspiration.—Herbert Kasper

Herbert Kasper has made his name as a designer by working predominantly for one company, Joan Leslie in New York, whom he joined in 1963. In 1980 he became vice-president of the company as well as designer, creating high fashion looks that reflect trends but are commercial and wearable. A private customer, Joanne Carson (then the wife of talk-show host Johnny) described his clothes as being both feminine and sexy: "He's got a totally female concept," she enthused, adding that he knew how to put together the perfect interchangeable wardrobe for her various excursions abroad.

Kasper is a designer who really cares about his customer. He wants the person who buys a dress to enjoy it and return for more. His satisfaction comes from seeing a woman look and feel good in his clothes. His reputation has always been that of a respectable craftsman who honours all levels of production involved in creating fashion, from design to manufacture.

After military service in World War II, where he designed costumes for the troupe shows in which he took part as a chorus boy, Kasper enrolled at Parsons School of Design in New York. He then spent two years in Paris perfecting his skills, with a short period at l'École de la Chambre Syndicale de la Couture, Paris and positions at Jacques Fath and Marcel Rochas. Returning to the United States he worked for the milliner Mr. Fred, where his reputation grew. In his next position as dress designer for a company called Penart, the department store Lord and Taylor in New York, who were promoting American designers, said they wanted to feature his work; he became known as Kasper of Penart. His talent was for making inexpensive clothes look exquisite and expensive, which endeared him to several other Seventh Avenue manufacturers in the 1950s.

Kasper's forte has always been dresses, but a designer's job involves adapting to the demands of the market and in the early 1970s he opened a sportswear division for Joan Leslie, J. L. Sport. Part of his fashion philosophy has been that clothes should always work together, so he often found it difficult to differentiate between these two lines when designing. A coat for Joan Leslie Dresses, he once declared, could work equally well with the less expensive separates line for J. L. Sport.

While working in Paris, Kasper noted that women spent a lot of money on custom-made clothes, ordering several outfits for different occasions. He formed a philosophy based on these observations that individual garments can be mixed and matched with many others to create an outfit, a sportswear concept that has become a way of life in the United States today.

Kasper has always been a great socialite. His social life inspires his work because it gives him an insight into how people live, their attitudes, and changing tastes. As a designer he is happy with his work, regarding each creation as one of his own children, which in a way justifies his devotion to his craft.—KEVIN ALMOND

Kawakubo, Rei

Japanese designer

Born *Tokyo, 1942.*

Education *Graduated in fine arts, Keio University, Tokyo, 1964.*

Career *Worked in advertising department, Asahi Kasei textile firm, 1964-66; free-lance designer, 1967-69; founder-designer, Comme des Garçons, 1969, firm incorporated, 1973; menswear line Homme introduced, 1978; Tricot knitwear and Robe de Chambre lines introduced, 1981; first Paris boutique opened, 1981; Comme des Garçons, S.A. ready-to-wear subsidiary formed, 1982, New York subsidiary formed, 1986; furniture collection launched, 1983; Homme Plus collection introduced, 1984; men's Paris bou-*

Rei Kawakubo: Comme des Garçons, Fall/Winter 1984/85. *Photograph by Peter Lindbergh.*

tique opened, 1986; Homme Deux and Noir collections introduced, 1987; Comme des Garçons Six magazine published, from 1988; Tokyo flagship store opened, 1989.

Exhibitions *A New Wave in Fashion: Three Japanese Designers, Phoenix, Arizona, Art Museum, 1983; Mode et Photo, Comme des Garçons, Centre Georges Pompidou, Paris, 1986; Three Women: Madeleine Vionnet, Claire McCardell and Rei Kawakubo, Fashion Institute of Technology, New York, 1987; Essence of Quality, Kyoto Costume Institute, Tokyo, 1993.*

Awards *Mainichi Newspaper Fashion Award, 1983, 1988; Fashion Group Night of the Stars Award, New York, 1986; Chevalier de L'Ordre des Arts et des Lettres, Paris, 1993.*

Address *Comme des Garçons, 5-11-5 Minamiaoyama, Minato-ku Tokyo 107, Japan.*

My approach to fashion design is influenced by my daily life . . . my search for new means of expression.

I feel that recently there has been a little more of an interest towards those who look for new ideas and who are searching for a new sense of values. My wish is to be able to continue my search for the new.—

—Rei Kawakubo

Rei Kawakubo's work is both paradox and ideological imperative. Minimal, monochromatic and modernist, her approach to fashion design challenges conventional beauty without forgoing stylish cloth, cut, and color. Her clothing is not so much about the body as the space around the body and the metaphor of self. Architectonic in conception and decidedly abstract, the clothing nevertheless derives from Japanese traditional wear.

Kawakubo emerged as a clothing designer by an indirect route, from both a training in fine art at Keio University in Tokyo and work in advertising for Asahi Kasei, a major chemical company that produced acrylic fibres—promoted through fashionable clothing. In 1967 she became a free-lance stylist, a rarity in Japan at the time. Kawakubo's dissatisfaction with available clothes for the fashion shoots provided the impetus for designing her own garments. She launched the Comme des Garçons women's collection in Tokyo in 1975 with her first shop in Minami-Aoyama and her first catalog the same year. It was an especially fertile period for Japanese fashion design, with the concurrent rise of Issey Miyake and Yohji Yamamoto.

Kawakubo's themes combine the essence of Japanese traditional work-end streetwear, its simplicity of style, fabric, and color, with an admiration for modern architecture, especially the purism of Le Corbusier and Tadao Ando. Translated into clothing's rational construction, these affinities emphasize the idea of garment—the garment as a construction in space, essentially a structure to live in. The tradition of the kimono, with its architectural silhouette off the body and its many-layered complexity of body wrappings, combines with a graphic approach that is flat and abstract. It is a disarming look that requires a cognitive leap in wearability and social function.

The building block of Kawakubo's design is the fabric, the thread that produces the clothing structure. Her long-standing collaboration with specialty weaver Hiroshi Matsushita has allowed her to reformulate the actual fabric on the loom, the complexities of the weave, the imperfections, the texture of the fabric. Her 1981 launch of the Comme des Garçons line in Paris marked her first international exposure and the introduction of her loom-distressed weaves. What have been referred to as "rag-picker" clothes, a homage to the spontaneity and inventiveness of street people, was based on fabric innovation—cloth that crumpled and wrapped, that draped coarsely as layers, folded and buttoned at random. Most notable of these was her so-called "lace" knitwear of 1982, where sweaters were purposely knitted to incorporate various-sized holes that appear as rips and tears or intentionally intricate webs. This was an attack on lingering Victorianism in fashion, on the conventional, the precise and the tight-laced. It offered a rational argument for anti-form at a time when minimalism had lapsed into decorativeness.

Kawakubo's use of monochromatic black as her signature is analytical and subtle rather than sensual and brash. Black, which is often perceived as flattering, assumes the status of a non-color—an absence rather than a presence. Her intent is to reject clothes as mere decoration for the body. Even with the later introduction of saturated color in the late 1980s lines, in which her clothes became slimmer. Black was still a basic—evident in the Noir line, as well as in Homme and Homme Plus, her menswear collections.

Her control of the presentation of Comme des Garçons in photography, catwalk shows, the design of store interiors, catalogs, and most recently a magazine, is integral to the design concept that extends from the clothing. Kawakubo was the first to use non-professional models, art world personalities, and film celebrities, both in photography for catalogs and in catwalk shows. Her early catalogs from the 1970s featured noted figures from Japanese art and literature. The 1988 introduction of the quarto-sized biannual magazine _Six_ (for sixth sense) replaced the Comme des Garçons catalogs and pushed Kawakubo's anti-fashion ideas to extreme. These photographic essays became enigmatic vehicles for stream-of-consciousness, surrealism, exoticism, and Zen, that which informs Kawakubo's sensibility and, ultimately, in a semiotic way, is imbued in her fashion designs. Rei Kawakubo's ideas have explored the realm of possibilities associated with the production and selling of clothing. Her control of the environment of her stores from the sparse design of the interiors, on which she collaborates with architect Takao Kawasaki, to the industrial racks and shelves, to the way the sales people act and dress, even now to the furnishings, which she designs and sells, is total and defining. Kawakubo's art is one of extending the boundaries of self-presentation and self-awareness into an environment of multivalent signs. It is an extension of fashion design into the realism of metaphysic, of "self in landscape," of which the clothing is a bare trace.—SARAH BODINE

Kelly, Patrick

American designer working in Paris

Born _Vicksburg, Mississippi, 24 September 1954._

Education _Studied art history and black history at Jackson State University, Jackson, Mississippi, and fashion design at Parsons School of Design, New York._

Career _Held various jobs in Atlanta, Georgia, including window dresser, Rive Gauche boutique, instructor, Barbizon School of Modeling, vintage clothing store proprietor, mid-1970s. Moved to Paris, 1980; costume designer, Le Palais club, c.1980-81, also free-lance designer, 1980-90; Patrick Kelly, Paris, formed, and first ready-to-wear collection introduced, 1985; also free-lance sportswear designer, Benetton, 1986; opened first boutique in Paris, produced first couture collection, sold worldwide rights to ready-to-wear collections, 1987._

Died _(in Paris) 1 January 1990._

A published "Love List" for designer Patrick Kelly included "fried chicken," "foie gras," and "pearls" (*Women's Wear Daily,* 1 March 1990). Kelly's designs celebrated pride in his spiritual upbringing in the American South and a tourist-like adoration of Paris. Not for the faint-hearted, his specialty was form-fitting knits irreverently decorated with oversized and mismatched buttons, watermelons, black baby dolls, and huge rhinestones densely silhouetting the Eiffel Tower.

Wearing too-big overalls and a biker's cap emblazoned "Paris," Kelly engendered folklore as important as the clothing he designed. Growing up in Mississippi, taught sewing by his grandmother, selling vintage clothing in Atlanta, failing to be hired on New York's Seventh Avenue . . . a one-way ticket to Paris from a model/friend resulted in his being discovered while selling his own designs in a Paris flea market.

Kelly was exotic and different. He and his clothing charmed the French and the rest of the world, and he was the first American ever admitted to the elite Chambre Syndicale de la Couture Parisienne, the group of Paris-based designers permitted to show collections in the Louvre. Exuberantly witty, his first show at the Louvre began with Kelly spray painting a large red heart on a white canvas, and included dresses entitled "Jungle Lisa Loves Tarzan," a spoof of Mona Lisa featuring leopard-print gowns.

Kelly's designs remained unpretentious yet sexy, affordable while glamorous. Dresses were fun and uncontrived, yet Kelly paid great attention to design details. Bold, theatrical details such as white topstitching on black, low necklines, and dice buttons on a pin-striped business dress, silver fringe on a western skirt, and vibrant color combinations make one want to shimmy just looking at them. Kelly's art was in embellishment of women, young and old. Trims become jewelry; collars and hemlines become frames. Frills are exaggerated, enlarged, unexpected, and re-thought, saucily decorating what would otherwise be rather simple designs.

A love-in atmosphere prevailed at an April 1989 show and lecture for students at New York's Fashion Institute of Technology. A standing-room-only crowd screamed, laughed, and applauded Kelly—his effervescence and his happiness were contagious. He showed a sassy and smart collection, including a tight black mini dress with shiny multicolored buttons outlining a perfect heart on the buttocks; wide, notched, off-the-shoulder collars; leopard-print trench coats and turtlenecked body suits; multicolored scarves suspended from the hip, swaying below abbreviated hemlines; and a *trompe l'oeil* bustier of buttons on a fitted mini dress. Kelly's models danced, even smiled, down the catwalk, delighted to be wearing his clothing (they modeled this show for free). The audience was delighted to be there: the clothing and designer seemed to be welcoming everyone to a good party, and everyone had a good time.

Kelly's personal attention to detail, his love of design, his spirit, sold his clothing. He stated "the ultimate goal is selling," but he did more than just sell. Wearing a Patrick Kelly dress meant embracing one's past, doing the best with what you have, triumphing over failure, and laughing at one self. One could be part of Patrick Kelly's fairy tale and celebrate his *joie de vivre.*—JANE BURNS

Kemper, Randy

American designer

Born *Philadelphia, 22 August 1959.*

Education *Attended Parsons School of Design.*

Career *Worked as a designer for J.G. Hook, Philadelphia, 1980-81; Givenchy, Paris, 1981-82; Hanae Mori, New York City, 1983-84; Bill Blass, New York City, 1984-86; established own design firm, New York City, 1987.*

Address *530 Seventh Avenue, New York, New York, 10018.*

Anne-Marie Schiro, writing in the *New York Times* (March 28, 1996), noted, "Randy Kemper has come a long way as a designer and now seems to have finally found his niche. . . his fall collection is pure and simple, with lean jackets over shirts and wrapped blouses, dresses with elliptical seaming and buttonless coats tossed over slim-cut pants." Kemper's quintessential traits as a designer are modernist clarity and wearer's comfort. He is at his best when he is eliminating anything superfluous from the garment and finding the capacity of one button to close a garment or a means to suppress buttons under a fly front. Earlier, Bernadine Morris (*New York Times*, October 8, 1989) encapsulated Kemper's style: "His clothes have a low-key sophistication and are not overpowering; everything has a fresh, upbeat quality." With minor deviations, his work since establishing his own company in 1987 has been about a graceful simplicity in working clothing for women and in temperately sophisticated evening and leisure apparel. His style models would be Katherine Hepburn or Lauren Bacall with a touch of the working Jacqueline Kennedy Onassis on the side.

Following Parsons School of Design and early work with Bill Blass and Givenchy, both of whom are exemplars to Kemper's chic but plain style and paradigms to Kemper's easygoing affability and personal charm, Kemper established a small business in New York that achieved some recognition. Bernadine Morris (*New York Times*, December 26, 1989) immediately acclaimed Kemper for "soft and subtle" clothing with "a look of quality." Kemper's great talent is in quality, his clothes generally looking better in their utmost simplicity and wearability than most clothing at the same price-point (Kemper's sole/signature line is moderately priced). Kemper himself said of his spring 1996 collection that it was founded on "equal measures of innovation and restraint."

Kemper had the great good fortune and agonizing misfortune to have been a preferred designer of Hillary Rodham Clinton even before 1992. While Clinton had bought Kemper's clothing through a Little Rock dress shop and had never met the designer, Kemper was skyrocketed into recognition in 1993 due to Clinton's interest in his work. In 1993, just as the world watched, Kemper created the graceless faux pas of a young designer, remembering the early 1970s in tie-dyes, but Kemper has otherwise kept his vision steady on easing and erasings, paring his clothing down. Ironically, Kemper's tie-dyed shift was editorially used in Italian *Glamour* (January 1994), an unusual international recognition for the designer even as it was an anomaly for his design interests.

If Kemper has come a long way in the past ten years, his glaringly spotlighted progress has been remarkably principled in the ethos of sportswear. He told Morris (October 8, 1989), "When designers start out, they tend to work too hard to make a statement. I tend to go for clothes that look elegant and sleek and have as few seams as they need to make them work." In this restriction to the structural essence as the sole decoration, Kemper has been steadfast. Yet one could argue that modern sportswear in the tradition of Claire McCardell, Anne Klein, and Halston has always sought this grail of pared-down design. What Kemper has managed to confer in addition to this austerity is a consistent sense of cheerful, confident clothes. His clothing is easy to wear: in 1993, when Kemper was in the spotlight for his association with Clinton, he was one of the leading sportswear designers in America to resist the ubiquity of the blazer which was on the wane and moved to elongated vest and the slinky proportions of longer jackets. His mood has always been idealist and positive, avoiding plainness, and offering a way to be dressed in working style with no sacrifice to the long-held values of style and comfort. When Kemper went a little Hollywood for fall 1994, the *New York Times* (April 7, 1994) chided and congratulated, "Randy Kemper gave his clothes a lot of fancy Hollywood names, disguising the fact that the makes great coats, jackets, and separates." Despite occasional kleig lights and political hot lights, Kemper is one of the great sportswear designers in America, conscious of separates, wardrobe-building, and the presence of quality in ordinary clothes. His spring 1996 press kit proclaimed, with justice: "With new formulas for dressing emerging in the Nineties, Randy Kemper has designed his Spring 1996 collection to be not only of the finest quality of fabrication and tailoring, but equally as important, he has kept his fashion equations simple: Jacket + Dress = Suit, Shell + Skirt = Dress." Such ingenious equations in wardrobe-building and ingratiating proportions in soft separates characterize Kemper's easy harmony in modern dress.—RICHARD MARTIN

Kenzo

Japanese designer working in Paris

Born   *Kenzo Takada in Tokyo, 27 February 1939.*

Education   *Studied at the Bunka College of Fashion.*

Career   *Designer for Sanai department store; pattern designer Soen magazine, Tokyo, 1960-64; free-lance designer, Paris, from 1965, selling to Féraud, Rodier and several department stores; designer for Pisanti; established Jungle Jap boutique in Paris, 1970; Rue Cherche Midi Boutique opened, 1972; Kenzo-Paris boutique established, New York, 1983; menswear line launched, 1983; boutiques opened in Paris, Aix en Provence, Bordeaux, Lille, Lyon, Saint-Tropez, Copenhagen, London, Milano, and Tokyo, 1984-85; menswear and womenswear lines, Kenzo Jeans, and junior line, Kenzo Jungle, both launched, 1986; Kenzo Bed Linen and Bath Wear line launched, 1987; boutiques opened in Rome, New York, 1987; established childrenswear, line, 1987; womenswear line, Kenzo City launched, 1988; boutique opened in Brussels, 1989, and in Stockholm, 1990; line of bath products line Le Bain launched, 1990; boutique opened in Hong Kong, 1990, Bangkok, 1991, and Singapore, 1991; Kenzo Maison line launched, 1992; Bambou line launched, 1994. Perfumes: Kenzo, 1988; Parfum d'Été, 1992. Also: costume designer for opera, film director.*

Awards   *Soen Prize, 1960; Fashion Editors Club of Japan Prize, 1972; Bath Museum of Costume Dress of the Year Award, 1976, 1977; Chevalier de l'Ordre des Arts et des Lettres, 1984.*

Address   *54 rue Étienne Marcel, 75001 Paris, France.*

In 1986, Kenzo [Takada] called his menswear collection "Around the World in Eighty Days," but that expedition had long been underway in Kenzo's clothes for women and men. Significantly, for more than 20 years, Kenzo has been the most prominent traveller in fashion, but also the most multicultural and the most syncretistic, insisting on the diversity and compatibility of ethnic styles and cultural options from all parts of the world. Kenzo has steadfastly mixed styles. This Japanese tourist has rightly perceived and selected from all cultures and styles. In 1978, he told *Women's Wear Daily* (17 February 1978),"I like to use African patterns and Japanese patterns together." Kenzo interprets style and specific costume elements of various parts of the world, assimilating them into a peaceful internationalism more radical than other designers. Thus, the spring-summer 1975 Chinese coolie look was combined with Portuguese purses, copious Riviera awning-striped beach shirts, and T-shirt dresses for full cultural diversity. In 1973, Romanian peasant skirts became his inspiration, as did Mexican *rebozos* and heavy Scandinavian sweaters. In fall 1976, he was inspired by Native Americans in a highly textural, colorful, and feather-inflected collection. In spring-summer 1984, his collection was based chiefly on North Africa, with elements of an excursion to India for a modified Nehru suit. For spring-summer 1979, the Egyptian look became the front-page headline of *Women's Wear Daily,*"Kenzo barges up the Nile." *Wunderkind* and celebrity in 1970s fashion, Kenzo never fixed on one look, but has preferred to view fashion as a creative, continuous adventure. Shyly, Kenzo said in 1978: "It pleases me when people say I have influence. But I am influenced by the world that says I influence it. The world I live in is my influence."

Kenzo. *Photograph by Friedmann Hauss.*

Other influences include American popular culture: Chinese tunics and wrappings, especially at the low-swung waist, batiks of East Asia, European peasant aprons and smocks, and Japanese woven textiles. For his 40th birthday, the designer became Minnie Mouse; his spring-summer 1988 menswear collection was a homage to Al Capone. Asked by Joan Quinn about travels and ethnic clothing, Kenzo replied: "I prefer to travel only for vacations. I don't go around looking for influences. The energy arrives." In fact, Kenzo serves as "the prototype of the young designer, the designer with a sense of humor about fashion, culture, and life, as well as a lively curiosity about clothing itself," as Caroline Milbank described, precisely because his theme collections and almost volcanic change imply a continuous stream of ideas. Kenzo, after all, emerged first as a designer of poor-boy-style skinny sweaters. Like Elsa Schiaparelli who likewise began with ingenious knits, he has become a prodigious continuing talent. His fashion references seem never to be imposed upon clothing, but are reasonable as a consequence of his design exploration: the low-slung waist returned Kenzo to casual, boyish styles of the skirt even as he acknowledged ethnic sources. Military and ecclesiastical looks in 1978 simply streamlined and simplified his style.

In addition, Kenzo has been fascinated by painting, drawing upon Wassily Kandinsky and David Hockney for inspiration, as well as calligraphy. His pallet has always been internationally vibrant, filled with the ethnic eruption of Fauvism, play of pattern, and unorthodox color combinations.

Is the work of this influential Japanese designer, born in Japan in 1939 and living in France since 1965, merely a kind of ethic parade in which the designer as a kind of latter-day Haliburton plunders the vocabularies of regional styles to remain exciting and innovative? Or, is there in Kenzo's synthesis of many aesthetics a creative mix, synergy, and energy that we might understand as the best product of multicultural awareness? After all, there were many fashion designers in the 1970s who used ethnic expressions merely to be hip.

Kenzo's work, in fact, argues strongly for the harmony of cultural influences, the most disparate and distinct expressions of dress coming together in the styles of a designer who has himself raised barbed issues of ethnicity in insisting upon "Jap" for his early collections, encouraging a racist pejorative to be converted into a positive identity.

Kenzo demonstrates a sustained aesthetic of absorption, assimilating many global influences into an integrated and wholly modern style of his own. The flamboyance of Kenzo's art and life captured the popular imagination of fashion in the 1970s, but his abiding and exemplary contribution is his ability to digest many style traits and to achieve a powerful composite. In 1978, Kenzo told André Leon Tally, "One needs a lot of folly to work in fashion" (*Women's Wear Daily*, New York, 17 February 1978). It is that sense of exuberance, creative excitement, and caprice that has marked Kenzo's work for more than two decades. Claude Montana once commented, "Kenzo gives much more to fashion than all the couturiers lumped together." Indubitably, Kenzo epitomized fashion energy and imagination in the 1970s: his brilliant creative assimilation brought street initiative and global creativity to fashion.—RICHARD MARTIN

Khanh, Emmanuelle

French designer

Born *Renée Mezière in Paris, 12 September 1937.*

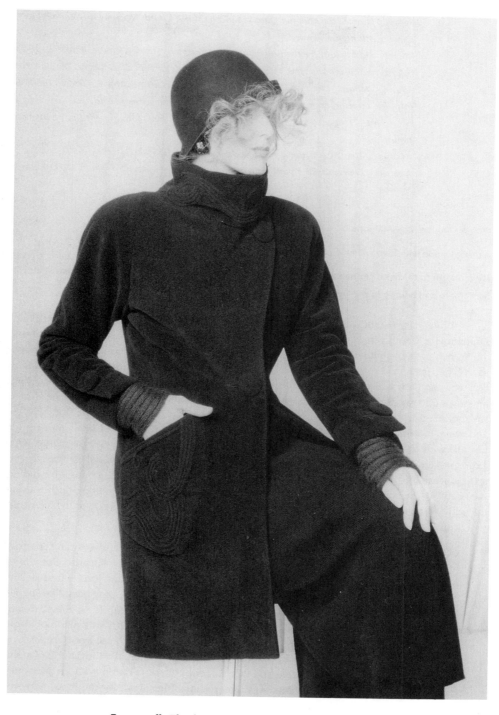

Emmanuelle Khanh: Winter 1994. *Photograph by H. Meister.*

Family   Married the designer Quasar Khanh (Manh Khanh Nguyen) in 1957; children: Othello, Atlantique-Venus.

Career   Mannequin for the Balenciaga and Givenchy fashion houses, Paris, 1957-63; began creating own designs, 1962; created collections for Belletête, Missoni, Dorothée Bis, Laura, Cacharel, Pierre d'Alby, Krizia, Max Mara, and Le Bistrot du Tricot, 1963-69; founder, director, Emmanuelle Khanh label and fashion garment and accessory company, from 1971; opened first Paris boutique, 1977; President, Emmanuelle Khanh International, 1987.

Awards   Named Chevalier des Arts et des Lettres, Paris, 1986.

Address   Emmanuelle Khanh International, 39 avenue Victor Hugo, 75116 Paris, France.

Women inspire me—fashions bore me.

A model made with love will skip off to the person who will live with it.

My strength is to make clothes which are timeless. To create clothes for me is a wonderful way to participate and belong to my era.—Emmanuelle Khanh

While Mary Quant was revolutionizing fashion in England at the beginning of the 1960s, Emmanuelle Khanh was at the vanguard of the young French ready-to-wear movement. From the French pronunciation of the Beatles' "yeah, yeah, yeah," the emerging clothes were known as "yé yé" fashion. Having modelled for Balenciaga and Givenchy in the late 1950s, Khanh believed the time was right for rebellion against the strictures of haute couture and to begin making attractive clothing for the masses. Her individuality quickly caught on in France, where she modelled and sold the clothes herself. Soon her modern fashions reached the United States and were in demand in major department stores. The clothes Khanh had been making for herself, with the help of her husband, Quasar Khanh, were noticed by *Elle* magazine. This exposure led to Khanh's collaboration with another ex-Balenciaga model to design the groundbreaking "Emmachristie" collection in 1962. Khanh criticized haute couture for hiding the beauty of the body. For her own designs, she emphasized femininity by cutting clothes along the body's curves, to follow the movement of the body, unlike Balenciaga's gowns, which could practically stand alone, regardless of the woman's body within them.

Khanh created an architecturally classic mode with a twist: careful seaming, narrow armholes, a slim, close to the body "droop" silhouette. Her suits had the surprise element of skirts that were actually culottes. Innovations included dog-eared collars, long, fitted jackets with droopy collars, blouses and dresses with collars consisting of overlapping petal-like shapes along a U-shaped opening. Khanh also had a democratic approach to fabric. She used denim and tie-dyeing, chenille, and plastic. A characteristic evening top in 1965 was made of crêpe appliquéd with fluorescent plastic circles. Khanh often used the Shetland wools and Harris tweeds that had long been favored by middle-class Frenchwomen. In the late 1960s she introduced ready-to-wear furs, and tulle and lace lingerie. In cooperation with the Missonis, Khanh made fashions from Italian knit fabrics. The results of her work for the Paris ready-to-wear house of Cacharel, and her work with designer Dorothée Bis, resulted in dresses with a long, slim, flowing 1930s feeling. The use of Romanian hand embroidery became a hallmark of the clothes which Khanh produced under her own label. Keeping pace with the ethnic trend of the 1970s, Khanh created short, loose, peasant-style dresses out of colorful Indian gauze fabrics. Feminine blouses would be trimmed with scalloped embroidered edges, short skirts would be frilled, and lace would be used to trim soft linen in her designs of that period.

Later, during the 1970s, Khanh turned to designing knitwear and skiwear. A casual summer look consisted of a wide, striped cotton skirt, buttoned down the front, worn with a matching halter top and wedged-heeled shoes of matching fabric. The matching shoes were a couture touch for ready-to-wear. During the next decade Khanh continued to free-lance, making soft, individualistic fashions, bouncing creative ideas off her engineer, inventor, and interior-designer husband.

Khanh's signature boldly-rimmed glasses have been successfully marketed, as have the clear plastic umbrellas she designed. One hundred and fifty boutiques around the world attest to her lasting popularity. In the 1980s her clothes had a retro feeling about them, with extended shoulders and cinched waistlines that flattered the figure. One outfit featured a very long, very loose camel hair coat falling freely from the shoulders, caught about the waist by a narrow leather belt, worn over a soft dark-brown wool jersey jumpsuit. For Jet Lag Showroom in 1990, Khanh designed a suit consisting of a waist-length tightly fitting jacket, worn with a long full flannel skirt. She continued in the 1990s to create comfortable, simple jackets and coats for special orders from the firm.—THERESE DUZINKIEWICZ BAKER

Kieselstein–Cord, Barry

American jewelry and accessories designer

Born   *New York, 6 November 1948.*

Education   *Studied at Parsons School of Design, New York University, and the American Craft Institute.*

Family   *Married Elisabeth Anne (CeCe) Eddy in 1974; daughter: Elisabeth.*

Career   *Worked as art director/producer for various advertising agencies, 1966-70; founded company, 1972; divisions include jewelry, belts, handbags (from 1991), gloves, and home furnishings and accessories. Opened in-store boutiques at Bergdorf Goodman, New York, 1985; Neiman Marcus, Beverly Hills, 1990, and Mitsukishi, Tokyo, 1990; has also opened shops in Italy, Germany, and Switzerland. Also: Artist; Director of Council of Fashion Designers of America, 1987.*

Collections   *Metropolitan Museum of Art, New York; Louisiana State Museum.*

Awards   *Hollywood Radio & Television Society Award, 1965; two Art Directors Club Awards, New York, late 1960s; Illustrators Society Award, New York, c.1967; Coty American Fashion Critics Award, 1979, 1984; Council of Fashion Designers of America Award, 1981.*

Address   *119 West 40th Street, New York, New York 10018, USA.*

My life as an artist started when I was about eight. My primary interest at that moment was directed toward North American Indian art. This was my first influence between the ages of eight and 14. I produced large-scale carvings and effigies and interpretations. Between 14 and 22 my focus had switched to painting and metalwork. At 14 I had also started to bury objects and metal in the ground to

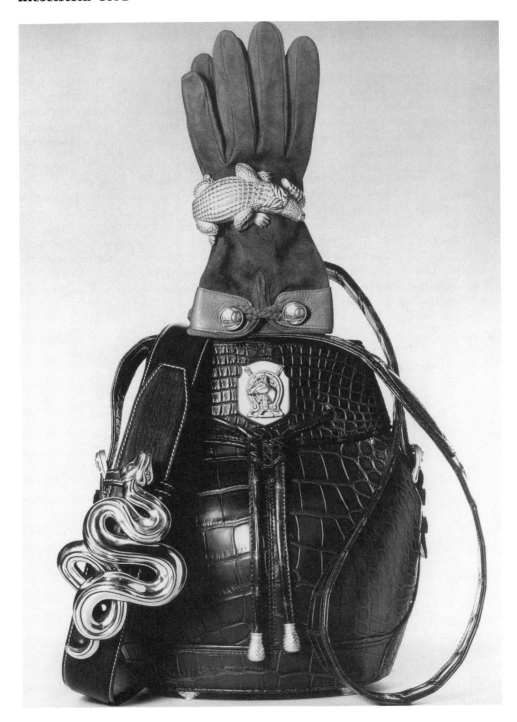

Barry Kieselstein-Cord: 1993; large serpent buckle on teal leather; large alligator bracelet; suede camel gloves; small western alligator tack sack.

observe color and patina changes. From the earliest moments I can recall fascination with all past cultures and an intense attraction to art and architecture, not surprising as in their youth my mother had been an illustrator and father an architect. I still hold these fascinations and occasionally some recall slips into my work. I have rarely ever looked at the ornamentation of other artists; my primary influences come from entire cultures and periods.

I am not influenced by fashion, preferring to be an influencer. Some of my most successful collections took three to five years to create the impact needed to make them commercially successful—really my most successful pieces I could not give away until people developed a new appreciation for my directions. Naturally this has produced my greatest reward (influencing direction) as an artist. My intent is to capture the illusive mental image—a single example is if you are riding in a car down a country road at a good speed, and think you see something wonderful. You stop your car and back up to discover what it was, only to find a jumble that your mind saw as a completed image. That is my creative process: to capture the illusive image that was the correlation between the speed, your mind's eye, and what you thought you'd seen; to make it three-dimensional; and to fill space with something new that was not there before this creation. As to contemporary fashion, the present mode of "anything goes" is quite wonderful. One can live out one's fantasy, bring it out of the closet and, if in good taste, be really very chic. I do like black ties on men and sexy elegant evening gowns on beautiful women. It quickens the pulse. . . .—Barry Kieselstein-Cord

In his affirmation "I don't make jewelry; I do sculptures for the body," Barry Kieselstein-Cord has described the independence and the ambition of his work. Like Elsa Peretti and other contemporary designers of jewelry, Kieselstein-Cord has sought to define an art that is autonomous from fashion, boldly sculptural in a way that makes a clear distinction from the wondrous but miniaturized repertory of a designer like Miriam Haskell, and historically aware without being subservient to past styles. His scarab *minaudiere,* for example, is indebted to ancient Egypt, as well as to the art deco Egyptian revival, but with the curtly reduced modernism that characterizes his work. His landmark—in law as in art, as their copyright was legally upheld from accessories pirates—belt buckles, the Vaquero, and the Winchester, are both of the Old West, but transmitted through art nouveau curvilinear interpretation. In fact, it is hard not to call Kieselstein-Cord's work jewelry, even as he avoids the term with "bodywork" or "sculpture," but the feeling is undeniably different from that of most jewelry. The designer argues that it comes from all the sculpture having as its Platonic ideal some large, even monumental form, surpassing its role on the human body.

Kieselstein-Cord has been one of the critical designers who, from the 1970s, has offered a jewelry that aspires to the condition of sculpture, allowing shapes to reclaim their ancient expressive, even spiritual/prophylactic, aspect in allowing jewelry to become something more than trivial adornment. After expressing his admiration for Easter Island statues, the designer told André Leon Talley, "I also like things which are sophisticated in an innately primitive way. Things that are transformed into a past and present that you can't identify. I like some of Miró's giant sculptures, some by Lipchitz, Noguchi, and Brancusi. The last thing I look at for inspiration is jewelry of any kind or period." Peretti, Robert Lee Morris, and Tina Chow would all probably adhere to the same spiritual striving and monumental desire for jewelry. Kieselstein-Cord had liberated jewelry from being paltry and precious in scale.

Similarly, Kieselstein-Cord disavows fashion as an influence, maintaining that jewelry must hold its separate aesthetic and power. "My accessories are not meant to be fashion," he told Jill Newman (*Women's Wear Daily Accessories Magazine*, January 1990). "They are designed to augment fashion. Things made of precious metal are meant to last forever and a day." Indeed, many of Kieselstein-Cord's designs have been of such enduring interest that they continue to be produced, while some collectors wait for each new sculptural edition in the manner of collecting any other artistic production. The Winchester belt buckle first produced in 1976 is still produced. In the early 1980s, he produced accessories for the home. Kieselstein-Cord's work has recently expanded in a line of high-quality handbags.

If Kieselstein-Cord takes his art seriously enough to declare it sculpture and not jewelry, he is nonetheless playful enough to realize diverse properties of materials and to bring some elements of non-western culture to the vocabulary of jewelry. In 1976, for example, a coiled choker of silk cord was accented with a gold orb; gold was used with tortoise-shell hair combs. In the same year, he created a splendidly reeling art nouveau antelope *minaudiere* that he engraved on the gold body to create a Florentine finish. A 1981 duck bandolier was a little Pancho Villa, a little nursery frieze for a fantastic equivocation in jewelry. John Duka declared his spring 1981 belt buckles "postmodern," perhaps the first time that appellation was used for accessories. Bold concha belts, Celtic interlace, and Gauguin-inspired shapes have been featured in his collections.

Kieselstein-Cord began his work in the 1970s, when American alternative culture might have convinced almost any marijuana-smoking hippie of the probity of body sculpture—and he even used cowboys and Indians to prove the point. What Kieselstein-Cord has done is more important and far-reaching: he has convinced all of us of the probity of body sculpture, spiritual and symbolic; he has enlarged the tradition of jewelry, giving it a chunky, palpable integrity; he has declared jewelry sovereign from fashion; and he has given jewelry and related accessories a standard of luxury along with a contemporary vocabulary.—RICHARD MARTIN

Klein, Anne

American designer

Born *Hannah Golofsky in Brooklyn, New York, 7 June 1923.*

Education *Studied art at Girls' Commercial High School, New York, and fashion at Traphagen School, New York, 1937-38.*

Family *Married Ben Klein (divorced, 1958); married Matthew Rubenstein in 1963.*

Career *Designer, Varden Petites, New York, 1938-40; designer, women's fashions for Maurice Rentner, 1940-47; founder and partner with Ben Klein, Junior Sophisticates, 1948-66; Anne Klein and Co., and Anne Klein Studio design firms established, c.1965.*

Exhibitions *Versailles, 1973; American Fashion on the World Stage, Metropolitan Museum of Art, New York, 1993.*

Awards *Mademoiselle Merit Award, 1954; Coty American Fashion Critics Award, 1955, 1969, 1971; Neiman Marcus Award, 1959, 1969; Lord and Taylor Award, 1964; National Cotton Council Award, 1965.*

Died *(in New York) 19 March 1974. Firm continued after her death with designers Donna Karan (to 1984), Louis Dell'Olio (to 1993), and Richard Tyler (from 1993).*

Address *205 West 39th St, New York, New York, 10018, USA.*

Known as an American designer, Anne Klein often bragged that she had never seen a European collection. Klein's philosophy was "not with what clothes might be but what they must be." Anne Klein's career spanned three decades and her contributions to the industry were many. Like Claire McCardell before her, Anne Klein helped to establish casual but elegant sportswear as defining American fashion.

Most notably, Klein transformed the junior-sized market from little-girl clothes designed with buttons and bows to clothes with a more sophisticated adult look. She also recognized that clothes for juniors should be designed for size rather than age. By analyzing the lifestyles of young women, Klein realized that the fashions offered to them did not reflect their needs. In 1948, Klein and her first husband, Ben Klein, opened Junior Sophisticates, a company dedicated to this market, thus expanding the industry. Her first collection for Junior Sophisticates featured the skimmer dress with jacket; full, longer skirts; small waists; and pleated plaid skirts with blazers.

During the mid-1960s, Klein free-lanced for Mallory Leathers, where she established leather as a reputable dress fabric in the ready-to-wear market. She designed leather separates in bright colors and smartly styled silhouettes.

In 1968 Anne Klein and Company and Anne Klein Studio were opened by Klein and her second husband, Chip Rubenstein. Focusing on sportswear with elegant styling, Klein established the concept of separates dressing. In doing this, she was teaching women a new way to dress. Klein proclaimed: "Do not buy haphazardly, but rather with a theme of coordination." In the showing of the collections as well as in the stores, Klein emphasized how interchangeable the clothes were. Her designs were sold in boutiques called Anne Klein Corners, which were in major department stores. This marked the beginnings of the individual designer shops within retail environments. Accessories also became an important part of the overall look. Klein designed belts, chains, shoes, and scarves which complemented her clothes.

Anne Klein focused on the needs of the American business woman in many of her collections for Anne Klein and Company. She relied on her own instincts to understand the diverse needs of the 1960s woman. By simplifying clothing, and showing women how to coordinate separates and accessorize, Klein taught the American woman how to dress with a minimum amount of fuss. The result was a finished, sophisticated look. The classic blazer was the central garment with shirtdresses, long midis and trousers introduced as well.

Anne Klein died in 1974. Designers Donna Karan, Louis Dell'Olio, and Richard Tyler continued as the designers at Anne Klein & Co. Anne Klein reformed the junior market and expanded the concept of separates dressing to define sportswear and the American Look.—MARGO SEAMAN

Klein, Calvin
American designer

Born *Bronx, New York, 19 November 1942.*
Education *Studied at Fashion Institute of Technology, New York, 1959-62.*

Family   *Married Jayne Centre in 1964 (divorced); daughter: Marci; married Kelly Rector in 1986.*

Career   *Assistant designer, Dan Millstein, New York, 1962-64; free-lance designer, New York, 1964-68; Calvin Klein Co. formed in partnership with Barry Schwartz, 1968, company reorganized, 1991. Fragrances include Obsession, 1985, and Eternity, 1988.*

Awards   *Coty American Fashion Critics Award, 1973, 1974, 1975; Bath Museum of Costume Dress of the Year Award, 1980; Council of Fashion Designers of America Award, 1993.*

Address   *205 West 39th St, New York, New York 10018, USA.*

Indisputable genius in marketing, recognized wizard in fashion financing, charismatic image-maker and image himself, Calvin Klein is the quintessential American fashion expression of the last quarter of the 20th century. The energy of his identification with jeans in the late 1970s and early 1980s, his later frontiers of underwear, and his consistent edge and eye in advertising image in print and media have rendered him a vivid figure in the landscape of American cultural life. A sleazy, potboiler biography of Klein in 1994 was titled *Obsession: The Lives and Times of Calvin Klein* (New York, 1994), taking its title from one of his fragrance and beauty products; its reference to "lives" sprung from lurid insinuations, but also testified to Klein's professional daring in being chameleon and index to American needs and desires. Years before, Michael Gross had already described Klein's life in *New York* magazine (8 August 1988) as "an extraordinary odyssey—a sort of one-man pilgrimage through the social history of modern America." Klein is homegrown hero to young America, the elusive image of the creator as mega-power and carnal charmer, the recurrent American worship of a tragic grandeur in those few who achieve absolute power in a democracy and who practice sexual thrall in a Puritan ethic. In 25 years as a top designer, Klein has established himself as a veritable obsession. He has only intensified that stature in spiralling success that challenges, yet flourishes in, the very visible arenas of fashion's dilation into culture.

Is Klein a designer? Suffused with aura and surrounded by negotiation—commercial and social—Klein might seem to have sacrificed his essential métier as a designer. Significantly, he has not. His sensibility for minimalist aesthetics, in an active lifestyle configuration with the ethos of sportswear, is as evident today as it ever was. Klein's clothing is as judicious as his marketing is advanced: streamlined pattern to be worn with ease prevails, even as he has looked at Madeleine Vionnet in the 1990s as assiduously as he considered, modulated Halston's and Giorgio di Sant'Angelo's radical innovations in the 1970s, and absorbed Armani's sober luxury in the 1980s. Klein's best eveningwear gives a first impression of delicacy and refinement, but the chaste construction—characteristically avoiding linings and complications—and the more durable and accommodating fabrics than one had imagined come into play as the wearer enjoys an unexpected freedom and mobility. Klein has made a virtue of all the cost-cutting, production-saving emendations that Seventh Avenue always wanted to make to save money; he has put the few high expenses in fabric at a conspicuous level of visibility and tactility, thus maximizing the economic effect.

Klein's fashion is the quintessence of American fashion expression and taste: his minimal construction promotes mass manufacturing; his ease allows comfortable dressing in all sizes and shapes; his penchant for quality wool, cashmere, cotton, and other feel-good textile luxuries affirms a sense of luxury in clothes otherwise so undistinguished in their simplicity as to pass unnoticed. While in a 1994 press statement Klein avows that "Everything begins with the cut," one knows that we are not thinking of cut and construction in the traditional fashion measure of Vionnet or Madame Grès. Klein's spare cut is not truly architectural; it is unobtrusive, or, in Bernadine Morris's words, "without frills" (*New York Times,* 1 May 1985). When the Council of Fashion Designers of America honored Katharine Hepburn in 1986, Klein made the presentation, one of true affinity, speaking to her traits of the "hard-working and independent woman who was never afraid to be comfortable" and whose penchant for trousers went from "scandalous" in the 1930s to "sensational" style in the 1980s.

Arguably, even Klein's marketing of jeans, underwear, and fragrance has been consistent in its aggressive, even opportunistic, address to gender and sexuality. Beginning with 1980 television advertising conceived by Richard Avedon and Klein using young model Brooke Shields, Klein has steadily set and stretched the parameters of American acceptance of overt sensuality in promotion of fashion and in public display ranging from national television campaigns to Times Square (New York) billboards to print media. Significantly, Klein's campaigns have been progressive, seeming in each instance to build upon and move beyond the first provocation and the inevitable acceptance of the prior campaign. Defining the public protocols of the 1980s and 1990s, Klein has made a distinct cultural contribution in advertising alone. Transporting fashion sensibility to clothing classifications prodigiously latent in sexuality such as jeans and underwear, Klein has likewise established the possibility of assertive sensuality and its designer personification in heretofore undeclared dominions of apparel. Cleaving gender needs and identities in fragrances in the 1980s through his Escape lines introduced in 1991-92, Klein launched the first major campaign for a shared gender fragrance in 1994.

James Brady wrote of Klein (*Parade,* 26 October 1986): "His success is so enormous, his income so vast, his lifestyle so lavish, that we tend to forget that in life there are no free rides." America distrusts its creative artists; America denies its geniuses in marketing and promotion; America violates its tokens of sexual license; America devours its heroes with zoological exigency. Controversy surrounds Klein as much as does celebrity. But it is incontrovertible that Klein has altered the landscape of modern American fashion and its perception as only a genius and a giant can. In an epoch of uncertainty and recriminations, Klein's imperfect, but ever-upward course of design actions has prompted dispute and jealousy, but there can be no contest to his incorporation of our time in his cleanly minimalist clothing and in the bodies that he has instinctively defined in media imagery to inhabit the clothes.—RICHARD MARTIN

Kobayashi, Yukio

Japanese designer

Career *Designer, menswear line, Monsieur Nicole line, for Matsuda.*
Address *(Matsuda) 3-13-11 Higashi, Shibuya-ku, Tokyo 150, Japan.*

Memory, both in the collective and crystalline form of analytical history and in the most vaporous ether of personal recollection, is the primary concern of Yukio Kobayashi's menswear for Matsuda. Memory mingles in Kobayashi's work with a desire for literary expression. Language blurts out irrepressibly in the work in frequent words, letters, and numbers. A lapel, for instance, may vanish into linear design or letters may become a surrealist free-fall of pattern. Literature abides in another way: the clothing is laden with an evocative knowledge of the

Yukio Kobayashi: For Matsuda, Fall/Winter 1993. *Photograph by Guy Marineau.*

tangible literary past, as if sartorial costuming for a Merchant-Ivory film (Kobayashi's 1984 collections had reflected movie-star elegance from the 1940s).

Kobayashi builds his clothing on the dandy's proposition that all clothing is to be seen in a self-conscious spectatorship. Tailored clothing explores a repertory of early 20th-century menswear with erudition; sportswear is supple and minimal, sometimes suggesting the Renaissance, Beau Brummel languor, or anticipating Utopia. Without contradiction to his historicism, Kobayashi is an apostle of advanced technology in synthetic fibers, often in startling juxtaposition with traditional materials and craft-domain handwork. The knowledge that manifestly animates Kobayashi's aesthetic has made Matsuda menswear favored apparel for artists and intellectuals; the *boulevardier* dandyism of the clothing is due to its intellectual edge. Peter Fressola characterized Kobayashi's work for Matsuda Men almost as an acquired, special taste in *DNR* (5 November 1986): "If you have never liked Matsuda, chances are good that you never will. But this designer has inspired the loyalty of a great many who willingly suspend judgment in favor of the rich, romantic, almost decadent aesthetic that is the world of his design." In literary traits and propensities, audacious style eclecticism, and dandy-like exactness, Kobayashi is creating the most romantic menswear of our time. Kobayashi's clothing is like learned, earnest, university discourse. Language specifically plays a role in meandering letters and in the adaptations of Matsuda's interest in speaking vestments. But design is also used ontologically: shapes, design standards, and menswear paradigms are acknowledged as principles in Kobayashi's work.

Kobayashi's aesthetic is invariably elegant, but he achieves his elegance not solely through refined materials, but through the tactile satisfactions of fabric and pattern. A Norfolk jacket, a favorite template of Kobayashi's design, is transformed by blocks of pattern at differing scale; robust outerwear becomes luxurious by the swelled proportions of the collar; in the 1990s, trousers are transfigured by their uninflected plainness, flat-front and cropped just above the ankle. Kobayashi mediates between the inherent elegance of his style and a simple sincerity of the design: he treats the basics of clothing, allows jackets to move with loose fit, explores soft velvety and corduroy materials, gives the gentle irony of tweed and houndstooth and plaids at all scales, and even in fall/winter 1992 uses a patchwork theme derived from childhood memories of his mother sewing patches on his play-worn trousers. *DNR* (5 February 1992) called the Kobayashi fall 1992 menswear "a modern, down-to-earth, *very* Matsuda look," capturing its unpretentiousness. Even argyle pattern, Donegal tweeds, jackets with suppressed waists, and other usurpations of the aristocracy seem common, comfortable, and friendly again. Thus, Kobayashi achieves the dandy's grace with none of the dandy's disdain or arrogance: rugged materials, comfort and vernacular borrowings are essential to his design. England and Scotland are the motherland of Kobayashi's historicist vision.

In brilliant command of menswear history, Kobayashi favors early 20th-century clothing, the time of menswear codification. Nonetheless, he is capable of reflecting with *bravura* elegance on Victorian *tartanitis* and in creating revelers from a Venetian masked carnival in modern form. Responding to a question in *Details,* Kobayashi said: "The early part of the century was a time when the way people thought about clothes was radically changing. But the period I enjoy speculating about most is the future." Without such a sense of late-modern invention and adventure, the components of Kobayashi's style might seem to fall into clever, but tiring, eclecticism. Instead, he keeps a sharp analytical edge and an unremitting sense of the new and vanguard about his clothing. After all, almost all other menswear designers have recourse to the same body of Anglophilic and Edwardian styles that inspire Kobayashi, but his energy is quicker, more intellectual, and more transforming. He does not succumb to the British Empire: he takes a sense of history and invests it in his personal memories and choices. In this, he divests the clothing of its colonialism: Kobayashi makes the tradition his own.

Few designers, especially in menswear, possess Kobayashi's consistency and intensity of vision. In this work the past becomes the present. He practises a cognitive historicism of styles, but insists on the freshness of the new garment. He functions with aesthetic opinion and conviction in the market of menswear. His style makes use of memory, even nostalgia, but he is creating advanced, manifestly modern clothing in the romantic tradition.—RICHARD MARTIN

Kors, Michael

American designer

Born *Long Island, New York, 9 August 1959.*

Education *Studied fashion design at Fashion Institute of Technology, New York, 1977.*

Career *Sales assistant, at Lothar's boutique, New York, 1977-78 (whilst studying at FIT), then designer and display director, 1978-80; established own label for women's sports-wear, 1981; also designer for Lyle & Scott, 1989; lower priced "Kors" line and menswear collection introduced, 1990; designer, womenswear collection for Erreuno J, from 1990; bridge line discontinued, company reorganized, 1993.*

Awards *Dupont American Original Award, 1983.*

Address *119 West 24th Street, New York, New York 10011, USA.*

Perhaps the best summary of Michael Kors was offered by Woody Hochswender (*New York Times,* 1 November 1988) when he said, "Mr Kors showed that simple doesn't have to be zero." Kors is inherently a minimalist working within a sportswear tradition. In this, he perpetuates and advances ideas of Halston, including a strong sexuality. He particularly flatters the gym-toned body of the late 1980s and early 1990s in stretchy, simple dresses that call attention to the body within. Minimalists in art and architecture might seem to remove themselves from the figure and human proportion; the irony is that a fashion minimalist like Kors draws attention to the figure within.

Moreover, while he has shown pattern, Kors prefers neutral color fields and emphasizes the apparel of the fabric with luxurious wools and cashmere for fall-winter and stretch and cotton for spring-summer. Leather in shirts, skirts, and jackets is essential for any Kors fall-winter collection; trousers are critical in all collections; and layering is important, even light layers in spring-summer collections. Kors spoke the language of separates in arguing to Bernadine Morris (*New York Times,* 28 April 1992), "Store buyers are zeroing in on the idea that women will probably not be shopping for entire new wardrobes. A single piece or two that will enliven everything else is what they will be searching for. And leather fills the bill—suede for times they are in a softer mood, smooth leather when they feel more aggressive." Kors's distinctive position as a leading minimalist in late-20th-century sportswear is achieved by his precise harmonics of color and fabrications in separates. In this, he predicts a reduced as well as reductive wardrobe, but one that has its own correlations and unanimity.

There is some affinity between Kors and Donna Karan, both creating innovative body suits, sensual stretch skirts and tops, and other sportswear elements, as well as borrowings from menswear. In fact, Karan and Kors are somewhat similar in their menswear collections as well. They share the dubious distinction of both offering bodyshirts (underpants attached to shirts) in menswear collections for fall 1992. If anything, Kors's minimalism is a little more referential than Karan's: he has deliberately evoked the glamour and sportiness of the 1930s, the "Belafonte" shirt of the 1950s, or vinyl late-1960s clothing. Despite his proclivity to the most simple in shapes, he produces clothes that are undeniably romantic (and Kors admits to loving the movies, telling Wendy Goodman (in *HG,* October 1991) that he had only two choices in life, movie star or fashion designer).

Of Claire McCardell, Kors acknowledges that he looked at her clothes in old magazines. "They were timeless. And she was the first designer to look not to Paris for inspiration but to the needs of the American woman." A spring-summer silk shantung scarf blazer by Kors reminds one of the McCardell twists and ties, but with all the sleek romance of a Noel Coward drawing room. Like the other sportswear designers, he learns from and responds to his clients and potential customers. He told Bart Boehlert (in *Connoisseur,* August 1988) that he likes to talk with women from his office, customers, and his mother, and ask what they most want in clothing.

His sportswear-based pragmatism is particularly effective as a monitor to the sexuality of his clothing. A bare Kors dress or jumpsuit may be audaciously sexy, but toned down with a neutral jacket or other cover-up, it can become suitable for the office. Conversely, Kors can take a simple skirt and blouse from the office setting into hot evening life with the addition of a leather jacket and a satin swing jacket. Only partly facetiously, he told Woody Hochswender (*New York Times,* 9 September 1990) of his comfortable and chic Kors line, "In Texas they call it carpool couture. They all want to wear something pretty for the carpool." Kors creates the pretty, the sexy, and the highly practical, a mastery in the harmonic balance of American sportswear.—RICHARD MARTIN

Kouyaté, Lamine (for Xüly Bet)

Malian fashion designer working in Paris

Born *Bamako, Mali, c. 1963, son of a diplomat and a doctor. Moved to Paris, c.1986.*
Education *Studied architecture at Architecture School of Strasbourg, France, and at La Villette, Paris.*
Career *Designs under Xüly Bet label, based in Kouyaté's Funkin' Fashion Factory, Paris; became known for recycled, patched-together clothing.*
Address *L'Hôpital Ephémère, 2, rue Carpeaux, 18e Paris, France.*

In a Paris collections report under the rubric "The Last Word," *Women's Wear Daily* (14 March 1994) recounted: "Deadly heat, a grating live band and groupies lounging on the floor. . . . But it wasn't a Grateful Dead concert—just Xüly Bet's *défilé* at La Samaritaine department store." Lamine Kouyaté, designing for his label Xüly Bet, has all the characteristics of an avant-garde and disestablishment fashion, but one that at least assumes a fashion system and that even shows good likelihood of becoming a positive and lasting element of the fashion system.

Recycling, collage, rags to riches economics, exposed seams and construction, a profoundly African sensibility and artistic temperament all seem at odds with Establishment fashion, but have, in fact, brought Xüly Bet to the mainstream and major recognition. Lauded as a fashion post-modernist and deconstructivist, Kouyaté's fashion coincides only with the intellectual postulation; his design creativity is more intuitive and personal, founded in his childhood in Mali, Africa, and the necessarily pastiched view of the world that he perceived in a former French colony. The 1993 Xüly Bet collection was based on torn, dismembered, and reassembled surplus and flea-market clothing, each a one-of-a-kind invention from the "given" of a distressed or discarded fashion object. His urban picturesque includes cropped jackets, bold African prints, graphics, and graffiti lacerated and reassembled, and long dresses that defy their own length in haphazard apertures, visible seaming, and a charming sense of coming apart. Kouyaté's dilapidated dresses and clothes are a romantic, enchanted vision.

As Kouyaté told Amy Spindler (*New York Times,* 2 May 1993), "At home, all the products come from foreign places. They're imported from everywhere, made for a different world, with another culture in mind. A sweater arrives in one of the hottest moments of the year. So you cut the sleeves off it to make it cooler. Or a woman will get a magazine with a Chanel suit in it, and she'll ask a tailor to make it out of African fabric. It completely redirects the look." Adaptation and alteration are paramount in Xüly Bet's work, beginning with the patchwork of distressed, repaired, and patched garments of 1993 and his 1994 compounds of cultures and fabrics. Like the Futurist demand that sculpture relinquish its pedestal, material unity, and high-art status, Kouyaté's fashion demands that high fashion come to the streets, flea markets, and collage medium to renew itself. It is, of course, a demolition for the purpose or rejuvenation, but an extreme of ruin that some find difficult to accept. Yet few could deny the beauty of Kouyaté's vision: sensuous patchwork, often skintight, gives the dress a sense of tattoo or body decoration more than of party dressing; his 1993 show sent African models out in Caucasian-colored "skin-tone" Band-Aids to reinforce the impression of scarification and the necessary politics of adornment. If Kouyaté's oeuvre shares principles with Martin Margiela's pensive and poetic deconstruction in fashion and both owe some debt to Rei Kawakubo's pioneering deconstructions of the early 1980s and again in the late 1980s, Kouyaté's African roots and sensibility set him apart, mingling rich pattern mix with the concept of collage. Kouyaté requires different eyes— the Xüly Bet name means the equivalent of "keep your eyes open," as with alertness and wonderment—and a Western willingness to accept an African aesthetic.

The reluctance to accept fully Kouyaté's innovative work resides less in its *épater les bourgeois* scorn for tradition and deliberate inversion of the economic order, for both of these are standard gambits of fashion novelty. The greater difficulty is probably in seeing improvised and aesthetically coarse (in Western terms and fashion's propensity to refinement) creation of fashion. But what Kouyaté proves is that the colonial disadvantage that he might supposedly have begun with is an opportunity and offers its own aesthetic. The lesson to old imperialisms is obvious; and fashion must know better than to be one of the ruined empires. A few tatters, some exposed junctures, and disheveled first impressions may be tonic and certainly far more interesting than an inflexible and rarefied status for fashion. Like Jean-Michel Basquiat's brilliant and lasting impact on American art, Kouyaté is showing the "real thing" of an African taste rendered in his own meeting with Western terms, not merely rich peasants or tourist views of a third world pageantry. Kouyaté's aesthetic is irrefutably an eye-opener for fashion.—RICHARD MARTIN

Lacroix, Christian

French fashion designer

Born *Christian Marie Marc Lacroix in Arles, France, 16 May 1951.*

Education *Studied art history at Paul Valéry University, Montpellier, and museum studies at the Sorbonne, Paris, 1973-76.*

Family *Married Françoise Rosensthiel in 1974.*

Career *Free-lance fashion sketcher, 1976-78; assistant at Hermès, Paris, 1978-80; assistant to Guy Paulin, 1980; designer and Artistic Director, house of Patou, 1981-87. Opened own couture and ready-to-wear house, 1987; Christian Lacroix haute couture and Boutique salons established in Paris, 1987; cruise collection developed, 1988; ready-to-wear collection designed for Genny, 1988; followed by menswear collection and boutique; seven accessory lines introduced, from 1989; line of ties and hosiery introduced, 1992; perfume, C'est la Vie! launched, 1990. Also designed costumes for American Ballet Theater's Gaieté Parisienne, New York, 1988.*

Awards *Dé d'Or Award, 1986, 1988; Council of Fashion Designers of America Award, 1987.*

Address *73 rue du Faubourg St Honoré, 75008 Paris, France.*

There is a prevalent myth in French haute couture that only once every decade does a new star emerge. Writer Nicholas Coleridge traced this path of succession from Paul Poiret, to Chanel, to Balenciaga, to Saint Laurent, then Lagerfeld (*The Fashion Conspiracy,* London 1988). Judging by the buzz and excitement that preceded the launch of his first collection in the Salon Impérial Suite of the Hotel Intercontinental in July 1987, there could be no doubt that the new star was Christian Lacroix.

Quite why Lacroix became the new star of couture is debatable but his timing was definitely right. There had been no opening of a couture house since 1961 with Saint Laurent. (Karl Lagerfeld became a star by resuscitating the established house of Chanel.) As the chairman

Christian Lacroix: Fall/Winter 1994/95.

and financial director of the new house, Paul Audrain was to declare, "We had a very strong presentiment that the climate was right for a new couture house." New social and cultural changes had reversed the values of the 1970s; the jeans and T-shirt dressing, so prevalent during that decade, had changed. A new sexual identity had emerged. The entrepreneurial spirit of the 1980s created new money and Lacroix's debut was in time to capitalize on this trend.

Christian Lacroix had begun his career with an aspiration to be a museum curator. After moving to Paris from Arles in the early 1970s he met his future wife Françoise Rosensthiel who encouraged his interest in fashion which led to his taking positions at Hermès and Guy Paulin. He became the designer for Jean Patou in 1981, revitalizing the flagging couture house and upping sales from 30 dresses a season to a hundred. He seduced the fashion press with spectacular shows, reviving fashion staples such as the frou-frou petticoat and the puffball skirt. It was in 1987, with the backing of five million francs from the textile conglomerate Financière Agache, that Lacroix opened his new couture house.

As a designer Lacroix throws caution to the wind, providing the sort of luxurious product that, at first, justified the amount of "new money" spent on him. His collections are always an exotic, lavish cornucopia of influences, ranging from the primitive, rough naïveté of the paintings of the Cobra movement, to a homage to Lady Diana Cooper, to modern gypsies, travellers, and nomads. He uses the most luxurious fabrics in often unexpected mixes or even patchwork, embroidered brocades, fur, re-embroidered lace, ethnic prints and embroideries, even gold embroidery. Nothing is considered too expensive or too *outré* to be included in the clothes.

An extravagant technicolour musical from the golden age of Hollywood would perhaps be an understatement when describing the impact of a Lacroix collection. As an artist he is not afraid to plunder junk shops, museums, the theatre and opera, or the glamour of the bullfight to create designs that astound, yet are always stylish in their eclectic clutter.

There are many strong retrospective 1950s, 1960s and 1970s references in a Lacroix collection: the detached hauteur or waif-like gestures of fashion models from the period. The unapproachable allure of movie stars like Tippi Hedren or Capucine, or real-life personalities who embody these qualities, all inspire his designs, often resulting in eccentric accessories, colours, and poses.

Lacroix recognizes that contemporary couture is often only a public relations exercise for money-spinning ventures such as perfume or licensing deals that use a designer name to sell a product. However, Lacroix is fully aware of the value couture has in pushing fashion, projecting a dream, and making dramatically important fashion statements. This is essential if fashion is to survive commercially because the ready-to-wear and mass-market manufacturers always see designers as the inspirations that direct the movement of fashion. Before his first show Lacroix seemed to synthesize this point of view when he said, "I want to get back to the position where the couture becomes a kind of laboratory of ideas, the way it was with Schiaparelli 40 years ago."—KEVIN ALMOND

Lagerfeld, Karl

German designer

Born *Hamburg, 10 September 1938. Immigrated to Paris in 1952.*

Career *Design assistant at Balmain, 1955-58; art director, Patou, 1958-63; free-lance designer for Chloë, Krizia, Ballantyne, Timwear, Charles Jourdan, Valentino, Fendi, Cadette, Max Mara and others, from 1964; director of collections and ready-to-wear, Chanel, from 1983; Karl Lagerfeld and KL ready-to-wear firms established in Paris and Germany, 1984; Karl Lagerfeld, S.A., acquired by Chloë parent company, Dunhill, 1992; created fragrances Lagerfeld, for Elizabeth Arden, 1975, Chloé-Lagerfeld for men, 1978, KL for women, 1983, KL for men, 1984. Also photographer and stage designer.*

Exhibitions *Karl Lagerfeld: Fotografien, Galerie Hans Mayer, Dusseldorf, 1989.*

Awards *Second prize, International Wool Secretariat design contest, 1954; Neiman Marcus Award, 1980; Bath Museum of Costume Dress of the Year Award, 1981; Council of Fashion Designers of America Award, 1991; Fashion Footwear Association of New York Award, 1991.*

Address *14 Boulevard de la Madeleine, 75008 Paris, France.*

Universally recognized as one of the most prolific and high-profile designers of the last 20 years, Karl Lagerfeld has maintained his reputation through consistently strong work for the numerous lines he produces every year. Each label has its own distinct look, while clearly bearing the bold, uncompromising Lagerfeld signature that guarantees the success of everything he produces.

Moving between the six main collections he designs with consummate ease, he displays the skills he learned from his couture background in his fine tailoring and flashes of surreal detailing. He functions best as a catalyst, re-invigorating labels and broadening their customer base. Since 1983 he has most spectacularly demonstrated this capability at Chanel, where, despite some criticism, Lagerfeld has brought the label to the pinnacle of high fashion. He has produced endless innovative variations on the signature tweed suits that often mix street style references, for example, teaming the traditional jacket with denim mini skirts (1991), with the signature Chanel gilt buttons and chains. He stretches the look to embrace younger customers' tastes, with club-influenced black fishnet bodystockings, the traditional Chanel camellia placed cheekily over the breasts, and hefty lace-up boots set against flowing georgette skirts and leather jackets. This combination of wit with recognizable Chanel symbols has rejuvenated the house, making Lagerfeld's fashion word an aspirational message to a new generation. His experiments are at their most fantastic in the vibrant lines of the couture show, made more accessible in the ready-to-wear range. Only Lagerfeld could put the Chanel label on underpants (1993) and camellia-trimmed cotton vests (1992) to make them the most talked-about elements of the Paris collections. This quirkiness is underpinned by the quality of his designs and the mix of classic separates that are always an undercurrent in his work.

His own name label KL highlights these skills. Bold tailoring, easy-to-wear cardigan jackets in his favourite bright colours, combined with softly shaped knitwear, show the breadth of his talents and ensure the longevity of his appeal. If his more outrageous combinations of references at Chanel have enabled him to outlive the excesses of the 1970s that trapped some of his contemporaries, then his clever manipulation of fabric and colour prolongs the life of his clothes still further.

During the 1970s his work for Chloë was equally influential, his love of eveningwear coming to the fore, albeit in a more restrained form than at Chanel. The main look of this period was flowing pastel chiffon draped onto the body to give a highly feminine feel and trimmed with silk flowers. He recreated this style for his return to the label in spring-summer 1993, complete with Afro-wig-wearing models. At first coolly received by the fashion press, it went on to inspire many with its floaty silhouette and flower-child air, reviving ethereal dresses with no linings, unnecessary seams, or extraneous detail.

While he continues to move from label to label, never quite losing the free-lance mentality of his early days, it is only the occasional lack of editing in his collections that betrays how widely his talents are spread. Idea follows idea, frequently inspired by his current model muse as he re-interprets garments to create very modern styles. At Fendi this desire to continually push forward to greater modernity, absorbing the influences around him and seeking greater perfection in his work, led to his taking the furriers' trade a step further. The lightness of touch that had established his name as early as 1970 led him to strip the Fendi sisters' signature fur coats to the thinnest possible layer. He removed the need for heavy linings by treating the pelts to produce supple lightweight coats shown in 1973 with raglan sleeves and tie belts, which complemented the sporty feel of the knitwear he also produces for the company.

Lagerfeld's position in fashion history is assured. He is equally skilled in his bold strokes at Chanel as in his delicate shaping at Fendi and Chloë, or in the vibrant classics of his own lines. His skill as a designer has enabled him to push the discipline further by combining the immediacy of ready-to-wear with the splendour and elegance of couture.—REBECCA ARNOLD

Lane, Kenneth Jay
American jewelery and accessories designer

Born *Detroit, Michigan, 22 April 1932.*
Education *Studied at the University of Michigan, 1950-52, and at Rhode Island School of Design, Providence, 1953-54.*
Family *Married Nicola Samuel Waymouth in 1975 (divorced, 1977).*
Career *Art staff member, Vogue (New York), 1954-55; assistant designer, Delman Shoes, New York, 1956-58; associate designer, Christian Dior Shoes, New York, 1958-63; founder, designer, Kenneth Jay Lane, New York, from 1963. Kenneth Jay Lane shops located in the United States, Great Britain, France, and Austria.*
Awards *Coty American Fashion Critics Award, 1967; Harper's Bazaar International Award, 1967; Tobé Coburn Award, 1966; Maremodo di Capri-Tiberio d'Oro Award, 1967; Neiman Marcus Award, 1968; Swarovski Award, 1969; Brides Magazine Award, 1990.*
Address *20 West 37th Street, New York, New York 10018, USA.*

Acclaimed by *Time* Magazine as "the undisputed King of Costume jewelry" and called "one of the three great costume jewelers of the 20th century" by *Women's Wear Daily*, Kenneth Jay Lane transformed a previously undistinguished field into the height of fashion.

Kenneth Jay Lane.

"I believe that every woman has the right to be glamorous and have always believed that a woman can be just as glamorous in costume jewelry as million dollar bangles and beads," he once said. "Style has little to do with money and expensive possessions; attitude and flair make all the difference."

Born in Detroit, Kenneth Jay Lane attended the University of Michigan for two years, then came east to earn a degree in advertising design from the Rhode Island School of Design. After a brief stint in the art department at *Vogue* in New York, he went on to become the fashion coordinator at Delman Shoes, New York. Later, while working as an associate designer for Christian Dior Shoes, he spent part of each summer in Paris under the tutelage of the preeminent French shoe designer, Roger Vivier. He also designed a shoe collection for Arnold Scaasi in New York. In 1963, while adorning shoes with rhinestones and jeweled ornaments, he began to experiment with making jewelry.

"A whole new group of beautiful people began to exist," Lane said. "They started dressing up and costume jewelry was rather dull. I believed it didn't have to be." The thought that fake jewelry could be as beautiful as the real thing grew on Lane. He bought some plastic bangles at the dime store, covered them with rhinestones, crystals, leopard and zebra patterns and stripes, and a new era in costume jewelry was born.

In 1963, while still designing shoes, he worked nights and weekends, creating jewelry. "I started moonlighting jewelry," he said. Since he was being paid by Genesco, Delman's parent firm, to design shoes, "I thought it would be in better taste to use my own initials and not my name for jewelry." His work was enthusiastically received, written about and photographed by the fashion magazines. Neiman Marcus in Dallas and Bonwit Teller, New York placed orders for rhinestone earrings. Within a year, his jewelry was bringing in 2000 dollars a month wholesale, and by June 1964, sales had risen to 10,000 dollars a month wholesale. His part-time jewelry business became a full-time career. In 1969 Kenneth Jay Lane Inc. became part of Kenton Corporation, an organization that includes Cartier, Valentino, Mark Cross, and other well known names in fashion. Lane repurchased the company in 1972.

Lane considers himself a fine jeweler, and eschews the traditional methods of making costume jewelry. First, he fabricates his designs in wax by carving or twisting the metal. He often sets the designs with opulent stones highlighted by their cut and rich colors. Many of these stones, particularly the larger ones, he has created for himself. "I want to make real jewelry with not-real materials," he noted. He sees plastic as the modern medium: lightweight, available in every color, and perfect for simulating real gems. He likes to see his jewelry intermixed with the real gems worn by his international roster of celebrity customers. Lane is proud of the fidelity of his reproductions and claims that some of "faque" stones look better than the real ones.

"I work in less commercial ways than most manufacturers of costume jewelry," says Lane. He is realistic about the source of his designs. "My designs are all original—original from someone," he said. "There are original ideas, but a lot of good designing is editorial, choosing what is available idea-wise and applying these ideas practically. I think it's called 'having the eye'. It isn't necessarily reinventing the wheel."

Lane is as much a showman as talented designer. In addition to receiving numerous fashion awards, his jewelry was regularly featured on several soap operas, including *Another World, The Guiding Light,* and *Days of Our Lives.* He has also created jewelry for the Costume Institute exhibitions at the Metropolitan Museum of Art, New York.

In addition to being a fixture on the social circuit, Lane is frequently named on the International Best Dressed Men's List. "All you need is one person and you can meet the world," he said. Dinner-partner and friend to some of the world's most fashionable women, his clients have included Jacqueline Kennedy Onassis, Princess Margaret, the Duchess of Windsor, Elizabeth Taylor, Audrey Hepburn, Nancy Reagan, Joan Collins, Babe Paley, Brooke Astor, and Lee Radziwill Ross. Ex-First Lady Barbara Bush wore his "pearls" to her husband's inauguration, and that triple-strand has become an integral part of her signature style. Recently, he sent his 21-dollar saxophone pin to First Lady Hillary Rodham Clinton, to whom he wrote: "Looking forward to eight years of sweet music."

In 1993 Kenneth Jay Lane celebrated his 30th anniversary in business. The *New York Times* called him "the man who made costume jewelry chic and, more important to his bank account, readily available to what is loosely referred to as the masses. Chanel had done it earlier, but to a more affluent clientèle" (27 June 1993). Lane now has 20 stores in the United States, Canada, and Europe and recently celebrated his second year selling fashion on QVC, the cable television home-shopping network.—JANET MARKARIAN

Lang, Helmut

Austrian designer

Born *Vienna, Austria, 10 March 1956.*

Career *Grew up in Austrian Alps and Vienna; became acquainted with Viennese art scene; established own fashion studio in Vienna, 1977; made-to-measure shop opened in Vienna, 1979; developed ready-to-wear collections, 1984-86. Presented Helmut Lang womenswear, 1986, and Helmut Lang menswear, 1987, as part of Paris Fashion Week. Established license business, 1988. Moved several times between Paris and Vienna, 1988-93. Professor of Fashion Masterclass, University of Applied Arts, Vienna, since 1993. Other lines include Helmut Lang Men's Shoes, 1995, Helmut Lang Men's Underwear, 1996, and Helmut Lang Jeans, 1996. Opened franchise shops in Munich, Vienna, Milan, 1995-96.*

Collection *Museum of Applied Arts, Vienna.*

Addresses *P.O. Box 133, A-1013 Vienna, Austria. Press Office, c/o Michele Montagne, 184 rue St Maur, F-75010 Paris, France.*

At a moment of conflicting demands, people want modernity and identity, street style and savviness. Fashion now is fast, downbeat, and relentlessly urban. Because of that, I have been developing a particular vision; what I call a non-referential view of fashion. It is all about today. It has to do with my personality, with my life and with the idea that quality doesn't go out of style every six months. Working effectively with fashion means adding pieces to a continuing story, evolving fluently year after year. The basis of really effortless style is found in minimal exaggeration. A perfect economy of cut and exacting attention to finish is sometimes lost to the careless eye, which gives it precisely the sort of anonymous status that the truly knowing admire. If you have to ask, you don't get it, in either sense. Downbeat elegance is founded in precise proportions and clean tailoring; balancing hi-tech fabrics with real

Helmut Lang: 1994/55; reflecting jeans and cowboy boots painted with red nail polish.
Photograph by Jürgen Teller.

clothing. The result is fashion put into a different context to become something known, unknown.—
Helmut Lang

An attenuated, urban aesthetic, embodied by subtle mixes of luxury fabrics and post-punk synthetics, dominates Helmut Lang's confident designs. Both his men's and womenswear is uncompromisingly modern: stark minimalist pieces in sombre city shades are combined with harsh metallics and slippery transparent layers, questioning the restrictions of traditional tailored clothing.

Although Lang's work is avant-garde, he is unafraid to use sharply cut suiting, lending it an etiolated androgyny; with a punk-like disregard for accepted fabric use, as cigarette trousers and three buttoned jackets come in shiny PVC with clingy net T-shirts worn beneath. He enjoys the surprise of such cheap fabrics being lent a certain chic through their combination with their more luxurious counterparts, and often backs silk with nylon to give a liquid, shifting opacity to column dresses and spaghetti-strapped slips.

For all the deconstructed glamour of his clothes, they remain essentially understated, drawing their interest from the layering of opaques and transparents in sinuous strong lines, rather than unnecessary details which might dull their impact. Even the sexuality of his figure-hugging womenswear is tempered by a nonchalance and apparent disregard for the impact the clothes have. This parallels the growing sense of independence and confidence of women over the 15 years Lang has been designing.

If his stylistic reference points originated touching the past, then his distillation of them is always utterly contemporary. In line with, and often ahead of, current trends, he honed his skills during the 1980s, contradicting the decade's often overblown characteristics and charming first the Parisian, then the international fashion scene, which was impressed by the modernity of his work. He remains a hero of the *cognoscenti,* influencing mainstream fashion.

The simplicity of the cut of his garments is deceptive though. The slim mannish-shaped trousers he favours for women may be timeless enough, but the surprise of rendering them in hot red stretch synthetic in 1992 and creating an urban warrior look with halter top and toning boned breast-plate meant they appealed to the stylishly unconventional, who were unafraid to slip from day to night, informal to formal, disregarding the normal restrictions of what is appropriate to wear.

His emphasis on the importance of the innovative use of textiles is as prevalent in his menswear. He has been at the forefront of the shift of feeling in this area, which has gathered momentum during the 1990s. He has pushed for a crossover of fabrics from womenswear and a narrower line, shown in 19th-century cut three-piece single breasted suits, more attuned to the times than the big triangular silhouette of the 1980s. His deconstructed closefit tops with visible seaming and layered angora tank tops over untucked shirts increased his popularity as fashion became tired of its own overpowering dogma in the early 1990s.

Lang's work continues to maintain a high profile in fashion magazines. The deceptive simplicity of his clothes, complicated by his constant comparisons of clear and opaque, matt and shiny, silk-smooth and plastic-hard, has carried him successfully into the 1990s and, indeed, has enabled him to be part of a movement in fashion towards a redefinition of glamour and beauty. This revelling in texture and surface effect with raw dark and bright colours brings together the confrontation of the emaciated punk aesthetic with sophisticated restrained tailoring, producing a mature sense of negligent chic.—REBECCA ARNOLD

Lanvin

French fashion house

Founded in Paris in 1890 by Jeanne Lanvin (1867-1946) offering custom children's clothing; women's clothing offered, from 1909; men's clothing, from 1926; and women's sportswear, furs and accessories; women's ready-to-wear, from 1982. Fragrances: My Sin, 1925; Arpège, 1927; Scandal, 1931; Runeur, 1934; Pretexts, 1937; Crescendo, 1960. Products also included women's toiletries and cosmetics. Designers for the House of Lanvin have included Antonio del Castillo (active, 1950-62), Jules-François Crahay (active, 1963-85), Maryll Lanvin (from 1982), Claude Montana (1990), and Dominique Morlotti (from 1992).

Exhibitions *Paris Couture—Années Trente, Musée de la Mode et du Costume, Palais Galliera, Paris.*

Collections *Victoria and Albert Museum, London; Fashion Institute of Technology, New York; Costume Institute of the Metropolitan Museum of Art, New York; Musée de la Mode et du Costume, Paris; Musée des Arts de la Mode, Paris.*

Awards *Jeanne Lanvin, recipient, Chevalier de la Légion d'Honneur, 1926; Officier de la Légion d'Honneur, 1938.*

Address *15, 22 rue du Faubourg St.-Honoré, 75008 Paris, France.*

The youthful look identified with Lanvin came from her earliest couture, children's dresses; the many decorations were inspired by a trip to Spain during her childhood. The memory of the play on shadows and light would influence her choice of embroidery, such as multi-needle sewing machines stitching and quilting. She had three embroidery *ateliers*. Beading and appliqué were also applied. With dyes she ombréed textiles. She had her own dye works—Lanvin Blue inspired by stained glass was developed there. These decorations were applied to all categories: millinery, couture, menswear, and accessories.

Lanvin did not drape or sketch, but gave verbal instructions to the sketchers. Approved drawings were sent to *ateliers* for execution. Although Art Déco-style embroideries continued well into the 1930s, ideas come from all periods of art. She found inspiration everywhere—from her painting collection containing Vuillard, Renoir, Fantin-Latour, and Odilon Redon—from books, fruit, gardens, museums, travel, and costume collections. She had her own costume archives dating 1848-1925. Nothing was taken literally but interpreted. The chemise as women's dress was introduced in 1913. Her best known innovation, the *robe de style*, was an adaptation of the 18th-century pannier. Introduced in the 1920s, repeated in a variety of fabrics: silk taffeta, velvet, metallic lace with organdy, chiffon, and net. New models were presented for two decades.

She showed tea gowns, dinner pajamas, dolman wraps, hooded capes, and Zouave bloomer skirts that were either youthful, classic, or romantic. Her clear colors were subtle and feminine: begonia, fuchsia, cerise, almond green, periwinkle blue, cornflower blue. Silver was combined with black or white.

Adjusting to World War II, she created the split coat for bicycling and bright colored felt gas-mask cases. During the Liberation, she presented showings for American soldiers. Her family continued the business after her death. Antonio del Castillo, arriving in 1950, attempted to adapt to the house image. His Spanish background influenced his choice of brighter colors, light and heavy combinations of fabrics, and more severe sophisticated styles. His successor, Jules-François Crahay, returned to the collections the youthful quality which remains today.—BETTY KIRKE

Lars, Byron
American designer

Born *Oakland, California, 19 January 1965.*
Education *Studied at the Brooks Fashion Institute, Long Beach, California, 1983-85, and at the Fashion Institute of Technology, New York, 1986-87; selected to represent USA at the International Concours des Jeunes Créateurs de Mode, Paris, 1986, and at the Festival du Lin, Monte Carlo, 1989.*
Career *Free-lance sketcher and pattern maker, Kevan Hall, Gary Gatyas, Ronaldus Shamask, Nancy Crystal Blouse Co., New York, 1986-91. Showed first collection, 1991; also designer, En Vogue fashion collection, from 1993.*
Exhibitions *Byron Lars' Illustrations, Ambassador Gallery, New York, 1992.*
Awards *Vogue Cecil Beaton Award for illustration, London, 1990.*
Address *202 West 40th Street, New York, New York 10018, USA.*

The career of Byron Lars took wing with his fall 1992 collection inspired by legendary aviatrix Amelia Earhart, but Lars had already been for several years one of the most closely watched and praised newcomers in New York. If the fall 1992 collection consolidated his reputation (and not coincidentally his business circumstances, including backing from C. Itoh & Company), it was built on the same strengths that had characterized his earlier work. Appropriating from menswear, with a special interest in the man's dress shirt and in stripes and patterns especially associated with menswear, melding isolated elements of exaggeration with conventional dress in a dry irony, and responding concomitantly to high fashion and street influences, Lars has developed a signature style while still in his twenties. According to Anne-Marie Schiro (*New York Times,* 7 June 1992), stores "love his clothes, which can be quirky yet classic, streetwise but never vulgar. His inspiration may come from baseball or aviation, from rappers or schoolgirls. And the accessories are outrageous: caps with oversize crowns and two-foot-long peaks, lunch boxes or boom boxes as handbags. They make you smile." The references of Lars's clothing are easily identified and wholly likable in a quintessentially American mix of the orthodox and heretical, a flip view of fashion history and sources that can take the most wonderful plaids of the north woods and bring them into urban baseball-cap insouciance. A fall 1992 greatcoat with airplanes and parachutes bespeaks East Asia in the simplicity of its design and in the integrity of its shaping into the trajectories of the planes.

The designer Jeffrey Banks called Lars "the African-American Christian Francis Roth," relating Lars's visual resolution of content incongruity to Roth's paradoxes of sophisticated

Byron Lars.

innocence in clothing. Roth and Lars share yet another characteristic: they are both consummate masters of the cut, enjoying the construction of the garment almost in the manner of the couture. Lars is not making a mere joke of the man's shirt cross-dressed for a woman, but takes the shirt tail as a constructive element, reshapes the bust, and deconstructs, as it were, the man's shirt to be worn by a woman. It is as much a *tour de force* in construction as it is an apt idea of 1990s gender transaction. If Byron Lars's clothes were merely facetious, they would succeed as great fun. But they succeed as great fashion because they are beautifully cut.

In adapting menswear, Lars is attentive to feminine outcomes, offering a kind of enhanced sensuality in the presence of male and female in one garment. In many instances, peplums emphasize waist and hips (but not with the 1980s power look) and the sartorial nuancing of shirt and jacket for women directs attention to a broadened expanse of the bust. Often including even the man's tie, the result is unequivocally feminine when Lars includes a built-in bra for shaping. Even as he used airplane motifs in textiles in his epochal fall 1992 collection, his fantasy was not a little boy's: aviator jackets had a curvaceous femininity approximating Azzedine Alaia (also taking advantage of exposed seams as force lines and body-hugging allure); shorts, short skirts, and leggings emphasized the female. A duck hunter's outfit in plaid (with a duck decoy made into a handbag), seemingly destined for the L.L. Bean catalog before a perverse, savvy drollery rendered it chic, was featured in the "Tribute to the Black Fashion Museum" exhibition at the Fashion Institute of Technology, New York, in spring 1992.

Even before the Earhart collection, Lars was influenced by the 1940s. His twists of menswear in the best Rosie-the-Riveter tradition, and his fascination with the sarong, recall the period. Both shirts and sarongs depend upon tying, a sense of the improvised wrap, that the designer builds into the garment, but may read for the viewer as a kind of improvisation. In this, Lars also has a great antecedent in Claire McCardell, whose lifelong interest in casual wraps is similar to Lars's fascination with the shaping and informality afforded by tying.

If still a prodigy today, Lars began as a fashion designer in tenth grade when he designed the baggy pants he wanted for himself. Little more than a decade later, Lars is making clever yet important clothes, wearable ideas, wondrous social transplants and mutations, and some of the most sensitively and sensuously cut garments in America.—RICHARD MARTIN

Laug, André
French designer working in Italy

Born *Alsace, France, 29 December 1931.*
Career *Moved to Paris, 1958, to begin working for Raphäel fashion house; designer, Nina Ricci, Paris, early 1960s. Worked free-lance, from 1962, selling designs to Venet; also collaborating with Courrèges until 1963, when he moved to Rome. Designed nine collections of haute couture and five of ready-to-wear for Maria Antonelli, 1964-68; opened own couture house And showed own collection, Rome, 1968.*
Died *(in Rome) December 1984. House continued after his death.*
Address *81 Piazza di Spagna, 00187 Rome, Italy.*

Women's Wear Daily (20 July 1978) reported on a retailer's response to André Laug's couture collection: "The suits, the suits, the suits. His suits are divine. I love everything in black and black with gray—and there's a lot of it. These clothes are so neat, so technically perfect, so sharp. I could not be happier." For the client of keenest interest in impeccable tailoring along with a kind of restraint and temperate elegance about her style, Laug was the perfect expression of the Roman couture. From the 1960s until his death in 1984, Laug produced definitive collections of Roman style combining expertise in tailoring and the richest materials with a sober moderation.

For the American clientèle in particular, his suits held a *Daisy Miller* enchantment in an equilibrium between European sensuality and luxury and American simplicity. Americans may have, in general, expected the fireworks of extravagant Roman couture in the 1970s, but Laug provided an aesthetic closer to *Roman Holiday,* a reserved beauty. Moreover, the designer's success in the couture occasioned a lively, if somewhat less characteristic, ready-to-wear business in the late 1970s and 1980s.

Tailored clothing by Laug was sufficiently elegant to move from cocktails to evening. A simple Laug black jacket with mushroom-like shoulders could have worked for daywear, but clearly would pass as evening dress. In his final collection, a charcoal quilted wool and silk evening jacket with black velvet trousers could have sufficed for an elegant day as much as for evening. Laug knew the ethos of casual clothing in the 1970s and created an eveningwear that accommodated the social change of the period toward informality. His American clientèle was typically old-guard and even conservative, the high-quality and high-comfort sense of the Philadelphia Main Line (his discreet good taste sold especially well at Nan Duskin in Philadelphia). As Bernadine Morris noted, "His designs were not the spectacular kind that change the shape of fashion. They were conservative day and evening clothes, which made women feel comfortable. They reflected the way Mr. Laug himself dressed, like a banker."

Trustworthy chic of Laug's kind has often been compared to men's wear in opposition to the fluctuations of women's fashion in the 1970s. By avoiding excess, in allowing for a mix of day and evening elements, Laug allowed his clients to develop a sensible, abiding wardrobe. Like menswear, trousers and jackets were basic for both day and evening. Jackets were clearly tailored for women with a defined waist. Ironically, Laug's design interests and his personal sense of forbearance were pursued by many other designers by the time of Laug's death at the age of 53. His love of black was almost the same as the prevalence of fashion black in the 1980s. The swanky luxury of Laug's understated garments began with the textiles, lining jackets with rich and vivid textiles that inflect the relative moderation of the exterior. Further, the abstemious chic of a Laug suit would assume apparent luxury as accompanied by its silk blouse.

In the subtle distinctions among those designers who influence their colleagues and establish wardrobes for the most stylish women, as opposed to the most flamboyant and visible, André Laug represents the achievement of fashion as a well-bred, well-made design art. His catwalk shows were extravagant and showy, but not so the clothing. He sought no vanguard and claimed no new invention, but he made undeniably beautiful clothing for the most selective clients practicing a lifestyle of utmost urbanity and discretion.—RICHARD MARTIN

Lauren, Ralph
American designer

Born   *Ralph Lifschitz, in the Bronx, New York, 14 October 1939.*

Ralph Lauren: Robert Redford in *The Great Gatsby* (1974), costumes designed by Lauren.
Photograph: Paramount, courtesy of The Kobal Collection.

Education *Studied business science, City College of New York, late 1950s.*

Military Service *Served in the U.S. Army, 1962-64.*

Family *Married Ricky Low-Beer, c. 1964; children: Andrew, David, and Dylan.*

Career *Part-time sales assistant, Alexanders stores, New York, 1956-57; assistant menswear buyer, Allied Stores, New York, 1958-61; salesman, Bloomingdale's and Brooks Brothers, New York, 1962; road salesman in New England for A. Rivetz neckwear manufacturer, Boston, c.1964-66; designer, Polo Neckwear Division, Beau Brummel, New York, 1967; founder, designer and chairman, Polo Fashions, New York, from 1968; Ralph Lauren Womenswear, from 1971; Polo Leather Goods, from 1979; Polo/Ralph Lauren Luggage, from 1982; Polo Ralph Lauren Corp., from 1986; diffusion line, Chaps, introduced 1972; Ralph, Double RL, and Polo Sport lines introduced, 1993; established Polo/Ralph Lauren stores in Beverly Hills, 1971, Lawrence, Massachusetts, 1983, Paris, 1986, flagship store in New York, 1986, Costa Mesa, California, 1987, East Hampton, New York, 1989; Polo Sport, New York, 1993; launched fragrances Polo and Lauren, 1978, Chaps and Tuxedo, 1979, Safari, 1990, Polo Crest, 1991.*

Exhibitions *Retrospective, Denver Art Museum, Colorado, 1983.*

Collection *Fashion Institute of Technology, New York.*

Awards *Coty American Fashion Critics Award, 1970, 1973, 1974, 1976, 1977, 1981, 1984; Neiman Marcus Distinguished Service Award, 1971; American Printed Fabrics Council "Tommy" Award, 1977; Council of Fashion Designers of America Award, 1981; Coty Hall of Fame Award, 1981; Retailer of the Year Award, 1986, 1992; Museum of American Folk Art Pioneering Excellence Award, 1988; Council of Fashion Designers of America Lifetime Achievement Award, 1992; Woolmark Award, 1992.*

Address *650 Madison Avenue, New York, New York 10022, USA.*

Style, as opposed to fashion, is the major imperative underlying Ralph Lauren's work. Initially a designer of the high-quality ties that started the Polo label, Lauren soon directed his talents to menswear. Inspired by such notable dressers as the Duke of Windsor, Cary Grant, and Fred Astaire, he began to produce classic lines derivative of the elegant man-about-town or the country squire of a bygone age. A love of the fashions of the F. Scott Fitzgerald era led him to introduce wide neckties and bold shirt patterns. In 1974 he achieved world acclaim as the designer of the men's fashions in the film version of F. Scott Fitzgerald's novel *The Great Gatsby*.

When he turned to womenswear, he applied the same qualities of timeless elegance to his designs. By using uniformly high-quality tweeds, by tailoring down men's trousers and jackets, and by producing shirts in finer cottons, Lauren created clothes for the active woman of the 1970s, as epitomized in the Annie Hall look. These classic, tailored garments have changed little since they were first introduced but continue to epitomize long-lasting quality and style.

Another side of Ralph Lauren is seen in his Roughwear. Directly inspired by the tradition of America's past, this takes the form of long tweed or plain skirts combined with colorful, hand-knitted, Fair Isle or sampler sweaters, tartan scarves, trilby hats, and lumberjack's wind cheaters and brushed cotton shirts. The origins are easy to trace, but the result is an updated, truly American style. Romantic touches of Edwardian and Victorian times occur in lace-trimmed jabots and large collars delicately held together with aging cameo brooches. Shades of the classic English riding costume appear in his tailored tweed jackets. Lauren's contribution to fashion can perhaps best be summed up on the names that he gave to his cosmetics introduced in 1981: "Day," "Night," and "Active."

In the 1990s he continued to tune into contemporary life. The Double RL label featured new, high quality clothes that looked old as a response to the craze for the vintage and second hand. For increasingly fitness-conscious women he produced informal clothes with a strong fashion input.

His skill and experience has enabled him to design for women and men, their children, and their homes. The Rhinelander store on Madison Avenue, New York City, reflects his total lifestyle approach. As a native New Yorker, Lauren has promoted a truly American casual style in his prairie look, while developing classic, uncluttered lines that have brought him international fame along with his colleagues Calvin Klein and Perry Ellis. For Ralph Lauren, fashion is something that lasts for more than one season. It is this timelessness, abetted by inspirations deep in the soil of America's past, that distinguishes his work and won him a Lifetime Achievement award from the Council of Fashion Designers of America in 1992.—HAZEL CLARK

Léger, Hervé

French fashion designer

Born *Bapaume, Pas de Calais, France, 1957.*

Education *Studied Arts Plastiques in Paris until 1975.*

Career *Designed hats for Venus et Neptune, Pablo Delia, Dick Brandsma, 1975-77; assistant for Tan Giudicelli, couture and ready-to-wear, 1977-80; assistant to Karl Lagerfeld, furs, ready-to-wear, swimsuits and accessories at Fendi, Rome, 1980-82; designer Chanel, 1982-83; designer for Cadette, Milan, 1983-85; founded own company, MCH Diffusion, 1985; opened boutique in rue Pelican, Paris, assistant at Lanvin for couture and ready-to-wear, and assistant to Dianne von Furstenberg, 1985; designed fur collection for Chloé, 1987; designed accessory collection for Swarovski (Vattens, Austria), 1988-92; same year designed ready-to-wear collections for Charles Jourdan; partnership with Mumm, 1992; first ready-to-wear collection for Hervé Léger SA, 1993. Also: designed theatre costumes for The Troyens, Milan, 1992, and Trois Ballets, Opéra de Paris, 1994.*

Address *29, rue de Faubourg Saint-Honoré, 75008 Paris, France.*

In interviews I try systematically to dodge the connotation "artist, designer." The French word *créateur* seems to me particularly bombastic. I usually avoid theories on fashion in terms of "art" and I hate definitions on style. On the other hand I always insist on the quality of my work. People will always appreciate quality. Quoting Madeleine Vionnet, to her niece, I used to say, "we are not rich enough to buy cheap."

The quality "hand-sewn," "good investment," "good value," is a rather original attitude when one thinks about it. The dissertation on fashion has a tendency to glorify the short-lived, the novel, the whim, ostentatious consumption rather than the everlasting. I think it's a pity.

Two consumer types exist for me: the first, "crazy about fashion," "fashion victim," will irrevocably conform to the fashion of the designers and systematically adopt their outlook.

The second type of woman, the one I prefer, is fed up with the vagaries of fashion. She will not act as a guinea pig for the designer's "experiments." She does not give a damn about the trends, she refuses to be a feminine clothes hanger.

My fashion is made for that woman, to help her to express herself. I do not use woman to express my world vision.—Hervé Léger

If any designer heralded the shift away from the deconstructed, loose, long shapes of the early 1990s it was Hervé Léger. His clothes, based on the deceptively simple principles of Lycra and Spandex-rich fabrics pulling the body into the desired hourglass shape, have made him the darling of the fashion world. Tired of the austerity of recession dressing and eager for a contrary style which would revive a sense of glamour and flatter the wearer with its overblown femininity, Léger's work has been warmly embraced both by fashion opinion makers and the rock stars, models and minor royalty who are his most publicized clients.

He takes the 1980s cliché of "underwear as outerwear" to its logical conclusion by imbuing his dresses with the properties formally associated with foundation garments: the ability to mould the body and keep it in place. They enhance the figure, metamorphosing the wearer into cartoon-like proportions with full bust and hips. If this exaggeratedly feminine image is in direct contradiction to the narrow adolescent silhouette which had preceded and, indeed, runs in parallel with Léger's vision, it has nevertheless struck a chord with women wishing to relish their sexuality and unafraid to display their redefined body in the late 20th-century equivalent to tight laced corsetry.

Chiming in with the post-feminist doctrine of Naomi Wolf and Camille Paglia, which promotes the reclaiming of the right to enhance and emphasize the figure, this trend, labelled new glamour, is unashamed in its devotion to the female form. It is the latter which undoubtedly inspires Léger, his creations geared towards maximizing the purity of the curving lines of his models.

His most obvious predecessor is the Algerian designer Azzedine Alaia, who rose to fame in the late 1980s with his clingy Lycra creations, which Léger so clearly refers to in the overt sexiness of his own work. Léger, however, has developed the style further, exploiting the stretchy qualities of Lycra and Spandex to the full, so that the dresses are more restrictive and better able to maintain the desired shape. His signature outfits, known as "bender" dresses, are composed of narrow strips of these elastic materials combined with rayon, which are sewn horizontally like bandages to form the whole shape of the garment, sometimes with extra bands curving over the hips and across the bust to add emphasis. Even on the hanger, therefore, they have a three-dimensional quality, so reliant are they on the Olympian figure they at once create and emulate.

He produces innumerable variations of this style, all equally flattering, the fabric eliminating any faults in the figure to produce smooth hourglasses. For all their glamour his clothes avoid brashness through their lack of any unnecessary detail or decoration; their interest is in their shaping and the subtle Parisian tones in which they are produced. He concentrates on classic black, navy, white, and cream, tempered by stripes of burnt orange on halter dresses reminiscent of 1930s swimwear and delicate pastels with dark bodices.

Transforming women into Amazonian figures or goddess-like nymphs, his name has gained importance as the 1990s have progressed, especially as in the middle of the decade there is an increasing desire to express rather than obscure the potential sexuality of clothing. His dresses (and his work is predominantly the shapely one-piece) blur distinctions of day or eveningwear, since his designs are all equally glamorous.

Even when not using his moulding Lycra strips, his clothing still aspires to a feminine ideal. Full-length coats were given subtle emphasis in his autumn-winter 1994 collection—coats with curved satin inserts stretching from bust to waist set into their matt silhouettes to draw the eye to this area, held together with two tiny hooks to enable flashes of bare skin and fluid satin floor length skirts as the wearer moved. Grecian-inspired halter neck dresses with little floating chiffon skirts were also sculpted with tiny pleats to produce a similar effect.

Léger's concentration on the ability of clothing to create the desired flattering silhouette, through manipulation of fabrics and eye-arresting details, owes its legacy to his couture background. His time at great houses like Chanel, Fendi, and Chloé enabled him to witness the power of a thoughtfully-cut ensemble to transform the wearer. His homage to the goddess-like form has touched on the 1990s desire to demonstrate beauty through strong, clear lines and sexually-changed imagery which his clinging dresses so literally embody.—REBECCA ARNOLD

Leiber, Judith

American handbag and accessories designer

Born *Judith Peto in Budapest, 11 January 1921.*

Education *Educated in England, 1938-39; apprenticed with Hungarian Handbag Guild, 1939, became journeyman and first woman Meister.*

Family *Married Gerson Leiber in 1946.*

Career *Immigrated to the United States and moved to New York, 1947. Designer in New York for Nettie Rosenstein, 1948-60, Richard Kort, 1960-61, and Morris Moskowitz Co., 1961-62; launched own firm, 1963.*

Exhibition *The Artist and Artisan: Gerson and Judith Leiber, Fine Arts Museum of Long Island, 1991.*

Awards *Swarovski Great Designer Award; Coty American Fashion Critics Award, 1973; Neiman Marcus Award, Dallas, 1980; Foundation for the Fashion Industries Award, New York, 1991; Silver Slipper Award, Houston Museum of Fine Arts Costume Institute, 1991; Handbag Designer of the Year Award, 1992; Council of Fashion Designers of America Award, 1993; Council of Fashion Designers of America Lifetime Achievement Award, 1994.*

Address *20 West 33rd Street, New York, New York 10001, USA.*

I love to design beautiful objects that can be worn of course, whether it is made of alligator, ostrich, lizard or silk, or a great metal box/*minaudière* that can be held in the lady's hand. Top quality is a great concern and it pleases me greatly to keep that paramount.

Judith Leiber.

Leiber

Today's fashions really cry out for beautiful accessories, be they belts, handbags or great jewelry.—Judith Leiber

Judith Leiber talks of herself as a technician and prides herself on the Budapest-trained craft tradition that she exemplifies and continues. But her skill and the consummate perfection of her workshop are only one aspect of the recognition of her work. She is steadfast in advancing the artistic possibility of the handbag and she is unceasing in her own artistic pursuit of the handbag. Yet, as Mary Peacock averred, "a sense of whimsy is integral to Leiber's vision" and the committed pursuit of craft is matched with a stylish wit and the cultural cleverness that is akin to craft's creativity. A Leiber handbag is aN item of expert handwork and engineering, but it is also a charm, a potent amulet, and a beguiling object of beauty.

Technique is central to the Leiber concept. A Leiber *minaudière,* for example, might seem at first glance like a Christmas tree ornament, but in technique is more like an ecclesiastical censer, an object of perfection intended for long-lasting use. Her watermelon and citrus slices are farm fresh in their juicy hand-set rhinestone design, but these are fruits that will never perish. As Cathryn Jakobson describes the sound and impeccable impact of closing a Leiber handbag, "The engineering is perfect: it is like closing the door on an excellent automobile" (*Manhattan Inc.,* February 1986). Leiber's product may be jewel-like and ladylike in scale, but Leiber collectors are rightly as proud and avid about these small objects as any possessor of a Rolls Royce. There is perhaps one drawback to the Leiber evening bags: they hold very little. But Leiber's aesthetic more than mitigates the possible problem. If going out is a matter of saddlebags and gross excess, then Leiber's sweet purses and precious objects are not the answer. But if there is any truthful measure that the best things come in small packages, Leiber's beautiful clutches make the maxim true. In fact, Leiber's characteristic evening bags compound their delicacy in scale with their solid form: these hardly seem, despite their elegance, to be places of cash and chattel. Leiber has achieved a carrier that is neither wallet nor winnings: it is something intimate and personal. Indeed, many collectors of Leiber's evening bags present them as sculptural display when they are not in service as eveningwear.

The ideas for the bags come from a variety of sources. Arguably, little is invented *ex nihilo* in Leiber's work, but is instead understood and applied from other arts to the bag. Leiber acknowledges that she loves finding objects in museums and even the objects in paintings that lend themselves to her imaginative formation as the handbag, realizing the capability of an object to serve as a container. Leiber's version of Fabergé eggs at substantial, but less than Romanov, prices are inherently about containment, but her inventions of the three-dimensional bunch of grapes or the frogs that open up or Chinese Foo dogs with hollow insides are her own invention. Leiber has also looked to the arts of the East, especially *netsuke* purse toggles, for their wondrous world of invented objects and miniatures from nature. Leiber's first jeweled evening bag was a metal teardrop purse, an ironic play on the soft shape of the purse or moneybag converted into a hard form.

Handbags by Leiber for the day employ beautiful reptile and ostrich skins, antique Japanese *obis,* and extraordinary embroideries. In the daytime bags, Leiber uses not only the softest materials and a colorist's palette, even in skins, but lightens the touch with supple pleats, braid, and whimsical trims and closings. Leiber makes elegantly simple envelope bags accented by a single point or line of decoration.

Bernadine Morris says of Leiber's evening bags, "Women with an awareness of fashion consider them the finishing touch when they dress up for big evenings." (*New York Times*, 18 December 1990). The importance of Morris's observation is that the handbag is not thereby subsumed into an ensemble, but perceived as the accessory that fulfils all that has gone before in *maquillage* and dress: the finishing touch is the independent object that realizes the potential of all the preceding elements. Leiber never makes a subservient bag, but the autonomous object that, whether egg, *minaudière*, or piggy is the finality and *finesse* of style. In this, Leiber observes fashion as critically and cognizantly as she scours art for her selection of objects, but she never creates a tartan to be coordinated to a textile or a frog or other animal to fit into an established environment of garments. Rather, she creates commodities that enhance dress and create style because they are self-sufficient. Leiber creates objects that are undeniably, despite the creator's modesty, sculptures on a small scale, style at its finale, ultimate objects.—RICHARD MARTIN

Leser, Tina

American designer

Born *Christine Wetherill Shillard-Smith in Philadelphia, Pennsylvania, 12 December 1910.*

Education *Studied art at the Pennsylvania Academy of Fine Arts, the School of Industrial Arts, Philadelphia, and at the Sorbonne.*

Family *Married Curtin Leser in 1931 (divorced, 1936); married James J. Howley in 1948; daughter: Georgina.*

Career *Sold designs through her own shop in Honolulu, Hawaii, 1935-42; also formed a company in New York, 1941-43; designer, Edwin H. Foreman Company, New York, 1943-53; designer, Tina Leser, Inc., New York, 1953-64; designed Signet men's ties, 1949, Stafford Wear men's sportswear, 1950, and industrial uniforms for Ramsey Sportswear Company, 1953; retired briefly, 1964-66; retired permanently, 1982.*

Awards *Fashion Critics Award, New York, 1944; Neiman Marcus Award, Dallas, 1945; Coty American Fashion Critics Award, 1945; Sports Illustrated Sportswear Design Award, 1956, 1957; US Chamber of Commerce Citation, 1957; Philadelphia Festival of the Arts Fashion Award, 1962. Member, National Society of Arts and Letters Fashion Group.*

Died *(in Sands Point, New York) 24 January 1986.*

Tina Leser was an early and very successful proponent of an American design aesthetic inspired by textiles and clothing from non-Western cultures. She travelled through Asia, India, and Africa as a child, and lived in Hawaii after her first marriage in 1931, which may explain the ease with which she later adapted influences from those areas into her designs. Although she is remembered today primarily for that gift, her success was not confined to that genre, but also encompassed references to other folk and historical traditions.

Her earliest work was done in Hawaii, where she opened a shop in 1935 selling high quality ready-to-wear and playclothes of her own design. She used Hawaiian and Filipino fabrics, and even hand block-printed sailcloth. In 1940 she brought her work to New York where she was to open her own firm, but only began to be a force in fashion in 1943, when she joined the Edwin H. Foreman sportswear firm as designer.

Leser's work during World War II reflected the fabric scarcities of the wartime economy, and the limits of wartime travel. From Mexico she derived a printed flannel jacket with sequined trim; from Guatemala a strapless dress made from a handwoven blanket. Sarong-styled dresses and wrap skirts were an important part of her design vocabulary at this time, possibly stemming from her years in Hawaii. She varied these with less exotic styles, such as a tartan cotton playsuit with a matching shawl and kilted skirt, and wonderful wool flannel calf-length overalls—offspring of a very American idiom.

From the first Leser emphasized an uncluttered mode, and by the end of the war she had won awards from both Neiman Marcus and Coty for her contributions to American fashion. She had also widened her horizons to include India—very much in the news in the immediate post-war years—with her *dhoti* pants-dress, available in several versions for a variety of occasions. The facility with which she could adapt one model into many styles can be attributed to her artist's eye for proportion, and clean balance between line and form.

What was, in theory, an around-the-world honeymoon trip with her second husband in 1949 became, in practice, a way for Leser to collect fabrics, clothing, and antiques from a multitude of cultures. She based designs on objects as varied as an English game table, Siamese priests' robes, an Italian peasant's vest, and a Manchu coat. Her mature work, from this date on, displayed a consistent sense of humour and intelligence in her choice of references.

Her collections included many "play" pieces but also contained relaxed day and evening clothes eminently suited to the needs and budgets of many post-war American women. Her variation on the ubiquitous 1950s sweater twinset was a halter with an embellished cardigan, and she is also credited with introducing the cashmere sweater dress. Sensitivity to the realities of life for working women induced her, in 1953, to design a line of industrial uniforms for Ramsey Sportswear Co. The trim fitting separates included a skirt to be worn over uniform slacks on the way to or from work.

Her fabric choices as well as her fashion inspirations were wide-ranging. Indian sari silks, Pringle woollens, Boussac floral prints, and embroidered Moygashel linens shared her stage with cottons from Fuller fabrics' "Modern Masters" print series, Hope Skillman wovens, Galey & Lord ginghams, and Wesley Simpson prints. She championed denim as a fashion fabric, using it in 1945 for a two-piece swimsuit trimmed with chenille "bedspread flowers," in 1949 for coolie trousers and sleeveless jacket, and in the mid-1950s for a strapless bodice and wide cuffed pants. American bandanna prints or tablecloth fabrics were as likely to show up in her work as copies of Persian brocades, and they might equally be used for playsuits or cocktail dresses. One butterfly patterned batik print turned up as a swimsuit and cover-up skirt, capri trousers and strapless top, a sarong dress, and even as binding on a cardigan sweater.

Leser remained active throughout the 1960s and into the 1970s, maintaining her flair for sportswear, loungewear, and bathing suits. Some of her best pieces from this period were slim toreador or stirrup trousers worn with long, boxy sweaters or baby-doll tunics, and her coordinated bathing suits and cover-ups remained strong. The details of her designs, however, are rather less important than the spirit she brought to them. Many young American designers carry on the referential style Leser helped establish, creating, as she did, something uniquely American from a melting-pot of cultural sources.—MADELYN SHAW

Mackie, Bob

American designer

Born *Robert Gordon Mackie in Monterey Park, California, 24 March 1940.*
Education *Studied advertising and illustration at Pasadena City College, c.1957-58, and costume design at Chouinard Art Institute, Los Angeles, 1958-60.*
Family *Married Marianne Wolford in 1960 (divorced, 1963); son: Robin.*
Career *Sketch artist for film designers Frank Thompson, Jean Louis and Edith Head, 1960-63; worked in television as assistant designer to Ray Aghayan, receiving his first screen credit for The Judy Garland Show, 1963; designer for The King Family Show, 1965, Mitzi Gaynor's night club acts, from 1966, The Carol Burnett Show, 1967-78, The Sonny and Cher Comedy Hour, 1971-74, and The Sonny and Cher Show, 1976-77; designed swimwear for Cole of California, 1976; independent designer of ready-to-wear fashions, with own label Bob Mackie Originals, New York, from 1982.*
Awards *Emmy Award, 1967 (with Ray Aghayan), 1969, 1976, 1978, 1985; Costume Designers Guild Award, 1968; American Fashion Award, 1975.*
Address *Bob Mackie Originals, 225 West 29th, New York, New York 10001, U.S.A.*

Bob Mackie is one of a handful of designers to work with success in the related but disparate fields of theater and fashion design. Mackie is probably best known for the wittily revealing, glamorous beaded and feathered ensembles he has designed for the actress and singer Cher since the early 1970s. This collaborative image remains so strong that to visualize Cher is to see her dressed by Mackie. His true genius as an interpretative designer, however, can best be seen in his work for comedienne Carol Burnett. For 11 years Mackie designed costumes and wigs for Burnett's weekly variety show, including full-scale production numbers to showcase guest artists: elaborate parodies of such classic cult films as *Sunset Boulevard* or *Mildred Pierce*. These character sketches were written for Burnett's company of regular performers and on-going stories starring Burnett as one of her various alter egos. In Mrs Wiggins, for example, Mackie and Burnett created the archetypal "keep busy while doing nothing" secretary, complete with over-long fingernails, brass spittoon-colored perm, stiletto heels and a skirt so tight that walking seemed doubtful and sitting impossible. In this case the costume first defined the character and thus gave direction to the ensuing scripts. Visually, audiences were led away from the personality of the performer and towards that of the character portrayed. By contrast, Bob Mackie's designs for guest artists always enhanced their visual trademarks, so that the personalities remained the focus, supported by wig and costume, even when they played comic or character roles.

When he turned to ready-to-wear in 1982, Mackie's name had been before the television viewing public for 15 years. Women who had admired the casual but elegant tailored outfits Carol Burnett wore to open and close her show or the dramatic allure of Cher's gowns formed an eager and ready market for the first designs from Bob Mackie Originals. The fashion press took rather longer to convince that the aptly dubbed "sultan of sequins, rajah of rhinestones" had the necessary seriousness of purpose to sustain a career on Seventh Avenue. In fact, Mackie has always designed day and evening clothing in addition to his theatrical work. As early as 1969 he and partners Ray Aghayan and Elizabeth Courtney established their Beverly Hills boutique, Elizabeth the First, which in turn spawned the short-lived wholesale firm Ray Aghayan/Bob Mackie.

In his 1979 book, *Dressing for Glamor,* Mackie states his belief that glamor is ". . . a state of mind, a feeling of self-confidence." His strength as a designer is an intuitive understanding of what makes a woman feel self-confident and well dressed: solid craftsmanship, attention to detail, clothes which combine wit and artistry with a sense of flair and drama.—WHITNEY BLAUSEN

Mad Carpentier
American design house

Founded by Mad Maltezos and Suzie Carpentier in Paris, January 1939 (taking over from Vionnet after her retirement). House closed, 1957.

There were many diaspora far more urgent and desperate in the late 1930s than that which led to the creation of the house of Mad Carpentier in January 1940. The firm's two partners—Mad Maltezos and Suzie Carpentier—banded together when Madeleine Vionnet, their former employer, closed in 1939. In the unexamined cliché in fashion history and for a number of clients, the two women represented a continuation of Vionnet's bias cut and elegance in fashion combined with a discreet social model, always proper. Twins seized from a most inspired rib, two women balanced to equal one, and perseverance through the war years established an inexorable mythology around Mad Carpentier. Picken and Miller write passionately, "When it was almost impossible to think of luxury, of the richness of colors, of the beauty of fabrics, in a city without joy and without light, of deserted nights when there was no life except that of hope, these two talented women carried on" (New York, 1956).

Like Antoine de Saint-Exupéry heroines, Maltezos, designer and creative spirit, and Carpentier, refined and cordial proprietress, formerly a Vionnet *vendeuse,* sustained some of the ideas of Vionnet in soft evening clothes, but there were two special and autonomous distinctions for Mad Carpentier. In the late 1940s, Mad Carpentier created evening dresses of extraordinary historical fantasy, attenuating the body with *faux* bustles and creating the new sumptuousness of post-war evening clothes determined chiefly by silhouette. If these gowns did not achieve the flamboyant success of Fath and Dior in the same years, it is because the Mad Carpentier gowns are too redolent of the past and failed to capture the spirit of the "new" that was necessary to the marketing and imagination of the post-war era. Though Fath and Dior were both influenced by the past, the Belle Epoque could scarcely be revived in this era without, at least, the veneer of the newest and most extravagant. A Mad Carpentier gown photographed in *L'Officiel* (Christmas 1947) has New Look traits, but maintains the aura of a Victorian past.

The other hallmark of the house of Mad Carpentier was its most remarkable coats, long surpassing the Vionnet tradition. The bravura shapes of Mad Carpentier coats in robust textures were immensely popular in the 1940s and 1950s independent of the Vionnet tradition. In particular, the coats were much imitated by Seventh Avenue, New York manufacturers, often rivalling the ever-popular Balenciaga coats for copying. B. Altman & Co., New York, for example, advertised a Romantically sweeping long coat with high collar as "Mad Carpentier's famous coat . . . beautifully copied in all-wool fleece" in *Vogue,* January 1947. Amplitude, rugged materials, and the swaggering grandeur of riding coats gave both assertiveness and grace to the Mad Carpentier coats.

Indubitably, the Vionnet tradition was maintained in ease, a desire for easy shaping and even for tying. In the dresses, the full three-dimensionality emphasized by Vionnet was often compromised by an interest in details at the side, as if to reinstate planarity, but in the coats, the effect was to create soft, large volumes. It was the negligent, comfortable ease that made the coats so eminently susceptible to copying by the American manufacturers who avoided the greatest refinements of tailoring to duplicate pieces that could be mass-marketed. *Women's Wear Daily* (14 April 1948) reported that "the firm has gone its quiet way, and now ranks as a house for clothes of distinctive character rather than one taking an active or publicized role in the general development of the Paris couture. Carpentier clothes have the handmade air of Vionnet, but do not always follow the bias technique of that school of dressmaking."

Linked to Vionnet's innovations in dressmaking, but in fact functioning with little inclination to their inventiveness, Mad Carpentier turned out to be a house of the most traditional dresses, genteel tailoring, and of sensational coats. Its understated, highly proper sensibility was at odds with advanced and aggressive post-war fashion and only in the exuberance of its sculptural coats did the imagination and reputation soar.—RICHARD MARTIN

Mainbocher

American designer

Born *Main Rousseau Bocher in Chicago, Illinois, 24 October 1890. Adopted name Mainbocher, c.1929.*

Education *Studied at the Lewis Institute, Chicago, 1907; studied design, Chicago Academy of Fine Arts, 1908-09, and at the Art Students' League, New York, 1909-11; attended University of Chicago, 1911, and Königliche Kunstgewerbemuseum, Munich, 1911-12; studied painting with E. A. Taylor, Paris, 1913-14; also studied piano and opera.*

Military Service *In the American Ambulance Corps, and Intelligence Corps, Paris, 1917-18.*

Mainbocher: 1938. *Photograph by Eugène Rubin.*

Career *Lithographer, part-time, New York, 1909-11; sketch artist for clothing manufacturer E. L. Mayer, New York, 1914-17; illustrator, Harper's Bazaar, Paris, 1917-21; fashion correspondent, then editor, French Vogue, 1922-29; established couturier firm, Paris, 1930-39, and New York, 1939-71; also designed stage costumes, from 1932, and uniforms for American WAVES (US Navy), 1942; American Girl Scouts, 1946; American Red Cross, 1948; US Women's Marine Corps, 1951.*

Collections *Mainbocher sketchbooks, Costume Institute, Metropolitan Museum of Art.*

Died *(in New York) 27 December 1976.*

The snob appeal of patronizing an American couturier with a French sounding name, extremely successful in Paris for a decade before his arrival in the United States, appealed to the socially élite trade in 1940 New York. No less appealing was the fact that Mainbocher had designed the Duchess of Windsor's trousseau upon her marriage in 1937. In 1930, after several years as editor of French *Vogue,* Mainbocher suddenly decided to channel his artistic sensibilities into the establishment of a couture salon in Paris. Editorial experience enabled him to sense what would become fashionable, and to package himself as an exclusive designer to the wealthy and the titled. From the start, he specialized in simple, conservative, elegant, and extremely expensive fashions, the luxury of cut, materials, and workmanship that could only be recognized by those in the know. Most importantly, the clothes, exquisitely finished inside and out, gave self-confidence to the women who wore them.

Mainbocher considered his contemporary Chanel too plebeian, and Schiaparelli too avant-garde. Instead, he admired Vionnet and borrowed her bias-cut technique for his own simple slip evening dresses in the 1930s. A very similar slip design was employed by Mainbocher, as he was known in New York, 20 years later, produced in a signature elegant silk velvet fabric. From Augustabernard, another 1920s French dress designer, Mainbocher was inspired not only to form his name, but to use godets in skirts, and shoulder bows to catch the folds of draped bodices. Frequent Mainbocher suit treatments in the 1930s included short capelet effects or dropped shoulders widening into full sleeves. The designer knew his clientèle personally and designed for the lives they led, specializing in evening clothes. For resort wear he ventured into a mix-and-match ensemble consisting of matching top, skirt, bathing suit, and hat. Slim, demure black wool dresses for daytime would sport white chiffon interest at the throat. While Mainbocher did use some Japanese-like kimonos as eveningwear during this period, his hallmark was non-aggressive, not exaggerated or period dressing. A touch of labor-intensive luxury would be bestowed by all-over sequins on an evening jacket or on a bare top worn discreetly under a jacket. The grayish-blue, "Wallis blue," of the Duchess of Windsor's wedding dress, as well as the long, fluid crêpe dress itself, was widely copied. The simple, conservative elegance of Mainbocher's style, feminine but not fussy, suited perfectly the slim, severe good looks of the Duchess and wealthy women like her. Additionally, she was honoring a fellow American.

In 1934, Mainbocher introduced the boned strapless bodice, and, just before the war that forced him to leave Paris, a waist cincher, forming tiny waisted, pleated skirted dresses that presaged Dior's post-war New Look. Mainbocher's arrival in New York coincided perfectly with the city's élite's love for French couture, for he epitomized that, yet satisfied their patriotism because he was actually an American. Society matrons such as C. Z. Guest and the Vanderbilts, stage actresses such as Mary Martin, avidly patronized this "most expensive custom dressmaker" who made women look and feel exquisitely well-bred. Accedance to wartime economies resulted in Mainbocher's short evening dresses, and versatile cashmere sweaters, beaded, lined in silk, and closed by jeweled buttons, designed to keep women warm in their bare evening gowns. Another practical wartime innovation, the "glamor belt," an apron-like, sequined or bead-encrusted accessory, could be added to embellish any plain costume. Practically gratis, Mainbocher designed uniforms for the US Women's Marine Corps, the WAVES (Navy), the American Red Cross, and the Girl Scouts.

As the years progressed, Mainbocher continued to design exclusively on a made-to-order basis, refusing to license his name. La Galerie, a department in his salon, did make to order clothes in standard sizes, a compromise for busy women without time for lengthy fittings. The reverse snobbery of the humble pastel gingham or cotton piqué used for fancy dresses appealed to Mainbocher's clientèle, as did refined tweed suits with subtle dressmaker touches: curved bands or self fabric appliqués, worn with coordinating bare-armed blouses. A Mainbocher standby was the little black "nothing" sheath dress. By the 1950s and 1960s, Old Guard Mainbocher customers enjoyed wearing impeccably made classic coats and suits of wool, often fur-lined, in the midst of nouveau-riche ostentation. The typical ladylike daytime Mainbocher look was accessorized by a plain velvet bow in the hair instead of a hat, a choker of several strands of real pearls, white gloves, and plain pumps with matching handbag. The integrity of luxurious fabrics, intricate cut, quality workmanship and materials, elegance and classicism, were cherished and worn for years by Mainbocher's upper crust customers.—THERESE DUZINKIEWICZ BAKER

Mandelli, Mariuccia (for Krizia)

Italian fashion designer

Born *Bergamo, Italy, 1933.*

Family *Married Aldo Pinto.*

Career *Worked as a teacher, Milan, 1952-54, designer and founder with Flora Dolci, of Krizia fashion firm, Milan, from 1954: founded Kriziamaglia knitwear, 1966, and Kriziababy children's clothes, 1968: subsequently established Krizia boutiques, in Milan, Tokyo, London, New York, Detroit, Houston, etc.*

Exhibitions Italian Revolution, *La Jolla Museum of Art, California, 1982;* 40 Years of Italian Fashion, *Trump Tower, New York, 1983.*

Awards *Fashion Press Award, Florence, 1964.*

Address *Via Agnelli 12, 20100 Milan, Italy.*

The success of the Milanese boutique called Krizia, and, in fact, the prominence of Milanese fashion that has occurred during the 1980s and 1990s, are both largely due to the efforts of Krizia's founder and designer, Mariuccia Mandelli. Mandelli is one of the originators of the major contrast trend of Milan in which a simple, classic tailoring is punctuated with original and amusing accents to create a new face for stylish ready-to-wear fashion that is both eminently wearable and exuberantly youthful.

Among Krizia's early, important presentations was a showing at Orsini's on the invitation of Jean Rosenberg, vice-president of Bendel's. It was on this occasion that Mandelli was labeled

"Crazy Krizia" by the fashion press for her combinations of simple shapes with madcap details. In 1976 Bergdorf Goodman featured stock by Krizia and other Milanese designers, providing the final step necessary for the Italians' rise to the forefront.

Representative of what has been called Krizia's "rough and sweet" look are Mandelli's 1977 outfittings consisting of nylon undershirts topped by matching rose-colored or dove-gray mohair bedjackets or cardigans in open-knit weaves and worn with dropped-waist ballerina skirts of scalloped lace. Mandelli's daywear tends toward the practical; she has, for example, put elastic waistbands on her skirts for comfortable ease of movement, and her 1982 group of sport suits of loose tweeds and checks are plain, loose, and stylized. Mandelli's use of her signature "improbable contrasts," however, abound most openly in her evening clothes, such as the mixes of satin skirts with sporty Angora sweaters that appeared in 1978. In that same year, she also presented her simple slip dress accompanied by characteristic touches of humourous flamboyance such as a long, feathered stole or quilted jacket of satin faced in a different shade of the same color.

Mandelli has often used jodhpur pants. One 1977 outfit consisted of loose, draping jodhpurs in silk charmeuse worn with a lacy, mohair camisole, the whole enlivened by the glowing berry colors she featured that year. Also among Mandelli's original fashion accomplishments is her development of what she named "harmonica pleats," which combine vertical and horizontal pleatings.

Outstanding among Mandelli's designs are her knits, which include items such as her 1977 lacy, mushroom-colored evening sweater teamed with double-scarf of silk taffeta and eyelet taffeta and jodhpur pants. In 1981 she showed subtly sophisticated shiny knits and white angoras bedecked with yokes of pearls. Often appearing on Mandelli's knitwear are her signature animal motifs. In 1978 there was a jacquard crepe blouse with the front view of a tiger on its front and rear-tiger-view on its back. In her 1980 collection, there were colorful knits featuring parrots and toucans; short knit dresses included a one-piece version sporting the front half of a leopard and a two-piece style revealing the leopard's rear half. Not limiting herself to knitwear, Mandelli also put highly colorful birds and parrots on that season's summer tote bags and shoulder purses. For 1984, it's the dalmatian, sharing the scene with more streamlined suits and double-dresses such as a back-buttoned flare over a little bit longer slim skirt.

From the start, Krizia's Mariuccia Mandelli has continuously based her highly original designs on nervy eccentricity and wit that have earned her a prominent place in the recent Milanese force that has successfully nudged ready-to-wear fashion in a new direction.—BARBARA CAVALIERE

Marcasiano, Mary Jane

American designer

Born *Morristown, New Jersey, 23 September 1955.*

Education *Attended Montclair State College, Montclair, New Jersey; graduated from Parsons School of Design, New York, 1978.*

Mary Jane Marcasiano. *Photograph by Jean Michel Cazabat.*

Career   *Showed first collection, 1979; launched Mary Jane Marcasiano Company, New York, from 1980; introduced menswear line, 1982; licenses from 1985 include shoes, jewelry.*

Exhibitions   *All American: A Sportswear Tradition, Fashion Institute of Technology, April-June 1985.*

Collections Fashion Institute of Technology, New York City.

Awards   *Cartier Stargazer Award, 1981; Wool Knit Association Award, 1983; Dupont Award, 1983; Cutty Sark Award, 1984.*

Address   *138 Spring St, New York, New York 10018, USA.*

My design philosophy and how I want to look as a woman have always been intertwined.

My first collection came out of a desire to wear something that didn't exist yet. There is always a dual purpose when I design—the aesthetics of the line and color have to coexist with wearability. Therefore, I test all the yarns and fabrics first on myself.

Color is where I start when I'm working on a new collection, simultaneously matching color with the surface of the yarn or fabric to enhance the color impact. My goal is to create a wearable surface of color, texture and light. My shapes are simple. I like the ease of knitwear, giving enough room for the garment to move around the body, both covering and revealing it. Necklines are very important to my designs. I use simple geometric shapes to create a presentation of the face, neck, and decolleté.

I am designing for the lifestyle of the modern woman who needs clothes that can take her from day into evening, cold to warm weather, sexy to serious.

I want a woman to be as comfortable in all of my designs as she is wearing her favorite sweater. Complete knitwear dressing combined with Lycra blend stretch fabrics are how I achieve this.

I don't impose a "look" on my customer—my customer has her own style or I help her to discover her own. This is one of the great satisfactions in designing.—Mary Jane Marcasiano

Mary Jane Marcasiano began her business as primarily a sweater knit house, a focus she has maintained throughout her years in business. The company, which is located in the Soho district of New York, has grown and now includes woven fabrics as well as knits. When beginning a new collection, Marcasiano starts with color, simultaneously matching the color with the yarn or fabric to enhance the impact of the completed look. The yarns she prefers are rayon, cotton, silk, linen, and blends of these fibers. In woven fabrics, rayons and silks are favored owing to their lightness and drapeability. At a more experimental level she also utilizes yarns and fabrics with Lycra and superior uses of polyester and nylon. Her ultimate goal is to create a wearable surface of color, texture, and light. Shapes are always simple, as required by the needs of her specific knitwear designs. Beginning with the neckline, Marcasiano uses a variety of geometric shapes to create a pleasing presentation of the face, neck, and decolleté. The ease of wearing her knitwear as well as the woven elements of the collection allow the garments to flow around the body, both covering and revealing it.

Throughout the years Marcasiano's designs have been influenced by a wide variety of historical and artistic movements. The ancient cultures of Egypt, North Africa, Greece, and

Rome, with clothes that were the ultimate in simplicity, are an obvious influence on her minimalist designs. Etruscan and Roman jewelry and the Neo-Etruscan movement in Europe have also influenced her designs.

Her target market is women who buy designer price clothing, appreciate quality, comfort, and ease in their garments. Many professional women, women in the arts as well as women involved in the fashion industry, wear the Marcasiano label. Exclusive department stores such as Bergdorf Goodman in New York and Neiman Marcus, Dallas, have recognized Marcasiano's talent for understanding and designing for the American woman.

In her desire to create beautiful and wearable knitwear, Marcasiano follows in the footsteps of women designers such as Coco Chanel, Sonia Rykiel, and Dorothy Bis; typical of women designers in Europe who have influenced her work. Her personal innovations in the advancement of knit dressing in America through the use of unusual yarns, stitches, and simplification of the shape of sweaters, is an inspiration to a new generation of young independent designers working on their own.—ROBERTA HOCHBERGER GRUBER

Margiela, Martin
Belgian designer

Born *Louvain, Belgium, 9 April 1957.*
Education *Royale Académie of Fine Art, Antwerp, 1977-80.*
Career *Free-lance designer, Milan, 1980-81; free-lance fashion stylist, Antwerp, 1982-85; design assistant to Gaultier, 1985-87; showed first major collection under own label in Paris, 1988; knitwear line manufactured by Miss Deanna SpA, Italy, launched 1992.*
Exhibitions *Le monde selon ses créateurs, Musée de la Mode et du Costume, Palais Galliera, Paris, 1991; Infra-Apparel, Metropolitan Museum of Art, 1993.*
Address *13 Boulevard St Denis, 75002 Paris, France.*

a creativity : unfailing and inexhaustible (force) where everything fits

an energy : that makes things move

an extremity : that calls into question again

an action : carried out and provoking reactions

a force : that every time again provokes emotions

a fantasy : that makes one dream

a sensitivity : that makes you want to be part of it

a proposal : everyone has the choice to interpret

a subtlety : that makes everything possible

a sensuality : that makes everything acceptable

an authenticity : that restores the true or right values of things again

M

ᴊfashion

a professionalism : that makes one interested, curious, and inquisitive

a positivity : that gives hope for the future.—Jenny Meirens for Martin Margiela

Martin Margiela is a powerful new talent in avant-garde fashion. Formerly an assistant to Jean-Paul Gaultier, the Belgian-born Margiela showed his first collection in 1989 and immediately achieved cult status. He was heralded as fashion's latest "bad boy" genius and the most notorious exponent of *la mode destroy*. He dislikes the term "destroy fashion" and has insisted that he does not regard it as destructive when he slashes old clothes. On the contrary, he told *Elle* (April 1991), it is his way of "bringing them back to life in a different form."

The idea of cutting up clothes goes back to the ripped T-shirts of the Punks and the subsequent street style of slicing jeans with razor blades. But the new deconstruction goes much further. Margiela has unravelled old army socks and made them into sweaters, transformed tulle ballgowns into jackets, recut second-hand black leather coats in the form of dresses, even made plastic laundry bags into clothes. He has designed jackets—beautifully tailored and lined with three different kinds of fabrics—with the sleeves ripped off.

Although conservative members of the fashion industry cringed, young trend-setters enthusiastically embraced the radical new look, which has nothing to do with traditional forms of ostentatious elegance and everything to do with creativity and what Margiela calls "authenticity." Exposed linings and frayed threads testify to the internal construction of the garments, while the deliberate deconstruction of garments implicitly raises questions about our assumptions regarding fashion. Detached sleeves, for example, hark back to the way clothes were made in the Middle Ages, when mercenaries first slashed their silken garments. A cloven-toed boot-shoe and fingers laced in ribbons are rebellious statements in a world of high fashion orthodoxy.

The freedom of Margiela's imagination also evokes the sartorial liberty of the 1970s (a decade that Margiela views in a positive light), especially in contrast to the opulent and conservative 1980s. Like the hippies who pillaged flea-markets, Margiela gives a second life to old and rejected garments, recycling them, and giving a priority to individual creativity rather than consumerism. Opposed to the status-hungry cult of the designer, so ubiquitous in the 1980s, Margiela chose for his label a blank piece of white fabric and he resists talking to the press about what his clothes "mean."

Clothing per se interests him less than how styles are created and interpreted. In this respect, he is very much a conceptual and post-modern designer. Yet, like his former mentor, Gaultier, Margiela is an excellent tailor who really knows how to sew, and his clothes, although undeniably strange, are beautifully (de)constructed.

Margiela's aesthetic also extends to his fashion shows. He staged one show in an abandoned lot in a poor immigrant neighborhood of Paris, with local children dancing down the improvised catwalk along with the models. Another show was held at a Salvation Army hall, at the edge of the city, so that an international crew of fashion journalists found themselves wandering around, hopelessly lost, trying to read the hand-drawn map—and when they finally made it there, having to perch on second-hand furniture and drink wine in plastic cups. More recently, he held two simultaneous shows (one of all black clothes, the other white) at the edge of a cemetery, with crowds of admirers fighting to get in.

Symbolically powerful colors like black, white, and red dominate Margiela's palette. In his *atelier* are posted dictionary definitions of these colors, with red, for example, being associated with wine, blood, and rubies. His *atelier* itself, on the Boulevard Saint Denis, is near the red-light district of Paris. Like his clothes, his studio is a masterpiece of *bricolage*. Graffiti decorate the walls and the floors are covered with xeroxes of old magazine and newspaper articles, which on close inspection turn out to be reviews of his collections.

Margiela was one of six avant-garde designers to be featured in the 1991 exhibition *Le monde selon ses créateurs* [*The World according to its Creators*] at the Musée de la Mode et du Costume, Paris. Like Jean-Paul Gaultier, Vivienne Westwood, and Rei Kawakubo, Martin Margiela boldly moves fashion forward towards an unknown future.—VALERIE STEELE

Matsuda, Mitsuhiro

Japanese designer

Born *Tokyo, 1934.*

Education *Graduated from Waseda University, 1958; graduated with degree in fashion design from Bunka College of Fashion, 1961.*

Career *Ready-to-wear designer, Sanai Company, Japan, 1961-67; traveled to Paris and the USA, 1965; free-lance designer; formed own company, Nicole, Ltd., Tokyo, 1971; introduced divisions Monsieur Nicole, 1974, Madame Nicole, 1976, Chambre de Nicole, 1978, Nicole Club, 1982, Nicole Club for Men, 1984, Séduction de Nicole, 1986; cosmetics line introduced, 1987; formed Matsuda, USA, and opened boutiques, New York, 1982, Hong Kong, 1982, and Paris, 1987. Also worked in planning room of San-Ai Co., Ltd and publisher of Nicole Times.*

Awards *So-en Prize.*

Address *3-13-11 Higashi, Shibuya-ku, Tokyo 150, Japan.*

Mitsuhiro Matsuda's design is picturesque, evoking historical passages and a profound sense of connection with the past and place, but at the same time a transformation through Matsuda's personal style. *Women's Wear Daily* (29 November 1989) commented, "Few can tread the fine line between sophistication and adventure the way Mitsuhiro Matsuda does." In fact, the comparable designer is probably Romeo Gigli who brings a like erudition, yet transfiguration to his clothing. Matsuda, of course, precedes Gigli and also differs from him in an essential way: despite the whimsical romance of his clothing which could seem to suit a Brontë heroine, Matsuda observes a stern rule of practicality borrowed from menswear. His basic canon of separate elements, the signature Matsuda silk blouse, jackets (generally elongated), trousers of various kinds, vests, and sweater often elaborated with embroidery or other textural play, affords a versatile set of components in the sportswear tradition. Eminently pragmatic, but irrepressibly romantic and sensuous (even in appropriations of menswear to womenswear). Matsuda has defined a kind of practical aesthetic dress of the late 20th century.

In the mid-1960s, Matsuda and Kenzo sailed from Japan to Europe to make their way to Paris, the great beacon of fashion. After some six months, Matsuda returned to Japan with no money, while Kenzo stayed. Matsuda's aesthetic and cultural allegiance outside of Japan is not to Paris, but to England and America. His first company outside of Nicole Co. in Japan was Matsuda

Mitsuhiro Matsuda: Fall/Winter 1992/93. *Photograph by Guy Marineau.*

USA which opened a Madison Avenue boutique in 1982. Matsuda has delved into the Anglo-American sportswear traditions as ardently as any designer, even as much as Ralph Lauren. What differentiates Matsuda from Lauren, though, is his critical, slightly adverse, edge on examining the traditions. His famous fall 1982 collections showed the impeccable tailoring of the English jackets, heavy trousers, layering, and indulgent textiles of the English countryside for men now adapted to women, but with the almost impish heterogeneity of canvas aprons that served both as working-class signs and as reminders of the transference from male to female, female to male. That is, the apron customarily signifies the female; Matsuda both breaks and then re-employs the customary index of apron to female. In this scholarly and mischievous transgression, Matsuda declared his clothing to be free of mere continuation; he is one who interprets and alters, not merely observes. In this, Matsuda may be said to express his position as one of the foremost among the first generation of Japanese designers to function in the international arena of fashion. But Western critics would be myopic to believe that Matsuda, or any other Japanese designer of his era, creates an Asian international design out of late acquaintance or foreign feeling from Western clothing which had been present in Japan since the Meiji period. Matsuda, for example, knows and feels Anglo-American dress viscerally and intellectually (though his initial intention was to design textiles for *kimonos*). He has allowed himself critical revision, not mere continuity.

In fall-winter 1984, Matsuda's collections were seemingly inspired by Edwardian England; in fall-winter 1985, the collections seemed to step out of Burne-Jones's paintings; while the Moroccan embroideries of 1989 could costume a Paul Bowles novel. Matsuda's inherent picture-making of the garment, his ability to see it as a spectator as much as creator, is most evident in his propensity to fashion-illustration elongated forms, often seeming more like the Barbier illustrations of style than the garments Barbier, fashion illustrator of the 1920s, depicted. There is a further literary aspect to Matsuda's work in his preoccupation with words and letters. Matsuda's work has been favoured by artists, writers, and other creatives who have recognized a kinship with this most literary image-making style and who enjoy the practicality of clothing that mixes so easily, even improvisationally, with other separates.

There is a synaesthesia about Matsuda's work. In fall-winter 1992, he created a homage to jazz saxophonist Miles Davis. His collections are regularly presented as performance and are often affiliated with dance or visual arts. His advertising and photography have been collaborative art, often presenting the clothing in secondary status to the picture. His boutiques project the absolute austerity of the design and yet showcase the lasciviousness of Matsuda's details. Matsuda's work is unmistakable; his clients are ardently loyal; his work is profoundly progressive. In such characteristics, there is the sureness of the artist, uncompromising and singular in style.—RICHARD MARTIN

Maxwell, Vera

American designer

> **Born** *Vera Huppe in New York, 22 April 1903.*
>
> **Family** *Married Raymond J. Maxwell in 1924 (divorced, 1937); son: R. John Maxwell; married Carlisle H. Johnson (divorced, 1945).*
>
> **Career** *Danced with the Metropolitan Opera Ballet, 1919-24; studied tailoring in London and worked as a fitting model before beginning to design in 1929; designed for*

New York wholesale firms, including Adler & Adler, Max Milstein, Glenhurst, 1930s and 1940s; designer of sports and tailored clothes, Brows, Jacobson & Linde, from 1937; launched firm, Vera Maxwell Originals, New York, 1947; closed firm, 1985; designed collection for Peter Lynne division, Gulf Enterprises, 1986.

Exhibitions *Smithsonian Institution, Washington, D.C., 1970 (retrospective); Museum of the City of New York, 1978 (retrospective).*

Awards *Coty American Fashion Critics Award, 1951; Neiman Marcus Award, Dallas, 1955.*

Throughout her long career, Vera Maxwell held steadfastly to her belief that good design is timeless. Decade after decade her collections bore the fruit of this philosophy. In 1935 her career was launched with the goal of achieving softer tailoring in women's suits. The silhouette of those early designs would be quite fashionable today. In 1937 she joined Brows, Jacobson & Linde as a designer of sports and tailored clothes. Active sportswear was her specialty with emphasis on skiing, riding, and the shorts, jackets, slacks, and skirts that are the foundation of American sportswear separates and the staple of the industry. She was most famous for her suits and topcoats, worn for both the city and the country, and characterized by excellent tailoring, choice fabrics, beautiful colors, and pragmatism. One suit, designed under her own label in 1948, a year after she opened her own business, was designed for travelling. Called "the original flight suit," it consisted of a brown and white Irish tweed coat with a plastic lined pocket for carrying a washcloth and toothbrush, worn over slacks and blouse of a coordinating cocoa wool jersey. Ease of movement and comfort while travelling were of great importance, but the effectiveness of the design, with the close fitting jersey and the fingertip length full coat, have given this particular costume a timeless modernity.

Influences on Vera Maxwell's designs have come from many sources. One of her early memories is of a visit to Vienna with her father, an *aide-de-camp* to the Emperor Franz Joseph, where she was impressed with the beautifully dressed military officers. She herself has said that Chanel was an important influence. Long considered a classicist by the industry, her clothes are usually described as "handsome, interesting, and eminently wearable," as they were in a *New York Times* article on 25 November 1964. In 1960, on the occasion of the 25th anniversary of her entry into the fashion business, she pulled together her favorite designs of the past and discovered that she had trouble identifying them by year, an indication of what she has called the "constant" element in her work. In 1935 she visited Albert Einstein and was inspired by his Harris tweed jacket which she adapted and paired with a gray flannel skirt and pants, giving an important boost to the concept of separates and what she called the "weekend wardrobe." During the 1940s she designed a coverall, which she considered the first jumpsuit, for the women doing war work at the Sperry Gyroscope Corporation. In 1951 she was honored with a Coty Special Award, and in 1955 the Neiman Marcus Award, both during one of her most prolific decades. In 1970 she was given a retrospective at the Smithsonian Institution. Ever concerned with attractive and convenient clothes and wardrobes that could travel well, and ever on the lookout for new means to achieve them, in 1971 she took a significant risk to purchase 30,000 yards of a new fabric called Ultrasuede produced by a company in Japan. Initially buyers were afraid to purchase clothes made of the new material, but time proved Maxwell right and the fabric became identified with her designs.

Until the day she closed her business, early in 1985, Vera Maxwell had a loyal following of fashion conscious women who sought the timeless wearability of her clothes. She ranks among the top of the group of craftspeople-designers who flourished during the 1930s and 1940s in New York and who created the well-tailored but casual look long associated with American fashion.—JEAN DRUESEDOW

McCardell, Claire

American designer

Born *Frederick, Maryland, 24 May 1905.*

Education *Attended Hood College, Maryland, 1923-25, and Parsons School of Design, New York and Paris, 1926-29.*

Family *Married Irving D. Harris in 1943.*

Career *Fashion model, knitwear designer, Robert Turk, Inc., New York, 1929-31; designer, Townley Frocks, New York, 1931-38; designer, Hattie Carnegie, New York, 1938-40; designer, Claire McCardell for Townley Frocks, New York, 1940-58; children's line, Baby McCardells, introduced, 1956.*

Exhibitions *Retrospective, Frank Perls Gallery, Beverly Hills, California, 1953; Innovative Contemporary Fashion: Adri and McCardell, Smithsonian Institution, Washington, D.C., 1971; Three Women: Madeleine Vionnet, Claire McCardell and Rei Kawakubo, Fashion Institute of Technology, New York, 1987.*

Awards *Mademoiselle Merit Award, 1943; Coty American Fashion Critics Award, 1944, 1958; Neiman Marcus Award, 1948; Women's National Press Club Award, 1950; Parsons Medal for Distinguished Achievement, 1956.*

Died *(in New York) 22 March 1958.*

Claire McCardell was the founder of American ready-to-wear fashion, and in doing so defined what has become known as the American Look. She created casual, but sophisticated clothes with a functional design, which reflected the lifestyles of the American woman. McCardell's design philosophy was that clothes should be practical, comfortable, and feminine. Capitalizing on the World War II restrictions on the availability of French fashions and fabrics, McCardell designed simple, inexpensive clothes under the label Townley Frocks by Claire McCardell and later Claire McCardell Clothes by Townley.

The first successful silhouette McCardell designed was the Monastic, a dartless, waistless, bias-cut, tent style dress that could be worn with or without a belt. McCardell had several other successful designs which stayed in her collections, with slight changes, for years. In 1942, McCardell introduced the Popover, a wrap around, unstructured, utilitarian denim dress to be worn over smarter clothes. This garment was made in response to a request by *Harper's Bazaar* for clothing for those women whose hired help had left for wartime factory work. The Popover evolved, in later collections, into dresses, coats, beach wraps, and hostess dresses.

McCardell was known for many other innovations and she experimented with unconventional fabrics for various silhouettes. Her wool jersey bathing suits and cotton diaper swimsuit are examples of non-traditional fabric use. Madras cotton halter-style full-length hostess gowns were shown for evening. Her design trademarks were double top-stitching, brass hardware replacing buttons with decorative hooks, spaghetti ties, large patch pockets, and Empire waists. McCardell also brought denim to the fashion forefront as a dress fabric, as well as mattress ticking, calicos, and wool fleece. Manmade fibers, too, were a source of innovation. She also loved leotards, hoods, pedal pushers, and dirndl skirts. Surprising color combinations were indicative of McCardell's work.

Ever resourceful, McCardell viewed the 1940s wartime restrictions as challenging. Shoes were heavily rationed, so McCardell promoted the ballet slipper as street wear, often covered in coordinating or matching fabrics to her clothing ensembles.

The inspirations for McCardell's designs were many. She relied primarily on her own intuition as a woman, believing that many other women had the same needs for their wardrobes. "Most of my ideas," stated McCardell, "come from trying to solve my own problems." She sought to find solutions by analyzing the various needs of women, concluding that essentially clothes must be functional. While skiing she found her head became quite cold and thus designed winter playclothes with hoods. She recognized that cars and airplanes had changed the American travel lifestyle dramatically. Women needed clothes which would travel well. Accordingly, McCardell designed a six-piece interchangeable, coordinated wardrobe of separates which would enable the woman who traveled to produce many combinations from just a few garments.

McCardell rarely looked to contemporary French fashion for inspiration, as many other American designers did before and after World War II. She recognized the differing needs of the American woman from the European couture client and the potential of the larger ready-to-wear market in the United States. In this way she was able to define the American style of casual elegance. In 1926, during her sophomore year at Parsons School of Design, New York, McCardell studied in Paris. Whilst there she was able to buy samples from the French couturier Madeleine Vionnet and study the pattern and cut of her garments. Vionnet's influence is evident in McCardell's work; though McCardell did not work in the couture tradition, she was able to create ready-to-wear by simplifying Vionnet's cut. She incorporated the bias cut into her designs, both for aesthetic as well as functional effects. From Vionnet, McCardell said she learned "the way clothes worked, the way they felt."

The beauty of McCardell's clothes lay in the cut which then produced a clean, functional garment. Her clothes accentuated the female form without artificial understructures and padding. Rather than use shoulder pads, McCardell used the cut of the sleeve to enhance the shoulder. Relying on the bias cut, she created fitted bodices and swimsuits which flattered the wearer. Full circle skirts, neatly belted or sashed at the waist without crinolines underneath, a mandatory accessory for the New Look, created the illusion of the wasp waist. McCardell clothes often had adjustable components, such as drawstring necklines and waists, to accommodate many different body types.

Claire McCardell's greatest contribution to fashion history was in creating and defining the American Look. Her inspiration is evident in the work of many contemporary fashion designers.—MARGO SEAMAN

McFadden, Mary

American designer

Born *New York City, 1 October 1938.*

Education *Studied at the École Lubec, 1955-56, and at the Sorbonne, Paris, 1956-57; studied fashion at the Traphagen School of Design, New York, summer 1956; studied sociology at Columbia University and at the New School for Social Research, New York, 1958-60.*

Family *Married Philip Harari in 1965 (divorced); daughter: Justine; married Frank McEwan in 1968 (divorced, 1970); married Armin Schmidt in 1981 (divorced); married Kohle Yohannan in 1988 (divorced).*

Career *Director of Public Relations, Dior New York, 1962-64; merchandising editor, Vogue, South Africa, 1964-65; travel and political columnist, Rand Daily Mail, South Africa, 1965-68; founder, Vukutu sculpture workshop, Rhodesia, 1968-70; also free-lance editor for My Fair Lady, Cape Town, and Vogue, Paris, 1968-70; special projects editor, American Vogue, New York, 1970; free-lance fashion and jewelry designer, New York, from 1973; Marii pleated fabric patented, 1975; president, Mary McFadden Inc., from 1976; home furnishings line introduced, 1978; lower priced line manufactured by Jack Mulqueen, from 1980; Mary McFadden Knitwear Company, launched 1981. Also film costume designer for Zooni, 1993.*

Exhibitions *A Passion for Fashion: The Mortimer Collection, Wadsworth Atheneum, Hartford, Connecticut, 1993.*

Awards *Coty American Fashion Critics Award, 1976, 1978, 1979; Audemars Piquet Fashion Award, 1976; Rex Award, 1977; Moore College of Art Award, Philadelphia, 1977; Pennsylvania Governor's Award, 1977; Roscoe Award, 1978; Presidential Fellows Award, Rhode Island School of Design, 1979; Neiman Marcus Award, 1979; Doctor of Fine Arts, Miami International Fine Arts College, 1984; American Printed Fabrics Council Tommy Award, 1991.*

Address *240 West 35th St., New York, New York 10001, USA.*

With an artist's sensitivity to color, harmony, and proportion, Mary McFadden has been successfully designing decidedly original clothing for nearly 20 years. Her distinctive garments reflect an avid study of ancient and ethnic cultures. Inspired by the art and artifacts of Greece, Byzantium, South America and China, among others, as well as the distant cultures encountered during her own travels around the world, McFadden has built a foundation of pure, timeless silhouettes to which she adds exotic details, decorations, in stunning fabrics, to culminate in elegant and flattering results.

When *Vogue* featured McFadden's simple tunics made of African prints and Oriental silks, clothes she had fashioned for herself out of necessity during her years spent in South Africa, the effect created sensation. While trousers had become accepted as daytime workwear during the 1970s, women were resigned to spongy polyester double-knits in mundane sherbet colors. McFadden's tunics, worn over silk Chinese pants, offered the comfort of natural fabrics and the eye appeal of vibrant colors and patterns. McFadden's first collection included quilted *kimono*-shaped jackets, flowing silk or chiffon trousers topped by loose togas made of stylized batik prints depicting Indonesian flowers and dragons, themes she was to repeat in a more luxurious manner in the fall of 1992. Bold, chunky, African-inspired jewelry made from various metals, plastic, and coral accented the eclectic mix.

Shimmering tunics resembling the shapes and patterns of butterfly wings followed, as McFadden developed her famous *"marii"* pleating, recalling Fortuny's silk pleated fabrics, which were, in turn, based upon ancient Greek and Egyptian pleating. McFadden's pleated evening gowns were ideal for her wealthy, jet-setting clientèle because, being made of satin-backed polyester, they could retain their pleats through hand washing and travel. McFadden's awareness of modern technology had succeeded in making the pleats permanent.

Even her less expensive clothes, offered in the late 1970s, maintained an exotic feeling through the use of hand-painting on challis and suede, macramé yokes, quilting, and grosgrain ribbon binding. Herself a striking model for her creations, McFadden presented some black and white outfits in every collection, echoing her own straight black hair and very pale skin. Drama was created by the contrast, texture, and richness of fabric. The same sense of sophistication was imbued into McFadden's bedding and table linen licensing. During the late 1970s her more expensive line of dresses included chiffon embroidered in gold, silver, and gold lamé, gold washed silks, foreshadowing the opulence of the 1980s. McFadden continued to design bold sculptured jewelry and braided belts to tie her gowns closer to the body or to use as edgings. Bolero jackets featured details from Portuguese tiles, an example of McFadden's ability to focus on a detail of a work of art, enlarge the motif, and incorporate it into her design.

Ever sensitive to the interplay of textures, the designer punctuates her columns of fine vertical pleating with beaded cuffs and collars, jewel encrusted panels, draped diagonals. Many of her garments come close to the surface richness of the art-to-wear movement but, eschewing the social statements inherent in the movement, her work is instead wearable art, to be collected and taken out to wear as one might precious jewelry. As evocative of the past as some of McFadden's designs may be, they stop short of looking like costumes. Pattern-upon-pattern mosaics of gold embroidery on sheer silk may highlight a Gustav Klimt-inspired collection, but the clothes are always modern.

Despite the vagaries of fashion, McFadden has maintained a consistent aesthetic. Her clothes offer something for almost everyone who can afford them. They are pretty and always have some interesting detail that will cause comment when the self-assured woman who wears them makes an entrance. McFadden herself has recommended "chiffons for the heavy figures, the pleats for the thin ones, the velvets for everyone." By the end of the 1980s, McFadden had experimented with showing slits of bare skin in between swaths of pleated strips composing the bodices of her gowns. The columns closely outlined the curves of fit figures, for the cult of the body was in full swing. The designer shortened her skirts to above the knees, flippy skirts of rows of layered pleats dancing beneath sequined tops. A striking short dress in the spring of 1992 had a skirt encrusted with beads forming a panel from a Tiffany wisteria window, belted with a beaded belt beneath a diagonally *"marii"* pleated sleeveless bodice. Her Japanese collection followed, the mystery of the Orient conveyed through embroidered snakes and sinuous blossoms.

It may well be said about Mary McFadden that "she walks in beauty" as she continues to wear her own designs. She was recently seen in a luminous cascading white Ionic *chiton,* delicately bordered with glitter, in which she appeared to be the most glamorous caryatid of all.—THERESE DUZINKIEWICZ BAKER

McQueen, Alexander
British designer

Alexander McQueen knows the archetype of the avant-garde designer. Exciting controversy, especially in his 1995 "Highland Rape" runway show with models made up to seem bloodied in torn lace dresses; challenging authority, especially in his "bumster" low-rise and slashed-buttocks pants and skirts of 1995 and 1996; and provoking predictable shock with bare or barely covered breasts, McQueen offers a textbook study in the development of an avant-garde sensibility. Perhaps the model would work nowhere in the last quarter of the twentieth century with such clockwork (or *Clockwork Orange*) accuracy as in England, where Vivienne Westwood and John Galliano have already blazed a well-worn trail from embattled Scots to Establishment Britain to 18th-century revivals to expected obscenity and finally to facile fame. McQueen complements his slightly nasty, edgy temperament to displease with an ingratiating interest in the business and success of fashion. Of his spring 1996 collection, a coalition of polite and impolite clothes, McQueen told William Middleton and James Fallon (*W*, December 1995): "I wanted the audience to see a side of McQueen they've never seen before: wearable clothes. It's a fine balance. I'm trying to keep my artistic integrity and still sell as much as I can." McQueen's paradox is pronounced inasmuch as much of his clothing sets out to repel and be transgressive. Even his slashed skirts and dresses seem more wounded and even misogynistic than Saint Laurent's delicacy of apertures or Versace's brilliant apertures. McQueen's adolescent rudeness (he mooned one runway audience instead of taking customary bows) pervades the audacity of the artistic gestures that he makes, even when he exerts his tailor's discipline or uses an innovative material in the manner of his one-time employer Koji Tatsuno.

As Ingrid Sischy summarized (*The New Yorker*, 1 April 1996), "McQueen's most notorious articles of clothing are pants called bumsters: they lower the waistline, make people look taller, and reveal rear cleavage." Such bumsters are indubitably inspired by the 1980s and 1990s street style of young people—especially young men—wearing jeans low on the hip in the unbelted manner of convicts. If one readily identifies the source, along with the perennial plumber's butt, one can wonder if McQueen has created bona fide design or art from this perception of street style as the real revolutionaries such as Rei Kawakubo and Jean Paul Gaultier have done. McQueen plays to the journalists and editors, easy targets for frissons of self-conscious vangardism; Amy Spindler (*New York Times*, 30 March 1996) enthused that McQueen "has the ability to astonish with his imagination," concluding that he is "a brilliant designer, a fantastic tailor and a hopeless romantic, bad boy or no." Despite early training as a teenager in Savile Row, little evidence of that discipline obtains in McQueen's 1990s clothing and McQueen's alleged romance is little more than a banality of bad-boyism, masculinist by insinuation, adolescently mean by another insinuation, and careless by fabrication.

Withal, there is reason to be intrigued by McQueen's work. His tracings of lace on nylon net cover and uncover the body—thus included in the exhibition "Bare Witness" at the

Metropolitan Museum of Art (1996)—either politely or impolitely and were shown on the runway with panties. In this instance, we know that Saint Laurent and others have created delicate strategies of lace and net that are far more seductive and chivalrous. McQueen's gray suit with slashes below the buttocks surprises us with the intrusion to the body, but we know that Gaultier had done more in the "Express Yourself" clothing as worn by Madonna, allowing decisive apertures in a man's gray flannel suit to become the expressive garment of a powerful woman. McQueen's composites of lace and corset remember Westwood too distinctly to constitute an idea in their own right. Ironically, McQueen goes beyond polite Elizabethan slashings wherever he places them on the body to gash the dress and to seemingly violate its sanctity. Not unprecedented and reminiscent of Schiaparelli's "tear-illusion" dress (1938), McQueen's slashes take on the aesthetic savagery of Lucio Fontana or Antoni Tapies, gashing the cloth in the manner of a wound. McQueen's lacerations seem more referential than the garment-knowing changes wrought by the Deconstructivists of the early to mid-1990s. Importantly, McQueen implies a human story more poignant and important than a mere structural suture.

McQueen told Jessica Kerwin (*Women's Wear Daily*, 28 March 1996), "I have to make a living from what I do, so there's a part to the collection that's more ready-to-wear with jackets and trousers, and alpaca coats. Then you have the more avant-garde part that's more about innovation and design. But I never want to design things that no one will wear." It is such a balance between his little insurrections and his wearable clothing that will determine McQueen's viability as a designer, now formidably backed by a corporation MA Commerciale. McQueen makes disquieting clothing of a familiar kind. His energy is admirable, but the designer has yet to reconcile some fashion skills with his acumen to affront. Fashion, which too often flatters, can always learn from a renegade. In the waning of the deconstructivist impulse in fashion led by Martin Margiela and Anne Demeulemeester, McQueen is poised to offer constructive and controversial fashion if only he will heed his own remark to Middleton and Fallon, "I'm not a man with a chip on my shoulder."—RICHARD MARTIN

Miller, Nicole

American designer

Born *Lenox, Massachusetts, 1952.*

Education *Graduated from Rhode Island School of Design, Providence, Rhode Island attended École de la Chambre Syndicale Parisienne as a third-year student at RISD.*

Career *Designer, Rain Cheetahs, New York, 1975; head designer for Bud Konheim, P.J. Walsh women's fashion company, New York, 1975-82; in partnership with Konheim, company renamed Nicole Miller, 1982; launched line of men's accessories, c.1987, footwear, 1992; fragrance and cosmetics collection introduced, 1993; licenses include socks and tights, from 1991, jeans, from 1992, also handbags and men's formal wear; opened boutiques in New York, 1987, Mexico City and Naples, Florida, 1991, Barcelona, Tokyo and Osaka, 1992, Seville, 1992, Los Angeles, 1993.*

Awards *Dallas Fashion Award, 1991; Girl Scouts of America Award, New York, 1994.*

Address *525 Seventh Avenue, New York, New York 10018, USA.*

Nicole Miller.

Immense talent as a designer, fun, and an astute sense of fashion are the key to Nicole Miller's success. Miller is a hands-on designer, who pays particular attention to clothing construction throughout the entire design process. Her studies at a haute couture school in Paris taught her the importance of a well engineered and well fitting garment. Realizing that few women have perfect bodies, she makes certain the body looks its best, camouflaging problem areas. Because of simple but unique details and superior cut, a woman wearing a Nicole Miller garment is assured of always looking her best.

Nicole Miller has had her own women's line of clothing for over ten years. The company is primarily known for her great looking dresses in both solid and printed fabrics. However, due to an over-abundance of leftover fabric from a line of unsuccessful dresses, she opted to make the conversational black silk print, featuring colored ticket stubs in the foreground, into the Nicole Miller necktie sensation. Thus, the Nicole Miller line of men's accessories was born. This dark cloud turned out to have a platinum lining and Miller has blossomed into a leading men's accessory manufacturer. Presently the Miller ties, shirts, boxer shorts and robes account for 20 percent of its business. Men choose flashy tie patterns because they want to feel good. That is the whole reason for the fashion.

Inspiration for her prints can come from anywhere. After seeing the off-Broadway hit *Song of Singapore,* Miller decided to create a special silk print in honor of the show. Nicole Miller presently employs 40 artists who develop graphics to please consumers from all walks of life. Designs incorporate everything from assorted candy, animals or vegetables, to the sports collection, featuring basketballs, footballs, or baseballs. These prints have become so influential that knockoffs can be found at every level of the marketplace.

Miller has been prolific in other areas of design as well. She was involved in designing costumes for the Brooklyn Academy of Music's New Wave festival tribute to the late Carmen Miranda. Inspiration for the costumes was the peasant clothing of the Bahia region of Brazil that Miller had visited.

Although she has received a great deal of publicity for her prints, Nicole Miller's reputation has actually been built with her dramatic pared-down silhouettes and her striking use of graphics. Some examples are her curvy, strapless pale linen chambray dresses, and her short white rompers and dresses stitched in red like a baseball. Flattering fit and drop-dead designs are not Miller's only strong points. She is one of the few American designers with fashion's sixth sense for setting the trends without resorting to fads. Nicole Miller's clothes are young and fresh. In a time where many of the baby boomers have become more conservative, the Miller customer remains forever young.—ROBERTA H. GRUBER

Missoni
Italian knitwear and fashion house

Founded in Gallarate, Varese, Italy, 1953, by Ottavio Missoni (born in Dalmatia, 11 February 1921) and Rosita (Jelmini) Missoni (born in Lombardy, 20 November 1931). First collection produced for Rinascente Stores, 1954; Missoni label introduced, from 1958; first Paris showing, 1967; Missoni SpA workshop and factory established, Sumirago,

Missoni

Missoni.

1968; first New York showing, 1969; first boutiques opened, Milan and New York, 1976; fragrance line introduced, 1981; Missoni Uomo and Missoni Sport lines introduced, 1985.

Exhibitions *Solo exhibition, Il Naviglio Gallery, Venice, 1975; retrospective, La Rotonda Gallery, Milan, and the Whitney Museum, New York, 1978; solo exhibition, Galleria del Naviglio, Milan, and the University of California, Berkeley, 1981; retrospective, Ridotto/Pergola Theatre, Pitti Immagine Filati, Florence, 1994.*

Awards *Neiman Marcus Award, 1973; Bath Museum of Costume Dress of the Year Award, 1974; American Printed Fabric Council Tommy Award, 1976; Gold Medal of Civic Merit Award, Milan, 1979; Fragrance Foundation Award, 1982; Tai Missoni given Arancia Award, 1986; Rosita Missoni named Commendatore al Merito della Repubblica Italiana, 1986; Fashion Group International Design Award, 1991; Munich Mode-Woche Award, 1992.*

Address *Via Luigi Rossi 52, 21040 Sumirago (Varese), Italy.*

Missoni exemplifies success in a specific fashion area, knitwear for men and women. In the knitwear business since 1953, the business begun by Ottavio (Tai) and Rosita Missoni took off with recognition by Anna Piaggi in 1965 and was through the 1960s and 1970s one of the landmark enterprises of the Italian renaissance in post-war fashion products. In 1968 and 1969, Missoni garnered worldwide attention for knit dresses, coats, and sweaters that revived the sensational appeal of knits in the 1920s. From a start in producing the finest knits at a moment when both the Establishment and anti-Establishment were looking for poor-boy sweaters and the liquid ease of knits, the Missoni repertory now includes pullovers, long coats, chemises, and knit trousers and skirts. Even more, in the 1970s, the Missonis' deliberate allegiance to Milan heralded that city's eminence as a fashion center and helped create Milan fashion week. In spring 1967, at the Pitti collections in Florence, Rosita had been discouraged by the visibility of the models' bras under the thin knit dresses; she had the models remove their bras for the Missoni show. Stage lights made the clothes seem transparent and the showing became a *cause célèbre* in Italy. While it does not seem that the Missonis were banned from the Pitti showings thereafter, they defected to Milan and took with them a certain sense of Milan's most worldly view of fashion.

Primarily creators of exceptional knitwear, Missoni has been noted as an art as much as a business. Technology provides a range of fluid knits and special effects, but the identifying and indescribable aspect of the Missoni knits is color, the affinity to art. Most importantly, Missoni brought a vivid sense of imagination to knits, rescuing them from the heirlooms and old-fashioned aspects of handknits and from the conventional sameness of many machine-knitted products. Like many Italian products of the post-war period, the value of the product was not in its handwork, but in the unquestionable supremacy of design attained through machine. Today computers and sophisticated machines make the Missoni knits that are thought of as artisan production, so exceptional are their colors, so extraordinary do such knits seem to be in texture as in color. Today, Missoni knits seem as intrinsic to Italian style as Ravenna mosaics, likewise brilliant in elements and creative of color fields beyond their discrete *tesserae* or components. The knits have also proved as successful in menswear, sweaters in particular, as in women's apparel.

Tai Missoni's introduction to the knitwear business was as an athlete. Knitwear was for active sports, but by 1958 a striped Missoni knit shirtdress was produced and the crossover from sports to casual living was underway. The sports heritage remains in some graphic boldness, including stripes and zig-zags and even patchwork, that read with distinctness across a room. What enhances Missoni for daywear and even for evening (especially with Lurex) is the subtleties within. In fact, the Missonis have often pointed out that they deny fashion. Rosita told Elsa Klensch: "Our philosophy since we went into business has been that a piece of clothing should be like a work of art. It should not be bought for a special occasion or because it's in fashion, but because a woman likes it . . . and feels she could wear it forever" (*New York Post,* 24 May 1978). Little the Missonis have produced depends upon fashion. Instead their knits seem perennial. Their color multivalence works to the same effect: a Missoni design might be worn with a favored color one season and still be compatible with other colors in other seasons. Moreover, the color partakes of a convention of abstract painting and satisfies for many a sense of being modern through abstract pattern. Thus, Bernadine Morris's declaration that the Missonis "have elevated knitted clothes to a form of art" is not as startling as it might seem. (*New York Times,* 26 March, 1979). If they have done so, they have made that advancement because they realized that modern design is a synergy between machine and art. In fact, Missoni knits became in the 1970s and 1980s such visible status symbols that they might easily have become telling symbols of the time. Continued change has kept Missoni a vital force in the field of fashion that they self-consciously ignore to create enduring clothes.—RICHARD MARTIN

Miyake, Issey
Japanese designer

Born *Kazumaru Miyake in Hiroshima, 22 April 1938.*

Education *Studied at Tama Art University, Tokyo, 1959-63, and at École de la Chambre Syndicale de la Couture Parisienne, 1965.*

Career *Design assistant, Guy Laroche, 1966-68, and Givenchy, 1968-69; designer, Geoffrey Beene in New York, 1969-70; established Miyake Design Studio in Tokyo, 1970; also director, Issey Miyake International, Issey Miyake and Associates, Issey Miyake Europe, Issey Miyake USA, and Issey Miyake On Limits. Lines include Issey Sport, Plantation, and Pleats Please (introduced, 1993); fragrances: L'Eau de Missey, intro-duced, 1993, L'Eau d'Issey pour Homme, introduced, 1995; first US boutique opened in New York, 1988. Also theater designer, from 1980.*

Exhibitions *Issey Miyake in the Museum, Seibu Musem, Tokyo, 1977; Les Tissus Imprimés d'Issey Miyake, Musée de l'Impression sur Étoffes, Mulhouse, 1979; Intimate Architecture: Contemporary Clothing, Massachusetts Institute of Technology, 1982; Bodyworks, inter-national touring exhibition, 1983; A New Wave in Fashion: Three Japanese Designers, Phoenix Art Museum, Arizona, 1983; À Un, Musée des Arts Décoratifs, Paris, 1988: Issey Miyake Pleats Please, Touko Museum of Contemporary Art, Tokyo, 1990; Twist, Naoshima Contemporary Art Museum, 1992.*

Awards *Japan Fashion Editors Club Award, 1974; Mainichi Newspaper Fashion Award, 1976, 1984; Pratt Institute Design Excellence Award, New York, 1979; Council of Fashion Designers of America Award, 1983; Neiman Marcus Award, 1984; Officier de l'Ordre des*

Issey Miyake. "Paradise Lost," Spring/Summer 1977. *Photograph by Noriaki Yokosuka.*

Arts et Lettres, France, 1989; Honorary Doctorate, Royal College of Art, London, 1993; Hiroshima Art Prize, 1991; Chevalier de l'Ordre National de la Legion d'Honneur, Paris, 1993.

Address   *1-23 Ohyamacho, Shibuya-ku, Tokyo 151, Japan.*

Architect Arata Isozaki begins his essay in Issey Miyake's *East Meets West* with the question, "What are clothes?" The question, perhaps too fundamental and unnecessary for most designers, is the matrix of Issey Miyake's clothing. More, possibly, than any other designer of the century, Miyake has inquired into the nature of apparel, investigating adornment and dress functions from all parts of the world and from all uses and in all forms, to speculate about clothing. Aroused to question fashion's viability in the social revolution he observed in Paris in 1968, Miyake has sought a clothing of particular lifestyle utility, of renewed coalition with textile integrity, and of wholly reconsidered form. In exploring ideas that emanate from the technology of cloth, Miyake has created great geometries that surpass the body, the most effortless play of drapery on the bias and accommodating the body in motion since his paragon Madeleine Vionnet, and the folds and waffles of a first-phase cubism followed by a crushed, irregular form of fluid dressing. His highly successful "Windcoats" wrap the wearer in an abundance of cloth, but also generate marvelously transformative shapes when compressed, or billowing and extended. In these efforts, Miyake has created garments redolent of human history, but largely unprecedented in the history of dress, so committed is he to fashion that expresses and realizes life in the latter years of the 20th century. He is, without question, aesthetically the most visionary fashion designer of the second half of this period, often seeming to abandon commercial ideas of dress for the more extravagantly new and ideal experiments.

Characteristic examples demonstrate the designer's incomparable sense of experiment and innovation. In 1976, a knit square with sleeves becomes, as if by a magician's transmogrification, a coat with matching bikini. His 1982 rattan body sculpture is an ironically externalized cage of the body for which it serves instead as an ideal pattern of ribs and structural lines. Yet he also returns to kimono textiles as the basis for new textile design and fabrication and even experiments with paper and other materials to find the right medium for apparel. His fall/winter 1989-90 pleated collection partakes of a radical Cubist vision of the human body and of its movement, whereas the 1990s commitment to irregularly pleated fabric suggests a fashion possibility in disparity to any existing idea of dress. Is Miyake's insight so thoroughly Utopian and visionary as to defy a current fashion use? Despite idealist propensity and a highly original and conceptual nature, Miyake has appealed to a clientèle of forward thinkers and designers who wear the clothing with a zeal and identity of the creative enterprise and energy with which they are vested.

Miyake transcends the garments. Like Duchamp, he gives to his work interpretative issues and contexts that contribute to their meaning, acknowledging the garments as prolific signs. Thus, his books *East Meets West* (Tokyo, 1978) and *Bodyworks* (Tokyo, 1983), accompanied by these and other museum exhibitions, have placed a reading and meaning on the works that become inextricably involved with the sign-value of the garment. Miyake can be anthropologically basic; again and again, he returns to tattooing as a basic body adornment, rendered in clothing and tights and bodysuits. He relishes the juxtaposition between the most rustic and basic and the most advanced, almost to prove human history a circle rather a linear progression. But he is also the theorist ascribing to his clothing a plethora of signifying and significant thoughts. No other designer—with the possible exception of the more laconic Geoffrey Beene, for whom Miyake worked briefly and with whom he maintains a mutual admiration—interprets his work as deliberately and thoughtfully as Miyake.

Such allusiveness and context would have little value were it not for the abiding principles of Miyake's work. He relies upon the body as unerringly as a dancer might. He demands a freedom of motion that reveals its genesis in 1968. The experiments, then, of materials and design cannot impede motion, but can only enhance it, as do the aerodynamic works of the 1980s and 1990s. If Miyake's concept of the body is the root of all of his thinking, it is a highly conceptual, reasoned body. His books have customarily shown friends and clients—young and old-wearing the clothing. They come from East and West; they do not possess the perfect anatomy and streamlined physique of body sculptures and bustiers, but they are in some way ideals to Miyake. He intends clothing to be the dress of the intellectually and emotionally peerless. His is an uncommon, even unprecedented fashion idealism. In *Couture: The Great Designers*, Caroline Rennolds Milbank classifies Miyake among "Realists": he is no realist; he is our most compelling dreamer and visionary.—RICHARD MARTIN

Mizrahi, Isaac

American designer

Born *New York City, 14 October 1961.*

Education *Graduated from Parsons School of Design, New York, 1982.*

Career *Assistant designer, Perry Ellis, New York, 1982-83; womenswear designer, Jeffrey Banks, New York, 1984; designer, Calvin Klein, New York, 1985-87; formed own company, 1987; menswear collection introduced, 1990; added accessories line, 1992, and handbags, 1993.*

Awards *Council of Fashion Designers of America Award, 1988, 1989; Fashion Industry Foundation Award, 1990; Michaelangelo Shoe Award, New York, 1993.*

Address *104 Wooster Street, New York, New York 10012, USA.*

Isaac Mizrahi worked, upon graduation from Parsons School of Design, for Perry Ellis, Jeffrey Banks, and Calvin Klein. When he started his own business in 1987, he knew intimately the world of American sportswear at its best, but his work refines the sportswear model by a special sense of sophistication and glamor. His ideals, beyond those he worked for, are such American purists as Norell, Halston, Beene, and McCardell, each a designer of utmost sophistication. Suzy Menkes analyzed in 1990: "The clean colors and Ivy League image of Perry Ellis sportswear might seem to be the seminal influence on Mizrahi. But he himself claims inspiration from his mother's wardrobe of all-American designers, especially the glamorous simplicity of Norman Norell." (*International Herald Tribune*, 17 April 1990).

It is as if Mizrahi is most challenged by distilling the most well-bred form of each garment to an understated glamor, whether tartan taken to a sensuous evening gown but still buckled as if Balmoral livery; pocketbooks and luggage ingeniously incorporated into clothing with the practical pocket panache of McCardell; or versions of high style in adaptations of men's bathrobes or sweatshirting used for evening. While Mizrahi is often commended for the youthfulness of his clothing, the praise is properly for the freshness of his perception, his ability to recalculate a classic, not just a market for young women. His interest in the Empire waistline;

his practicality of wardrobe separates in combination; and his leaps between day and evening address all women equally. In the 1990s, many designers and manufacturers have seen the value in simplification: Mizrahi seeks the pure in tandem with the cosmopolitan.

When Sarah Mower described Mizrahi as "that rare thing in contemporary design: a life-enhancing intelligence on the loose," she rightly characterized his revisionist, rational, distilling, pure vision ("Isaac Mizrahi," *Vogue* [London], September 1989). With his fall 1988 collection Mizrahi was immediately recognized by the *New York Times* as "this year's hottest new designer" in combinations of color (for example, rust and mustard and orange-peel and pink) that were unusual, alpaca and other luxury materials, and the diversity of silhouettes from baby-doll dresses to evening jumpsuits to long dresses. Mizrahi had immediately demonstrated the range of a commercially viable designer while at the same time demonstrating his simplifying glamor and the cool, nonchalant charm of his smart (intellectually and aesthetically) clothing. The spa collection of 1988 included rompers and baseball jackets and playsuits as well as the debonair excess of trousers with paperbag waist. His spring 1989 collection assembled sources from all over the fashion spectrum to create a unified vision of elegance and appeal. The fall 1989 collection featured tartan (later developed by Mizrahi for costumes for a Twyla Tharp production for the American Ballet Theater in 1990) with most extraordinary accompaniment. In a notable instance, *New York* (21 August 1989) showed Mizrahi's tartan dress with his raccoon-trimmed silk taffeta parka in a perfect assembly of wild and urbane.

In 1990, Mizrahi showed a short-lived menswear line and sustained his color studies, creating double-faced wools and sportswear elements in watercolor-like colors, delicate yet deliberate. Spring 1990 was a typical Mizrahi transmogrification. Black and white pattern recalling both art déco and the 1960s was, in fact, derived from costume for the Ballets Russes. In 1991, Mizrahi's themes were American, creating a kind of Puritan revival in dresses with collars and bows in spring/summer 1991—like Norell in the early 1970s, but with more Massachusetts Bay Colony (American orthodoxy) than Norell's more demure version—and an American ethnic parade in fall 1991, including Native American dress and a notable totem-pole dress inspired by Native American art.

Mizrahi's drive to find the most sophisticated version of each concept he develops is the *leitmotif* of his work. His spring 1991 collection examined motifs of the 1960s, but with a clever sharpness not observed in other designers of the same year looking back to the period. In 1991, his tube dresses with flounces were inspired by Norell, but manifestly given proportion by Mizrahi. McCardell's audacious applications of cotton piqué are extended by Mizrahi's love of the same material and Halston's radical simplicity is inevitably a source for any designer longing to return to essential form. Mizrahi's color fields owe their consciousness to Perry Ellis, but the particular color sensibility is Mizrahi's. Mizrahi's immaculate, ingenious modernism is as clearly aware of sources as it is pushed toward the clarification of form.

Mizrahi has referred to his style as a "classic New York look," which presumably means a casual American idiom, but inflected with big-city reserve and refinement. Indeed, Mizrahi captures something of Manhattan chic and glamor of the 1940s and 1950s. It is perhaps the best description for fashion which is otherwise often indescribably beautiful in subtlety and sophistication.—RICHARD MARTIN

Molyneux, Edward H.

British designer

Born Hampstead, London, 5 September 1891.

Military Service Served as captain in the British Army during World War I.

Career Worked for the couturier Lucile in London and the USA, 1911-14; opened own house, Paris, 1919; added branches in Monte Carlo, 1925, Cannes, 1927, and London, 1932; moved business to London, 1939-1946; returned to Paris, added furs, perfume, lingerie and millinery, 1946-49; turned business over to Jacques Griffe and retired, 1950; reopened as Studio Molyneux, Paris, 1965; retired permanently soon thereafter. Fragrances include Numéro Cinq, 1926, Vivre, 1930, and Rue Royale, 1943.

Died (in Monte Carlo), 23 March 1974.

Captain Edward Molyneux embodied the style he created in the 1920s and 1930s, an idle, slim ("never too rich or too thin"), elegant style on the verge of dissipation, at the edge of the outrageous, and always refined. His friendship with Noel Coward was *kismet,* two personifications of the elegant style that made both drawing-room comedy and its grace. Caroline Milbank describes, "Molyneux was the designer to whom a fashionable woman would turn if she wanted to be absolutely 'right' without being utterly predictable in the Twenties and Thirties" (*Couture: The Great Designers,* New York 1985). Indeed, Molyneux's ineffable decorum had come as a privilege of his own style liberation from Lucile, Lady Duff Gordon. Lucile's trademark was her rich proliferation of fine details and adornment. One would not characterize Lucile as florid, but one would certainly characterize Molyneux as chaste. (In fact, his military self-presentation and English background made him seem even more Spartan in the world of French couture.) Molyneux banned all superfluous decoration in an early and intuited version of modernist International Style akin to the architecture of the period. He was a "modern" in his adoration of line and avoidance of excessive decoration. He was a "modern," not only in his engaging manner, but in his identification with style simplicity, his love of luxurious materials, and his embrace of modern circumstances, including the automobile. While his work is most often in black, navy blue, beige, and grey, he had the sophistication as an art collector to collect late Impressionist and Post-Impressionist paintings, shown in 1952 at the National Gallery of Art in Washington, D.C. and subsequently sold to Ailsa Mellon Bruce and later bequeathed to the National Gallery. He could love those bourgeois scenes of beauty. But he also created motoring outfits and easy-to-wear slip-like evening dresses for the leisure class of his time and superbly cut evening pajamas that could have costumed any Noel Coward comedy. Molyneux would be a designer successful at designing for and determining the lifestyle of his own social class, participant-observer in what Pierre Balmain called Molyneux's international set. His curious Franco-English snobbism belonged to a time and place. Indeed, Molyneux's two post-World War II business enterprises were of limited success, so fully was he the product and model of a world already forgotten.

The modern charm of Molyneux's creation was appreciated by Pierre Balmain who apprenticed with Molyneux in Paris. Balmain writes of his regret on departing that first job in the late 1930s and "that temple of subdued elegance. For if the magazines were filled with photographs of Schiaparelli's eccentricities, the world's well-dressed women wore the inimitable two-pieces, and tailored suits with pleated skirts, bearing the label of Molyneux" (*My Years and Seasons,* London 1964). Indeed, there is always a schism between the fashion that claims public attention and even the attention of the élite and that couture clothing that is so consistent, reserved, even understated that it is barely noticed by the fashion press, yet is the manifestation of a conservative, continuous style. Molyneux designed for the theater and was a friend of Gertrude Lawrence who wore his clothing with a West End and Broadway panache, but the costumes never subsumed the actress. Molyneux's international set wore his tailored suits by day, but also could be seen at night in one or both nightclubs owned by Molyneux in partnership with hostess Elsa Maxwell wearing furs, long gowns, beaded chemises, and other elegant outfits by the designer.

Today the designer who mingles with his clients is often criticized for social climbing. There is no evidence that such charges were placed against Molyneux as he moved so effortlessly and with *soigné* flair among the ladies that he dressed. Ernestine Carter called him "dashing and debonair," comparing him to Fred Astaire (*Magic Names of Fashion,* New York 1980). Further, that he dressed women of the greatest propriety and restraint made it clear that, in dwelling among them, he was of like sensibility and shared spirit. It was Molyneux's place in international café-society that allowed him to cavort with Noel Coward and that gave the sobriety of his design its sense of belonging. Given that fashion went through so many changes and excesses in the 1920s and 1930s, Molyneux was a constant model of cool elegance.—RICHARD MARTIN

Montana, Claude

French designer

Born *Paris, 29 June 1949.*

Education *Studied chemistry and law.*

Family *Married Wallis Franken in 1993.*

Career *Free-lance jewelry designer, London, 1971-72; designer, with Michelle Costas, ready-to-wear and accessories line for Idéal-Cuir, Paris, 1973; assistant designer, 1973, and head designer, 1974, MacDouglas Leathers, Paris; free-lance designer, Complice, Ferrer y Sentis Knitwear, Paris, from 1975; founded own company, 1979; Hommes Montana presented, 1981; first boutique opened, Paris, 1983; Montana Pour Femme fragrance introduced, 1986; Parfum d'Homme introduced, 1989; Parfum d'Elle introduced, 1990; designer in charge of haute couture, Lanvin, 1989-92; continues ready-to-wear collections under own name: diffusion line introduced, 1991.*

Exhibitions *Intimate Architecture: Contemporary Clothing Design, Hayden Gallery, Massachusetts Institute of Technology, 1982.*

Awards *Prix Medicis, 1989; Fragrance Foundation Award, 1990; Golden Thimble Award, 1990, 1991.*

Address *131 rue St Denis, 75001 Paris, France.*

In the late 1970s and 1980s Claude Montana was known for an *outré* silhouette and commanding sense of aggression that made him both *enfant terrible* in a cultural sense and yet fashion's most devoted adherent in design. Padded shoulders and leathers seemed to some observers a misogynist's view of women in the manner of a cartoon. To others, however, the same style renewed the shoulder-accented horizontal of Constructivism, or even the influence of Balenciaga's surgically acute cut. Little wonder, then, that Montana said in an interview in 1989, "I'm like a battlefield inside, a mass of contradictions." More than ever, Montana has proved in the late 1980s and 1990s how contradictory and how complex his style is, incapable of the kinds of knee-jerk reactions that many critics had initially. Few designers have been as virulently attacked as Montana has, sometimes for "gay-clone" proclivities to leather, for supposed misogyny, for impractical clothing, for excessive accoutrements. Leather jackets borrowed from menswear—bikers and the military—caused strong controversy in the American press and market in the 1980s when Montana appropriated them. A decade later, Ralph Lauren, Donna Karan, Calvin Klein, and Byron Lars were working with similar looks to no protest (and Saint Laurent had long borrowed from the male wardrobe to only mild demurral).

Few designers today can be equally admired for the surety of cut, the sensuousness of appearance, the femininity that is beneath the bold forms, the luxurious seductions of fabrics more varied than leather alone, and the continuous and consummate mastery of a fashion design that always plays between the abstract forms of art and the conventions of clothing. Indeed, Constructivism is a strong influence on Montana's work. Top-heavy geometry twirling into a narrow skirt or pencil-thin trousers was not commonplace until Montana offered the option. Reductive by nature, Montana has vacillated in terms of accessorizing, particularly in the mid-1980s, but by the 1990s he clearly preferred an austerity about clothing, approximating the linear probity and arc-based sculptural form. Like Constructivist drawings for the stage, Montana's designs come to life in the animation of gyrating proportions, often with exaggerated shoulders or collars, almost invariably with a very narrow waist, and the spin of a peplum over a narrow skirt. Cocoon coats could seem to be the nimbus of abstraction; spiralling line, alternately clinging to the body and spinning away, seemed a gesture of whole cloth, unpieced.

Montana's principal aesthetic contribution is silhouette; nonetheless, his materials, beginning historically with leather, and his color palette are beautiful and sensuous. What became the power look in women's clothing in the mid-1980s is derived from Montana's aesthetic, so persuasive was it as an option for assertive presence without sacrifice of the female form. Based on circuiting spirals and a few strong lines realized on the body, Montana's aesthetic was described by some critics as being too Space Age or futuristic, but recognized by its advocates for its invocation of the principles of Futurist abstraction. Moreover, after a signal collection for fall-winter 1984, in which Montana toned down the most extreme aspects of his style, he remained true to his aesthetic principles and interests, demonstrating that they were not merely the radical forms they had seemed at first, but the fundamental forms that fashion had known since Thayatt and Exter, Adrian and Balenciaga. As early as 1979, when many might have dismissed him as an iconoclast, Montana admitted to André Leon Talley of his admiration for Vionnet and Madame Grès, likewise two designers of utmost simplicity of form (*Women's Wear Daily,* 13 March 1978).

What had been extreme now seems pure. Even in that convention, Montana has emulated avant-garde art. As an artist-designer, he sustains his own predilections. For example, the gargantuan shoulders are reduced in the late 1980s and great, oversized collars keep the outspoken gesture to the top. Robert Knafo (*Connoisseur,* November 1988) describes that transition: "casting out the sharp-shouldered, fearsomely assertive Montana woman, installing in her place a mellower, softer-edged, more romantic figure, although no less self-assured." Indeed, it is some of the referentiality of fashion—association we make with clothing types and image—that has attributed the controversial profile to Montana as a designer. More importantly, he has been a steadfast practitioner of a kind of isolated, non-referential abstraction, obdurately and passionately and compellingly exploring fashion at its most distinct cut. Montana's design survival as a classic figure and a model with lasting impact on other advanced designers in modern fashion attests to that design primacy and perseverance.—RICHARD MARTIN

Mori, Hanae

Japanese designer

Born *Tokyo, 8 January 1926.*

Education *Graduated in literature from Tokyo Christian Women's University, 1947.*

Family *Married Kei Mori; children: Akira and Kei.*

Career *First atelier in Shinjuko, Tokyo, 1951; costume designer for films, 1954-c.1961; first New York fashion show, 1965; showed in Monaco and Paris, 1975; haute couture collection and haute couture house established in Paris and member of Le Chambre Syndicale de la Haute Couture Parisienne, 1977; Hanae Mori Boutique in Faubourg St. Honor, Paris, 1985; designer of costumes for La Scala, Milan; designer of costumes for Paris Opera Ballet, 1986; Hanae Mori Boutique launched, Monte Carlo, 1989. Shows in Paris, Budapest, Moscow and Kuala Lumpur, 1990; shows in Lausanne and Taipei, and member of Japan Olympic Committee and chairman of Cultural Affairs Promotion Committee of Tokyo Chamber of Commerce and Industry, 1991.*

Exhibitions *Avant-garde Japon, Centre Pompidou, Paris, 1986; Hanae Mori: 35 Years in Fashion, Tokyo, 1989, Monte Carlo, 1990, and Paris, 1990; Diana Vreeland: Immoderate Style, Metropolitan Museum of Art, New York, 1993-94; Japonism in Fashion, Kyoto Costume Institute, 1994; Japanese Design: A Survey Since 1950, Philadelphia Museum of Art, 1994; Orientalism, Metropolitan Museum of Art, New York, 1994-95.*

Awards *Neiman Marcus Award, 1973; Medaille d'Argent, City of Paris, 1978; The Symbol of Man Award, Minnesota Museum, 1978; Croix de Chevalier des Arts et Lettres, 1984; Purple Ribbon Decoration, Japan, 1988; Asahi Prize as pioneer of Japanese Fashion, 1988; named Chevalier de la Légion d'Honneur, 1989; Person of Cultural Merit, Japan, 1989.*

Address *6-1, 3 Chome, Kita-Aoyama, Minato-ku, Tokyo, Japan.*

I design primarily to enhance our lifestyle and make it richer and more enjoyable. Expression changes with the times. But the essence does not change. The history of the world is the story of men and women—how men relate to women and how they live. I would like to express that great sense of existence in clothing. I have been in pursuit of that all through my life. For women, something that encompasses truly valuable things have elegance at their core. This is something I have been trying to find out.

I am true to my identity. I keep trying to be myself. I am Japanese. In Japan there is this beauty by itself which has been nurtured by tradition—fashion is an international language. What I have been trying to do is to express the wonderful beauty of Japan using international language.—Hanae Mori

Hanae Mori. *Photograph by Hiro.*

A delicate sense of feminine beauty, stemming from Hanae Mori's Japanese heritage, is married to an artistic use of colour and fabric in all her work. She treads a careful line, balancing Eastern influences with Western ideals to produce consistently successful couture and ready-to-wear lines with international customers. If her clothes lack the more outrageous, attention grabbing qualities of some of her couture counterparts, they compensate with the economy of their cut and base their appeal on the practical needs of the wealthy metropolitan women who wear them.

By stepping outside current trends and concentrating on conservative, but always feminine daywear, Mori has established a niche for herself in the Parisian fashion arena. Integral to this is the sense of the longevity of her easy to wear separates, which even in the ready-to-wear line retain a delicacy of touch through the textiles used. Floating silk dresses, in simple shirtwaist shapes, were shown for spring-summer 1989, covered in powdery pastel flowers standing out from a black background and coupled with abbreviated blossom pink jackets. They encapsulated Mori's design principles by conveying femininity and practicality.

Mori elaborates on the basic tenets of combining fine fabrics and flattering cut, adding her own feel for the dramatic to her eye-catching eveningwear. For this Mori makes optimum use of the lustrous printed textiles produced by her husband, and designed especially for her work. Although there is an air of restrained elegance to much of her design, symbolized by the fragile butterfly motif by which she is known, her eveningwear often breaks into more vibrant realms. In 1981 she produced a languorous silk mousseline dress, the vampish leopard print and deep *décolleté* of which were balanced by the soft, sinuous fall of the fabric. Other examples use bright hot colours, juxtaposed in one ensemble to provide interest, bringing a strong Japanese feel to their narrow hues, which frequently hark back to the kimono for their silhouette and cut. It is in this area that her work is most inspired, bringing together European tailoring and Japanese colour and ideals of beauty. She uses the Japanese love of asymmetry to further develop her style and the linear patterns she prints on to her distinctive silks. She exploits the natural appeal of such fabrics with a well defined sense of cut to illuminate her realistic styles. By doing so, Mori is providing both an alternative to and a definite rejection of the type of elaborate couture confections which mould the female form into fantastical shapes, ignoring the woman beneath the fabric.

The other main strand to her design is her close involvement in the arts. Her early costuming of innumerable Japanese films enabled her sense of colour to evolve, using each primary hued textile to represent a different emotion, and sharpened her sense of the dramatic effect of dress. This has grown in her work for opera and ballet, her clothing for which has drawn on her love of delicacy and poise counterpointed with strong coloration and arresting mixes of the two worlds her design principles straddle.

A firm grasp of the value of these cross cultural reference points has enabled Mori to establish herself in Paris couture and therefore develop an international market. Her understanding of the needs of contemporary women has lent a practical slant to her simple shaped, wearable clothes, while her theatrical preoccupations and Japanese background have inspired her love of rich, tactile fabrics in vibrant prints and colours which are the hallmark of her design.—REBECCA ARNOLD

Morris, Robert Lee

American jewelry and accessories designer

Born *Nuremburg, Germany, 7 July 1947.*

Education *Graduated from Beloit College, Beloit, Wisconsin.*

Career *Showed first collection in 1972; owner and manager, Artwear Gallery, 1977-93; Robert Lee Morris Necessities mail order catalogue introduced, 1993. Also: packaging designer, Elizabeth Arden, New York, from 1992.*

Exhibitions *Artwear Gallery, New York, 1992; Good as Gold: Alternative Materials in American Jewelry, 1981-85 (Smithsonian Institution international touring exhibition); retrospective, Fashion Institute of Technology, New York, 1995.*

Awards *Coty American Fashion Critics Award, 1981; Council of Fashion Designers of America Award, 1985; International Gold Council Award, 1987; Woolmark Award, 1992; American Accessories Achievement Award, 1992.*

Address *161 Sixth Avenue, New York, New York 10013, USA.*

My jewelry is a distant cousin of ancient armor (those smooth, sensual body-conscious constructions that employ ingenious mechanics to allow for fluid movement). My inspiration has never been clothing or fashion trends, but rather, the human need for personal intimacy, with tokens of spiritual potential that amulets and talismans provide.

I constantly seek to fine-tune, focus, purify, and strengthen my style, to make it more clear, more recognizable, and more understandable by people of any and all cultures. Mass fashion jewelry, in my mind, is purely decorative, employing a cacophony of glittery values to achieve a dazzling effect. This is as much a part of human culture as the bright plumage of birds, and will remain with us, as it should. But, it has always been against this world that I design my work; placing value on classicism and heirloom status over the thrill of temporary trends. My forms and shapes lead my concepts. My concepts are generally anthropological and my attitude is "less is more."—Robert Lee Morris

"Wearable art" as created by Robert Lee Morris has become a symbol of style among young, modern, rebellious, sexy, and chic individuals. Morris has redefined the way people perceive jewelry. Morris entered the fashion scene some 20 years ago and has transformed the contemporary jewelry industry by drawing on symbols from antiquity in ways that underscore their relevance to our lives today. He remains fascinated by the meaning of art, the role of jewelry as a talisman of the spirit. Morris maintains a keen appreciation of a pure, powerful aesthetic.

Morris is more like a student of culture than a fashion trend setter. He originally planned a career in anthropology, but recognizing his artistic talents, combined his favorite disciplines through the craft of jewelry making. As a self-taught artist, Morris developed his distinctive "Etruscan" gold finish by layering pure 24-carat gold over brass. As opposed to the high shine of 18-carat gold jewelry, the matt yellow gold has an unusual muted glow. Along the same lines Morris created a green patina—a crude finish with the look of weathered stone. These creations not only established his style but filled a gap between costume jewelry and the "really real stuff." His bold, minimalistic, sculptural forms quickly became popular in the early 1970s, where he

ROBERT LEE MORRIS

Robert Lee Morris: 1996; sterling silver square link bracelet.

was initially represented by the Sculpture to Wear Gallery at the Plaza Hotel in New York. Sales of his designs immediately outpaced such masters as Picasso, Braque, Calder, Max Ernst and Man Ray. His Celtic crosses, cuffs, collars, disc belts, and heart shaped brooches are treasured by the stylish glitterati. This list includes Hollywood celebrities, heavy metal rock stars, rich urban bikers, as well as businessmen and women who are eager to express their individuality.

In 1977, Morris launched an entire modern jewelry movement when he opened Artwear. At Artwear, Morris created a showcase "for artists focusing on jewelry as their prime medium," and attracted public interest through merchandising techniques that were as unique as the gallery's overall concept. The jewelry was displayed on dramatic plaster body-casts resembling sculptural relics of ancient civilizations. This concept was based on his belief that jewelry "comes alive on the body." He also developed an image catalog, featuring models covered in mud, sand, and flour, which instantly became a collectors' item.

In addition to being a successful jewelry designer and businessman, Morris designs handbags, belts, scarves, amulets, sconces, candlesticks, picture frames, packaging for beauty products (the latter for Elizabeth Arden) as well as his own fragrance, *Verdigris,* named for the ancient color which has become a signature of his mythic style.

Robert Lee Morris has continually sought out new avenues for expression, collaborating with such designers and contemporaries as Calvin Klein, Geoffrey Beene, Karl Lagerfeld, and Donna Karan. In his own collections, he has invented a clean, pure, uniquely American style— launching such trends as "bold gold" and the green patina verdigris—while as founder of the gallery Artwear, he has fostered an entire generation of modern jewelry makers.—ROBERTA H. GRUBER

Moschino, Franco

Italian designer

Born *Abbiategrasso, 1950.*

Education *Studied fine art, Accademia delle Belle Arti, Milan, 1968-71.*

Career *Free-lance designer and illustrator, Milan, 1969-70; sketcher for Versace, 1971-77; designer for Italian company Cadette, 1977-82. Founded own company Moonshadow in 1983; launched Moschino COUTURE!, 1983; introduced diffusion line, CHEAP & CHIC, 1988; launched UOMO, menswear collection, 1986, and CHEAP & CHIC UOMO, 1991; also lines of underwear, swimwear, jeans, children's clothes, accessories; fragrance for women Moschino introduced, 1987, and OK-KO men's fragrance, 1991.*

Exhibitions *X Years of Kaos! (retrospective), Museo della Permanente, Milan, 1993-94.*

Died *18 September 1994.*

Address *Moonshadow SpA, Via Ceradini 11/A, 20129 Milan, Italy.*

"Fashion is full of chic" believes Franco Moschino, an ironic statement coming from one of Europe's most successful designers.

Based in Milan, Moschino originally studied fine art, with ambitions to be a painter, but came to see that tailoring and fabrics could be just as valid a means of expression as paint and canvas. Consequently, his first job in fashion was with the Cadette label, for whom in 1977 he produced a simple range of stylish clothes.

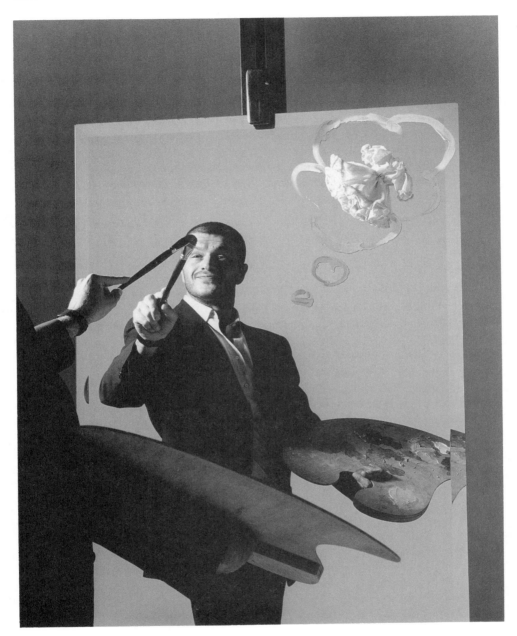

Franco Moschino: "Self Portrait."

Starting his own label in 1982, Moschino used his experience in the Italian fashion industry as a source for his philosophical ideas evolving a set of tactics designed to shake the fashion establishment out of its complacency. Much to his amazement, he was embraced with open arms as a new iconoclast by the very people he despised.

Essentially Moschino was picking up where Schiaparelli had left off, displaying an interest in the Surrealist tactic of displacement—he has for a long time professed a love of Magritte's use of the juxtaposition of incongruous imagery to produce a surreality. This is aptly shown in designs such as his quilted black denim mini with plastic fried eggs decorating the hemline, quilted jacket decorated with bottle tops, plug-socket drop earrings, and bodices made out of safety pins. Moschino's 1989 fun fur collection included a winter coat of stitched together teddybear pelts and a scorch-mark printed silk shirt saying "too much ironing."

Although dubbed the Gaultier of Italian fashion, Moschino responds to fashion different-ly. Unlike Jean-Paul Gaultier who is interested in playing around with the shapes and the fabrics of fashion, Moschino uses basic forms and traditional methods of construction to produce wearable, sexy clothes, cut to flatter and beautifully made. Dismissing his approach as visual and superficial, Moschino stresses that he is a decorator, completely disinterested in clothing construction.

Believing he can criticize the business more effectively from the inside, the underlying theme of his oeuvre is the parodying of so-called fashion victims, those prepared to be seen in the most ridiculous clothes if they are the latest style, and a general protest against the materialism of capitalism. He does this with visual gags like a triple pearl choker with attached croissant or the Rolex necklace—the pearls and Rolex being traditional ways of displaying wealth—and by mixing cheap plastics with expensive fur.

This parodying of the conspicuous consumers of fashion was continued in 1990 with his use of jokey logos on a series of garments like the cashmere jacket with the words "Expensive jacket" embroidered in gold across its back, or "Bull chic" on a matador style outfit. Designs such as these were supposed to make the wearer feel duped into spending vast amounts of money on designer clothing, but after achieving a vast amount of publicity, the people he was attacking flocked to buy his clothes. The iconoclasm of Moschino was destined to become the choicest thing on the catwalk.

Calling for a "Stop to the Fashion System" through his advertising in high fashion magazines, Moschino displays a classic Dada stance, for an end to the fashion system would mean the destruction of his own empire which now encompasses not just Moschino Couture! but the successful Cheap and Chic range—a diffusion line which is not actually all that cheap—and ranges of underwear, swimwear, jeans, children's clothes, accessories, and fragrances, the men's sold in a double-ended bottle so it can't stand up and the women's advertised with a model drinking it through a straw rather than dabbing it behind her ears.

Known for his theatrical fashion shows (in the past his models have impersonated Tina Turner and Princess Margaret), Moschino mixes up and twists classic styles and wrenches them into the present by using humour, for example a Chanel-type suit is restyled with gold clothes pegs for buttons. It will be interesting to see how far he can go before his insults are taken seriously. At one collection he pointedly mocked the top fashion editors by leaving moo-boxes on their seats, implying they were dull bovines with not an original thought in their heads, but they applauded all the more.

Moschino's ambition is to destroy the dictates of fashion so that people can please themselves with what they choose to wear, and to begin producing more anonymous clothes once he has finished with engineering the downfall of the industry. The irony is that the irony of Moschino has become its own status symbol, but his belief that fashion should be fun is valid and allows people to break the rules, if only in a way that is acceptable.—CAROLINE COX

Mugler, Thierry

French designer

Born *Strasbourg, Alsace, 1948.*
Education *Studied at the Lycée Fustel de Coulange, 1960-65, and at the School of Fine Arts, Strasbourg, 1966-67.*
Career *Dancer, Opéra de Rhin, Strasbourg, 1965-66; assistant designer, Gudule boutique, Paris, 1966-67; designer, André Peters, London, 1968-69; free-lance designer, Milan, Paris, 1970-73; created Café de Paris fashion collection, Paris, 1973; founder, Thierry Mugler, 1974, owner from 1986; Thierry Mugler Perfumes created, 1990, Angel fragrance introduced, 1992; first couture collection shown, 1992. Also professional photographer, from 1967.*
Address *130 rue du Faubourg St. Honoré, 75008 Paris, France.*

Rich in iconography, the work of Thierry Mugler has, since 1974, exploited wit and drama to convey an imaginary narrative which is at once erotic, amusing, and unsettling. His clothing spans the spectrum from vulgar ornamentalism to the most rigorous minimalism, denying the possibility of defining a Mugler style.

It is Mugler's imagery which most clearly identifies him within high fashion. His sources include Hollywood glamour, science-fiction, sexual fetishism, political history, Detroit car styling of the 1950s, and various periods in the history of art and decoration. In this way, his work reflects the eclecticism of the art world during the 1970s and 1980s. Mugler has taken a particular delight in industrial styling which he displayed in the precise geometries of ornamental detail and through his vocabulary of thematic references, which have included the jet age forms used in the fantastic automobiles devised by Harley Earl for General Motors during the 1950s.

Clothing designs which operate as costumes in a dramatic narrative have reinforced the importance of Mugler's link with the cinema, and particularly with the American film costumes of designers such as Edith Head, Travis Banton, and Adrian. A love of glamour was evident in his extravagant 1992 collection, redolent of 1950s fashion at its most lavish, and photographed among the Baroque roof sculptures of the old city of Prague.

His interest in romance and the bizarre has often run counter to political ideologies. Against a backdrop of feminist reinterpretation of the female image, Mugler has adopted an ironic, post-modern stance and exploited an array of erotic icons as themes for his collections. Difficult to characterize and appearing to work in opposition to current fashion and intellectual trends, Mugler has remained a controversial figure on the fashion scene.

Mugler's photographic talent may prove to be as important as his fashion designs. A book of his photographs, *Thierry Mugler, Photographer,* published in 1988, contained images comparable in their artifice, explosive glamour, and formal control to the cinematic images of Peter Greenaway. His photographs exploit grand vistas, deep interior spaces, and heroic monuments as settings upon which models perch like tiny ornaments, strongly defined by the extravagant outline of their costumes and asserting their presence through dramatic pose and gesture. His fashion photographs provide a narrative framework for Mugler's clothes while relegating them to the role of costume within a larger dramatic context. The broad-shouldered Russian collection of 1986, for example, was presented against backgrounds of heroic Soviet monuments or sweeping landscapes reminiscent of earlier 20th-century Social Realist painting and poster art.

Mugler has also made photographic collages repeating and emphasizing the formal elements of his clothes in kaleidoscopic compositions which revealed his interest in abstract aesthetics. These images were conceived as pure works of art, in which the clothing became an element of the creative whole.

Mugler's clothes are designed to be performed in. His major catwalk shows are choreographed like the great Hollywood musicals of Busby Berkeley. Later exhibitions have been held in huge sports stadia, emulating the highly charged atmosphere of rock concerts. Mugler designs the off-stage wardrobes of rock celebrities such as Madonna, as well as dressing famous women, like Danielle Mitterand, who require a more dignified appearance.

Whether aggressively vulgar or caricatures of sobriety, Mugler's designs are consistently body conscious. His clothes can be read as essays in the aesthetic potential of extreme proportions; shoulder widths three times head height, wasp waists, and panniered hips are among the repertoire of distortions and exaggerations of the human figure to be found among his designs. Mugler's eight annual collections, for both women and men, consistently aim to provoke through their challenging themes and flamboyant formal qualities.—GREGORY VOTOLATO

Muir, Jean

British designer

Born *Jean Elizabeth Muir in London, c.1933.*

Education *Dame Harper School, Bedford.*

Family *Married actor Harry Leuckert.*

Career *Sales assistant in lingerie and made-to-measure departments, Liberty, London, 1950-55; studied fashion drawing, and also modelled, at evening classes, St Martin's School of Art, London. Joined Jacqmar. Joined Jaeger, 1956-63. Sent to study knitwear design and manufacture, especially jersey. Visited Paris collections. Joined Courtaulds, 1966-69. Formed own label, Jane & Jane, 1967. Formed, with husband co-director, Jean Muir Ltd, 1986. Sold majority interest to Coats Paton group; bought back 75% stake in company, 1989. Jean Muir department in Jaeger's flagship store, Regent Street, London.*

Awards *British Fashion Writers Group Dress of the Year Award, 1964; Harper's Bazaar Trophy; Ambassador Award for Achievement, 1965; Maison Blanche Rex Awards, 1967, 1968, 1974, 1976; Churchman's Fashion Designer of the Year Award, 1970; Royal Society of Arts Royal Designer for Industry, 1972; elected fellow of RSA; Neiman Marcus Award, 1973; elected Fellow of Chartered Society of Designers, 1978; Bath Museum of Costume*

Dress of the Year Award, 1979; named Honorary Doctor, Royal College of Art, 1981; appointed to the Design Council, London, 1983; made a Commander of the Order of the British Empire, 1984; Honorary Degree, Doctor of Literature, University of Newcastle; awarded Hommage de la Mode, Fédération Française du Prêt-à-Porter Féminin; British Fashion Council Award for Services to Industry, 1985; Chartered Society of Designers Medal; Textile Institute Design Medal, 1987; Australian Bicentennial Award, 1988; The Ford Award, 1989.

Died *(in London) 28 May 1995.*

Jean Muir was noted for simple, flattering, and extremely feminine clothes that were sophisticated yet retain a hand crafted look with diligent attention to detail. Her favourite fabrics, jersey, angora, wool crêpe, suede, and soft leather, reappeared time after time, regardless of trends. Her more famous clients included the actresses Joanna Lumley and Patricia Hodge and writers and artists such as Lady Antonia Fraser and Bridget Riley.

Muir was renowned for being a designer who produces clothes women really want to wear and feel comfortable in. She achieved this by modelling all the clothes and toiles herself at fittings, an advantage she believed she had over male designers. "If you are going to make clothes, the first thing you have to understand is the female anatomy. When I try on a dress I can feel if something is wrong, I can tell if it's not sitting properly on the shoulders or the bust or the hip. I could not tell these things if I saw it on a stand," she explained.

There was an air of the fashion headmistress in Jean Muir's approach; her steadfast opinions could not be budged. Her tone was unrelenting when she stressed a need to restore a sense of pride in the technique of making clothes and her passion for "art, craft and design and the upholding of standards and quality, maintaining them and setting new ones." She believed fashion was not art but industry. The word fashion, she said, suggested the "transient and the superficial," hardly the best attributes for a commercial business.

Jean Muir described her work as being based on intuition, aesthetic appreciation, and mathematical technical expertise. Never at the cutting edge of fashion, the clothes were timeless, understated, and often dateless. Like Fortuny or Chanel, the company based its look on the evolution of a singular theme, a soft, supple fluidity of cut that creates the form of a garment.

In person Jean Muir epitomized the type of woman for whom she likes to design. The writer Antonia Fraser described her as a "Modish Puck." A white, powdered face with a mouth slashed in crimson lipstick. A wiry, bird-like frame always dressed in navy calf-length jersey dresses, with black stockings and Granny shoes. In her studio Muir had a reputation for perfectionism and exacting standards in all aspects of production. "There are tremendous activities involved in the making of clothes," she declared in a television interview, with such conviction that the viewer is left in no doubt about her sincerity.

In the annals of fashion history Jean Muir should be remembered as a designer who liberated the body. While many designers have forced bodies into structured tailoring, boning, or restrictive interfaced fabrics, Muir's fluid and easy clothes have always provided an emancipated alternative; devoid of structure and underpinning, the clothes remain womanly and melodious.—KEVIN ALMOND

Natori, Josie Cruz

American designer

Born *Josie Cruz in Manila, 9 May 1947.*

Education *Studied at Manhattanville College, Bronxville, New York, 1964-68, B.A., economics.*

Family *Married Ken Natori in 1971; son: Kenneth.*

Career *Stockbroker, Bache Securities, New York and the Philippines, 1968-71; investment banker, vice-president, Merrill Lynch, New York, 1971-77; founder, designer, Natori Company, women's lingerie and daywear, from 1977; at-homewear introduced, 1983; boudoir accessories and footwear lines introduced, 1984; bed and bath collections introduced, 1991.*

Awards *Harriet Alger Award, 1987; Girls' Clubs of America Award, 1990; Laboratory Institute of Merchandising Award, 1990; National Organization of Women Legal Defense and Education Fund Buddy Award, 1990.*

Address *40 East 34th Street, New York, New York 10016, USA.*

Josie Natori provides a new model of the business of fashion. She presides (along with her husband Ken) over a business, but disavows the designation "designer." But that is a practice like traditional American post-war fashion production. What is unprecedented about Natori as a person and businesswoman is the degree of her vision and tenacity: Natori has taken lingerie from a barely visible inner layer of fashion to the entirety of fashion, including many major international licenses. As a visionary, she purports simply to answer the client's question of "how or where should I wear this?" with "wherever you want," granting lingerie an opportunity to enter into every aspect of attire. Recognizing that, in the 1980s, her lingerie was being increasingly exposed by the women who purchased it, she created garments that are lingerie inspired for public clothing.

Josie Cruz Natori: Double georgette mid-calf gown with lace appliqué.

Realizing that lingerie by the 1990s was the visible and wide foundation of the clothing pyramid, Natori was involved in almost every aspect of fashion. To build a major fashion house from the base of lingerie is unparalleled, visionary, and a sign of the very late 20th century in its ambition and success. The resulting neologist crossover category "innerwear-as-outerwear" has never been the corporate slogan, though it might serve. Natori has brought boudoir apparel out of the bedroom, perhaps inevitably so at a moment in culture when all heretofore-privileged and private matters of the bedroom have become the public discourse.

Perhaps Puritanism and body reticence have fought the concept of fashion developing from the inside out, but contemporary culture has taken to Natori's vision of the beautiful details of lingerie being exposed within a fashion vocabulary largely denied ornamentation. Natori has brought back to apparel a richness of detail that she herself remembered from Philippine embroideries and appliqúes. That is, contemporary ready-to-wear had so eschewed ornamentation as a function of expense (and technical capability) and modernist streamlining that contemporary fashion may seem stark. Lingerie's abiding interest in ornament returns techniques, but also provides the connection to detailing and ornament. In fact, Natori had first approached a Bloomingdale's buyer about making shirts; Natori's destiny was set when the buyer recommended that she make them longer to be sold as nightshirts. Further, Natori shrewdly assesses the culture of the body, bringing stretch and bodysuits to the realm of lingerie and back to playwear, as well as the possibilities of feminine self-expression to dress for public circumstances.

Josie Natori neither supposes nor proposes that the clothing she designs be mistaken for career wear, the operative description for much apparel of the 1980s. Instead, she realizes the affiliation between private clothing, body expression, and eveningwear, all manifesting the body and all committed to comfort and to some degree of seduction and sensual pleasure. To some, Natori might seem anti-feminist; she argues, of course, that she is the true feminist in delighting in and extending the category endemic to feminine traits and the female body. Woody Hochswender quotes Josie Natori as exculpating her clothing from the male fantasies of lingerie, saying: "It's really a way for the woman to express herself. We've made women feel good without feeling sleazy" (*New York Times,* 3 January 1989). Indeed, all apparel addresses wearer and spectator; Natori's reassessment of the innerwear category is as viable as any patriarchal paradigm of male spectatorship.

"Think of Katharine Hepburn, answering her doorbell," Natori offered to Deborah Hofmann, giving evocative pedigree to the ease-without-sleaze that she makes of her innerwear-as-outerwear. Natori is a perfect exemplar for the woman who asserts authority in contemporary fashion: her first career was in investment banking; she herself wears couture (generally a tailored jacket and skirt) in impeccable taste; she makes her way and her company's way in the fashion market with unmistakable respect for the woman who wears her clothing, even more than for the grizzled, outmoded categories and classes of retailing. Natori's business acumen and design sensibility seem unerringly and culturally right: she is creating a fashion that satisfies women's feelings and practical needs in a culture and era of precious privacy and of women's expression of themselves.—RICHARD MARTIN

Norell, Norman

American designer

Born *Norman David Levinson in Noblesville, Indiana, 20 April 1900.*
Education *Studied illustration at Parsons School of Design, New York, 1919; fashion design at Pratt Institute, Brooklyn, New York, 1920-22.*
Career *Costume designer, Paramount Pictures, Long Island, New York, 1922-23; theatrical costume designer, 1924-28; designer, Hattie Carnegie, New York, 1928-40; partner, designer, Traina-Norell company, New York, 1941-60; director, Norman Norell, New York, 1960-72.*
Exhibitions *Norman Norell retrospective, Metropolitan Museum of Art, New York, 1972.*
Awards *Neiman Marcus Award, Dallas, Texas, 1942; Coty American Fashion Critics Award, 1943, 1951, 1956, 1958, 1966; Parsons Medal for Distinguished Achievement, 1956; Sunday Times International Fashion Award, London, 1963; City of New York Bronze Medallion, 1972; honorary Doctor of Fine Arts, Pratt Institute, 1962.*
Died *(in New York) 25 October 1972.*

Simple, well-made clothes that would last and remain fashionable for many years became the hallmark of Norman Norell, the first American designer to win the respect of Parisian couturiers. He gained a reputation for flattering design while Traina, whose well-heeled clientèle appreciated the snob appeal of pared down day clothes and dramatic eveningwear. From his early years with Hattie Carnegie, Norell learned all about meticulous cut, fit, and quality fabrics. Regular trips to Paris exposed him to the standards of couture that made French clothes the epitome of high fashion. Norell had the unique ability to translate the characteristics of couture into American ready-to-wear. He did inspect each model garment individually, carefully, in the tradition of a couturier, and was just as demanding in proper fabrication and finish. The prices of "Norells," especially after he went into business on his own, easily rivalled those of Paris creations, but they were worth it. The clothes lasted, and their classicism made them timeless.

Certain characteristics of Norell's designs were developed early on and remained constant throughout his career. Wool jersey shirtwaist dresses with demure bowed collars were a radical departure from splashy floral daydresses of the 1940s. World War II restrictions on yardages and materials coincided with Norell's penchant for spare silhouettes, echoing his favourite period, the 1920s. Long before Paris was promoting the chemise in the 1950s, Norell was offering short, straight, low-waisted shapes during the war years. For evening, Norell looked to the flashy glamor of his days designing costumes for vaudeville. Glittering *paillettes,* which were not rationed, would be splashed on evening skirts—paired with sweater tops for comfort in unheated rooms—or on coats. Later, the lavish use of all-out glamor sequins evolved into Norell's signature shimmering "mermaid" evening dresses, form-fitting, round-necked and short sleeved. The round neckline, plain instead of the then popular draped, became one of the features of Norell's designs of which he was most proud. "I hope I have helped women dress more simply," was his goal. He used revealing bathing suit necklines for evening as well, with sable trim or jeweled buttons for contrast. Variations on these themes continued throughout the years, even after trousersuits became a regular part of Norell's repertoire.

Striking in their simplicity, Norell suits would skim the body, making the wearer the focus of attention rather than the clothes. Daytime drama came from bold, clear colors such as red, black, beige, bright orange or pale blue, punctuated by large, plain contrasting buttons. Stripes, dots, and checks were the only patterns, although Norell was credited with introducing leopard prints in the 1940s, again, years before they became widespread in use. Norell's faithful clients hailed his clothes as some of the most comfortable they had ever worn.

Early exposure to men's clothing in Norell's father's haberdashery business no doubt led to the adaptation of the menswear practicality. An outstanding example was the sleeveless jacket over a bowed blouse and slim woolen skirt, developed after Norell became aware of the comfort of his own sleeveless vest worn for work. As in men's clothing, pockets and buttons were always functional. Norell created a sensation with the culotte-skirted wool flannel day suit with which he launched his own independent label in 1960. His sophisticated clientèle welcomed the ease of movement allowed by this daring design. As the 1960s progressed, Norell presented another masculine-influenced garment, the jumpsuit, but in soft or luxurious fabrics for evening. Just as durability and excellent workmanship were integral to the best menswear, so they were to Norell's. Men's dress was traditionally slow to change; Norell stayed with his same basic designs, continually refining them over the years. He developed the idea that there should be only one center of interest in an outfit, and designed only what he liked.

What he liked was frequently copied, both domestically and overseas. The short, flippy, gored, ice-skater skirt was copied by Paris. Aware of piracy in the fashion business, Norell offered working sketches of the culotte suit free of charge to the trade to ensure that at least his design would be copied correctly. This integrity earned him a place as the foremost American designer of his time. Unlike most ready-to-wear that would be altered at the last moment for ease of manufacture, no changes were allowed after Norell had approved a garment. His impeccable taste was evident not only in the clothes, but in his simple life: meals at Schrafft's and Hamburger Heaven, quiet evenings at home, sketching in his modern duplex apartment, unpublicized daily visits to assist fashion design students at Parsons School of Design.

As the designer whose reputation gained new respect for the Seventh Avenue garment industry, Norell was the first designer to receive the Coty Award, and the first to be elected to the Coty Award Hall of Fame. True to his innate integrity, he attempted to return his third Winnie award when he learned that judging was done without judges having actually seen designers' collections. Norell promoted American fashion as founder and president of the Council of Fashion Designers of America, but also by giving fledgling milliners their start in his black-tie, special event fashion shows. Halston and Adolfo designed hats for Norell, for, as in couture, Norell insisted upon unity of costume to include accessories.

As the "Dean of American Fashion," Norell was the first to have his name on a dress label, and the first to produce a successful American fragrance, *Norell,* with a designer name. Some of his clothes can be seen in the films *That Touch of Mink* and *The Wheeler Dealers.* Show business personalities and social leaders throughout the country treasured their "Norells" for years.—THERESE DUZINKIEWICZ BAKER

Oldham, Todd

American designer

Born *Corpus Christi, Texas, 1961.*

Education *No formal training in design.*

Career *Worked in the alterations department, Polo/Ralph Lauren, Dallas, Texas, 1980; showed first collection, in Dallas, 1981; partner and designer, L-7 company, New York, incorporating Times 7 women's shirt collection, from 1988; signature Todd Oldham collection reintroduced with backing from Onward Kashiyama Company, 1989; line of handbags introduced, 1991; Todd Oldham patterns produced for Vogue Patterns, 1992; footwear line introduced, 1993.*

Awards *Council of Fashion Designers of America Perry Ellis Award, 1991.*

Address *120 Wooster St. #3FL-SF, New York, New York 10012-5200, USA.*

Todd Oldham is to fashion design as Andy Warhol was to art and Keith Haring was to graphic design. He creates an essential belief system, an orbit, and an aura about himself as much as he creates artifacts. A home-grown American shaman and phenomenon who always thanks his "Granny" in show credits, Oldham succeeds half as Tom Sawyer, half as Leonardo. He is the winsome maverick who never offends, but always titillates and beguiles. Rising among the American fashion designers of the late 1980s, after moving to New York in 1988, Oldham was initially one among many talented newcomers, though he had already established his workshops in Texas in the early 1980s. His work was distinguished by a funky, ingenious and ingenuous, "outsider" art sense of whimsy and surprise. He is always colorful, figuratively if not literally. Fashion's propensity to sameness and to the jaded *Weltschmerz* of the New York design sensibility was suddenly confronted with buttons of Schiaparelli-esque eccentricity, unabashed good-humor drag queens on the runway, and madly "bad-taste" conglomerations of colors and materials. His aesthetic is patchwork and pastiche; he is cued into popular culture, both the grass roots populist kind and in the 1990s media sense, cleverly converting the abject into the art object. His Wooster Street store in New York could at first be confused for a Middle-American thrift shop. While a master of madcap prints, Oldham has also collaborated with artists Ruben Toledo and Kenny Scharf on designs.

Oldham is distinctive, but always regarded as a bellwether. In 1996, amidst declarations of the return of color, Oldham's multi-colored shifts were repeatedly singled out for high color, abstract pattern, and bold design. Color and surface embellishment are the chief traits of Oldham's work: he is little concerned with the silhouette and conventionally keeps to basic shapes allowing—like Schiaparelli—all of his creativity to be exercised on the rich surface. In 1992, Macy's in New York advertised Oldham's madras-simulating grid skirt in sequins to be worn with his white cotton blouse with gigantic and cartoonish ladybugs. In the same year, he showed on the runway a beaded leopard skirt, leopard beret and blouse, with a tufted vest and a quilted, tuft-printed coat on top, a trompe-l'oeil mix of the Princess and the Pea and "Wild Kingdom" that is unforgettable. Named in 1994 as consultant to Escada, Oldham's immediate impact has been to introduce unabashed color and decorative delight to a wardrobe otherwise somewhat staid. Beginning with his "Times 7" line, Oldham has always produced buttons, accessories, and ornamentation to great success, allowing not only his pastiche, but the client's creative participation. When Oldham received the Council of Fashion Designers of America's Perry Ellis Award for Fashion Talent for 1991, the program notes observed, "Just 30 years old and with no formal training as a designer, Oldham has turned his three-year-old company into a fun house of design. Seemingly as happy-go-lucky as his clothes, Oldham clearly believes in mixing business with pleasure." Oldham's business-with-pleasure mix of the respectful with the impertinent has an irresistible appeal in an era when clothing must go from workplace to home to social occasion.

Oldham is eclectic and zany. Woody Hochswender, reviewing Oldham's fall 1991 collection in the *New York Times* (April 11, 1991) called it "a whirlwind round-the-world tour— by plane, flying carpet and Greyhound." All of these vehicles are part of Oldham's ardent vagabondage. In 1991, his Byzantine and Guell-Park mosaics made from Lamontage synthetic-fiber felting were a small art history of elite monuments. The bus route is more likely for Oldham's Genie dress (1991) with cut-out midriff and sides articulated in gold braid and plastic stones in which he invokes Orientalism, but most specifically remembers the "I Dream of Jeannie" television series. His museums of good and bad taste have incorporated both the Mona Lisa onto a skirt and Kitsch horse paintings onto sequined jackets. In 1995-96, a serape print became a pants suit and evening dresses were based on mechanics' coveralls.

Yet Oldham is more than *enfant terrible*. In 1995, Roy Campbell wrote in the *Philadelphia Inquirer* (April 6, 1995), "Oldham is the glam-king of cartoony couture, one-minute-of-fame fashions that are perfect in circles shaped by MTV but have little relevance beyond that. His shows in past seasons were video-bite circus spectacles with female impersonators and gag-heavy clothes." But Campbell's assessment of the fall 1995 collection was that Oldham "had no drag queens, few gags, and plenty of wearable design." Later, Suzy Menkes reported in the *International Herald Tribune* (November 2, 1995) that Oldham "overcame the excesses of Halloween and the pre-show hype .... Oldham staged a strong show that enlivened the season." Like Warhol and Haring, Oldham has come to command an important economic empire as well as a social and aesthetic orbit. He imparts, as he always has, a seriousness of purpose to the work and canniness to its ambitions, even as he avoids the dull or the aggressive. A sweet innocence obtains at the core of the imagination that is as compelling in its Texas drawl and outrageous pastiche as one artist's sheepishness or another's struggle to donate his graphics to the subway system. Appraising Oldham's career and status in 1995, Amy M. Spindler (*New York Times*, April 6, 1995) saw the "overwhelmingly, uncompromisingly creative mind" of earlier work a little tempered by commerce, maturity, fragrances, and designer-jeans license. She concluded, "Mr. Oldham has grown up . . . efficiently setting up for richer, wider horizons." Thus, the American frontier for the native spirit.

In a telling series of images, Oldham undressed partially or wholly for photographs, first for the downtown New York *Paper* (September 1994), shirtless with cowboy hat, then undressed for the uptown and up-scale New York magazine *Avenue* (March 1995) naked for an article entitled "The Natural," and then appeared ostensibly naked with a model in anti-fur advertising in 1995-96 for PETA, one of the designer's favorite causes. Consciously or unconsciously, Oldham is the all-American boy, the genuine talent of frankness, genius, and mischief. Huckleberry Finn makes clothes and inexorably they are great clothes.—RICHARD MARTIN

Ozbek, Rifat

British designer

Born *Istanbul, 11 July 1953.*

Education *Studied architecture at Liverpool University, 1970-72; studied fashion design at St. Martin's School of Art, London, 1974-77.*

Military Service *Performed national military service in Turkey, 1977.*

Career *Worked with Walter Albini for Trell, Milan, 1978-80; designer for Monsoon, London, 1980-84; established own firm, Ozbek, 1984; second line, O, renamed Future Ozbek, established, 1987. Production under licence by Aeffe SpA, Italy, from 1988; launched New Age collection, 1989.*

Exhibitions *Fellini: I Costumi e le Mode, Pecci Museum, Prato, Italy, and Stedeligk Museum, Amsterdam, both 1994; V & A: Street Style; From Sidewalk to Catwalk, 1940 to Tomorrow, 1994-95; Customised Levi's Denim Jacket for Benefit for Diffa/Dallas Collection, 1990, 1991, 1992.*

Awards *Woman Magazine Designer Award, 1986; British Fashion Council Designer of the Year Award, London, 1988, 1992; British Glamour Award, 1989.*

Address *18 Haunch of Venison Yard, London W1Y 1AF, England.*

My collections always have an element of ethnic and modern feeling.—Rifat Ozbek

One of Britain's few truly international designers, Rifat Ozbek draws on London street style and his own Turkish origins to produce sophisticated clothes which successfully amalgamate diverse sources and keep him at the forefront of new developments in style. Ozbek restyles the classic shapes of Western couture, using multi-cultural decorative references like the traditional stitching of the *djellabah* and kaftan to outline garments such as A-line linen dresses. He became renowned in the 1980s for a series of lavishly embroidered black cocktail suits which appeared with different themes each season, such as gold bows and tassels or Daliesque lips.

After leaving Turkey at the age of 17, Ozbek trained as an architect at Liverpool University, cutting his studies short after deciding he was more interested in decorating the surfaces of buildings than learning the methods of construction needed in order for his architectural projects

Rifat Ozbek: Autumn/Winter 1992; black velvet ottoman cropped vest with shot taffeta skirt.

to remain standing. This interest in the decoration of classic shapes, rather than breaking the barriers of garment construction, was expressed in his first clothing designs which appeared in 1984.

Ozbek graduated from St. Martin's School of Art, London, in 1977 and went on to work for three years at Monsoon, a company known for creating popular styles based on non-Western originals. Ozbek assimilated all these ideas and became known in the mid-1980s for his combinations of motifs and shapes from different cultures and juxtapositions of unusual fabrics, creating not just a straight pastiche of ethnic, but an arresting amalgamation of eclectic sources such as Africa, the Far East, ballet, and the Ottoman Empire.

At this time his skillfully tailored clothes were fashioned out of luxurious fabrics like moiré silks and taffeta, with an amazing palette of colours of turquoise, purples, and fuchsia. His sophisticated and understated designs developed into an easily recognizable style, using heavy fabrics like gabardine or cashmere to structure the top half of an outfit combined with lighter materials below, like silks or jersey. This elegant look was supplanted by a more overtly sexy one in 1988, where the multi-cultural aesthetic was taken to new levels with the use of a diverse array of eclectic material. His confidence in dealing with a number of different non-Western sources was displayed in this significant collection with garments showing their origins in Senegal, Tibet, and Afghanistan, an ethnic look made urbane for the fashion consumer. The collection included sarong skirts and gold chain belts, midriff tops, and boleros embroidered with crescent moons and stars, hipster trousers, and tasselled bras worn on the catwalk by models who resembled Turkish belly dancers.

In the 1990s Ozbek has become more heavily influenced by the club scene and his White Collection of 1990 caught the mood of the times. Acknowledging the New Age and Green consumerist tendencies of his audience, Ozbek created a range of easy to wear separates based on tracksuits and other sports clothing to be worn as club gear. This collection was in complete antithesis to the hard metropolitan chic of 1980s power dressing and paved the way for hooded sweatshirt tops and trainers appearing in the catwalk collections of other designers that year. The clothes were a stark bright white, displaying New Age slogans like "Nirvana." Unlike designers who have used white before, such as the "yé yé" designers of the 1960s who employed white to glorify science and technology, Ozbek used the colour, without irony, to profess a faith in the concept of a New Age and a belief that a return to the spiritual would improve the quality of life in the city and save the planet.

This was an anti-fashion which became the fashionable look of the early 1990s. Casual, baggy clothes, making reference to sports and black youth subcultures, were worn with sequined money belts and baseball caps and Ozbek was lauded as a designer in touch with the street.

His popularity has continued in the 1990s with the Urban Cowgirl look of fringed suede tops, hotpants, and North American Indian jewellery, his mock bone fronts on waistcoats and evening gowns, and the Confederate look incorporating tailed or cropped military jackets.—CAROLINE COX

Parnis, Mollie

American designer

Born *Sara Rosen Parnis, in Brooklyn, New York, 18 March 1902.*
Education *Briefly studied law, Hunter College, New York.*
Family *Married Leon Livingston (originally Levinson) in 1930.*
Career *After high school, worked in sales for a blouse manufacturer, then as stylist for David Westheim Company, New York, c.1928-30. Parnis-Livingston ready-to-wear established, New York, 1933; launched own label, 1940s; boutique line added, 1970; Mollie Parnis Studio Collection ready-to-wear line added, 1979; firm closed, 1984; first loungewear collection, Mollie Parnis at Home, designed for Chevette, New York, 1985. Molly Parnis Livingston Foundation established, 1984.*
Died *(in New York), 18 July 1992.*

Mollie Parnis belongs to the first generation of American fashion designers to be known to the public by name rather than by affiliation to a department store. Her clothing became standard in the wardrobes of conservative businesswomen and socialites of the mid-20th century. Parnis herself was one of these women; she understood what women wanted to wear and what they required to appear appropriately dressed, yet feminine.

Mollie Parnis was a success in the fashion industry from the start. During her first job as a salesperson for a blouse manufacturer, she showed a keen interest in design details, as well as a good sense of what might sell. She was promoted to a design position with the firm in a short period of time. Her ability to determine what fashion would be successful served her throughout her career, spanning over 50 years in the industry. When she and her husband, Leon Livingston, started their own business just prior to World War II, the prospects for any new clothing wholesaler seemed dim. However, they knew that one of the keys to success is specialization, so Parnis-Livingston limited its line to women's dresses and suits which were immediately successful.

The look of Mollie Parnis clothes was conservative and classic. In the 1950s she was known for her shirtwaist dresses and suits in luxurious-looking fabrics that spanned seasons and made the transition from office to dinner. She also employed whimsical, all-American combinations such as menswear wool with silk fringe in some of her evening dresses. Though not always a design innovator, she was a consistent provider of well-made, highly wearable clothes. She interpreted the contemporary silhouette with her conservative good taste and her sensibility to the busy American woman's desires and needs.

United States First Ladies, from Mamie Eisenhower to Rosalyn Carter, were customers of Mollie Parnis's. One dress in particular received national attention in April 1955 when Mrs. Eisenhower arrived at a Washington reception wearing a Mollie Parnis shirtwaist of blue and green printed taffeta, only to be greeted by another woman in the same dress. Parnis expressed her embarrassment over the situation, but explained to the *New York Times:* "I do not sell directly to any wearer, nor do I usually make one of a kind; that is what makes this country a great democracy. But I do feel that the First Lady should have something special." (1 April 1955). There had been minor variations made to Mrs. Eisenhower's dress alone, but approximately 90 dresses of the similar style were shipped to stores around the United States.

Though other designers were hired by the firm eventually, Parnis remained the originator of themes and ideas, and the final editor of her design staff's creations. Eleanor Lambert described her as having "an architect's eye for proportion" and the ability to endow mass-produced clothing with a custom-made look. Like many designers who are successful in the long run, she avoided trendy looks in the service of her customers who came to expect from her clothing what was fashionable for more than one season. Mollie Parnis used her own life as inspiration and guide for her work. She stated her design philosophy in *Fashion: The Inside Story:* "Being a designer is being a personality. It's creating a look that you like, that your friends like, that belongs to the life that you know." (Barbaralee Diamonstein, New York 1985). Parnis's life exemplified the successful and civic-minded businesswoman in New York. In addition to her career as an award-winning fashion designer, she founded several philanthropic organizations. Through her design work and her membership in such organizations as the Council of Fashion Designers of America, she played a role in the promotion and success of the American fashion industry.—MELINDA WATT

Patou, Jean
French designer/company

Company founded by Jean Patou (1887-1936). Patou worked in small dressmaking business, Parry, before World War I, producing first collection, 1914. Captain of Zouaves during World War I. Returned to fashion, launching first couture collection, 1919; moved to rue St Florentin, Paris, 1922; visited USA, brought back six American models, 1924; dressed tennis star Suzanne Lenglen; opened sports shop; created perfume house, 1925; introduced Princess line, 1929. Perfumes include Amour Amour, que sais-je, Adieu Sagesse, 1925, Chaldée, 1927, Moment Suprême, 1929, Joy, 1930, Divine Folie, 1933, Normandie, 1935, Vacances, 1936, Colony, 1938, l'Heure Attendue, 1946, Caline, 1964, 1000, 1972, Eau de Patou, 1976, Patou pour Homme, 1980, and Sublime, 1992; Parfums Patou established in London, Milan, Geneva, Hong Kong, and Australasia, by 1982.

Jean Patou by Marc Bohan, Haute Couture, Fall/Winter 1954.

Patou

Brother-in-law, Raymond Barbas, took over business on death of Patou, 1936. Designers for the house have included Bohan (1954-56), Lagerfeld (1960-63), Goma (1963-73), Tarlazzi (1973-77), Gonzalès (1977-82), and Lacroix (1982-87).

Address   7 rue St. Florentin, Paris, 75008 France.

Since its origin, the House of Jean Patou has always associated fashion (1919) and perfumery (1925) activities. I think that there are numerous similarities in the care given to these two industries, notably in the domaine of know-how, innovation, the constant research for quality and in the intervention of a highly qualified work-force.

Forever the forerunner, Jean Patou has always understood the tastes and aspirations of his contemporaries. Whilst he was the primary influence in women's sportswear and creator of the first knitted bathing-suits, he was also the first Couturier to use his monogram as a design feature. For Jean Patou, "the modern woman leads an active life, and the creator must therefore dress her accordingly, in the most simple way, whilst maintaining her charm and femininity."

It is in this sense that the stylists that have succeeded Jean Patou have worked. They have created original and striking collections, with no limits, maintaining the label's prestigious aura, its liberty and quality. I think that fashion should reflect a woman's desires, should not constrain her but allow her to live with her epoch.—Jean de Moüy

Fashion history records that Jean Patou is best known for *Joy,* the world's most expensive perfume, and for his famous Cubist sweaters. His contributions to fashion were, however, much more substantial and far reaching. His genius was his ability to interpret the times in which he lived and translate the ideals of that era into fashion. In Paris, during the 1920s, couture was evolving from serving a few wealthy clients into a huge autonomous industry and Patou recognized couture's tremendous potential, both in France and in the United States. Patou helped expand the industry by introducing sportswear, expanding his business into the American market, emphasizing accessories and, like Paul Poiret, offering his customers a signature perfume.

The 1920s ideal woman was youthful, physically fit, and healthy looking. The truly athletic woman was realized in Suzanne Lenglen, the 1921 Wimbledon tennis star, who wore Patou clothes both on and off the court. The benefits gained by the sports stars and other celebrities publicizing Patou's designs were many. Patou also provided a complete wardrobe for the American female aviator, Ruth Elder, as well as many well-known stage stars. The Patou customers, most of whom did not play sports, sought to emulate this new look. Patou recognized the need for clothes for the sports participant, the spectator, and for those wishing to appear athletic, both in Europe and in the United States. In 1925, he opened a Paris boutique called Le Coin des Sports where he devoted, in the House of Patou, a series of rooms each to an individual sport. The complete, accessorized outfit was available for aviation, riding, fishing, tennis, golf, and yachting, among others. Also, recognizing the importance of leisure and travel to his customers, Patou opened salons in the resort areas, Deauville and Biarritz, where off-the-rack items such as sweater sets, swimsuits, and accessories were available.

After expanding his business in France, Patou realized the potential for the fashion industry in the United States. Patou admired the long, lean lines of the American silhouette. In 1925 he travelled to New York and hired six women to return to Paris with him and work as mannequins. This well-publicized action made the couture more accessible to the Americans, thus improving his overall market share and profits. The French sought to emulate this silhouette as well, making Patou one of the best-known names in fashion.

Patou's design philosophy was influenced by sportswear, continuing the theme of casual elegance into day and evening ensembles. He believed in beautiful but functional clothes which reflected the personality of the wearer. Patou never felt that fashion should dictate. The cut of the clothes was simple, often accented with architectural seam lines, embroidery detail, and attention to fabric, trims, and finishings. By collaborating with textile mills on design and color, Patou was able to create exclusive colors through thread-dyeing methods, thus eliminating exact copies by lesser competitors. Patou also developed a swimsuit fabric which resisted shrinkage and fading, pleasing both swimmer and sun worshipper. Design inspirations included Russian embroideries, antique textiles, and modern art.

By interpreting the surrounding art movements and cultural ideas into his designs, Patou created such classics as the Cubist sweaters. The sweater sets figured prominently in his business. By adding coordinating skirts, scarves, hats, and other accessories, he increased his overall sales. Patou revolutionized the knitting industry with machine production, which meant greater productivity and greater profits. The casual fit of sweater and sportswear, in general, was financially beneficial as it required fewer fittings and less overall production time. Patou also applied his own monogram to his sportswear designs—the first visible designer label.

The rivalry between Patou and Chanel is by now well known. It was intense and perhaps fueled both of their successful careers. Their visions for the modern woman were quite similar, and although it is Chanel that fashion history has credited with many of the silhouette and conceptual changes of 1920s fashions, it was Patou who, in 1929, dropped the hemline and raised the waistline. Chanel quickly followed suit.

The House of Patou prospered during the Depression but Patou himself was unable to interpret the 1930s as he had so successfully captured the 1920s. He died in 1936, a relatively young man. Patou had demonstrated a brilliant business sense which was ultimately undermined by his destructive gambling tendencies. The company is still in family hands and is now headed by the grand-nephew of Jean Patou.—MARGO SEAMAN

Paulin, Guy
French designer

Born *Lorraine, France in 1946 (one source says 1945).*
Career *Free-lance designer for Prisunic, Jimper, Dorothée Bis, Paraphernalia, Mic Mac, Byblos, and others, prior to establishing own house, 1970s-84, and 1986-89; designer, Chloé, 1984-86; designer, Tiktiner, 1990.*
Died *Paris, 1990.*

Guy Paulin began his career as a free-lance designer of women's ready-to-wear in Paris. Though he had no formal training he was hired as a design assistant to Jacqueline Jacobson at

Dorothée Bis, where he first worked with knits. He then signed a contract with Paraphernalia, a chain of franchised stores in New York, where he rubbed shoulders with other young designers of the time: Mary Quant, Betsey Johnson, Emmanuelle Khanh, and Lison Bonfils. A shy, quick-witted conversationalist and lover of 1950s American Abstract Expressionist paintings, Paulin believed fashion to be part of life, an essential component of the French l'art de vivre. He claimed to be most inspired by Katherine Hepburn—a mature, free-spirited soul who eschewed fashion trends and projected her own sense of personal style, and his clothing designs were often acclaimed for their gentle and unpretentious lines, reminiscent of classic American sportswear.

On returning to Paris after his New York sojourn, Guy Paulin received an enthusiastic press response for the simple, feminine clothes he designed for various clients. He worked for the next two decades in France and Italy, designing for Bercher, Biga, P. Blume, Byblos, Sport Max for Max Mara, Mic-Mac, PEP and Rodier. Before establishing his own business, he was known to juggle as many as 13 different ready-to-wear collections, designed anonymously, in a single season. His designs were marked by simplicity of line, softness of color, and ease of movement—from loose sportswear separates to classic suits and cocktail dresses.

In 1984, he succeeded Karl Lagerfeld as director of design at Chloé, claiming that his appointment was "a dream." At Chloé he adapted his unerring fashion sense into a look he called "as French as French cuisine—an image of a young couture, of ready-to-wear with the finesse of couture but with a very young spirit behind it." But his casual, relaxed, and individualistic styles were not completely welcomed by Chloé's tradition-minded customers, and he resigned after overseeing only a few collections.

The disappointment he experienced at Chloé did not deter him: between 1985 and 1990 he created S.A. Guy Paulin design studio, the principal clients being Byblos and Mic-Mac; took back the direction of his own house and signed two licensing contracts with the groups Kanematsu Gosho and Yoshida, establishing himself in Japan; and signed on as part-time artistic director of Tiktiner, a French ready to-wear manufacturer. During this period he designed a range of classic garments, including clingy knit dresses, feminine pin-striped suits, pretty floral 18th-century-inspired dresses, and simple one- and two-piece swimsuits. His clothes never strove for shock value, but remained reserved and feminine, with only the occasional theatrical accessory for emphasis, such as a "waistcoat" of multicolored cords draped across the breasts, or an oversized fringed straw hat.

Though not strictly an avant garde designer, Paulin considered himself one of a creative generation of createurs that included Thierry Mugler, Claude Montana, and the younger Jean-Paul Gaultier. Towards the end of his career he was investigating retro looks, such as 1940s-inspired tweed suits and neo-Baroque velvet gowns strewn with embroidery. His death in 1990 at the young age of 44 prompted waves of regret among his peers at the loss of such a talented, industrious, and benevolent designer and colleague.—KATHLEEN PATON

Peretti, Elsa

Italian designer working in New York

Born *Florence, 1 May 1940.*

Career *Language teacher in Gstaad, Switzerland, 1961; studied interior design in Rome; modeled in London, Paris, New York, mid-1960s; began designing jewelry for Halston*

and Sant'Angelo, New York, 1969; designer, Tiffany and Co., New York, from 1974; also packaging designer, Halston fragrances and cosmetics.

Exhibitions *Fifteen of My Fifty with Tiffany, Fashion Institute of Technology, New York, 1990.*

Awards *Coty American Fashion Critics Award, 1971; President's Fellow Award, Rhode Island School of Design, 1981; Fashion Group "Night of the Stars" Award, 1986; Cultured Pearl Industry Award, 1987.*

Address *727 Fifth Avenue, New York, New York 10022, USA.*

"Style," Elsa Peretti says, "is to be simple." Peretti can deliver a brusque maxim in her husky voice with a Chanel imperiousness and a Montesquieu-like incisiveness. Her knowledge of style is perhaps so vivid because it comes intuitively from a career in modeling, friendships with fashion designers, interest in sculptural adornment, and a fascination with the crafts that go into jewelry. Her quest is for expressive, perfect form, even if it happens to look imperfect at first. Touch—the hand of making and of holding—is foremost. She has brilliantly expanded the materials and repertory of jewelry, assuring that it is a modern tradition, but also guaranteeing that it preserves special crafts of the past. Her art evades any particular place in the world, drawing upon Japanese traditions, Surrealism, and modernist design; it is an art so vagrant its only home is in the heart.

Peretti explores nature with a biologist's acumen and an artist's discrimination. The simplicity of her forms resides in the fact that she selects the quintessential form from among those found in nature, never settling on the median or most familiar, but striving for the essence. Her hearts, for instance, are never of a trite Valentine's Day familiarity; rather, they cleave to the hand with shaped, hand-held warmth. That the heart necklace hangs from its chain in asymmetry as the chain passes through the middle, gives it the quirk of love and the aberration of art that Peretti admires.

Reminding us that Chanel never forgot that she was a peasant, Peretti, too, never forgets the simple things of life. Her suite of beans is ineffably ordinary, yet they are extraordinary in their craft, in their scaling to hand, and in their finest materials. Her bottles are common; Peretti transfigures the crude practicality into an elegant simplicity. "The design," said Peretti, "is full of common sense. Of course I'm slow, I have to crystallize a form, find the essence."

In the 1990 catalogue *Fifteen of My Fifty with Tiffany,* I wrote: "A transcendental aspect haunts Peretti's work; she hints at our affinity to nature even as she plucks the perfect form from the cartload of nature's abundance and art's options. Peretti returns us in her absolute objects to a Garden of Paradise. There, all form has its lingering memory and every shape is the definitive best." (Richard Martin, Tiffany/Fashion Institute of Technology, New York 1990).

Peretti's sensibility is deeply touched by her professional and personal friendships with Halston and Giorgio di Sant'Angelo, no less so after the death of both designers. As a model, Peretti had known both. Halston's minimalism is a touchstone for Peretti, not only in the opportunity for her demonstrative forms to stand out in the ensemble of such simple luxury in dress, but also in the obdurate minimalism of her own design. From Giorgio di Sant'Angelo, Peretti's spirit is of incorporating regional materials in an aggregate at once a composite of many sources and a refinement of them in modern terms.

Generous in acknowledging such designers and in expressing her pleasure in cooperating with craftspeople in the fulfilment of her work, Peretti cannot disguise her own remarkable ability, which she sometimes passes off as craft, to distil form and ideas. The sabotage of her belts is that their sources are in the stable, not in haberdashery: Peretti's attention in 1969 to a leather horse girth inspired a belt without mechanisms, working by the unadorned looping to fulfil the function of the belt. Her tableware is fit for a peasant table, before chopsticks or other utensils: she has created the perfect setting for Picasso's *Blind Man's Meal* to transform it to Tiffany grace without ever compromising its rudimentary, manual presence.

Characteristically, when Peretti confronted the precious materials of diamonds, she flouted convention and offered the affordable—and revolutionary—"Diamonds by the Yard," giving even the desired stone a degree of access and of animation. Of that insouciant success, a landmark of 1970s design, Peretti says modestly, "My objective is to design according to one's financial possibilities." Few would earlier have imagined a leading jewelry designer to coming up with such a frank and sensitive view of the product or the consumer. In fact, it is one of Peretti's triumphs to restore to jewelry a vitality it had lost in the 1960s and early 1970s.

"My love for bones has nothing macabre about it," Peretti says. Indeed, Peretti's sensibility is one of unmitigated joy. Her fruits are prime produce; her sea life is a miracle of abundance; her scorpions and snakes are never scary, but seem instead to be mementoes of exhilaration; her handbags long to be clutched; even her teardrops adapted for earrings, pendants, and even pen-clips are never melancholic. They are tears of joy created by a designer who zealously celebrates life.—RICHARD MARTIN

Picasso, Paloma

French designer

Born *Paris, 19 April 1949, daughter of Pablo Picasso and Françoise Gilot.*

Education *Attended University of Paris, Sorbonne, and University of Nanterre; studied jewelry design and fabrication.*

Family *Married Rafael Lopez-Cambil (aka Lopez-Sanchez), 1978.*

Career *Fashion jewelry designer for Yves Saint Laurent, 1969; jewelry for Zolotas, 1971; designed costumes and sets for Lopez-Cambil's Parisian productions L'Interprétation, 1975, Success, 1978. Teamed with Mr. Lopez-Cambil to create Paloma Picasso brand, including jewelry for Tiffany & Co., 1980; introduced fragrance Paloma and cosmetics Mes Jours, Mes Nuits, 1984, Minataure, 1992; designed men's and women's accessories for Lopez-Cambil, Ltd., 1987; hosiery for Grupo Synkro; eyewear for Carrera; bone china, crystal, silverware, and tiles for Villeroy & Boch; household linens for KBC; fabrics and wall coverings for Motif. Paloma Picasso boutiques opened in Japan and Hong Kong.*

Address *Lopez-Cambil Ltd., 37 West 57th Street, New York, New York 10019, USA.*

With such a name, one could hardly fail to be noticed. And since her marriage, her name has an even more exotic ring—Paloma Picasso Lopez-Sanchez. The daughter of Pablo Picasso, however, is undoubtedly a personality and exciting talent in her own right. Visually arresting with striking features, she consistently wears her signature red lipstick to emphasize her white skin and thick, black hair. She is a newsworthy and photogenic participator in the world's fashion circuit. This, combined with her creative talent, makes her ideally suited to the needs of the modern world where a high profile and excellent social and professional contacts can be an integral part of success.

Paloma Picasso is truly international. Placed in the front row of the Paris and Milan couture collections, she visits the smartest restaurants, the interior decorations of her apartments are publicized, and her choice of garments is recorded in society publications throughout the world. Social gatherings are considered incomplete without her, and she numbers many celebrities amongst her circle.

Professionally, she is an individual designer who uses her assets to great effect in marketing and promoting her ideas. Her jewelry and perfume are particularly noteworthy, demonstrating a modernity and panache that single them out as something special. Her name and the colour red are used as essential ingredients of her work. Her name, meaning "dove," is distinctive, and when used skillfully, a good name has always been an advantage if cleverly exploited.

Paloma Picasso was born and educated in Paris. Formally trained as a jewelry designer, her interest was possibly kindled by childhood memories of the glass beads seen on the island of Murano in Venice and an early fascination with sparkling colours. Initially she was involved in costume design for the theatre, where her originality and exotic pieces attracted much attention. An invitation from Yves Saint Laurent to create a collection of jewelry for his couture house ensured that her work was widely seen, and in 1972 her gold designs for the Greek company Zolotas achieved further recognition and acclaim.

Tiffany and Co. of New York, founded in 1837 as a fancy goods store, has built an international reputation as a high class jeweler, specializing in gemstones and precious metals. In 1980 Paloma created the first of several imaginative and vibrant collections for the company. The signature pieces are unusual in their colour combinations and use of polished surfaces. The shapes are bold and vigorous and enhanced the clothing with which they may be worn. Striking and exciting, her jewelry, although always of the moment, seems to have the timeless quality that sets apart true creativity.

Paloma Picasso's other notable creative contribution to fashion appeals to another sense. The highly successful and distinctive fragrance *Paloma,* with its dynamic red and black packaging and strikingly shaped bottle, is a lingering and suitable evocative tribute to this individual and intriguing personality.—MARGO SEAMAN

Porter, Thea

British designer

Born *Dorothea Naomi Seale in Jerusalem, 24 December 1927. Raised in Damascus, Syria.*

Education *Studied French and Old English at London University, 1949-50; studied art at Royal Holloway College, Egham, Surrey.*

Family *Married Robert Porter in 1953 (divorced, 1967); daughter: Venetia.*

Career *Lived in Beirut, 1953-c.1962; established Greek Street, Soho, boutique selling textiles from the Near East and clothing of her own design, 1967-69; also maintained a*

Thea Porter. *Photograph by Ken Howard.*

shop in Paris, 1976-79; in-store Thea Porter boutique created at Henri Bendel specialty store, New York, 1969. Free-lance fashion, textile and interior designer, London, from 1969.

Awards   *English Fashion Designer of the Year Award, 1972.*
Address   *13 Bolton St., London W1Y 7PA, England.*

Having lived in the Middle East as a child, Thea Porter based her fashion aesthetic upon the ethnic clothing she encountered there. During the late 1960s, fashion revolutions of many kinds were taking place, one of which was the new romanticism mirroring the romantic view of the East common to Victorian England. Hippie types went to Porter's store in Greek Street, Soho, London, to purchase Middle Eastern imports to decorate their homes, true to the spirit of 19th-century artists who created a complete atmosphere in their immediate environment that included loose aesthetic robes echoing distant lands and other time periods. Porter's shop offered pillows and cushions made from fancy Middle Eastern textiles as well as antique caftans. These dresses sold so well that Porter began to design them herself to meet the demand.

An ancient, loosely cut ankle length garment, the caftan lent itself to opulent decoration and luxurious fabrics. Porter's evening gowns were made from silks, brocades, velvets, even crêpe de chine and filmy chiffon, embellished with metallic embroidery and spangles or braid. While not strictly native costume reproductions, the caftans captured the spirit of mysterious harem allure. Wealthy international clients like Elizabeth Taylor, Barbra Streisand, and the Empress of Iran comprised Porter's clientèle, as much for the exoticism of the clothes, as no doubt for the comfort. Porter had long admired Arabic clothing, entranced by the rich embroideries and fabrics, in shapes that produced a protected and secure feeling of being able to hide in one's clothes while feeling like a princess, in the richness of execution of her romantic fantasies.

Porter's nostalgic sensibilities also extended toward the Renaissance and the Edwardian periods. During the 1970s she offered high-waisted midi- or maxi-dresses with voluminous sleeves. These simple historic shapes also lent themselves to luxurious brocades, tapestries, velvets, and embroidery. Her Edwardian looks featured vintage trimmings, and sailor-collared or lacy dresses recalling the last days of the Imperial Russian Grand Duchesses. Porter claimed Chekhov as an influence as well as art déco. Gypsy dresses with their full-flounced skirts allowed for romantic play of colorful patterned fabrics. Again, the shapes were easy, flattering.

Much as Poiret brought Eastern exoticism to a turbulent era, so Porter reflected rapid fashion change toward individuality, coupled with comforting escapism. Even her knit collection, developed for the chilly English climate, included caftan-type dresses, skirt and cardigan sets, and culottes in bright, cheerful colors. By the 1980s Porter had dressed many well-known personalities in her couture and expensive ready-to-wear, including the Beatles, Donovan, Princess Margaret, and Jessye Norman. Her designs allowed the expression of artistic inclinations, while allowing the wearer a shield from the too-scrutinizing eyes of the public.—THERESE DUZINKIEWICZ BAKER

Prada

Italian fashion house

Luxury leather goods company founded by Mario Prada and brother. Mario Prada born in Milan, Italy in 1913. Taken over by granddaughter Miuccia Bianchi Prada. Studied political science, earning Ph.D.; studied mime at Piccolo Teatro di Milano. Worked briefly for the Communist Party. Began designing for company, early 1980s. First London boutique launched, 1994.

Fratelli Prada was established as a purveyor of fine quality leather goods and imported items in Milan, Italy in 1913, by Mario Prada and his brother. For most of this century, affluent clients have been offered the requirements of fine living, in an atmosphere immersed in the refined opulence of Milan's Galleria Vittorio Emmanuele boutique. The *oggetti di lusso* or luxury items have included steamer trunks, Hartman luggage made in America, handbags from Austria, silver objects from London, crystal, tortoise, and shell accessories as well as now obsolete articles made from exquisite materials. Mario Prada traveled throughout Europe in order to familiarize himself with those materials and elements which would build his essential concepts of style and luxury.

Attracted to these same aspects but integrating her own design philosophy, his granddaughter, Miuccia Bianchi Prada, proceeded to enrich and expand this inherited legacy in 1978. Initially she had dismissed any involvement with the family business as less important than the goals she had set for herself. She received a degree in political science, followed by a period of study in mime at the Piccolo Teatro di Milano in preparation for a career in acting. By her mid-20s she was a committed participant in the political activities of the 1970s in Milan. Though one who had always drawn inspiration from history, "she also refused to reject that part of herself." She was taught to value quality materials and craftsmanship, in a city noted for traditional tailor's *ateliers* and elegant fabric showrooms.

Her personal convictions and this serious aspect of her education probably attributed to her belief that women are successful designers because clothing today must express what many women deeply feel. This philosophy has resulted in clothing not preoccupied with sex appeal. What appears to be restrained design quite surprisingly feels exceptional on the body. There has continued to be a nonconforming aspect of beauty in all her collections. This was important to the continuance of Mario Prada's vision of fashion in a full and creative context, capable of making the artisan's qualities come alive in a contemporary spirit.

In 1978 Miuccia Prada, with her distinctive regard for clothing, accessories, and footwear, began to develop and market an innovative line of fashion accessories eventually followed by a line of ready-to-wear clothes and footwear. In a magazine article, she was quoted as saying that her designs had freedom of movement, freedom from definition, and freedom from constriction. Bohemians, the avant-garde, the beatniks had been constant motifs in her designs. Many of her designs are based on the northern Italian tradition of having clothes beautifully made by local tailors and seamstresses. Her philosophy of dress also includes aspects developed and influenced by her own free spirited personality. In fact, a recent and approving magazine writer remarked that "her clothes don't necessarily have misfit connotations, nor are particularly for young women, they're like uniforms for the slightly disenfranchised." In the 1970s she was among the first to produce a practical, lightweight, nylon backpack and other hand-held bags of the same waterproof material. Disregarding season and occasion, the metal stamped Prada logo and brilliant palette combined tassels and leather trim. Black was, without a doubt, the stylish choice. She states that she does not focus on inventing but rethinks the company's traditions in a different fashion, "I believe that every form is an archetype of the past."

In their Milanese headquarters, Miuccia Prada and her husband, business partner Patrizio Bertelli, oversee all aspects of the company. Collections are presented there as well as the occasional cultural event. In their Tuscan factory, near Arezzo, prototypes are sampled and all stages of design and technology are controlled. The firm, I Pelletieri D'Italia S.A. (IPI), produces and distributes the various lines. It was to this Bertelli-owned factory that Miuccia Prada was originally attracted when she researched improved manufacturing techniques. The firm continues to research all possible methods to make an industrial product look like the unique work of an artisan. The company Fratelli Prada continues to manufacture leather goods; suede trimmed with *passementerie* and silk tassels, leather wallets embossed with constructivist motifs, jewelry rolls in suede-lined calf skin, boxy pigskin suitcases, and key rings with leather medallions. Beginning with autumn/winter 1989, ready-to-wear was presented in the calm and stately atmosphere of the Palazzo Manusardi headquarters. Admittedly inspirational to her first collections of black and white dresses and sportswear, were the predominantly stylish and lonely characters in films by Michelangelo Antonioni. "Prada is a reflection of Miuccia's taste, about being a connoisseur rather than a consumer," is an excerpt from a magazine interview. Her first footwear collections combined classicism with elements of the avant-garde in such styles as spectator oxfords and embroidered and bejeweled suede slippers.

Signora Prada begins developing her seasonal repertory with the concept that no single style is appropriate for one occasion. She offers her international clientele an open minded regard for style. In 1994 there were 45 Fratelli Prada retail stores worldwide and two Miu Miu stores. In the Fratelli Prada store in the Galleria, the original mahogany and brass fittings reflect luxury and tradition. On two floors, garments, accessories, footwear, and the recent addition of menswear, express refinement, grace and gentility as they fuse the past with the modern present. In one of her statements on design she confesses that combining opposites in unconventional ways such as refinement with primitive, and natural with machine made helped to produce the collections in her name-sake store Miu Miu. In 1992, inspired by items in her own wardrobe closet, she created this bohemian, artsy-craftsy collection of patchwork and crocheted garments, saddle bags, and sheepskin jackets, clogs, and boots. She based the new and fresh line on rough finishes, natural colors, and materials reflecting the artisan's craft, stylish in the small boutiques of the 1960s. Her choices of fabrics usually associated with haute couture have been cut into streamlined sportswear such as silk *faille* trenchcoats, double faced cashmere suits, and nylon parkas trimmed in mink. "In the end," she says, "fabric is fabric. What is really new is the way you treat it and put the pieces together."—GILLION SKELLENGER

Pucci, Emilio

Italian designer

Born *Marchese Emilio Pucci di Barsento in Naples, 20 November 1914.*

Emilio Pucci: Spring/Summer 1992.

Education   *Educated at the University of Milan, 1933-35, University of Georgia, 1935-36, Reed College, Portland, Oregon, 1936-37; M.A., 1937; Ph.D., University of Florence, 1941.*

Family   *Married Cristina Nannini di Casabianca in 1959; children: Alessandro, Laudomia.*

Military Service   *Bomber pilot in the Italian Air Force, 1938-42.*

Career   *Women's skiwear designer, White Stag, for Lord and Taylor department store, 1948; free-lance fashion designer, from 1949; first Pucci shop established in Capri, 1949, and Rome, Elba, Montecatini, from 1950; President, Emilio Pucci Srl, Florence, and Emilio Pucci, New York, from 1950; vice-president for design and merchandising, Formfit International, 1960s. Also Olympic skier, 1934.*

Awards   *Neiman Marcus Award, 1954, 1967; Sports Illustrated Award, 1955, 1961; Burdine Fashion Award, 1955; The Sunday Times Award, London, 1963; Association of Industrial Design Award, Milan, 1968; Drexel University Award, Philadelphia, 1975; Italy-Austria Award, 1977; Knighthood, Rome, 1982; Medaille de la Ville de Paris, 1985; Council of Fashion Designers of America Award, 1990.*

Died   *(in Florence, Italy) 29 November 1992.*

Address   *Palazzo Pucci, via dei Pucci 6, Florence, Italy.*

Rising out of the ashes of European fashion after World War II, Emilio Pucci brought a spectrum of carefree colours to the rationed continent. His sportswear beginnings lent a casual air to his work, a welcome relief from recent austerity and a new meaning to the term "resort wear." The swirling freestyle patterns and fluid fabrics he used became internationally recognized and desired, copied by many but rivalled by few.

American Tina Lesser may have been earlier with her hand-painted silks, but Pucci quickly made them his own, covering the fine lustrous fabric with optical fantasies of geometric shapes. His colour range came straight from an Aegean horizon, turquoise and ultramarine set against sea green and lime, or hot fuchsia and sunflower yellow. Pucci swept away the repetitive sailor styles and tailored linens of cruisewear and brought in a new air of ease and luxury with his breezy separates. He capitalized on the lull in British and French couture after the war that benefitted many American and Italian designers, and dressed the fashionable *mondaine* in bold ready-to-wear.

The government-backed presentations of Italian designers of the late 1940s provided an aristocratic Florentine backdrop for Pucci's collections, which were soon popular internationally, and he became increasingly aware of the importance of the American market to his success. His characteristic style was best seen in slim-legged trousers in fruity shades, which provided a sexy foil to loose-hanging tunics and classic shirts left to hang outside the waistband.

His collections encompassed more than just stylish but jaunty daywear. In 1961 he showed simple evening dresses with deep V-shape panels set into their sophisticated bias cut silhouette. The 1960s was the decade that saw his greatest success, his psychedelic pattern printed silks being seen everywhere. They were, and continue to be, worn by celebrities, from Marilyn Monroe, to Jackie Kennedy, and to Madonna, all seduced by the light touch of his designs.

As his reputation grew, his distinctive patterns were aspired to by many; a Pucci scarf or vivid silk handbag providing the cachet of luxury. His name was seen on everything from gloves to small ornaments. However, by the 1970s his work, like that of other big fashion houses, seemed less in tune with the times. During the 1980s, Pucci ranges seemed irrelevant to the weighty tailored severity that preoccupied the fashion world. It was not until the start of the 1990s that the pure whirling colours of the Pucci label (by then directed by his daughter, Laudomia) were again universally embraced. His signature shapes and vivid patterns had already inspired a generation of Italian designers, notably Gianni Versace and Franco Moschino, and in 1991 the reinvigorated Pucci look was everywhere. It had been translated into the modern essentials: clingy leggings, catsuits, and stretch polo necks which continued the sexy feel of his work and contrasted perfectly with his airy shirts. His clothes sold out across the world as a new, younger audience took up the label, perpetuating its popularity, albeit on a less high profile level after the initial Pucci mania of that year.

The eclectic use of surface pattern and innovative colour combinations that distinguish Pucci's work have been widely emulated throughout the fashion strata. His use of colour adds a feeling of movement to his clothes, while the quality fabrics he uses enhance the fluid line. The classic separates he designed continue to be successful, while the addition of newer styles ensures that the label will continue to provide a vibrant note to fashion in the 1990s.—REBECCA ARNOLD

Pulitzer, Lilly

American designer

> **Born** *Lillian McKim in Roslyn, New York.*
>
> **Family** *Married Herbert (Pete) Pulitzer; children: Minnie, Liza; married Enrigue Rousseau.*
>
> **Career** *Formed business in Palm Beach, Florida, for sale of women's shifts, 1959; president, Lilly Pulitzer, Inc., 1961-84; children's dresses, called "Minnies," introduced, 1962; Pulitzer Jeans introduced, 1963; Men's Stuff line introduced, 1969; business closed, 1984; rights to women's line purchased by Sugartown Worldwide, 1993.*

According to the legend, it all began with an orange juice stand begun by a bored (and rich) housewife in October 1959. The boss brought a dozen dresses she made (actually her dressmaker made them, but that's not so Horatio Alger) from fabric bought at Woolworth's down to the stand and sold them off a pipe-rack. "I started it as a lark," Pulitzer remembered years later to Lorna Koski of *W*, "I just knew what I liked." Within five years, it seemed as if every woman in America had at least one "Lilly" and more or less lived in the comfortable lifestyle of the "Lilly."

Fashion—design and business—respects quintessence. For many, fashion is a business of knock-offs and copying, but there are gestures that epitomize and that captivate for their ability to distil a fashion idea. The "Lilly," designed by Lilly Pulitzer, is the fashion cipher for the shift or chemise, an unarticulated little dress, that may better serve to represent the chemise than its Balenciaga invention, its countless couture permutations, or its striving variations in the mass market. Publisher John Fairchild wrote in 1965, "Watch the chemise make a comeback with the masses. The élite have never given it up. Just look at the Lilly, those chemises designed by Lilly Pulitzer, who has a gold mine in those little nothing, beautiful print chemises which she turns out by the carloads in her Miami, Florida, factory. All the top stores clamor for them—the same fashion they had on their markdown racks a few years back. The only difference is the "Lilly" is lined and the shape controlled" (*The Fashionable Savages*, New York). There is, however, always a big difference between the uncomplicated Diane Von Furstenberg wrap dress, the

Halston Ultrasuede shirtwaist or other icons of style, and all the competition. Pulitzer invented nothing; she is hardly a designer; Fairchild is right to call them "little nothing" dresses; but she gave a uniform to the early-to-mid-1960s.

The barren non-design of the "Lilly" was its allure. A perky, bright, and unpretentious shift in polished cotton chintz met an American need for personal style amidst homogenous culture. Eleanor Lambert describes its evolution, "first a 'snob' uniform, then a general fashion craze" (*World of Fashion,* New York, 1976). Pulitzer is a powerful family name in America and the associations with Palm Beach's largely vestigial grandeur made vague allusion to wealth and aristocracy, but the dress was eminently accessible. In fact, one of the elements of its popularity was that it appealed not only across class lines, but across all ages of women, serving young women who might aspire to more than "Laugh-In" shifts and style and to women of a certain age who found the simplified form a kind of chaste elegance, especially in an era influenced by the easy and unadorned grace of First Lady Jacqueline Kennedy. As Marylin Bender reports, "the fact that Jacqueline, Ethel and Joan Kennedy were Lilly-fans didn't hurt at all" (*The Beautiful People,* New York, 1976). In fact, the history of the Lilly must be seen in the context of Jacqueline Kennedy's allure in American style, allowing high style to become an acceptable middle-class American grace, whether in décor or clothes and personal style.

Bender quotes Pulitzer as saying, "The great thing about the Lilly is that you wear practically nothing underneath." In this inner simplicity as well as the outward simplicity in silhouette and bold tropical print, Pulitzer understood her time as much as she understood herself. Reportedly, Pulitzer had worked with her dressmaker to come up with an alternative to trousers for the leisure life of Palm Beach, as she felt she did not look good in trousers. The alternative arrived at was nothing more than the classic housedress, sanctioned a little by Balenciaga's 1950s chemise, brightened by the tropical palette, and rarefied by the connection to grand lifestyle.

While Pulitzer diversified her business founded in such serendipity, especially with success in a girl's version known as the Minnie, the essential garment of the business was always the "Lilly," its basic design modulated three times a year to ensure a freshness—akin to the principles of the orange-juice stand—in the product. But the "Lilly" was treated by designer and consumer alike as a classic, not something to be significantly tampered with. In 1993, Pulitzer re-established the business, backed by Sugartown International, after a ten-year hiatus.

Only in America could the "Lilly" have happened as it did: a triumph of non-design; an aristocratic aura bestowed on a distinctly non-aristocratic idea; a dress that at a modest $30 to $75 retail exemplified its time. In fact, the mid-1960s youth-quake, with its extreme mini-dresses followed by paper dresses and other experiments and social temperaments, made the "Lilly" recede with accustomed dignity quite rapidly into its historical moment of the first half of the 1960s, where it abides, an icon.—RICHARD MARTIN

Quant, Mary

British designer

Born *London, 11 February 1934.*

Education *Studied art and design at Goldsmith's College of Art, London University, 1952-55.*

Family *Married Alexander Plunket Greene in 1957 (died, 1990); son: Orlando.*

Career *Fashion designer, from 1955; established Bazaar boutique and Alexander's restaurant, London, 1955; founder, director, Mary Quant Ginger Group wholesale design and manufacturing firm, 1963, and Mary Quant, Ltd., 1963; cosmetics line introduced, 1966; Mary Quant Japan franchise shops established, 1983; has designed for JC Penney, Puritan Fashions, Alligator Rainwear, Kangol, Dupont Europe, Staffordshire Potteries, etc. Member, Design Council, London, from 1971.*

Exhibitions *Mary Quant's London, Museum of London, 1973.*

Awards *Woman of the Year Award, London, 1963; The Sunday Times International Fashion Award, London, 1963; Bath Museum of Costume Dress of the Year Award, 1963; Maison Blanche Rex Award, New Orleans, 1964; Piavola d'Oro Award, 1966; Chartered Society of Designers Medal, 1966; Officer, Order of the British Empire, 1966; Fellow, Chartered Society of Designers, 1967; Royal Designer for Industry, Royal Society of Arts, 1969; British Fashion Council Hall of Fame Award, 1990; Senior Fellow, Royal College of Art, London, 1991.*

Address *3 Ives St., London SW3 2NE, England.*

The name Mary Quant is synonymous with 1960s fashion. Quant's designs initiated a look for the newly emerging teen and twenty market enabling young women to establish their own identity and put Britain on the international fashion map.

Quant

Quant did not study fashion. Following parental advice she enrolled in an Art Teacher's Diploma course at Goldsmith's College, London University, but she was not committed to teaching. In the evenings she went to pattern cutting classes. Her fashion career began in 1955, in the workrooms of the London milliner, Erik. Also that year she opened her boutique, Bazaar in the King's Road, Chelsea, in partnership with her future husband, Alexander Plunket-Greene. The idea was to give the so-called Chelsea Set "a *bouillabaisse* of clothes and accessories." Mary was the buyer, but she soon found that what she wanted was not available. The solution was obvious, but not easy. Twenty-one years old, with little fashion experience, Quant started manufacturing from her bedsit. Using revamped Butterick patterns and fabrics bought retail at Harrods, she created a look for the Chelsea girl. Her customers were hardly younger than herself and she knew what they wanted. Her ideas took off in a big way, on both sides of the Atlantic.

The Americans loved the London Look. So much so that in 1957 Quant signed a contract with JC Penney to create clothes and underwear for the wholesale market. American coordinates convinced her that separates were versatile and ideal for the young. To reach more of the British market in 1958 she launched the Ginger Group, a mass-produced version of the look, with US manufacturer Steinberg's. In the same year she was nominated Woman of the Year in Britain and *The Sunday Times* in London gave her their International Fashion Award.

Quant created a total look based on simple shapes and bold fashion statements. She hijacked the beatnik style of the late 1950s: dark stockings, flat shoes, and polo necks became obligatory for the girl in the street. The pinafore dress, based on the traditional British school tunic, was transformed as one of the most useful garments of the early 1960s. Hemlines rose higher and higher. Quant's mini skirts reached thigh level, in 1965, and everyone followed. Courrèges confirmed that the time was right by launching his couture version in Paris but Quant needed no confirmation: 1965 was the year of her whistlestop tour to the United States. With 30 outfits and her own models, she showed in 12 cities in 14 days. Sporting mini skirts and Vidal Sassoon's five-point geometric haircuts, the models ran and danced down the catwalk. It was the epitome of Swinging London and it took America by storm.

Quant's talents did not go unnoticed in higher places. In 1966 she was awarded the OBE for services to fashion and went to Buckingham Palace wearing a mini skirt. Her cosmetics range was launched that year. Recognizable by the familiar daisy logo, Quant cosmetics were an international success. Later taken over by Max Factor, they were retailed in 90 countries. She also experimented with new materials including PVC and nylon, to create outerwear, shoes, tights, and swimwear.

In the early 1970s Quant moved out of the mass market and began to work for a wider age group, chiefly for export to the United States and Europe. Her range of merchandise expanded to include household goods, toys, and furnishings. Mary Quant at Home, launched on the US market in 1983, included franchised home furnishings and even wine. By the end of the 1980s her designs were again reaching the British mass market, through the pages of the Great Universal Stores/Kays mail order catalogues.

Mary Quant remains a genuine fashion innovator. She has adjusted to change. The 1960s designer for the youth explosion became a creator for the 1980s lifestyle boom. Her market had grown up with her and she was able to anticipate its demands. Quant is truly a designer of her time.—HAZEL CLARK

Rabanne, Paco

French designer

Born *Francisco Rabaneda Cuervo in San Sebastian, Spain, 18 February 1934; raised in France.*

Education *Studied architecture at l'École Nationale des Beaux-Arts, Paris, 1952-55.*

Career *Presented first haute couture collection, 12 Experimental Dresses, Paris, 1964; home furnishing and tableware lines introduced, 1981; men's ready-to-ear line introduced, 1983; women's ready-to-wear line introduced, 1990; leather goods line introduced, 1991. Opened first shop in Paris, 1990. Fragrances include Calandre, c. late 1960s, Paco Rabanne pour Homme, 1973, Metal, 1979, La Nuit, 1985, Sport, 1985, Tenere, 1988; men's skin care line launched, 1984. Holds over 140 licenses.*

Exhibitions *Body Covering, Museum of Contemporary Crafts, New York, 1968.*

Awards *Beauty Products Industry Award, 1969; Fragrance Foundation Recognition Award, 1974; L'Aiguille d'Or Award, 1977; Dé d'Or Award, 1990; made Chevalier de la Légion d'Honneur, 1989; made Officier de l'Ordre d'Isabelle la Catholique (Spain), 1989.*

Address *23 rue du Cherche-Midi, 75006 Paris, France.*

It comes as no surprise, on viewing the designs of Paco Rabanne, to hear that he prefers to be described as an engineer rather than a couturier. Son of the chief seamstress at Balenciaga (a designer famed for his intricate techniques of construction), Rabanne, after studying architecture, made his name in the 1960s with a series of bizarre, futuristic garments made out of incongruous materials. When viewed on the catwalk they seemed space-age prototypes rather than high fashion garments.

Believing that the only new frontier left in fashion was the discovery and utilization of new materials, rather than the old couture method of changing lines from season to season, Rabanne totally broke with tradition, experimenting with plastic and aluminium, to create some of the most eccentric yet influential garments of the 1960s.

It was estimated that by 1966 Rabanne was using 30 thousand metres of Rhodoid plastic per month in such designs as bib necklaces made of phosphorescent plastic discs strung together with fine wire and whole dresses of the same material linked by metal chains. When he had exhausted the possibilities of plastic, Rabanne created a contemporary version of chainmail using tiny triangles of aluminium and leather held together with flexible wire rings to construct a series of simple shift mini dresses.

The delight of his designs comes in the use of disparate materials not previously considered appropriate for use in clothing, or the displacing of traditional materials in order to produce strange juxtapositions of colour and texture. For instance, he was one of the first designers to combine knits, leather, and fur, using combinations like a cape made of triangles of matte silver leather with black ponyskin or a coat teaming curly white lamb and white leather.

It could be said that in the 1970s and 1980s the name Paco Rabanne became associated with male toiletries rather than for the intriguing experimentation he had been carrying out. In fact, Rabanne relies on the sales of his successful line of skinscents—including *Calandre, Paco,* and *Metal*—in order to finance his more technological projects. In 1971 he collaborated with Louis Giffard, an authority on flow-moulding techniques, to produce a raincoat moulded entirely in one piece of plastic. Even the buttons were part of the same process, moulded directly into the garment and fitting into pressed-out pieces on the other side of the coat.

In the 1990s, with a 1960s renaissance in full swing, the inventive calibre of Paco Rabanne has been rediscovered. His latest collections are concentrating on stretch jersey, cotton and viscose fabrics in metallic hues, still accessorized by enormous pieces of jewellery.

The high modernism of his 1960s designs seems touchingly innocent when viewed through the jaded eyes of the 1990s. Science and technology in contemporary culture signify something far removed from the faith and hope in the future that Rabanne was expressing with his self-consciously space age materials. His designs give less a sense of the future than imbue us with feelings of nostalgia for the optimism in new technology embraced in the aesthetics of 1960s design.—CAROLINE COX

Restivo, Mary Ann
American designer

Born *South Orange, New Jersey, 28 September 1940.*

Education *Studied retailing at College of St. Elizabeth, Morristown, New Jersey, 1958-60, and design at Fashion Institute of Technology, New York, 1960-61, with associate degree in Applied Arts.*

Family *Married Saul Rosen in 1978.*

Career *Trainee, Abby Michael junior sportswear house, New York, 1961; designer for New York firms Bernard Levine, Petti for Jack Winter, Something Special, Sports Sophisticates, and Mary Ann Restivo for Genre, 1962-74; for Cisco Casuals, head designer, women's blouse division, Dior New York, 1974-80; launched own firm, Mary Ann Restivo, Inc., 1980; sold company to Leslie Fay Corporation, 1988; designer, Mary Ann Restivo division, Leslie Fay Corporation, 1988-92; independent design consultant, from 1993.*

Awards *Hecht Company Young Designers Award, Washington, D.C., 1968; Mortimer C. Ritter Award, Fashion Institute of Technology, 1973; awarded Honorary Doctor of Humanities, College of Saint Elizabeth, 1986; Alumnus of the Year Award, American Association of Community and Junior Colleges, 1992; Ellis Island Medal of Honor Award, 1993.*

"People need fashionably sensible clothes," asserted Mary Ann Restivo to *People* magazine in the midst of the era of late 1980s excesses. *People* replied that Restivo is "emerging . . . as the saviour of the stylish but sane professional woman." Career and professional dressing are the appropriate context for Restivo's work, not only in terms of her clientéle, but in terms of the clothing's emphasis on good fit, excellent materials and manufacture, personal luxury without ostentation, and wearable good taste.

Bernadine Morris, a likely champion of Restivo's work in her commitment to American sportswear, wrote of Restivo that she "tries to walk the tightrope between clothes that are subdued and those that attract attention." The attention that a Restivo garment attracts is primarily for its flattering image to the client. Restivo emphasizes fit, with some camouflage to the hips, appealing to women in sizes six, eight, and ten. As the designer argues in the tradition of sportswear, no woman should feel squeezed into the clothing, but should have mobility for her own sense of elegance and self-confidence, as well as the functions of dressing for careers in which one outfit may suffice from home to office to evening. In the 1980s, Restivo's work directly coincided with the perceived need of women of middle- and upper-management to wear clothing that was sufficiently sensible to the office without merely adapting menswear. Other American designers came to the same conviction in the 1980s, but Restivo was one of the first to create stylish career dressing and to establish it as the cornerstone of her business.

In a 1993 lecture at the Italian Trade Commission in New York, Restivo spoke passionately of her love of textile resourcing, finding the best materials for her garments and permitting the textiles to determine the clothes. Arguing that every collection begins with its textile resources, Restivo uses wool jersey, cashmere, and other luxuries of texture and vision throughout her collections.

Through the 1980s, jackets were an important element of all Restivo collections, even for resort. Like most designers of the period, Restivo made her jackets softer and softer, choosing the textiles for unconstructed jackets still capable of the fresh self-confidence required by women in the place of business. Dresses play an important part in Restivo's ideal of the career wardrobe, but resort collections also permit trousers and her jackets in elegant proportions work as part of tailored suits or as separates. Restivo told Morris (*New York Times*, 8 May 1990) at the apogee of the well-tailored business jacket: "The jacket is the key. When you start to develop your collection, you begin with the jacket then build everything else around it. You work out the skirts or the pants and the blouses and sweaters." Restivo added: "It is interesting to me that when store buyers come to buy the collection, they follow the same procedure. When customers go shopping for their fall clothes, they will probably do the same thing."

Restivo's acuity to the customer has always been an essential part of her business, begun in 1981. The loyalty of her clients is legendary. When the Restivo line was abruptly dropped by Leslie Fay in the early 1990s, clients pursued the designer herself to be sure that they would not be cut off from their favorite clothing. Restivo's client empathy is undeniably important in the success of a woman designer creating for like-minded sensible women of business and style.

Gloria Steinem once said of Restivo's clothes that they are "the kind of clothes that, after you've died, another woman would find in a thrift shop and like." Such enduring good taste and clothing recycling may thwart the image of fashion as a place of excess and fickle change. Indeed, Restivo's clothing fosters another, more sensible, more purposeful, undeniably beautiful concept of fashion.—RICHARD MARTIN

Rhodes, Zandra

British designer

Born *Zandra Lindsey Rhodes in Chatham, Kent, 19 September 1940.*

Education *Studied textile design, Medway College of Art, 1959-61, and Royal College of Art, 1961-64.*

Career *Established dressmaking firm with Sylvia Ayton, London, 1964, and textile design studio with Alexander McIntyre, 1965; partner, designer, Fulham Clothes Shop, 1967-68; free-lance designer, 1968-75; director, Zandra Rhodes UK Ltd, and Zandra Rhodes Shops Ltd, from 1975; launched ready-to-wear collections, in Australia, 1979, and in Britain, 1984. Has also designed bedlinens and household textiles.*

Exhibitions *Zandra Rhodes: A Retrospective with Artworks, Art Museum of Santa Cruz, California, 1983.*

Awards *English Fashion Designer of the Year Award, 1972; Moore College of Art Award, Philadelphia, 1978; DFA, International Fine Arts College of Miami, 1977; Royal Designer for Industry, Royal Society of Arts, 1977.*

Address *87 Richforth Street, London W6 7HJ, England.*

Zandra Rhodes is an artist whose medium is printed textiles. Working in a calligraphic style uniquely her own, she designs airy prints from which she produces floating, romantic garments whose cut evolves from the logic and placement of the print itself. Rhodes has no imitators; her work is instantly recognizable.

In a field where novelty is prized, Rhodes's work over the years is remarkable for its consistency. Because the shapes of her garments are fanciful and fantastical, using volume to display the textile to its best advantage, her clothes do not date. Rhodes's references are timeless: T-shaped gowns of printed chiffon belted in satin; the full pleated skirts and long gathered sleeves of Ukrainian festival dress; off-the-shoulder tabards finished with a fringe of dagging; children's smocking re-interpreted in silk jersey. Zandra Rhodes's clothes are extravagantly feminine, delicate, and mysterious, created, as one writer has observed, for "contemporary Titanias."

Each collection of prints evolves as a thoughtful response to a personal vision. Drawing on traditional historic sources, on images from nature, from popular culture, and from her own past, Rhodes sketches an object over and again, entering into a dialogue with it as the sketches become increasingly abstract and a personal statement emerges. Only at that point are a series of these personal images combined until the right composition presents itself to be translated into the final screen print. The print determines how the garment will be cut. Rhodes was not trained as a draper or cutter and she has not been bound by the concept of symmetry, conventional seam placement, or internal shaping. Many of Rhodes's dresses are cut flat or with minimal shaping,

**Zandra Rhodes. From the collection Unfinished Symphony, 1995. Modelled by Lisa B.; shoes by Red or Dead;
bag by Lulu Guiness; hair by Michael John.** *Photograph by Rose Beddington;* © *Zandra Rhodes.*

sometimes incorporating floating panels which follow the undulations of the patterned textile. She favours large repeats on silk chiffon or silk net and as the garment falls in on itself against the body it creates mysterious shapes and soft, misty layers not easily known. Rhodes is without doubt one of the most gifted and original designers of the late 20th century.—WHITNEY BLAUSEN

Ricci, Nina

French designer/company

Couture house founded by Nina Ricci (1883-1970) and son Robert Ricci (1905-88) in Paris, 1932. First ready-to-wear collection shown, 1964; men's collection introduced, 1986; first boutique opened, Paris, 1979; men's boutique, Ricci-Club, opened, Paris, 1986; cosmetics line, Le Teint Ricci, introduced, 1992. Fragrances include Coeur de Joie, 1945, L'Air du Temps, 1948, Capricci, 1961, Farouche, 1974, Signoricci, 1975, Fleur de Fleurs, 1980, Nina, 1987, Ricci-Club, 1989.

Awards *Mme. Ricci awarded Chevalier de la Légion d'Honneur; Fragrance Foundation Hall of Fame Award, 1982; Fragrance Foundation Perennial Success Award, 1988; Dé d'Or Award, 1987; Bijorca d'Or Award, 1987, 1988; Vénus de la Beauté, 1990; Trophée International Pardum/Couture, 1991; Prix d'Excellence "Créativité" 92, 1992; Trophée de la Beauté de Dépêche Mode, 1992; Prix Européen de la P.L.V., 1992; l'Oscar du Mécénat d'Entreprises, 1993.*
Address *39, avenue Montaigne, 75008 Paris, France.*

To make women beautiful, to bring out the charm of each one's personality. But also to make life more beautiful . . . that has always been my ambition, and that is the underlying philosophy of NINA RICCI.—
—Robert Ricci

Nina Ricci is established as one of the longest running Parisian couture houses. Unlike her peers, Elsa Schiaparelli and Chanel, Ricci's reputation does not rest on a revolutionary fashion statement. Instead, she was successful because she provided an understated, chic look for elegant and wealthy society women, always classic, yet intoxicatingly feminine.

When it came to designing clothes, Nina Ricci relied greatly on her feminine intuition. She worked directly on to the model and designed by draping the actual fabric, which she felt gave her the answer to what the dress would become. Creating clothes was simply a matter of solving problems and in the 1930s she described several of them; she had to find an extra special, elegant detail that would render a dress a client's favourite and achieve a maximum ease and lightness that did not encumber the wearer when moving or dancing.

Much of the detailing in Nina Ricci's clothes reflected her ultra-feminine approach, the flattering effects of gathers, tucks, and drapery and an attention to décolleté and figure-hugging details like fitting dresses below the waist. She was clever and original in her use of fabric, cutting plaids and tartans on the bias for evening dresses and a black silk border print fabric so that the print was avidly displayed over the bust, leaving the rest of the dress to become a straight column of fabric.

Nina Ricci: Spring/Summer 1996. *Photograph by Guy Marineau.*

Ricci had been a successful designer for other houses before she decided to open her own house with her son Robert in 1932. At the age of 49, this could have been a risky venture but the gamble paid off as the company rapidly grew in size and stature during its first decade. By 1939 they occupied eleven floors in three buildings, a stark contrast to their humble beginnings in one room at 20 boulevard des Capucines, Paris.

Nina Ricci retired from the business in the early 1950s, leaving the field open to her son Robert who has since pursued his own ambitious plans for the house. An excellent businessman, Robert Ricci has established many divisions and licensees for the Ricci name. A fragrance, *Coeur de Joie*, was introduced in 1945, followed by the now classic *L'Air du Temps*. Later such fragrances as *Coeur de Joie, L'Air du Temps, Fleur de Fleurs,* and *Nina* were successively marketed. Sunglasses alone were reported to be grossing six million dollars in the late 1970s and by 1979 the house had become firmly established in the former Kodak Mansion, opposite the House of Dior on avenue Montaigne, Paris.

Robert Ricci has also been successful in his choice of recent designers for the house. The Belgian designer Jules François Crahay was named Head Designer in 1954 and made his debut with a collection that paid homage to Nina Ricci's trademark feminine look. Carrie Donovan from *The New York Times* described it as "a collection that was feminine in the extreme—beautiful of coloring and fabric, unbizarre and elegant." Crahay was succeeded in 1963 by Gérard Pipart, who remains today as designer of both the couture and boutique collections, turning out typically Ricci clothes in the most beautiful laces, tailored fabrics, appliqué, and natural fibres.—KEVIN ALMOND

Richmond, John

British designer

Born *Manchester, England, 1960.*

Education *Graduated from Kingston Polytechnic, 1982.*

Family *Married Angie Hill; son: Harley D; daughter: Phoenix.*

Career *Free-lance designer in England for Lano Lano, Ursula Hudson, Fiorucci, Joseph Tricot, and Pin Up for Deni Cler, 1982-84; designer and partner with Maria Cornejo, Richmond-Cornejo, London, 1984-87; John Richmod Man and John Richmond Woman collections introduced, 1987; lower priced Destroy collection introduced, 1990; Destroy Denim collection introduced 1991; first London boutique opened, 1992.*

Address *Proudheights Ltd, 25 Battersea Bridge Road, London SW11 3BA, England.*

The twin icons of popular rebellion, rock music, and biker chic, are combined with good tailoring and attention to detail to make John Richmond's designs a success, commercially and critically. He is one of the most business-minded of his British counterparts, steadily building up his clothing range while others have fallen prey to financial and production problems. His designs have developed along the lines initiated during his partnership with Maria Cornejo, with certain motifs being carried through. These make his work instantly recognizable and, he says, justify the use of the Destroy slogan as a brand name for his cheaper lines, instead of promoting it as a diffusion range.

His womenswear shows the use of sharp tailoring with subversive twists which carry out the motto of "Destroy, Disorientate, Disorder," so often emblazoned on his garments, as he tries to challenge accepted design conventions and expectations. Richmond's clothes are always sexy and brazen, leading many stylists and pop stars to reach for his styles when wanting to create an image that is striking and memorable. Well-cut jackets, often in hot fruity colours, are combined with fetish motifs. Bondage chains, zips, and leather inserts hark back to punk, although the sophistication of the style and the quality of the fabric make the overall look far more contemporary. His Tattoo sleeve tops and biker jackets were seen everywhere, even inspiring a vogue for the real thing among some London clubbers.

These design details also highlighted another side of his more subversive work. The macho tattoos he juxtaposed with transparent georgette wrap tops in the late 1980s questioned sexual stereotypes, something he continues in his menswear, where bright shiny fabrics are used for long-jacketed suits, and net is set against hard leather. These are perhaps a reflection of the vulnerable, slightly camp edge possessed by many of the rock 'n' roll heroes that inspire him, impossibly masculine images at the same time tempered by a glam-rock glitziness, or the feminine twist of a soft shiny fabric. Although the anarchy symbols he so often uses challenge, they never lead to his creating clothes that are unwearable or unsellable. A suit may be made with bondage trousers as a witty edge to a traditional design, but the fine Prince of Wales check of the fabric still makes it seem stylish and desirable.

Richmond's Destroy and Destroy Denim labels have the same pop star/rock chic feel, yet retain the quality of design of his main line, relying mainly on Lycra, denim, and splashes of leatherette to produce a sportswear influence and clubby feel. Jeans in denim and biker jackets form the basis of this collection, although sharp suits also feature, with 1970s glam rock again an influence: feather boa-like trim around coats and jackets and tight sequin tops for both men and women. Later collections have shown a growing maturity in style and widening of influences, in couture-inspired jackets with gilt buttons and quilted linings and sleek slit skirts, still with the distinctive Richmond elements like shiny leggings and the contrast platform heels of the boots designed for Shelly's, the popular London footwear chain.

John Richmond is undoubtedly one of the forerunners of contemporary British fashion, a dedication to which is shown in the part he takes in "5th Circle" with four other menswear designers who want to build on and develop Britain's innovative talents. His slick marketing techniques and his ability to reflect contemporary moods in his designs make him one of the most exciting and prominent of his country's designers. Many believe his business sense will ensure his future success, something which is often as important for survival as the production of consistently good designs.—REBECCA ARNOLD

Rochas, Marcel

French designer

Born *Paris, 1902.*

Career *Opened fashion house in rue Faubourg St-Honoré, Paris, 1924. Moved to avenue Matignon, 1931. Perfumes include: Femme, 1945, Madame Rochas, 1960, and Mystère, 1978.*

Died *(in Paris) 1955.*

In the sometimes indeterminate world of fashion, Marcel Rochas was determined and decisive. He operated with a business acumen and cultural strategy (including the fashion designer as a conspicuous social mixer) that caused him in the post-war period to doubt the continued vitality and interest of the couture and to turn resolutely to his boutique operation and lucrative fragrance business. His motto was "Youth, Simplicity, and Personality," alternatively reported in the *New York Herald Tribune* (3 August 1948) as "elegance, simplicity, and youth," but it was in many ways the characteristic of personality that differentiated Rochas from other designers of his era. Rochas's initial fame came in the 1920s and rested on his *tailleur,* accompanied with supple skirts with the fullness and articulation of godets. In 1942, five years before the Dior New Look, Rochas had offered a new corset to create the *guépière,* or wasp waist, anticipating the return of the extreme femininity that enchanted him. Caroline Rennolds Milbank describes, "The Rochas output is characterized by a calculated originality" (New York, 1985). This reserved encomium is perhaps just for a designer of obsession with feminine beauty, but also with a commercial perspicacity.

Originality was, however, important for Rochas, if only as a sign of rights and attribute of value rather than of real creative initiative. In the 1930s, he was already selling ready-to-wear and made-to-order clothes in his New York store. He claimed to have invented the word "slacks" in the early 1930s, along with originating the idea to include gray flannel slacks as part of a suit. In an era when women's trousers were limited to extreme informality or recreation, Rochas's trousers suit was highly advanced if not revolutionary. His clothing was not cautious, but it was in its way circumspect, even the vaunted "inventions" coming with a social justification. For Rochas, "original" and "invention" were key words in the vocabulary of fashion selling.

The wide shoulders of the 1930s were created by several designers more or less simultaneously. He continuously played on the shoulders as a sign of the feminine: a fall/winter 1947 evening gown, for instance, invents broad shoulders through a capelet-like scarf attached to the bodice. Bolero jackets of the 1940s are lighter in construction than Balenciaga's inspirations direct from Spain; rather, Rochas is interested in the effect of the enhanced shoulders to pad and to frame. Likewise, a 1949 *robe du soir* dips to a bouquet of silk camellias at the bust, but caps the shoulders and frames the face with a flaring lightness. Shoulders look like the soaring roof of Le Corbusier's architecture at Ronchamp. In other instances, grand white collars perform the same role of dilating the impression of the shoulders and in providing a sweet, portrait-like framing for the face. The *New York Herald Tribune* described in 1948, "white collars in Queen Cristina [sic] and Louis XIII manner with points on shoulders are shown on many dresses for every occasion." *Women's Wear Daily* (29 January 1948) reported of Rochas, "this house is very modern but with the modernity which carries with it a tradition linking it with the fashion picture of the day. There is always an air of excitement in his collections which are designed to enhance the charm of women." Rochas claimed his *robe Bali,* with pronounced shoulders, to have been inspired by the Balinese dance costumes he had seen at the 1931 *Exposition Coloniale:* what he learned from Asian dress was the light float of a prominent shoulder, but he reinforced the idea with constant recourse to portrait collars and cognate enhancement of the head and shoulders.

If Rochas's anatomical obsession was the shoulder, his second favorite was the arm. He often embellished the sleeves in suits and coats, and his coats from the 1940s, which tended to be voluminous and drapey, were characterized by large sleeves. Loose blouson effects were more than carried over into the excess of sleeves as well as an interest in full backs.

Picken and Miller record, "Conscious of the changes in fashion, Rochas was the first to give up his heavy burden of the haute couture collections and to restrict his present activities to his boutique which specializes not only in accessories, but also in separates." Lace used in packaging affirmed the luxury textiles and laces that Rochas used in his couture, especially the corset. In fact, Rochas's accessories tended toward a chic wit, less self-conscious than Schiaparelli, but similarly inventive and imaginative. Anticipating Cardin and the marketing orientation of fashion and beauty, Rochas was a visionary. His feminine designs still conformed to a traditional fashion ideal, but Rochas's eye was on the future. At his death in 1954, he had not fully achieved the synthesis of design and marketing that would become the dynamic of late 20th-century fashion, but he was definitely a believer and a pioneer.—RICHARD MARTIN

Roehm, Carolyne

American designer

Born *Jane Carolyne Smith in Kirksville, Missouri, 7 May 1951.*

Education *Graduated from Washington University, St Louis, 1973.*

Family *Married Axel Roehm in 1978 (divorced, 1981); married Henry Kravis in 1985 (divorced).*

Career *Designer, Mrs sportswear by Kellwood Co. for Sears, Roebuck & Co., c.1973; designer, Oscar de la Renta licensees, including Miss "O" line, New York, 1974-84; launched own deluxe ready-to-wear firm, New York, 1985; added couture line, 1988, and footwear, 1989; closed house, 1991-93; launched mail order clothing, accessories and gift collection, 1993, with related in-store boutiques at Saks Fifth Avenue. Also: President, Council of Fashion Designers of America, 1989.*

Awards *Pratt Institute Award, 1991.*

Address *550 7th Avenue, New York, New York 10018, USA.*

Carolyne Roehm is an American designer who creates clothes for men to love and women to find flattering. She is a person with a passion for designing beautiful, feminine clothes in luxurious materials, who takes great care with the details. She opened the doors of her own ready-to-wear and couture design firm in 1985, only to close them six years later.

Designing clothes was a lifelong passion for Jane Carolyne Smith Roehm. After studying fashion design at Washington University, she spent a year designing polyester sportswear for Kellwood Co., a company that supplied Sears, before working for Oscar de la Renta, holding pins and serving as his fitting model. She learned the details of classic couture from him, and later designed the Miss "O" line. After ten years with de la Renta, she formed her own design firm known as Carolyne Roehm, Inc.

She designs for women, like herself, who have money and who live an active life, involved with benefits and social events, but who might also work. She is known for well-detailed, finely constructed, feminine clothes which are created to make women feel elegant. Fabrics are rich: cashmere, satin, velvet, and suede. Details might include *trapunto* stitching, embroidery, or leather trim. Roehm's eveningwear is glamorous, fairy tale-like, to be seen in at social occasions and photographed in at charity events. The dresses could be cut full and made of rich fabrics, reminiscent of those worn in the aristocratic portraits of the artist Franz Winterhalter, or sleek, sensuous columns that recall John Singer Sargent's *Madame X*. Although best known for her glamorous eveningwear, half of her design work is in everyday wear. She creates sporty separates, dresses, coats, hats, and shoes. In all circumstances, Roehm's design work is known for quality and fit.

Carolyne Roehm can be numbered among the working rich. Her former husband, Henry Kravis, financed her design firm before they were married. After she was married she did not have to work, but she was driven. She designed her collections and used her organizational skills to support charity events. As president of the Council of Fashion Designers of America, Roehm guided the organization as they became a major supporter of AIDS research. She served as her own fitting model and appeared in her own advertising campaigns.

In 1991, for personal reasons, Carolyne Roehm closed her design business, Carolyne Roehm, Inc. From 1991 to 1994, she maintained a small office and staff, created a mail-order business, and produced clothes for private customers only. It remains to be seen whether Roehm returns on a larger scale to the field she graced with her feminine, glamorous designs.—NANCY HOUSE

Roth, Christian Francis

American designer

Born *New York City, 12 February 1969.*

Education *Special student, Fashion Institute of Technology, New York, 1986-87; studied fashion design at Parsons School of Design, New York, 1987-88.*

Career *Apprentice, later employee, of Koos Van den Akker; produced first small collection in Van den Akker's studio, 1988; showed first full collection, 1990.*

Awards *Council of Fashion Designers of America Perry Ellis Award, 1990.*

Address *18 East 17th Street, New York, New York 10003, USA.*

In 1990, a week after his first show and at the young age of 21, Christian Francis Roth was heralded by *Women's Wear Daily* as Seventh Avenue's latest boy wonder. Acclaim came stiflingly early for Roth. *Vanity Fair* had already photographed Roth with his ingenious dress-form dress (now in the collection of the Metropolitan Museum of Art) in August 1989 and in *The New Yorker* of 29 January 1990, Holly Brubach proclaimed of Roth's designs, "These clothes would look first-rate in Paris or Milan or Timbuktu. It is already too late to call him promising. There is, in his clothes, nothing more to wait for." Such immoderate and unanimous praise could only be withering to many young artists, but Christian Francis Roth earned the adulation and has only gone on to warrant further accolades. Yet, after the last hurrah and congratulations, there is the designer who works as a consummate technician in a tightly circumscribed aesthetic. He reaches not for the gold ring of commercial success and recognition like other designers, but instead for a level of virtuosity and quiet quality in his work.

Roth is an artist as evidenced by his vocabulary of forms conversant with such artistic elements as Surrealist *trompe l'oeil,* used in the dress-form dress (1989) and his wool jersey dress with illusionistic inset collar, cuffs, and belt (1991). Pop Art-derived concepts from consumer culture are represented in the spring 1990 Cartoon collection featuring daffy squiggles and suits with buttons that look as though they were spilled out of M & M candy bags. His breakfast suit (1990) breaks some eggs and prepares them sunny-side up, while his Rothola crayon outfits play with the children's toy for making art, and his scribbles and pencil shaving skirt and jacket provide the means for artistic delineation. His 1990-91 wrought-iron (or, as he says, "Roth-iron") fence dress (also a jacket and jumpsuit) is partly indebted to the artist Jim Dine, while the dollar bill dress, which wraps the body in oversized bills, owes more than a buck to Andy Warhol. His spring-summer 1991 collection included a suite of brilliantly colored dresses inspired by Matisse's *découpages*.

Admitting such debts does not diminish Roth's luster and originality, however, for each artistic enterprise is different, and Roth has scrupulously chosen to take from art only that which he accommodates to the construction of clothing. His inlaid panels, sometimes compared to the finest marquetry, are a skilled fabrication in the pattern of the garment. While some fashion designers have sought to poach on art's prestige and to steal some aesthetic thunder, Roth has committed only the most discriminating, transmogrifying larceny, flattering both art and fashion. In fact, his concern in integrating the scribbles into the form of the garment is more integral to his medium than the cartoon appropriations of Pop Art. When he brings Matisse's cutouts to dressmaking, he does so not as surface decoration, but as pattern pieces to create the three-dimensional shape of the garment.

Roth's small collections are likewise developed with the concentration and formal intensity of musical form. His fall 1992 collection studied menswear. The lyrical spring 1992 collections included cocktail dresses that set up a 1950s bar and became the drinks themselves as well as a black cotton sateen dress with a diamond ring homage to Marilyn Monroe. In fall-winter 1991, his principal studies were Amish quilts which Roth translated from the spiral concentricity of flat quilt patterns into the piecing of dresses and circle skirts. Combining some techniques of color blocks with the rich harmonies of American quilts, the collection emphasized Roth's handmade warmth and beauty. Accompanying the quilt patterns, Roth provided a congenial coterie of hoboes in a trickle-up theory of fashion, the hoboes' improvisations of patches becoming Roth's elegant and equally affable piecing for clients not accustomed to a trackside way of life.

Like Geoffrey Beene, whom he admires, Christian Francis Roth is an American designer of extravagant gift who has chosen the almost scholastic life of precious technician and exacting artist. With the unceasing patience and quest of an artist, Roth has achieved in measure and modesty what others cannot attain in magnitude.—RICHARD MARTIN

Rowley, Cynthia
American designer

Born *Barrington, Illinois, 29 July 1958.*
Education *Studied art at Arizona State University, graduated from the Art Institute of Chicago, 1981.*
Family *Married Tom Sullivan, 1988 (died, 1994).*
Career *Senior at the Art Institute when she sold an 18-piece collection to Marshall Fields. Moved to New York, 1983, business incorporated, 1988. Designed costumes for dance troupes and films (including Three of Hearts and Dream Lover). Produces shoes, ready-to-*

wear, sportswear, dresses. Introduced line of girl's dresses, 1991. Taught at Parsons School of Design, New York, 1992-93; critic at Fashion Institute of Technology, New York City, 1992-94, and at Marist College, New York, 1994.

Exhibitions   *Objects of their Appreciation, Interart Center, New York City, 1993; Linen exhibition, Fashion Institute of Technology, New York, 1993; Dupont/Lycra exhibition, Fashion Institute of Technology, New York 1994.*

Collections   *Metropolitan Museum of Art Fashion Video Library, New York; Fashion Institute of Technology Permanent Collection, New York; Fashion Resource Center, Chicago Art Institute.*

Awards   *New York Finalist, "Entrepreneur of the Year," Forbes magazine, 1994.*

Address   *550 Seventh Avenue, 19th Floor, New York, New York, USA.*

The underlying thing about my clothing is that I always think about a woman's shape. Sometimes it's a basic shape that everyone understands, but I try to make it a bit more fun. I definitely have a sense of whimsy with everything. I like clothes that are very feminine, but with an added twist. I also think that a

Cynthia Rowley.

woman shouldn't have to spend a lot for great clothes. Maybe it's my Midwestern practicality coming through, but I feel there's always a need for great dresses at good prices.

For me, inspiration is very personal. A lot of what I design is inspired by where I grew up. I often do a play on the classics: tiny crop twin sets, mixed-match plaids, and polo dresses. Like everyone growing up in the suburbs, television was my link to fashion coolness—it's where I got my first sense of glamour. My clothing reflects these classics but with wit and originality.—Cynthia Rowley

Cynthia Rowley does not think that clothes should be taken too seriously; nor does she believe that style and individuality must necessarily go hand in hand with a high price tag. Rowley is known for a line of dresses which are charming, easily affordable, and utterly distinctive. This winning combination has enabled her sales to double twice within the past three years, while some of her better known colleagues have had to retrench.

Rowley's clothes reflect her well-developed sense of play. Drawing on shared and familiar elements of popular American culture, she elevates the mundane, rethinking and transforming the cliché to produce garments which arrest and amuse. Yet she is careful not to push a joke too far. These are clothes with a sense of humor for daily use, not novelty items to be quickly discarded.

For fall 1992, Rowley showed a long, snap fronted sleeveless dress of quilted rayon and acetate satin worn over a matching ribbed cotton turtleneck. The reference to the classic hunter's vest was simultaneously reinforced and subverted by a six-pack of Budweiser slung low on the model's hip.

To commemorate the 100th anniversary of the bottle cap, Rowley scattered them across the front of a sleeveless cotton sweater, one half of a twin set with an eye catching twist. Her spring 1993 collection included sundresses of classic red and white tablecloth checks, supported by straps made from plastic fruits and vegetables. "I definitely like to have a little sense of whimsy with everything," she said in a 1992 interview with the *Chicago Sun-Times*.

Rowley's more traditional dresses also incorporate styling elements not often seen at her end of the market. A halter dress becomes suitable for the office when cut from classic pinstripes and paired with a white shirt. She understands that the basics need not bore and that an imaginative dialogue between cut and fabric can produce distinctive clothing in any price range.—WHITNEY BLAUSEN

Rykiel, Sonia

French designer

Born   *Sonia Flis in Paris, 25 May 1930.*

Education   *Attended high school in Neuilly sur Seine.*

Family   *Married Sam Rykiel in 1953; children: Nathalie and Jean-Philippe.*

Career   *Free-lance designer for Laura boutique, Paris, 1962; first Paris boutique opened, 1968; household linens boutique opened, Paris, 1975; Sonia Rykiel Enfant boutique opened, Paris, 1987; cosmetics line introduced in Japan, 1987; Rykiel Homme boutique opened, Paris, 1989; Inscription Rykiel collection, designed by Nathalie Rykiel, intro-*

Sonia Rykiel: Spring/Summer 1994. *Photograph by Graziano Ferrari.*

duced, 1989; new flagship boutique opened, Paris, 1990; menswear collection, Rykiel Homme introduced, 1990; second Inscription Rykiel boutique opened, Paris, 1990; Rykiel Homme boutique opened, Paris, 1992; footwear collection launched, 1992; Sonia Rykiel fragrance introduced 1993. Also columnist for Femme from 1983.

Exhibitions   Sonia Rykiel, 20 Ans de Mode (retrospective), Galeries Lafayette, Paris, and Seibo Shibuya department store, Tokyo, 1987; retrospective, the Orangerie, Palais du Luxembourg, 1993.

Awards   French Ministry of Culture Croix des Arts et des Lettres, 1983; named Chevalier de la Légion d'Honneur, 1985; Fashion Oscar, Paris, 1985; Officier de l'Ordre de Arts et des Lettres, 1993.

Address   175 boulevard Saint Germain, 75006 Paris, France.

First I destroyed, undid what I had made. I wasn't satisfied with it. It wasn't me. It didn't relate to me. It was fashion, but it wasn't my fashion. I wanted to abolish the laws, the rules. I wanted to undo, overflow, exceed fashion. I wanted to unfold, unwind it. I wanted a lifestyle appropriate to the woman I was . . . this woman-symphony who was living the life of a woman mingled with the life of a worker.

I wanted airplane-style, travel-style, luggage-style. I saw myself as a woman on the go, surrounded by bags and children . . . so I imagined "kangaroo-clothes," stackable, collapsible, movable, with no right side, no wrong side, and no hem. Clothes to be worn in the daytime that I could refine at night. I put "fashion" aside to create "non-fashion."—Sonia Rykiel

The French ready-to-wear designer Sonia Rykiel is a compelling presence whose intellect and individuality are apparent in her clothes. With her small bones and trademark mane of hair, she is probably her own best model, projecting assurance and energy. She began designing with no previous experience when, as the pregnant wife of the owner of *Laura*, a fashionable boutique, she was unable to find maternity clothes she liked. Continuing to design knitwear for *Laura*, she soon carved a niche for herself designing for well-to-do and sophisticated modern French women.

By 1964, she had been nicknamed "The Queen of Knitwear" in the United States, where an ardent following developed for her knits, which were sold in trend-setting stores like Henri Bendel and Bloomingdale's in New York. For those women who were rich and thin enough to wear them, these skinny sweaters, with their high armholes, imparted instant chic. Part of their appeal lay in their distinctive colors and striped patterns. Black, navy, gray, and beige are still standards, but there was also a unique Rykiel palette of muted tones; for example, stripes of grayed seafoam green and grayed teal. Although she herself does not wear red (she wears black, considering it a uniform), Rykiel still uses it consistently, with the shade changing from season to season.

Today, Sonia Rykiel continues to design a complete range of clothes and accessories for women, drawn from her experience and her fantasies, which she encourages women to appropriate and adapt whilst inventing and re-inventing themselves. In addition to knits and jerseys, she uses crêpe for soft clothes, and woven tweeds and plaids for a more structured day look. Evening fantasies are best expressed in lightweight black luxury fabrics, often combined with sequins, metallic thread, embroidery, or elaborate combinations incorporating velvet.

Physical fitness is implicit in Sonia Rykiel's idea of modern femininity, so it is no surprise that the innermost layers of the knitted or jersey separates at the heart of her collections continue to be body conscious, if not figure hugging. They range in style from skimpy, narrow-shouldered pullovers with recognizable Rykiel detailing, to drop-shouldered tunics, to cardigans both short and boxy, and long and flowing. The detailing itself can be as soft as ruffles and bows, or as hard as nail heads. Although certain themes like cropped wide-leg trousers recur, the skirts and trousers that accompany the sweaters sometimes reflect the fashion of the moment, as in the short skirt worn with a classic Rykiel sweater which was featured by the *New York Times Magazine* in Patricia McColl's Spring 1988 Fashion Preview, subtitled "The Byword Is Short." The sweater is a fine example of another important facet of her work: the dress, sweater, or accessory as bulletin board. As befits the author of four books, Sonia Rykiel began in the 1970s to incorporate words into her art. Across the stomach of a slinky 1977 dress is emblazoned the word "MODE." The next year saw the fronts or backs of sweaters variously inscribed "2," "TOI," "MOI" and "NU," "FÊTE," and "PLAISIR," among others. Nor has English been slighted: "ARTIST," "READY," "TRADITIONS," "BLACK TIE," and "BLACK IS THE BEST" are among the many examples. Not even eveningwear is sacrosanct: a 1983 ensemble with a sheer black lace bodice and black crêpe sleeves and skirt is encircled with a rhinestone studded belt which reads "SPECIAL EDITION EVENING DREAMS." Nonetheless, the most frequent words to appear are "Sonia Rykiel," and simply "Rykiel."

Rykiel was an early exponent of deconstruction. Made of the finest quality wool yarns, sometimes mixed with angora, her knits are frequently designed with reverse seams. She also innovated the use of lockstitched hems. Since the early 1980s Sonia Rykiel has also produced at least two casual lines a year in cotton velours, a fluid, sensual fabric well suited to uncluttered silhouettes. Each season there is at least one dress, in addition to trousers, pullovers, cardigans, and jackets, many of which have reverse seams. They are offered in several solid colors, in stripes and, occasionally, in prints. Like other clothes of illusory simplicity, they have often been unsuccessfully copied.

Another Rykiel specialty is outerwear. Her coats, whether in fine woolens, or in highly coveted fake fur, tend to be voluminous. Along with these and her accessories line, other Rykiel enterprises include children's and menswear lines and perfumes. The entire Rykiel design output is available in the lifestyle boutique on Boulevard Saint Germain which opened in 1990. Sonia Rykiel is a worthy successor to the Chanel tradition: a strong, ultra-feminine, articulate intellectual with a flair for simplicity and self-promotion, who has shown herself capable of both refined innovation and commercial success.—ARLENE C. COOPER

Saint Laurent, Yves

French designer

Born *Yves Henri Donat Mathieu Saint Laurent in Oran, Algeria, 1 August 1936.*

Education *Studied at L'École de la Chambre Syndicale de la Couture, 1954.*

Career *Independent clothing stylist, Paris, 1953-54; designer and partner, 1954-57, chief designer, Dior, Paris, 1957-60; founder, designer, Yves Saint Laurent, Paris, from 1962; Rive Gauche ready-to-wear line introduced, 1966; menswear line introduced, 1974; fragrances: Y (1965), Rive Gauche, Opium, Paris; firm purchased by Elf-Sanofi SA, 1993. Also film and theatre designer from 1959.*

Exhibitions *Yves Saint Laurent, Metropolitan Museum of Art, 1983; Yves Saint Laurent et le Théâtre, Musée des Arts de la Mode, Paris, 1986; Yves Saint Laurent, 28 Ans de Création, Musée des Arts de la Mode, 1986; retrospective, Art Gallery of New South Wales, Sydney, Australia, 1987.*

Awards *International Wool Secretariat Award, 1954; Neiman Marcus Award, 1958; Harper's Bazaar Award, 1966; Council of Fashion Designers of America Award, 1981.*

Address *5 avenue Marceau, 75116 Paris, France.*

A great adaptor, Yves Saint Laurent responds in his designs to history, art, and literature. Vast ranges of themes are incorporated into his work, from the Ballet Russes to the writings of Marcel Proust, who inspired his taffeta gowns of 1971; the paintings of Picasso to the minimalist work of Mondrian and the de Stijl movement, shown in the primary colours of his geometrically blocked wool jersey dresses of 1965.

Saint Laurent has a great love of the theatre. He has designed costumes for many stage productions during his long career and the theatre is an important source of ideas for his couture collections. Flamboyant ensembles, such as the Shakespeare wedding dress of brocade and damask of 1980 and his extravagant series of garments inspired by a romantic vision of Russian dress, reflect his passion for theatrical costume.

Less successful have been his attempts to engage with counter-cultural movements such as the 1960 collection based on the bohemian Left Bank look. The criticism levelled by the press on being confronted with the avant garde on the couture catwalk led to Saint Laurent's replacement as head designer for Dior, even though his 1958 trapeze line had been an enormous success and he had been fêted as the saviour of Parisian couture. At this time the House of Dior was responsible for nearly 50 per cent of France's fashion exports, so there was a heavy burden of financial responsibility on Saint Laurent's shoulders.

The 1960 collection appropriated the Left Bank style with knitted turtlenecks and black leather jackets, crocodile jackets with mink collars, and—a design which was to crop up again and again in his repertoire—the fur jacket with knitted sleeves. In 1968 Saint Laurent produced a tailored trouser collection reflecting his sympathy with the cause of the student marchers who had brought the streets of Paris to a standstill. The clothes were black and accessorized with headbands and Indian fringes. The use of politics as a decorative device hung uneasily on garments such as the fur duffle coat with gold toggles, giving the designs a paradoxical quality that was later expressed in such collections as the Rich Fantasy Peasant of 1976, which helped in internationalizing a sanitized ethnic look.

Where Saint Laurent sets the standards for world fashion is in his feminizing of the basic shapes of the male wardrobe. Like Chanel before him, he responded to the subtleties of masculine tailoring, seeking to provide a similar sort of style for women, and produced a whole series of elegant day clothes, such as the shirt dress, which became a staple of the sophisticated woman's wardrobe of the 1970s. Saint Laurent is justly acclaimed for his sharply tailored suits with skirts or trousers, *le smoking* (a simple black suit with satin lapels based on the male tuxedo, which became an alternative to the frothily feminine evening gown), safari jackets, brass buttoned pea jackets, flying suits—in fact many of the chic classics of post-war women's style.

Saint Laurent's designs contain no rigid shaping or over-elaborate cutting but depend on a perfection of line and a masterful understanding of printed textiles and the use of luxurious materials. He works with the silk printers Abraham to produce glowing fabric designs which incorporate a brilliant palette of clashing colours such as hot pink, violet, and sapphire blue. A sharp contrast is produced with his simple, practical daywear and romantic, exotic eveningwear, which is more obviously seductive with its extensive beadwork, embroidery, satin, and sheer fabrics such as silk chiffon.

Less interested in fashion than in style, Saint Laurent is a classicist, designing elegant, tasteful, and sophisticated dress, perfectly hand-crafted in the manner of the old couturiers. He is, however, prepared to use industrial methods to produce his Rive Gauche ready-to-wear line, created in 1966, and sold in his own franchised chain of boutiques. He acknowledges in ready-to-wear that mechanically produced garments could never achieve the same standards of fit and tailoring so must be designed differently—a realistic approach which accounts for the success of the range.

There has been a radical change in the small company founded by Yves Saint Laurent and his business partner Pierre Bergé in 1961. It has become a massive financial conglomerate with a stock market listing on the Paris Bourse, the result of valuable licensing deals Yves Saint Laurent has negotiated to allow his signature to grace such items as designer perfume. His is a name that has become a symbol of classic design.—CAROLINE COX

Sanchez, Fernando

Spanish designer working in New York

Born *Spain, 1934.*

Education *Studied fashion, École de la Chambre Syndicale de la Couture Parisienne, 1951-53.*

Career *Assistant designer, Maggy Rouff, Paris, 1953-56; designer, Hirsh of Brussels, c.1956-58; designer for Dior boutiques, and Dior lingerie and knitwear licensees, Paris, Germany, Denmark and the United States, 1960s; designer, Revillon, New York and Paris, 1961-73 and 1984-85; established own lingerie firm, New York, 1973; introduced ready-to-wear line, 1980; also designer for Vanity Fair, from 1984.*

Awards *Winner, International Wool Secretariat Competition, 1954; Coty American Fashion Critics Award, 1975, 1981; Coty Special Award for Lingerie, 1974, 1977; Council of Fashion Designers of America Award, 1981.*

Address *5 West 19th Street, New York, New York 10011, USA.*

Born of a Spanish father and a Flemish mother, Sanchez began his career in high fashion ready-to-wear in Paris after studying at the École de la Chambre Syndicale de la Couture. He started out at the house of Dior, where he produced knitwear, lingerie, and accessories for the prestigious company's chain of boutiques. From there he moved to design assistant at Yves Saint Laurent before starting up his own company in 1974, after a period of working in both New York and Paris. With a name already established for extravagant and exotic fur designs for Revillon, he rapidly built on his reputation through the creation of elegant, easy separates with an ambiguous functionality—they had no obvious place in the formal etiquette of dress. Such clothes as his soft, fluid camisoles with matching pyjama trousers and wrapped jackets or overshirts could be worn just as easily to bed as to dinner at an upmarket restaurant. He was quickly assimilated into the circle of New York fashion designers, which at the time included Halston, Calvin Klein, and Mary McFadden.

Sanchez's experimentation with separates dressing struck a chord amongst affluent American women in the 1970s and seemed to fit the notion of independent femininity which had filtered into fashion imagery and marketing. The ideal of self-reliant womanhood was superficially acknowledged in the whole concept of separates—the idea of putting together garments in one's own individual way, rather than being dictated into sporting a designer look from head to toe. However, Sanchez's separates, like those of other American designers, were always created with an organic whole in mind.

In the 1980s Sanchez was recognized for his use of lace appliqué which appeared extensively on his nightwear, and the fan motif became his trademark as was the bold use of synthetics and vibrant colour. His more contemporary forays into the high fashion ready-to-wear market follow the same lines as his original, understated and elegant look with its basis in the language of lingerie, for which he received a Coty Special Award in 1974 and 1977. The whole concept of underwear as outerwear, so current since the mid-1980s, seems especially suited to Sanchez who has been experimenting within precisely those parameters since the early 1970s, although in a less obvious fashion than Jean-Paul Gaultier or Dolce e Gabbana. His latest designs are sleek, flirty slip dresses for the same sort of fashionably wealthy woman who, like her counterpart in the 1970s, does not want to stand out from the crowd.—CAROLINE COX

Sander, Jil

German designer

Born *Heidemarie Jiline Sander in Wesselburen, Germany, 1943.*

Education *Graduated from Krefeld School of Textiles, near Düsseldorf, 1963; foreign exchange student, University of Los Angeles, 1963-64.*

Career *Fashion journalist, McCall's, Los Angeles, and for Constanze and Petra magazines, Hamburg (Director of Promotions for the latter), 1964-68; free-lance clothing designer, 1968-73; opened first Jil Sander boutique, Hamburg, 1968; founded Jil Sander Moden, Hamburg, 1969; showed first women's collection, 1973; founded Jil Sander GmbH, 1978; introduced fragrance and cosmetics line, 1979; Jil Sander furs introduced, 1982; leather and eyewear collections introduced, 1984; Jil Sander GmbH converted to public corporation, Jil Sander AG, 1989; opened Paris boutique, 1993; showed first menswear collection, 1993. Perfumes include Woman Pure, Woman II, Woman III, Man Pure, Man II, Man III, and Man IV.*

Awards *Fil d'Or Award, 1980, 1981, 1982, 1983, 1984, 1985; City of Munich Fashion Award, 1983; Vif-Journal Silberne Eule, 1983; Fédération Française du Prêt à Porter Feminin Award, 1985; Aguja de Oro Award, Madrid, 1986; Forum Preis, 1989.*

Address *Osterfeldstrasse 32-34, 2000 Hamburg 54, Germany.*

Jil Sander has often been described as the Queen of German fashion, but her style and ambitions are international. Her company headquarters are in the north German city of Hamburg, but her clothes are manufactured in Milan, were she showed for almost a decade before changing her venue to Paris. A self-made success story, Sander designs for independent, intelligent women around the world. She produces fragrances for both men and women, and since 1993, she has also produced a men's line.

Sander has a strong, modern sensibility, and her style may be described as luxurious minimalism, on the edge of forward. There are no frills or fads in Sander's world. Everything irrelevant is eliminated. Like Giorgio Armani, she is one of the fashion world's most austere purists, a creator of designs that are so clean they seem stripped down to the bone. Yet it is not entirely accurate to describe her clothes as classic, because this would imply that they are static, and Sander has never repeated a best-selling design from the previous season's collection.

"I find 'timeless' classic terribly boring," Sander told German *Vogue* (January 1990). "A classic is an excuse, because one is too lazy to confront the spirit of the time." Her own style of classicism always has a modern edge, and the woman who wears Sander's clothes "knows perfectly well what is 'in' this season, and has consciously reduced [it] to suit herself." Sander loves fashion and change, and believes that other women feel the same way. "We don't buy a new coat because we are cold. We buy things that animate, that give us a good feeling."

Sander is one of the most important women designers working in the world today, and she believes that there are definitely differences between the male and female design sensibilities.

Male designers, Sander told *Mirabella* (June 1991), tend to "see things more decoratively—more from the outside. I want to know how I feel in my clothes." She tries on all the clothes in her women's collection herself, to ensure that they look and feel exactly right. They have the high quality of the best menswear; they are beautifully tailored, and made from menswear-derived fabrics, often her own luxury fiber blends, such as wool-silk or linen-silk. Yet her palette tends towards pale neutrals, which read as both strong and feminine.

Sander's combination of masculine and feminine design elements results in clothes that feel comfortable and look powerful, but are also sexy in a subtle way. Her version of understated chic is not cheap, however. "If you want quality, it costs," she bluntly told *Mirabella*'s journalist. (Her women's suits range from $1,500 to $6,500.) Think more and buy less, she advised. "People have already consumed too much." But, as journalist Melissa Drier observed, Sander's clothes give women the same confidence that a hand-tailored suit gives a man.

The words "strong" and "powerful" occur frequently in Sander's conversation, revealing something of her own personality, as well as her design aesthetic and her ideal customer. "A powerful women, a woman who knows who she is—I would say that is more interesting than a doll with the most beautiful nose in the world," she told *Marie Claire* (August 1991). Meanwhile, as if to complement the strong modern woman, Sander has called her men's fragrance *Feeling Man*.

Sander has no sympathy for the old-fashioned concept of woman as sex kitten or status symbol. "It is possible to have a very sexy feeling without looking like a sex kitten," she told *W* (30 September-7 October 1991). A woman wearing an austere, brown wool trouser-suit can look and feel sexy, she believes. The typical *alta-moda* woman might not be happy in Sander's clothes, but many women today do want clothes that express a liberated sensibility and a modern sensuality.

What is important, Sander emphasizes, is that fashion should underline the wearer's personality. Her own best model, Sander often appears in her advertisements, looking like what she is: an attractive and intelligent adult.—VALERIE STEELE

Scaasi, Arnold

American designer

> **Born** *Arnold Isaacs in Montreal, 8 May 1931.*
>
> **Education** *Studied fashion design at École Cotnoir Capponi, Montreal, 1953, and at the École de la Chambre Syndicale de la Haute Couture Parisienne, 1954-55; apprenticed one year with Paquin.*
>
> **Career** *Moved to New York and worked with Charles James, 1951-53; free-lance designer in New York working for Dressmaker Casuals and Lilly Daché, 1955-57; opened own business, 1957; president and designer, Arnold Scaasi, Inc., from 1962; designer, Scaasi couture collections, from 1962; designer, ready-to-wear collections, 1962-63, 1969, and from 1984. Signature fragrance introduced, 1989.*
>
> **Exhibitions** *Retrospective, 1975, New York State Theater, Lincoln Center, New York.*

Arnold Scaasi.

Awards *Coty American Fashion Critics Award, 1958; Neiman Marcus Award, 1959; Council of Fashion Designers of America Award, 1987; Pratt Institute Design Award, 1989; Dallas International Apparel Fashion Excellence Award, 1992.*
Address *681 Fifth Ave., New York, New York 10022-4209, USA.*

Clothes should be worn to make one feel good, to flatter and as a statement of personality. The overall effect should always be a well-groomed look, not sloppy. Even if someone is not a great beauty or has some bad features, one should always try to look the best one can—at all times. This is not a matter of self-indulgence. When you know you look your best, you face the day and the world with great self-assurance. It's most important that one chooses clothes that work for their lifestyle, both financially and psychologically. Obviously, do not choose a dance dress if you don't go to dances but choose the best fitting trousers if they work into your lifestyle.

I try to design clothes that will flatter the female form. I create clothes that are pretty, usually with an interesting mix of fabrics. I like luxurious fabrics, great quality for day, opulence for evening dresses. I AM DEFINITELY NOT A MINIMALIST DESIGNER! Clothes with some adornment are more interesting to look at and more fun to wear.

I believe that clothes should touch and define the body at least in one spot. Most of my clothes have a defined waist and hipline, with some movement below the hip. Bustlines are always defined and I prefer, and am known for low decolletage—either off-the-shoulder, strapless or simply scooped-out necklines. Sweetheart necklines are also flattering and I use them constantly.

Throughout my career I have dressed many celebrities—Barbra Streisand, Claudette Colbert, Elizabeth Taylor, Dame Margot Fonteyn, Mary Tyler Moore, Joan Sutherland, Aretha Franklin, and Barbara Bush to name a few. I believe it is more graceful to wear a long evening dress for "public" appearances than a short one, especially on stage. Evening pajamas are sometimes interesting and accomplish the same graceful movement.

I prefer using color to black and white though sometimes black and/or white are most dramatic. Shades of red, pink, turquoise, violet and sapphire blue can be more flattering and exciting to look at.

At one point in my career I used an enormous amount of printed fabrics and found them wonderful to work with. However, in recent seasons my eye has changed and the prints seemed to have faded from fashion. Before long, the print craze will probably return as women—and designers—get bored with solid fabrics. In place of prints we are using more embroideries to give texture and life to the fabrics.

Lastly, clothes should be fun with a dash of fantasy. Scaasi creations are the champagne and caviar of the fashion world, as a very prominent Queen once said, "Let them eat cake!" I do hope I won't have my head chopped off for these thoughts!—Arnold Scaasi

As a young apprentice to Charles James during the early 1950s, Scaasi was imprinted by James's concentration on "building" an evening dress as a sculpture. This early training led Scaasi to construct dresses in the round and to approach design as three-dimensional form. The influence of Charles James has been a life-long inspiration for Scaasi. Another stimulus for Scaasi was the richness of the fabrics and furs used during the 1950s, when the prerequisite for women was to be perfectly dressed from head to toe.

Scaasi began rethink his objectives after juggling a career during the late 1950s and early 1960s that included menswear, children's wear, and costume jewelry, in addition to ladies' ready-to-wear and custom designs. He decided to focus strategically on couture dressmaking at a time when Paris couture was beginning to suffer. It was 1964 when Scaasi debuted his collection of eveningwear. He was able to take the freedom of the youth-obsessed 1960s and channel the energy into designs that featured keen attention to details and the workmanship of couture dressing.

Scaasi emphasized sequins, fringe, and feathers as trims, substituting new fabrics to create an ostentatious signature style that included mini dresses, trouser suits, and the use of transparency. Barbra Streisand wore a memorable Scaasi creation to the 1969 Academy Awards. His customers are often the celebrated rich and famous—Elizabeth Taylor, Ivana Trump, Blaine Trump, Joan Rivers, Barbara Walters, and many other glamorous clients favor Scaasi.

During the 1970s, styles changed to a more body-conscious, pared-down way of dressing. Scaasi, true to form, turned to dressing women who still loved to be noticed, such as the artist Louise Nevelson. It made sense to Scaasi to continue to create what he was known for and what he loved to do. The basis of his work is a combination of cut, color sensibility, and fabric selections that recall a past elegance yet speak to his clients' most current desires.

The 1980s, the Reagan era, ushered in a renaissance of upscale dressing which was perfect for the Scaasi touch. He dressed First Lady Barbara Bush for the Inaugural Ball and designed her wardrobe for the week of festivities. Never one to concern himself with everyday dressing, Scaasi dresses the urban woman who attends parties, galas, charity balls, and elaborate dinners. His customer is of a certain affluence and has a personality that enables her to wear a Scaasi creation. Often described as lavish, sumptuous, and magical, Scaasi's evening gowns are worn for making a sensational entrance.—MYRA WALKER

Scherrer, Jean-Louis

French designer

Born *Paris c. 1936.*

Education *Studied ballet, Conservatoire de Danse Classique, Paris, and fashion, Chambre Syndicale de la Couture Parisienne.*

Career *Assistant at Christian Dior, 1955-57, and to Saint Laurent at Dior after Dior's death, 1957-59. Left to design for Louis Féraud, 1959-61. Founded Jean Louis Scherrer label, 1962 (left company in 1992); ready-to-wear collection and Scherrer Boutique ready-to-wear lines introduced, 1971; signature fragrance, 1979; Scherrer 2 perfume, 1986; bath line, 1981; diffusion line, Scherrer City, 1992.*

Awards *Dé d'Or Award, Paris, 1980.*

Address *51 avenue Montaigne, 75008 Paris, France.*

His early training as a dancer exposed Jean-Louis Scherrer to theatrical costumes and prepared him to later design clothes that would suit the public roles of women connected with politics, theatre, and the arts, as well as the more private roles lived by the wives of wealthy Arabs, whose patronage accounted for 30 per cent of the income of the House of Scherrer.

From an early apprenticeship with Christian Dior in Paris, Scherrer learned the basics of cutting and draping, alongside young Yves Saint Laurent. When Saint Laurent inherited the house of Dior, Scherrer successfully started his own haute couture establishment during a period when critics foretold the demise of traditional couture. He quickly became known for designs described as classic, restrained, sophisticated, and sexy but not vulgar. His customers read like a roster of the world's wealthiest women: Mme Anne-Aymone Giscard d'Estaing, wife of the then President of France, as well as his daughter, Valerie-Anne Montassier; Baronness Thyssen; Olympia and Nadine de Rothschild; Queen Noor, the wife of the King of Jordan; Patricia Kennedy Lawford; Isabelle d'Ornano; Ann Getty; Nan Kempner; Françoise Sagan; Michèle Morgan; Raquel Welch; and Sophia Loren.

In the mid-1970s over a hundred American stores, including Bergdorf Goodman in New York, carried Scherrer. Chiffon evening dresses, often accented with sequinned embroideries, have long been a staple. De luxe ready-to-wear was often in the Scherrer Boutique line. These were simpler clothes, more moderately priced than the thousands of dollars of the couture, but still expensive-looking. One such boutique outfit, modeled by Scherrer's daughter Laetitia, featured a leopard print shaped blazer jacket with matching leopard *cloche* hat, worn with a slim black leather skirt.

Scherrer was not a maker of trends, but of refined de luxe versions of trends. When everyone was showing tiered flounced skirts during the 1980s, Scherrer made a restrained version that just grazed the knee and was topped by a long-sleeved, shirt-collared bodice, in luxurious silk. A prime example of Scherrer's hallmark "exotically pampered appearance" was a lavishly embroidered coat in mink-bordered beige cashmere, hooded, reminiscent of Anna Karenina and following in the footsteps of Saint Laurent's revolutionary Russian-inspired looks of the late 1970s. In fact, Scherrer often borrowed exotic details from the East. Chinoiserie and Mongolian-inspired coats and jackets frequently appeared in his collections. At the apex of 1980s opulence in couture, Scherrer indulged in pearl-decorated rajah jackets, tunics, and trousers. In a spirit of Arabian Nights fantasy much like Paul Poiret's, jeweled and feathered turbans completed the ensembles. Other evening looks included beaded taffeta ballgowns or paisley patterned lamé dresses topped with jewel-embroidered jackets. The old-fashioned grand couture hand-worked and hand-embroidered traditions were preserved. Beading was by Lesage.

Even day clothes featured opulent touches: velvet appliqués on wool, or gold piping on trenchcoats. Chiffon and silk were used for dresses and skirts; leathers and furs decorated coats. While hemlines rose during the remainder of the decade, Scherrer continued to show calf-length skirts. For him, surface texture and sumptuous workmanship were more important than innovative lines. The longer, covered-up fashions satisfied his customers' modesty requirements, dictated by Islamic law, while also proclaiming their wealth and status.

Into the 1990s Scherrer continued to employ luxury materials and to explore a variety of trends: long, short, bright colors (a departure from conservative beiges, grays, and white), patchwork prints, plaids, jumpsuits, feminine versions of men's suits and hunting attire. The Scherrer boutique continued to offer sleek, toned down versions of the high fashion items in over a hundred markets in 25 countries. In Europe and Japan men's and women's Jean-Louis

Scherrer accessories could be obtained. A bestselling signature perfume launched in 1979 was followed by a spicy floral haute couture perfume, *Scherrer 2*, in 1986.

Despite financial difficulties that resulted in the 1992 firing of Scherrer from the firm he founded, Jean-Louis Scherrer SA plans a menswear collection, Jean-Louis Scherrer Monsieur, for spring/summer, consistent with the designer's high quality image.—THERESE DUZINKIEWICZ BAKER

Schön, Mila

Yugoslavian designer working in Italy

Born *Maria Carmen Nutrizio Schön in Trau, Dalmatia, Yugoslavia, 1919. Raised in Trieste and Milan, Italy.*

Career *Opened atelier, Milan, 1958; first showed own custom designs, 1965; first boutique for womenswear opened, at No. 2, via Montenapoleone, Milan, 1966; launched Linea Uomo line of menswear, alongside opening of new boutique, Mila Schön Uomo, at No. 6, via Montenapoleone, 1972; Mila Schön 2, second company, set up in 1973 to produce and distribute Alta Moda Pronta, Miss Schön, and Mila Schön Uomo lines; launched perfume, Mila Schön, 1978; established Mila Schön Japan, company for distribution of products in Japan; took over running of company in Como, Italy, for the manufacture and distribution of textiles for all Mila Schön lines, 1983; Aqua Schön swimwear collection introduced, 1984; opened first U.S. shop, Beverly Hills, 1986. Also produced shoes, stockings, furnishings, eyewear. Long-standing collaboration with Mantuan goldsmith Loris Abate, who designed jewellery and buttons for Mila Schön collections from 1959; Moved to Florence.*

Address *Via Montenapoleone, Milan.*

Mila Schön's interest in high fashion began when she became a personal client of Balenciaga. Her family were wealthy Yugoslav aristocrats who had fled to Italy to escape the communist regime. Living the life of a wealthy Italian demanded an elegant wardrobe and Schön's natural grace and good taste made her an excellent couture client. She must have studied the business thoroughly during her fittings because, when the family fortunes were lost, she turned to the fashion industry in order to make a living.

Business began in 1959 when Schön was 35, with a small atelier in Milan, where Parisian models were basically adapted and copied, combining Balenciaga's austerity of cut with Dior's versatility, plus a hint of Schiaparelli's wit. By the mid-1960s Schön was showing more original work at trade fairs in Florence and Rome, establishing a reputation as a perfectionist who worked within the constraints of a classic design structure. Her tailoring is particularly distinctive, executed with faultless attention to detail and cut in her favourite double-faced wools. The resultant clothes were and are highly sophisticated and sold at the top end of ready-to-wear or in the Mila Schön boutiques in Rome, Florence, and Milan. Small wonder that clients have included wealthy socialites like Jacqueline Kennedy Onassis, her sister Lee Radziwill Ross, and Babe Paley.

Mila Schön describes her company slogan as being "Not how much, but how." This is reflective of her attitude towards high quality and taste. The company decided to translate the

Mila Schön: Fall/Winter 1994/95.

DOC (controlled origin denomination), a quality mark used in the wine business, for use on their clothes, denoting the company's attitude towards perfection. Mila Schön is also very selective when it comes to choosing clients in order to retain quality. She trades on what she describes as a "medium circulation basis," so that when any side of her business is seen to make a marked profit, therefore operating beyond its limits, she starts a new company to accommodate it.

There have been several diffusion lines and licensees since the company's inception. In line with the Mila Schön business philosophy, all these products are marketed and sold through separately formed companies. Mila Schön Due is a less expensive ready-to-wear line; Mila Schön Uomo is the men's range. There is also a swimwear range, Aqua Schön, and a sunglasses range, Schön Ottica. Ties, scarves, fabrics, handbags, belts, and the perfume *Mila Schön*, are also produced.

Mila Schön is one of the most respected and established names in Italian fashion. She represents faultless design standards that are classic, flattering, and sometimes highly imaginative, and she ranks alongside Genny, Fendi, and Valentino in clientèle and prestige.—KEVIN ALMOND

Shamask, Ronaldus

Dutch designer working in New York

Born *Amsterdam, 24 November 1945. Raised in Australia.*

Education *Trained as an architect, self-taught in fashion design.*

Career *Window display designer, Melbourne, Australia, 1963-66; fashion illustrator for The Times and The Observer, London, 1967-68; theatrical designer, Company of Man performance group, Buffalo, New York, 1968-71; free-lance interior and clothing designer, New York, 1971-77; designer, Moss Shamask fashion company, New York, 1978-90; opened Moss on Madison Avenue boutique, New York, 1979, closed, 1986; introduced first menswear collection, 1985; showed new collection under his own name, and formed new company, SUSA (Shamask USA), 1990.*

Exhibitions *Intimate Architecture: Contemporary Clothing Design, Massachusetts Institute of Technology, Cambridge, Mass., 1982; Infra-Apparel, Metropolitan Museum of Art, New York, 1993.*

Awards *American Fashion Critics Coty Award, 1981; Council of Fashion Designers of America Award, 1987; Confédération Internationale du Lin Fil d'Or Award, 1987, 1989; Woolmark Award, 1989.*

Address *c/o Revlon, 625 Madison Avenue, New York, New York 10022, USA.*

Peter Carlsen perceived Ronaldus Shamask's design in a most interesting and prophetic way. Carlsen claimed, "Shamask dresses an élite—the largely self-appointed élite comprising the devotees of high style. Certainly, his work is part of a way of life that is bound up with living in Manhattan; his clothes are meant to be worn in lofts, to downtown openings, are meant to signal to other members of what might be called the esthetic establishment their wearers' good standing in its ranks. . . . What Charles James was to 1940s New York, Shamask was to the late 1970s and early 1980s." (*Contemporary Designers*, Detroit 1984). Shamask creates intellectual/esthetic dress and therefore dresses, perhaps inescapably, intellectuals and esthetically minded individuals.

Recognized initially in a feature article by John Duka in the *New York Times Magazine* (16 August 1981) and subsequently in an exhibition, *Intimate Architecture: Contemporary Clothing Design* at the Massachusetts Institute of Technology in May-June 1982, Shamask was *wunderkind* of the architectural rubric. But people do not wear buildings. Nor is Shamask's design genuinely analogous to architecture. Rather, he is an immensely idiosyncratic and adventuresome designer with a sensibility for minimalism, a cant to the East, and a depth of conviction about fashion that often makes his work seem more utopian than commercially viable. And he denies the classification of architecture with every inventive fold and has enough folds and tucks to be a perfect master of origami creasing and gathering. He dispenses with the non-essential as a rigorous architect might, but he also enjoys the body as only the most Vitruvian builder would; and he mingles international traditions and possibilities with the inventiveness of a Lafcadio Hearn.

Shamask seeks a purity in fashion that others would not even warrant: his pursuit can seem too severe to some and austerely perfect to others. Anne-Marie Schiro wrote (*New York Times,* 4 November 1988), "At a time when many American designers are sticking to the classics, Mr. Shamask went a different route, showing styles that most women do not already have in their closets. Of course, they are not clothes for most women but for those with a flair for fashion and a desire to look different." His design is deliberate, but its visual rewards can be equally deliberate as well.

His fall 1981 two-piece coat with a visible spiraling seam may be more sophisticated in construction than most wearers or viewers would wish to know, though others such as Balenciaga and Geoffrey Beene have similarly designed to the utmost chastity of form. His 1979 linen ensemble literally unbuttons pockets down their sides to become part of the fold of the garment. In such gestures, Shamask stands in synthesis of two traditions: reductivism and the complications of details that constitute many multi-layered, multivalent cultures of clothing. His Japanese-inspired *hakima* trousers were featured in the "Japonisme" exhibition of the Kyoto Costume Institute at the Kyoto National Museum in 1994; his sensibility is shaped by Japanese esthetics. Shamask participates in a rarefied international culture that recognizes fashion as an art and seeks its participation with dance, theater, architecture, and all visual arts. He creates fashion worthy of such a status.

In the 1990s, Shamask has devoted himself to menswear where his talent for the building of clothing has been shown to advantage. Ruth Gilbert in *New York Magazine* (24 February 1992) acclaimed his tailored clothing "perfect fits." Earlier, Shamask had told *Esquire* (September 1987) "men are less interested in applied decoration than in the logical engineering of clothes."

Even in menswear, it may always be that Shamask has ardent admirers and a circle of devoted wearers without having vast commercial impact. His may not be an easily likable esthetic, but it definitely is a high art of dress, one highly informed by intelligence.—RICHARD MARTIN

Simonetta

Italian designer

Born *Duchess Simonetta Colonna di Cesaro in Rome, 10 April 1922.*
Family *Married Count Galaezzo Visconti in 1944 (divorced); daughter: Verde; married Alberto Fabiani in 1953 (divorced); son: Bardo.*

Simonetta

Career *Design studio opened, Rome, 1946-62 and 1965; partner, designer, Simonetta et Fabiani, Paris, 1962-65; Incanto fragrance introduced, 1955; traveled in India, in the 1960s and 1970s, establishing a colony for the care of lepers and a craft training program, 1973-76.*

Address *8 via Cadore, 41012 Caroi (MO), Italy.*

Eugenia Sheppard (*New York Herald Tribune*, 14 November 1951) called Simonetta the "youngest, liveliest member of the up and coming Italian Couture," commending the breadth of her collection from a two-part playsuit with cummerbund and bloomer shorts to a silk shantung dress-suit with tiered collar to her short and long eveningwear. By 1951, with ardent advocacy from American *Vogue* and Bergdorf Goodman, Simonetta was one of the best-known names in America for the new Italian post-war fashion.

Simonetta had presented her first collection in Rome in 1946. An aristocrat, she had been interned by the Mussolini government for anti-Fascist activities; the further pluckiness of starting up her couture business so immediately after the war was a sign of Simonetta's dauntless determination. A press release for her 1946 collection read in part: "To understand how difficult it was to open a *maison de couture* and have a show with 14 models just after the liberation of Rome by the Allies, one must remember the general situation at that time. Materials and trimmings were very scarce. The most surprising and common materials had to be used to make the extraordinary collection—dish cloths, gardeners' aprons, butlers' uniforms, strings and ribbons, and everything that could be found on the market." It was a humble beginning for an aristocrat dreaming of a high style.

The glamour of a politically-correct aristocrat improvising an Italian post-war renaissance was of hypnotic charm to the American market. Moreover, Simonetta's youthful style held a special appeal, especially in buoyant silk cocktail dresses and her elegant débutante dresses and ball gowns of the 1950s, with their emphasis on the bust. Equally popular were the daywear, sportswear, and coats, with coats in particular providing a favored inspiration for Seventh Avenue copying. She could rival Balenciaga in coats and suits of robust materials, cut with precision and minimal detailing to draw attention to one salient feature. Like Balenciaga, she favored cape-like sleeve treatments that gave the coats a dramatic sense of volume, especially in photographs. Further, she shared with Balenciaga a preference for the seven-eighths sleeve in coats, allowing for the display of gloves and jewelry. For the American market, these popular attributes constituted an idea of ease and mobility, but they also lent themselves to facile imitation and copying. In 1962, when Simonetta and her husband Alberto Fabiani moved to Paris and established Simonetta et Fabiani, the enterprise was less successful.

Her distinguished international clientèle included Audrey Hepburn, Clare Booth Luce, Eleanor Lambert, Lauren Bacall, and Jacqueline Kennedy Onassis. As Aurora Fiorentini Capitani and Stefania Ricci observed in *The Sala Bianca*, "the collections by Simonetta were invariably met with success, in terms of the public and in terms of sales, because they translated the image of a naturally chic woman, with essential lines, elevated by one simple feature, a knot or a raised neck, and corresponded in every way to the personality of the Roman designer" (Milan 1992). Simonetta was often photographed in her clothing and served in some ways as her own best model. She lived the life Americans dreamed of as portrayed in such movies as *Roman Holiday*. If Simonetta was the ideal model for her clothing in the 1940s and 1950s, exemplifying practicality and young elegance, she later epitomized another cultural transformation as she forsook fashion to devote herself to philanthropy and spirituality, working with lepers in India in the 1970s and 1980s. In the 1990s, she returned to Rome, interested in reviewing and collecting her fashion work for a museum.

Simonetta's life seems to have been, more than most, culturally keyed. If it was in any way a destiny granted with privilege, it was also a destiny seized. Her fashion recognized the possibility of renewed elegance in post-war Italian and American life as well as the practicality of designing for distinctly modern women.—RICHARD MARTIN

Smith, Willi

American designer

Born *Willi Donnell Smith in Philadelphia, 29 February 1948.*

Education *Studied fashion illustration, Philadelphia Museum College of Art, 1962-65; studied fashion design, Parsons School of Design, New York, 1965-67.*

Career *Worked as fashion illustrator with designers Arnold Scaasi and Bobbi Brooks, New York, 1965-69; free-lance designer, working in New York, for Digits Inc., sportswear company, Talbott, Bobbie Brooks, 1967-76; with Laurie Mallet established company, WilliWear, Ltd, 1976; added WilliWear men's collection, 1978; first store opened posthumously, Paris, 1987. Also: designed for McCall's, Kroll Associates, Bedford Stuyvesant Workshop, etc. Lecturer, art history, Fashion Institute, London.*

Awards *International Mannequins Designer of the Year Award, New York, 1978; Coty American Fashion Critics Award, 1983; 23 February named Willi Smith Day in New York City, 1988.*

Died *(in New York City) 17 April 1987.*

Without respect for race, Willi Smith was one of the most talented designers of his era. With respect to race, he was indisputably, as *New York Daily News* fashion writer Liz Rittersporn wrote at his death in 1987, "the most successful black designer in fashion history." Smith chafed at the attention given to the anomaly of his being a black designer, yet he acknowledged some advantages in sensibility in being an African-American: "Being Black has a lot to do with my being a good designer. My eye will go quicker to what a pimp is wearing than to someone in a gray suit and tie. Most of these designers who have to run to Paris for color and fabric combinations should go to church on Sunday in Harlem. It's all right there." It was all right there for Smith as a quintessentially American designer, of the people and for the people, with a vivid sense of style democracy and eclectic mix.

Perhaps in part due to his Indian cottons and colors, perhaps to his inexhaustible appeal to youth, perhaps just due to his own wit and sense of loose fit, Smith excelled in clothing for summer; his winter collections were especially notable for oversized coats based on classic shapes. Was it wit, racial marginalization, or happy style foolishness that made a WilliWear coat so capacious, its lapels just a little too great, and its time-honored style just hit the edge of loopy?

His WilliWear News for fall 1986 proclaimed with irony his intention to get "serious" with the fall collection. In a sense, Smith never was serious, preferring instead a lively incongruity and surprising mix that he learned from observation and that he refined in affordable clothing made in India. WilliWear, the company he founded with Laurie Mallet in 1976, went from $30,000 in sales in its first year to $25 million in 1986. His soft, baggy looks did not require sophisticated tailoring and benefitted from the Indian textiles that he chose for their supple hand, easy care and comfortable aging, and indescribably indefinite colors. Smith's slouchy softness was a "real people" look, marketed at modest costs with great impact in the 1980s as the informality of designer jeans and other casual wear was replaced by the kind of alternative that Smith's design offered: a drapey silhouette for comfortable clothing with style. While primarily a designer of women's clothing, WilliWear was also influential in men's clothing. In July 1983, he created the clothes for Edwin Schlossberg on his marriage to Caroline Kennedy: Smith designed blue-violet linen blazers to be worn with white slacks and white buck shoes for the groom's party; the groom wore a navy linen double-breasted suit with a silver linen tie, outfits that were both traditional and slightly spoofy and outrageous enough to notice and enjoy.

George James in an obituary in the *New York Times* quotes Smith: "I don't design clothes for the Queen, but for the people who wave at her as she goes by." In Smith's designs there was no equivocation: sportswear was for fun and comfort. He knew this, having first worked for Arnold Scaasi in a rarefied world of fancy dress. Later, he worked for Bobbie Brooks and Digits, among others, but it was on his own, first in a business with his sister Toukie, and later in WilliWear, that Smith found his own voice designing what he affably called "street couture" without apology. Smith created uniforms for the workers on Christo's Pont Neuf, Paris wrapping in 1985. In fact, Smith's work arguably anticipates much that has become casual style in America in the late 1980s and 1990s through The Gap and A/X—loose, slouchy oversizing and mixable possibilities. Hilton Als eulogized Smith in the *Village Voice*, "As both designer and person, Willi embodied all that was the brightest, best, and most youthful in spirit in his field. . . . That a WilliWear garment was simple to care for italicized the designer's democratic urge: to clothe people as simply, beautifully, and inexpensively as possible" (28 April 1987). In a tragically short life terminated by an AIDS-related death at 39, Smith made little issue or complaint of the social disadvantage and difficulty of being an African-American committed to making a mass-market clothing business—he simply proceeded to make an exemplary life of innovative design that both earned him the Coty Award in 1983 and countless fans of his sportswear style who may never have known—or cared—whether he was Black, White, or any other color.—RICHARD MARTIN

Spook, Per
Norwegian fashion designer

Born *Oslo, Norway, 1939.*
Education *Studied at School of Fine Arts, Oslo, and École de la Chambre Syndicale, Paris.*
Career *Arrived in Paris, 1957, and joined house of Dior soon afterwards. Worked as free-lancer with Yves Saint Laurent and Louis Féraud. Opened own house, 1977. Produces haute couture and ready-to-wear.*
Awards *Golden Needle (Chambre Syndicale, Paris), 1978; Golden Thimble, 1979.*
Address *6 rue François 1er, 615008 Paris, France.*

Per Spook came to Paris in the late 1950s after graduating from the Oslo School of Fine Arts. For him Paris had been a lifelong ambition, the place to go for anyone wanting to work in the fashion industry. After studying at L'École de la Chambre Syndicale de la Couture in Paris, he embarked on a long career as an apprentice and free-lance designer. Experience with revered houses like Yves Saint Laurent, Christian Dior, and Louis Féraud gave him a taste for the haute couture and specialized fashion that created a sensation when he opened his own house at the age of 38 in 1977.

Per Spook clothes were instantly applauded for their new, soft shapes and colour. He established a hallmark for well-cut clothes that were elegantly understated but upheld the characteristics of quality, individuality, and wearability. Distinctive innovations have been his versatile long dresses that include a device that allows them to be taken up for daywear then let down again for an evening look; his Ile de Wight dress, a square-cut white linen dress embroidered with abstract black squares; his Crumple clothes made from a fabric that allows the clothes to fold into a small bundle and pack away without creasing. He also likes to design versatile mix-and-match outfits that can unite to create ensembles ranging from glamorous cocktailwear to daywear.

When it comes to ready-to-wear, the ideal Per Spook customer is a woman who is both realistic and practical. She is active, up to date and, with her international lifestyle and career, needs clothes that are graceful and polished, but also witty and lively. With his couture clothes Per Spook likes to combine his own creativity with the individual personality of a client. He recognizes that each client has a different set of needs and fantasies about how they want to look. Even if designer and client have opposing ideas, it is always possible to create a united design.

Per Spook collections are often fanciful and evoke romantic images of society lifestyles in the 1920s and 1930s. The clothes have a strong resort feel, suggesting leisured times at Deauville or on the Lido at Venice. Figure prints on expensive crêpes and asymmetric details on cross-over crêpe mini dresses have been popular, as have saucy nautical stripes, abstract polka dots and geometrics, like black and white checkerboard jackets or long sequin shift dresses in geometric-patterned fabrics. They evoke references to fashion icons of the past, an updated Duchess of Windsor, Marlene Dietrich or the 1950s model Dovima.

Per Spook's other artistic interests are noteworthy and undoubtedly inspirational when it comes to fashion design, and his design interests are not exclusively fashion oriented. He is an accomplished painter, sculptor, and photographer. Interiors, textiles, and product design capture his imagination and are barometers of inspiration and observation that help form and develop his creative fashion ideas.

In his career Per Spook has been recognized with several fashion awards, including the Chambre Syndicale's Golden Needle and Golden Thimble awards. Ultimately it is in couture that Per Spook excels. To a designer, haute couture is often the inventive lifeblood of the industry, where creativity is unhampered by the limitations of expense or market. Per Spook's approach is down to earth. He enjoys creating couture that combines practicality and realism with creativity and aesthetic vision.—KEVIN ALMOND

Sprouse, Stephen
American designer

Born *Obio, 1953.*

Education *Attended Rhode Island School of Design for three months.*

Sprouse

Career   *Worked briefly for Halston and for Bill Blass; showed first collection, 1983; out of business, 1985-87; showed three lines, S, Post Punk Dress for Success and Stephen Sprouse in own shop, 1987; satellite shop opened, Beverly Hills, 1988; out of business, 1988-92; designer, introducing Cyber Punk line, Bloomingdale's, 1992.*

A much lauded figure on the New York fashion scene in the early 1980s, Stephen Sprouse must be one of the most notorious success-failure stories in the American fashion business. One of a number of designers with their roots in the rural backwaters of Indiana, Sprouse shares his origins with Norman Norell, Bill Blass, and Halston, for whom he worked briefly in the early 1970s. Reputedly already displaying a precocious talent by the age of 12 when he designed leopard-print jumpsuits, Sprouse went on to study for a mere three months at the Rhode Island School of Design before hitting the New York scene as a rock photographer.

In the late 1970s, Sprouse made his name by designing stage clothes for Debbie Harry of the pop group Blondie, having met her in the kitchen of the flats they were sharing in New York's Bowery. His designs included ripped T-shirts, minis, and leotards, paving the way for the first of his collections in 1983.

Sprouse's clothes display a nostalgia for the New York underground of the 1960s, particularly Andy Warhol and the Factory aesthetic, and he almost designs with Edie Sedgewick or Ultra Violet in mind. Revisionist rather than retro, the garments are a witty caricature of the wildest excesses of 1960s fashion, harking back to the days of Betsey Johnson at Paraphernalia, yet tempered by Sprouse's New Wave sensibilities.

Sprouse uses synthetic fabrics, neon hues, and striking graphic prints to give his basic shapes visual appeal, contrasting day-glo colours with black jersey separates such as T-shirts and minis. Press attention has focused primarily on his use of sequins shown on jackets, thigh high boots, and his signature single shoulder strap dresses worn with matching bra tops.

The influence of André Courrèges and Rudi Gernreich is obvious in his use of cutout panels revealing parts of the female torso such as the waist or midriff, or in his redefinition of that staple of the 1960s male wardrobe, the Nehru jacket, coloured hot punk pink by Sprouse in 1985.

Acknowledging the clichés of youthful rebellion, Sprouse toys with items of subcultural style which through overuse in popular imagery have become mainstream. A prime example of this approach is the motorcycle jacket which Sprouse experiments with endlessly, covering it with sequins, 1960s iconography, or pseudo-slang. His use of logos, which seem to be making reference to some magical teenage argot, bemused audiences in 1988 when the meaningless phrase Glab Flack was emblazoned over clothes shown on the catwalk.

Arguably his best work, as worn and publicized extensively by the rock singer Debbie Harry, was the collection in 1983 on which Sprouse collaborated with the celebrated New York graffiti artist Keith Haring to produce day-glo prints of hand-painted scribbles, imagery lifted straight from the subway walls. Matching outfits of miniskirts and tights or shirts and flares for men made the wearer look as if he or she had been caught full force in the fire of a spray can.

Sprouse's designs are strictly club clothes, street fashion at couture prices as a result of the expensive fabrics, applied decoration and handfinishing applied to every garment. He is one of a rare breed of American designers using post-war American history as his source, rather than deferring to European influence and as such should be recognized as an original.—CAROLINE COX

Sui, Anna

American designer

Born *Dearborn Heights, Michigan, c.1955.*

Education *Studied at Parsons School of Design, New York, c.1973-75.*

Career *Stylist for photographer Steven Meisel and for junior sportswear firms in New York, 1970s to 1981; sportswear designer, Simultanee, New York, 1981; also designed own line, from 1980; formed own company, New York, 1983; first runway show, 1991; menswear line added, 1992; opened in-store boutique, Macy's, and first free-standing boutique, New York, 1992; second boutique opened, Hollywood, 1993.*

Awards *Perry Ellis Award, 1993.*

Address *275 West 39th Street, New York, New York 10018, USA.*

When Anna Sui started her own apparel company in 1980, her mission was to sell clothes to every rock 'n' roll store in the country. "It was right after the punk rock thing and I was so into that," said the designer, who has earned a reputation for bringing a designer's sensibility to wild-child, rock 'n' roll clothes with a vintage spin.

One of three children of Chinese immigrants, Sui knew she wanted to be a clothing designer since she was a little girl growing up in Detroit in the late 1950s and 1960s. She came to New York to attend Parsons School of Design after graduating from high school in the early 1970s—an era whose music-inspired fashion scene, mix-it-up attitude, and free-spirited energy has influenced Sui to a great degree. At Parsons Sui met photographer Steven Meisel—her counterpart in styling ventures then and now.

Upon graduation from Parsons, Sui's first job was with the now-defunct junior sportswear firm Bobbie Brooks, where she worked as a design assistant for about a year. After working for other firms over several years, Sui landed at Glenora, a firm the designer described as "very hip at the time." There she was able to experiment with her interest in clothing with a historical bent, made modern by mixing fresh colors and new shapes with vintage elements.

In 1980, prompted by friends and the praise she received as a stylist for Meisel's shoots for the Italian fashion magazine *Lei,* she started her own company. Greatly influenced by New York's punk scene of the 1970s, Sui's main focus was on selling her funky styles to rock 'n' roll stores, though she continued as a stylist for Meisel. This changed around 1987, when the designer decided to "get serious about being a designer," as she recalled. She moved her line into the Annette B showroom, owned by Annette Breindel, a no-nonsense woman known for nurturing young designers. "Annette helped me enormously," said Sui. "She helped me build my dress business first because that's what she saw as a worthwhile area."

Building that category is what allowed Sui to move her business out of her apartment and into a loft workspace in the garment district of New York. In 1991, Sui staged her first major fashion show during New York show week. Her friends—supermodels Naomi Campbell, Linda Evangelista, and Christy Turlington—walked Sui's runway for free, in exchange for clothes. Influenced by the shows of Thierry Mugler and Jean Paul Gaultier, the designer created a show that was as much about music and theatre as about clothing. She now reigns as the queen of the fashion show extravaganza.

Sui's collection is now sold in many major department and specialty stores, as well as her own two stores—one in New York and one in Los Angeles. Priced moderately, the collection reflects Sui's current concern: "To continue to make these clothes accessible to the people I want wearing them."—MARY ELLEN GORDON

Sybilla
Spanish designer

Born *Sybilla Sorondo in New York, 1963, to Polish/Argentinian parents; moved to Madrid, age seven; moved to Paris, 1980.*

Family *Married Enrique Sirera in 1992; son: Lucas.*

Career *Apprentice cutter and seamstress, Yves Saint Laurent, 1980; returned to Madrid, 1981, making made-to-measure clothes for friends; first collection, Madrid, 1983; also made first shoe collection; signed production and international distribution agreement with Spanish company, for women's ready-to-wear, 1985; presented first collections in Milan, Paris, New York, 1985. Head designer, Programas Exterioras SA, Madrid, from 1985. Sybilla boutique opened, Madrid, 1987. Signed with Italian company Gibo for women's ready-to-wear, 1987. Begins producing knitwear with Italian company ICAP, 1988; same year starts producing women's shoes and bags with Spanish company Farrutx; also starts designing carpets with German company Vorwerk. Agrees to exclusive license in Japan with Itokin, 1989; opens new shops in Paris and Tokyo, 1991. Opened 20*

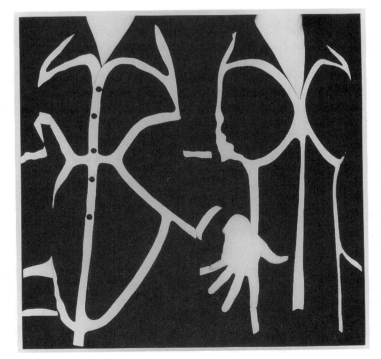

Sybilla. *Photograph by Julio Limia.*

in-store outlets in Japan. Also designs household items, tableware (for Bidasoa of Spain), childrenswear and accessories. Autumn/winter 1993-94 launched second line for younger people, with 20 shops, called Jocomomola.

Exhibitions *50 años de moda, Cuartel de Conde Duque, Madrid, 1987; Le monde selon ses créateurs, Musée de la Mode et du Costume, Paris, 1991.*

Collections *Museo de la Moda, Barcelona; Musée de la Mode et du Costume, Paris; Fashion Institute of Technology, New York.*

Awards *Premio Balenciaga, Best Young Designer of the Year, Spain, 1987; Prix Fil d'Or, France, 1987.*

Address *Jorge Juan 12, 28001 Madrid, Spain.*

I guess that people try to dress up in a way that represents themselves. Somehow we all "paint" our skin with clothes, copying an inner image of ourselves. If you are able to get to this point, you can forget what you are wearing, you can overcome your own image . . . at this moment the peace and serenity that you show outside can be condsidered elegance.—Sybilla

Sybilla has been widely acclaimed as the most exciting designer to have emerged from Spain since Balenciaga. She was born in 1963 in New York City, the daughter of an Argentine diplomat. Her mother was a Polish aristocrat who worked as a fashion designer under the name "Countess Sybilla of Saks Fifth Avenue." When she was seven years old her family moved to Madrid, and she considers herself thoroughly Spanish; her clothes, she says, are also very Spanish—"not *olé olé*' but Spanish in the classical sense.

She served a brief apprenticeship in Paris at the couture *atelier* of Yves Saint Laurent, but recoiled at what she regarded as the "snobbish, cold, and professional" aspects of French fashion. "Paris scares me. 'Fashion' is too serious. In Spain, you can still play." Like filmmaker Pedro Almodovar, Sybilla is a member of the post-Franco generation that launched a creative explosion in the 1980s. "We were the first generation after Franco died, and we tried to be different and creative," recalled Sybilla. With success came greater professionalism. In 1987, Italian fashion manufacturer Gibo began producing Sybilla's clothes en masse in Italy.

At the end of the 1980s, Sybilla became famous for creating what she called "weird and outrageous designs"—such as sculpted dresses with wired hems. But there is also a soft feeling to many of her clothes, which derives both from the colors (tobacco, pumpkin, pale green) and from a tendency towards biomorphic shapes. "The dresses of Sybilla remind you of when you were a child and your mother would tell you fairy stories," says Almodovar actress Rossy de Palma. "But in her dresses you live that, like a dream."—VALERIE STEELE

Tam, Vivienne

Chinese-born American designer

Born *Canton, China, 7 December 1962.*

Education *Hong Kong Polytechnic, B.A.*

Career *Travelled extensively and worked in London before settling in New York in 1981; owner East Wind Code Ltd. since 1983.*

Awards *Vogue Designer of the Month, March 1995; Featured Designer, Fashion Week 1997, Hong Kong Trade Development Council.*

Vivienne Tam is a fresh, irreverent, even occasionally unpredictable designer. Working under her own name since 1981, Tam is yet hard to characterize, so driven is she by enthusiasms as varied as her global travels and the anthropological options and expressions of apparel, her commitment to East-meets-West amalgamations, and her demanding interest in new textiles and fabrications. There is a restless, curious energy to Tam as a person; her design work conveys the same exuberant vivacity. While her most famous collection is indubitably her Mao designs of 1994, Tam has otherwise explored Impressionism, Op Art (especially for fall 1995), and florals from East and West. In notes to her fall 1996 collection, Tam proposes "the luxury of ancient China, the palette of the French Impressionist and the mood of 1930s Berlin." Even if Tam does not always unite all such elements, and would perhaps best be wary of Weimar Germany, her will to pastiche and reconciliation is distinct and spirited. Born in Canton, Tam was brought up in Hong Kong, worked in London, and has settled in New York, though travel remains an important part of her designing *modus operandi*. Crochet, pleating, and other hand-referenced skills always play a part in her design, though her propensity is to be modern in silhouette and materials. Tam is manifestly smart and modern, while wistfully nostalgic and eclectic. Her spring 1996 collection included prints taken from Ming Dynasty plates depicting naked couples in varieties of copulation.

Tam's brave old world resides in handicraft traditions and in remembering old styles. Her brave new world is an often sleek technology. Straddling the two and serving both is Tam's enthusiasm for eclectic arts and aesthetic cultures. The 1994 Mao images on garments are perhaps political as Debra Gendel (*Los Angeles Times*, November 7, 1994) alleges, "Tam's beautiful Audrey Hepburn cocktail dresses, imprinted with black-and-white photographic images of Mao, reflect her own position on the leader of [the] old regime. 'He did some positive things and he did some negative things.'" But Tam's irreverent Maos are also an homage to Warhol. Some images with pink lips, pigtails more *The Color Purple* than *Quotations from Chairman Mao*, a bee poised menacingly on Mao's nose, Mao with clerical collar (holy Mao tee), and propaganda icons covered with sequins are all more ironic and artistic than mere politics. Tam's idealistic globalism transcends politics and offers a more enchanted, peaceful world.

Tam's cosmopolitan disposition means that she never creates mere retro or facile modernism like some of her contemporaries. Everything is assimilated and absorbed for Tam; she is definitely her own creation. Explaining her start in New York to Anne-Marie Schiro (*New York Times*, January 17, 1995), Tam recalls, "I had a strong conviction that anyone who saw my designs would like them." Such faith is the heart of Tam's designing and of her rare individuality as a designer committed to medium-priced clothing. She told Schiro, "The day I became an American, I was in this room with hundreds of people from all over the world. It was so

Vivienne Tam. *Photograph by Marilynn K. Yee/New York Times.*

wonderful to think that they were all bringing their cultures here. America is a place where you can express yourself and be yourself." Cannily, Tam is no patriot of banal homogeneity and no designer of such; her savvy thinking and beliefs are evident in clothing that suggests tolerance, global acumen, and a Fourth-of-July faith in individual expression tonic in the 1990s.—RICHARD MARTIN

Thomass, Chantal

French designer

Born   *Chantal Genty in Malakoff, Seine, 4 September 1947.*

Family   *Married Bruce Thomass in 1967; children: Louise, Robin.*

Career   *Free-lance designer selling to Dorothée Bis, 1966-71; Partner, Ter et Bantine boutique, Paris, 1967, renamed Chantal Thomass, 1975; introduced lingerie and hosiery collections, 1975, maternity wear, 1981, children's clothing line, from c.1982; signed partnership with World Company for distribution, licensing and boutiques in Japan, 1985; second boutique for clothing and household accessories opened, Paris, 1991.*

Awards   *named Chevalier des Arts et Lettres.*

Address   *100, rue du Cherche Midi, 75006 Paris, France.*

Chantal Thomass. *Photograph by Sylvie Barin.*

Chantal Thomass has built a reputation for her tantalizing, flirtatious clothes. Much of her work pays a titillating homage to exotic underwear; there is, however, never a blatant display of overt sexuality. Instead there is always a hint of the naughty schoolgirl or a sensuous allusion to the charms of the teenage seductress, like Carole Baker in *Baby Doll,* or Sue Lyon in *Lolita.* The clothes are often fitted or skimpy, trimmed in frills, ribbons, and flounces, and always produced in the most sophisticated fabrics.

Chantal Thomass has had no formal training in fashion design but as a child dressing up proved enough of a motivation for her to design her own clothes, which were made up by her mother. She began her fashion career at 18, designing clothes for girls of her own age. A year later she married Bruce Thomass, who had studied at the École des Beaux Arts in Paris. Together, they formed a small fashion company called Ter et Bantine that manufactured and sold young and unusual clothes. They created dresses from hand-painted scarves, designed by Bruce, and succeeded in selling them to Dorothée Bis. Thomass also designed dresses with flounced pinafores, schoolgirl collars, and balloon sleeves that were sold from their first boutique on Boulevard Saint Germain in 1967. Actress and French cultural symbol Brigitte Bardot became a regular customer, as did designer Jacqueline Jacobson, who ordered over a hundred dresses in one season alone!

The business was sufficiently successful for the pair to found the Chantal Thomass label in 1975, with Chantal as creative director and Bruce as licensing and sales director. As the profile of the company rose so did the price of the clothes, although they retained their young, enchanting, and highly feminine style.

Thomass declares herself to be motivated by the progression of her own life. Her pregnancy in 1981 led her to develop a line of maternity clothes. As her daughter began growing, Thomass developed a childrenswear division that retained many of the distinctive and theatrical elements of her mainline collections. The company moved into licensing in 1985, joining forces with the Japanese group World as a financial partner. Licensed products that are available throughout Europe and Japan include: fine leather goods, tights, women's shoes, eyewear, watches, children's ready-to-wear, scarves, lingerie, and swimwear. There are now 12 boutiques throughout France, two in Paris.

Chantal Thomass retains her eminence by reflecting fashion changes and adapting her look to suit the prevalent mood. A youthful feel to her clothes keeps her in the forefront of leading Paris-based designers.—KEVIN ALMOND

Toi, Zang

American designer

Born *Malaysia, 11 June 1961.*

Education *Studied fashion design at Parsons School of Design, New York, 1981-83.*

Career *Production associate, Mary Jane Marcasiano, New York, 1982-87; free-lance designer, Ronaldus Shamask, New York, 1988; opened own business, 1989, introduced diffusion line, Z, 1992.*

Exhibitions *Fashion Institute of Technology Museum.*

Zang Toi: 1996.

Toi

Awards   *Mouton-Cadet Young Designer Award for outstanding achievement in the arts, 1990.*

Address   *30 West 57th Street, New York, New York 10019, USA.*

At the house of Toi, it all starts with color. Lavish hues of chartreuse, red, and hot pink . . . theoretically should never be seen together. Here they have been combined masterfully with a flair and wit that has won the hearts of both critics and customers alike!!!

Breaking the rules is what I do best. I try not to limit my thinking to the way things have been done before—my customers have come to expect the unexpected. Pioneering in dressing up good old all-American denim in splashy red and hot pink stitched with metalic gold stitching into sexy suits and little bustier dress is the chicest way to dress.

The Zang Toi's formula is creating glamourous tailored, classic sportswear with a dramatic twist. With a surprising mixed palette and signature design finishes. Evening at Zang Toi means haute fantasy with a dash of old Hollywood glamour.

It is always a dream of mine to merge my fashion sense with fine food. The magic words here are food is like fashion; clothes are just a piece of cloth until you add the decoration and the look, then it becomes fashion. The same with food, once you start decorating it becomes appetizing. My personal philosophy is that beautiful food and clothes should always be a part of life.—Zang Toi

Zang Toi has the dubious distinction of being a featured designer in a *Newsday* article of 3 October 1990, "Fashion's New Kids: On the Block," and of being a principal in Nina Darnton's article "The New York Brat Pack" in the 29 April 1991 issue of *Newsweek*. In the *Newsweek* article, Zang Toi has the last word, telling Darnton, "I think women are looking for good prices and styles that are new—not just young people in the same mold as the current stars." Likewise, in the *Newsday* article, Zang Toi's pragmatic and sensible remarks form the article's conclusion when he says, "There are so many young designers who are eager to be stars right away. But ego can be the worst killer to any young designer. You can't let the press and the hype go to your head. If the work doesn't meet the demand and the quality, it doesn't mean anything."

Toi's work resoundingly meets demand and determines desires and styles in the early 1990s. The gifted young designer has demonstrated a color sensibility related not only to Asian textiles (the collection that earned him the Mouton-Cadet Young Designer Award was inspired by Southeast Asian textiles, with rich batiks and embroideries), but perhaps equally to Matisse in his vibrant palette. Toi's color is often and aptly compared to Christian Lacroix's. But Toi has brought his tinted exuberance not, as Lacroix, to almost baroque forms of highly elaborated couture, but to serviceable sportswear separates. For Lacroix, arguably the delectation is in the whole and is a design by ensemble. In Toi's work, the delights are in the elements. Even within, his ingenious and impertinent buttons and extravagant details give punctuation with whimsy. Well-cut jackets, saucy skirts and shorts, spunky sarong skirts with ornament, wonderful vests and trousers provide a sensible dressing from constituents rich in color and texture. It is as if Albers's color cards and Matisse paper cutouts and the richest textile patterns (often with the exquisite horror vacui excess associated with Southeast Asian textiles) have come together in three-dimensional and living form in Toi's beautiful designs. As much as Toi loves glamour, he has also created a diffusion line, Z, launched in 1992, that luxuriates in denim and less expensive fabrication.

Toi did not set out to be a designer. Growing up as the youngest son of seven children of a grocer in a small town in Malaysia, Toi loved sketching and drawing, but dreamed of being an architect or interior designer. His love of fashion came later and always in conjunction with cuisine and other pleasurable arts. He admits to wanting to combine fashion and running a restaurant. Like many designers, however, a lifetime interest in classic movie glamor and stars such as Audrey Hepburn encourage his fashion interests. The Malay tradewinds have always brought rich interactions of British colonialism (apparent in Toi's schoolboy stripes), Chinese, Indonesian, and other converging possibilities. Exoticism and pragmatic synthesis seem to come effortlessly to Toi.

In the West, we have traditionally enjoyed an adulation of the new and Zang Toi is a new designer. But his merit and interest reside in the fact that his design is distinguished not by novelty but by his intense commitment to color. His fashion draws eclectically and with an absorbing anachronism on history and global fashion, always keeping his international eye for color. His practicality and sensitivity to the consumer are hallmarks of smart design for the 1990s. Infinitely personable and charming, Toi also partakes of a Western tradition of the designer as social mixer and gregarious personality. Lauren Ezersky wrote, "I love Zang. Everybody loves Zang. He truly is one of the nicest designers on the scene today. And his designs are as fabulous as his gams, which he displays on a regular basis by wearing shorts" (*Paper,* October 1992).

If he is a new kid on the color block, Toi has the characteristics of precocious aptitude and wise business acumen. Frank de Caro said ungrammatically of Malaysian-born Toi and of his success, "if anyone is the Next Big Thing, it's him" (*Newsday,* New York, 29 April 1991). One could wish that all proclaimed as new and the Next Big Thing were as solid, as self-aware, and as sensible in design exploration and innovation as Zang Toi.—RICHARD MARTIN

Toledo, Isabel

Cuban designer working in the United States

Born *Cuba, 9 April 1961.*

Education *Studied painting and ceramics, then fashion design at the Fashion Institute of Technology and Parsons School of Design, New York.*

Family *Married Ruben Toledo in 1984.*

Career *Showed first collection, 1985.*

Awards *Coty American Fashion Critics "Winnie" Award.*

Address *31 West 31st St, New York, New York 10018, USA.*

The United States is better known for the mass-production of clothing than for nourishing avant-garde talent. Isabel Toledo is one of the few cutting-edge designers working in New York, and financial success has been a long time coming. When she began designing professionally in 1986, Toledo was immediately recognized as a powerful talent; her clothes were featured in magazines like *Vogue* and *Harper's Bazaar* and sold in prestigious stores like Bendel's of New York. Since then, however, she has had legal difficulties with a financial backer, as well as problems with American retail store executives.

Isabel Toledo did not sell a single piece of clothing at retail in the United States for three years in the early 1990s. She and her husband, artist Ruben Toledo, told *Women's Wear Daily* that they just could not afford to take orders from stores that refuse to provide half payment up front. Meanwhile, store buyers worried that her line was too "experimental" for the American market. She survived on the business from sales in Japan and Paris. "It makes sense for us to sell to Japanese and European accounts because when they give you an order, they give you the money," she said. She also had the patronage of about 60 devoted private clients, who are attracted by what she calls her penchant for "practicality disguised as fantasy."

Through it all, Isabel Toledo has been a cult figure among fashion enthusiasts. Her fellow designers admire her tremendously. Todd Oldham calls her "one of America's greatest resources." Both Marc Jacobs and Christian Francis Roth have praised her "incredible" talent and urged retailers to advance her money. Journalists agree: "Best overall collection for our money was Isabel Toledo, who ignored the market and concentrated on a well-edited, very weird, internal vision," raved a reporter for the *Village Voice*. Toledo is a "great designer . . . travelling on that new American highway of fashion," argues Kim Hastreiter of *Paper*. Recently, she has begun to achieve the financial recognition that she deserves, and her clothes are now available in Barneys New York (Manhattan, Chicago, and Beverly Hills).

Toledo designs clothes that are structured, even architectural, and sometimes (as she says) "rather severe—a lot of black and strong shapes." She has always started with a shape, usually a circle or a curved line: a circle skirt, a curved bra, a flared apron overskirt, the sweeping arc of a coat. "I'm not a fashion designer," insists Toledo. "I'm a seamstress. I really love the technique of sewing more than anything else." She believes that it is crucial to know fashion from the inside: through cutting, draping, pattern-making and sewing. Among the designers she admires are women like Madeleine Vionnet and Madame Grès, who also worked in three dimensions rather than from a flat sketch. Toledo sees definite advantages in being a woman designer, because they "experience" the way the clothing feels. Men, she believes, tend to be more "decorators of clothing."

Like Claire McCardell, creator in the 1940s of the "American look," the Cuban-born Toledo uses classic materials such as denim and cotton flannel plaid in a modern way. Although inventive tailoring is characteristic of her work, her clothes are not for "an office type of person," she admits, but for someone like herself: artistic and feminine. There is also a futuristic element in her work, which she sees as being related to her experiences as an immigrant to a new country. Unlike many designers, Toledo is not interested in recycling styles from the past, preferring to experiment with the basic materials of her art, and to explore the future of fashion.

Ruben Toledo once did an illustration, "Fashion history goes on strike!" which depicted the styles of the past (from New Look to Mod) marching in a demonstration with signs demanding: "Let us rest in peace! No more retro! Look forward, not backwards!" That sums up Isabel Toledo's approach to fashion.—VALERIE STEELE

Treacy, Philip
Irish designer working in England

Born   *Ireland.*

Education   *Attended Royal College of Art.*

Career *Hat designer; has worked for such designers as Karl Lagerfeld, Marc Bohan, and Rifat Ozbek; produces hats for various couture houses and ready-to-wear firms, including the Philip Treacy for Right Impression label.*

Address *c/o Public relations office, Marie-Helene de Taillac, 69 Elizabeth Street, London SW1, England.*

Ex-Royal College of Art student Philip Treacy was recognized as a talented milliner even before graduating from college where his final show was sponsored by *Harper's and Queen* magazine, London. In the two years since leaving college, Irish-born Treacy has moved to the forefront of the fashion world, producing hats for some of the most prestigious couture and ready-to-wear designers, including Karl Lagerfeld at Chanel, Marc Bohan at Hartnell, and Rifat Ozbek. Described as the Rembrandt of millinery by the established hat designer, Shirley Hex, Treacy's monumental creations for the fashion catwalks often receive as much publicity as the outfits for which they were designed.

Treacy's millinery designs reflect his unquestionably vivid imagination, drawing upon diverse subjects such as surrealism, the dance of Martha Graham, as well as religious and historical imagery. Treacy asserts that to create a modern hat does not require space age influences, preferring to plunder the past for inspiration and then make it appear totally new. A floral hat by Philip Treacy is a crash helmet covered in flowers and butterflies, the traditional guardsman's busby is completely transformed in yellow ostrich feathers, a towering turban is created by an intricately wrapped blanket with fringed edging, a large cluster of black coq feathers are tied together with white feathers to form a brim and crown. Treacy's hats, like those of other British milliners, are often described as eccentric. Treacy attributes this eccentricity to the fact that the British are associated with idiosyncrasy but says that he does not set out to create deliberately unusual hats. Using what he describes as "boring" fabrics, Treacy begins working upon these materials with different treatments—feathers, for example, are singed so that they take on the appearance of very fine gossamer.

An important factor in Treacy's work is his mastery of highly skilled traditional millinery techniques which ensure the correct balance, fit, and proportion for the hat which he concedes are as much mathematical as aesthetic. It is this artisan approach, with the emphasis on craft and technique, that characterizes much of Treacy's work. Treacy currently produces hats for nine different companies—three couture houses and six ready-to-wear firms, one of which is the Philip Treacy for Right Impression label designed for his backer. Treacy's ability to work at all levels of the market, from the costly couture creations to the less expensive ready-to-wear field, illustrates his versatility as a designer for whom price barriers are seen as a challenge rather than an obstacle.

While Treacy's use of imagery and visual effects for his millinery creations is a vital element in his success, fashion critic Brenda Polan claims that Treacy's mastery of technique is what singles him out as a great milliner, stating, "The balance of his hats, their swooping and curving, is perfect. A Treacy hat sits naturally upon the head, its proportions complementing those of the body, its horizontal and vertical lines extending and dramatizing the planes of the face. It is a perfection only an obsessive can achieve."—CATHERINE WORAM

Trigère, Pauline

American designer

Born *Paris, France, 4 November 1912.*

Education *Jules Ferry and Victor Hugo Colleges, Paris, 1923-28.*

Family *Married Lazar Radley in 1929 (separated); children: Jean-Pierre, Philippe.*

Career *Immigrated to the United States, 1937, naturalized, 1942. Trainee clothing cutter, Martial et Armand, Paris, 1928-29; assistant cutter, fitter, in father's tailoring business, Paris, 1929-32; free-lance designer, Paris, 1933-36; design assistant, Ben Gershel, New York, 1937; assistant to Travis Banton, Hattie Carnegie fashion house, New York, 1937-42; co-founder, designer, House of Trigère, from 1942.*

Awards *Coty American Fashion Critics Award, 1949, 1951, 1959; Neiman Marcus Award, Dallas, 1950; National Cotton Council of America Award, 1951; Filene Award, Boston, 1959; Silver Medal, City of Paris, 1972.*

Address *550 Seventh Avenue, New York, New York 10018, USA.*

I've always found it difficult to talk or write about FASHION. I think FASHION—clothes, garments—should be enjoyed and worn, and certainly fill a certain purpose in one's life.

I also think that for me, doing it for 50 years or more, proved that I have done it somewhat right.

I love my work, I love designing, I love folding, draping, molding the fabric in my hands and producing new shapes, new designs.

I have never gone up-up, or down-down like a yo-yo. I have tried to keep my women, my customers, happy in their Trigère clothes—hoping that they bought them and wore them with pleasure, and that they were right for their lives—PTA, business meetings, concerts, theater, etc.

In thinking back, I don't think that I would have enjoyed anything else but doing collection after collection, four to five times a year—(oh yes, maybe I could have been an architect, or yes, yes, most certainly a surgeon . . .).—Pauline Trigère

Pauline Trigère is more than a designer of women's clothing, she is a fabric artisan. Trigère left her native France in 1937 and arrived in New York with practical training gathered from her parents' tailoring shop and the Parisian couture house of Martial et Armand, plus a natural talent for working with fabric. She started her own business in 1942 with a collection of just 12 dresses. During World War II, when the American fashion industry was cut off from inspiration normally coming from Paris, Trigère's combination of French elegance and American practicality proved successful. Her constant commitment to excellent design and workmanship has kept her in business for over 50 years.

During the 1940s Trigère become known especially for her impeccable and imaginative tailoring of women's suits and coats. She made use of all weights of wool, from sheer crêpes for eveningwear to thick tweeds for daytime coats. She was recognized early in her career as an innovator for such fashions as evening dresses made of wool or cotton, reversible coats and capes in all shapes and sizes. Another characteristic Trigère feature is the luxurious touch of fur

Pauline Trigère: 1990; white doubleface wool suit with strapless gold embroidered top.
Photograph by Gideon Levin.

trim at necklines, cuffs, and hems. Before the 1960s, her palette was fairly subdued and she rarely used printed fabrics; during the 1960s and 1970s she began to use more prints and softer fabrics, always retaining a tailored touch. Her use of prints is bold and deliberate, the pattern is often used to complement the structure of the piece. Notwithstanding her extensive use of wool and tailoring techniques, Trigère's clothing is unmistakably feminine. She rarely makes use of menswear details.

While she is an acknowledged innovator of fashions, she is also know for repeating and perfecting her most successful themes. For example, her princess line dress which appears in her collections consistently is considered to have no equal, and her rhinestone bra top, first introduced in 1967, was revived in 1985 and 1992.

Throughout the evolution of fashion in the last half-century, Trigère has worked within the mainstream while retaining her signature style. Simple elegance and timelessness are descriptions often applied to her work, but style is not her only concern. She insists on the highest quality of materials to assure that her clothing will serve her customers for years to come. Her collections are carefully planned so that many pieces will work together, and complement past seasons' collections.

Trigère's work has been compared to that of two legendary French couturiers, Cristobal Balenciaga and Madeleine Vionnet. These designers were known for employing complex and unusual construction techniques to create simple, elegant silhouettes. Trigère herself rarely sketches her ideas; like Balenciaga and Vionnet she designs by draping and cutting the actual fabric on a dress form or live model. The fabric itself is an important part of Trigère's design process. It is her inspiration and her guide as it reveals what it is capable of doing. Trigère's continued involvement with the creative process and her insistence on quality make her unique on New York's Seventh Avenue.—MELINDA L. WATT

Tyler, Richard

Australian designer working in Los Angeles

Born *Sunshine, Australia, c.1948, son of a factory foreman and a seamstress.*

Family *Married Doris Taylor (divorced); married Lisa Trafficante, 1989; children: (first marriage) Sheriden; (second marriage) Edward.*

Career *Opened store, Zippity-doo-dah, in Melbourne, Australia, late 1960s; designed outfits for rock and roll stars, early 1970s; designed and traveled with Rod Stewart's "Blondes Have More Fun" tour, 1978; started the Richard Tyler collection with wife and partner Lisa Trafficante, late 1980s; opened Los Angeles showroom, Tyler Trafficante, 1988; opened New York City showroom, 1992; named head designer for Anne Klein & Company, 1993; left Anne Klein & Company, 1994.*

Awards *Council of Fashion Designers of America New Talent award, 1993; Council of Fashion Designers of America Womenswear Designer of the Year award, 1994.*

"At my age, I'm thrilled," 46-year-old Richard Tyler told *People* magazine when he won the Council of Fashion Designers of America New Talent award in 1993. Just one year later he walked away with the Council's Womenswear Designer of the Year award—one of the fashion world's highest honors. While Tyler's fame may have come later in life than other designers, it has quickly grown, earning him the respect of his peers and the devotion of his customers.

Much of Tyler's initial success was due to his celebrity clients. Julia Roberts, Janet Jackson, Sigourney Weaver, and Oprah Winfrey are just a few of the stars who have publicly praised the exemplary quality and fit of his clothes. "That's the age-old recipe for success in fashion: get the right people to wear your clothes," Patrick McCarthy, the executive editor of *Women's Wear Daily,* told *Newsweek.* While his famous clients might draw new customers in, it is Tyler's attention to detail and fine tailoring that keeps his business growing. Everything on a Richard Tyler piece of clothing is done by hand. Identical and precise buttonholes are a hallmark of his collection, and his fabrics—the finest wools, silks, and linens—boast such details as individual stripes sewn onto the cloth with silk threads.

Tyler was born in Sunshine, Australia, just outside of Melbourne. His mother was a costumer with the Melbourne Ballet, and also sewed wedding dresses, men's suits, and clerical robes. Tyler's father was a plastics factory foreman with one of the best wardrobes in town. It was through his mother that Tyler learned his love for fine quality tailoring. At age 16, Tyler decided to drop out of school and began work as a tailor at a shop that was known for outfitting the Australian prime minister. He also spent some time at a factory, cutting out bras. At the age of 18, with his mother's help, Tyler opened his own store, Zippity-doo-dah, in a run-down section of Melbourne. His father paid the bills and his mother sewed his designs in the back room.

By the 1970s Tyler's shop was beginning to attract a steady clientele. Australian celebrities, and such touring rock and roll stars as Cher, Elton John, and Alice Cooper, began to seek out his lycra and sequined outfits. During this time Tyler married Doris Taylor. The marriage lasted ten years, and they had a son, Sheriden, born in the late 1970s. After Tyler's mother died in 1976, he made many trips to London, continuing to dress rock and roll stars.

In 1978 Rod Stewart asked Tyler to design his "Blondes Have More Fun" tour. When the show stopped in Los Angeles, Tyler fell in love with the city and decided to make it his home. He continued to design for performers, including Supertramp, the Bee Gees, the Go-Gos, and Diana Ross. But as costume demands became increasingly outrageous in the mid-1980s, Tyler began to drop his work for the stars. He stayed in Los Angeles, doing odd jobs and trading his gardening and sewing skills for rent at his friends' guest houses.

Tyler then spent two years in Oslo, Norway, but ended up back in Los Angeles in 1987, with his last $100 and a plane ticket home to Australia. The night before he was to fly home, he met Lisa Trafficante, an actress and businesswoman, who would change his life forever. Together Tyler and Trafficante would soon form a partnership that enabled them to establish the Richard Tyler line of clothing. Trafficante urged Tyler to follow his strengths and design finely tailored menswear. She took it upon herself to come up with a business plan and the necessary capital.

Tyler's clothes were so bold that many buyers thought their customers wouldn't buy them. It was during their last appointment of the day, at the boutique If in SoHo, that Tyler and Trafficante received their first order. If's customers were immediately drawn to Tyler's work, and within two years Chativari in New York City and Wilkes Bashford in San Francisco were also buying from Tyler. In 1988 Trafficante persuaded Tyler that they needed to open their own showroom in Los Angeles. With the backing of Trafficante's sister Michelle and investor Gordon DeVol, they bought a drapery-manufacturing building in an out-of-the-way part of town. They gutted the interior of the art-deco building and created a bare, contemporary setting for Tyler's fashion-forward designs.

The store was named Tyler Trafficante, and it was there that Tyler first became known for his trademark fitted jackets. Diana Rico, writing for *GQ,* described the transformation felt after trying on a Tyler jacket: "Its dashing cut and construction are so comfortable that you feel as though you're barely wearing anything at all. The sensuous silk lining and luxurious hand-tailored details bespeak an old-world emphasis on fine craftsmanship, while the stagy lapels, offbeat colors and elongated silhouette give the piece a daring rock and roll edge."

Although the showroom started without a women's section, so many women came in off the street requesting clothes that the next season Tyler began designing for them. It was the demand for women's clothes that really sparked the growth of Tyler Trafficante. Within five years they had one of the hottest stores in Los Angeles.

In 1992 Tyler decided it was time to introduce his line to New York. The New York fashion world welcomed Tyler and the press lauded his debut show in March of 1993. The reviews were barely in when he was contacted by the upscale women's sportswear line, Anne Klein & Company, asking him to sign on as their new design director. Many in the fashion world questioned the pairing of Tyler, known for his bold, sexy designs, with Klein, a label that manufactures traditional, conservative career clothes for women. The first year Tyler began designing for Anne Klein, store orders rose 30 percent. Despite the immediate jump in sales, the reviews of the Anne Klein line were mixed.

In December of 1994 Anne Klein and Tyler parted company. There were a number of problems that plagued his tenure with Anne Klein. Tyler had difficulty controlling quality and price: his demand for impeccable quality raised the price of an Anne Klein jacket by 15 percent. In addition, he was not used to overseeing a huge staff of patternmakers, tailors, design assistants, and dressmakers. Many speculated that the overriding reason for Tyler's termination, however, was that in his attempt to attract a younger customer, he made too many changes too soon and turned off Klein's traditional customers.

Industry insiders have no doubt, however, that Tyler will rebound. He is known as a survivor. He left Anne Klein with a reported $2.1 million buyout of his contract. In the near future, Tyler plans to launch a secondary line, with a lower price point so that more women can afford his clothes. His tenure with Anne Klein only served to increase his visibility and will undoubtedly help when he launches his new line. As for the quality of the clothes in this new line, Tyler promises that there will be no compromise. As always, his collection will begin with his tailoring skills. "In Richard's work a detail always becomes a major theme in the collection," Trafficante told *Vogue.* "Some designers have theatrical themes, but he has the way he makes his clothes as his theme." The Richard Tyler label continues to grow in popularity, and services accounts all over the globe. The key to Tyler's success was given in *Vogue:* "My mother always said if you have great quality, women will come back."—MOLLY SEVERSON

Ungaro, Emanuel

French designer

Born *Aix-en-Provence, 13 February 1933.*

Career *Worked in his father's tailoring business, Aix-en-Provence, 1951-54; stylist, Maison Camps tailors, Paris, 1955-57; designer, Balenciaga, Paris, 1958-64; head of design, Balenciaga, Madrid, 1959-61; designer, Courrèges, 1964-65; established own firm, 1965; Ungaro Parallèle ready-to-wear collection introduced, 1968; menswear collection added, 1975; sportswear line, Emanuel, introduced, 1991; Ungaro perfume introduced, 1977, signature fragrance introduced, 1991; other fragrances include Diva, 1983 and Senso, 1987.*

Awards *Neiman Marcus Award, Dallas, 1969.*

Address *2 avenue Montaigne, 75008 Paris, France.*

Upon celebrating 25 years of success in couture, Ungaro could look back and see that he had indeed accomplished his goal of "seducing the woman." His early training in the *atelier* of Balenciaga taught Ungaro about line and color. He still refers to what he learned about draping directly on the model. Later, working with Courrèges, Ungaro participated in the Space Age hard chic of his mentor. It was later suggested that many of Courrèges's successful designs might have been attributed to Ungaro, who created metal bras, skimpy cutout A-line dresses, and white boots in a hard, futuristic manner that even Ungaro himself later dismissed as "false modernism." The influence of two years with Courrèges carried over into the early years of Ungaro's work on his own. He continued to make young, "kicky" fashions, dresses, and coats in bold, interlaced geometrics. His turtleneck and leggings worn underneath a sleeveless pinafore was a 1960s look that was resurrected by other designers to great popularity 20 years later. With the advantage of textile designer Sonia Knapp's artistic fabric designs, Ungaro gradually developed a softness of line that was to fully develop a decade later. Of his early designs, Ungaro prefers to say little, but chenille daisy appliquéd see-through trouser-suits speak for themselves.

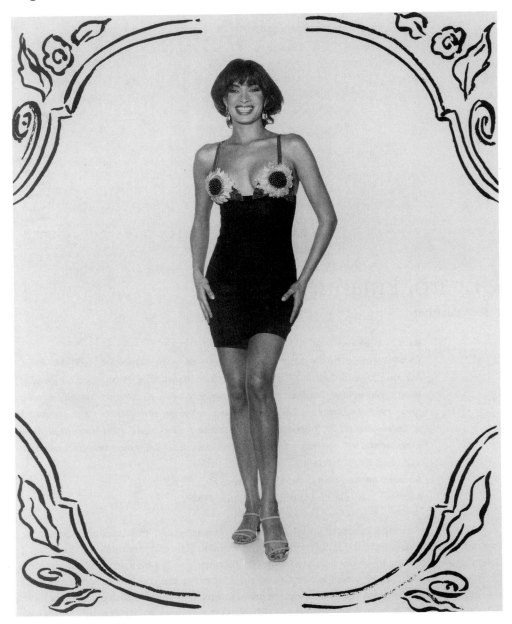

Emanuel Ungaro: Spring 1992; black linen daisy applique sundress.

Toward the end of the 1970s, Ungaro began to experiment with the then-taboo mixing of textures and prints, of which he has become the master. Knapp's fabrics had evolved into more painterly, impressionistic florals, abstract smears, luminous colors. In daytime clothing Ungaro would pair a paisley blouse with a plaid suit, or a striped top worn under a tweed jacket with glen plaid trousers. In 1980, this daring approach found full expression in a collection of casual but complex ensembles, featuring fantasy printed, gold-edged jackets over sheer lace blouses, luxuriant paisley shawls wrapped over quilted, fur-lined cardigans, solid chiffon blouses paired with half-patterned, half-striped skirts. For evening, embellished velvet burnooses or wrapped paisley dresses, trimmed in black lace, completed this unusual eclectic look, offered through Ungaro's expensive ready-to-wear line, Parallèle. This risk taking had its early appearance in Ungaro couture, and has continued to the present day. The clothes were designed for women who chose and combined their outfits without regard to what others would think. In the wake of the drab "dress for success" uniform, Ungaro's vision offered the self-confident woman, or one who was not dependent upon conformity for job security, the opportunity for a more personal, individual look. Knapp's special fabrics made the mixtures work. Her colors were rich, with underlying coordinate properties that were not easy to duplicate. Over the years many designers have borrowed from Ungaro's ideas, with varying degrees of success.

Borrowing from the East, in 1981, Ungaro layered fluid chinoiserie patterned tunics over contrasting colorways skirts, draped with tasseled shawls of tiny floral and undulating lines in a riot of colors. The sensual, covered-up looks suggested Gustav Klimt's paintings in their profusion of mosaic colors and patterns. Cummerbund-bound floral skirts topped with lacy blouses under boleros showed a folkloric influence, though less literal than Saint Laurent's Russians a few years before.

Ungaro's designs have been intended to convey sex appeal without being vulgar. He has said that when doing a dress he would always ask himself if the woman in the dress would be seductive. Women and music are his inspiration. One can only guess if a particular collection has been created while Ungaro was listening to Mozart, Beethoven, Wagner, Stravinsky, or Ravel. Certainly his designs possess the contrast and harmony, repose and counterpoint of a musical composition. By the mid-1980s an Ungaro dress could be immediately identified by its diagonally draped and shirred skirt, wide shoulders gathered into gigot sleeves buttoned at the wrist, wrapped V-neckline, jewel-toned silk jacquard fabric. Ungaro wedding dresses were of pale pastel crêpe, sculpted, diagonally draped and caught with self-fabric flowers. At this time he introduced the short black-skirted suit with colorful jackets, both printed and plain. This look continues to be universally chic. To add to the seductiveness of his ensembles, Ungaro's models wore veiled elongated pillbox hats, pushed down over the eyes, an accessory resurrected a decade later for fall.

By 1985 Ungaro seemed to achieve a new serenity, the result of his thoughts and dreams. Since then he has repeated with variations the sleek curvaceous silhouettes, the fluid construction, ingenious cut, original color sense, and print and pattern mixtures without ever becoming boring. The self-confident Ungaro customer is also appealingly vulnerable because the fabric and cut subtly reveal her body. A flirtation with the short bubble floral skirt followed Lacroix's introduction of that silhouette, but Ungaro became even more wildly successful with his short, tightly wrapped dress. Late 1980s spring dresses featured short flounced skirts, big puffed sleeves, and bold solids or florals. Ungaro called his style a "new Baroque." Fall 1989 ball gowns were gypsy inspired, with floor-length bouffant floral skirts trimmed with polka dotted ruffles and black lace, puffed sleeved jackets of contrasting florals trimmed with velvet and jewels. In 1990 folkloric flowers trimmed a cape worn over a short black leather skirt and deep red jacket. Voluminous Victorian bustled plaid skirts on strapless evening dresses highlighted Ungaro's 1991 couture, while padded Central Asian coats were offered through his ready-to-wear line. After a cheerful, bouffant skirted spring, Ungaro presented a more somber, but no less luxurious, collection for the fall of 1992. Ungaro Parallèle continued to produce feminine floral brocade dresses and vibrant plaid suits interwoven with gold threads. In 1991 the lower priced Emanuel line was launched, with the famous tight and short Ungaro silhouette typified by a thigh-high shirred houndstooth dress with high neck and long sleeves.

Certainly the body-hugging Ungaro designs require a trim figure, but all the shoulder and hip emphasis can also be flattering to many figures by simulating an hourglass shape. Diagonal lines have a slimming effect. Some of Ungaro's spring dresses have merely skimmed the body, hiding flaws. Slit skirts have flatteringly shown off still-good legs. Ever in search of pleasing the woman, of following his dream, Ungaro has endured because his clothes show profound appreciation and respect for women.—THERESE DUZINKIEWICZ BAKER

Valentina

American designer

Born   *Valentina Sanina in Kiev, Russia, 1 May 1904.*
Education   *Studied drama in Kiev, 1917-19.*
Family   *Married George Schlee in 1921 (died, 1971).*
Career   *Dancer, Chauve Souris Theater, Paris, 1922-23; moved to New York, 1923. Opened small couture house, 1925, incorporated as Valentina Gowns, Inc., 1928; introduced perfume My Own, 1950; firm closed, 1957. Also: theater designer, leading ladies' gowns, 1934-54, 1964.*
Died   *(in New York) 14 September 1989.*

Madame Valentina was as exotic as her name. A Russian emigrée, she attracted attention in New York after her arrival in 1923 by looking like a woman at a time when women were trying to look like young boys. For dining in fashionable restaurants or attending the theater and parties with her theater producer husband George Schlee, Valentina wore her own designs—long, high necked, long sleeved gowns with natural waistlines, made of flowing black velvet—in contrast to the short, waistless, beaded flapper fashions that prevailed. Instead of bobbed hair, Valentina emphasized high cheekbones and large soulful eyes by wearing her long blonde hair in a high chignon. Slavic reserve, thick Russian accent, expressive hands, and movement with a dancer's grace completed the personality. She was her own best model and maintained a consistency of appearance throughout her long career.

Interest in Valentina's unusual clothes led to the establishment of Valentina Gowns, Inc. in 1928, on New York's upper East side. Success was immediate. Valentina's clients included luminaries from the theater, opera, ballet, society, and film. Greta Garbo, whom Valentina was said to resemble ("I am the Gothic version"), was one of her customers. Each of Valentina's customers, who numbered no more than 200 at any one time, was granted personal attention. Valentina insisted that she alone knew what was best for the customer and made last-minute changes in color or detail if necessary. Fashion editors were exasperated by Valentina's insistence upon selecting and modeling her clothes herself, but, ultimately, Valentina was right. Her business remained successful for 30 years. Valentina's sophisticated color sense, influenced by Léon Bakst, gravitated toward subtle earth tones, "off-colors," monochromatic schemes, and the ubiquitous black. An evening dress with a bolero might be made of three shades of grey. In the 1950s Valentina began using variations of deep colors of damask and brocade. From a visit to Greece, Valentina learned proportion, which lent an architectural dignity to her gowns. Her couture was original, intricately cut and fitted, and avoided the popular practice of copying French haute couture.

With an innate flair for the dramatic, Valentina successfully designed for the theater. Beginning with a play starring Judith Anderson in 1933, Valentina was known for her ability to suit the character, whether on or off the stage. Critic Brooks Atkinson commented, "Valentina has designed clothes that act before a line is spoken." The clothes she created for Katharine Hepburn in the 1939 stage play, *The Philadelphia Story,* remained in demand by her customers for five years. Timelessness of design was essential. In the 1930s and 1940s Valentina introduced hoods and snoods as headcoverings, wimple-like effects (flattering to mature throats) swathed around tall, medieval-inspired head-dresses. The diamond and emerald Maltese cross brooch she wore almost constantly was widely copied. Drawing inspiration from fine art in European galleries, Valentina created striking evening ensembles along Renaissance lines; a white crêpe floor-length gown fastened down the bodice with small self-fabric bows, topped by a three-quarter length beige wool cape, lined with gold brocade and fastened with an antique gold chain was one example.

Only the wealthy could afford Valentina. A minimum price of 250 dollars was charged per dress in the 1930s, with an average price of 600 dollars in the mid-1950s. Valentina preferred to sell entire wardrobes, presenting a unified look from formal to casual. For ease of travel she introduced the concept of a few coordinating pieces: blouse, bare top, skirt, shorts, and scarf that could be mixed and matched. Valentina disdained fussy, frilly ornamentation, silk flowers, or sequins, relying instead on exquisite line. During the 1930s she borrowed Oriental details such as *obi* sashes and Indian striped embroidery used as sleeve accents. A favorite casual accessory was a coolie hat tied under the chin. In the 1940s she promoted a look that was slightly softer than the popular, mannish, broad-shouldered silhouette, and she introduced the short evening dress, while promoting ballet slippers, which were not rationed, worn with dark rayon stockings.

Valentina's working costume often consisted of a simple black long-sleeved dress with a versatile neckline, cut so it could be pinned high with a contrasting pin, or folded down and worn with a long scarf draped about the head or shoulders for evening. A slice of colored satin lining would be turned *en revers* for contrast with the black. By the 1950s Valentina's evening gowns featured increasingly *décolletage* necklines. Her casual ruffled handkerchief linen blouses, worn with pleated skirts, were widely copied, as were her aproned organdie party dresses. The supple matte fabrics favored by Valentina included crêpe cut on the bias for daytime, wool and satin crêpes, chiffons and damasks. Elegant wraparound silhouettes were created for coats, one of which featured three layers of progressively longer capes falling from the shoulders. Valentina's idiosyncratic, though classic, fashions also included evening gowns with one bare shoulder, the other long-sleeved, dolman sleeves, large fur hats made from sable, the only fur she would accept. Plain necklines lent themselves well to showcasing her client's jewelry.

Often called "America's most glamorous dressmaker," Valentina was recognized to be one of the United States' top couturiers and theater costume designers. She retired in 1957, and died in 1989.—THERESE DUZINKIEWICZ BAKER

Valentino

Italian designer

Born *Valentino Garavani in Voghera, Italy, 11 May 1932.*

Education *Studied French and fashion design, Accademia dell'Arte, Milan, to 1948; studied at the Chambre Syndicale de la Couture, 1949-51.*

Career *Assistant designer, Jean Dessès, 1950-55, and Guy Laroche, 1956-58; assistant to Princess Irene Galitzine, 1959; business established, Rome, 1960; company owned by Kenton Corporation, 1968-73, repurchased by Valentino, 1973; showed first ready-to-wear collection, 1962; Valentino Più, interior décor, textile and gift company established, 1973; ready-to-wear boutiques established, Paris, 1968, Rome, 1972, 1988, Milan, 1979, London, 1987; menswear collection introduced, 1972; signature fragrance introduced, 1978.*

Exhibitions *Italian Re-Evolution, La Jolla Art Museum, California, 1982; retrospective, Capitoline Museum, Rome, 1991, and New York, 1992.*

Awards *Neiman Marcus Award, 1967; National Italian American Foundation Award, 1989.*

Address *Piazza Mignanelli 22, 00187 Rome, Italy.*

Both a reverent hush and an excited clamor surround the Italian designer Valentino simultaneously. He enjoys the patronage of a long established clientèle of wealthy and aristocratic women, yet his clothes are never staid and always express a fresh, current style. His collections and his lifestyle embody the grandeur and serenity of eternal Rome, where he works from his salon near the Spanish Steps, and at the same time represent the up-to-the-minute point of view of a jet-setting citizen of the world. In 1991 Valentino celebrated 30 years in business. The anniversary was celebrated in characteristically Valentino style in Rome with a magnificent retrospective exhibition, a lavish formal dinner, and an all-night dance party. The press reported this event with detailed descriptions of the proceedings and participants, who had flown in from around the globe to pay homage to the designer they devoutly refer to as "The Chic." Valentino's various homes, in London, Capri, Gstaad, and New York, are regularly featured in magazines and newspapers, an indication that "Valentino" is not just a style of dressing, but rather a style of living.

In 1960, when Valentino opened his first salon in the Via Condotti, Rome was the center of fashion in Italy. The ready-to-wear designers of Milan, the industrial center, did not come to prominence until a decade later. Thus the fashion world in Italy was the world of the couture in Rome. After having served as an apprentice in Paris for five years with Jean Dessès and two years with Guy Laroche, Valentino's design foundation was firmly set in the haute couture tradition of quality, luxury, and a dose of extravagance. He immediately began to attract clients who came to him for his finely crafted, colorful, and elegant designs. By the mid-1960s he introduced his signature trousersuits for day and evening.

In 1968 he created a sensation with his White Collection which featured short dresses shown with lace stockings and simple flat shoes. That same year Jacqueline Kennedy chose a lace-trimmed silk two-piece dress with a short pleated skirt, for her marriage to Aristotle Onassis. Red has become Valentino's signature color, a rich shade of crimson with vibrant overtones of orange. He uses it throughout his collections, especially in his lavish evening designs, which are characterized by magnificent embroideries and meticulous detailing. A section of his retrospective exhibition was devoted to evening jackets covered entirely in elaborately beaded decorations. Typical Valentino details include scalloped trims and hems, raglan sleeves, circular ruffles, complex plays of proportion, and extravagant pattern and texture mixes; for example, the combination of lace, velvet, and houndstooth in a single outfit.

Valentino's devotees flock to him for couture and ready-to-wear and a vast array of products and accessories including menswear, innerwear, leather goods, eyewear, furs, and perfumes. He reaches the youth market through his Oliver line of clothes that are casual but still marked with distinctively refined Valentino sensibility. He produces a special collection of eveningwear called Valentino Night, in which the luxury of his couture designs is adapted for a wider audience. All of his designs, throughout all of his collections, express a singularly opulent view of the world. Valentino's sensibility embraces both timelessness and originality, filtered through a dedication to a luxurious way of life and the commitment to express that lifestyle in his collections.—ALAN E. ROSENBERG

Van den Akker, Koos

American designer

Born *The Hague, Netherlands, 16 March 1939.*

Education *Studied at the Netherlands Royal Academy of Art, 1956-58; worked in department stores in The Hague and in Paris; studied fashion at L'École Guerre Lavigne, Paris, 1961.*

Military Service *Served in the Royal Dutch Army, 1958-60.*

Career *Apprenticed at Dior, Paris, 1963-65; returned to The Hague and maintained own boutique, 1965-68; immigrated to the United States, 1968, naturalized, 1982; lingerie designer, Eve Stillman, New York, 1969-70; free-lance designer, from 1971; first New York boutique established, Columbus Avenue, 1971-75; relocated to Madison Avenue, 1975; opened second shop, Beverly Hills, California, 1978; opened second New York boutique, 1979; added line of handbags, 1986; introduced diffusion line, Hot House, 1983. Also: designer of bedlinen, lingerie and home furnishings.*

Awards *Gold Coast Award, 1978; American Printed Fabrics Council "Tommy," Award, 1983.*

Address *550 7th Avenue, 18th Floor, New York, New York 10018, USA.*

Koos Van Den Akker is known for his painterly delight in mixing colors, patterns, and textures in unusual, often one of a kind, garments. Since his arrival in the United States in 1968 with just a sewing machine, he has been delighting clients who want something a bit different to wear. His styles have not changed much, simple shapes being more amenable to rich surface manipulations. Having learned the basics of good fit and cut as an apprentice with the house of Christian Dior, Van Den Akker was able to proceed confidently with the fabric collages which have become his signature. Although his Koos garments recall the art-to-wear movement, they remain free of the sometimes heavy-handed messages inherent in the artifacts that seem more suitable for gallery walls: they are meant to be worn and appreciated for their beauty.

Conservatively styled suits consisting of cardigan jackets and gored skirts might be covered with textured mixtures of fur, quilted fabric, leather strips, or pieces of wool. A dress of lace might be dramatized by bold appliqué. As many as six materials might be combined in collages of cotton, wool, furs, tweeds, sequins, and leather. Some of the results are reminiscent of grandmother's "crazy quilt," but they are carried out with a true designer's skill and artistic sensitivity. Indeed, Van Den Akker has admitted that the designs just flow, working themselves out through the process of creation, perhaps reflecting a hereditary affinity with Dutch national costume.

Six years at The Hague selling his own custom-made dresses in a boutique gained Van Den Akker the experience to open a Madison Avenue shop, one in Beverly Hills, and a men's boutique during the 1970s. In 1983 he presented a moderately priced collection, Hot House. By 1986 he was designing lingerie, daytime and evening clothes, furs, sheets, and home furnishings. Women's clothes were made of beautiful fabrics with colorful print and lace inserts, sometimes following the lines of the garments in harmony and balance, other times contrasting shapes versus line. During the 1980s Van Den Akker collected a following among show business personalities including Gloria Vanderbilt, who at one point surrounded herself with patchwork, Elizabeth Taylor, Cher, Madeleine Kahn, Barbara Walters, Marilyn Horne, and Glenn Close. Bill Cosby wore Van Den Akker's sweaters on *The Cosby Show*.

Van Den Akker has been eager to share the joy he attains from his craft. Designer Christian Francis Roth was his apprentice for several years before venturing on his own. In late 1989 Van Den Akker showed the home-sewing public how to make their own creative clothing in a detailed article in *Threads Magazine*. The next year signaled a broadening of his range to include simpler ready-to-wear sportswear: tweed dresses and coats, coats of blanket materials, matching suede jackets and skirts, and short floral dresses with just a hint of the Koos play with fabrics in a mixed-print collar.

Van Den Akker continues to refine his artistry, developing a ready-to-wear sportswear collection for DeWilde that is more subtle and interchangeable. Toned-down collage effects and texture appliqués lend interest to classic pieces in wool and cashmere, even sheer georgette.—THERESE DUZINKIEWICZ BAKER

Vass, Joan
American designer

Born *New York City, 19 May 1925.*
Education *Attended Vassar College and graduated in philosophy from the University of Wisconsin, 1942; did graduate work in aesthetics at the University of Buffalo.*
Family *Children from first marriage: Richard, Sara, Jason.*

Career *Assistant curator, drawing and prints, the Museum of Modern Art, New York; free-lance editor, Harry N. Abrams publishing house, New York; columnist, Art in America, New York. Began designing hand knits in the early 1970s with sales to Henri Bendel, New York; company incorporated as Joan Vass, Inc., 1977; labels include Joan Vass Sporting, Joan Vass New York, men's and women's clothing; Joan Vass USA, lower priced women's line, introduced, 1984; Joan Vass USA For Men introduced, 1988; New York flagship store opened, 1989.*

Awards *Smithsonian Institution, Extraordinary Women in Fashion Award, 1978; Coty American Fashion Critics Award, 1979, 1981; Prince Machiavelli Prix de Cachet Award, 1980.*

Address *485 Seventh Avenue, New York, New York 10018, USA.*

Joan Vass is an American designer who believes the only purpose for a label in a piece of clothing is to show which way to put it on. Her easy-to-wear designs for both men and women are beautifully crafted, in simple, elegant lines.

In college, Vass studied philosophy and aesthetics. She worked as an assistant curator of drawings and prints at the Museum of Modern Art in New York. At the same time she edited art books for Harry N. Abrams and wrote columns about art auctions for *Art in America*.

Joan Vass began a cottage industry in the early 1970s when she brought her personal interest in hand knits and crochet to women who needed an outlet for their marketable skills. Vass created designs for hats and mufflers which these women crocheted. Marketed at Henri Bendel, New York, they quickly sold out. She went on to create designs for sweaters for both men and women, having them produced under the label Joan Vass New York. Vass provided the designs, the yarns and buttons if necessary. Her cadre of workers, ranging in age from 20-70, came from a variety of backgrounds including housewives and artists. They would knit, crochet, or hand-loom the design, incorporating their personal style. The production for this line was limited, selective, and not accessible to everyone. The Joan Vass New York line continues today with some of the original craftspeople still creating the designs provided by Joan Vass. It remains a small-volume, selective design business which now includes woven materials. All of the designs from the past are still available to be produced.

The return to natural fibers, the individuality in American fashion expression, the use of knits for more than just the travel wardrobe, plus a new-found appreciation for hand-made items during the 1970s all helped create a welcoming environment for Vass's designs. Her work was unique, practical, and beautifully crafted.

Vass created her own company in 1977. In the 1980s, a mid-priced licensed line was first produced on a large scale by the Signal Knitting Mills in South Carolina. Working with Joan Vass designs these clothes carry the label Joan Vass USA. They are made of beautiful fine-gauged, natural fiber, knitted and woven fabrics. Today there is a third design line called Joan Vass Sporting. This is a more casual line which includes more details. Though natural fibers are still used, the designs also use some of the new synthetic fibers such as chinchilla, a 100 percent polyester fabric.

Whether Joan Vass New York, Joan Vass USA, or Joan Vass Sporting, the designs she creates are simple and easy to wear. They are predominantly made of natural fibers, usually in subtle colors, in unstructured shapes. There are no extras such as shoulder pads. Besides sweaters, she designs trousers, skirts, and shorts and dresses. Her stated aim is to produce interchangeable, ageless designs which evolve from season to season. Reviews in the *Daily News Record* describe Vass's designs as classic. When the clothes are old, she wants them to be worn for gardening.

In an interview for *House and Garden,* Vass says, "If you notice me I am not well-dressed" (Johnathan Etra, "Vass Horizons," January 1989). She feels that style is something that lasts. This does not preclude a sense of humor in her design work, as she has been inspired by iguanas and has created bizarre and funny hats. Joan Vass is an American woman who has strong ideas and concerns which are reflected in her designs.—NANCY HOUSE

Venet, Philippe

French fashion designer

Born *Lyons, France, 22 May 1929.*
Education *Apprentice tailor, age 14, at Pierre Court, Lyons, until 1948.*
Military Service *Served in French Army, 1948-50.*
Career *Assistant designer Schiaparelli, Paris, 1951-53; master tailor for Givenchy, 1953-62. Established Philippe Venet couture house, Paris, 1962; launched menswear collection, 1990s.*
Awards *Dé d'Or, Paris, 1985.*
Address *62 rue Francois 1er, 75008 Paris, France.*

Philippe Venet had a long apprenticeship in fashion before opening his own couture house in 1962, at the age of 33. Born in Lyons, France, he was apprenticed at 14 to an established and respected dressmaker in the town, Pierre Court, where he was taught about fabric, manufacture, and cut, as well as learning the rudiments of tailoring, a major feature of his later work. Pierre Court held the rights to the Balenciaga label and it was Venet's association with this Parisian couture house that led him to the fashion capital to pursue his design career.

His first job was at the house of Schiaparelli. Elsa Schiaparelli had been one of the most important and influential designers of the 1930s, when her witty surrealist and avant-garde designs broke new ground in fashion. By the 1950s, however, Schiaparelli's influence was waning and the house was soon to close. For Venet the job was a stepping stone in his career. It was at Schiaparelli that he met the young Hubert de Givenchy, who was also an employee. When Givenchy opened his own couture house in 1953, he employed Venet as his master tailor.

The 1950s were Givenchy's heyday, a success to which Philippe Venet undoubtedly contributed. Givenchy is perhaps most notable for his association with Audrey Hepburn whom he first dressed in the 1954 film *Sabrina Fair*. Together, the design house and actress created a gamine look that typified the style of the late 1950s and 1960s. It was young elegance, long-legged and sophisticated, ranging from Audrey's beatnik look in the 1957 film *Funny Face,* to her little black dress look in the 1961 film *Breakfast at Tiffany's*.

Philippe Venet finally opened his own couture house at 62 rue François 1er in 1962. His experience and respect for the traditions of haute couture were a mainstay of his work from the beginning, as were his superb tailoring skills. His cut is always innovative and imaginative and a range of beautifully cut and tailored coats have always featured in a collection. Distinctive pieces from the 1960s were his kite coats, plastic diamonds attached edge to edge to thick white, short, and full length coats. A strong coat theme from the 1970s was geometry, oversize capes and jackets in flannel and reversible wools, with square and dolman sleeves and triangular pocket details. His suits and coats in the 1980s and 1990s are romantic and flirtatious, in refreshing colours.

Venet's eveningwear is often inspired by flora and fauna. In a black organza dress, the skirt is folded into layered petals and secured with a belt. A baby doll dress is made from a country garden flower-print taffeta, strapless and suspended by a huge bow at the bust. The overall look is romantic but sophisticated, smart but with a hint of naughtiness, and designed for a wealthy clientèle.

Venet was awarded the Dé d'Or Award in January 1985. This award not only recognized his aesthetic contribution to the fashion industry but applauded the detailed attention he brings to every aspect of the business; closely monitoring the creation of each outfit and personally attending all the fittings.

Today Venet divides his time between France and the United States. A third of his clients are American, and he presents a collection once a year in both Los Angeles and New York. Expansion of the business in the 1990s has included a menswear line to complement the womenswear ranges.—KEVIN ALMOND

Versace, Gianni

Italian designer

Born *Reggio Calabria, Italy, 2 December 1946.*

Education *Studied architecture, Calabria, 1964-67.*

Career *Designer and buyer in Paris and London, for his mother's dressmaking studio, 1968-72; free-lance designer, Callaghan, Complice, Genny, Milan, 1972-77; formed own company, Milan, 1978; showed first womenswear collection, 1978, first menswear collection, 1979; signature fragrance introduced, 1981; home furnishings collection launched, 1993. Also theatrical costume designer, La Scala and Bejart Ballet, from 1982.*

Exhibitions *Galleria Rizzardi, Milan, 1982; Studio La Città, Verona, 1983; Galerie Focus, Munich, 1983; Gianni Versace: dialogues de mode, Palais Galliera, Paris, 1986; retrospective, Fashion Institute of Technology, New York, 1992-93.*

Awards *Occhio d'Oro Award, Milan, 1982, 1984, 1990, 1991; Cutty Sark Award, 1983, 1988; Council of Fashion Designers of America International Award, 1993.*

Address *Via Gesu, 20121 Milan, Italy.*

Gianni Versace's work is both metaphorical opera and real clothing, the first in its larger-than-life exuberance and design *bravura* and the latter in its unpretentious, practical application to the comfort of the wearer and the expressiveness of the body. Versace has made all the world a stage for flamboyant and fascinating costume with the knowledgeable pageantry of the Renaissance, a Fellini-like sensuality of burlesque, and the brilliant notes of operatic color and silhouette. Richly cultivated in historical materials and vividly committed to the hedonism of late 20th-century culture, Versace creates a distinctive, at-the-edge design that achieves the aesthetic limit of the avant-garde and the commercial success of viable apparel. As Peter Carlsen argued in 1979, a Versace garment is of its time, is part of a "pure" design continuum pursued by Versace, and incorporates elements of history. (*Gentleman's Quarterly,* August 1979.)

Versace has expressed his admiration for Poiret, the fashion revolutionary who in a brief *éclat* of design genius combined a theatrical fantasy with *legerdemain* eclecticism. Similarly, Versace functions as a kind of impresario to his own style, commanding authority over his image and advertising, menswear, womenswear, and other products. His apparel design is character-ized by a particular interest in bias, itself a means of revealing the body in dramatic, sexy clothing for women. His embroideries (and metal mesh) harken back to the art déco, but also come forward to the conversationals of recent magazine covers. Likewise, his fascination with black-and-white grids and alternations recalls the 1920s and 1930s. His abundant swathings suggest Vionnet, Madame Grès, and North Africa. Line is important, with many Versace suits, dresses, and coats marked by lines as if the bound edges of fabric would in outline define waistlines, shoulders, or center front. Like any great prestidigitator on stage, Versace is also concerned with metamorphic clothing; that which can be worn or perceived in several different ways. In these respects, it is clear that the Milanese designer looks to Tokyo as well as to Milan and Paris. His metallics, trousers for women (ranging from voluminous pantaloons to cigarette-trouser leg wrappings), leather for women, and chunky, glittery accessories have created an image of women as a cross between Amazon and siren.

The boldness of silhouette in his womenswear is only reinforced in his work with photographers to represent the clothing, generally against a pure white field to grant further starkness and aggressiveness. But, in person and in the individual item, Versace's clothing is far less *diva* and dominatrix than it might seem. Versace's jewel-like colors, his line in geometry in pattern, his recurrent fascination with the asymmetrical collars engendered by bias, and his flamboyant juxtapositions of pattern are elegant traits. Likewise, Versace employs luxurious textiles, a proclivity to classical references, bias in its mediation between the hard edge of geometry and the soft rendering of the body (even as practised in trousers on the bias), and such combinations as leather reversible to wool, embroidery-encrusted bodies and soft flowing skirts, and anomalous fashion history in skirt-trouser combinations with blazer and wrapped waist, a piquant pastiche of fashion elements. When Diana Vreeland reportedly commended Versace, saying that no one could wrap cloth like him and that wearing a Versace blouse made her feel 20 years old again, Vreeland identified the bias as his most trenchant attribute and as a trait precious in fashion history since Vionnet.

Versace's menswear is also accented by leather, body wrapping for sensuality, audacious silhouette, and oversizing for comfort. Even in menswear, Versace plays with asymmetry and the bias-influenced continuous rotation around the body, rather than a disjunctive front and back. Versace's menswear in particular is sometimes criticized as being futuristic with its big shoulders and technological detailing seeming to suggest science fiction. However, Versace employs the most elegant menswear materials in a loose, capacious drape that defies any outer-space uniforms. Rather, his design recalls Thayaht and the Futurist ideal of clothing fully realized for the first time with sensuality and practicality.

Versace is an encyclopaedist of classical tradition. His insistence upon directing all aspects of the fashion communication, his books and exhibitions interpreting his one work, and his theatrical work in its virtuoso diversity testify to a philosophy of fashion as expressed in his exhibition and book *Gianni Versace: L'abito per pensare*. Versace is neither a secluded scholastic, though, nor merely the glittery dresser of stars and celebrities that some have perceived. The truth is somewhere in between, in a design imagination of brilliant theatrical insight, probing and analytical interest in bias, and a desire to reconcile the use of fashion history with the making of a clothing aesthetic for today. Versace has brought theatrical delirium and delight to the classical tradition in a way that reminds us of the ceaseless energy and entertainment of human adornment. In Versace, a dynamic classicism survives and a jubilant theater triumphs.—RICHARD MARTIN

Vionnet, Madeleine

French designer

Born *Chilleurs-aux-Bois, 22 June 1876.*

Family *Married in 1893 (divorced, 1894); one child (died); married Dmitri Netchvolodov in 1925 (divorced, 1955).*

Career *Dressmaker's apprentice, Aubervilliers, 1888-93; dressmaker, House of Vincent, Paris, 1893-95; cutter, then head of workroom, Kate Reilly, London, 1895-1900; saleswoman, Bechoff David, Paris, 1900-01; head of studios under Marie Gerber, Callot Soeurs, Paris, 1901-05; designer, Doucet, 1905-11; designer, Maison Vionnet, 1912-14, 1919-39; retired, 1940.*

Exhibitions *Three Women: Madeleine Vionnet, Claire McCardell and Rei Kawakubo, Fashion Institute of Technology, New York, 1987; retrospective, Musée de Marseille, 1991.*

Died *(in Paris) 2 March 1975.*

Bruce Chatwin once commented: "A Vionnet dress looks [like] nothing in the hand. It contains no artificial stiffening and flops limply on the hanger" (*The Sunday Times Magazine,* London 4 March 1973). Vionnet's inexorable synergy is the body in the dress. Her draping on the bias gave stretch to the fabric, a fully three-dimensional and even gyroscopic geometry to the garment, and a fluid dynamic of the body in motion as radical as Cubism and Futurism in their panoramas on the body. Her work inevitably prompts the analogy to sculpture in its palpable revelation of the form within. Some accused Vionnet of a shocking *déshabillé,* but Vionnet was seeking only the awareness of volume. Chatwin wrote: "No-one knew better how to drape a torso in the round. She handled fabric as a master sculptor realises the possibilities latent in a marble block; and like a sculptor too she understood the subtle beauty of the female body in motion and that graceful movements were enhanced by asymmetry of cut."

The only rigidity that ever obtained for Vionnet was her definite sense of self: she closed her couture house in 1939, although she lived until 1975. She lamented the work of other designers and disdained much that occurred in fashion as unprincipled and unworthy; and she was a true believer in the modern, scorning unnecessary adornment, seeking structural principles, demanding plain perfection. Fernand Léger said that one of the finest things to see in Paris was Vionnet cutting. He used to go there when he felt depleted in his own work.

Vionnet draped on a reduced-scale mannequin. There she played her cloth in the enhanced elasticity of its diagonal bias to create the garment. In creating the idea in miniature, Vionnet may have surpassed any sense of weight of the fabric and achieved her ideal and effortless rotation around the body in a most logical way. When the same garments achieved human proportion, their sheerness, the avoidance of decorative complication, the absence of planes front and back, and the supple elegance of fabric that caresses the body in a continuous peregrination were distinctive of Vionnet.

While bias cut was quickly emulated in the Paris couture, Vionnet's concepts of draping were not pursued only by Claire McCardell (who bought Vionnets to study their technique) before World War II, Geoffrey Beene, Halston, and other Americans in the 1960s and 1970s, Azzedine Alaïa in France, and Japanese designers Issey Miyake and Rei Kawakubo in the 1970s and 1980s (alerted to Vionnet by her strong presence in *The 10s, 20s, 30s* exhibition organized by Diana Vreeland at The Costume Institute of the Metropolitan Museum of Art in 1973-74).

One of Vionnet's most-quoted aphorisms is "when a woman smiles, her dress must smile with her." By making the dress dependent on the form of the wearer rather than an armature of its own, Vionnet assured the indivisibility of the woman and the garment. It is as if she created a skin or a shell rather than the independent form of a dress. Like many designers of her time, Vionnet's external references were chiefly to classical art and her dresses could resemble the wet drapery of classical statues and their cling and crêpey volutes of drapery.

At Doucet, she had discarded the layer of the underdress. In her own work, Vionnet eliminated interfacing in order to keep silhouette and fabric pliant; she brought the vocabulary of lingerie to the surface in her *détente* of all structure; she avoided any intrusion into fabric that could be avoided. Darts are generally eliminated. In a characteristic example, her "honeycomb dress," all structure resided in the manipulation of fabric to create the honeycomb, a pattern that emanates the silhouette. Elsewhere, faggoting and drawnwork displace the need for darts or other impositions and employ a decorative field to generate the desired form of the garment. The fluidity of cowl neckline, the chiffon handkerchief dress, and hemstiched blouse were trademarks and soft symbols of a virtuoso designer.

In insisting on the presence of a body and on celebrating the body within clothing, Vionnet is an early-century revolutionary in the manner of Diaghilev, Isadora Duncan, and Picasso. But there is also a deeply hermetic aspect to Vionnet who remains, despite the prodigious research revelations of Betty Kirke, a designer's designer, so subtle are the secrets of composition, despite the outright drama of being one of the most revolutionary and important fashion designers of the century.—RICHARD MARTIN

Vittadini, Adrienne

American designer

Born *Adrienne Toth, in Budapest, Hungary, 1944. Immigrated to the United States, 1956.*

Education *Studied at the Moore College of Art, Philadelphia, 1962-66; received academic scholarship to apprentice with Louis Feraud, Paris, 1965.*

Family *Married Gianluigi Vittadini in 1972.*

Career *Designer, Sport Tempo, New York, 1967; designer, SW1 line for Rosanna division, Warnaco, New York, 1968-71; designer, Adrienne Vittadini collection for Avanzara division, Kimberly Knits, New York, 1976-79; with partner Victor Coopersmith, established own firm, AVVC, 1979, bought out partner, renamed company Adrienne Vittadini,*

1982; formed Vopco Inc., franchising company, New York, 1987. First boutique opened, Beverly Hills, California, 1987. Also designer, Adrienne Vittadini swimwear collection for Cole of California.

Awards Coty American Fashion Critics Award, 1984.

Address 1441 Broadway, New York, New York 10018, USA.

To the industry and the fashion press, Hungarian-born Adrienne Vittadini is known as the Queen of Knits. In 1979, after working with several knitwear firms, Vittadini started her own knitwear company, always asserting that knitwear is more than just sweaters. As a knitwear designer she is also a textile as well as a fashion designer. Vittadini maintains, "creating fabrics, then silhouettes, is the essence of fashion." She begins with a concept or theme for a collection, based on a mood or a feeling, which she then connects with a particular inspiration. The inspiration can evolve from an individual artist, an artistic movement, or her travels. Once she decides on a theme, intense research in libraries, museums, books, and magazines begins. Her collections have been inspired by the works of Alexander Calder, Pablo Picasso, Joan Miró, and Max Bill as well as Norwegian design and early Russian embroidery. She also taps into contemporary pop culture for ideas, such as the line she designed based on the cartoon character Dick Tracy.

After establishing a theme, Vittadini creates the knit fabric by selecting and creating unusually textured yarns with Italian yarn spinners. She then oversees the dyeing to obtain her own distinctive colorings and often supervises the initial samples off the knitting machines. Once the color and pattern are finalized, the fit, finishing, and quality are considered. This allows her to maintain a sense of control over the design process from start to finish. Vittadini likens this entire process to painting, relating to her background in fine arts study at Moore College of Art in Philadelphia.

The Vittadini look is characterized by knitwear that is of all-natural fiber, a certain practical, casual ease, and contemporary design with a feminine appeal. Her trademark knit silhouettes are loose-fit sweaters worn over short skirts, sophisticated ensembles, and sweater dresses which can all be interchanged. Vittadini asserts that knits are the most modern way of dressing. In her collections, she balances her love of European elegance in design with American practicality and ease by creating clothes which are "feminine without fussiness, a certain cleanness and pureness without hardness." Vittadini's simple knit silhouettes create a seductive look as they mold to the shape of the body.

First and foremost, Vittadini design is defined by the textile. She has expanded the knitwear industry by inventing and developing new computer knitting techniques in textures, prints, and patterns as well as shapes and colors. Vittadini cites Lycra as the most important development in knitwear. She uses it as a technological and functional tool to keep shape in her knits—especially trousers. Vittadini has expanded the fabrics used in her collections to include wovens, prints, suedes, and leathers. Her lines now include licensing arrangements for cotton swimwear, accessories, girlswear, sleepwear, sunglasses, home furnishings, wallcoverings, and decorative fabrics. Roughly 60 per cent of her line is knits.

Adrienne Vittadini has always stressed the advantage she has as a woman designer. She states that, because she is a woman, she knows innately what other women want: clothes which reflect their modern lifestyles.

For many years, knits were looked upon by the industry as dowdy. Since Vittadini revolutionized the power of knits, many Seventh Avenue companies now include knits in their collections. By promoting the ease and practicality of knits as well as the fact they travel well, the Vittadini customer is both suburban and city, housewife and businesswomen, with a diverse set of needs from clothes. Adrienne Vittadini has recognized the importance of sportswear to her American customer by offering a quality, well-designed product.—MARGO SEAMAN

Vivier, Roger
French footwear designer

Born *Paris, 13 November 1913.*

Education *Studied sculpture at l'École des Beaux Arts, Paris.*

Military Service *Performed military service, 1938-39.*

Career *Designed shoe collection for friend's shoe factory. Opened own atelier, 1937, designing for Pinet and Bally in France, Miller and Delman in USA, Rayne and Turner in United Kingdom; designed exclusively for Delman, New York, 1940-41 and 1945-47. Studied millinery, 1942; opened New York store, Suzanne and Roger, with milliner Suzanne Remy, 1945; returned to Paris, 1947, designing free-lance; designed for Dior's new shoe department, 1953-63; showed signature collections, from 1963; reopened own business in Paris, 1963. Designs collections for couture houses, including Grès, St Laurent, Ungaro, and Balmain.*

Exhibitions *Musée des Arts de la Mode, Paris, 1987 (retrospective).*

Awards *Neiman Marcus Award, 1961; Daniel & Fischer Award; Riberio d'Oro.*

Roger Vivier has been perhaps the most innovative shoe designer of the 20th century. Vivier's shoes have had the remarkable ability to seem avant-garde yet destined at the same time to become classics. He has maintained an eye for the cutting edge of fashion for nearly six decades. Vivier looks back into the history of fashion and forward to the disciplines of engineering and science for inspiration. The shoes may seem shocking at first; however, it is the way that they complete the silhouette that has made Vivier so coveted by top fashion designers of the 20th century. With a sophisticated eye for line, form, and the use of innovative materials, Vivier has created footwear which has been worn by some of the most stylish and prestigious people of the 20th century, among them red *faux* snakeskin boots for Diana Vreeland, gold kidskin shoes studded with rubies for the coronation of the Queen of England, "Ball of Diamonds" shoes for Marlene Dietrich.

Vivier has worked with some of the most innovative fashion designers of the 20th century: these have included Elsa Schiaparelli, Christian Dior, and Yves Saint Laurent, at the height of their careers. Schiaparelli was the first designer to include Vivier's shoes in her collection. Vivier was working for the American firm Delman at the time. Delman rejected Vivier's sketch of the shocking platform shoe which Schiaparelli included in her 1938 collection. In 1947 Vivier began to work for Christian Dior. The New Look by Dior brought new emphasis to the ankle and foot. Vivier created a number of new heel shapes for Dior, including the stiletto and the comma heel. During their ten-year association, Dior and Vivier created a golden era of design. In the 1960s Vivier created the low heeled "pilgrim pump" with a square silver buckle. This shoe is often cited as fashion's most copied shoe.

Vivier was one of the first designers to use clear plastic in the design of shoes. His first plastic designs were created in the late 1940s after World War II; however, in the early 1960s he created entire collections in plastic. Vivier popularized the acceptance of the thigh-high *cuissarde* boot in the mid-1960s, a fashion which had been considered unacceptable for women since the time of Joan of Arc (Trasko, Mary, New York 1989). Vivier teamed with Delman again in 1992. The mood of his collections continues to be imaginative and forward thinking. Drawing his inspiration from nature, contemporary fashion, the history of fashion, painting, and literature, Vivier has updated some of his earlier designs and he is constantly creating new designs which challenge the ideas of shoe design.

Vivier studied sculpture at the École des Beaux-Arts in Paris and later apprenticed at a shoe factory. It was this solid base of training in both aesthetics and technical skills that led Vivier to become known for precision fit as well as innovative design. A *Vogue* ad for his shoes in 1953 educates the viewer to look beyond the design. Showing the shoes embraced in callipers and other precision tools the ad reads, "Now study the heel. It announces an entirely new principle— the heel moved forward, where it carries the body's weight better." In another ad from *Vogue* (1954) the experience of owning a pair of Vivier shoes is likened to owning a couturier suit or dress, "a perfection of fit and workmanship." Vivier's shoes not only have the ability to complete a silhouette with an eloquence that makes a whole, but the beauty of their line, form, and craftsmanship make them creations that stand alone as objects of art. Vivier's strong combination of design and craftsmanship allows his shoes to stand prominently in the permanent collections of some of the world's most prestigious museums: the Costume Institute of the Metropolitan Museum of Art, New York; the Victoria and Albert Museum, London; and the Musée du Costume et de la Mode of the Louvre, Paris.—DENNITA SEWELL

Von Furstenberg, Diane

Belgian designer working in the United States

Born *Diane Michelle Halfin in Brussels, 31 December 1946.*

Education *Studied at the University of Madrid, graduated in economics, University of Geneva.*

Family *Married Prince Egon Von Furstenberg in 1969 (divorced, 1983); children: Alexandre, Tatiana.*

Career *Immigrated to the United States, 1969; owner, designer, Diane Von Furstenberg Studio, 1970-77, and from 1985; established couture house, 1984-88; signature cosmetics line produced, 1977-83; Tatiana fragrance introduced, 1977.*

Awards *Fragrance Foundation Award, 1977; City of Hope Spirit of Life Award, Los Angeles, 1983; Savvy Magazine Award, New York, 1984, 1985, 1986, 1987, 1988; Einstein College of Medicine Spirit of Achievement Award, New York, 1984; Mayor of the City of New York's Statue of Liberty Medal, 1986.*

Address *745 Fifth Avenue, suite 2400, New York, New York, 10151, USA.*

I got into fashion almost by accident, inspired to create the pieces I wanted, but couldn't find, in my own wardrobe. From my original 1970s knit wrap dress, to my new 1990s stretch "sock dress," I believe in marrying fashion and function—chic style and easy comfort, maximum impact and minimum fuss.

Today I look to the modern woman. Pulled in many different directions in the course of a day, she juggles multiple roles depending on the situation, but always knows who she is and what's really important in her life.

I like to say that "I design a line the way I pack a suitcase," visualizing all of the different places I'm going to be, and then creating the appropriate outfits. My clothing must be timeless and versatile, so that a few simple pieces add up to many different looks. I think building a wardrobe should be like compiling a scrapbook of your life—over the years you accumulate favorite pieces, like old friends, that you always come back to for their unfailing ability to make you feel safe or confident, sexy or secure, depending on what you need.

Fabrics are key, since they're like a second skin, and should always be soft to the touch and breatheable. Colors should be beautiful and harmonious, and silhouettes simple, allowing the body to move freely. All in all, clothes should complement a woman, the perfect accessories to her beauty and lifestyle.—Diane Von Furstenburg

When Diane Von Furstenburg married Prince Egon Von Furstenburg in 1969, she became Princess Diane Von Furstenburg. This aristocratic title proved no mean asset when she embarked on a fashion career in 1969, after moving from Europe with her husband to the United States. The cachet of "Princess" on a label proved especially potent to American buyers, aware of the American public's fascination with titles.

Putting the preeminence of rank aside, Von Furstenburg began her career with no fashion training. Her qualifications were a degree in economics from the University of Geneva and a fluency in five languages. She did, however, have a knowledge of international high society and culture. For a short period after her marriage both she and her husband were celebrities amongst the party-going jet set of the late 1960s, and for a time there was not a party that they did not attend. Von Furstenburg started her business during this period with a range of simple dresses that she had made up in Italy. They were a reaction to the jeans dressing so prevalent then, providing an easy, elegant alternative for women who wanted to wear a dress. Selling the clothes herself by tugging a sample rail around various American stores, she became an immediate success and a known designer name almost overnight.

Her philosophy was simple: she wanted to create elegant ease for all women. "There was a need for my things, for very simple dresses everyone could wear," she said in an interview for the book *The Fashion Makers* (New York 1978). Both slim and large women could wear the clothes, senator's wives or secretaries. They were sexy and chic regardless of the customer because they were designed to be sexy, accessible, and easy-to-wear.

Von Furstenburg's business quickly flourished and expanded. Highly successful lines of cosmetics, scent, handbags, shoes, jewellery, table linen, furs, stationery, wallpaper, and designs for *Vogue Patterns* were produced. She even produced a *Book of Beauty* in 1976 which detailed many of her philosophies towards life and design. She established herself as a liberated role model for many women. When she declared, "You don't sit around in little white gloves and big hats and try to look fashionable. You have a job, a husband or lover and children," she was stressing the practicality with style needed to adapt to modern life, which in many ways sums up her design philosophy.

Von Furstenberg

Von Furstenburg resumed her business in the 1990s selling via television. Her contribution to fashion rests on a universal practicality. She believes in the importance of finding a style that is right for the individual, which is why many of her collections have featured very simple, flattering clothes. They can be dressed up or dressed down and are versatile enough for all sorts of women to feel attractive in. "Stick with them," she advises her customers when they have found Diane Von Furstenburg clothes to suit them.—KEVIN ALMOND

Weitz, John

American fashion and industrial designer

Born *Berlin, Germany, 25 May 1923; immigrated to Britain, 1934, and to the United States, 1940; naturalized American, 1943.*

Education *Studied at The Hall School, 1936, at St. Paul's School, London, 1936-39; apprenticed to Edward Molyneux, Paris, 1939-40.*

Family *Married Susan Kohner, 1964; children: Paul and Christopher; also, children Robert and Karen, from a previous marriage.*

Military Service *Served in the United States Army, 1943-46; became Captain.*

Career *Designer of women's sportswear, working with several companies in London and New York, until 1954; founder-designer and chairman, John Weitz Designs, Inc., men's fashion designs, New York, from 1954. Also a yachtsman and ex-race car driver.*

Awards *Sports Illustrated Award, 1959; NBC Today Award, 1960; Caswell-Massey Awards, 1963-66; Harper's Bazaar Medallion, New York, 1966; Moscow Diploma, 1967; Coty American Fashion Critics Award, 1974; Cartier Design Award, 1981; Mayor's Liberty Medal, New York, 1986; First Class Order of Merit, Germany, 1988; Dallas Menswear Mart Award, 1990; Fashion Institute of Technology President's Award, New York, 1990.*

Address *600 Madison Avenue, New York, New York 10022, USA.*

John Weitz explained to *The Boston Globe* (9 April 1989) that he never wears a formal dress shirt with his tuxedo. "I wear white business shirts. I can't take the time to fiddle with front studs. The last thing I want is to be controlled by fashion." No one would say—and certainly no one would dare say in his presence—that Weitz is controlled by fashion. Rather, he has treated fashion as a chosen field, one among many. He abandoned the competitive field of womenswear for a mannerly, self-invented calling in menswear. Even there, he has stayed slightly aloof, choosing to be the debonair gentleman rather than fashion victim/victimizer. He has become two rare personalities: a late New York intellectual and a natural aristocrat who has seen aristocracies disintegrate, but who persists in imagining new ones.

Since the 1940s, Weitz has spoken a gentlemanly common sense about fashion for men and women. First encouraged by Dorothy Shaver of Lord & Taylor (New York) in the 1940s to pursue women's sportswear with his demanding sense of a contemporary post-war lifestyle, Weitz carried his marrow of American practicality within the genteel spirit of his own European and English cultivation. A polymath, as much a man of letters and ideas as of fashion, once an adventurer who drove race cars and was solicited to portray James Bond, a paragon of elegance often compared in appearance to Gregory Peck and Cary Grant, Weitz is a consummate gentleman in the sometimes less than genteel world of fashion.

While his great achievements in apparel in the 1950s were women's sportswear, he became one of the first men's fashion designers in the early 1960s, shifting his emphasis to this field for its capability to fulfil his interest in classic looks, utmost practicality, and no-nonsense durability. Until Giorgio Armani and Ralph Lauren in the late 1970s and 1980s, no designer was as faithful as Weitz to menswear as the germinal center of design and of a practical approach to

John Weitz.

wardrobe. In personal style as well as his design, Weitz exemplifies the refined, but unpretentious, good taste that comes of humane attention to what is important in life, with clothing following as a consequence of those values. Even in the extreme years of menswear in the late 1960s and early 1970s, Weitz's vision was always tempered.

If Weitz was first a visionary of the disciplines of sportswear for women in America, creating car coats, playsuits, jeans, button-down shirts for women in pink satin, and other practical items in the 1950s, he transferred his allegiance to menswear at the early moment in 1962-63 when a number of designers recognized for women's apparel were testing the waters of menswear, among them Geoffrey Beene and Bill Blass in America, Hardy Amies in England, and Pierre Cardin in France. Weitz alone gave his primary attention to menswear, a field where his own principal ideas had first come from observing the Duke of Windsor. Long before absorbing and ultimately creating the ethos of sportswear, Weitz had been an assistant to Molyneux in London. There, he was a part of fashion that was fastidious, client-driven, and rich in protocol and money. When asked in _Interview_ (March 1983) if he considered himself a couturier, Weitz replied, "Good God, no. I'm a modern-day creature that emerged from an old couture assistant into a sort of inventive concept, which I don't mind at all." Weitz is his own creation: his acumen for business and licensing has enabled him to build an empire in menswear and cognate products with, in fact, a minimum of participation from the designer. His own engaging and cosmopolitan charm establishes only the guidelines for product development. In many ways, Weitz was the first to be such a designer: god-like prime cause, thereafter far removed from the world of his own creation. Weitz makes a point, however, of wearing his own clothes: this is a matter of honor for a man of boyscout, even knightly, integrity. With selfeffacing grace, he explained this phenomenon to Cecelia Capuzzi Simon in _The New York Observer_ (10 September 1990): "You can survive beautifully being dead. I had no intention of taking that as a specific or as a quantum leap into the future. Now, eventually I have to perform that."

Alive and well, Weitz offers a graceful conceptual model of a fashion designer. To some, Weitz exemplifies effete or feigned aristocratism. But he is rather more of the special individuals Paul Fussell described in _Class_ (1983) as "X," an open class that many could join though they have not understood that they have been invited. This class resembles E. M. Forster's "aristocracy of the sensitive, the considerate, and the plucky" who are "sensitive for others as well as themselves . . . considerate without being fussy." That's John Weitz.—RICHARD MARTIN

Westwood, Vivienne

British designer

> **Born** _Vivienne Isabel Swire in Glossop, Derbyshire, 8 April 1941._
>
> **Education** _Studied one term at Harrow Art School, then trained as a teacher._
>
> **Family** _Children: Ben, Joseph._
>
> **Career** _Taught school before working as designer, from c.1971. With partner Malcolm McLaren, proprietor of boutique variously named Let It Rock, 1971, Too Fast to Live, Too Young to Die, 1972, Sex, 1974, Seditionaries, 1977, and World's End, from 1980; second shop, Nostalgia of Mud, opened, 1982; Mayfair shop opened, 1990. First showed under own name, 1982; first full menswear collection launched, 1990. Professor of fashion, Academy of Applied Arts, Vienna, 1989-91._

Vivienne Westwood.

Exhibitions *Retrospective, Galerie Buchholz & Schipper, Cologne, 1991; retrospective, Bordeaux, 1992.*

Awards *British Designer of the Year Award, 1990, 1991; Order of the British Empire (OBE), 1992.*

Address *Unit 3, Old School House, The Lanterns, Bridge Lane, Battersea, London SW11 3AD, England.*

Vivienne Westwood's clothes have been described as perverse, irrelevant, and unwearable. Westwood's creations have also been described as brilliant, subversive, and incredibly influential. Westwood is unquestionably among the most important fashion designers of the late 20th century.

Westwood will go down in history as the fashion designer most closely associated with the punks, a youth subculture that developed in England in the 1970s. Although her influence extends far beyond that era, Westwood's relationship with the punk subculture is critically important to an understanding of her style. Just as the mods and hippies had developed their own styles of dress and music, so did the punks. But whereas the hippies extolled love and peace, the punks emphasized sex and violence. Punk was about nihilism, blankness and chaos, and sexual deviancy, especially sadomasochism and fetishism. The classic punk style featured safety pins piercing cheeks or lips, spiky hairstyles, and deliberately revolting clothes, which often appropriated the illicit paraphernalia of pornography.

Westwood captured the essence of confrontational anti-fashion long before other designers recognized the subversive power of punk style. In the 1970s Westwood and her partner Malcolm McLaren had a shop in London successively named Let It Rock (1971), Too Fast to Live, Too Young To Die (1972), Sex (1974), and Seditionaries (1977). In the beginning the emphasis was on a 1950s-revival look derived from the delinquent styles of 1950s youth culture. "I was making Malcolm Teddy Boy clothes," recalled Westwood. "Remember, I was a first time round Teddy Girl." In 1972 the shop was renamed after the slogan on a biker's leather jacket, heralding the new brutalism that would soon spread throughout both street fashion and high fashion. Black leather evoked not only anti-social bikers like the Hell's Angels, but also sadomasochistic sex, which was then widely regarded as "the last taboo."

Westwood's Bondage collection of 1976 was particularly important. Working primarily in black, especially black leather and rubber, she designed clothes that were studded, buckled, strapped, chained, and zippered. Westwood talked to people who were into sadomasochistic sex and researched the "equipment" that they used: "I had to ask myself, why this extreme form of dress? Not that I strapped myself up and had sex like that. But on the other hand I also didn't want to liberally *understand* why people did it. I wanted to get hold of those extreme articles of clothing and feel what it was like to wear them." Taken from the hidden sexual subculture that spawned it and flaunted it on the street, bondage fashion began to take on a new range of meanings: "The bondage clothes were ostensibly restricting but when you put them on they gave you a feeling of freedom."

Sex was "one of the all-time greatest shops in history," recalled pop star Adam Ant. The shop sign was in padded pink letters and the window was covered, except for a small opening, through which one could peep and see items like pornographic T-shirts. Westwood, in fact, was prosecuted and convicted for selling a T-shirt depicting two cowboys with exposed penises.

Other T-shirts referred to child molesting and rape, or bore aggressive slogans like "Destroy" superimposed over a swastika and an image of the Queen.

Sex was implicitly political for Westwood; when she renamed the shop Seditionaries, it was to show "the necessity to *seduce* people into revolt." Westwood insisted: "Sex is fashion." Deliberately torn clothing was inspired by old movie stills of "film stars looking really sexy in ripped clothes." She also launched the fashion for underwear as outerwear, showing bras worn *over* dresses. From the beginning she exploited the erotic potential of extreme shoe fashions, from leopard-print stiletto-heeled pumps to towering platform shoes and boots with multiple straps and buckles.

"When we finished punk rock we started looking at other cultures," recalled Westwood. "Up till then we'd only been concerned with emotionally charged rebellious English youth movements. . . . We looked at all the cults that we felt had this power." The result was the Pirates Collection of 1981, which heralded the beginning of the New Romantics Movement. The Pirates Collection utilized historical revivalism, 18th-century shirts and hats, rather than fetishism, but like the sexual deviant, the pirate also evoked the mystique of the romantic rebel as outcast and criminal. Meanwhile, in 1980 the shop was renamed World's End, and in 1981 Westwood began to show her collections in Paris, finally recognized internationally as a major designer.

Like pirates and highwaymen, Westwood and McLaren wanted "to plunder the world of its ideas." The Savages Collection (1982) showed Westwood gravitating toward a "tribal" look; the name was deliberately offensive and shocking; the clothes were oversized, in rough fabrics, and with exposed seams. Subsequent collections, like Buffalo, Hoboes, Witches, and Punkature, continued Westwood's postmodern collage of disparate objects and images. Models dressed in layers of mud-colored, torn clothing, with rags in their hair—and bras worn over their dresses.

In 1985 Westwood launched her "mini-crini," a short hooped skirt inspired by the Victorian crinoline, and styled with a tailored jacket and platform shoes. "I take something from the past which has a sort of vitality that has never been exploited—like the crinoline," she said. Westwood insisted that "there was never a fashion *invented* that was more sexy, especially in the big Victorian form."

She also revived the corset, another much maligned item of Victoriana—and an icon of fetish fashion. "I never thought it powerful to be like a second-rate man," said Westwood. "Feminine is stronger." Certainly her corsets and crinolines forced people to reexplore the meaning of controversial fashions. As she moved into the late 1980s and early 1990s, Westwood continued to transgress boundaries, not least by rejecting her earlier faith in anti-establishment style in favour of a subversive take on power dressing. Like "Miss Marple on acid," Westwood appropriated twinsets and tweeds, and even the traditional symbols of royal authority.—VALERIE STEELE

Workers for Freedom

British design firm

Founded October 1985 by Richard Nott (born in Hastings, England, 3 October 1947) and Graham Fraser (born in Bournemouth, 20 July 1948). Nott studied at Kingston University; design assistant to Valentino, Rome, 1972-75; principal lecturer, Kingston University Fashion School, 1975-85. Fraser studied accountancy and fashion retailing; worked as buyer/accountant, Feathers Boutique, London, 1970-71; assistant buyer, Harrods, London, 1975-78; buyer for Wallis Shops, London, 1978-81; advertising manager, Fortnum and Mason, London, 1981-82; fashion director, Liberty, London, 1982-85. Nott and Fraser operated first Workers for Freedom shop, Soho, London, 1985-92; introduced mens- and womenswear wholesale collections for Littlewoods Home Shopping catalogue, beginning in summer 1993; womenswear collection for A-Wear, Dublin, summer 1994.

Exhibitions   *Dayton Hudson, Minneapolis, USA, 1991; Fenit, São Paolo, Brazil, 1992.*
Awards   *British Fashion Council Designers of the Year Award, 1990; Viyella Designer of the Year Award, 1990.*
Address   *6 Spice Court, Ivory Square, Plantation Wharf, London SW11 3UE, England.*

Graham Fraser and Richard Nott launched their company, Workers for Freedom, in 1985, leaving behind their respective former careers as merchandising manager for fashion and accessories at Liberty in London and principal fashion lecturer at Kingston University in Surrey. Nott came from an art school background, and also worked for three years as design assistant to Valentino in Rome.

The company name was chosen to emphasize what they saw as their freedom from the large companies for whom they had previously worked. Their former experience in the fashion field left them well qualified to set up their own fashion company which, amongst other things, earned them the title Designer of the Year at the British Fashion Awards in 1990. The reason behind the formation of their own label, according to Nott and Fraser, was their mutual disillusion with what was happening in the field of menswear design at that time and their aversion to very "preppy" styles with little or no decorative adornment. Their first collection, which was sold through their retail shop in Lower John Street in London's Soho district, was comprised solely of menswear. The garment that was to become their hallmark was the embroidered shirt, in black on white or white on black combinations. The success of this first collection, which attracted both male and female customers, prompted Workers for Freedom to extend the next collection to womenswear, at the request of the American and Japanese buyers who bought their collections.

Nott and Fraser have always stressed that their designs are outside mainstream fashion trends, and that their customers are not concerned with being in fashion. The evolutionary nature of their designs has meant that each season the customer may add an outfit or single garment to those from previous collections. Nott describes Workers for Freedom's clothes as being "very gentle" and admits that at one point during the 1980s, with the advent of designers like Christian Lacroix, their designs seemed somewhat out of place with what was happening in fashion as a whole.

According to Richard Nott, who is responsible for designing the collections (Fraser handles the administrative and promotions side), the inspiration for his designs has always come from the fabric itself, which ultimately determines the shape or form of the garment. Nott views each garment within a collection as an individual piece, since he does not start out to create a certain look. Each garment is designed as a separate item and the collection is styled afterwards. At this point a certain garment, such as a shorter skirt for example, may be added if it is deemed necessary. The fabric for which Workers for Freedom is best recognized is silk, which they have

411

used continually both in its plain state and in Nott's textile prints. Their signature colours have always been subtle, with a predominant use of black, brown, ivory, and indigo blue.

In October 1991 Workers for Freedom began working for Littlewoods mail order catalogue, for whom they have continued to design a separate collection each season. The Littlewoods connection is viewed by Nott and Fraser as being rather like a diffusion collection, which is produced at a lower price range and also helps maintain their name at High Street level. This has left them free to make the mainline collection to be what they describe as more rarefied, since the sportswear element is now incorporated into other ranges such as Littlewoods and a collection for A-Wear shops in Ireland, which is distributed by the company Brown Thomas.

The decision by Workers for Freedom to move to France in 1992 attracted a considerable amount of publicity from the British press. Nott and Fraser had sold their shop in Soho and considered moving the business to Toulouse where they found a château that they decided to buy and establish the company base there. This fell through when the exchange rate dropped and they found themselves unable to sell their London house. During this period Nott and Fraser kept a low profile, did not produce a collection for fall/winter 1993 and moved the company headquarters to Battersea, South London. The six-month break from producing a collection enabled a reevaluation period for Workers for Freedom, and their succeeding collections indicate a definite change in direction. Their signature use of embroidery has been dropped ("because everyone has it now," says Nott), and there is an emphasis on shape using bias-cutting that Nott sees as the new softer alternative to stretch Lycra fabrics. The fall/winter collection for 1994-95 by Workers for Freedom was produced entirely in black and brown, without embroidery or other form of decoration.

Having always considered themselves to be on the outside of high fashion, it is somewhat ironic that the gentle, almost handcrafted image perpetrated by Workers for Freedom has become totally relevant to fashion in the 1990s, with the final demise of power dressing that dominated fashion in the late 1980s.—CATHERINE WORAM

Yamamoto, Kansai

Japanese designer

Born *Yokohama, 1944.*

Education *Studied civil engineering and English, Nippon University; graduated from Bunka College of Fashion, 1967.*

Career *Apprenticed with Junko Koshino and Hosano; designer, Hisashi Hosono, c.1968-71; opened firm, Yamamoto Kansai Company, Ltd., Tokyo, and showed first collection, London, 1971; first Paris showing, 1975; opened Kansai Boutique, Paris, 1977.*

Awards *Soen Prize, Bunka College of Fashion, 1967; Fashion Editors Award, Tokyo, 1977.*

Address *4-3-15 Jungumae, Shibuya-ku, Tokyo 150, Japan.*

Kansai Yamamoto's presentation of his fall-winter 1981-82 collection was divided into 14 parts, among them "Peruvian Geometry," "Sarraku" (Japanese 17th-century painter), "Korean Tiger," "Ainu," and "Sea Foam, 5 Men Kabuki Play." Kansai declared in the accompanying program notes: "True originality is almost impossible to imitate as it is the expression of the creator's personal experience and cultural environment. As a Japanese, I always seek the 'oriental quality' that is within me." Yet, Kansai's personal sensibility is a single aspect of Orientalism and reflects a style relatively little known in the West in Asian forms, but comparable to many traditions of the West. Kansai is Kabuki in his overt theatricality, flamboyant sense of gesture and design, and brilliant colorful design as much to be read from afar as admired at close range. Leonard Koren said, "For Kansai, fashion means creating a festival-like feeling using brightly colored clothes with bold design motifs inspired by the *kimono*, traditional Japanese festival wear, and military clothes" (*New Fashion Japan,* Tokyo 1984). Gaudy by desire, larger-than-life by theatre's intensity, and virtually to Japanese culture what Pop style was to Anglo-American culture, Kansai has consistently cultivated a fashion of fantastic images, extravagant imagination, and sensuous approach to both tradition and a view of the future.

Unabashed entertainer and impresario (long a familiar product spokesman on television in Japan), Kansai achieved cult status in Japan in the 1970s for his worldly transmission of Japanese culture. Kansai's selections of favor in his indigenous culture have not been the refined natural dispositions of materials so much favored in the West as the alternative to Western materialism, but the aspects of Japan that are expressive, grandly symbolic, and vernacular. In fact, Kansai's work has often been controversial in Japan inasmuch as it is thought to promote and exploit images of Japanese vulgarity internationally. Is Kansai creating an "airport art," expensive exoticism for the West that still thinks of an East Asia of bright colors, lanterned festivals, Kabuki masks, and fabulist stories with dragons and tigers? Kansai seems poised between traditional Japanese culture, the Pop sensibility of the late 20th century, and a longing for a millennial future. Central to Kansai's work is his delight in mass entertainment and popular culture, a sense of both following and leading the ordinary population whether in graphic T-shirts or the convenience of knitwear. His stadium coats are the hyperbole of an American sportswear vocabulary; his fall-winter 1979 stegosaurus coat, with shoulder and sleeves built into a crenellation of triangles, harkens back to animal tales and prehistory; his fish and bird forms seem exotic, but merge with spiky punk. His silhouettes for both menswear and womenswear are extreme, suggesting either the most wondrous last *samurai* or the most magnificent first warriors for intergalactic futures; and his appliqués have been in the ambiguous realm between primitive art and 20th-century abstraction.

In a West frightened by Japanese militarism (no Yukio Mishima, but no Buddhist monk either, Kansai has drawn inspiration from firemen's uniforms and other easily identified work vestments traditional in Japanese subcultures of conformity) and prone to disregard any popular culture if not its own, Kansai became a designer of special, but limited, interest in the 1980s. His less-than-solemn work is anathema to some, celebratory to others. Cerebral, spiritual, aestheticized Japan (as represented by Issey Miyake or Rei Kawakubo) seemed more ideal, especially to the West. Kansai's plebeian flash was for many in the West the worst of two worlds.

Kansai's sensibility, however, is universal. If he was the first fashion designer to bring Kabuki circus-like joy and impertinence and Japanese common culture to international fashion, he has remained a significant figure in espousing such conspicuous love of theatre, love of life, love of exaggeration. His aggrandizements begin in delight and exuberance and end in celebration of the most universal kind. They benefit from a relationship to costume, though Kansai is always grounded in the wearability of his clothing. They often function as happy graphic signs, emblems of the most bold in fashion. On the opening of his Madison Avenue boutique in 1985, Kansai remarked to *Women's Wear Daily,* "My clothes are no good for someone who loves chicness." If we understand chic to be slightly haughty and narrowly sophisticated, Kansai misses the mark by express intention. Rather, he is seeking an earthy, populist ideal of clothing created in the grand gesture for the great audience. "I am making happiness for people with my clothes," he told *Women's Wear Daily* in 1985. "If you walk through Central Park in them you create a 'wow.'" Kansai achieves exclamatory, spectacular visual statement. Wow!—RICHARD MARTIN

Yamamoto, Yohji

Japanese designer

Born *Yokohama, Japan, 1943.*

Education *Graduated in Law, Keio University, 1966; studied at Bunka College of Fashion, Tokyo, 1966-68, won Soen and Endu prizes; earned scholarship to Paris, 1968, studied fashion, 1968-70.*

Career *Designer, custom clothing, Tokyo, from 1970; formed ready-to-wear company, 1972; showed first collection, Tokyo, 1976; launched men's line, 1984; Yohji Yamamoto design studio, Tokyo, established, 1988; also opened Paris boutique.*

Exhibitions *A New Wave in Fashion: 3 Japanese Designers, Phoenix Art Museum, Arizona, 1983.*

Awards *Fashion Editors Club Award, Tokyo, 1982; Mainichi Grand Prize, 1984.*

Address *San Shin Building 1, 1-22-11 Higashi Shibuya-ku, Tokyo, Japan.*

Part of a pioneering fashion sensibility that erupted onto the Parisian catwalks of the early 1980s, Yohji Yamamoto has a philosophical approach to fashion that makes him interested in more than just covering the body: there has to be some interaction between the body, the wearer, and the essential spirit of the designer. With Issey Miyake and Rei Kawakubo, Yamamoto is exploring new ways of dressing by synthesizing Western clothing archetypes and indigenous Japanese clothing. Refusing to accept traditional ideas of female sexual display and reacting against the Western notion of female glamour as expressed in titillating figure-hugging garments, Yamamoto employs a method of layering, draping, and wrapping the body, disguising it with somber, unstructured, swathed garments based on the *kimono* that ignore the usual accentuation points.

Uncompromising to Western eyes, Yamamoto is in fact investigating the traditional Japanese conviction in beauty being not naturally given but expressed through the manipulation of the possibilities of the colours and materials of garments. Consequently, Yamamoto's clothing construction is viewed in the round rather than vertically, not from the neck down as in Western fashion, but a rectilinear, two dimensional approach that explores the visual appeal of asymmetry, the notion of the picturesque that plays an important part in Japanese design philosophy where irregular forms are appreciated for their lack of artifice and thus closeness to nature. Therefore, Yamamoto's garments have strange flaps, pockets, and layers, lopsided collars and hems, set off by the body in motion, and the labels inside are inscribed with the epithet, "There is nothing so boring as a neat and tidy look."

By not referring to Western fashion but to a fixed form of Japanese dress that has been developed and refined over the centuries, Yamamoto produces anti-fashion—non-directional garments that ignore contemporary Western developments of the silhouette but influence Western designers in turn. Beauty is more indefinable, to be found in the texture of materials rather than applied decoration, with the use of fabrics like linen and rayon that have been deliberately chosen and developed for their likelihood of wrinkling and heavy knitted surfaces. Like a number of Japanese designers, Yamamoto is interested in developing new materials.

Yamamoto's source material is idiosyncratic and derives from a vast library that he draws on for inspiration. One book to which he consistently refers is a collection of photographs by August Sander, a photographer based in Cologne in the early 20th century, who took photographs of representative types in the everyday clothes that sharply reflect their lives. Yamamoto is also inspired by utilitarian outfits such as the protective clothing worn by women munitions workers in the 1940s, and has been known to reproduce the coat lapel worn by Jean-Paul Sartre discovered in an old photograph.

Yamamoto

Notable for his relentless use of black, a colour traditionally associated in Japanese culture with the farmer and the spirit of the *samurai,* Yamamoto's move into navy and purple in the 1980s was shortlived—he found it roused too many complicated emotions for him!

His company, launched in 1976, now produces the experimental, idiosyncratic Yohji Yamamoto line, the Y and Y line for men that is moderately priced and extremely successful, made up of an easy to wear mixture of integrated separates and the Workshop line of casual leisurewear.—CAROLINE COX

Zegna, Ermenegildo

Italian designer/company

Company founded in 1910 by Ermenegildo Zegna (1892-66) in Trivero, Biellese Alps, Italy. Ermenegildo turned business over to sons, Aldo and Angelo, who expanded into ready-to-wear clothing, menswear line, 1960s; opened branches in Spain, France, Germany, Austria, United States, Japan, and United Kingdom; group-controlled production units opened in Spain and Switzerland, 1968. Company specialises in menswear fabrics in natural raw materials, ready-to-wear for men: suits, jackets, trousers, shirts, ties, accessories. First U.S. boutique launched, 1989; fragrance, Zegna; E.Z. line, designed by Kim Herring, launched 1993. From 1980s, Angelo's son Gildo became responsible for Formalwear Division; Aldo's son Paolo became President of the Textile Division; Gildo's sister Anna responsible for image and communication of the Group and Zegna shops worldwide; Benedetta, Angelo's youngest daughter, responsible for coordinating the fully owned and franchised Zegna stores in Italy. Oasi Zegna, land recovery program, Trivero, launched, 1993, to provide sports and leisure facilities to visitors and local population.

Exhibitions   *Made in Italy, Pier 84, New York, 1988; Wool Bicentennial, Barcelona, 1990; The Meandering Pattern in Brocades and Silk, Milan, 1990-91; and at the Fashion Institute of Technology, New York, 1992.*

Collections   *The Power House Museum, Sydney; Museo della Scienza e della Tecnica, Milan.*

Awards   *Cavaliere del Lavoro (to Ermenegildo Zegna), 1930.*

Address   *Via Pietro Verri 3, 20121 Milan, Italy.*

Our style is classical but modern; international but deeply rooted in the Italian tradition. It is a style which fully respects the individual personality of each of our clients, based on care over details,

Ermenegildo Zegna: Spring/Summer 1995; single-breasted three-button suit, cotton shirt, silk tie.
Photograph by Aldo Fallai.

comfort, and personalization of our products. It is for this reason that we offer a "made-to-measure" service which is capable of satisfying even the most demanding and sophisticated consumers. And while we are talking of service, we also guarantee the post-sale of our customers' wardrobes, because Zegna products are faithful companions designed to last, deserving all of the care and attention that can be given them.

Finally, Zegna is also characterized by its sensitivity and respect for the environment. As early as 1930, Ermenegildo Zegna established and financed a vast project for the reclamation of the mountain overlooking Trivero, the village in the Alpine foothills of Biella where Zegna's headquarters are located. And now, following in the footsteps of the company's founder, the younger generations of the family have created *Oasi Zegna*, a project designed to protect nature over an area of about 100 square kilometres.—Ermenegildo Zegna

Ermenegildo Zegna was founded in 1910 as a company which created and produced woolen fabrics.

With the passing of time, the subsequent generations of the family encouraged the diversification of the company's activities, leading to the introduction of a complete line of menswear. Our philosophy has always been based on quality and the search for excellence.

What makes Zegna unique is the fact that it is the only company of its type in the world specialized in the direct purchase of natural raw materials on their markets of origin, with a totally verticalized creative and production cycle going from raw materials to cloths, clothing and accessories, which are internationally distributed through Zegna's salespoints and other selected menswear shops.

"Our typical client believes in understated classic styles," says Gilda Zegna. "That's why they like Ermenegildo Zegna." Ermenegildo Zegna is not a brand of radical fashion statements; on the contrary, very classic tailoring, rich and supple fabrics, and obsessive attention to detail make Ermenegildo Zegna the Rolls Royce of menswear, and image Zegna is quick to reinforce. All their marketing and advertising copy speaks of wool spun into strands so fine that one kilo stretches 150,000 metres, hand-sewn buttons, and the hand pressing of each jacket before leaving the factory. The latter, we are told, takes 45 minutes, but then suit prices are high. Ermenegildo Zegna has built a reputation on catering only to the richest of businessmen, well-established celebrities, and the world's royalty.

So how does Zegna differentiate from the hundreds of companies vying for this same market sector? Zegna clothes are quintessentially English, from the suits of a world-class banker to the casualwear of a world-beating yachtsman or horsemaster. The fabrics are Italian, made for lightweight softness and presoaked in the waters of the Italian Alps, whose mineral-free quality has been sought after by Italian cloth merchants since the middle ages. The craftsmanship is Swiss—accurate, precise, always correct. Colours change year on year. Winter 1993 was brick, brown, tobacco, evergreen, billiard green, emerald. Winter 1994 was eye-blue, cobalt, stone grey, tobacco, some red, more browns. Raw materials are taken from the world over—wool from Australia, cashmere from China, mohair from South Africa. Although most upmarket men's fashionwear use similar resources and methods, when one discovers that Zegna's preferred cashmere is that of a Chinese goat, aged between three and five years, one understands that these are not just professionals but inspired visionaries of men's clothing.

The fact remains that Ermenegildo Zegna is successful in a highly competitive sector. The market for men's suits costing over one thousand dollars is, in 1994, considered one million units per year. Ermenegildo Zegna currently sells 300,000 such suits or 30 percent of the market. To maintain and grow in this sector, their marketing is more than just subtle. Ermenegildo Zegna sponsors a yacht race at Portofino, Italy. The sponsorship is discrete, no banners and posters, just models walking through the crowd wearing Zegna blazers with the small white EZ motif. The seat covers for the Saab 9000 car are made by Zegna. Saab salesmen are drilled in the virtues and qualities of Zegna fabrics, information passed on to Saab buyers. Above all, Zegna mails sample swatches, possible combinations jackets, ties, and shirts to their best customers, several times a year. Perhaps Zegna's strength is its size; they remain resolutely small and claim to have no desire to be a popular brand.

In recent years, however, Zegna has started to expand into new markets with soft suits, the casual cut, and mix 'n' match coordinates now so popular in the United States, France, and Italy. Specifically for the United States market, Zegna designs sportswear to compete with Hugo Boss, Giorgio Armani, and Calvin Klein: shirts, slacks, and sports and outerwear jackets are all aimed at the 35 plus market. To complete a man's wardrobe, Zegna makes natural cotton undergarments, high quality corporate gifts (for example, Paco Rabanne ties), and more recently a fragrance.

Ermenegildo Zegna's originality lies in its manufacturing process. Unusually, the company is completely vertically integrated. It buys its own raw materials, makes its own fabrics, designs its own clothes, and runs its own boutiques. The company is forward-looking, yet steeped in tradition. It uses the most advanced databases to maintain and update customer measurements, purchases, and personal details. Satellite communication allows such data to be transferred at the touch of a button from Singapore to Switzerland. A Computer-Aided Design (CAD) program is used to adjust a pattern to the customer. Yet wool fabrics are washed and suits finished by hand. Salesmen visit businessmen in their offices and homes. And still Zegna looks for improved speed in delivering clothes or bringing a new collection to market.

Perhaps Zegna's unique strength is the family that holds this tight-knit, perfectionist company together. The Zegna company employs both sons of Ermenegildo Zegna and five of his eight grandchildren. As yet there is no indication that such reliance on home-grown talent has led to stagnation. If anything, the enthusiasm of the young Zegnas, educated in universities and colleges across Europe, is tempered and modeled by the experience of the older family members. Gilda Zegna, quoting an Italian proverb, essentially states the company's philosophy: "Qui va piano, va sano, e va lontano" ("He who goes slowly, goes safely, and will last longest").—SALLY ANNE MELIA

Zoran

American designer

Born *Zoran Ladicorbic in Banat, Yugoslavia, 1947. Immigrated to the United States, 1971.*

Education *Studied architecture at the University of Belgrade.*

Career *Worked variously in New York as coat checker at Candy Store club, salesman at Balmain boutique, accessory designer for Scott Barrie, salesman and designer for Julio,*

1971-76. Free-lance designer in New York, from 1976; first collection shown, 1977; Washington, D.C. showroom established, 1982; also maintains studio in Milan.

Zoran Ladicorbic was born in Banat, Yugoslavia in 1947. The designer, who goes by his first name, was trained in his native country as an architect, and a love of geometric shapes and straight lines is evident in his clothing design.

Zoran came to the United States in 1972. Although he had no formal education in fashion, he worked for the first few years in retail. He was also an accessories designer for the 1970s women's fashion designer, Scott Barrie.

In 1976 Zoran started his own collection, using only the best and most luxurious fabrics. Cashmere, satin, velvet, and high-quality wool are staples of his collection. He creates two collections a year, spring and fall, and shows them in his New York loft-workplace located in the downtown SoHo neighborhood.

He is obsessive about cutting and finishing a garment. His clothes create a feeling of luxury through perfect craftsmanship and materials, not through ostentatious embellishment, bright color, or showy fabrics. He uses the same muted color palette over and over: black and white, ivory, gray, and navy, with an occasional washed-out pastel such as pale pink or celery thrown in to liven the mix.

Zoran has kept to this minimalist aesthetic even during the more flamboyant 1980s. In the somewhat more abashed 1990s, his designs have gathered more momentum and his customer base has increased. His designs are not cheap, but he has a loyal following that snaps up his designs year after year. Among the Zoran devotees are model-actresses such as Lauren Hutton, Candice Bergen, and Isabella Rossellini, the painter Jennifer Hartley, socialite Amanda Burden, and Tipper Gore, the U.S. vice-president's wife. His clothes are sold by high-level, slightly avant-garde stores such as Barney's and Henri Bendel in New York, as well as out of his workplace.

Zoran believes that his typical customer visits him once a year and buys several thousand dollars' worth of pieces at one time. Like the color palette, the silhouettes vary only slightly from season to season. Core pieces include a cardigan jacket, a T-shirt, crewneck cashmere sweaters, loose trousers, loose shorts, and a sarong skirt, which the designer claims he wore himself for a year to make sure the fit was correct.

The designer eschews the typical New York fashion life. He prefers solitude and is said to keep a constant supply of Stolichnaya vodka close at hand at all times of the day. He has an apartment in New York and a house in the resort community of Naples, Florida.—JANET OZZARD

APPENDIX: BRIEF ENTRIES

This section contains brief descriptions of a number of fashion houses, designers, merchandisers, photographers, and other figures who have also made important contributions to the world of fashion.

Adri (1934-) American designer, especially of ingeniously simplified sportswear.

Agha, Mehemmed Fehmy (1896-1978) Ukraine-born American graphic designer and art director of *Vogue*, 1929-1943.

Akira [Maki] (1949-) Japanese-American designer, custom-made and ready-to-wear.

Ally Capellino British design firm [Alison Lloyd and Jono Plate], founded 1979.

Antonelli, Maria (1903-1969) Rome-based designer prominent in the new Italian fashion of the 1950s, an accomplished dressmaker, but also famous for coats and suits.

Antonio [Lopez] (1943-1987) American fashion illustrator whose tour-de-force stylistic range of images in the *New York Times, Vanity*, and *Interview* imbued fashion with panache and spirit.

Aquascutum British design firm, specializing in rainwear and accessories, founded 1851.

Arai, Junichi (1932-) Japanese textile designer, specializing in innovative hand weaving.

Aujard, Christian (1945-1977) French ready-to-wear designer who started menswear and womenswear boutiques.

Avedon, Richard (1923-) Photographer whose fashion photographs in *Harper's Bazaar* defined the 1940s and 1950s and whose audacious body images in *Vogue* in the late 1960 defined that era.

Ayton, Sylvia (1937-) British ready-to-wear designer, working chiefly under other labels, and fashion teacher.

Azagury, Jacques (1956-) French fashion designer, with special affinity for glamorous style, working in London.

Banana Republic American retailer founded by Mel and Patricia Ziegler in 1978 with safari theme, now the better-quality stores owned by The Gap.

Banks, Jeff (1943-) British designer, retailer, and BBC television personality.

Banks, Jeffrey (1955-) American designer, chiefly of classic, colorful men's sportswear.

Banton, Travis (1894-1958) Film costume designer famous for his Paramount Pictures work in the 1930s.

Barnett, Sheridan (1951-) British ready-to-wear designer.

423

Barocco, Rocco (Rocco Muscariello) (1944-) Italian designer working in Rome, known for luxury ready-to-wear clothing and accessories.

Bastille, Franck-Joseph (1964-) French artist-designer creating one-of-a-kind and conventional dress.

L. L. Bean American clothing manufacturer and mail order company founded 1912. Purveys reliable outdoor and spores clothing for a variety of uses.

Beaton, Cecil (1904-1980) Artist, illustrator, costume and set designer (most notably *My Fair Lady*), royal photographer, and fashion collector-advisor.

Benetton Italian sportswear company, founded 1968, with shops spread globally and famous advertising images by Oliviero Toscani.

Beretta, Anne-Marie (1937-) French fashion designer with international design contracts, recognized for her sculptural coats.

Bianchini-Férier High-end French textile company, founded ca. 1880, Lyon. A supplier to the couture.

Dorothée Bis French ready-to-wear company, famous for chic knits, founded by Elie and Jacqueline Jacobson in 1962.

Black, Sandy (1951-) British knitwear designer, known for complicated, often whimsical sweaters and wraps.

Blair, Alistair (1956-) British designer and design consultant on the Continent, characterized by sophisticated high style.

Blumarine Italian ready-to-wear house founded 1977, designed by Anna Molinari.

Bogner German sportswear company founded 1936 by Willy Bogner, Sr., for skiwear; now, chiefly skiwear and sportswear—graphic and high-tech.

Boss, Hugo German workwear company founded 1923 has expanded to be a comprehensive menswear firm, including sportswear and tailored clothing.

Brioni Italian menswear company founded for tailored menswear, 1945; epitome of Roman tailoring for men.

Brodovitch, Alexei (1898-1971) Russian-born graphic designer who, in 1934 to 1958, served as art director of *Harper's Bazaar* in an animated graphic modernism; collaborated with and introduced many artists.

Brooks Brothers Classic American clothier, principally menswear, in business since 1818.

Burberry British design house, focussed on classic rainwear inspired by founder Thomas Burberry's waterproof coat, 1856.

Capucci, Roberto (1930-) Italian designer of strong theatrical and three-dimensional imagination.

Casely-Hayford, Joe (1956-) British designer for rock groups and ready-to-wear.

Catalina California swimwear company founded 1907.

Caumont, Jean Baptiste (1932-) French designer working in Italian ready-to-wear.

Cesarani, Sal (1939-) American designer, chiefly of menswear.

Champion American active-sportswear manufacturer, founded 1919 by Abe and Bill Fainbloom, most notable for its sweatshirts.

Charles, Caroline (1943?-) British designer first recognized with "Swinging London," but an abiding force in British fashion.

Chase, Edna Woolman (1877-1957) From 1914 to 1952, Editor of *Vogue*.

Cipullo, Aldo (1936-1984) Rome-born American jewelry designer whose most famous creation was the 1960s Cartier love bracelet with screw mechanism and accompanying screwdriver.

Clark, Ossie (1942-) Artistic London menswear and womenswear designer.

Clergerie, Robert (1934-) French footwear designer.

Cole of California Swimwear company founded by Fred Cole in 1923; under Cole and designer Margit Fellegi, major innovations in swimwear (including 1962 "scandal suit"); now directed by Anne Cole.

Coleman, Nick Young British designer, chiefly menswear inspired by street and rock styles.

Connolly, Sybil (1921-) Welsh-born designer; her simple silhouettes show off well-chosen and luxurious textiles, including many Irish wools and linens, popular for at-home entertaining and day to evening transitions.

Conran, Jasper (1959-) British designer from famous design family and likewise of mainstream good taste.

Corneliani Italian menswear firm founded in the 1930s; in the 1980s and 1990s, producing for Corneliani label and other designer labels.

Correggiari, Giorgio (1943-) Italian designer.

Costa, Victor (1935-) American designer famous for copying and adapting designs to his own strong sense of theater.

Costelloe, Paul (1945-) Irish designer, famous for his fabrics, especially staunch wools and Irish linens.

Coveri, Enrico (1952-1990) Italian sportswear designer known for bright pallette and youthful styles.

C.P. Company Italian sportswear company inspired by American active sports and team uniforms.

Crahay, Jules Francois (1917-1988) French designer working, most importantly, as lead designer for Nina Ricci, 1952-63; Lanvin, 1964-84.

Creed, Charles (1909-1966) Of a family of London tailors going back to the 18th century, Creed created a comprehensive fashion enterprise with both couture and ready-to-wear in the 1950s and 1960s.

Cunningham, Bill (1929?-) Since the 1970s, steadfast fashion photographer for the *New York Times* in a unique shrewdly observed chronicle of high fashion, party life, and street fashion; a Baudelaire to the late twentieth century.

Dahl-Wolfe, Louise (1895-1989) American fashion photographer, chiefly for *Harper's Bazaar*, beginning in the 1930s.

Dallas, Sarah (1951-) British knitwear designer.

Danskin American hosiery manufacturer, begun 1923, known for dance tights translated in the late 1950s and since to recreational clothing.

Dell'Olio, Louis (1948-) American sportswear designer; co-designer of Anne Klein from 1974-1985 with Donna Karan; designer of Anne Klein in highly successful years, 1985-1993.

de Meyer, Baron Adolf (1868-1949) Fashion writer and photographer, perhaps the inventor of the medium in work for *Vogue* and *Vanity Fair* before World War I; soft-focus photographs, but a sharp insight into fashion.

Dennis, Pamela (1960-) American designer, specializing in eveningwear.

de Prémonville, Myrène (1949-) French designer of women's suits and separates.

de Ribes, Jacqueline (1931-) French socialite and designer.

de Senneville, Elisabeth (1946-) French fashion designer of artistic sensibility.

Dominguez, Adolfo Spanish menswear designer.

Duke, Randolph (1958-) American sportswear designer, first in swimwear, and continuing the transitions among swimwear, exercise wear, and stretch leisurewear.

Eiseman, Florence (1899-1988) Childrenswear designer known for traditional, playful attire for children.

Eisen, Mark (1958-) Born in South Africa, American designer of spare-silhouette, body-revealing designer sportswear.

English Eccentrics British textile and fashion company founded 1982 by Helen and Judy Littman. Whimsical, artistic textile designs.

Erreuno Italian ready-to-wear company founded in Milan in 1971 by Ermanno and Graziella Ronchi.

Erté [RT: Romain de Tirtoff] (1892-1990) Theatre and fashion illustrator and costume/scenic designer, including many fashion magazine illustrations and covers.

Escada German firm devoted to elegant sportswear and luxury accessories founded by Wolfgang and Margarethe Ley in 1976.

Esprit Initially founded 1968 by Susie and Doug Tompkins, a no-fuss sportswear company emphasizing family values and sprightly colors.

Esterel, Jacques (1918-1974) French couture designer adventuresome in the 1960s and 1970s.

Estevez, Luis (1930-) Cuban-American designer known for supple, flowing eveningwear.

Fabrice (1951-) Haitian-born American designer known for floating and beaded evening gowns.

appendix

Farhi, Nicole (1946-) British designer, born in France, recognizable for soft 1980s and 1990s dress-reform styles.

Fassett, Kaffe (1937-) American-born knitwear designer working in London, creating colorful art-to-wear knits.

Fenn Wright and Manson London design house founded in 1974 by Trevor Wright, Colin Fenn, and Glen Manson, specializing in classic design in quality materials.

Ferretti, Alberta (1950-) Italian designer and fashion businesswoman creating her signature collection as well as producing and distributing other designers including Moschino and Ozbek.

Fielden, David British designer, once with a boutique on King's Road, appealing to a bold, glamorous clientele.

Flett, John (1963-1991) British designer of dazzling creative success in the 1980s.

Flusser, Alan American menswear designer and writer espousing traditional values in menswear.

Fogarty, Brigid (1948-) British knitwear designer, known for cozy mohairs and handknits.

Fortuny, Mariano (1871-1949) Spanish-born designer working in Venice identifying himself as scientist and inventor. From 1907, pleated Delphos gowns, printed velvet capes, caftans, and djellabahs.

Freis, Diane American fashion designer working in Hong Kong.

French Connection British design house first for womenswear, now men and children as well, founded by Stephen Marks, 1969.

Freud, Bella (1961-) A former assistant to Vivienne Westwood, British designer known for her strong, quirky vision.

Fujiwara, Giuliano Japanese-born designer making avant-garde menswear in Milan.

The Gap Founded by Donald and Doris Fisher as a jeans retailer in 1969, now a leading American retailer; modernist interiors, simple design, shopping convenience, fashion basics; now, Gap, BabyGap, GapKids, Old Navy, Banana Republic.

Garratt, Sandra (1951-) American designer, especially of knits and separates.

George, Jennifer (1959-) American designer of quality sportswear.

Gibb, Bill (1943-1988) Scottish-born London designer of colorful *Gesamtkunstwerk* dressing expressive of flamboyant London in the 1970s.

Godely, Georgina (1955-) London designer of imaginative clothing often reshaping the human body to principles of abstraction.

Griffe, Jacques (1917-) Protegé of Vionnet, French designer espousing soft draping and color, influential from the 1940s to the 1960s.

Gruppo GFT Italian menswear manufacturer founded in Turin in 1887, now worldwide.

Guess American jeans and sportswear company founded by the Marciano family, 1981.

Guillemin, Olivier (1961-) French designer trained at the cutting-edge Studio Bercot, attuned to advanced design.

Harp, Holly (1939-1995) American designer, first of hippie styles, growing into romantic dressing.

Hawes, Elizabeth (1903-1971) Maverick American designer and acerbic fashion critic and writer.

Head, Edith (1907-1981) American film costume designer for Paramount and Universal Studios.

Hechter, Daniel (1938-) French ready-to-wear designer.

Henderson, Gordon (1957-) American designer of easy sportswear.

Herman, Stan American designer of Mr. Mort (1961-1971), sportswear, utility uniforms for corporations and airlines, and, since 1991, President of the Council of Fashion Designers of America.

Hermès French design house founded in Paris in 1837; from equestrian leather to a full range of apparel, accessories, and luggage.

Hogg, Pam British avant-garde fashion designer.

Peter Hoggard British firm founded by Michelle Hoggard and Peter Leather in 1983, specializing in one-of-a-kind artistic clothing.

Hope, Emma (1962-) British footwear designer.

Horn, Carol (1936-) American sportswear and knit designer.

Horst, Horst P. (1906-) Fashion and interiors photographer active from the 1930s into the 1990s.

Howell, Margaret (1946-) British menswear and women's ready-to-wear designer.

Hoyningen-Huené, George (1900-1968) Fashion photographer for *Vogue* and *Harper's Bazaar*.

Irié, Sueo (1946-) Japanese designer working in France.

Isani Korean-American design team of Jun Kim and Soyon Kim, founded 1988.

Jaeger British fashion house founded 1884 by Lewis Tomalin based on the rational, healthy dress theories of Dr. Gustav Jaeger; now more chic and classic than merely "sanitary."

Jansen, Jan Dutch shoe designer, often conceptual and artistic.

Jantzen American swimwear company, founded in Oregon as Portland Knitting Company by John A. Zentbauer, C. Ray Zentbauer, and Carl C. Jantzen, which rightly advertised in the 1920s: "the suit that changed bathing to swimming."

Joseph [Ettedgui] (1938-) Morrocan-born London fashion and retailing entrepreneur; his spare 1980s boutiques and cafes epitomized a sleek modern lifestyle.

Jovine, Andrea (1955-) American designer of better sportswear with a sensibility for spare, elegant form and no superfluous adornment.

Julian, Alexander (1948-) American designer, chiefly menswear and subtle coloristic domestic objects.

Kaiserman, Bill (1942-) American designer, principally menswear, working in Italy.

Kaplan, Jacques (1924-) French-American furrier and are collector whose keen interest in contemporary art sponsored artist-designed fur coats.

Kloss, John (1937-1987) American designer, chiefly of lingerie and cross-over lingerie looks as street dress.

Knecht, Gabriele (1938-) German-born American designer of architecturally conceived clothing.

Konishi, Yoshiyuki Japanese designer of extraordinarily complex and colorful knits, especially men's sweaters inspired by kilims and architectural decoration.

Koshino, Hiroko (1937-) Japanese designer of kimono-wrapped garment accommodated to Western sensibilities.

Koshino, Junko (1939-) Japanese designer, most notable for graphic team and business uniforms keenly aware of new technology and comfort.

Koshino, Michiko (1950-) Japanese designer working in London, including club-scene advanced clothing.

Lachasse British couture house founded 1928, renowned for tailored suits and coats; since 1981, a comprehensive fashion house with boutique.

Lacoste French sportswear company founded 1933 by René Lacoste, now a broad range of sportswear, but beginning with the famous Lacoste knit tennis shirt with alligator monogram.

Lam, Ragence (1951-) Hong Kong designer.

Laroche, Guy (1923-1989) French couture and ready-to-wear designer, working for Jean Dessès 1950-57, then Guy Laroche Couture beginning 1961, also men's and women's ready-to-wear.

Lee, Mickey Chinese designer and fashion consultant for ready-to-wear, working in Hong Kong.

Lehl, Jurgen (1944-) German designer working in Japan, notable for developing exceptional textiles.

Lelong, Lucien (1889-1958) French couture and ready-to-wear designer who distinguished himself in service as president of the Chambre Syndicale de la Couture 1937-1947, resisting German Occupation efforts to transport couture to Berlin.

Lempica, Lolita French fashion designer specializing in naughty, fun, party-dress clothing of enormous energy and imagination.

Leva, Michael (1961-) American sportswear designer.

Levi-Strauss From Gold-Rush 1850s jeans to diverse classic and fashion-sensitive jeans and leisurewear, this definitive fashion manufacturer has built an empire, still headquartered in San Francisco, on denim and good common sense.

René Lezard German fashion company of men's and women's ready-to-wear founded by Thomas Schaefer in 1978.

Liberman, Alexander (1912-) Russian-born American sculptor, photographer, and Art Director of *Vogue* from 1942 to 1994; since 1994, Deputy Chairman of Condé Nast Publications.

Liberty of London Merchant Arthur Lazenby Liberty established his London department store in 1875 as an Orientalist emporium dedicated to advance Aesthetic dress and related dress reform and the fusions between Eastern and Western dress; still a Regent Street store.

Linard, Stephen (1959-) British designer working in music and club-scene styles.

Ma, Walter (1951-) Hong Kong designer influential throughout South Asia and Australia.

I. Magnin San Francisco department store founded by Mary Ann Magnin in 1876; after broad expansion in California, contraction in the 1980s and 1990s.

Mann, Judy (1946-) Chinese ready-to-wear designer and retailer born and working in Hong Kong.

Marimekko Finnish textile, interiors, and clothing firm founded by Armi Ratia and Viljo Ratia in Helsinki in 1951 and representing Finnish modernism; enormously popular internationally in its simplicity and graphic boldness.

Marina Rinaldi Founded in 1980 as part of the Max Mara Group, a division devoted to larger sizes without sacrifice of style.

Marongiu, Marcel (1962-) French ready-to-wear designer.

Maxfield Parrish British design label founded by designer Nigel Preston in 1972; most recognized for sheepskin, suede, and leather garments.

Max Mara Italian high-fashion company founded by Achille Maramotti in 1951.

McClintock, Jessica (1930-) American sportswear designer, first for Gunne Sax, later for eponymous company known for fresh, but romantic, style.

Meyer, Gene (1954-) American designer, an assistant to Geoffrey Beene from 1978-1989,

chiefly making menswear, notable for the geometric-optic neckties and polka dots and geometry in sportswear.

Model, Philippe (1956-) French footwear and accessories designer.

Mondi German fashion and accessory company founded by Herwig Zahm in 1967.

Moreni, Popy (1947-) Italian designer working in Paris known for witty, youthful styles.

Morlotti, Dominique (1950-) Versatile French designer working for Lapidus, Dior and Dior Monsieur, and Lanvin.

Morton, Digby (1906-1983) Dublin-born London designer, first of sportswear for Lachasse, but best known for Digby Morton tailored clothing often employing Irish tweeds.

Moses, Rebecca (1958-) American designer of sportswear with a sensibility for the fluid and elegant; since 1992, working in Italy for Genny and her own collection.

Muji Japanese design and retail company founded 1983; rejecting the Japanese zeal for designer labels, Muji is a contraction of an expression "no-brand quality goods," meaning generic high quality.

Mulberry British fashion and accessory firm founded by Joan and Roger Saul in 1971.

Munkacsi, Martin (1896-1963) Photojournalist who created images of figures in motion, applying these principles to animated fashion images for *Harper's Bazaar*.

Nast, Condé (1873-1942) Flamboyant American publishing magnate who established with Condé Nast Publications the viability of style and fashion publications *Vanity Fair* and *Vogue*.

Navarro, Sara (1957-) Spanish footwear designer.

Neuville, Charlotte (1951-) American sportswear designer.

New Republic American company known for retro-influenced menswear (with special affinities for the Edwardian era and the 1950s) founded by designer Thomas Oatman in 1981.

Newton, Helmut German fashion photographer of unabashed sexuality, notable in French *Vogue* in the 1970s.

Next British manufacturer and retailer founded in 1981 by George Davies for good-taste fashion basics, comparable to The Gap in the United States.

Nikos Men's swimwear, exercisewear, and underwear company created by Nikos Apostolopoulos; scent "Sculpture" complements the highly homoerotic menswear.

Oldfield, Bruce (1950-) British designer of traditional fashion grandeur.

Olive, Frank (1929-1995) American milliner.

Oliver, André (1932-1993) French creator of menswear and colleague of Pierre Cardin in both couture and ready-to-wear.

Ong, Benny (1949-) Singaporean/British designer working in London, known for eveningwear.

Packham, Jenny (1965-) British designer, known for luxurious textiles

Paquin French couture house, long directed by Mme. Paquin; closed 1956.

Parkinson, Norman (1913-1990) English fashion photographer, most notably in British *Vogue* and *Town & Country*.

Pedlar, Sylvia (1901-1972) American lingerie designer.

Penn, Irving (1917-) Fashion and still-life photographer.

Pepe Anglo-American jeans and casualwear manufacturer founded in the 1980s.

Perris, Bernard (1936-) French couture and ready-to-wear designer.

Pfister, Andrea (1942-) Italian footwear designer working in Paris.

Piguet, Robert (1901-1953) Swiss-born French designer important in the 1930s and 1940s.

Pipart, Gerard (1933-) French designer working for Nina Ricci.

Plunkett, Walter (1902-1982) Film costume designer for RKO Studios, later free-lance.

Pollen, Arabella (1961-) British designer.

Pomodoro, Carmelo (1956-1992) American sportswear designer.

Price, Anthony (1945-) British designer with proclivity to romantic Hollywood-style glamour.

Pringle of Scotland A Scottish hosiery business since 1815, Pringle is known for its traditional Scottish knitwear, wools, and hosiery.

Rayne, Sir Edward (1922-1992) British footwear designer and manufacturer.

Georges Rech French ready-to-wear design house founded by Georges Rech in Paris in 1960.

Red or Dead British ready-to-wear and footwear company founded 1982 by Wayne and Geraldine Hemmingway, with clothing as politically intense as the name implies.

Reese, Tracy (1964-) American sportswear designer.

Rentner, Maurice (1889-1958) American Seventh-Avenue manufacturer.

Richard, Kenneth (1965-) American better-sportswear designer devoted to interchangeable separates.

Roberts, Patricia (1945-) British knitwear designer.

Robinson, Bill (1948-1993) American menswear designer.

Rodier Founded by Eugene Rodier in 1848 for creating Kashmir shawls, a French textile and clothing company.

Rouff, Maggy [Maggy Besancon de Wagner] (1896-1971) French couture designer from 1929 until her retirement in 1948 with her business continued by her daughter through the late 1960s.

Ruggeri, Cinzia (1945-) Italian ready-to-wear designer of strong artistic referencing and sensibility.

Sachs, Gloria (1927?-) American sportswear, knitwear, and sweater designer known for her innovative and artistic wools.

Schiaparelli, Elsa (1890-1973) Roman-born French designer known especially for her tailored clothing, extravagant embroidery, and sensitivity to Surrealism in the 1930s, including collaborations with Salvador Dali and Jean Cocteau.

Schnurer, Carolyn (1908-) American sportswear designer, influenced by world travel to create kimono and caftan derivations for beachwear and sportswear.

Sharaff, Irene (1910-1993) American film and stage costume designer, especially of MGM musicals.

Shilling, David (1956-) British milliner much favored at Ascot for exuberant hats.

Simpson, Adele (1904-1995) American designer who created flattering suits, dresses, and coats; dressed First Ladies Eisenhower, Johnson, Nixon, and Carter.

Sitbon, Martine (1952-) French designer.

Sitbon, Sophie (1961-) French designer.

Smith, Graham (1938-) British milliner.

Smith, Paul (1946-) British designer of classic menswear often with an ironic twist.

Snow, Carmel Irish-born American editor of *Vogue*, 1929-32; then fashion editor and editor, *Harper's Bazaar*, 1932-57.

Stavropoloulos, George Peter (1920-1990) Greek-American designer, most noted for diaphanous chiffon eveningwear.

Stefanel Italian sportswear manufacturer and retailer founded in Treviso in 1959 by Carlo Stefanel.

Steichen, Edward (1879-1973) Luxembourg-born American photographer working in fashion in the 1920s toward a more straightforward, crisp fashion image.

Steiger, Walter (1942-) Swiss footwear designer working in Paris.

Stock, Robert (1946-) American rugged-wear and men's sportswear designer.

Storey, Helen (1959-) Roman-born British avant-garde designer.

Strenesse Group German fashion house founded by Gerd Strehle in 1968.

Sung, Alfred (1948-) China-born Canadian ready-to-wear and menswear designer.

Tang, William Chinese designer working in Hong Kong.

Tassell, Gustave (1926-) American designer of custom-made and ready-to-wear clothing, including stint (1972-76) as chief designer for Norell after Norell's death.

Telford, Rodney Vaughn (1967-) American sportswear designer, born in South Africa.

Tice, Bill (1942-1995) American lingerie and loungewear designer.

Tiel, Vicky (1943-) American designer working in France, specializing in sultry, seductive cocktailwear and eveningwear.

Tiffeau, Jacques (1927-1988) French designer, chiefly of ready-to-wear.

Tiktiner French fashion house founded by Dina Tiktiner Viterbo in Nice in 1949.

Tilley, Monika (1934-) Austrian-born American swimwear and sportswear designer.

Timney Fowler British textile design firm making distinctive textiles for apparel and home, especially whimsical conversationals, founded in London in 1979 by Sue Timney and Grahame Fowler.

Tinling, Ted (1910-1990) British sportswear designer, specializing in tennis attire.

Torii, Yuki (1943-) Japanese fashion designer.

Torrente French ready-to-wear house founded by designer Mme. Torrente Mett in the 1960s.

Transport British footwear firm founded by Jimmy Sarvea in 1970.

Trussardi Italian leather goods and accessories manufacturer founded as a glove-making firm by Dante Trussardi in Bergamo in 1910; now quality fashion and accessories for men and women.

Tuffin, Sally (1938-) British ready-to-wear designer, first designing for Tuffin and Foale in the 1960s, with keen sense of street style and fashion excitement.

Underwood, Patricia (1947-) British millinery designer working in New York.

Unger, Kay (1945-) American designer specializing in women's clothing for the office and sportswear.

Van den Akker, Koos (1939-) Dutch-born American designer of distinctive art clothing, especially graphic and surprising sweaters.

Venturi, Gian Marco (1955?-) Italian fashion designer, chiefly stylish ready-to-wear and a small line of menswear.

Verdu, Joaquin Spanish designer, specializing in knits.

Verino, Roberto (1945-) Spanish designer, known for leatherwear.

Victor, Sally (1905-1977) American milliner.

Victorio y Lucchino Spanish design company favoring influences of Spanish traditional dress, founded 1972 by Jose Luis Medina de Corral and Jose Victor Rodriguez Caro in Seville.

Vionnet, Madeleine (1876-1975) French couture designer, known for bias dresses of utmost simplicity and design daring in the 1920s and 1930s; not active as a designer after 1939.

Vollbracht, Michaele (1947-) American artist, illustrator, interior designer and fashion designer.

Vreeland, Diana (1906?-1989) American editor and fashion leader, fashion editor for *Harper's Bazaar*, 1937-62; editor, *Vogue*, 1962-71; consultant, The Costume Institute, The Metropolitan Museum of Art, 1972-89.

Louis Vuitton French luggage, leather, and accessories firm founded by Louis Vuitton in Paris in 1854.

Walker, Catherine French designer working in London.

Whistles British retailer founded by Lucille Lewin in London in 1976.

Whittal and Shon American millinery firm founded by Eliot Whittal and Richard Shon in 1986.

Yeohlee [Teng] (1955?-) Malaysian-born American designer, noted for her geometric cuts and simplicity.

Yuki [Gnyuki Torimaru] (1940?-) Japanese-born designer working in London known for draping and bias-cut eveningwear.

appendix

NATIONALITY INDEX

fashion

AMERICAN
Abboud, Joseph
Adolfo
Adrian, Gilbert
Alfaro, Victor
Allard, Linda
Anthony, John
Badgley Mischka
Barnes, Jhane
Barrie, Scott
Bartlett, John
Beene, Geoffrey
Blass, Bill
Brigance, Tom
Brooks, Donald
Bruce, Liza
Burrows, Stephen
Carnegie, Hattie
Cashin, Bonnie
Cassini, Oleg
Cesarani, Sal
Claiborne, Liz
Daché, Lilly
di Sant'Angelo, Giorgio
Ellis, Perry
Fezza, Andrew
Fogarty, Anne
Galanos, James
Gernreich, Rudi
Halston
Hardwick, Cathy

Heisel, Sylvia
Hilfiger, Tommy
Jacobs, Marc
James, Charles
Javits, Eric
Joan & David
John, John P.
Johnson, Betsey
Kahng, Gemma
Kamali, Norma
Karan, Donna
Kasper, Herbert
Kelly, Patrick
Kemper, Randy
Kieselstein-Cord,
    Barry
Klein, Anne
Klein, Calvin
Kors, Michael
Lane, Kenneth Jay
Lars, Byron
Lauren, Ralph
Leiber, Judith
Leser, Tina
Mackie, Bob
Mad Carpentier
Mainbocher
Marcasiano, Mary Jane
Maxwell, Vera
McCardell, Claire
McFadden, Mary
Miller, Nicole

Mizrahi, Isaac
Morris, Robert Lee
Natori, Josie Cruz
Norell, Norman
Oldham, Todd
Parnis, Mollie
Pulitzer, Lilly
Restivo, Mary Ann
Roehm, Carolyne
Roth, Christian Francis
Rowley, Cynthia
Scaasi, Arnold
Smith, Willi
Sprouse, Stephen
Sui, Anna
Tam, Vivienne
Toi, Zang
Trigère, Pauline
Valentina
Van den Akker, Koos
Vass, Joan
Vittadini, Adrienne
Weitz, John
Zoran

AUSTRALIAN
Tyler, Richard

AUSTRIAN
Lang, Helmut

BELGIAN
Bikkembergs, Dirk

Demeulemeester, Ann
Margiela, Martin
Von Furstenberg,
    Diane

BRITISH
Amies, Hardy
Ashley, Laura
Bellville Sassoon-
    Lorcan Mullany
Bodymap
Dagworthy, Wendy
Emanuel, David and
    Elizabeth
Galliano, John
Ghost
Hamnett, Katharine
Hartnell, Norman
Hulanicki, Barbara
Jackson, Betty
Jones, Stephen
McQueen, Alexander
Molyneux, Edward H.
Muir, Jean
Ozbek, Rifat
Porter, Thea
Quant, Mary
Rhodes, Zandra
Richmond, John
Westwood, Vivienne
Workers For Freedom

nationality index

CANADIAN
Cox, Patrick

CHINESE
Feng, Han

CUBAN
Toledo, Isabel

DOMINICAN
De la Renta, Oscar

DUTCH
Shamask, Ronaldus

FRENCH
Agnès B.
Alaia, Azzedine
Balmain, Pierre
Bohan, Marc
Cacharel, Jean
Cardin, Pierre
Carven
Castelbajac, Jean-
　Charles de
Chanel, "Coco"
　Gabriel Bonheur
Chloé
Courrèges, André
Dessès, Jean
Dior, Christian
Fath, Jacques
Féraud, Louis
Gaultier, Jean-Paul

Girbaud, Marithé &
　François
Givenchy, Hubert de
Grès, Madame
Heim, Jacques
Jourdan, Charles
Khanh, Emmanuelle
Lacroix, Christian
Lanvin
Laug, André
Léger, Hervé
Montana, Claude
Mugler, Thierry
Patou, Jean
Paulin, Guy
Picasso, Paloma
Rabanne, Paco
Ricci, Nina
Rochas, Marcel
Rykiel, Sonia
Saint Laurent, Yves
Scherrer, Jean-Louis
Thomass, Chantal
Ungaro, Emanuel
Venet, Philippe
Vionnet, Madeleine
Vivier, Roger

GERMAN
Escada
Joop, Wolfgang
Lagerfeld, Karl

Sander, Jil

IRISH
Treacy, Philip

ITALIAN
Albini, Walter
Armani, Giorgio
Biagiotti, Laura
Byblos
Calugi e Giannelli
Cerruti, Nino
Dolce & Gabbana
Fendi
Ferragamo, Salvatore
Ferré, Gianfranco
Fiorucci, Elio
Fontana
Genny SpA
Gigli, Romeo
Gucci
Mandelli, Mariuccia
　(for Krizia)
Missoni
Moschino, Franco
Peretti, Elsa
Prada
Pucci, Emilio
Simonetta
Valentino
Versace, Gianni
Zegna, Ermenegildo

JAPANESE
Kawakubo, Rei
Kenzo
Kobayashi, Yukio
Matsuda, Mitsuhiro
Miyake, Issey
Mori, Hanae
Yamamoto, Kansai
Yamamoto, Yohji

MALIAN
Kouyaté, Lamine (for
　Xüly Bet)

NORWEGIAN
Spook, Per

RUSSIAN
Galitzine, Irene

SPANISH
Balenciaga, Cristobal
Blahnik, Manolo
Fortuny (y Madrazo),
　Mariano
Sanchez, Fernando
Sybilla

VENEZUELAN
Herrera, Carolina

YUGOSLAVIAN
Schön, Mila

Almond, Kevin Fashion director, Leeds College of Art and Design. Designer, Enrico Coveri, 1988-89, assistant designer, Woman Hautwell Ltd., 1989-90. Senior lecturer in fashion/fashion promotions, University of Central Lancashire, 1990-94. Contributor of "Camp Dressing" article to *Components of Dress*, 1988. *Essays:* John Anthony; Scott Barrie; Bellville Sassoon-Lorcan Mullany; Bodymap; Jean Cacharel; Oleg Cassini; Wendy Dagworthy; Oscar de la Renta; Christian Dior; Escada; Louis Féraud; Gianfranco Ferré; Norman Hartnell; Betty Jackson; Donna Karan; Herbert Kasper; Christian Lacroix; Guy Laroche; Jean Muir; Nina Ricci; Mila Schön; Per Spook; Chantal Thomass; Philippe Venet; Diane Von Furstenberg.

Arnold, Rebecca Lecturer in fashion history and cultural theory, Kent Institute of Art and Design. *Essays:* Dirk Bikkembergs; Marc Bohan; Liza Bruce; Chloé; Ann Demeulemeester; Dolce & Gabbana; John Galliano; Romeo Gigli; Karl Lagerfeld; Helmut Lang; Hervé Léger; Hanae Mori; Emilio Pucci; John Richmond.

Arsenault, Andrea Professor of Fashion Design, School of the Art Institute of Chicago. Designer. Former chair of the fashion department, and the faculty senate, School of the Art Institute of Chicago. Contributor, *Jean Charles de Castelbajac Album;* contributor and advisor, *Con-*temporary *Designers* and *Contemporary Masterworks*. *Essay:* Jean-Charles de Castelbajac.

Baker, Therese Duzinkiewicz Associate professor/extended campus librarian, Western Kentucky University, Bowling Green, Kentucky. Author of journal articles on library service for off-campus students. Book reviewer in decorative arts for *Library Journal*. Contributor to *Dictionary of American Biography*. *Essays:* Gilbert Adrian; Norma Kamali; Emmanuelle Khanh; Mainbocher; Mary McFadden; Norman Norell; Thea Porter; Jean-Louis Scherrer; Emanuel Ungaro; Valentina; Koos Van Den Akker.

Blausen, Whitney Independent writer and researcher. Former administrator, the Costume Collection, Theatre Development fund. Contributor of numerous articles to various periodicals, journals, and books, including *Theatre Crafts International, Fiber Arts, Surface Design Journal, Dictionaire de la mode au xxc siècle*, 1995, *50 American Designers*, 1995, and *Dictionary of Women Artists*, 1996. *Essays:* Donald Brooks; Bonnie Cashin; Betsey Johnson; Bob Mackie; Zandra Rhodes; Cynthia Rowley.

Bodine, Sarah (with Michael Dunas) Independent lecturer and writer in design and craft studies and criticism. Teacher, senior thesis studio, University of the Arts. Visiting lecturer and critic at various institutions, including Cleveland Institute of Art, Akron University, Tyler

School of Art, RISD, Cranbrook Academy of Art, University of Michigan, Alfred University, Massachusetts College of Art, Parsons School of Design, Miami University, and Moore College of Art. Whitney Library of Design, 1973-79. Editor, *Metalsmith,* 1979-92; editorial director, Documents of American Design, 1988-91. Contributor to numerous periodicals and volumes, including *Industrial Design* and *Design Book Review. Essays:* Agnès B; Rei Kawakubo.

Brown, Mary Carol   Free-lance essayist based in England. *Essays:* Laura Ashley; "Coco" Gabriel Bonheur Chanel; Salvatore Ferragamo.

Burns, Jane   B.A. in ecology and environmental studies, University of Georgia; studied fashion design at Fashion Institute of Technology. Designed Christmas windows for Hermès, New York; worked as a dresser for the Macy's Thanksgiving Day parade. *Essays:* Badgley Mischka; Patrick Kelly.

Carlano, Marianne T.   Formerly curator of costume and textiles at both the Wadsworth Atheneum in Hartford and the Museum of Fine Arts, Boston. Textile scholar. Author of catalogue essays and articles in *Art Journal* and *Arts Magazine. Essays:* Joseph Abboud.

Cavaliere, Barbara   Free-lance writer on art and design, New York City. Associate editor, *Womanart* magazine, 1976-78; contributing editor, *Arts Magazine,* 1976-83. Fellowship in art criticism, National Endowment for the Arts, 1979-80. Author of exhibition catalogues. *Essay:* Mariuccia Mandelli.

Clark, Hazel   Head of School of Design, Hong Kong Polytechnic University, Hong Kong. Contributor to various journals, including *Journal of Design History, Design, Design Week, Design Review, Monument,* and *Women's Art Journal.* Author of "Selling Design and Craft" and "Footprints Textile Printing Workshop" in *Women Designing: Redefining Design in Britain between the Wars,* 1994. *Essays:* Ralph Lauren; Mary Quant.

Coleman, Elizabeth A.   Curator, textiles and costumes, Museum of Fine Arts, Houston, Texas; former curator of costumes and textiles, Brooklyn Museum. Adjunct professor, Fashion Institute of Technology, New York. Rice University Fellow. Author of *The Genius of Charles James,* 1982, and *The Opulent Era: Fashions of Worth, Doucet, and Pingat,* 1989. *Essay:* Charles James.

Cooper, Arlene C.   Consulting curator, European textiles and shawls, Museum for Textiles, Toronto, Ontario, Canada. President, Arlene C. Cooper Consulting (consultant to museums and private collectors of shawls, European textiles, and 20th-century fashion). Senior research assistant for textiles, department of European sculpture and decorative arts, Metropolitan Museum of Art. Author of "The Kashmir Shawl and Its Derivatives in North American Collections," 1987, and "How Madame Grès Sculpts with Fabric," in *Great Sewn Clothes from Threads* magazine, 1991. *Essays:* Hubert de Givenchy; Sonia Rykiel.

Cox, Caroline   Free-lance essayist based in England. *Essays:* Azzedine Alaia; Giorgio Armani; Pierre Cardin; André Courrèges; Jean-Paul Gaultier; Rudi Gernreich; Franco Moschino; Rifat Ozbek; Paco Rabanne; Yves Saint Laurent; Fernando Sanchez; Stephen Sprouse; Yohji Yamamoto.

Druesedow, Jean L.   Director, Kent State University Museum. Associate curator in charge, the Costume Institute, Metropolitan Museum of Art, New York, 1984-92. Adjunct full professor, New York University. Author of *Jno. J. Mitchell Co. Men's Fashion Illustrations from the Turn of the Century,* 1990, and "Who Wears the Pants," chapter in *Androgyny,* 1992. *Essays:* Vera Maxwell.

Ehrlich, Doreen   Tutor in art and design history, Hillcroft College. Author of *Twentieth Century Painting,* 1989, and *The Bauhaus,* 1991. *Essay:* Liz Claiborne.

Flux, Alan J.   Free-lance essayist. *Essays:* Lilly Daché; Stephen Jones.

Gordon, Mary Ellen   Free-lance writer. Associate editor, *Women's Wear Daily,* 1989-94. Contributor to periodicals, including *Elle, Self, InStyle,* and *Paper Magazine. Essay:* Anna Sui.

Gruber, Roberta Hochberger   Assistant professor, fashion design, Drexel University. Co-director, design arts gallery, Drexel University. Free-lance designer and fashion illustrator. Curator of several exhibitions, including *Fashion Imagery,* 1991, *Hat Formation,* 1993, and *Designer Sketchbook,* 1995. *Essays:* Mariano (y Madrazo) Fortuny; Nicole Miller; Robert Lee Morris.

Hill, Chris   Senior lecturer, Cordwainers College, London. Company Director, Fancy Footwork Ltd. *Essays:* Patrick Cox; Charles Jourdan.

House, Nancy Adjunct faculty, art history, Wilmington College; also taught at Ohio State University and Salem State College, Massachusetts. *Essays:* Anne Fogarty; Joan & David; Carolyne Roehm; Joan Vass.

Kirke, Betty Retired head conservator, Edwarde C. Blum Design Laboratory, Fashion Institute of Technology. Created and taught graduate curriculum in costume conservation at Fashion Institute of Technology in the 1980s. Author of *Vionnet*, 1991. *Essays:* Lanvin.

Markarian, Janet Textile specialist. Taught textile studies at many colleges and universities. Taught master's program at the Costume Institute, Metropolitan Museum of Art, and New York University. Worked in the Metropolitan Museum's Ratti Textile Center, 1995. *Essays:* Linda Allard; Kenneth Jay Lane.

Marsh, Lisa Sportswear reporter with *Women's Wear Daily*. *Essays:* Perry Ellis; David and Elizabeth Emanuel.

Martin, Richard Curator, the Costume Institute, Metropolitan Museum of Art. Among numerous other posts: editor of *Arts Magazine*, 1974-88; editor of *Textile & Text*, 1988-92. Executive director of the Shirley Goodman Resource Center, 1980-93, and professor of art history, 1973-93, at the Fashion Institute of Technology. Taught at Columbia University, New York University, School of Visual Arts, the Juilliard School, Parsons School of Design, and the School of the Art Institute of Chicago. Books include *Fashion and Surrealism* and *The New Urban Landscape*. More than 300 essays have appeared in various journals, including *Vogue* (Munich), *Journal of American Culture, Los Angeles Times, International Herald Tribune,* and *Artforum*. *Essays:* Walter Albini; Victor Alfaro; Cristobal Balenciaga; Jhane Barnes; John Bartlett; Geoffrey Beene; Laura Biagiotti; Bill Blass; Tom Brigance; Stephen Burrows; Byblos; Calugi e Giannelli; Nino Cerruti; Han Feng; Andrew Fezza; Fontana; Irene Galitzine; Marithé & François Girbaud; Madame Grès; Halston; Jacques Heim; Gordon Henderson; Tommy Hilfiger; Marc Jacobs; Eric Javits; John P. John; Wolfgang Joop; Gemma Kahng; Kenzo; Barry Kieselstein-Cord; Calvin Klein; Yukio Kobayashi; Michael Kors; Lamine Kouyaté; Byron Lars; André Laug; Judith Leiber; Mad Carpentier; Mitsuhiro Matsuda; Missoni; Issey Miyake; Isaac Mizrahi; Edward H. Molyneux; Claude Montana; Josie Cruz Natori; Todd Oldham; Elsa Peretti; Lilly Pulitzer; Mary Ann Restivo; Marcel Rochas; Christian Francis Roth; Ronaldus Shamask; Simonetta; Willi Smith; Zang Toi; Gianni Versace; Madeleine Vionnet; John Weitz; Kansai Yamamoto.

Melia, Sally Anne Science and culture free-lance journalist and author. Contributor to *St. James Guide to Fantasy Writers*, 1994, *Larousse Encyclopedia*, 1995, *Lexus Dictionary of French Life and Culture,* 1995; author of celebrity interviews and articles for magazines in the United Kingdom and the United States, including *SF Chronicle* and *Interzone*. *Essays:* Ermenegildo Zegna.

Ozzard, Janet Graduate of Bryn Mawr College; M.A. in fashion history, Fashion Institute of Technology. Reporter for *Women's Wear Daily*. *Essay:* Zoran.

Paton, Kathleen Writer, researcher, and editor specializing in cultural history. Free-lance graphic designer, since 1988. M.A. in museum studies, State University of New York, Fashion Institute of Technology, 1993. Research and essays for *In A Rising Public Voice: Women in Politics Worldwide*. *Essay:* Guy Paulin.

Pattison, Angela Lecturer in design. Program leader, Cordwainers College. International design consultant. Trained as a fashion designer in the early 1960s. Specializes in trend predictions, fashion forecasting, and designing footwear and accessories with major manufacturers and retailers throughout the world. *Essays:* Manolo Blahnik; Elio Fiorucci.

Rosenberg, Alan E. Studied fashion design at the Fashion Institute of Technology and art history at Hunter College of the City University of New York. Director of the Metropolitan Historic Structures Association for several years. Studying for master's degree in museum studies, Fashion Institute of Technology. *Essays:* Adolfo; Carven; Valentino.

Seaman, Margo Graduate of the College of Wooster; master's degrees from the Fashion Institute of Technology and Bank Street College of Education. Teacher and free-lance writer. *Essays:* Pierre Balmain; Carolina Herrera; Anne Klein; Claire McCardell; Jean Patou; Paloma Picasso; Adrienne Vittadini.

Severson, Molly Free-lance writer. *Essay:* Richard Tyler.

Sewell, Dennita Graduate of the University of Missouri and Yale School of Drama. Collections manager in the Costume Institute, Metropolitan Museum of Art, since 1992. *Essays:* Cathy Hardwick; Roger Vivier.

Shaw, Madelyn Collections manager, the Textile Museum, Washington, D.C. Former member of the curatorial staff, the Museum at the Fashion Institute of Technology, New York, and the Gallery of Cora Ginsburg, Inc., New York. Instructor, Boston University School of Theatre Arts, Boston, Massachusetts. Also involved in free-lance exhibition consultation and preparation. Contributor to *A World of Costume and Textiles: A Handbook of the Collection*, 1988, and of "Women's Flying Clothing: 1910-1940," in *Cutter's Research Journal*, 1992-93. *Essays:* Hattie Carnegie; Jean Dessès; Tina Leser.

Skellenger, Gillion Free-lance wallpaper and fabric designer, Chicago. Instructor, fashion department, School of the Art Institute of Chicago, beginning in 1977. *Essay:* Prada.

Steele, Valerie Author and professor at New York's Fashion Institute of Technology. Author of *Fashion and Eroticism*, 1985, *Paris Fashion*, 1988, *Women of Fashion*, 1991, and *Fetish: Fashion, Sex and Power*, 1995. Co-editor of *Men and Women: Dressing the Part*, 1989. *Essays:* Jacques Fath; Martin Margiela; Jil Sander; Sybilla; Isabel Toledo; Vivienne Westwood.

Triggs, Teal Course leader, School of Graphic Design, Ravensbourne College of Design and Communication, London. Design historian. Editor, *Communicating Design*, 1995, and (post-conference publication) *Rear Window: American and European Graphic Design*, 1995. Author of "Framing Masculinity: Herb Ritts, Bruce Weber and the Body Perfect" in *Chic Thrills: A Fashion Reader*, 1992. Contributor of articles to numerous periodicals and books, including *Eye* magazine, *Visible Language*, *Contemporary Designers*, and *Contemporary Masterworks*. *Essays:* Sylvia Heisel.

Votolato, Gregory Essayist. Head of art history department, Buckinghamshire College, High Wycombe. *Essays:* Barbara Hulanicki; Thierry Mugler.

Walker, Myra J. Associate professor of fashion history, School of Visual Arts at the University of North Texas in Denton. Director, Texas Fashion Collection. Curator, "The Art of Fashion: The Radical Sixties," Kimbell Art Museum, 1990. Exhibition organizer, JC Penney national headquarters, 1993-95. Specialist in 20th-century fashion history. *Essays:* Giorgio di Sant'Angelo; Arnold Scaasi.

Watt, Melinda L. Study storage assistant, the Costume Institute, Metropolitan Museum of Art. M.A. in costume studies from New York University. *Essays:* Pauline Trigère.

Woram, Catherine Free-lance fashion writer/stylist. Author of *Wedding Dress Style*, 1993. *Essays:* Hardy Amies; Fendi; Genny Spa; Ghost; Gucci; Katharine Hamnett; Philip Treacy; Workers for Freedom.